ABSTRACTS OF CAPE GIRARDEAU COUNTY DEEDS

BOOKS A/B-F, 1797-1826

Abstracted by Bill Eddleman
French translations by Jane Randol Jackson, M.A., French

This book is dedicated to the late Jean Adams, for all the work she did for the Cape Girardeau Co. Genealogical Society, and for her work in making Southeast Missouri records available to genealogists; and the late Jane Randol Jackson, first county archivist of Cape Girardeau County, for all her work in making local records available for research.

The Cape Girardeau County Genealogical Society issued an earlier version of this book in 2000.

Southern Historical Press, Inc.
Greenville, South Carolina

This volume was reproduced
from a personal copy located in
the Publishers private library

Please direct all correspondence and book orders to:
SOUTHERN HISTORICAL PRESS, Inc.
PO Box 1267
Greenville, SC   29602-1267

Copyright 2024 by:
    Southern Historical Press, Inc.
ISBN #978-1-63914-314-6
Printed in the United States of America

ABSTRACTS OF CAPE GIRARDEAU CO. DEED BOOKS A/B-F, 1797-1826

The deeds abstracted herein have also been the subject of a transcription of Book 1 of the Indirect Index to Cape Girardeau Co. Deeds (Adams, Jean. undated. Indirect land transactions, 1805-1828. Privately printed, Cape Girardeau, Mo.). This index covers Deed Books A-F and part of Book G. The index does not mention land descriptions, relationships, nor witnesses, and so this book provides complete abstracts for these deeds. The deeds contained herein were transacted between 1797 and 1826, and were recorded between 14 June 1805 and 22 May 1826. We used microfilm of the original deed books to abstract these deeds. For Deed Book A and Deed Book B, we used an 1870 copy of the combined deed books (the originals are still available in the Cape Girardeau County Recorder's Office, but are harder to read).

In this transcription, we have tried to list all names mentioned in the deed, including grantor(s), grantee(s), original patentees or grantees, neighbors, witnesses, officials, slaves, or those owed debts. Spellings are as they appear in the deed book. Question marks (?) denote the text was illegible or unclear. We include some information as comments, or obtained it from other sources, and these appear enclosed in [ ]. Names are transcribed exactly as they appear in the deeds, so please be aware when searching for your ancestor that spellings may vary (e.g., Randall for Randol, Billue for Bellew, Hubbell for Hubble). The intent of these abstracts is to point researchers toward information they may need on their ancestors, and *one should always consult digitized deedbooks, microfilm, or the original deed books* to insure accuracy and to obtain a complete description of the transaction(s). Other agreements other than the purchase of land are included in the deed book, including land grants, marriages, mortgages, powers of attorney, pre-nuptial agreements, delinquent tax lists, personal property transfers, agreements to pay debts, posting of bonds, and estate partitions. Any errors or misinterpretations are ours and ours alone.

Most of these abstracts were prepared using the microfilm of Deed Books A, B, C, D, E, and F, filmed by the Church of Jesus Christ of Latter Day Saints, and available from the LDS Family History Library in Salt Lake City, its local branches, or from the Missouri State Archives (#C1231 and #C1232). Digital copies of the deeds are also accessible via FamilySearch, the Missouri State Archives County and Municipal Records, and the Cape Girardeau County Recorder's Office via ArcaSearch. Copies of the three plats included in the five books are included.

Deed abstracts in this book are in the following format:

1. A serial number assigned to each deed *for indexing purposes only*.
2. The page number in the deed book.
3. The execution date as mentioned in the deed.
4. The name or names of the grantor(s), or sellers, followed by their town, county, and state of residence. If no location appears, then the grantor(s) are from Cape Girardeau County. The word "same" denotes that the grantor is the same as in the preceding deed.
5. After the word "to", the names or names of the grantee(s), or buyers, followed by their place of residence. Again, if no location appears, then the grantee(s) are from Cape Girardeau County. The word "same" denotes that the grantee is the same as in the preceding deed.
6. Following the phase "For the sum of..", the sale price in dollars or other consideration (such as "for love and affection").
7. The amount of land in acres or arpens/arpents, or the words "mortgage on" and the amount of land. A __ indicates the area of land is not given in the deed.
8. If mentioned, the watercourse on which the land is located, the lot number, survey number, U. S. Land Office description, or some description of the land. If mentioned, previous history of land ownership may also be given.
9. If given, adjacent land ownership by description or owners' names.
10. Any information about court cases, debts owed, or other details given in the deed.
11. Following "Signed:" is the spelling of the names of the grantor(s) as signed. If the granter(s) signed with a mark, an (x) is inserted between the given and surname; as John (x) Doe. Unique marks are typed with a similar symbol, because these may allow identification of an

individual; as John (D) Doe. Except for German signatures, signatures in these deed books were actually copied by the clerk, and are not original signatures.

12. Following "Wit:" or "Test:" or "Proved:" is the name of the witnesses, legal authorities who witnessed the deed (usually a justice of the peace) and their title, and/or those who proved the deed in court. The latter rarely appears in these deed books.

13. The date the deed was recorded. Rarely, this may be over 30 years after execution of the deed.

Abbreviations Used:

Adminr - administrator	JP - justice of the peace
Atty. - attorney	RD - relinquished dower rights
CCP - Court of Common Pleas	Recr - recorder
Co. - county	Rng - range
Directions - abbreviated using 1 or 2 letters	Sd - said
(e.g., S - south, SE - southeast)	Sec - section
Dist - district	St - street
Execr - executor	Terr - territory
JCCP - Justice of the Court of Common Pleas	Twp - township

Glossary of Terms Used in the Abstracts

Acre - A measure of land comprising 160 square rods, or 4,840 square yards, or 43,560 square feet.

Agent - An individual who represents another from whom he has derived authority.

Administrator - A person appointed by the court to administer the estate of a deceased person who left no will; that is, who died intestate.

Appurtenance - That which belongs to something else; something which passes with land, such as a right-of-way.

Arpen/Arpent - A measure of land area used by French authorities; equal to about 0.85 acres.

Attorney in fact - Anyone who is appointed to act for another in a particular situation or transaction not of a legal nature. See Power of Attorney.

Bond - Money or property paid to an individual or authority such as a court to guarantee that the grantor will perform an action that has been agreed upon; examples are guarantees of court appearances or promises to execute a deed.

Chain - A distance of 66 feet.

Commissioners - Group of individuals appointed by a court authority to perform a specific legal task, such as partition of an estate or sale of real estate belonging to a deceased person.

Confirmation - A land claim that was confirmed by the Board of Commissioners; most of these claims were made prior to the purchase of Louisiana from France in 1803. Also, a land title issued by Spanish or French authorities that was issued after an individual had occupied, possessed, or cultivated the land for 10 years.

Dower - The right which a wife has in her husband's estate at his death. Under common law, this was 1/3 of the value of all lands which her husband had owned during their marriage. Thus, in land transfers, the grantor's wife would have to relinquish (give up) her dower rights so the grantee could gain clear title to the land. Otherwise, she would have the right to claim her dower rights on the land at a later date.

Et al. - And others.

Executor - A person named in a will to carry out its provisions.

Foreclosure - A court process instituted by a mortgagee on or lien creditor to defeat any interest or redemption which the debtor/owner may have in the property.

Grant/Land Grant - A process by which a government gives land to an individual.

Grantee - the individual receiving property; for most deeds, the buyer of the land.

Grantor - the individual disposing of property; for most deeds, the seller of the land.

Head Right - Land granted to an individual by a government in exchange for settling and improving that land (that is, land granted "per head"). In Cape Girardeau Co., this was land granted by the Spanish Government to American settlers who agreed to settle in the District.

Improvement - Changes an individual makes in a parcel of land; such as buildings, clearing fields, etc. Oftentimes, individuals had to show proof of improvements in order to have land entries confirmed.

Infant - any person not of full legal age; a minor.

Intestate - A person who dies without making a legal will.

Moiety - Half of anything.

Mortgage - A conditional transfer of legal title to real or personal property as security for payment of a debt.

Partition, Partition Deed - The dividing of real property among all joint owners according to their respective rights.

Patent - First title to a land parcel, issued by a federal government. This document is issued at the conclusion of the land grant process, or after a cash sale at the U. S. Land Office. Patents were issued by Spanish, French, or U. S. governments.

Perch - A distance of 16 1/2 feet; same as a pole or rod.

Plat - A map of a tract, sometimes showing its location in relation to neighboring land owners.

Pole - A distance of 16 1/2 feet; same as a perch or rod.

Power of Attorney - The bestowal of the authority to act as an attorney in fact.

Preemption, Preemption Right - Legal claim to a parcel of land obtained by a settler (or squatter) who had cultivated a land tract prior to the opening of the Jackson Land Office in 1823. The settler had a right to purchase the land and obtain clear title after the land office opened. Most parcels were 40 or 80 acres. Preemptions were oftentimes sold prior to obtaining a patent, so the original patentee may not have been the original "owner" of a land parcel.

Quit Claim Deed - A deed given when the grantee already has, or claims, complete or partial title to the premises and the grantor has a possible interest that otherwise would constitute a question upon the title.

Rod - A distance of 16 1/2 feet; same as a perch or pole.

Settlement Right - Land granted to an individual for settling on a tract prior to the Louisiana Purchase. In the Cape Girardeau District, individuals were granted such land based on their wealth and importance, the size of their family, and their ability to cultivate land, but few settlement rights exceeded 800 arpents. The only cost was for fees and surveying. See Confirmation, Head Right.

Sheriff's Deed - A deed that is executed by the sheriff or other official acting in that capacity; used in cases where land was seized to pay a debt or satisfy a judgment in court.

Test. - Attest; the witness to a deed swears to that deed in court, or swears to the signature of the grantor(s).

Trust Deed - A deed that places the title to real estate in one or more trustees to secure payment of a debt. The property could then be sold by the trustee(s) in the case of default, with the debt to be paid from the proceeds.

Writ of fieri facias - a document issued by a Court that directs the Sheriff or other official acting in that capacity to levy the amount of a judgment from the goods and chattels (including land) of the person against whom the court made its judgment.

Writ of Scire faci - the Sheriff or other official acting in that capacity returns to the Court stating he has given notice to the parties against whom a writ has been issued.

A Brief History of Land Disbursement in Cape Girardeau County

Prior to the Louisiana Purchase, French and Spanish authorities did not offer lands for sale in upper Louisiana (Houck 1908). Rather, the Governor and Ordonnateur made grants of land to qualifying individuals. In 1770, under Spanish dominion, the Governor alone was authorized to make grants of land. Land grants were to be make to actual settlers entering the province intending to "establish" themselves. The authority to make land grants changed to the Royal Intendant by Royal decree in 1798, and new rules for land grants were issued in 1799. Immigrants were specified as, "...Catholics, of the class of farmers and artisans.", and must have possessed some property and be of good character. If they were married, they were granted 200 arpens of land. Fifty additional arpens were granted for each child, and 20 arpens for each negro slave, brought in by the settler. No lands were to be granted to unmarried strangers, not farmers, and without property in negroes, or merchandise or money, until they had resided in the province for four years. On the recommendation of a farmer, any unmarried man could secure a grant if the farmer were willing to give his daughter's hand in marriage to the man. Land grants were to be adjacent, to prevent attacks by Indians and facilitate enforcement of justice. Grants ranged from 200-500 arpens for poor settlers, to 30,000 arpens or more for services rendered, in the case of Louis Lorimier for example. There were fees associated with granting title to the lands. Grant and land records of Cape Girardeau District of the Spanish regime are housed in part at the Missouri Historical Society and have been microfilmed, and a few of these are recorded in these deed books.

Grants and the accompanying surveys were often done in a careless manner, making for difficulties in securing title after the Louisiana Purchase. The U. S. Board of Land Commissioners had to confirm French and Spanish land grants after the Louisiana Purchase, and the resulting testimony can oftentimes have information of genealogical interest. Some of these grants remained unconfirmed until the 1830s, so the "cheap land" many of the grantees received may not have been so inexpensive in the long run! These are contained in the *American State Papers, Public Lands* (index in McMullin 1976) and *Missouri Land Claims* (New Orleans: Polyanthos Press, 1976; a reprint of a Congressional document). The survey numbers for some of these land grants are included in several of the deeds abstracted in this book. The prolonged deliberations of the Land Commission delayed opening of a land office in the Cape Girardeau County area. Additionally, the New Madrid earthquakes of 1811-1912 delayed opening of a land office (Luebking 1997). The first U. S. land records other than the Land Commission proceedings involve an 1815 law granting scrip for up to 640 acres to sufferers in "injured lands" damaged by the earthquake, and the Jackson Land Office opened only after settlement of all of these claims.

The policy of the U. S. Government regarding land differed substantially from Spanish policy. Land was to be sold, rather than granted, and there were few stipulations on buyers. Survey of the public lands had to precede sale of lands. The survey system as developed by the U. S. Land Office divided lands into a series of townships, 6 miles on a side, and surveyed from a series of baselines (running E-W) and principal meridians (running N-S). Surveys of lands in Cape Girardeau County refer to the 5th Principal Meridian, and the baseline running through central Arkansas. Each township is numbered north or south from the baseline (e.g., Township 31 N), and is also described in relation to the principal meridian as east or west using ranges (e.g., Range 11 E). Townships are divided into 36 sections, usually 1 mile on a side and 640 acres, allowing additional description of land location (e.g., Section 18). Further description of land occurred by halving or quartering sections, and most land sales were for tracts of 40 or 80 acres or multiples thereof. For complete descriptions of the U. S. Land Office land system, see Greenwood (2017) or Luebking (1997).

Public lands sold through a number of land offices set up in the state. The first opened in 1818 in St. Louis, and the Jackson office opened on 31 December 1820. The date of earliest sales of lands in Cape Girardeau County are 1823, probably delayed by the paperwork process. Individuals lived on some of these lands for many years, as judged by tax records, land sales in this book, and known migration dates from other states. Sometimes these parcels in these abstracts are referred to as a "preemption" or a "preemption right". Once an individual filed for land, he/she had to obtain a patent on the land, and often had to provide supporting information on his/her family, improvements on the land, etc. Oftentimes, the applicant may not have been the original "owner", but owned the preemption right at the time they applied for the patent. The land office sent applications for patents to the General Land Office headquarters in Washington, D. C., which confirmed that all paperwork was in order and issued a patent, or first title deed. A credit system was an option for obtaining patents until 1820, or upon a cash down payment.

Cape Girardeau County Boundaries, 1804-1826

The designation of Cape Girardeau County as a district from a non-county area in the district of Louisiana occurred by proclamation of Gov. William Henry Harrison on 1 October 1804 (Houck 1908:379, Hast and Long 1984). The boundaries were Apple Creek on the north, the Tywappity

Bottoms on the south, Mississippi River on the east, and the western boundary of the Louisiana district on the west. The first county seat was at Cape Girardeau, designated on 1 January 1805. Boundary changes added land presently in Scott and Stoddard counties from New Madrid County on 1 July and 15 August 1806 from New Madrid County. At this time, the county was bounded on the north by Apple Creek and a line projected west to the west border of the county, south by 37 degrees N latitude (present-day central Scott County), and west by 94 degrees, 16 minutes W longitude (present-day eastern Barton and Jasper counties). The area first became a county of the newly-created Missouri Territory on 7 December 1812. Portions of northern Cape Girardeau County went to Ste. Genevieve and Washington counties, and portions of the southeastern part of the county were exchanged with New Madrid on 31 December 1813. The county seat moved to Jackson on 1 March 1814.

The vast western segment of Cape Girardeau County went in part to newly-formed Madison County on 1 January 1819, and the remainder to newly-formed Wayne County on 1 February 1819 (Hast and Long 1984, Thorndale and Dollarhide 1987). The western boundary at that time was partly the western boundary of present-day Bollinger County, partly on a line running along the headwaters of several creeks, and partly by Castor River. Cape Girardeau County remained as a county of the new State of Missouri at statehood on 10 August 1821. Portions of the southern part of the county went to newly-formed Scott County on 30 December 1824 and 16 February 1825. This was the configuration of the county at the end of the period covered by this book. Views of boundary changes are accessible at the Newberry Library's Atlas of Historical County Boundaries interactive map at: https://digital.newberry.org/ahcb/map/map.html#MO.

Because of the frequent boundary changes, and the large area covered by early Cape Girardeau County, researchers may find ancestors who lived in present-day Mississippi, Scott, Wayne, Madison, and Bollinger counties among these deeds. Many of the deeds recorded in early deed books concerned land in the Tywappity Bottom (present-day Scott County), and in old St. Francis township of Cape Girardeau County (parts of present-day Wayne and Madison counties). The farthest west any of these deeds extend is on Black River in present-day Wayne County. The presence of many Wayne County area deeds is particularly valuable in view of the near-total loss of Wayne County records in two courthouse fires prior to 1900.

References

Goodspeed Publishing Company. 1888. History of Southeast Missouri. Goodspeed Publishing Co., Chicago, Ill. [Reissued 1990 by Southern Historical Press, Greenville, South Carolina.]

Greenwood, Val D. 2017. The researcher's guide to American genealogy. 4th edition. Genealogical Publishing Co., Baltimore, Maryland.

Hast, Adele, and John H. Long. 1984. Historical atlas and chronology of county boundaries, 1788-1980. Vol. 4. Iowa, Missouri. Hermon Dunlap Smith Center for the History of Cartography, The Newberry Library. G. K. Hall & Co., Boston, Mass.

Houck, Louis. 1908. A history of Missouri. Vol. II. R. R. Donnelley & Sons Co., Chicago, Ill.

Luebking, Sandra H. 2006. Land records. Pages 241-288 *in* Loretto D. Szucs, and Sandra H. Luebking, editors. The source--a guidebook of American genealogy, 3rd edition. Ancestry, Inc., Salt Lake City, Utah.

McAllister, Anne W., and Kathy G. Sullivan. 1988. Lincoln County, North Carolina Court of Pleas and Quarter Sessions July 1796-January 1805. McAllister-Sullivan, Lenoir, N. Car.

McMullin, Philip W. 1993. Grassroots of America. Southern Historical Press, Greenville, S. Car.

Peoples, Minnie K. 1976. Definitions of real estate terms. North Carolina Genealogical Journal 2(1):34-37.

Thorndale, William, and William Dollarhide. 1987. Map guide to the U.S. federal censuses, 1790-1920. Genealogical Publishing Co., Baltimore, Md.

Acknowledgments: I owe debts of gratitude to a number of people for making this book possible. First, a special thanks to the late Jean Adams for graciously giving me the go-ahead to supersede her index book on early Cape Girardeau County deeds, and for sharing her long experience in Cape Girardeau County genealogy by proofreading the names. L. Havelock Jackson translated the portions of two deeds recorded in Spanish. The staff of the Cape Girardeau County Recorder's Office and Ms. Janet Robert, Recorder, were always helpful and cooperative in allowing access to records. Finally, I thank Hope and Chris Eddleman for being so patient while we were busily engaged in reading old script on the microfilm during many an evening.

Plats Appearing in the Deed Books

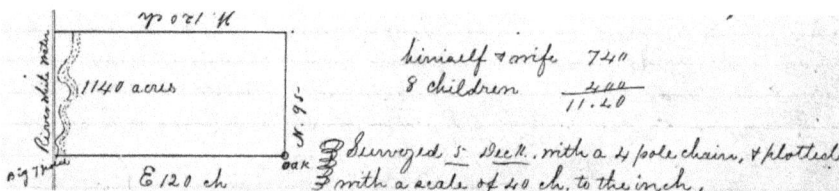

Figure 1. Plat of land grant of Adenston Rogers (Book AB: 83, Deed Abstract No. 128), surveyed 28 February 1806.

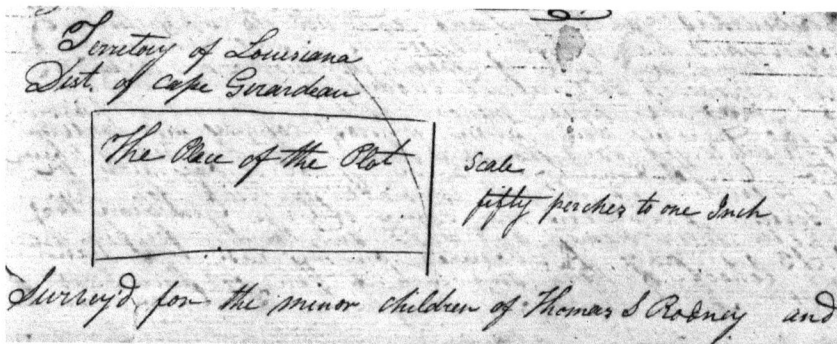

Figure 2. Plat of land surveyed for the minor children of Thomas S. Rodney (Book C: 273, Deed Abstract No. 512), surveyed 8-9 March 1811.

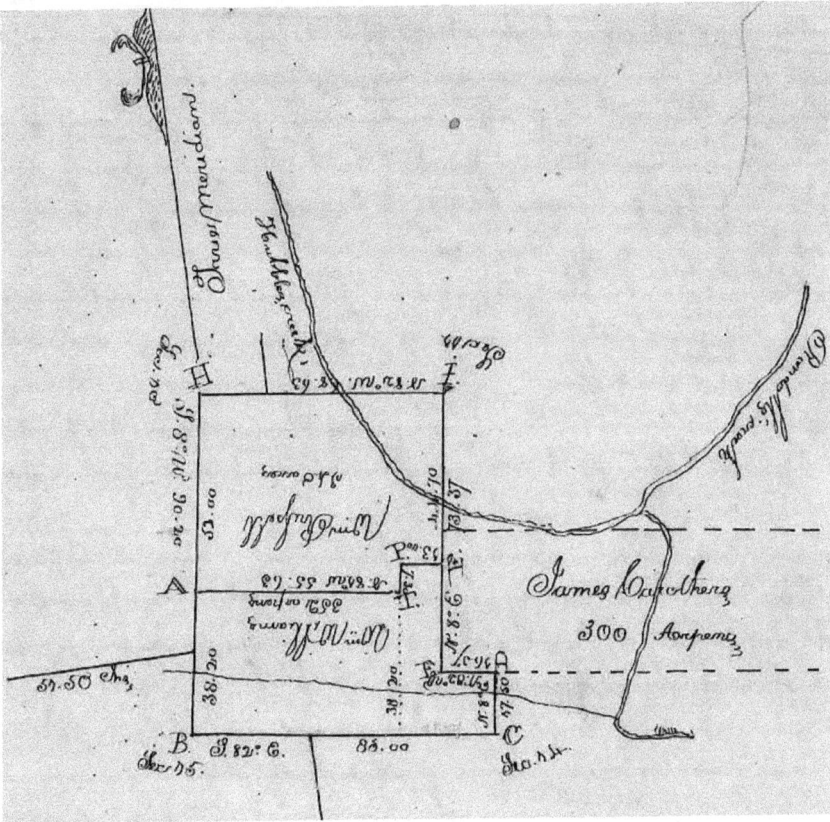

Figure 3. Plat of the land partition of William S. Russell and William Williams near the junction of Hubble and Randol creeks (Deed Book F: 224, Deed Abstract No. 1996) made 18 March 1822.

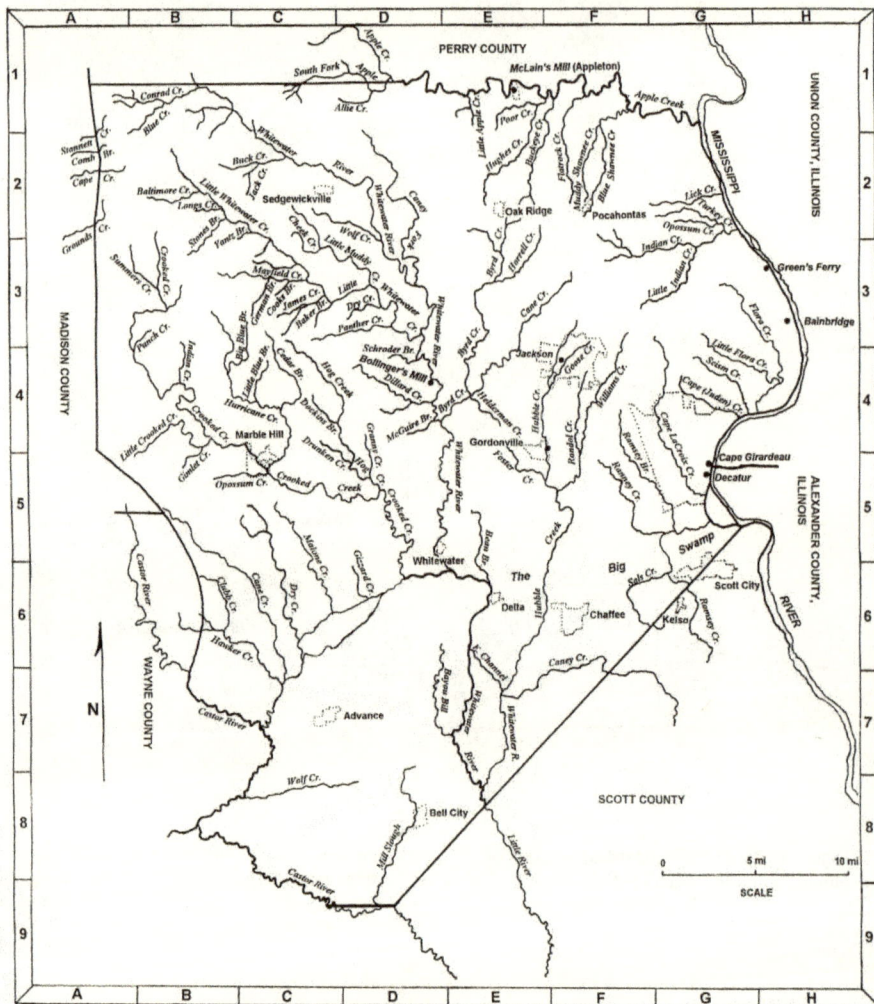

Map of the Cape Girardeau County area in 1826, showing boundaries at that time.

Index to Map of Cape Girardeau County in 1826

A
Allie Creek, D1
Advance, C7
Alexander County, Illinois, H5
Allie Creek, D1
Apple Creek, D1, E1, F1, G1
Appleton, E1

B
Bainbridge, G3
Baker Branch, C3
Baltimore Creek, B2
Bayou Bill, D7
Bean Branch, E5, E6
Bell City, D7
Big Blue Branch, C3, C4
Big Swamp, The, F5, F6, G5, G6
Blue Creek, B1
Blue Shawnee Creek, F2
Bollinger's Mill, D4
Buck Creek, C2
Buckeye Creek, E2, F1
Byrd Creek, E2, E3, E4

C
Cane Creek (Bollinger), B5, B6, C6
Cane Creek (Cape Girardeau), E3,E4, F3
Caney Creek, E7, F6, F7, G7
Caney Fork, D2, D3
Cape Creek (Bollinger), A2
Cape Creek (Cape Girardeau), G4
Cape Girardeau, G4, G5
Cape LaCroix Creek, G4, G5
Castor River, A5, A6, B5, B6, B7, B8, C7, C8, C9, D8
Cedar Branch, C4
Chaffee, F6
Cheek Creek, C2, C3
Clubb Creek, B6
Combs Branch, A2
Commerce, H6
Conrad Creek, B1

Cooks Branch, C3
Crooked Creek, B3, B4, C5, D5, D6

D
Decatur, G5
Delta, E6
Dillard Creek, D4
Dockins Branch, C4
Drunken Creek, C4, D5
Dry Creek (North), D3
Dry Creek (South), C5, C6

E
E. Channel Whitewater River, E6, E7

F
Flatrock Creek, F1, F2
Flora Creek, G3, H3, H4
Foster Creek, E5

G
German Branch, C3
Gimlet Creek, B5
Gizzard Creek, D6
Goose Creek, F4
Gordonville, E4
Granny Creek, D4, D5
Green's Ferry, G3
Grounds Creek, A2

H
Hawker Creek, B6, C6
Helderman Creek, E4
Hog Creek, C4, D4, D5
Horrell Creek, E3
Hubble Creek, E4, E6, E7, F4, F5
Hughes Creek, E2
Hurricane Creek, B3, B4, C4

I
Indian Creek (Bollinger), B4
Indian Creek (Cape Girardeau), F3, G3

J
Jack Creek, C2
Jackson, F4
James Creek, C3
Juden Creek, G4

K
Kelso, G6

L
Lick Creek, G2
Little Apple Creek, E1
Little Blue Branch, C4
Little Blue Creek
Little Crooked Creek, B4
Little Flora Creek, G4, H4
Little Indian Creek, G3
Little Muddy Creek, D3
Little River, E8, E9
Little Whitewater Creek, B2, C2, C3, D3
Longs Creek, B2

M
Madison County, A4
Malone Creek, C5, C6
Marble Hill, C4, C5
Mayfield Creek, C3
McGuire Branch, D4
McLain's Mill, E1
Mill Slough, D7, D8
Mississippi River, G1, G2, G4, G5, H3, H4, H5, H6, H7, H8
Muddy Shawnee Creek, F2

O
Oak Ridge, E2
Opossum Creek (Cape Girardeau), G2
Opossum Creek (Bollinger), B5, C5

P
Panther Creek, C3, D3
Perry County, E1
Pocahontas, F2
Poor Creek, E1
Punch Creek, B3

R
Ramsey Branch, F4, F5, G5
Ramsey Creek, G6
Randol Creek, F4, F5
Ranney Creek, F5

S
Sals Creek, F6, G6

Schroder Branch, D4
Scism Creek, G4
Scott City, G6
Scott County
Sedgewickville, C2
Shawnee Creek, F1
South Fork Apple Creek,
C1, D1
Stannett Creek, A1, A2
Stoddard County
Stones Branch, B2
Summers Creek, A3, B3

T
Turkey Creek, G2

U
Union County, Illinois,
H2

W
Wayne County, B7
Whitewater, D5
Whitewater River, C1,
C2, D2, D3, D4, D5, E4,
E5, E6, E7
Williams Creek, F4
Wolf Creek (North), C2,
D2
Wolf Creek (South), C8

Y
Yantz Branch, C2

1. Page 1. 2 Sep 1804. Benjamin **HARTGRAVE** to Peter **FRANKS**. For the sum of $156, a certain improvement where sd **HARTGRAVE** now lives. Signed Benjamin **HARTGRAVE**. Wit Jmes. (x) **MURPHY**, William **PAGE**. Title is assigned to Joseph **WALLER** on 20 Feb 1805. Signed Peter **FRANKS**. Test George **HENDERSON**, Christopher **HAYS**, Edw. F. **BOND**, Recr.. Rec 14 Jun 1805.

2. Page 1. 22 Feb 1805. Peter **FRANKS** to Joseph **WALLER**. For the sum of $__, 240 acres, more or less, being his improvement, entered in Louis **LORIMIER's** office in Feb 1802. Signed Peter **FRANKS**. Test Geo. **HENDERSON**, Christ. **HAYS**, U. S. Justice. Title is assigned to John **HARBISON** on 11 Jun 1805. Signed Joseph (x) **WALLER**. Wit Joseph M. **McFERRON**. Rec 14 Jun 1805.

3. Page 2. 22 Feb 1805. Andrew **FRANKS** to Joseph **WALLER**. For the sum of $__, the balance due him by the Spanish Government and granted to him by Louis **LORIMIER**, Commandant of Cape Girardeau. Signed Andrew (x) **FRANKS**. Test. Geo. **HENDERSON**, Christ. **HAYS**. Title is assigned to Jno. **HARBISON** for value received on 10 Jun 1805 (written on back of the deed). Signed Joseph (x) **WALLER**. Wit Joseph **McFERRON**. Rec 4 Jun 1805.

4. Page 3. 29 Mar [1802]. Alexander **ANDREW** to John **McGEE**. For the sum of $14 for survey and $3 on sd **ANDREW's** account with Louis **LORIMIER**, 240 acres on the waters of Stephen Byrd's Creek, adjoined on the W by Stephen **BYRD**, [S] by John **BYRD**, and N by James **BOYD**. Signed Alexander (C) **ANDREW**. Test Charles **McGEE**, Michael **QUINN**. Title assigned to Michael **QUINN** for value received on 6 Oct 1803. Signed Jno. **McGEE**. Test Hugh (__) **CONNELLY**, [illegible]. Rec 14 Jun 1805.

5. Page 3. 5 Oct 1804. Michael **QUINN**, merchant, to John **HAYS**, farmer. For a negro girl named **Mary** aged 5 years, and $100 in store goods; the land described in the preceding deed, granted to Alexander **ANDREW** by Zenon **TRUDO** Lent, Governor resident in St. Louis, on 5 Jan 1798. Sd grant describes land much farther down, adjoining Hubble's Mill, but sd **ANDREW** laid the grant on this land; being where sd **QUINN** now lives with Joseph and Mrs. **McGEE**. Sd **QUINN** guarantees the land against claims made by John **McGEE**, Joseph **McGEE**, or Sarah **McGEE**, wife of Jno.

McGEE. Signed Michael **QUINN**. Wit Geo. **HENDERSON**, Edwd. F. **BOND**, Recr., Christ. **HAYS**. Rec 14 Jun 1805.

6. Page 5. 1 Oct 1804. Elijah **WHITTAKER**, planter, to John **HAYS**. For one bay horse; 120 acres, being part of a tract of 500 arpens where he now lives and has improved, granted to sd **WHITTAKER** for himself and his family by the Spanish government, that he settled in 1800, beginning about the middle part of the woods between a little spring. The sd tract was granted as 250 acres for him and his wife, and 250 arpens for his five children, three girls and two sons. Signed Elijah (x) **WHITTAKER**. Wit Geo. **HENDERSON**, Elizabeth **NEELY**, Adam **LINDNER**. Rec 14 Jun 1805.

7. Page 6. 6 Jan 1805. Moses **BURNET** of the Ark. Dist. to Thomas W. **WATERS**. Power of attorney to ask, demand, and sue for damages and to recover 11 head of horses, mares, and colts taken by Lewis **LORIMIER**. Signed Moses (x) **BURNET**. Wit James **CURRIN**, John **LOYD**. Thos. **BALLEW** swears to **CURRIN** and **LOYD**. Rec 18 Jun 1805.

8. Page 6. 6 Apr 1805. Hezekiah **DICKSON** to John **GUETHING**. For the sum of $400, 300 arpens, being his head right from the Spanish government and joined by Jonathan **FORMAN**, William **HILL**, Charles **FALLENASH**, and James **ARREL**. His brother Lewis **DICKSON** serves as security. Signed Hezh. **DICKSON**, Lewis **DICKSON**. Wit B. **COUSINS** by Polite **MARDTE**. Rec 18 Jun 1805.

9. Page 7. 12 May 1804. William **DEAKINS** of New Madrid, Upper La. to Andrew **RAMSEY** senr. For the sum of $200, 250 arpens, more or less, joining Jonathan **FORMAN**, James **ARRELL**, Henry **SHARADIN**, and John **GUETHING**. Signed William **DEAKINS**. Wit Wm. **SMITH**, Enos **HANNAH**. Title is assigned to William **DAUGHERTY** for value received on 2 May 1803. Signed Andrew **RAMSEY**. Wit B. **COUSINS**, R. **WORTHINGTON**, J. C. **HARBISON**. Rec 18 Jun 1805.

10. Page 8. 14 Jun 1804. Samuel **BRADLEY** to Andrew **RAMSEY** senr. For the sum of $250, 300 arpens on the N side of the big swamp joining Solomon **THORN's** concession. Signed Saml. **BRADLEY**. Wit Morgan **BYRNS**, David **DONNARD**. Rec 18 Jun 1805.

11. Page 8. 14 May 1804. Solomon **THORN** to Andrew **RAMSEY**. For the sum of $220, 240 arpens, more or less, N of the Big Swamp, bounded on the W by Samuel **BRADLEY's** concession, E by a tract surveyed for Mary **FITZ GIBBONS**. Signed Solomon **THORN**. Wit Morgan **BYRN**, David **DONNARD**. Rec 18 Jun 1805.

12. Page 9. 3 Apr 1804. Timothy **CONNELLY** to Morgan **BYRNS**. For the sum of $400, payable by 15 Dec next, $100 in silver specie and $300 in pork, two tracts; 240 arpens, more or less, where he now resides, bounded on the W by Alexander **GUIBONY's** concession and E by a tract formerly surveyed for William **MOREFOOT**, now occupied by Samuel **BRADLEY**; and 150 arpens to the S and adjoining the first tract, that was allowed him by the Spanish Government for military and other public services. Signed Timothy **CONNELLY**. Wit B. **COUSINS**, Moses **BYRNE**. Rec 18 Jun 1805.

13. Page 10. 24 Apr 1801. Jonathan **DITCH** to John **GUETHING**. For the sum of $560, bond to convey 240 acres, W of and joining Samuel **TIPTON** and Willm. **BONER**, which is mortgaged to sd **GUETHING** for $281. Signed Jonathan **DITCH**. Wit B. **COUSIN**, timoin. Title is assigned to Andrew **RAMSEY** Senr for value received on 29 Apr 1805. Signed John **GUETHING**. Test B. **COUSINS**. Rec 18 Jun 1805.

14. Page 11. 5 Jan 1804. Daniel **ASHEMBRANER** to Frederic **LIMBAUCH** senr. For the sum of $25 Spanish, in silver coin, ___ acres on both sides of a branch of Little White River; joining the land of Daniel and Phillip **BOLLINGER**, Widow **SLOMGGER(?)**, Jeremiah **BONIG**, and vacant land. Signed Daniel (x) **ASHEMBRANER**. Wit Daniel **BOLLINGER**, Davald (x) **CRIZE**. Rec 18 Jun 1805.

15. Page 11. 30 Dec 1805. Wm. **JACKSON** to John **BYRD**. Transfer of his survey adjoining Wm. **BYRD**. Signed Wm. **JACKSON**. Wit B. **COZEN**. Rec 18 Jun 1805.

16. Page 11. 22 Jul 1805. John **HAYS'** ear mark is recorded as right ear cropped with one hole in it, and an under bit in the left ear. Signed Robert **GREEN** (JP). Rec 22 Jul 1805.

17. Page 12. 22 Jul 1805. Robert **GREEN's** ear mark is one crop and one under bit in the right

ear, and one over bit in the left ear. Signed Robert **GREEN**. Wit Ewd. F. **BOND**, Recr. Rec 22 Jul 1805.

18. Page 12. 12 May 1804. Edward **ROBERTSON** of this district, but actually living in New Madrid, to Andrew **RAMSEY** senr. For the sum of 1030 piastres, mortgage on 480 arpents of land; sd **ROBERTSON** owes the debt to sd **RAMSEY**. Signed Edw. (ER) **ROBERSON**. Wit John **GUETHING**, William **DEEKINS**, B. **COUSINS**. Rec 18 Jun 1805. [IN FRENCH]

19. Page 12. [no date] Andre **RAMSEY** Sr to Edward **ROBERSON**. Receipt of one 169 gallon still and another 83 gallon still, to make together 252 gallons at 1 ½ piastres per gallon; two black slaves for 600 piastres; a cow and calf for 30 piastres and 22 piastres; and a few diverse items; totaling 1030 piastres that sd **ROBERSON** owes **RAMSEY**. **ROBERSON** has not paid the loan made 24 Sep 1799 due 1 Jan 1801, so he forfeits the land described in the preceding deed (AB:12). Signed Edouard (ER) **ROBERSON**. Wit B. **COUSIN**, Andrew **RAMSEY** Jnr, L. **LORIMIER**. Rec 18 Jun 1805. [IN FRENCH]

20. Page 13. 8 Dec 1802. Daniel O **DUGGAN** to Edouard **ROBERSON** of New Madrid. For the sum of 300 piastres in a promissory note payable next Christmas, a plantation seven miles W of Cape Girardeau, bordered on the N by Joseph **WALLER** and John **ABERNATHY**, S by Samuel **RANDOL** son of Enos, W by Enos **RANDOLL**, and E by 300 arpens of vacant ground; being the same granted to sd **DUGGAN** on 1 Apr 1798 by Don Zenon **TRUDEAU**, Chief Commandant of Upper Louisiana, and surveyed 22 Apr 1798. Signed Daniel **DUGGAN**. Wit P. **ROCHEBLANE**, Hippolite **MAROT**, L. **LORIMIER**. Title is assigned to Medad **RANDOLL** for value received on 1 Jan 1804. Signed Edouard (ER) **ROBERSON**. Wit B. **COUSINS**, Jeremiah **THOMPSON**. Rec 18 Jun 1805. [IN FRENCH]

21. Page 15. 8 Dec 1802. Daniel O **DUGGAN** to Bartholemy **COUSINS**. Power of attorney to transfer 300 arpens that sd O **DUGGAN** sold to Edouard **ROBERSON**. Sd **DUGGAN** has not yet received title to the property and plans to leave the area. Signed Daniel **DUGGAN**. Wit P. **ROCHEBLANE**, Hippolite **MAROT**, L. **LORIMIER**. Rec 18 Jun 1805. [IN FRENCH]

22. Page 16. 6 May 1801. William **BONER** to Peirre **GODAIRE**. For the sum of $__, 60 arpens S of and joining sd **BONAR**, on which is a spring to which he reserves for himself and his descendants right of access in perpetuity. William **BONER** agrees to pay Peirre **GODAIRE** 500 piastres. Signed William (M) **BONAR**. Wit L. **LORIMIER**, Commandant. Rec 18 Jun 1805. [IN FRENCH]

23. Page 16. 25 Oct 1803. Benjamin **HARTGROVE** to Joseph **WALLER**. For the sum of $200, 500 acres where he now lives, being his head right; bounded by the surveys of John **RAMSEY**, Abraham **BIRD**, Mathew **HUBLE**, and Samuel **STRAUTHER**. Signed Benjamin **HARTGROVE**. Wit B. **COUSINS**, Geo. **DULCAEL**(?). Rec 27 Jun 1805.

24. Page 17. 25 Oct 1803. Same to James **BOYD**. Power of attorney to make a deed of conveyance for the land described in the preceding deed (AB:16) to Joseph **WALLER**, if a deed can be obtained. Signed Benjamin Hargroves. Wit B. **COUSINS**, L. **LORIMIER**, Commandant. Rec 27 Jun 1805.

25. Page 17. 4 Jul 1805. Joseph **WALLER**'s ear mark is one crop and one slit in the right ear, a half crop in the underside of the left ear. Signed Joseph ( ) **WALLER**. Test Edwd. F. **BOND**. Rec 21 Jul 1805.

26. Page 17. 18 Oct 1803. Joseph **WORTHINGTON** to William **STROTHER**. For the sum of $165, 278 arpens, more or less, to the E of Matthew **HUBBLE**, N of Samuel **STROTHER**, W of Simion **KENYON**, and S of Joseph **THOMPSON** and Jno. **RANDOLL**. Sd **WORTHINGTON** grants sd **STROTHER** power of attorney to get a formal deed, which has not been obtained. Signed Jos. **WORTHINGTON**. Wit B. **COUSINS**, Saml. **BRADLEY**. Title is assigned to John **HAYS** for value received on 13 Nov 1803. Signed Wm. **STROTHER**. Test. J. **BOYD**, Robt. **GREEN**. Rec 23 Jul 1805.

27. Page 18. 30 Dec 1801. Jno. **STOCKER** to Jno. **GIBBONEY**. For the sum of 350 piastres, mortgage on 350 arpens about 6 miles from Cape Girardeau, joining the grant of Abranda **GIBBONEY**. Sd **STOCKER** owes sd **GIBONEY** the debt payable in one year. Sd **STOCKER** may not sell anything for one year, and sd **GIBBONEY** may move onto the property and use the property. In the event sd **STOCKER** dies or leaves the area, Don Louis **LORIMIER** or Barthem **COUSINS** have power of attorney to deliver the title of land. Signed Jonathan **STOCKER**. Wit Barthme. **COUSIN**, surveyor, L. **LORIMIER** Jr., L. **LORIMIER**, commandant. Rec 18 Jun 1805. [IN FRENCH]

28. Page 20. 9 Apr 1805. Jonathan **FOREMAN** to Benjamin **TENNEL**. For the sum of $1, 1300 acres, more or less, on Hubble's Creek in three tracts; 700 acres, more or less, bounded by Jassee **CAIN**, etc.; and two tracts estimated at 540 acres, adjoining each other and improved by John **GUILDER** and **CAMPBELL** under the proclamation of his Catholic majesty for building a mill. Signed Jona. **FOREMAN**. Wit Edward (x) **HALE**, Julius **WICKER**. Test Robt. **GREEN**. Rec 9 Aug 1805.

29. Page 20. 28 Oct 1799. Charles **FALLENASH** to Dr. Chs Dehault **DELASUS**, Lieut. Col. & Gov of Upper Lousiana. Petition for land grant. Charles **FALLENASH** C. R. and father of a family, who crossed to this side of the river to become a subject of his Majesty, has with the agreement of **LORIMIER** , Commandant at Cape Girardeau, been placed provisionally on some land about 10 miles NW of Cape Girardeau. His family has three people: himself, his wife, and one child. Signed Charles **FALLENASH**. 31 Oct 1799. The land being requested belongs to the Crown, the person requesting the land appears deserving, and his family consists of himself, his wife and child. Signed L. **LORIMIER**. [SECTION IN SPANISH] 15 Dec 1799. The suppliant will be granted 250 arpens of level land as measured by the Royal Parisian system of linear measurement in accordance with the farmland in this province. The land bordered on the NW by lands owned by the Crown, S by the grant of Abraham **BYRD** and Santiago **MILLS**, and E by Jonathan **FOREMAN**. Rec 20 Feb 1802. Title is assigned to Edward **HALE** on 28 Mar 1804. Signed Charles ( ) **FALLENASH**. Wit Ben **GOODIN**, Rob **JONES**, Mary **ANDREW**. Rec 9 Aug 1805. [IN FRENCH AND SPANISH]

30. Page 22. 28 Mar 1804. Charles **FALLENASH** to Edward **HALE**. For the sum of $300, 250 acres Spanish measure, more or less, on Hubble's Creek, beginning on **FARMON**'s line. Signed Charles ( ) **FALLENASH**. Wit Ben **GOODIN**, Robert (x) **JONES**, Mary (x) **ANDREW**. Rec 9 Aug 1805.

31. Page 22. 5 Apr 1803. Peter **GODAIRE** to William **ROSS**. For the sum of $200, 240 acres on the bank of the Mississippi River, bounded above by William **LAND**, below by sd **ROSS**. Sd **GODAIRE** has not received the patent from the intendant, and he agrees to provide a better right so as to not be accountable any further than to relinquish his right. Signed Peter (x) **GODER**. Wit M. **JONES** Junr, Timothy **CONNELLY**, Edmond **HOGAN**. Title is assigned to John and Robert **GIBBONY** for value received on 20 Sep 1804. Signed William **ROSS**. Wit B. **COUSIN**, Surveyor, Peter (x) **GODER**. Rec 13 Aug 1805.

32. Page 23. 15 Jan 1805. Mary **FITZGIBBONS** of Ste. Genevieve to Roland **MERIDITH**. For the sum of $50, 200 arpens on the N edge of the Big Swamp, granted to her by the Spanish Government in 1798 and surveyed in 1799; bounded on the W by Solomon **THORN**. Signed Mary (x) **FITZGIBBONS**. Wit John **HAWKINS**, JP in Ste. Genevieve Dist., John **BURGET**, Arthur **MURPHY**. Rec 30 Sep 1805.

33. Page 24. 28 Feb 1805. Roland **MERIDITH** to George **HAYS**. Assignment of 200 acres as described in the preceding deed (AB:23). Signed Roland **MEREDETH**. Wit Geo. **HENDERSON**, John **HAYS**, Christr. **HAYS**, U. S. Justice. Rec 30 Sep 1805.

34. Page 24. 28 Feb 1805. Same to same. For the sum of $196 ½, bond to provide a warranty deed for 200 acres (AB:23). Signed Roland **MEREDITH**. Test Geo. **HENDERSON**, Jno. **HAYS**, Christr. **HAYS**. Rec 30 Sep 1805.

35. Page 25. 2 Oct 1799. Joseph **CHEVALIERS** to Carlos Dehault **DELASSUS**. Petition for land grant. Joseph **CHEVALIERS**, Jr. wants to build a dwelling and raise animals and requests a grant of 400 arpens of land. The suppliant hopes to receive this favor considering the good reputation of his father in this area and his faithful devotion to His Majesty, and wishes to live as a farmer. Made at La Nouvelle Bourbon. Signed Joseph (K) **CHEVALIER**. We, commandant **SOUGNE** of the Post of Nouvelle Bourbon certify to the Lt Gov of Upper Louisiana that the suppliant is deserving of receiving the land grant because of the good reputation and honesty of his family in the part of this Colony. He has been raised to be a farmer since his childhood here in La Nouvelle Bourbon. 6 Oct 1799. Don **DELASSUS DE LUZIENE**. [SECTION IN SPANISH] Carlos Dehault **DELASSUS** supports the supliant's request for a land grant. Signed Joseph (K) **CHEVALIER**. Rec 11 Jul 1805. Grant is transferred to Gabriel **NICOL** by exchange at St.

Michell on 21 Jan 1805. Signed Andre(X) **CHEVALLIER**. Title is assigned to John **HAYS** for $400. Signed Gabriel **NICOL**. Wit P. **CHEVALIER**, John __**CURTY**. Rec 22 Jul 1805. [IN FRENCH AND SPANISH]

36. Page 26. 9 Sep 1803. Jeptha **CORNELIUS** to Joseph **YOUNG**. For one dark roan mare, one year old last spring, __ acres above Stephen **BIRD**; to be transferred by 1 Apr. Signed Jeptha **CORNELIUS**, Josep **YOUNG**. Wit Stephn. **BYRD**, Jonathan **RICE**, Austin **YOUNG**, Phillip **YOUNG**. Rec 16 Oct 1805.

37. Page 26. 21 May 1804. Joseph **YOUNG** to Henry **HOWARD**. For the sum of $150, the land described in the preceding deed (AB:26), to be delivered on payment by 21 May. Signed Joseph **YOUNG** (also for receipt of $105 on 14 Sep, $20 on 16 Oct 1805, and in full on 16 Oct 1805), Henry **HOWARD**. Test Stephen **BYRD**, Solomon **THORN**. Rec 16 Oct 1805.

38. Page 27. 9 May 1805. Jonathan **HUBBLE**, son of Ithamar **HUBBLE**, to John **McCARTY**. For the sum of $150, all his and his family's right to land on the W side of White Water, which he claimed as his head right, settled, and improved in Jul 1803. Signed Jonathan (x) **HUBBLE**, son of Ithamer **HUBBLE**. Test John **THOMPSON**, Danl. **FRAZIER**; Christr. **HAYS** (JCCP). Rec 21 Oct 1805.

39. Page 27. 8 May 1805. Jonathan **HUBBLE** Junr to same. For the sum of $1000, bond to execute deed for land on White Water whereon he now lives, with his improvement, made in Jul 1803 by permission of Commandant **LORIMIER**, and head right; with possession to occur on 10 Dec next. Signed Jonn. (x) **HUBBLE** Junr. Test John **THOMPSON**, Christr. **HAYS** (JCCP). Rec 21 Oct 1805.

40. Page 28. 9 May 1805. John **SHIELDS** to John **THOMPSON**. For the sum of $20, a certain improvement lying between **GIBBONEE** and Tarrence **DYAL**, which sd **SHIELDS** made in Sep 1802. Signed John **SHIELDS**. Test John **McCARTY**, Christr. **HAYS** (JCCP). Rec 21 Oct 1805.

41. Page 29. 1 Feb 1804. William **STROTHER** of New Burboun Dist., Upper La., to David **DOWNARD**. For the sum of $120, 240 acres on Cane Creek, adjoining Jona. **FOREMAN**, Jno. **BOYD**, and others. Sd **STROTHER** is to pay the surveying fees. Signed Willim. **STROTHER**. Test John **McCARTY**, John **THOMPSON**, Christr. **HAYS** (JCCP). David

DOWNARD assigns title to John **McCARTY** on 3 Feb 1804. Signed David **DOWNARD**. Test Jno. **HAYS**. B. **COUSINS** certifies on 3 Jun 1804 that in Jan 1803, William **STROTHER** assumed the payment of surveyor's fees for a tract on Stephen Byrd's Creek granted to David **ANDREWS**, sd **ANDREWS** having sold his claim to sd **STROTHER**. Signed B. **COUSINS**. Rec 21 Oct 1805.

42. Page 30. 28 Jan 1805. James **ERLES** to John **BIRD**. For the sum of $58, 200 acres on White Water joining Peter **BLEW** on the S. Signed James **ARRELS**. Wit. Jas. **BOYD**, Jonathan **BUIS**, Thos. **MORGAN**, Jas. **COOPER**. Rec 23 Oct 1805.

43. Page 30. 18 Feb 1805. Hugh **CONNELLY** to John **BYRD**. For the sum of $800, 450 acres where he now lives. Signed Hugh (o) **CONNELLY**. Test James **COOPER**, Abraham **BYRD**, Joseph **YOUNG**. Rec 23 Oct 1805.

44. Page 30. 16 Jan 1805. James **COOPERS** to same. For the sum of $500, 350 acres, where he now lives and that he entered in the Spanish Land Office. Signed James **COOPERS**. Wit Abraham **BYRD**, Jno. **ZELIFROW**, Danl. **SULLIVAN**. Rec 23 Oct 1805.

45. Page 31. 15 Apr 1805. Samuel **DORSEY** to same. For the sum of $240, paid by one sorrel mare worth $150, one yoke of oxen worth $50, a cow and calf worth $12, and cash; 240 acres, more or less, lying on the road from William **DAUGHERTY**'s to sd **BYRD**; joined on the E by Jonathan **FOREMAN**, N by John **BOYD**, and W by B. **COUSUNG**. The consideration is due by (?) Jan next. Signed Samuel **DORSEY**. Test. James **WILKINSON**, John **SKEEN**. Rec 23 Oct 1805.

46. Page 31. 1 Nov 1804. William **JACKSON** to John and Stephen **BYRD**. For the sum of $91, 350 acres joining sd **BYRD** on the W and Josiah **LEE** on the N, granted to sd **JACKSON** for services rendered to the country and also being entitled to his draw of land as a Spanish subject. There is no competent title, so Stephen **BYRD** is to receive any confirmation of the grant and to convey the same to John **BYRD**. Signed William **JACKSON**. Test Saml. S. **KENNEDY**, Joseph **YOUNG**. Rec 23 Oct 1805.

47. Page 32. 23 Oct 1804. Josiah **LEE** to John **BYRD**. For the sum of $15.25, 200 acres, granted to sd **LEE** for his services, being the balance of his head right; beginning on his father's line five poles from sd **LEE**'s line. Signed Josiah **LEE**. Wit Joseph **YOUNG**, Jas. **COX**, Simion **KINON**, Henry **HATTER**. Rec 23 Oct 1805.

48. Page 32. 12 Apr 1802. Jacob **MYERS** and Kesiah, his wife, formerly the widow of Joseph **CRUTCHELOW**, to same. For the sum of $50, __ acres, being the improvement where sd **SCHUELOU** lived in his lifetime. Signed Jacob **MEYERS**, Kesiah (x) **MYERS**. Wit M. **JONES** Junr., Susannah **JONES**. Rec 23 Oct 1805.

49. Page 33. 2 Nov 1803. William **SMITH** to Joseph **WORTHINGTON**. For eight good second rate cows and calves, payable on 1 May next, ½ of 300 acres on Cane Creek along the road from [Cape Girardeau] to New Madrid about seven miles distant from Charles **FRIEND**'s plantation; being the same sold to him by Daniel **SEXTON**, to whom the entire 300 arpens was granted as his head right. Sd **SMITH** also obligates himself to purchase the other ½ of the 300 arpens for sd **WORTHINGTON**, and to have the tract surveyed and pay for any expense to secure a legal deed. Signed Wm. **SMITH**. Wit B. **COUSINS**, Saml. **BRADLEY**. Title is assigned to John **BYRD** on 22 Jul 1805. Signed Jos. **WORTHINGTON**. Test Joseph **YOUNG**, Samuel **PEW**. Rec 23 Oct 1805.

50. Page 34. 12 Jan 1805. Samuel J. **KENNEDY** to John **BYRD**. For the sum of $30, 400 acres beginning at the first narrows below where Kelley's Trace crosses Castor Creek; being his entry at the Spanish Land Office. Signed Saml. J. **KENNEDY**. Test Joseph **YOUNG**, Thomas **ARMSTRONG**. Rec 23 Oct 1805.

51. Page 34. 30 Mar 1805. Cornelius **EVERETT** to John **HAYS** and Jeremiah W. **STILL**. For the sum of £50, 250 acres which he has obtained from the Spanish Government. Signed Cornelius **EVERETT**. Wit Geo. **HENDERSON**, Jas. **BYRD**, Robert **GREEN**, David **GREEN**, Christr. **HAYS** (JCCP). Rec 23 Oct 1805.

52. Page 35. 7 Jul 1803. John **HAYS** to Samuel **DORSEY**. For the sum of $150 in good livestock, 245 acres adjoining John **McCARTY** on one side and Mr. **COURSANG** on the other. If sd parties shall not agree on the price of the livestock, then the assessment shall be left to two impartial judges. Signed John **HAYS**. Test John **McCARTY**, Robt. **HALL** (JCCP). Rec 23 Oct 1805.

53. Page 35. 22 Mar 1800. Joseph **CRITCHLOW** to John **HAYS**. For the sum of £10, the improvement where he now lives. John **HAYS** is to pay for surveying fees to Mr. **GOOSING**, and is receive the land by 1 May 1800. Signed Jo. **CHUTCHLAW**. Test Christr. **HAYS**, Henry **HAND**, Elizabeth **NEELY**. Sd **HAYS** is also to be allowed to work the place before 5 May. Signed J. **CRITCHLOW**. Wit Christr. **HAYS**, Elisabeth **NEELY**, Henry **HAND**, Robert **HALL** (JCCP). Rec 23 Oct 1805.

54. Page 36. 13 Aug 1803. Jacob **KELLEY** to John **McCARTY**. For the sum of $100, 550 acres on Byrd's Creek, adjoining sd **McCARTY** and B. **COUSIN**; being granted to him by the King of Spain. Signed Jacob **KELLEY**. Test John **THOMPSON**, John **HAYS**, Robt. **HALL** (JCCP). Rec 23 Oct 1805.

55. Page 36. 8 Jul 1804. David **McMURTREY** to Jessee **CAIN**. For the sum of $__, __ acres, being an improvement made by permission of the Commandant of the Dist., and lying between Jno. **GIBBONEY** and James **COX** senr. Signed David **McMURTREE**. Wit Lewis **LATHAM**, John **BOYD**, Enoch **SPINKS**, Christr. **HAYS** (JCCP). Title is assigned to David **DOWNARD** for value received on 4 Aug 1804. Signed Jessee **CAIN**. Test David **GREEN**, Nathan **McCARTY**. Wit Christr. **HAYS** (JCCP). Title is assigned to Jeremiah **THOMPSON** for value received on 12 Oct 1804. Signed David **DOWNARD**. Test John **THOMPSON**, Christr. **HAYS** (JCCP). Rec 23 Oct 1805.

56. Page 37. 6 Dec 1804. Same to Jeremiah **THOMPSON**. For the sum of $200, 300 arpens, more or less, between John **GUIBONEY** and James **COX**, being an improvement made by sd **McMURTREY** with the permission of the Commandant of the Dist. in fall 1802. Sd **THOMPSON** is to pay surveying and all other costs necessary to confirm title. Signed David **McMUTTREE**. Wit B. **COUSIN**, Robt. **HALE**, Chapman **HARRIS**. Title is assigned to William **MORRISON** for $300 on 7 May 1805. Signed Jeremiah **THOMPSON**. Wit Saml. **DORSEY**, Robt. **HALL** (JCCP). Rec 24 Oct 1805.

57. Page 38. 1 Oct 1804. Peter **BELLEW** to Jeremiah **CONWAY**. For the sum of $400, __ acres, being his head right and claim on the waters of White Water, joining land of Elijah **WELCH**. Signed Peter **BELLEW**. Wit Jas.

BOYD, Matt **HUBBLE**, Robt. **HALL**. Rec 25 Oct 1805.

58. Page 39. 8 Jan 1805. John **SMITH** to Jeremiah **THOMSON**. For the sum of $100, __ acres which he improved before 1803, adjoined on the N by Terrance **DEAL**, S by Jerry **SIMSON**, and W by John **JACOBS**. Signed John (x) **SMITH** (also signed for money received). Wit George **WELCH**, Saml. **DORSEY**. Title assigned to Abraham **BYRD** for value received on 19 Jun 1805. Signed Jerimiah **THOMSON**. Wit Dennis **SULLIVAN**, Saml. **BRADLEY**, Thomas **BALLEW** (JCCP). Rec 26 Oct 1805.

59. Page 40. 20 Oct 1801. David **ALLEN** to Benijah **LAUGHERTY**. For value received, assignment of his head right. Signed David **ALLING**. Test Siles **FLETCHER**. Rec 28 Oct 1805.

60. Page 40. 9 Jan 1804. Joseph **McGEE** of More Co., N. Car. to James **CURRIN**. Power of attorney to act for him in all cases, just the same as if he was when present himself in Cape Girardeau Dist., also to conduct his business E of the Mississippi River; that is, to open a road from the Ohio to the place he bought of William **SMITH** and establish a public ferry if convenient. Signed Joseph **McGEE**. Test William **ROSS**, Moses (x) **BURNETT**, Thos **BALLEW**. Rec 10 Dec 1805.

61. Page 40. 8 Nov 1805. Peter **WEAVER** to John **WEAVER**. For the sum of $400, 300 acres on the road leading from Jeremiah **THOMSON**'s to Cape Girardeau, about 1 ½ miles from sd **THOMSON**. Signed Peter (   ) **WEAVER**. Wit Jas. **BOYD**, Saml. **BRADLEY**, Jono. **FORMAN**, Christr. **HAYS** (JCCP). Rec 18 Dec 1805.

62. Page 41. 8 May 1805. Daniel **HUBBLE** to Doctr. Samuel **DORSEY**. For the sum of $125, __ acres on White Water that he improved before 20 Dec 1803. Signed Daniel (   ) **HUBBLE** (also for consideration received). Wit Wm. **MORRISON**, Horrace **AUSTIN**, Thos. **BALLEW** (JCCP). Rec 4 Jan 1806.

63. Page 42. 8 May 1805. Jonathan **HUBBLE** Junr. to same. For the sum of $200, __ acres on White Water, being his settlement right and that of his wife, one son, and two daughters, and which he improved before 20 Dec 1803. Signed Jonathan **HUBBLE** (and for cash received). Wit

Wm. **MORRISON**, Horace **AUSTIN**, Rufus **EASTON**, Judge of La. Terr.. Rec 4 Jan 1806.

64. Page 42. 2 Jun 1804. John **McCARTY** to same. For the sum of $500, bond to make a warranty deed within 12 months on 240 acres on Cain Creek adjoining Jonathan **FOREMAN**, John **BOYD**, and others. Signed John **McCARTY**. Wit Wm. **LOWERY**, John **THOMSON**, Thos. **BALLEW** (JCCP). Rec 4 Jan 1806.

65. Page 43. 8 May 1805. Horace **AUSTIN** to same. For the sum of $125, __ acres on White Water, being the same he improved before 20 Dec 1803. Signed Horace **AUSTIN** (and for money received). Wit Wm. **MORRISON**, Robert **HALL** (JCCP). Rec 31 Jan 1806.

66. Page 44. 14 Jun 1804. Translation of part of a list signed by Reason **BEMRIE**, then sindeck(?) at Tywapity, and a grant of lands granted by Mr. **PEREUX**, Commandant at New Madrid, dated 12 Jan 1802: Jessee **BOWDEN**, his wife, one boy, one girl, and one negro, 250 arpens. Signed Henry **PEROUX**, Commandant. The land is about ½ league from the Mississippi, joined by Widow Phe__ **JONES**, and vacant lands on three sides, fronting on King's Road. Signed Pierre Anto. **LAFORGE**. Title assigned to Danl. **MULLINS** for value received on 30 Mar 1805. Signed Jessee **BOWDEN**. Test Saml. **BRADLEY**, Ennas **HANNAH**. Title assigned to Capt. Stephen **BYRD** [for a sorrel horse named Taffee] on 12 Jul 1805. Signed Daniel (x) **MULLINS**. Test Saml. **BRADLEY**, James **SCOTT**. Rec 15 Feb 1805.

67. Page 44. 12 Jul 1805. Daniel **MULLINS** to Capt. Stephen **BYRD**. For the sum of $150 in Spanish milled dollars, bond to guarantee lawful title to the land described in the preceding deed (AB:44), should sd title not be obtained from the commission. Signed Stephen **BYRD**, Daniel (x) **MULLINS**. Wit Samul. **BRADLEY**, James **SCOTT**. Rec 15 Feb 1806.

68. Page 45. [1 Aug 1802.] Alexander **ANDREW** to William **MURPHY**. For __, his improvement and crop he made on the land adjoining John **McCARTY**. Signed Alexander (x) **ANDREW**. Test David **ANDREWS** (JCCP), Thos. **BALLEW**. Rec 17 Feb 1806.

69. Page 45. 11 Feb 1806. William **MURPHY** to John **McCARTY**. For the sum of $150, improvement made by Alexander **ANDREWS** in 1802, adjoining John **McCARTY**, James

BOYD, and others. Signed William **MURPHY**. Test Stephen **BYRD**, Wm. **DAUGHERTY**, Thos. **BALLEW**. Rec 17 Feb 1806.

70. Page 46. 2 Jun 1804. Doctr. Samuel **DORSEY** to same. For the sum of $500, bond to convey 240 acres on Byrd's Creek adjoining sd **McCARTY** and B. **COUSINS**, within 12 months. Signed Saml. **DORSEY**. Wit Wm. **LOWERZ**, Jno. **THOMSON**, Thos. **BALLEW** (JCCP). Rec 18 Feb 1806.

71. Page 46. No date. James **RANDOL** to John **DAUGHERTY**. For 50 gallons of whiskey, his right, title, claim, and interest for service done on an expedition under Leut. Col. Charles Dehault **LASURE** to New Madrid at the time the Indian was shot. The whiskey was delivered to him in a note on Andr. **RAMSEY** Senr., which note he received from sd **DAUGHERTY** as full pay from S. **DAUGHERTY**. If Bartholimew **COUSINS** will not survey the land, sd **RANDOL** agrees to return the note to John **DAUGHERTY**, and this obligation to be void. Signed James **RANDOL**. Wit Jas. **BOYD**, John **McCARTY**. Rec 18 Feb 1806.

72. Page 47. 19 Feb 1806. Josiah **LEE** to Anderson **NUNNERLY**, late of N. Car. For the sum of $350, __ acres on Byrd's Creek which he settled and improved before 20 Dec 1803; adjoined by Jno. **McCARTY**, George **CAVENDER**, and Josiah **LEE** Senr. Signed Josiah **LEE**. Wit Robt. **HALL** (JCCP), Saml. **DORSEY**. Rec 20 Feb 1806.

73. Page 47. 27 Jan 1806. Jesse **CAIN** to White **MATTACK**, merchant. For the sum of $500 in trade, except $50 in cash, 250 arpens, being part of his settlement right; bounded on the N by William **DEAKINS** and Jonathan **FOREMAN**, S by William **DAUGHERTY** and Robert **GREEN**, E by Andrew **RAMSEY** Senr. and W by Robert **GREEN**. Signed Jessee **CAIN**. Wit B. **COUSIN**, Louis **FOLLKEE**, Christr. **HAYS** (JCCP). Rec 6 Mar 1806.

74. Page 48. 5 Mar 1805. Alexander **BURTON** of Dutch Settlement, cordwainer, to Leonard **WELKER**. For the sum of $30, two tracts, 400 acres in the forks of two branches of Little White River, somewhat more than ½ mile above Michael **SHALE**; and 250 acres, more or less, being a grant received by sd **BURTON** five years earlier about 20 miles above where the River Ohio joins the Mississippi. Sd **BURTON** also promises to make 1000 rails of lawful size for the benefit of sd **WELKER** before he quits the land, and is to clear sd land and improvements until 1 Apr next, then to deliver sd land without protestation, hindrance, or trouble. Both parties bind themselves in the sum of $400, which sum to be obtained and recovered of them who break sd agreement. Signed Alexander **BURTON**, Leonard **WALKER**. Wit David (x) **BOLLINGER**, F. **LIMBAUGH** Senr. Rec 6 Mar 1806.

75. Page 49. 3 Jan 1806. Leonard **WALKER** to John **WIGHLE**. For the sum of $140, to be paid in two mares, one now on delivery and worth $70, the other worth at least $70 and to be delivered 1 Nov next, the land described in the preceding deed, with the agreement that sd **WALKER** will not answer for the grant on the Ohio and Mississippi, with further conditions that sd **WIGHLE** shall not neglect surveying of sd land. If the grant for the 400 acres shall not stand, then the mare to be returned and sd note abolished. Signed Leonard **WALKER**, John **WIGHLE**. Test Michael **LIMBAUGH**, Frederick **LIMBAUGH** Senr. Rec 6 Mar 1806.

76. Page 49. 21 Mar 1806. William **SMITH** to Daniel **SEXTON**, both of Tywapety Bottom. For the sum of $100, 10 French arpens on the Mississippi River in Tywopity Bottom as described: 3 arpens fronting on the river and ten arpens back; adjoining **SEXTON**'s land on the upper side, and known as Johnston's Lot. Signed Willm. **SMITH**. Wit John **BYRD**, Edwd. F. **BOND**. Rec 22 Mar 1806.

77. Page 50. 20 Jun 1803. Abrm. **BYRD** to Lemuel R. **CURREN** and Daniel **SEXTON**. Power of attorney to make a deed for 200 acres on the Mississippi River to James **CURREN**. Sd land adjoins Benj. **ROSE** above, and B. **COUSINS** below. Signed Abraham **BIRD**. Wit Robert **LANE**, Stephen (x) **QUINBY**, Thos **BALLEW** (JCCP). Rec 22 Mar 1806.

78. Page 51. 21 Mar 1806. Edwd. F. **BOND** to negro **Mathew**, formerly of Maryland. For diverse good causes, his manumission. Signed Edwd. F. **BOND**. Wit Christr. **HAYS** (JCCP), John **BYRD**. Rec 22 Mar 1806.

79. Page 51. 10 Aug 1804. Benjamin **ROSE** to Daniel **SEXTON**. Power of attorney to act and do for him regarding his land on the banks of the Mississippi River adjoining Lemuel **CHENEY** above, and Abraham **BYRD** below, in Tywappety Bottom; granted by Louis **LORIMIER** and returned to Gov. **TRUDO**.

Signed Benjamin **ROSE**. Test James **CURREN**, Thos. L. **NARRIS**. Rec 25 Mar 1806.

80. Page 52. 28 May 1804. Solomon **THORN** to Thomas **FULTON**. For an obligation from Waters & Hall for 500 gallons of whiskey, bond to pay $274 as follows: $110 2/3 in silver specie and $163 1/3 in fur. Stephen **BYRD** holds the surety bearing the date of the 24th instant. Signed Solomon **THORN**. Wit B. **COUSIN**, Timoin. Sd **FULTON** shall not make use of the surety until sd **THORN** fails to pay the note. Signed Stephen **BYRD**, Solomon **THORN**, Thomas **FULTON**. Test B. **COUSIN**. Rec 31 Mar 1806.

81. Page 52. 24 May 1804. **WATERS & HALL** to Solomon **THORN**. Agreement to pay 500 gallons of whiskey, 200 by next Mar, 200 by Mar following, and 100 by 1 Jan next; but should they have to pay to Louis **LORIMIER** any money due by sd **THORN**, then credit will be given on this note. Signed **WATERS & HALL**. Test Jack **REID**. [No recording date given.]

82. Page 52. 3 Apr 1806. Jeremiah **THOMSON** to John **THOMSON**. For the sum of $500, one negro woman named **Lydia** and two children, **Pherebe**, a girl, and **Andrew**, a boy. Signed Jeremiah **THOMSON**. Wit Edwd. F. **BOND**, Betsey **GIBSON**. Rec 3 Apr 1806.

83. Page 53. 19 Oct 1805. Henry **LAUSON** to Thomas W. **WATERS** & Co. Bill of sale for 45 head of hogs that Stephen **JONES** was to deliver to him and Zadock **McLURE**, to be paid 12 Aug past. If sd **JONES** does not deliver, then sd **WATERS** & Co. may bring suit in sd **LAUSON**'s name to recover the money. Signed Henry **LAUSON**. Test. R. **WORTHINGTON**, John **BYRD**. Rec 16 Apr 1806.

84. Page 53. 10 Dec 1805. Allen **McKINZIE** to Reuben **NORMAN**. For the sum of $25, 100 acres, being a grant to him from the Spanish Government, and entered in Don Louis **LORIMIER**'s books in 1802. Signed Allen **McKINSIE**. Wit Alexander **SUMMERS**, Mary (x) **WELCH**. Rec 19 Apr 1806.

85. Page 54. 6 Dec 1805. Jacob **FOSTER** to same. For the sum of $30, 150 acres granted to him by the Spanish Government and entered in Don Louis **LORIMIER**'s book in 1802. Signed Jacob (x) **FOSTER**. Wit Jeremiah **THOMSON**, John **LATHEM**. Rec 19 Apr 1806.

86. Page 54. 6 May 1806. Jeremiah **THOMSON** to Thomas **ENGLISH**. For the sum of $1, 600 arpens/acres, being the residue of 800 arpens/acres after 200 acres/arpens was sold to John **THOMSON**; bounded on the NE by Samuel **RANDALL** Jr., W by Andrew **FRANKS**, and S by **RENRON** and **COX**; being the same surveyed for Jeremiah **THOMSON** on 20 Apr 1798 by B. **COUSIN**. Signed J. **THOMSON**. Wit John **McCARTY**, Benja. **TENNILLE**, Robt. **HALL** (JCCP). Rec 6 Jun 1806.

87. Page 55. 22 Mar 1806. Lemuel **CHANEY** to Andrew **RAMSEY** Jur. For the sum of $500, mortgage on 240 arpens in Tywappity Bottom on the Mississippi River; joined on the N by Danl. **SEXTON**, S by James **BRADLEY**. Sd **CHANEY** owes a debt to sd **RAMSEY**. Signed Lemuel **CHENEY**. Wit Jno. C. **HARBINSON**, Uri **BROOKS**, Simeon **BLUNDRIDGE**, Delppeur **BROOKS**, Robt. **HALL** (JCCP). Rec 19 Jun 1806.

88. Page 56. 28 Dec 1805. Charles **BRADLEY** to Morgan **BYRNE**. For the sum of $150 to be paid as one mare valued at $100, $10 cash, and $40 in merchandise, payable on demand; 300 acres, being part of his settlement right. Sd **BRADLEY** agrees to lay off the land. Signed Charles **BRADLEY**, Morgan **BYRNE**. Wit Saml. **BRADLEY**, Luke **BYRNE**, Christ. **HAYS** (JCCP). Rec 24 Jun 1806.

89. Page 56. 22 Mar 1806. Samuel **BRADLEY** to same. For the sum of $300, __ acres on Bonar's Creek, where the mouth of Wever's spring branch empties into sd creek; being called his Bargain Tract. Signed Saml. **BRADLEY**. Test Moses **BYRNE**, Christ. **HAYS** (JCCP). Rec 24 Jun 1806.

90. Page 57. 24 Jun 1806. John **WYGLE** to Leonard **WELKER**. For a $70 note and a mare received by sd **WELKER** of sd **WYGLE**, a tract assigned to him by sd **WELKER**, and to sd **WELKER** by Alexander **BURTON**. Sd **WYGLE** is to retain use of the cabin and cleared land until 25 Dec next. Signed John **WIGLE**. Test John **BYRD**. Rec 10 Aug 1806.

91. Page 57. 5 Jun 1798. Moses **HURLAY** and Catharine **ROBINSON**. Marriage ceremony at 10:00 a.m. by Don Louis **LORIMIER**. Wit Solomon **THORN**, Andrew **RAMSEY**, Moses **HURLEY**, Wm. **DEAKINS**. Signed Catharine (x) **ROBERSON**, Edward (ER) **ROBERSON**,

Andrew **RAMSEY**, John **DOBBIN**. Rec 22 Oct 1805. [in French]

92. Page 58. 5 Jun 1710 [probably 1798]. William **MOREFOOT (MANHEAUT)** and Elisabeth **MARTIN**. Marriage ceremony at 10:00 a.m. Signed Wm. (x) **MAUPHET**, Catherine (x) **MARTIN**. Wit Solomon **THORN**, Andrew **RAMSEY**, John **DOBBIN**, Andrew **RAMSEY**. Rec 22 Oct 1805. [in French]

93. Page 58. 1 Aug 1799. Medad **RANDOL**, son of Enos **RANDOL**, and Debora **WALLER**, daughter of Joseph **WALLER**. Marriage ceremony at 10:00 a.m. by Don Louis **LORIMIER** at the home of Joseph **WALLER**. Signed Medad **RANDOL**, Deborah **RANDOL**, Joseph ( ) **WALLER**, Mrs. Annah ( ) **WALLER**, L. **LORIMIER**. Wit Wm. **THOMSON**, Andrew **RAMSEY**, Enos **RANDOL**, Thos. **BULL**, Samuel **RANDOLL**, Elisabeth **THOMSON**, Celia **THOMSON**, Saml. (x) **RANDOL** Senr. Rec 22 Oct 1805. [in French]

94. Page 59. 8 Aug 1799. Joseph **YOUNG** and Sarah **BYRD**, daughter of John **BYRD**. Marriage ceremony with signed consent of the parents, at 8:00 p.m. Signed Magdalen (x) **RUSSELL**, B. **COUSIN**, Joseph **YOUNG**, Sarah (x) **BYRD**, L. **LORIMIER**. Rec 22 Oct 1805. [in French]

95. Page 60. 19 Sep 1799. John **BOYD** from St. Andre on the Missouri and Elisth. **ANDREWS**. Marriage ceremony with signed consent of the parents. Signed John (C) **BOYD**, Elisabeth (S) **ANDREW**. Wit Alexander **ANDREW**, James (-) **MURPHY**, B. **COUSIN**, L. **LORIMIER**. [No recording date.] [in French]

96. Page 60. 23 Jan 1800. James **EARL** and Polly **SHERADINE**, legitimate daughter of Henry & Christina **SHARDINE**. Marriage ceremony at 10:00 a.m. Signed James **ARLE**, Polly (x) **SHARADIN**. Wit Moses **HURLEY**, Wm. **DAUGHERTY**, Joseph ( ) **WALLER**, L. **LORIMIER**. Rec 22 Oct 1805. [in French]

97. Page 61. 15 Apr 1800. Elijah **AVERITT** and Ann **BYRD**, widow of Amos **BYRD**. Marriage ceremony at 11:00 a.m. Signed Elijah (x) **AVERITT**, Anne (x) **BYRD**. Wit John **BYRD**, Jonathan **BUIS**, Henry **HALL**, Moses **BYRD**, Henry **SHARADIN**. Rec 22 Oct 1805. [in French]

98. Page 61. 12 Jun 1800. Dr. Saml. **DORSEY** of New Madrid, Mo. and Elizabeth **THOMSON**, daughter of Jeremiah **THOMSON** of Cape Girardeau. Marriage contract (9:00 a.m.). They will own everything jointly. Elizabeth **THOMSON**'s dowry in case of survival or separation is 2000 piastres and ¼ of personal property and real estate. Her dowry from her parents is valued at 1000 piastres. Signed Saml. **DORSEY**, Elisabeth **THOMSON**. Wit L. **LORIMIER**. Rec 22 Oct 1805. [in French]

99. Page 62. 12 Jun 1800. Doctr. Saml. **DORSEY** of New Mardrid, Mo. and Elisabeth **THOMSON**, daughter of Jeremiah **THOMSON** of Cape Girardeau. Marriage ceremony at 10:00 a.m. Signed Saml. **DORSEY**, Elisabeth **DORSEY**, L. **LORIMIER**. Wit Wm. **THOMSON**, Henry **SHARADIN**, John **McCARTY**, Jeremiah **THOMSON**. Rec 22 Oct 1805. [in French]

100. Page 62. 4 Feb 1799. Allen **McKINZIE** to Leney **RANDALL** (divorced from John **DURHAM** in Post Vincennes). Marriage ceremony at 10:00 a.m. Signed Allen **McKENZIE**, Helene ( ) **RANDOLL**, L. **LORIMIER**. Wit Wm. **THOMSON**, James **RANDLE**, Bettrey **RANDEL**, L. **LARGEAU**, Cealia **THOMSON**, Saml. **RANDOL**. Rec 22 Oct 1805. [in French]

101. Page 63. 27 Jan 1801. Joseph **BAKER** and Catherine **NYSWONGER**, daughter of Joseph & Catherine **NYSWONGER**. Marriage ceremony. Signed Joseph **BAKER**, Catherine (x) **NISWONGER**, L. **LORIMIER**. Wit Joseph **NYSWONGER**, Chronst. **OBATO**(?), Jeremiah **TANEY**. Rec 22 Oct 1805. [in French]

102. Page 63. 20 May 1801. James **RANDOLLS**, son of Enos **RANDOL** & Rebecca **RANDOL** to Ann **DOWTY**, daughter of Zachariah and Elizabeth **DOWTY**. Marriage ceremony. Signed James **RANDOLLS**, Anne ( ) **DOWTY**, L. **LORIMIER**. Wit James **DOWTY**, Saml. (x) **RANDOLL**, Saml. **RANDOLL**, Enos ( ) **RANDOL**, Marie ( ) **RODNEY**. Rec 22 Oct 1805. [in French]

103. Page 64. 9 ___ 1801. George **HAYS**, son of Christophe & Eve **HAYS** and Sarah **BYRD**, daughter of Amos & Sarah **BYRD**. Marriage ceremony. Signed George **HAYS**, Sally **BYRD**. Wit Joseph **YOUNG**, Polley **BYRD**, Abraham **BYRD**, L. **LORIMIER**, Stephen **BYRD**, John **HAYS**, Elizabeth (x) **BYRD**. Rec 22 Oct 1805. [in French]

104. Page 65. 10 Jul 1801. Danile **ASHABRANNER**, son of Urbin **ASHABRANNER** and Susannah **ANDERSON** of N. Car., U. S. A., Presbyterian faith, and Catharine **BOLLINGER**, daughter of Jon **BOLLINGER** and Catherine **FULBRIGHT** of Sinkhorn [Lincoln] Co., N. Car., Presbyterian faith. Marriage ceremony at Ste. Genevieve, Mo. The original is in the Ste. Genevieve Archives. Signed Daniel **ASHABRANNER**, Catherine **BULLINGER**, Maxmill. **CURE**. Wit John **BULLINGER**, Jos. **COCHRUN**, Will **FRIGG**, Moses **FERGUSON**. Rec 22 Oct 1805. [in French]

105. Page 65. 20 Sep 1800. John **JOHNSON** and Elizabeth **WILKINSON**, former wife of Henry **GUY**, Greene Co., Tenn., also a child raised by Juir John **WEIR**. Marriage ceremony at 10:00 a.m. Signed John (x) **JOHNSON**, Elisabeth (x) **WILKINSON**. Wit Nathan **WILKINSON**, Wm. **SMITH**, L. **LORIMIER**. Rec 22 Oct 1805. [in French]

106. Page 66. 10 Jul 1802. Marie **RANDOL**, widow of Samuel **RANDOL**, to Samuel **RANDOL**, for her children John age 6, and Jerry age 2. For the sum of 209 piastres and 6 rioux, mortgage on land. Sd Marie will keep this money for her children, for whom Samuel **RANDOL**, Jr. is legal guardian. Signed Saml. (x) **RANDEL**. Wit Solomon **THORN**, L. **LARGEAU**, L. **LORIMIER**. Rec 19 Aug 1805. [IN FRENCH]

107. Page 67. 18 Jul 1801. James **ROZEN** by L. **LORIMIER** to Richd. J. **WATERS**. For the sum of 64 piastres, 240 arpens on Cape La Cruche. Sold at public sale on 11 Dec 1799 by order of Don Carlos D'Hault **DELASSUS**, Lt Gov of Upper Louisiana, at the request of R. J **WATERS** of New Madrid. The sale was held three times and finally sold to **WATERS**, the only bidder. Signed L. **LORIMIER**. Wit Bartholomey **COUSINS**, Solomon **THORN**, Surveyors. Rec 19 Aug 1805. [IN FRENCH]

108. Page 68. 7 Mar 1806. Jeremiah **BANIGH** to George **WOLF**. For the sum of $25, 200 acres on both sides of Little Whitewater, being the NW part of nearly 800 acres surveyed to sd **BANIGH** by B. **COUSIN**, General Surveyor; where sd **BANIGH** now lives, and adjoining Fredc. **LIMBAUGH** Esqr. and others; beginning at a hickory tree N of the school house. Signed Jeremiah **BANIGH**. Wit John **MELLOY**, Michael **LIMBACH**, Fredc. **LIMBAUGH** srn (JP). Rec 22 Sep 1806.

109. Page 69. 23 Sep 1806. Morgan **BYRNS** to Saml. **BRADLEY**. Quit claim to the Bergen Tract; conditions relating to transfer of sd tract from sd **BRADLEY** to sd **BYRNS** having not been performed. Signed Morgan **BYRNE**. Test Mosses **BYRNE**, Josep **HUNTER**, L. **LORIMIER** (JCCP). Rec 25 Sep 1806.

110. Page 69. 5 Sep 1806. William **MURPHY** to John **GIBBONEY**. For the sum of $569.33 and one barrel of whiskey, __ acres on White Water River, which sd **MURPHY** was granted by the Spanish Government and improved and lived on in 1803. Sd **GIBBONY** obtained judgments of $537.50 and $31.83 against sd **MURPHY** at Sep 1806 Term of the Court of Common Pleas. Signed William (W) **MURPHY**. Wit Edward F. **BOND**, Thos. **BALLEW** (JCCP). Rec 26 Sep 1806.

111. Page 71. 22 Nov 1805. Enos **RANDOLLS** Jur to Edward F. **BOND**. For the sum of $100, 200 acres, part of a tract where he now lives and has an improvement; the sd land not to be taken from any cleared lands or improvements. Signed Enos (N) **RANDOLL**. Wit Betsey **GIBSON**, Arra Minter **GIBSON**, Christ. **HAYS** (JCCP). Rec 29 Sep 1806.

112. Page 71. 15 Oct 1805. Samuel D. **STROTHER** to James **RAMSEY**. For the sum of $400, 196 acres on Randoll's Creek, adjoined on the S by **MURPHY**'s old place and N by a tract sd **STROTHER** sold to **HARKLEROADS**. Signed S. D. **STROTHER**. Wit Saml. **BRADLEY**, Jereh. **SIMPSON**, L. **LORIMIER** (JCCP). Rec 1 Oct 1806.

113. Page 72. 23 Oct 1805. George **GROUNT** to Benjamin **SHELL**. For the sum of __, his improvement, made before 20 Dec 1803, near Daniel **BULLINGER**. Signed George **GRUND**. Wit Danl. **BULLINGER**, Henry **BULLINGER**, F. **LIMBAUGH** (JP). Rec 14 Oct 1806.

114. Page 73. 9 Oct 1804. Jacob **FOSTER** [senr], millright, to Benjamin **PATTERSON** of New Madrid Terr., yeoman. For the sum of $200, 200 acres, being ½ of the plantation where he now lives, beginning at the SW corner. Signed Jacob **FOSTER**. Wit George **CREATCH**, Jacob **FOSTER**. Title is assigned to George

CRAATH for $300 on 7 Nov 1804. Signed Benjn. **PATTERSON**. Wit Jno. B. **GOBEAU**, John **REED**. Title is assigned to John Bat. **GOBEAU** for 180 gallons of whiskey on 7 Nov 1804. Signed George **CRATH**. Test John **REED**, Benjamin **MYERS**. Title is assigned to James **EARLE** for value received on 19 Dec 1805. Signed John B. ($) **GOBEAU**. Wit Saml. **HANNA**. Title is assigned to Anthony **MADEN** on 4 Oct 1806. Signed James **EARL**. Wit Robt. **HALL** (JCCP). Rec 7 Nov 1806.

115. Page 74. 8 Oct 1806. Edward **ROBERTSON** of New Madrid Dist. to Belemus **HAYDEN** of Bourbon Co., Ken. For the sum of $400, 240 arpens on the waters of Hubble's Creek, claimed and conceded to John **LEESLEY** by the Spanish Government in 1798 and adjoining Ithamer **HUBBLE**'s mill seat and Joseph **FITE**. Signed Edwd. (ER) **ROBERTSON**. Wit Edwd. F. **BOND**, G. **HARTH**, Saml. **BRADLEY**, Robt. **HALL** (JCCP). Rec 11 Nov 1806.

116. Page 75. 10 Oct 1806. Joseph **THOMSON** to Webb **HAYDEN** of Franklin Co., Ken. For the sum of $3 per acre, ½ in cash and ½ in a bond, 260 acres/arpens where sd **THOMSON** now lives, bounded by Jos. **WORTHINGTON**'s old claim, Allen **McKENSIE**, Mathew **HUBBLE**, **KLINGINGSMITH**'s old place, etc. Signed Joseph **THOMPSON**. Wit Jerh. **SIMPSON**, Belemus **HAYDEN**, Jos. **WORTHINGTON**, Robt. **HALL**, (JCCP). Rec 11 Nov 1806.

117. Page 76. 16 Mar 1806. Samuel **DORSEY** to Thomas **BALLEW**. For the sum of $600, 400 arpens where he now lives, being the same sd **DORSEY** purchased from Thomas W. **WATERS**. Signed Saml. **DORSEY**. Test James **MORRISSON**, Robt. **HALL** (JCCP). Title is assigned to Robert **HALL** for value received on 8 Nov 1806. Signed Thos. **BALLEW**. Test Edwd. F. **BOND**, Robt. **HALL** (JCCP). Rec 11 Nov 1806.

118. Page 76. 25 Mar 1806. Hugh **CRISWELL** to William **WHITE**. For the sum of $1, 300 acres, more or less, being sd **CRISWELL**'s head right, adjoining **BALLEW**, Tash, **MORRISON**, Widow **MILLS**, and **RANDALLS**. Signed Hugh **CRISWELL**. Wit Benjn. **TENNILLE**, John **DAVIS**, Robt. **HALL** (JCCP). Rec 11 Nov 1806.

119. Page 77. 28 Dec 1804. Daniel **MULLINS** to Thomas W. **WATERS**. For the sum of $300, 300 acres, French measure, known as Gravely

Spring, being sd **MULLINS'** head right lying on the road to New Madrid about two miles from **FRIEND**'s, being the same formerly occupied by the Widow **SMITH**. Sd **WATERS** is to pay for surveying. Signed Daniel (x) **MULLINS**. Test. R[obert] **WORTHINGTON**, Hy. Polite **MAROTE**, Robt. **HALL** (JCCP). Rec 22 Nov 1806.

120. Page 78. 12 Apr 1804. John **TUCKER** and Fany **SMITH**. For the sum of $5000, marriage bond. Signed John **TUCKER**, Fany **SMITH**. Wit Thos. L. **NORRIS**, Lemuel **CHENEY**, Bird William **ROSS**, George **HACHER**, James **LUCAS**. Rec 19 Dec 1806.

121. Page 78. 12 Apr 1804. John **TUCKER** and Phaney **SMITH**. Marriage ceremony. Signed Jno. **TUCKER**, Phaney **SMITH**. Wit Thos. L. **NORRIS**, Lemuel **CHENEY**, Bird William **ROSS**. Rec 19 Dec 1806.

122. Page 78. 20 Dec 1806. John C. **HARBISON** to James **COTTLE**. For the sum of $110.10, 270 acres on the waters of Bonar's Creek, known as **BERGIN**'s old place, assigned by him to Samuel **BRADLEY**, and sold under an execution in favor of Francois **SIGO** against sd **BRADLEY** to the sd **HARBISON**. Signed John C. **HARBISON**. Wit A. **HADEN**, John **GUETHING**, Abraham **BYRD** (JCCP). Rec 23 Dec 1806.

123. Page 79. 13 Jul 1799. Samuel **RANDOLLS** to his daughter Elizabeth **RANDOLLS**. For taking care of her parents Samuel **RANDOL** Sr. and Maria **RANDOL** until their deaths, and her brother John, until he becomes of age, donation of land and personal property: four cows, six steers, one horse, 20 pigs, six sheep, one wagon, and diverse ploughing implements, along with a house and all household furnishings therein; also a flour mill and a mill for "sui" with about 20 arpens of cleared and fenced land--in general everything Samuel **RANDOL** possesses in the Post of Cape Girardeau. At the time sd John become of age, she will divide the estate in half with him. Signed Saml. (x) **RANDOL**, L. **LORIMIER**. Wit Willm. **THOMSON**, B. **COUSIN**. Will witnessed by B. **COUSINS** (Note: The donation of Samuel **RANDOLLS** to Elizabeth **RANDOLLS** was received 18 June 1805 from B. **COUSINS**. But I did not know the parties had mislaid it.) Signed L. **LORIMIER**. [No recording date given.] [IN FRENCH]

124. Page 80. 25 Feb 1806. William **MURPHY**, Daniel **BRANT**, Rozein **BAILY** and others to Ezekiel **ABLE**. For the sum of __, their settlement rights: William **MURPHY**, wife, four children--940 acres; Willm. **SMITH**, wife, six children--1040 acres; Danl. **BRANT**, wife, one child--790 acres; Rezin **BAILY**, wife--740 acres; Jas. **MURPHY**, wife, one child--790 acres; Francis **MURPHY**, wife, one child--790 acres; Jams. **SMITH**--640 acres; Jacob **SHERIDAN**--640 acres. Signed William **MURPHY**, William **SMITH**, Danl. **BRANT**, Rezen **BALY**, James **MURPHY**, Francis **MURPHY**, James **SMITH**, Jacob **SHEREDAN**, Will (U) **MURPHY**. Wit William **MURPHY**. Test Js. **BOYD**, Robt. **HALL** (JCCP), Dan **SULLIVAN** (as to William **MURPHY**), John **BYRD**. [no recording date given]

125. Page 81. 10 Mar 1806. Emas **BYRD** to James **WILKINSON**. For the sum of $400, two tracts; 350 arpens from the W side of the tract where he now lives; and 50 acres that he bought of Micheal O. **HOGAN** on the S of the first tract. Also, bond of $800 is given by sd **BYRD** to secure a lawful title. Signed Amos **BYRD**. Test. Joseph **YOUNG**, George **FRANKLIN**, Andrew P. **PATTERSON**, Stephen **MALONE**, John **BYRD** (JCCP). Rec 26 Dec 1806.

126. Page 81. 7 Oct 1806. Josiah **LEE** to Jacob **SKEEN**. For the sum of $150, two tracts; 120 arpens, being the lower end of his father's plantation; and 10 acres of the NW corner his own survey, to include a spring. Signed Josiah **LEE**. Test John **BYRD** (JCCP). Title is assigned to William **WILKINSON** for $174 on 7 Oct 1806. Signed Jacob **SKEEN**. Wit Christ. **HAYS** (JCCP). Rec 26 Dec 1806.

127. Page 82. 1 Jan 1807. John **McCARTY** to Nathan **McCARTY** and William **McCARTY**. For love and good will that he bears to his two sons, all his lands; one negro girl named **Violet**; one yoke of oxen and 14 head of other cattle; one mare; one small brown gelding; one cribb full of corn, supposed to contain 800 bushels; 64 head of hogs; three feather beds, with all the furniture; and all other furniture belonging to his house; also an inventory of sd property. Signed John **McCARTY**. Wit Dens. **SULLIVAN**, Thomas **FULTON**, Christ. **HAYS** (JCCP). Inventory of property lists land as 570 arpens granted to Jacob **KELLY** and transferred to sd **McCARTY**, 240 arpens granted to Joseph **CRUTCHELOW**, and 200 arpens improved by Alexr. **ANDREWS**. Rec 11 Jan 1807.

128. Page 83. 20 Nov 1806. Adenston **ROGERS** to Ithamar **HUBBLE**. For value received, 550 acres, on Whitewater River, being part of 1140 acres, the settlement right for himself, wife, and 8 children, claimed under 2nd Section of the Act of Congress, beginning at a bounded poplar with 2 blazes; bounded by Doctr. Samuel **DORSEY**. Survey recorded 28 Feb 1806. Signed Adenston **ROGERS**. Test Jno. **ABERNETHER**, A. **HADEN**, Christr. **HAYS** (JCCP). The Board of Commissioners for land claims confirms 500 arpens to sd **ROGERS** on 15 Apr 1806. Signed John B. C. **LUCAS**, Jas. L. **DONALDSON**. Wit Christ. **HAYS** (JCCP). Plat rec 12 Jan 1807, deed on 4 Feb 1807. [see Figure 1]

129. Page 84. 16 Jan 1807. Jeremiah **THOMSON** to John **THOMSON**. Acknowledgment of bill of sale (AB:52). Signed Thos. **BALLEW** (JCCP). Rec 16 Jan 1807.

130. Page 85. 21 Feb 1802. Micheal **BURGAN** to Samuel **BRADLEY**. For the sum of $70, the improvement where he last lived on the spring branch below Widow **WEAVER's**. Signed Michal **BERGAN**. Wit Daniel **DUGGAN**, M. **JONEIS** Junr. Title assigned to James **COTTLE** for value received on 22 Dec 1806. Signed Saml. **BRADLEY**. Test Jno. C. **HARBISON**, John **GUETHING**, Solomon **THORN**, Robert **HALL** (JCCP). Rec 16 Jan 1807.

131. Page 85. 6 Jan 1807. Bennijah **LAUGHERTY** to Joseph **WALLER**. Assignment of bill of sale from David **ALLING** for **ALLING's** head right on the Mississippi River, where sd **WALLER** now operates a ferry. Sd **LAUGHERTY** does not hold himself responsible for confirmation of title. Signed Bennijah **LAUGHERTY**, Joseph ( ) **WALLER**. Wit Edwd. F. **BOND**, Richad. **WALLER**. Rec 19 Jan 1807.

132. Page 86. 1 Jan 1807. Robert **CRUMP** to George **MILLER**. For the sum of $440, 350 acres on the middle fork of Crooked Creek, beginning at a white oak. Signed Robert **CRUMP**. Wit J. **BOYD**, Mathew **HUBBAL**, Thos. **BALLEW** (JCCP). Rec 5 Feb 1807.

133. Page 86. 6 Oct 1806. Jacob **FOSTER** Junr to Thos. S. **RODNEY**. For a valuable consideration, all his land claims for head right or settlement. Bond of $700 is posted by sd **FOSTER** to make as good a right as can be obtained for all lands granted to him. Signed Jacob (x) **FOSTER** Junr. Test Jesse (x)

TAYLOR, Martin **RODNEY**, John **BYRD** (JCCP). Rec 10 Feb 1807.

134. Page 87. 26 Dec 1806. Edward F. **BOND** to Benijah **LAUGHERTY**. For 10,000 staves of white oak for pipes, 200 acres which he purchased of Enos **RANDOLL** in 1805. Signed Edwd. F. **BOND**. Wit Christr. **HAYS** (JCCP). Rec 20 Feb 1807.

135. Page 88. 29 Mar 1806. Jeremiah **SIMPSON** to Mathew **SCRUGGS**. For the sum of $2000, bond to make title to 800 arpens and 40 perches joining the Big Swamp and Jacob **JACOBS'** land; being the same settled by sd **SIMPSON**, where he now lives, and being his head right. Signed Jeremiah **SIMPSON**. Test Samuel G. **DUNN**, Mathew **HUBBELL**, Thos. **BALLEW** (JCCP). Rec 21 Feb 1807.

136. Page 88. 8 Oct 1806. Isaac **FLANNERY** of Livingston Co., Ken. to James **CURRIN**. Power of attorney for consigning a bond given to him for a negro boy between 15 and 20 years of age, dated 7 Oct 1806 and due in 1808. Signed Isaac (A) **FLANNERY**. Test Zadok **McNUE**, Charles **FENLY**, Robt. **HALL** (JCCP). Rec 27 Feb 1807.

137. Page 89. 11 Jan 1805. William **SMITH** to Thos. W. **WATERS**. For the sum of $2000, 470 arpens known as Tarrapity on the River, joined on the S by land surveyed for Jno. **JOHNSON** and now occupied by Dr. **SEXTON**; except 10 arpens sold to sd **SEXTON**. Signed Wm. **SMITH**. Wit B. **COUSINS**, Andrew **RAMSEY**, L. **LORIMIER** (JCCP). Rec 27 Feb 1807.

138. Page 90. 9 Jun 1806. Daniel **SEXTON** and Thos. W. **WATERS**. Articles of agreement. For the sum of $1825, paid as follows: all accounts, notes, and debts due from sd **SEXTON** to sd **WATERS**; 10 young cows and calves or cows with calf worth $100 due by 1 May next; and the remainder in cattle, horses, mares, and colts; 250 arpens on the Mississippi River, being where sd **SEXTON** lately lived at the head of Tywapity Bottom, between Thomas W. **WATERS** and Lemael **CHANY**. Should agreement on the value of the stock not be obtained, the parties hereby bind themselves for $1650. Signed Thos. W. **WATERS**, Daniel **SEXTON**. Wit James **BRADY**, Jno. C. **HARBISON**, Abraham **BYRD** (JCCP). Rec 27 Feb 1807.

139. Page 91. 20 Jul 1805. Daniel **MULLINS** to Wm. **EDWARDS**, late of Ga. For the sum of

$900 and a negro girl, 300 arpens in Tywappity Bottom on the Mississippi, joining the land where sd **MULLINS** now lives, Thos. W. **WATERS**, and vacant land on the W. Sd **EDWARDS** to take possession of the land upon payment of $450, in the name of Reese **BOWIE** or Jesse **BOWDEN**. Should the U. S. not grant title, sd **MULLINS** to return the purchase price, and he posts bond of $1800 to do so. Signed Daniel (x) **MULLINS**. Test Thos. W. **WATERS**, James **CURRIN**, Robt. **HALL** (JCCP). Rec 27 Feb 1807.

140. Page 92. 5 Mar 1805. Moses **BURNET** to Thomas W. **WATERS**. For the sum of $500, 250 arpens, joining a tract formerly belonging to Reese **BOYEI** and vacant land, being sd **BURNET**'s head right. Signed Moses (x) **BURNET**. Wit James **CURRIN**, James **BRADY**, Robt. **HALL** (JCCP). Rec 27 Feb 1807.

141. Page 92. 8 Apr 1805. Robert **LANE** to James **CURRIN**. For the sum of __, bond to make a title to 250 acres on the Mississippi adjoining Josiah **QUINBY** below and Jacob **MIRES** above. Signed Robert **LANE**. Test James **BRADY**, James **WELBORN**, Robt. **HALL** (JCCP). Rec 27 Feb 1807.

142. Page 92. 10 Aug 1804. Benjn. **ROSSE** of Shelby Co., Ken. to Daniel **SEXTON**. For the sum of $300, 240 acres on the Mississippi in Tywappy Bottom, adjoining Lemuel **CHENEY** above and Abraham **BIRD** below. Signed Bej. **ROSSE**. Wit James **CURRIN**, Thos. L. **NORRIS**, Robt. **HALL** (JCCP). Title is assigned to Jacob **ZANOR** for value received on 8 Nov 1804. Signed Daniel **SEXTON**. Test James **CURRIN**. Title is assigned to Wm. **SMITH** for value received on 2 Mar 1805. Signed Jacob **ZENOE**. Test Thos. W. **WATERS**, Lemuel **CHENEY**. Title is assigned to James **BRADY** for value received on 19 Sep 1805. Signed Wm. **SMITH**. Test James **CURRIN**. Rec 27 Feb 1807.

143. Page 93. 18 Sep 1805. William **SMITH** to James **BRADY**. For the sum of $700 in the form of $250 in horses by Oct, $300 in merchandise, and $150 in goods; 240 acres joining Lemuel **CHANY** and **BIRD**. Signed Wm. **SMITH**, James **BRADY**. Test James **CURRIN**, Robt. **HALL** (JCCP). Rec 27 Feb 1807.

144. Page 94. 7 Jan 1804. Daniel **SEXTON** to Joseph **MAGEE**. For one rifle gun and $15, two tracts, one of 250 acres that he bought of John

SHORTER, including sd **SHORTER**'s head right and improvement; and 200 acres in the name of Jashuway **SEXTON**, between John **LOYD**'s and Charles **LOACASES**. Sd **MAGEE** is to pay the office fees. Signed Daniel **SEXTON**. Test James **CURRIN**, Moses (x) **BURNET**. Title is assigned to Thos. W. **WATERS** for value received on 26 Oct 1805. Signed James **CURRIN**, agent for Jos. **MAGEE**. Wit Robt. **HALL** (JCCP). Rec 6 Feb 1807.

145. Page 94. 30 Dec 1803. Mary **SMITH** to same. For the sum of $15, 300 acres, being her head right and land recorded at Lanelagru in Tywappity; between John **LOYD**'s and Charles **LOKUS** on both sides of the road. Sd **MAGEE** is to do the improvement and incur all expenses, and she appoints sd **MAGEE** as her lawful attorney to get the deed to sd land. Signed Mary (x) **SMITH**. Test James **CURRIN**, John **LOYD**. Title is assigned to Thomas W. **WATERS** for value received on 20 Aug 1805. Signed James **CURRIN**, agent for Jos. **MAGEE**. Wit Robt. **HALL** (JCCP). Rec 27 Feb 1807.

146. Page 95. 7 Feb 1807. Louis **LORIMIER** to John **RUSHER**. For the sum of $100, Lot No. 5, Range D in Cape Girardeau, bounded on the N by Harmony St, S by the public square, E by Spanish St, and W by Lorimier St. Signed L. **LORIMIER**. Test B. **COUSIN**, Christr. **HAYS** (JCCP). Title is assigned to Abraham **BYRD** on 3 Mar 1807 for $150. Signed John **RISHER**. Wit Robt. **GREEN**, Jos. **McFERRON**, Christr. **HAYS** (JCCP), John **BYRD**. Rec 5 Mar 1807.

147. Page 96. 6 Dec 1806. William **THOMSON** and Elizabeth **RANDOL**, his wife, of New Madrid Dist. to Samuel **RANDOL**. Exoneration from the terms of a deed of gift in favor of Elizabeth **RANDOL** executed about nine years ago, concerning the plantation where sd Samuel now lives. Signed Wm. **THOMSON**, Elizabeth **THOMSON**. Wit M. **AMOUREUSE**, JCCP in New Madrid Dist. Rec 5 Mar 1807.

148. Page 96. 28 Jan 1807. James **HANNA** to John **HANNA**. For the sum of $250, 250 arpens on the waters of Hubble's Creek between Abraham **BYRD**, John **GAITZ**, and Lewis **WOTH**, being part of 350 arpens granted to James **HANNA** by the U. S. Commissioners. Signed James (#) **HANNA**. Wit David **FARREL**, John **GIBONEY**, Christr. **HAYS** (JCCP). Rec 17 Mar 1807.

149. Page. 97. 1 Dec 1806. Joseph **WORTHINGTON** to Joseph **THOMPSON**. For the sum of $42 and his bail, mortgage on 1000 arpens adjoining John **GIBBONY**, Abraham **BYRD**, Jacob **JACOBS**, and others, until sd **WORTHINGTON** relieves sd **THOMPSON** in a case against sd **WORTHINGTON** by Waters & Hall, wherein he is bail for sd **WORTHINGTON**; and for $42 loaned. Signed Jos. **WORTHINGTON**. Wit Jas. **THOMPSON** Junr, Isaac **THOMPSON**, Christr. **HAYS** (JCCP). Rec 18 Mar 1807. [Marginal note: Full satisfaction received on 8 Feb 1810. Signed Rachel (x) **THOMPSON**, administr of Jos. **THOMPSON**. Test George **HENDERSON**, Recr..]

150. Page 98. 1 Dec 1806. Same to same. Deed of trust to sell the land described in the preceding deed (AB:97), or any part thereof, using the proceeds to pay Waters & Hall, lifting a mortgage on sd land, and the balance to be returned to sd **WORTHINGTON**. Signed Jos. **WORTHINGTON**. Wit Jos. **THOMPSON** Junr, Isaac **THOMPSON**, Christr. **HAYS** (JCCP). Rec 18 Mar 1807.

151. Page 98. 16 Jul 1806. Edwd. F. **BOND** to William **WHITE**. For one bay mare, five years old and 15 hands high, 120 acres, being part of a tract on or near the head waters of Randol's Creek conveyed to Jno. **HAYS** by Elijah **WHITTAKER** on 1 Oct 1804, and being part of sd **WHITTAKER**'s settlement right. Signed Edwd. F. **BOND**. Wit Eli **WHITE**, Betsey **GIBSON**, Christr. **HAYS** (JCCP). Rec 20 Mar 1807.

152. Page 99. 29 Oct 1806. Benjn. **TENNELLE** to John **DAVIS**. For the sum of $550, 232 arpens on a fork of Hubble's Creek leading to Col. **HAYS'**, bounded on the N by sd **TENNILLE**, E by Edward **HAILL**, W by Hugh **CRESSWELL**, and E by Henry **HAND**; formerly known as Jonathan **FOREMAN**'s mill tract, including the mill. Sd **TENNILLE** to return the consideration money plus interest should a lawful deed not be obtained from the U. S. Signed Benjn. **TENNILLE**. Wit Hugh **CRISWELL**, James **ARREL**, Robt. **GREEN** (JCCP). Rec 31 Mar 1807.

153. Page 100. 8 Apr 1806. William **WHITE** to John **BURNS**. Quit claim to 82 acres, more or less, that he purchased of Hugh **CRISWELL**; bounded by lands he purchased of sd **CRISWELL** and the widow **MILLS**, and James **RANDOL**. Signed William **WHITE**. Test.

Hugh **CRESWELL**, Benjn. **TENNILLE**, Robt. **GREEN** (JCCP). Rec 2 Apr 1807.

154. Page 101. 9 Feb 1807. Hugh **CRISWELL** to John **BURNS**. For the sum of $85, 86 acres, bounded on the E by land sold by sd **CRISWELL** to William **WHITE**, S by Lavena **MILLS**, W by James **RANDOL**, N by Lewis **TASHE**; being the same where sd **BURNS** now resides. Signed Hugh **CRESWELL**. Wit John **DAVIS**, James **ARREL**, Robt. **GREEN** (JCCP). Rec 2 Apr 1807.

155. Page 102. 13 Mar 1807. Benjamin **TENNILLE** to John **MARTIN**. For the sum of $1800, 600 acres English measure, more or less, on the waters of Hubble's Creek; bounded on the S by White **METLOCK**, E by **DOHERTY** and **ERREL**, N by **GUETHING** and William **HILL**, and W by **GREEN** and others. Sd land was confirmed to Jonathan **FOREMAN** and conveyed to sd **TENNILLE**. Signed Benjn. **TENNILLE**. Wit John **MARTIN**, Robt. **HALL** (JCCP). Rec 9 Apr 1807.

156. Page 103. 20 Mar 1806. Thomas **BALLEW** to James **MORROSON**. For the sum of __, 16 acres, being on the W boundary of the tract where sd **BALLEW** now lives, S of sd **MORROSON**'s improvement. Signed Thos. **BALLEW**. Test A. **HADEN**, Robt. **HALL** (JCCP). Rec 13 Apr 1807.

157. Page 103. 9 Mar 1804. Anthony **RANDOLL** and Enos **RANDOLL** to Thomas **BALLEW**. For the sum of $800, bond to make title to 250 acres, Spanish measure, on Hubble's Creek, being the same that Anthony **RANDOLL** settled and where he now lives, being the whole of his head right. Sd **BALLEW** to be in full possession of sd land until title is made. Signed Anthony (x) **RANDOLL**, Enos **RANDOL**. Test Robert **HALL**, Adam **McGEE**. Bond is assigned to James **MORRISON** and John **WILSON** on 11 Sep 1804. Signed Thos. **BALLEW**. Test Robt. **HALL** (JCCP), Ben **MORGAN**. Rec 13 Apr 1807.

158. Page 104. 2 Dec 1806. Benjamin **TENNILLE** to John **MARTIN**. For the sum of $3600, bond to make title to a tract of land where sd **TENNILLE** now lives, originally granted to Jonathan **FOREMAN**. Signed Benjn. **TENNILLE**. Wit Edward (x) **HAIL**, John **DAVIS**, Christr. **HAYS** (JCCP). Rec 16 Apr 1807.

159. Page 105. 22 Nov 1806. Louis **LORIMIER** to Louise **RODNEY**. For good and just motives and paternal affection for his daughter, now wife of Thomas **RODNEY**, Lot No. 5, Range E in Cape Girardeau; bounded on the E & W by two streets, on the S by Thos. **RODNEY**, and N by an unsold lot. Signed L. **LORIMIER**. Test B. **COUSIN**, John **GUETHING** (JP). Test 17 Apr 1807.

160. Page 105. 17 Oct 1806. Jacob **FOSTER** Junior to Martin **RODNEY**. For diverse good causes to his trusty and loving friend, power of attorney to convey his interest and claims in any land. Signed Jacob (x) **FOSTER**, Junr. Wit Josiah **HUNTER**, W. Right **TAYLOR**, John **BYRD** (JCCP). Rec 17 Apr 1807.

161. Page 106. 23 Jan 1807. Thomas **LEWIS** to Mathew **HUBBLE**. For the sum of $100, his head right and claim. Signed Thos. **LEWIS**. Wit John **CAMRON**, Robert **CRUMP**, Robt. **GREEN** (JCCP). Rec 18 Apr 1807.

162. Page 107. 16 Mar 1807. Henry **HATTEN** to Benijah **LAUGHERTY**. For the sum of $10, 250 acres on the Mississippi opposite the first inlet above old Cape Creek, being his head right received as a settler for eight years past, the improvement being made in 1802. Signed Henery **HATTIN**. Wit Charles **DEMOSS**, Jacob **HUDGENS**, Christr. **HAYS** (JCCP). Rec 30 Apr 1807.

163. Page 107. 1 Apr 1807. Robt. **HALL** to Robt. **ENGLISH**. For the sum of $800, 400 arpens, known as Frankes Improvement which sd **HALL** purchased of Saml. **DORSEY**; adjoining land that Thos. **BALLEW** bought of Enos **RANDOL**, James **MORRISON**, and Thos. **ENGLISH**. Signed Robt. **HALL**. Test Frederick **GIBLER**, Eli **WHITE**, Louis **LORIMIER** (JCCP). Rec 2 May 1807.

164. Page 108. 22 Nov 1806. John **McCARTY** to Robert **ENGLIS**. For the sum of $200, __ acres on the E side of White Water, settled by Jonithan **HUBBEL** Junr. Sd **McCARTY** is to cause title to be confirmed by the commissioners, or the deed to be null and void. Signed John **McCARTY**. Test John **THOMSON**, Josiah **LEE**, Robt. **GREEN** (JCCP). Rec 5 May 1807.

165. Page 108. 2 Nov 1804. Norris **MONDAY** to George **HAYS**. For the sum of £5, all his head right. Signed Noris (x) **MONDAY** (also signed for money received). Wit Christr. **HAYS**, John **HAYS**, Robt. **GREEN** (JCCP). Rec 30 May 1807.

166. Page 109. 15 Jul 1805. Jacob **ISOM** to Rufus **EASTON** of St. Louis, Mo. For the sum of $100, 640 acres on the headwaters of Anthony **RANDOL**'s Creek on the N side of sd **RANDOL**'s plantation, being the improvement right of Peter **BELLEW** and his family; bounded on the E by Henry **SHERIDAN**, W by James **DOTY**, and S by Henry **HAND**. Signed Jacob **ISOM**. Wit Bernd. **PRATTS**, Saml. **SOLOMON**, Otho **SHRADER**, Judge for Terr. of La.. Rec 8 Jun 1807.

167. Page 110. 7 Mar 1807. Daniel **MULLINS** to John C. **HARBISON**. For the sum of $300, 1/3 of 320 acres on the W bank of the Mississippi River in Tywappity, being where sd **MULLINS** now lives. Sd tract was granted to Sarah **WILLIAMSON**, wife of sd **MULLINS**, and the 1/3 part is to be laid off on the upper side of the tract, adjoining vacant lands and Robert **LANE**. Bond of $600 is posted to make a deed when sd **HARBISON** calls on sd **MULLINS**. Signed Daniel (x) **MULLINS**. Test Frederick **GIBLER**, Daniel F. **STEINBECK**, Charles **BRADLEY**, Christr. **HAYS** (JCCP). Rec 17 Jun 1807.

[End of original Deed Book A]

Finis 17 day of June 1807. Edwd. F. **BOND** . Recr.

[Beginning of original Deed Book B]

168. Page 111. 8 Oct 1806. John **HAYS** to Robert **ENGLISH**. For the sum of $2000, bond to make a title on 278 arpens on a branch of Randol's Creek, bounded on the N by Joseph **THOMPSON**, S by **HARKLEROAD**, E by **SMITH**, and W by unknown lands. The bond to be void when rights can be obtained from the U. S. Signed John **HAYS**. Wit William **HITT**, Benjn. **TENNILLE**, L. **LORIMIER** (JCCP). Rec 16 Jun 1807.

169. Page 111. 2 Mar 1807. Ezekiel **ABLE** to Jeremiah **ABLE**. For diverse and good causes to his beloved son, 11 tracts; 478 acres where he now lives, 245 acres on each side of Hubble's Creek joining James **DOTY**; 150 acres where John **FISHER** now lives on Hubble's Creek; 450 acres on the branches of Hubble's Creek where the widow **MURPHY** lives, joining sd **DOTY**; his right to the head right of James **CAMPBELL**, joining John **DAVIS'** Mill tract; his right to land purchased of William **HAND**

where John **TAYLOR** now lives, joining **HECKTOR** and Louis **DICKSON**; his right to land purchased of John **SHIELDS**, James **MURPHY**, and Francis **MURPHY**; John **SHIELDS'** improvement where he lived; Daniel **BRANT**, William **MURPHY**, Reason **BAYLES**, and John **SMITH's** improvement where he now lives, also James **SMITH** and George **MORGAN's** on White water; his improvement bought of William **WELLING** on St. Fransway River; Thomas **RING's** improvement on St. Fransway River; and Jacob & John **SHEREDEN's** improvement on White water. Signed Ezekiel **ABLE**. Wit John **BYRD** (JCCP). Rec 20 Jun 1807.

170. Page 112. 2 Mar 1807. Same to same. For the sum of $3750; 40 cattle; 40 sheep; 200 hogs now in the possession of Samuel **CAMPBELL**, John **SHIELDS**, and John **COOPER**; 7 salt kettles at sd **CAMPBELL's**; two bar skier(?) plows; two axes and two hoes; one cart in the possession of sd **CAMPBELL** living on St. Fransway; one plow and one hoe at John **COOPER's**; five horses and three mares; two stills, one holding 120 gallons, the other 70 gallons; one set of blacksmith tools in the possession of John C. **HARBISON**; eight feather beds and furniture; and all his household and farming tools; one waggon; and four pair of oxen. Signed Ezekiel **ABLE**. Wit John **BYRD** (JCCP). Rec 20 Jun 1807.

171. Page 113.. 2 Mar 1807. Same to same. For the sum of $1660, seven negro slaves; **Orman**, about 50 years old, and his wife **Rachel**, 20 years old; one woman named **Diner**, about 30 years old, and her three children, **Rose**, **Silay**, and **Frank**; and one boy about 12 years old named **Alexander**. Signed Ezekiel **ABLE**. Wit John **BYRD** (JCCP). Rec 20 Jun 1807.

172. Page 114. 30 Jul 1806. S. D. **STROTHER** to William **MATHEWS**. For the sum of $500, 240 acres where he now lives near Hubble's Mill, adjoined on the N by Martin **RODNEY**, and S by Joseph **FIGHT**. Signed S. D. **STROTHER**. Test. John **THOMSON**, John **HAYS**, Robt. **GREEN** (JCCP). Rec 15 Jul 1807.

173. Page 114. 18 Jul 1807. Mary **RANDOL** to Samuel G. **DUNN**. Power of attorney to collect a legacy or sum of money and other things bequeathed to her by the will of Francis **PIERPONT**, decd, late of Hardin Co., Ken., and which she is due as a daughter and heir of sd **PIERPONT**. Signed Mary (x) **RANDOL**. Wit L. **LORIMIER** (JCCP). Rec 20 Jul 1807.

174. Page 115. 18 Apr 1807. Louis **LORIMIER** to John **RANDOL**. For the sum of $100, Lot No. 6, Range D in Cape Girardeau, formerly occupied and improved by Anth. **HADEN** Esqr., and who has resigned his right to same; fronted on the E by the public square. Signed L. **LORIMIER**. Test B. **COUSIN**, Christr. **HAYS** (JCCP). Rec 20 Jul 1807.

175. Page 116. 26 Jul 1804. John **FREEMAN** [FOREMAN] to Michael **SHELL**. For the sum of $140, 400 arpens in the Dutch Settlement on Caney Creek, being his head right and improved by him in virtue of a Spanish grant; above and joining Leonard **WELKER**. Sd **SHELL** to pay costs of getting a final deed should the grant be confirmed. Signed John (x) **FOREMAN**. Wit B. **COUSIN**, Joseph **NISWONGER**, Christr. **HAYS** (JCCP). Rec 20 Jul 1807.

176. Page 117. 20 Mar 1806. S. D. **STROTHER** to Elizabeth **DRYBREAD**. For 240 acres of land within 3/4 mile of Eithamore **HOBLE's** Mill and all the buildings thereon, delivered by John **DRYBREAD**; one negro wench that he brought from the old states a few days past. Signed S. D. **STROTHER**, John (x) **DRYBREAD**, Mary (x) **DRYBREAD**. Wit Saml. **BRADLEY**, Joseph **THOMSON**, Martin **RODNEY**, Christr. **HAYS** (JCCP). Rec 4 Aug 1807.

177. Page 117. 29 Jul 1807. Louis **LORIMIER** to the Dist. of Cape Girardeau. In compliance with his proposal dated 13 Jan 1806 to have the seat of justice for the district on his land, 4 acres in Cape Girardeau, for the purpose of erecting public buildings thereon, including a court house and prison that have already been erected. Sd land is bounded on the E by Spanish St, W by Lorimier St, and divided into 2 equal parts by Themis St. Sd land is to remain forever common and public, never to be appropriated to private use. Signed L. **LORIMIER**. Test B. **COUSIN**. Rec 13 Aug 1807.

178. Page 119. 27 Sep 1806. Medad **RANDOLL** and Richard **WALLER** to John **HITT**. For the sum of $5000, bond to make title to 300 arpens, being where sd **RANDLE** now lives; bounded on the N by Joseph **WALLER** and John **ABERNATHIE**; S by Samuel **RANDOLE**, decd, son of Enos; W by Enos **RANDLE**; and being the same granted to Daniel O. **DUGGAN** on 1 Apr 1798. Signed Medad **RANDOL**, Richard **WALLER**. Wit Allen **McKINSE**, Thomas (T) **ENGLISH**, L. **LORIMIER** (JCCP). Rec 14 Aug 1807.

179. Page 120. 17 Sep 1806. Ithamore **HUBBLE** to Jeremiah **SIMSON**. For the sum of 4200 Spanish Mill dollars, bond to make title to 600 acres, joining Watlers **BURRIS** (?), Joseph **FIGHT**, John **DRYBREAD**, Martin **RODNEY**, Abraham **BYRD**, and Matthew **HUBBLE**; being the same where sd **HUBBLE** settled as his head right, and where Adence(?) **ROGERS** now lives. Sd **SIMSON** to take possession on 7 Oct next, and title to be made when the payment is made. Signed Ithamore (x) **HUBBLE**. Test John **THOMSON**, Abraham **BYRD**, Samuel G. **DUNN**, Christr. **HAYS** (JCCP). Rec 31 Aug 1807.

180. Page 121. 28 May 1807. Jeremiah **SIMPSON** and John **SIMPSON** to John **DUNN**. For the sum of $700, two negros, **Patrick** about 11 years old, and **Sheela** about 9 years old. Signed Jeremiah **SIMPSON**, John **SIMPSON**. Wit Dens. **SULLIVAN**, John **CAMERON**, Aaron **DAVIS**, Christr. **HAYS** (JCCP). Rec 31 Aug 1807.

181. Page 121. 3 Sep 1807. John **SIMPSON** and Jeremiah **SIMPSON** and Maryann, his wife, to Mathew **SCRUGGS**. For the sum of $1000, 800 arpens and 40 perches, beginning on a land mark; being a grant from his Catholic Majesty to Jeremiah **SIMPSON**, and assigned by him to John **SIMPSON**. Signed John **SIMPSON**, Jeremiah **SIMPSON**, Maryann ( ) **SIMPSON**. Wit Dens. **SULLIVAN**, Wm. **DUNN** (JP), Wright **DANIEL**, Enoch **EVANS**. Rec 29 Sep 1807.

182. Page 123. 29 Sep 1807. Benjamin **ANTHONY** of Lincoln Co., N. Car., yeoman, to Jeremiah **BANIGH [BENNICK]**, his father-in-law. For the sum of $1600, bond to build a house on land that sd **BANIGH** has conveyed on this date to sd **ANTHONY**; to add to buildings for the use of sd **BANIGH** and Margaretha, his wife, and those that live with them; provide them sufficient firewood, cut and hauled to the door, clothes for work or holidays, every sort of meat, butter and milk, cofee, whisky, and other victuals and substances agreeable to aged persons; to attend them with all care in health and sickness; and to provide them with sufficient meal bread and all necessaries during their lifetimes. Should any contest arise between sd **BANIGH** and sd **ANTHONY**, then three freeholders in the neighborhood, equally selected, shall settle the same. Signed Benj. **ANTHONY**. Wit [2 German signatures], Fred. **LIMBAUGH** Senr, John **BYRD** (JCCP). Rec 2 Oct 1807.

183. Page 125. 5 Oct 1807. Samuel **RANDOL** to Willm. **THOMSON** and Elizabeth, his wife. Deed of gift for one negro boy named **Joe**. Signed Samuel (x) **RANDOL**. Wit D. **SULLIVAN**, Nathan **McCARTY**, Christr. **HAYS** (JCCP). Rec 10 Oct 1807.

184. Page 125. 1 Dec 1806. Wm. **OGLE** to Louis **LORIMIER**. For the sum of $100 in silver coin of the U. S., mortgage on Lot No. 11, Range E in Cape Girardeau. The debt due with interest from 1 Jul next on 1 Jul 1808. Signed Wm. **OGLE**. Test Solomon **ELLIS**, B. **COUSIN**, Christr. **HAYS** (JCCP). Rec 23 Oct 1807. [Marginal note: Full satisfaction received on 24 Nov 1809. Signed Geo. C. C. **HARBISON**, atty. Test Geo. **HENDERSON**, Recr.]

185. Page 126. 1 Dec 1806. Solomon **ELLIS** to same. For the sum of $100 in silver coin, mortgage on Lot No. 10, Range E in Cape Girardeau, conveyed to him by sd **LORIMIER** in behalf of sd **ELLIS'** sons Erasmus and Allen. The debt to be paid by 1 Jul 1808. Signed Solomon **THORN**. Wit B. **COUSIN**, Wm. **OGLE**, Christr. **HAYS** (JCCP). Rec 23 Oct 1807.

186. Page 126. 1 Dec 1806. Same to same. For the sum of $100 in silver coin, mortgage on Lot No. 9, Range E in Cape Girardeau, conveyed to him by sd **LORIMIER** in behalf of his son James **ELLIS**. The debt to bear interest from 1 Jul next. Signed Solomon **ELLIS**. Test Wm. **OGLE**, B. **COUSIN**, Christr. **HAYS** (JCCP). Rec 23 Oct 1807.

187. Page 127. 14 Jul 1807. Ezekiel **ABLE** to same. For the sum of $100, mortgage on Lot No. 14, Range E in Cape Girardeau, to be paid within 12 months. Signed Ezekiel **ABLE**. Test B. **COUSIN**, Christr. **HAYS** (JCCP). Rec 23 Oct 1807.

188. Page 127. 11 Jul 1806. G. C. **HARTT** to same. For the sum of $100, mortgage on Lot No. 9, Range F, being the SE ¼ of the third square from the Mississippi River; bounded on the S by St Bellview and E by Lorimier St.; to be paid by 1 May next. Signed G. C. **HARTT**. Test B. **COUSIN**, Christr. **HAYS** (JCCP). Rec 23 Oct 1807.

189. Page 128. 20 Apr 1807. John and Samuel **RANDOL** to same. For the sum of $210 in silver specie, mortgage on a lot in Cape Girardeau joining the public square, being the same occupied and improved by Anthony **HADEN**, Esqr, who resigned his right to sd **RANDOL**s; the debt due by the end of May next. Signed John **RANDOL**, Samuel **RANDOL**. Wit B. **COUSIN**, Christr. **HAYS** (JCCP). Rec 23 Oct 1807. [Marginal note: Full satisfaction received 17 Jul 1817. Signed D. F. **STEINBECK**, adminr of Louis **LORIMIER**, decd. Wit J. **McFERRON**, Clerk.]

190. Page 129. 19 Dec 1806. John C. **HARBISON** to same. For the sum of $300, mortgage on Lot No. 8, Range F, and Lot Nos. 8 & 9, Range C in Cape Girardeau; the debt due by 1 May next. Signed Jno. C. **HARBISON**. Test B. **COUSIN**, Christr. **HAYS** (JCCP). Rec 23 Oct 1807.

191. Page 129. 1 Jul 1806. Andrew **RAMSEY** to same. For the sum of $200 in silver specie, mortgage on Lot Nos. 7 & 8, Range D in Cape Girardeau; the debt due in 12 months. Signed Andrew **RAMSEY**. Test Medad **RANDOL**, B. **COUSIN**, Christr. **HAYS** (JCCP). Rec 23 Oct 1807.

192. Page 130. 8 Jun 1807. William **WHITE** to same. For the sum of $100, mortgage on Lot No. 9, Range B in Cape Girardeau; the debt due by 1 May next. Signed Wm. **WHITE**. Test Wm. **NEELY**, B. **COUSIN**, Christr. **HAYS** (JCCP). Rec 23 Oct 1807.

193. Page 130. 1 Jul 1807. Charles G. **ELLIS** and Solomon **ELLIS** to same. For the sum of $100 in silver specie, mortgage on Lot No. 5, Range F in Cape Girardeau; the debt due by 1 Jul 1808. Sd **ELLIS**es are acting in behalf of Sarah **DAVIS**. Signed Charles G. **ELLIS**, Solomon **ELLIS**. Wit Wm. **OGLE**, B. **COUSIN**, Christr. **HAYS** (JCCP). Rec 23 Oct 1807. [Full satisfaction received on 24 Nov 1809. Signed Geo. C. C. **HARBISON**, attny. Test Geo. **HENDERSON**, Recr.]

194. Page 131. 9 Nov 1806. Elisha **ELLIS** and Solomon **ELLIS** to same. For the sum of $100 in silver specie, mortgage on Lot No. 8, Range E in Cape Girardeau; the debt due on 1 Jul 1808, or it will bear interest thereafter. Signed Elisha **ELLIS**, Solomon **ELLIS**. Wit Wm. **OGLE**, B. **COUSIN**, Christr. **HAYS** (JCCP). Rec 23 Oct 1807.

195. Page 132. 27 Mar 1806. Henry **HAND** to same. For the sum of $100, mortgage on a lot in Cape Girardeau; the debt due by 1 Nov next. Signed Henry **HAND**. Wit John **GIBONEY**, B.

COUSIN, Christr. **HAYS** (JCCP). Rec 23 Oct 1807.

196. Page 133. 22 Aug 1807. Joseph **SEAWELL** and William **NEELY** to same. For the sum of $150 in coin, mortgage on Lot No. 12, Range B in Cape Girardeau; the debt due on 9 May next. Signed Joseph **SEAWELL**, Wm. **NEELY**. Wit John **WILSON**, B. **COUSIN**, Christr. **HAYS** (JCCP). Rec 23 Oct 1807.

197. Page 133. 22 Aug 1805. Peter **GODAIR**, alias **Sonnette**, and Essix, his wife, to Bartholomew **COUSIN**. For the sum of $555, a negro boy slave named **Willis**, aged about 9 or 10 years, whom sd **GODAIR** purchased of David **HARRIS** on 11 Sep 1804. Signed Peter (x) **GODAIR**, alias **Sonnette**, Essexs **GODER**. Wit James **SCOTT**, Hypolite **MAROTE**. Rec 23 Oct 1807.

198. Page 134. 10 Jan 1803. L. **LORIMIER** to Bartholomew **COUSIN**. Gift of land in Cape Girardeau; bordered to the N by Solomon **THORN**, W by two streets, and E by the wagon road which goes along the river; including about ½ arpent with a house or cabin being about 18 feet long by 15 feet wide with a "galline" on the front, with a pole fence and other works on the site; being the same purchased from sd **THORN**, who acquired it from Samuel **BRADLEY**, to whom sd **LORIMIER** originally sold it. Signed Louis **LORIMIER**. Wit Don Dehault-**DELASSUS**, Camille **DELASSUS**, Fivis **VALLE**, Jr. Rec 23 Oct 1807. [IN FRENCH]

199. Page 135. 26 Aug 1807. Joseph **WORTHINGTON** to Joseph **THOMPSON** Senr. For the sum of $243, 284 arpens, 31 ½ perches (243 acres), as surveyed on 20 Dec 1805 for him as assignee of Henry **HALL**; bounded on the N by John **GUIBONY**, S by Jacob **JACOBS** and Terence **DIAL**, E by unappropriated lands, and W by Abraham and Thomson **BYRD**. Signed Jos. **WORTHINGTON**. Wit L. **LAPORTE**, Christr. **HAYS** (JCCP). Rec 18 Nov 1807.

200. Page 136. 29 Sep 1807. Samuel **RANDOLL**, and William and Elizabeth **THOMSON**, formerly of the Cape Girardeau Dist and now of the New Madrid Dist, to John **SHEPPARD**. For two negros and a horse, 300 arpens, French measure, more or less, on Randoll's Creek; bounded on the N by the heirs of Samuel **RANDOLL** Junr., decd, S by Jeremiah **THOMSON**, and W by the original grant of Enos **RANDOLL** Senr. Signed Saml.

(x) **RANDOL**, Wm. **THOMSON**, Elizabeth (x) **THOMSON**. Test Daniel **BRANT**, Enoch **EVANS** (JP). Rec 10 Nov 1807.

201. Page 137. 7 Oct 1807. Alexander **MILLIKIN** to John **ORDWAY**, both of Tywappity Twp. For the sum of $940, 350 arpens in Tywappity Twp on the Mississippi River, being the head right of sd **MILLIKIN**; bounded on the E by the Mississippi River, S by James **CURRIN**, W by Jesse **BOWDEN**, and N by John **LOYD**'s head right, now the property of sd **ORDWAY**. Signed Alexander **MILLIKIN**. Wit A. **HADEN**, Saml. **BRADLEY**, Christr. **HAYS** (JCCP). Rec 18 Nov 1807.

202. Page 138. 10 Oct 1807. John **LOYD** and Delily, his wife, to same, all of Tywappity Twp. For the sum of $225, 50 arpens on the W bank of the Mississippi River in Tywappity Twp, being the lower side of sd **LOYD**'s head right; bounded on the E by the Mississippi River, S by a line between sd **LOYD** and Alexander **MILLIKIN**, and W by vacant lands. Signed John **LOYD**, Delilah (x) **LOYD**. Wit Alexandr **MILLIKIN**, Wm. **LOYD**, Timothy (x) **HARRIS**, George (x) **SADLER**, Christr. **HAYS** (JCCP). Rec 18 Nov 1807.

203. Page 139. 10 Oct 1807. Same and same to same. For the sum of $300, 100 arpens in Tywappity Twp, being the part of his head right including the first improvements made on sd head right; bounded on the E by land sd **ORDWAY** purchased of Alexander **MILLIKIN**, S by Jesse **BOWDEN**'s head right, W by Congress lands, and N by Charles **FINLEY**. Signed John **LOYD**, Delilah (x) **LOYD**. Wit Alexandr **MILLIKIN**, W. **LOYD**, George (x) **SADLER**, Timothy (x) **HARRIS**, Christr **HAYS** (JCCP). Rec 18 Nov 1807.

204. Page 141. 6 Oct 1807. Alexander **MILLIKIN** to same. For the sum of $__, all the cattle and hogs that are on the plantation lately sold to sd **ORDWAY** on the Mississippi River in Tywappity Twp, except those reserved by contract. Sd **ORDWAY** is also to have the mark of sd **MILLIKIN**; a smooth crop of the left ear and under bit and a slit in the right ear. Signed Alexandr **MILLIKIN**. Wit Saml. **BRADLEY**, John **RANDOL**, Christr. **HAYS** (JCCP). Rec 18 Nov 1807.

205. Page 141. 9 Oct 1807. Roland **MERIDETH** of the Ste. Genevieve Dist to George **HAYS**. For the sum of $187, 240 acres, being his head right granted by Louis

LORIMIER, commandant. Signed Roland **MERIDETH**. Wit Geo **HENDERSON**, Nathan **McCARTY**, Christr. **HAYS** (JCCP). Rec 12 Dec 1807.

206. Page 142. 18 Sep 1807. William **LORIMIER** by Sheriff John **HAYS** to James **EVANS**, Esqr. For the sum of $121, 500 arpens back of the old Cape. Sold on 15 Sep 1807 in execution of two writs of fieri facias from Territorial Court, one obtained by James **ROBERTSON** against sd **LORIMIER** for $60.35 debt with 6% interest per annum from 17 Sep 1805 and $8.46 ½ costs; the other obtained by Waters & Hall for $56.96 and 5 mills in debt, $30 damages, and $7.12 costs. Signed John **HAYS**, Sheriff. Test Robt **GREEN** (JCCP), Thomas C. **SCOTT**, Common Pleas Court Clerk. Rec 16 Dec 1807.

207. Page 145. 22 Sep 1807. John C. **HARBISON** to Thomas **GRAHAM**. For 200 gallons of whiskey to be paid by 1 Jun or sooner and $50, deed for 3/4 of his lot. Signed Jno. C. **HARBISON**, Thos. **GRAHAM**. Wit James **EVANS**, Enoch **EVANS**, Christr. **HAYS** (JCCP). Rec 17 Dec 1807.

208. Page 145. 26 Dec 1806. Edward F. **BOND** to Betsy **GIBSON**. For the sum of $1, __ acres on Stephen **BYRD**'s Creek where sd **BOND** lives, and all the cattle, hogs, horses, and every other specious property rights and credits. Signed Edwd. F. **BOND**. Wit Christr. **HAYS** (JCCP). Rec 7 Dec 1807.

209. Page 146. 9 Mar 1807. Ebenezer **HUBBELL** and Ithamer **HUBBLE** to Maurice **YOUNG**. For the sum of $100, 200 acres or more, being an improvement on the W side of White Water, adjoining land formerly claimed by Jonathan **HUBBELL** Junr and now belonging to Dennis **SULLIVAN**. If a good title can be obtained to the land by Ebenezer **HUBBLE**, then he is bound for $600 to sd **YOUNG** to make a deed; otherwise sd **YOUNG** has no further demand, and must pay $200 to sd E. **HUBBELL**. Signed Ebenezer (x) **HUBBLE**, Ithamer (x) **HUBBLE**, Morris **YOUNG**. Wit Dens. **SULLIVAN**, Mary **HUBBLE**, John **BYRD** [JCCP]. Rec 30 Dec 1807.

210. Page 146. 24 Nov 1805. Thomas W. **WATERS** to Richard **DAVIS** of Frederick Co., Md. For the sum of $2400, bond to make a deed on 800 arpens on Mucklemurry Island, opposite to James **CURREN** in Tywappity Bottom, within 12 months or any time on demand, provided the commissioners confirm the concession. Signed Thos. W. **WATERS**. Wit James **BRADY**, Christr. **HAYS** (JCCP). Rec 31 Dec 1807.

211. Page 147. 4 Jan 1808. Richard **WALLER** and Medad **RANDOL** to William **WILLIAMS**. For the sum of $600, bond to execute a deed of conveyance, in fee simple, within 10 months, to an estimated 100 arpens, French measure, on both sides of the left-hand fork of Randoll's Mill Creek; adjoining Joseph **WALLER**, James **DOWTY**, John **ABERNATHIE**, and a field with a burned cabin where Thos. **GREEN** formerly tended the land; being the upper part of the old survey of sd **WALLER**, where he formerly lived. Should the land be more than 100 arpens, then sd **WILLIAMS** to pay at $3/arpen; if less than 100 arpens, then Richard **WALLER** is to make up the quantity or pay sd **WILLIAMS** for same. Signed Richard **WALLER**, Medad **RANDOL**. Test Geo. **HENDERSON**, James **ARREL**, Christr. **HAYS** (JCCP). Rec 5 Jan 1808.

212. Page 149. 31 Dec 1807. Stephen **QUIMBY** to Robert **QUIMBY**. For the sum of $746.16, one horse, 19 cattle, his crop of corne, all his household furneture and plantation utensels. Signed Stephen **QUIMBY**. Wit John (   ) **FRIEND**, Jacob **FRIEND**, Christr. **HAYS** (JCCP). Rec 11 Jan 1808.

213. Page 149. 15 Jul 1805. Jacob **ISOM** to Rufus **EASTON** of St. Louis, Mo. For the sum of $100, 640 acres on the head waters which run through John **GIBBONIE**'s land and adjoining James **COX**es' improvement on the S and sd **GIBBONIE** on the N, being the allowance to the wife and family of a settler, and the improvement right of David **McMOURTRY**, he having a wife and one child. Signed Jacob **ISOM**. Wit Saml. **SOLOMON**, Edwd. F. **BOND**, Otho **SHRADER**, Judge of La. Terr.. Rec 19 Jan 1808.

214. Page 150. 16 Oct 1807. Samuel **RANDOLL** to John **RANDOLL**. For a valuable consideration, one bay mare named Gin about eight years old (to be delivered now); a bay horse five years old; a yellow bay mare named Fanny with her two colts; two other two-year-old colts, both bay; a sorrel mare and her colt got by Cumberland Venture; a dark bay mare four years old; a sorrel mare two years old past; a yearling mare colt of sorrel kind; a dark brown mare name Poll; all his cattle and hogs now on the Indiana side of the Mississippi, all marked with a crop

off the left ear and an underbit in right ear. Signed Samuel (x) **RANDALL**. Test F. M. **HENRY**, Alexander **SCOTT**, Robt. **BLAIR** (JP). Rec 4 Feb 1808.

215. Page 151. 15 Nov 1807. Same to same. For the sum of $__, a waggon and hour horses which he purchased at the sale of Medad **RANDALL**. Signed Saml. (x) **RANDALL**. Test F. M. **HENRY**, Robt. **BLAIR** (JP). Rec 4 Feb 1808.

216. Page 151. 16 Oct 1807. Same to same. For a valuable consideration, a negro named **Jeffry**. Signed Samuel (x) **RANDALL**. Test F. M. **HENRY**, Alexander **SCOTT**, Robt. **BLAIR** (JP). Rec 4 Feb 1808.

217. Page 152. 1 Feb 1808. Charles **DEMOSS** to George **HAYS**. For the sum of $500, bond to execute a deed within 18 months for 100 acres; being the SW corner of a tract where sd **DEMOSS** now lives, adjoining sd **HAYS** and Christopher **HAYS**; and being the same conveyed by sd **DEMOSS** to Jeremiah W. **STILL** on 27 Dec 1804, by sd **STILL** to Abraham **BYRD** acting for Jacob **SKEAN** by an assignment dated 7 Nov 1805, and by him to sd **HAYS**. Sd **DEMOSS** has sold the land to sd **HAYS** for $100 on this date. Signed Charles **DEMOSS**. Test Geo. **HENDERSON**, John **HAYS**, Christr. **HAYS** (JCCP). Rec 4 Feb 1808.

218. Page 152. 27 Jan 1807. George **MORGAN** to James **EARL**. For the sum of $50, his improvement on the E side of White Water Creek, adjoined by Jeremiah **CONAWAY**. Signed George (M) **MORGAN**. Wit John **DAVIS**, Alex. **McDANIEL**, Christr. **HAYS** (JCCP). Rec 12 Feb 1808.

219. Page 153. 27 Jan 1807. Jeremiah **CONAWAY** to same. For the sum of $50, an improvement on the waters of White Water known as Round Pond Improvement, made by sd **CONAWAY**. Signed Jeremiah **CONAWAY**. Wit John **DAVIS**, Alex. **McDANIEL**, Christr. **HAYS** (JCCP). Rec 12 Feb 1808.

220. Page 154. 20 Feb 1808. Samuel **RANDOL**, William **THOMSON**, and Elizabeth **THOMSON** to John **SHEPPARD**. Deed proved in open court (AB:136). Signed Daniel **BRANT**. Wit Christr. **HAYS** (JCCP). Rec 20 Feb 1808.

221. Page 154. 15 Mar 1808. Meriwether **LEWIS**, Governor and Commander-in-chief of the Terr. of La., to Joseph **McFERRON**.

Appointment as Clerk of the Courts of Common Pleas and Quarter Sessions of the Dist of Cape Girardeau. Signed Meriwether **LEWIS**, Governor. Wit Frederick **BATES**, Secretary. Joseph **McFERRON** takes the oath as clerk of the Courts of Common Pleas and Quarter Sessions. Signed Joseph **McFERRON**. Wit Bernd. **PRATLE**. Rec 19 Mar 1808.

222. Page 155. 16 Mar 1808. Same to same. Commission to administer oaths of office to Justices of the Peace, and subordinate offices civil and military. Signed Meriwether **LEWIS**, Governor. Wit Frederick **BATES**, Secretary. Rec 19 Mar 1808.

223. Page 155. 1 Feb 1808. Charles **FRIEND** to Israel **FRIEND**. For certain good causes to his son Israel **FRIEND**, 400 arpens known by the name Jacob **BOGARD**; adjoined on the S by John **FRIEND** and E by Jonas **FRIEND**. Signed Charles **FRIEND**. Wit Andrew **RAMSEY**, Wm. **RAMSEY**, Andrew **RAMSEY**, James **RAMSEY**, John **BYRD** (JCCP). Rec 21 Mar 1808.

224. Page 156. 23 Sep 1807. John **LARK** to James **CURRIN**. Power of attorney to collect all debts that may be due within La. Terr., and to give receipts, pay moneys and to ratify any acts for him. Signed John **LARK**. Wit Jno. C. **HARBISON**, Ths. **HAWKINS**, Robert **BLAIR** (JP). Rec 22 Mar 1808.

225. Page 156. 12 Mar 1808. Louis **LORIMIER** to Frederick **GIBLER**. For the sum of $50, lot in Cape Girardeau, to the S and adjoining two lots formerly sold to and occupied by sd **GIBLER**. Signed L. **LORIMIER**. Test B. **COUSIN**, Christr. **HAYS** (JCCP). Rec 25 Mar 1808.

226. Page 157. 23 Jun 1806. Same to same. For the sum of $200 in a note obligatory and mortgage, two lots in Cape Girardeau on a branch heretofore considered the S boundary of the village, and ½ way from the mouth of sd branch to sd **LORIMIER**'s dwelling; bounded by streets on the N, E, and W, and S by unappropriated lots. Should sd **GIBLER** build a dam across the branch below, he is not to raise the water so as to drown any of the springs above sd branch. Signed L. **LORIMIER**. Wit Jn. **LAVALLEE**, B. **COUSIN**, Christr. **HAYS** (JCCP). Rec 25 Mar 1808.

227. Page 158. 18 Feb 1808. Robert **LANE** and Briget, his wife, to James **MONTGOMERY**. For the sum of $700, 450 arpens in Tywappity Bottom on the W side of the Mississippi River, being a Spanish Grant to sd **LANE** recorded in New Madrid, to include the improvement where they now live. Signed Robert **LANE**, Briget **LANE**. Wit Th. O. **FLETCHER**, Wilson **MONTGOMERY**, Christr. **HAYS** (JCCP). Rec 25 Mar 1808.

228. Page 159. 18 Feb 1808. James **MONTGOMERY** and Barbary, his wife, to Robert **LANE**. For the sum of $700, 350 arpens on the W bank of the Mississippi in Tywappity Bottom; being a Spanish Grant to Thomas **WELBORN** recorded in New Madrid, so as to include the improvement where sd **WELBORN** lives. Signed James **MONTGOMERY**, Barbary **MONTGOMERY**. Wit Thos. **FLETCHER**, Wilson **MONTGOMERY**, Christr. **HAYS** (JCCP). Rec 25 Mar 1808.

229. Page 160. 18 Jan 1808. Thomas **WELBORN** to James **MONTGOMERY**. For the sum of $700, two tracts on the W bank of the Mississippi in Tywappity Bottom; 250 arpens where sd **WELLBORN** now lives, being part of a Spanish Grant for 450 arpens to sd **WELLBORN** recorded in New Madrid; and 100 arpends granted to John **WELLBORN**, to include the balance of sd improvement and adjoining the 250 arpens. Signed Thos. **WELLBORN**. Wit James **CURRIN**, John **WELLBORN**, Robt. **GREEN** (JCCP). Rec 25 Mar 1808.

230. Page 161. 15 Dec 1807. James **BRADY** and James **CURRIN** of Tywappity Bottom to Richard **DAVIS** of Md. For the sum of $1240, bond to execute a deed by the last of Mar next, on a tract in Tywappity Bottom about ten miles below Mrs. **WATERS**, and about 1 ½ miles from the Mississippi River on the E boundary, being part of the settlement rights of Mary **SMITH** and Joshua **SEXTON**. Sd land is level and clear from swamps, and sd **DAVIS** has paid sd **BRADY** $620 for it. Signed James **BRADY**, James **CURRIN**. Wit Th. C. **SCOTT**, John **WILBURN**, Christr. **HAYS** (JCCP). Rec 25 Mar 1808.

231. Page 162. 22 Feb 1808. Josiah **QUIMBY** to Robert **QUIMBY**. For the sum of $1000, 200 arpens, more or less, in Tywappity Bottom, beginning at a boxelder near the Mississippi River. Signed Josiah **QUIMBY**. Wit A. **HADEN**, D. F. **STEINBECK**, Levi **WOLVERTON**, John **BYRD** (JCCP). Rec 26 Mar 1808.

232. Page 163. 22 Feb 1808. Stephen **QUIMBY** to same. For the sum of $1000, 200 arpens, more or less, in Tywappity Bottom, beginning at a boxelder and elm near the Mississippi River at the SE boundary of Josiah **QUIMBY**. Signed Stephen **QUIMBY**. Wit A. **HADEN**, D. F. **STEINBECK**, Levi **WOLVERTON**, John **BYRD** (JCCP). Rec 26 Mar 1808.

233. Page 164. 1 Apr 1808. Valetine **LOWR** (alias **LOHR**), bachelor, to Joseph **NISWONGER** Junr. For diverse good causes and considerations, him thereunto moving, and the sum of $800, 300 acres on the little fork E of Little White River granted to sd **LOHR** in 1804 by Louis **LORIMIER** and his agent **COUSANT**; adjoining Jacob **WELKER**, Rubn. **NORMAN**, and vacant land; also four head of horses; a sorrel horse about 15 years of age; a bay mare about five years old; sorrel of about two years; a colt of one year; a man's saddle and bridle; a ploughshare, colter, etc; two axes; one wedge; a grubing hew; a sickle; a steel drap; and all other articles of husbandry and household furniture too tedious to mention; subject to the payment of taxes. Signed Valetine (x) **LOWR** [also for money received]. Wit Martin (W) **DUMAS**, [German signature], John **BYRD** (JCCP). Rec 17 Apr 1808.

234. Page 166. 1 Oct 1807. Frederick **BATES**, Secretary of the Terr. of La., to Robert **BLAIR**, Esq. Commission as JP in Cape Girardeau Twp.. Signed Frederick **BATES**, Secretary of La. Terr.. Sd **BLAIR** is administered the oath of office by Th. C. **SCOTT**. Rec 19 Apr 1808.

235. Page 167. 9 Apr 1808. Andrew **RAMSEY** Junior to Jesse **SCRUGGS**. For the sum of $300, 229 arpens or 196 acres nearly, on the waters of Ramsey Creek; adjoining the heirs of Samuel **TIPTON**, land formerly belonging to William **BONER**, and land surveyed for David **HARRIS** and now occupied by Jno. C. **HARBISON**; being the same bought by sd **RAMSEY** of John **GUETHING**, and by him from Jonathan **DITCH**, who was granted it by the Spanish Government; excepting 6 acres sold heretofore to David **HARRIS** at the NW corner of the tract, and now occupied by sd **HARBISON**. Signed Andrew **RAMSEY**. Wit Enoch **EVANS** (JP), Andrew **RAMSEY**. Rec 27 Apr 1808.

236. Page 168. 18 Dec 1807. Tarence **DOYL** and Elizebeth, his wife, to Jesse **SCRUGG**. For the sum of $600, 310 arpens, being the improvement where they now live; being the same granted to sd **DOYL** by his Catholic Majesty. Signed Tarence (I) **DOYL**, Elezebeth (x) **DOYL**. Wit Charles **WALL**, Mathew **SCRUGGS**, John **SHIELDS**, Enoch **EVANS** (JP). Rec 27 Apr 1808.

237. Page 169. 28 Apr 1808. Daniel **SEXTON** and Nancy, his wife, of Ind. Terr., to Fanny **WATERS**, adminr of Thomas W. **WATERS**, decd. For the sum of $820, 250 arpens, 10 arpens of which originally belonged to William **SMITH**, in Tywappity Bottom where sd **SEXTON** formerly lived, lying on the Mississippi River between Mrs. **WATERS** and where Lemuel **CHENEY** formerly lived. Signed Daniel **SEXTON**, Nansy **SEXTON**. Wit James **CURRIN**, James **BRAYDY**, Christr. **HAYS** (JCCP). Rec 2 May 1808.

238. Page 170. 22 Nov 1807. Josiah **QUIMBY** to Stephen **QUIMBY**. For the sum of $400, 200 arpens; bounded on the S by Stephen **QUIMBY**, N by James **CUREN**, and E by the Mississippi River. Josiah **QUIMBY** also posts a bond of $1000 against any other claims. Signed Josiah **QUIMBY**. Test Stephen ( ) **JONES**, William **SOWLE**, Christr. **HAYS** (JCCP). Stephen **QUIMBY** assigns title to James **MOGOMERY** for value received on 7 Dec 1807. Signed Stephen **QUIMBY**. Wit William **SOWLE**, Phebe **SOWLE**. James **MONTGOMERY** assigns title to James **CURRIN**, etc. for value received on 10 Dec 1807. Signed James **MONTGOMERY**. Test James **WELLBORN**, Wm. **KELSO**. Wit Edmond **HOGAN** (JP), Christr. **HAYS** (JCCP). Rec 2 May 1808.

239. Page 171. 22 Apr 1808. Same to James **CURRIN**. Confirmation of the preceding deed and assignments. Sd **QUIMBY** had given a deed to Robert **QUIMBY** for the same land, but acknowledges he did so in a fraudulent manner to get clear of paying his debts and did not receive any value for the sd land. The deed to Robert **QUIMBY** is disowned. Signed Josiah **QUIMBY**. Test Edmond **HOGAN** (JP), James **BRADY**, Christr. **HAYS** (JCCP). Rec 2 May 1808.

240. Page 172. 15 Apr 1806. U. S. Commissioners of Land Claims to John **LATHAM**. Grant for 300 arpens, provided sd land is found vacant, his having cultivated sd land prior to and on 20 Dec 1803. Signed John B. C. **LUCAS**, Jas. S. **DONALDSON**, by the Board. John **LEATHAM** assigns the land to James **DOWTY** on 23 Oct 1806. Signed John (I) **LEATHAM**. Test David **HOLLEY**, James

COX Junr, Christr. **HAYS** (JCCP). Rec 27 May 1808.

241. Page 173. 29 Sep 1807. Jeremiah **BANIGH** [**BENNICK**] to Benjamin **ANTHONY**, his son-in-law, of Lincoln Co., N. Car. For the sum of $1600, bond to convey his right to 800 acres, more or less, being all his land in the Dutch Settlement, adjoining Peter **HARTLE**, Daniel **BOLLINGER**, Frederic **LIMBAUGH** Senr, and others, granted to him by the Spanish or French Governments. Sd **ANTHONY** is to abide by an obligation to support sd **BANIGH** and his wife (see AB:123), and is to pay all costs for confirming title. Signed Jeremiah **BANIGH** [in German]. Wit [German signature], Frederic **LIMBAUGH** Senr., Christr. **HAYS** (JCCP). Rec 30 May 1808.

242. Page 174. 26 May 1808. Solomon **ELLIS** Senr. and Elisha **ELLIS** to Erasmus **ELLIS**. For securing a payment of $3000 and the sum of $1, deed of trust for 240 arpens, more or less, on Ramsey's Creek, bounded on the N by the heirs of Saml. **TIPTON**, S by Peter **GODAIR**, E by Andrew **RAMSEY**, and W by a tract formerly granted to John **DITCH** and now owned by sd **RAMSEY**; also Lot No. 8 marked E and Lot No. 2 marked F in Cape Girardeau. Erasmus **ELLIS** is to sell the lands at public sale if Solomon and Elisha **ELLIS** do not pay the debt by 1 Jan 1809. Signed Solomon **ELLIS**, Elisha **ELLIS**. Wit Enoch **EVANS** (JP), Robt. **BLAIR** (JP). Rec 30 May 1808.

243. Page 175. 26 May 1808. Same and same to same. For securing the payment of $20,000 and the sum of $1, deed of trust on property; negro men including **Dick** 45 years of age, **Sam** about 30, **Ralph** about 20, **Harry** about 45, **Jacob** about 18, **Abraham** about 20, **Bob** about 19, **Neron** about 30; negro women including **Fanny** 60 years of age, **Genny** about 45, **Phillis** about 30, Ginny **WILSON** about 30, **Charity** about 30, **Jannet** about 20 and her infant, **Clory** about 25; negro girls including **Darcus** 18 years old, **Amy** about 16, **Sopha** aged 18, **Mint** about 12, **Cate** about 10, **Fanny** about 4, **Mary** about 3; negro boys including **Frederic** about 8 years old, **Isaac** about 10, **Jesse** about 2; also five sorrel horses; two black horses; two bay horses; one white horse and black mare; 70 head of neat cattle; 11 feather bed with furniture; five bed steads; 20 trunks; four folding tables; and 100 head of hogs. Erasmus **ELLIS** is to sell the property at public sale if Solomon and Elisha **ELLIS** do not pay the debt by 1 Jan 1809. Signed Solomon **ELLIS**, Elisha **ELLIS**. Wit Enoch

EVANS (JP), Robert **BLAIR** (JP). Rec 30 May 1808.

244. Page 177. 30 Mar 1807. David **FARRIL** to John and Robert **GIBONEY**. For the performance of making a title to a tract of land, bond on one black horse known as Forters ball, two cows and yearlings, and all his household furniture and farming utensils. Signed David **FARRIL**. Wit Josiah **HUNTER**, John (x) **HANNA**. David **FARRIL** to John and Robert **GIBONEY**. Quit claim to 250 arpens where he now lives. Signed David **FARRIL**. Wit Josiah **HUNTER**, John (x) **HANNA**, Robert **BLAIR** (JP), Enoch **EVANS** (JP). Rec 30 May 1808.

245. Page 178. 30 Mar 1807. Same to same and same. For the sum of $1000, bond to make a title to 250 arpens off the W end of the tract where he now lives. Signed David **FARRIL**. Wit Josiah **HUNTER**, John (x) **HANNA**, Robert **BLAIR** (JP), Enoch **EVANS** (JP). Rec 30 May 1808.

246. Page 179. 6 Sep 1805. James **MURPHY** to William **GARNER**. For the sum of $300, the head right and improvement where he now lives, bounded on the E by Mr. **CONAWAY**, and N and S by vacant land. Signed James (x) **MURPHY**. Wit Dens. **SULLIVAN**, David **FARRIL**, John **BYRD** (JCCP). Rec 1 Jun 1808.

247. Page 179. 27 May 1808. Thomas **MORGAN** appeared before John **ABERNATHIE**, JP for Cape Girardeau Twp, to swear he witnessed John **LATHAM**, formerly of the Cape Girardeau Dist, assign his title to 979 acres and some poles for value received on 23 Oct 1806 to James **DOWTY**. Signed Thos. **MORGAN**. Wit Jno. **ABERNETHIE** (JP). Rec 1 Jun 1808.

248. Page 180. 25 Jun 1808. William **HAND** to Ezekiel **ABLE**. For the sum of $100, a certain tract obtained by sd **HAND** from the commandant of the Cape Girardeau Dist. Signed Willim **HAND**. Wit Henry **HAND**, James **ARREL**, Enoch **SPINKS**, Christr. **HAYS** (JCCP). Title is assigned to Jeremiah **ABLE** for value received on 27 Jun 1808. Signed Ezekiel **ABLE**. Test Christr. **HAYS** (JCCP). Rec 1 Jun 1808.

249. Page 181. 19 Jun 1805. Articles of agreement between Thos. W. **WATERS** and Samuel **DORSEY** to exchange land. Sd **WATERS** owns 400 arpens, formerly owned by Andrew **FRANKS** and his head right, adjoining Thos. **BELEW**, Allen **McKINNY**, Jeremiah

THOMPSON, or vacant land, and a tract of DESHA's. Sd DORSEY exchanges to sd WATERS 800 acres, being his concession as old as 1799, to be laid in any part of the Cape Girardeau Dist on vacant land. Both agree to make lawful title to each other, but if it cannot be obtained, then the party not obtaining lawful title shall pay the other $600 and interest from 15 Apr past. Both make bond of $1200 to execute this agreement. Signed Thos. W. WATERS, Saml. DORSEY. Test John HAYS, Thos. BALLEW, Christr. HAYS (JCCP). Rec 1 Jun 1808.

250. Page 181. 9 Mar 1805. Andrew FRANKS to Louis LORIMIER. For the sum of $400, 400 arpents, more or less, about nine miles W of Cape Girardeau, joining the concessions of Enos RANDALL Senr, Allen McKINZIE, and Jno. SUMMERS Senr. Signed Andrew (A) FRANK. Wit Joseph McFERRON, John GUETHING, John BYRD (JCCP). Rec 1 Jun 1808.

251. Page 182. 29 Dec 1807. Daniel MULLINS and Sarah, his wife, to James BRADY, all of Tywappity Bottom. For the sum of $600, 213 1/3 acres on the W bank of the Mississippi River in Tywappity Bottom where sd MULLINS now lives, adjoining land confirmed to Reese BOWIE as his head right, and now claimed by William EDWARDS, and being 2/3 of the land that was to be confirmed to Sarah WILLIAMSON, now Sarah MULLINS, wife of Daniel. Signed Daniel (x) MULLINS, Saray (x) MULLINS. Wit Th. C. SCOTT, Richd. DAVIS, James CURRIN, John WELLBORN (JP). Rec 1 Jun 1808.

252. Page 183. 27 May 1804. Louis LORIMIER to Thomas W. WATERS. For the sum of $400, 400 arpens on the waters of Randalls Creek, being the same improved by Andrew FRANKS, adjoining Enos RANDALL Senr, Anthony RANDOLL, Jeremh. THOMPSON, Joseph THOMPSON, Allen McKINZIE, and John SUMMERS Senr. Signed L. LORIMIER. Wit B. COUSIN, Jack REID, John BYRD (JCCP). Rec 1 Jun 1808.

253. Page 184. 25 Apr 1808. Benjamin ROSE to James BRADY, both of Tywappity Bottom. For the sum of $700, 240 arpens granted to sd ROSE on the W bank of the Mississippi River in Tywappity Bottom, adjoining Samuel CHANEY on the upper line, Abraham BIRD on the lower line, and W by vacant land; being the same where Elizabeth LAWRANCE now lives. Signed Benj. ROSE. Wit James CURRIN, Ewd.

MATHEWS, Robt. GREEN (JCCP). Rec 1 Jun 1808.

254. Page 185. 29 Jan 1808. David ANDREW to William STROTHER of Ste. Genevieve Dist. In consequence of a former deed made by sd ANDREW to sd STROTHER, for which he gave full satisfaction, 240 arpens on Byrd's Creek, adjoining John MARTIN, John BOYD, and land claimed by Barthe. COUSIN. Signed David (x) ANDREW. Wit Dens. O. SULLIVAN, little Wm. DAUGHERTY, Robt. GREEN (JCCP). William STROTHER assigns title to John McCARTY for value received on 30 Jan 1808. Signed William STROTHER. Test. Hugh CRESWELL, Andrew LEEPER, John BYRD (JCCP). Rec 1 Jun 1808.

255. Page 186. 1 Apr 1807. Robert HALL to Robert ENGLISH. Assignment of title [land not described]. Signed Robt. HALL. Wit Anthony HADEN, Robt. GREEN (JCCP). Rec 1 Jun 1808.

256. Page 186. 8 Mar 1808. Jeremiah ABLE, Ezekiel ABLE, and Sarah, wife of Ezekiel ABLE, to William H. ASHLEY. For the sum of $2500, 480 arpens, bounded on the N by James ARRELL and Moses HURLEY, S by Thomas BULL, E by the King's Dominion, and W by William DEAKINS and Andrew RAMSEY Junr. Signed Jeremiah ABEL, Ezekiel ABEL, Sarah ABEL. Wit A. HADEN, James EVANS, John BYRD (JCCP). Rec 1 Jun 1808.

257. Page 187. 16 Mar 1808. Stephen QUIMBY by Sheriff John HAYS to James BRADY. For the sum of $234.50, 200 arpens in Tywappity Bottom. Sold on 21 Mar 1808 in execution of writ of fieri facias issued by Court of Common Pleas on 1 Dec 1807, in case of James BRADY, surviving partner of Thomas W. WATERS & Co., vs. Stephen QUIMBY for $85.25 debt, with interest at 6% per annum from 27 Feb 1807, and $6.65 costs. Signed John HAYS, Sheriff. Wit Joseph McFERRON, Clerk of Court of Common Pleas, Geo. HENDERSON, Robt. BLAIR. Rec 1 Jun 1808.

258. Page 189. 21 Mar 1801. James MILLS to Rees MERODETH. For the sum of $400, bond to make a deed for 150 acres where sd MILLS now lives by 1 Apr 1805. Signed James (x) MILLS. Wit Christr. HAYS, John GUETHING, George HAYS. [Following section IN FRENCH.] 1 Jun 1802. Sd MILLS will buy 150 arpents for 2000 piastres from Rolland MEREDITH, brother and heir of decd

Rees **MEREDITH**, as soon as Rolland **MEREDITH** obtains title to his land grant. [Remainder in ENGLISH.] Signed James (x) **MILLS**, Rolland **MERIDETH**, B. **COUSIN**, L. **LORIMIER**. Title to sd bond is assigned to John **MYRES** for value received on 27 Feb 1805. Signed Roland **MEREDITH**. Wit Christr. **HAYS** (JCCP). Title to sd bond is assigned to Hugh **CRESWELL** for value received on 10 Apr 1806. Signed John **MEYERS**. Test John **DAVIS**, John **BYRD** (JCCP). Title to sd bond is assigned to Ezekiel **ABLE** for value received on 22 Oct 1806. Signed Hugh **CRESWELL**. Test John **DAVIS**. Title to sd bond is assigned to Jeremiah **ABLE** for value received on 23 Oct 1806. Signed Ezekiel **ABLE**. Test John **DAVIS**. Title to sd bond is assigned to Jeremiah **WHETSON** for value received on 9 Oct 1807. Signed Jeremiah **ABLE**. Test John **DAVIS**. Rec 1 Jun 1808.

259. Page 191. 2 Jun 1808. Solomon **THORN** swears he executed the within instrument for the purposes herein mentioned. Signed Solomon **THORN**. Wit Robt. **GREEN** (JCCP). Rec 2 Jun 1808. [There is no additional information for this deed.]

260. Page 191. 4 Jun 1807. Francis **MURPHY** to Ezekiel **ABLE**. For the sum of $150, __ acres, being his whole head right and claim. Signed Francis (x) **MURPHY**. Wit David **FARRIL**, Alexander (x) **MURPHY**, Robt. **GREEN** (JCCP). Title is assigned to Jeremiah **ABLE** for value received on 2 Jul 1807. Signed Ezekiel **ABLE**. Wit Robt. **GREEN** (JCCP). Rec 2 Jun 1808.

261. Page 192. 10 Dec 1805. Jeremiah and John **THOMPSON** to William **VIRGEN**. For the sum of $450, 200 French acres, being where John **THOMSON** now lives, and part of the tract where Jeremiah **THOMSON** now lives. The grantors post bond of $900 to make a deed to the land. Signed Jeremiah **THOMSON**, John **THOMSON**. Test Saml. **DORSEY**, Joseph **DUNN**, John **McCARTY** (as to the signature of John **THOMSON**), Robt. **GREEN** (JCCP). Rec 2 Jun 1808.

262. Page 192. 4 Mar 1807. Ezekiel **ABLE** to Francis **MURPHY**. Agreement to return land he purchased of sd **MURPHY**. Signed Ezekiel **ABLE**. Test Robt. **HALL**, Medad **RANDOL**, John **DAVIS**. Title is assigned to James **RANDAL** on 2 Jan 1808. Signed Francis (x) **MURPHY**. Test A. **HADEN**, John **DAVIS** (JP, Bird Twp). Rec 2 Jun 1808.

263. Page 193. 21 Jan 1808. Francis **MURPHEY** to James **RANDOL**. For the sum of $240, 240 arpens on the waters of White Water, adjoining Jeremiah **CONAWAY**, and land formerly claimed by George **MORGAN** and now Ezekiel **ABLE**'s. If good title is not obtained from the U. S. A., then sd **RANDOL** is not bound to pay the money. Signed Francis (x) **MURPHEY**, James **RANDAL**. Test. A. **HADEN**, D. F. **STEINBECK**, Robt. **GREEN** (JCCP). Rec 2 Jun 1808.

264. Page 193. 18 Jun 1805. James **CAMBELL** to Ezekiel **ABLE**. For the sum of $150, his improvement and head right, claimed by him as a settler agreeable to the custom of Spain, on a creek above the tanyard formerly occupied by Reese **MEREDITH** and below Col. **HAYS**; also adjoins George **HAYS** on the lower side. Signed James **CAMBELL**. Wit Js. **BOYD**, P. **BURNS**, James **BYRD** (JCCP). Title is assigned to Jeremiah **ABLE** for value received on 2 May 1807. Signed Ezekiel **ABLE**. Wit John **BYRD** (JCCP). Rec 3 Jun 1808.

265. Page 194. 7 Mar 1808. Ithamar **HUBBLE** to John **STRONG**. For value received, 235 ½ arpens. Signed Ithamar (x) **HUBBLE**. Wit Enoch **EVANS**, Dens. O. **SULLIVAN**, Christr. **HAYS** (JCCP). Rec 3 Jun 1808.

266. Page 195. 7 Mar 1808. Same to same. For value received, 400 arpens. Signed Ithamar (x) **HUBBLE**. Wit Enoch **EVANS**, Dens. O. **SULLIVAN**, Christr. **HAYS** (JCCP). Rec 3 Jun 1808.

267. Page 195. 7 Mar 1808. Same to same. For value received, 235 ½ arpens. Signed Ithamar (x) **HUBBLE**. Wit Enoch **EVANS**, Dens. O. **SULLIVAN**, Christr. **HAYS** (JCCP). Rec 3 Jun 1808.

268. Page 195. 1 Mar 1808. Jeremiah **WHITSON** to Jonathan **BUIS**. For the sum of $500, 150 acres on a branch of Hubble's Mill Creek, adjoining Ezekiel **ABLE**, James **EARL**, and others. Signed Jeremiah **WHITSON**. Wit John **BYRD**, Dens. O. **SULLIVAN**, Robt. **GREEN** (JCCP). Rec 3 Jun 1808.

269. Page 196. 30 Apr 1805. Henry **SHARADEN** to Ezekiel **ABLE**. For value received, assignment of title to land. Signed Henry **SHARADEN**. Test Jone. **FOREMAN**, Js. **BOYD**, John **BYRD** (JCCP). Ezekiel **ABLE** assigns title to Wm. H. **ASHLEY** on 8 Mar 1808. Signed Ezekiel **ABLE**. Test A. **HADEN**,

James **EVANS**, Christr. **HAYS** (JCCP). Rec 3 Jun 1808.

270. Page 196. 8 Dec 1806. Jonathan **BUIS** to Joseph **WALLER**. For value received, articles of agreement in which sd **BUIS** gives up his claim to an improvement he made on the bank of the Mississippi River about three miles below where sd **WALLER** now lives, with his head right. Signed Jonathan **BUIS**, Joseph T. **WALLER**. Wit [German signature], Joseph **WALLER**, Robt. **GREEN** (JCCP). Rec 3 Jun 1808.

271. Page 197. 30 Apr 1805. Henry **SHARADEN** to Ezekiel **ABLE**. For value received, assignment of title to land. Signed Henry **SHARADEN**. Test Jone. **FOREMAN**, Js. **BOYD**, John **BYRD** (JCCP). Ezekiel **ABLE** assigns title to Jeremiah **ABLE** for value received on 1 May 1805. Signed Ezekiel **ABLE**. Title is assigned to Joshua **GOZA** for value received on 17 Dec 1807. Signed Ezekiel **ABLE**, Jeh. **ABLE**. Test Jos. **SEAWELL**, Lewis **LATHAM**, Christr. **HAYS** (JCCP). Rec 3 Jun 1808.

272. Page 197. 24 Jun 1804. Reson **BALY** to Terrens **DOIL** [Terrance **DOYLE**]. For the sum of __, 250 acres on the W side of Little White Water near Mr. **FRANKS**, who lives on the E side; being the head right and improvement of sd **BALEY**. Signed Rezin **BALEY**. Test Jacob **ISOM**, Jacob (x) **FRIEND**. Title is assigned to Daniel **BRANT** for value received on 1 Dec 1804. Signed Tarrance (I) **DOYLE**. Wit Thomas S. **RODNEY**, Moses **BYRNE**, John **SEAVERS**. Title is assigned to Ezekiel **ABLE** for value received on 2 Sep 1805. Signed Daniel **BRANT**. Test Js. **BOYD.**, John **BYRD** (JCCP). Title is assigned to Jeremiah **ABLE** for value received on 2 May 1807. Signed Ezekiel **ABLE**. Wit John **BYRD** (JCCP). Rec 3 Jun 1808.

273. Page 198. 17 Dec 1807. Ezekiel **ABLE** and Jeremiah **ABLE** acknowledge assignment of land to Joshua **GOZA** before Christopher **HAYS** (JCCP) (AB:197). Signed Christr. **HAYS** (JCCP). Rec 3 Jun 1808.

274. Page 198. 15 Dec 1805. Benijah **LAUGHERTY** to Joseph **WALLER**. For the sum of $100, 240 acres, being his claim and improvement with springs, etc., on the Mississippi River where sd **LAUGHERTY** now resides with his family, by virtue of David **ALLEN**'s head right. If sd **WALLER** cannot get lawful right to sd land, then sd **WALLER** nor

other persons shall have any recourse against sd **LAUGHERTY**. Sd **LAUGHERTY** to retain rights to staves or timbers for him, Stephen **BYRD**, and A. **BYRD**; as well as the right to other timbers to finish their boats, etc. Sd **LAUGHERTY** relinquishes any rights he has to his improvement on the opposite side of the river in Ind. Terr. to sd **WALLER**. Signed Benijah **LAUGHERTY**. Wit Jno. **ABERNETHIE**, John **BYRD** (JCCP). Rec 3 Jun 1808.

275. Page 199. 3 Jan 1807. David **FARRIL** to Josiah **HUNTER**. For the sum of $1.50 per acre, bond to make deed on 100 acres or less, on the E side of sd **FARRIL**'s survey by a conditional line not to exceed 20 poles W of the bayou. If sd land is not 100 acres, then the grantee can come W of the line to make it 100 acres. Signed David **FARRIL**. Test Enos **HANNAH**, John (x) **HANNAH**. Rec 3 Jun 1808.

276. Page 200. 16 May 1807. Josiah **HUNTER** to Robert **GIBONEY**. For value received, assignment of bond (AB:199). Signed Josiah **HUNTER**. Test John **SAVERS**, Peter **CRAIG**, John **BYRD** (JCCP). Enoch **EVANS** (JP) and Robert **BLAIR** (JP) attest to the bond executed by David **FARREL**. Rec 3 Jun 1808.

277. Page 200. 16 Mar 1804. Enas **RANDOL** and Medad **RANDOL** to Thomas **BALLEW**. For the sum of $1800, bond to make a deed on 480 acres, Spanish measure, on the waters of Hubble's Creek, being the tract where Enos **RANDOL** first settled and now lives; being his head right. Title is to be made as soon as Enos **RANDOL** obtains a legal right to the same, with possession by sd **BALLEW** to occur by 15 Sep next. Signed Enos **RANDOL**, Medad **RANDOL**. Wit Robert **HALL**, David **McMUTHRIE**, Enoch **EVANS** (JP), Robert **BLAIR** (JP). Title is assigned to Charles G. **ELLIS**, atty in fact for Gary **DAVIS**, for value received on 30 Jan 1807, excepting 16 acres on the W boundary reserved for James **MORRISON**. Signed Thos. **BALLEW**. Test Wm. **OGLE**, Enoch **EVANS** (JP). Rec 3 Jun 1808.

278. Page 201. 21 Apr 1808. James **ARREL** to John P. **EDONA** (**EDONER**) [**EDDINGER**]. For value received, assignment of title to a quit claim from George **MORGAN**. Signed James **ARREL**. Wit John **DAVIS** (JP), John **BYRD** (JCCP). Rec 3 Jun 1808.

279. Page 202. 2 Jun 1808. Robert **ENGLISH** to Joel **RENFROE**. For the sum of $1100, bond to make a deed on 278 arpens on a branch of Randol's Creek; bounded on the N by Joseph **THOMPSON**, S by **HARKLERODE**, E by land that was **SMITH**'s, and W by unknown. The deed to be made when sd **ENGLISH** obtains rights from the U. S. A. Signed Robert **ENGLISH**. Wit John **GUETHING**, John **BYRD** (JCCP). Rec 3 Jun 1808. [Marginal note: Full satisfaction received on 11 Aug 1827, and the deed to be null and void. Signed Joel **RENFROE**. Wit Hy. **SANFORD**, Clerk.]

280. Page 203. 18 May 1805. Joshua **VICKEROY** to James **GILBRETH**. For the sum of $100 [a rifle gun and note], one mile square on the W bank of the Mississippi at the foot of the hills in Tywappity Bottom, about ten miles S of Cape Girardeau, being a settlement right and actual cultivation of land prior to 1803, given by act of Congress on 2 Mar 1805 to his wife and family. Signed Joshua **VICKERY**. Wit Theophilus **HICKMAN**, O. **REED**. Miles **HOTCHKISS** swears to the signature of Oliver **REED**, and William **BOON** swears to the signatures of Oliver **REED** and Theophilus **HICKMAN** before J. **FINNEY**, JP in Randolph Co., Ind. Terr.. Rec 3 Jun 1808.

281. Page 204. 18 Feb 1806. Elijah **WELCH** to James **RAMSEY**. For ___, an improvement sd **WELCH** made on a tract claimed by sd **RAMSEY** on White Water. Sd **WELCH** made sd cultivation in Oct 1803. Signed Elijah (x) **WELCH**. Test Ens. **HANNAH**, Robt. **GREEN** (JCCP). Rec 3 Jun 1808.

282. Page 204. 27 Aug 1807. Robert **MORRISON**, Clerk of Randolph Co., Ind. Terr., swears that James **FINNEY** is a JP for sd Co.. Signed Robert **MORRISON**, Clerk, Randolph Co., Ind. Rec 3 Jun 1808.

283. Page 204. 3 Aug 1805. William **HARPER** to John **FARRIL**. For the sum of $100, his whole head right and claim. Signed William (H) **HARPER**. Test David **FARRIL**, Jacob (F) **FOSTER** Junior, John **BYRD** (JCCP). Rec 3 Jun 1808.

284. Page 205. 20 Jul 1807. Peter **GODAIR** to Enoch **EVANS** of Monongahela Co, Va. For the sum of $800, 260 arpens, more or less, on Ramsey's Creek, bounded on the N by And. **RAMSEY** Senr. and land sold by Wm. **BONER** to Solomon **ELLIS**, S by And. **RAMSEY** Junior and unappropriated lands, E by **RAMSEY** Senr and vacant lands, and W by sd **ELLIS** and And. **RAMSEY** Junr. Sd **GODAIR** purchased 60

arpens of the tract from William **BONER**, and 200 arpens was granted to him by the Spanish Government. Signed Peter (x) **GODAIR**. Wit B. **COUSIN**, Frederck **GIBLER**, Robert **BLAIR** (JP). Rec 3 Jun 1808.

285. Page 205. 19 Dec 1806. Samuel **BRADLEY** by Sheriff John **HAYS** to John C. **HARBISON**. For the sum of $100.10, 270 acres, more or less, bounded on the W by Peter Widow **WEAVER**, E by John **WEAVER** and Joseph **THOMSON**, and S by David **HARRIS**; late the property of sd **BRADLEY**, assignee of Michael **BURGON**. Sold in execution of writ of fieri facias against sd **BRADLEY** for debt of $60.44 and 5 mills and damages of $43.27 to Francois **VEGO**. Signed John **HAYS**, Sheriff. Wit Robt. **GREEN** (JCCP). Rec 4 Jun 1808.

286. Page 207. 4 Jun 1808. David **ANDREW** to William **STROTHER** of the Ste. Genevieve Dist. For the sum of $__, 240 arpens. Sd deed was executed on 29 Jan 1808, and proved by William **DAUGHERTY** before Robert **GREEN**, Esq on 1 Jun 1808 [AB:185]. The original deed omitted the word "hundred", and this rectifies that mistake. Signed David (x) **ANDREW**. Wit John **BYRD** (JCCP). Rec 4 Jun 1808.

287. Page 208. 8 Jan 1806. Andrew **RAMSEY** Sen to Emsly **JONES**. For a yoke of oxen, a white bull, two breeding sows and a barrow to weight 150 weight, and a yoke ring and steple; bond on 200 arpens in Tywappity Bottom in New Madrid Dist. Signed Andrew **RAMSEY**. Wit J. C. **HARBISON**, Peter **CRAIG**. Sd **JONES** received title from Edward **ROBESON**, and acknowledges he received full payment from sd **RAMSEY**. Signed Elmsley (x) **JONES**. Wit Jas. **GILBREATH**, Jos. **McFERRON**, Robert **BLAIR** (JP). Rec 4 Jun 1808.

288. Page 208. 13 Oct 1797. Louis **LORIMIER**, Commandant, to William **BIRD** of Tenn. For his farming and developing the land, 200 arpents with 8 arpents on the river about 7 miles below Cap a la Cruche; joining the land of Benjamin **ROZE**. Sd **BIRD** wishes to move to this side of the river with his family and slaves. Louis **LORIMIER** requests that the Lt Gov grant the land being requested on 15 Oct 1797. Antoine **SOULARD** said that the land is vacant and available on 2 Jan 1798, and granted to sd **BIRD**. Signed Zenon **TRUDEAU**. Rec 4 Jun 1808. [IN FRENCH]

289. Page 209. 10 Nov 1807. William **BIRD** to Henry **COCKERHAM**. For __, assignment of title to the land in the previous deed (AB:208). Signed William **BIRD**. Test James **CURRIN**, Robt. **BLAIR** (JP). Rec 4 Jun 1808.

290. Page 209. 25 Feb 1806. Samuel **DORSEY** to William **MORRISON** of Kaskaskia. For value received, assignment of title for land on White Water, written on the back of a conveyance from Daniel **HUBBLE** to Saml. **DORSEY** dated 4 Jan 1806 (AB:41). Signed Saml. **DORSEY**. Wit Robert **MORRISON**, Fras. **MOORE**, R. **BLAIR** (JP). Rec 6 Jun 1808.

291. Page 210. 5 Feb 1806. Same to same. For value received, assignment of title for land on White Water, written on the back of a conveyance from Jonathan **HUBBLE** to Saml. **DORSEY** dated 4 Jan 1806 (AB:42). Signed Saml. **DORSEY**. Wit Robert **MORRISON**, Fras. **MOORE**, R. **BLAIR** (JP). Rec 6 Jun 1808.

292. Page 210. 27 Mar 1807. William **BONER** and Catharine, his wife, to Solomon **ELLIS**. For the sum of $750, 240 arpens, more or less, on Ramsey's Creek, being the same granted to him in 15 Nov 1797 by the Spanish Government; bounded on the N by heirs of Saml. **TIPTON**, S by Peter **GODAIR**, E by And. **RAMSEY**, and W by a tract formerly granted to Jon. **DITCH** and now owned by sd **RAMSEY**. The grantees obligate themselves to make a sufficient deed when the tract is confirmed by the U. S. A. Signed William ( ) **BONER**, Catherine ( ) **BONER**. Wit B. **COUSIN**, Robt. **BLAIR** (JP). Rec 6 Jun 1808.

293. Page 211. 26 Feb 1806. Garah **DAVIS** of Columbia Co, Ga. to Charles G. **ELLIS**. For the great trust and confidence reposed by him in sd **ELLIS**, power of attorney for sd **ELLIS** to remove 10 negroes, horses, waggons, and different articles of household and kitchen furniture belonging to him, from Columbia Co., Ga. to Tenn., and use or sell sd property as he shall deem most prudent and advantageous, and to purchase land that he deems proper for the purpose of farming. Signed Garah **DAVIS**. Wit Wm. **OGLE**, F. W. **COBB**. Richard **DAVIS** swears to the signatures before R. **BLAIR** (JP). Rec 6 Jun 1808.

294. Page 212. 5 Dec 1804. Francois **BERTHIAUME** to Louis **LORIMIER**. For the sum of 210 piastres, his rights to 420 arpents granted to him by the Spanish government following the decree of 28 Dec 1799. Signed Francois (x) **BERTHIAUME**. Wit B. **COUSINS**, Surveyor, Robt. **GREEN** (JCCP). Rec 7 Jun 1808. [IN FRENCH]

295. Page 213. 18 Feb 1804. Hypolite **MAROTE** to same. For a lot in Cape Girardeau, 500 arpents he was granted on 10 Oct 1799 for services as baker for the expedition against the Indians, measured on the N by lowlands on two sides of the road to New Madrid, which will be better seen on the map that sd **LORIMIER** will receive. The lot is about 3/4 arpent, and **LORIMIER** measured it on the 30th of last month, as described in the paper he gave sd **MAROTE**. Sd **MAROT** will also receive money on account and pay on the balance he owes sd **LORIMIER**. Signed Hypolite **MAROTE**. Wit Pierre **MENARD**, B. **COUSIN**, Robt. **GREEN** (JCCP). Rec 7 Jun 1808. [IN FRENCH]

296. Page 214. 7 Jun 1808. Louis **LORIMIER** swears that George **HENDERSON** Esq. was one of the men who served in a military expedition to New Madrid in Dec 1802 and Jan following, which caused him to recommend him for 300 arpens of land in the Cape Girardeau Dist. as stated in the list of Concession A now possessed by the Board of Commissioners. Signed L. **LORIMIER**. Wit Robt. **GREEN**. Rec 7 Jun 1808.

297. Page 215. 17 Sep 1807. Isaac M. **BLEDSOE** to William H. **ASHLEY** of the Ste. Genevieve Dist. For the sum of $480, a negro man named **Titus**, about 25 years old. Signed Isaac M. **BLEDSOE**. Wit R. **WORTHINGTON**, Wm. **WHITE**, John **DAVIS** (JP). Rec 7 Jun 1808.

298. Page 215. 7 Dec 1805. Louis **LARGEAU**, decd, by Sheriff John **HAYS** to John C. **HARBISON**. For the sum of $0.10, the land claim of sd **LARGEAU**. Sold on an execution issued by the Court of the Ste. Genevieve Dist against sd **LARGEAU** and for Walter **FENWICK**. Signed John **HAYS**, Sheriff. Test Thos. S. **RODNEY**, Robt. **GREEN** (JCCP). Rec 7 Jun 1808.

299. Page 216. 18 Apr 1807. Daniel **THORN** to Solomon **THORN**. For the sum of $200, 480 arpens, known as the David **STRICKLAND** place, being granted to and improved by him. Signed Daniel (x) **THORN**. Wit Jno. C. **HARBISON**, Gm. **LORIMIER**, Robt. **GREEN** (JCCP). Title is assigned to **REINECKE & STEINBECK** on 26 Mar 1808.

Signed Solomon **THORN**. Wit Levi **WOLVERTON**, Robt. **GREEN** (JCCP). Rec 7 Jun 1808.

300. Page 216. 27 May 1808. Solomon **THORN** to **REINECKE** and **STEINBECK**. For value received, assignment of title for 600 arpens, and authorization for them to apply to the Board of Commissioners. Signed Solomon **THORN**. Wit John C. **HARBISON**, Levi **WOLVERTON**, Robt. **GREEN** (JCCP). Rec 7 Jun 1808.

301. Page 217. 16 Mar 1807. John **HAYS**, Sheriff, received $202.23 ½ of Andrew **RAMSEY** Junr, being the full amount of an execution in favor of Joseph **BROOKS** on Samuel **CHANEY**, sd **RAMSEY** being security for sd **CHANEY**. Signed John **HAYS**, Sheriff. Test Geo. **HENDERSON**, Robt. **GREEN** (JCCP). Rec 7 Jun 1808.

302. Page 217. 16 Jan 1808. Daniel **MULLINS** to John **SHEPPARD**. For the sum of $1000, bond to make a deed for 250 arpens on the bank of the Mississippi granted to Mallakiah **JONES**; bounded on the NW and NE by the Mississippi, SE by vacant land, and SW by John **BROOKS**, and assigned by a bond dated 4 Oct 1803 to John Nicholas **SHRUM**, and from sd **SHRUM** to sd **MULLINS** by a bond dated Apr 1806. Should the land not be confirmed to sd **MULLINS**, he is to pay $450 with interest from this date to sd **SHEPPARD**. Signed Daniel (x) **MULLINS**. Wit John **DAVIS**, Robt. **GREEN**, Christr. **HAYS** (JCCP). Rec 8 Jun 1808.

303. Page 218. 17 Jun 1806. Louis **LORIMIER** to Thomas **MORGAN**. For the sum of $100, $60 now and the balance per note bearing this date, lot in Cape Girardeau; bounded on the N by the public lot, W by an unappropriated lot, and also by a lot of B. **COUSIN**. Signed L. **LORIMIER**. Test A. **HADEN**, B. **COUSIN**, John **BYRD** (JCCP). Rec 8 Jun 1808.

304. Page 219. 9 May 1807. Same to Joseph **SEAWELL** and William **NEELY**. For the sum of $150, Lot No. 12, Range B in Cape Girardeau, and the NW ¼ of the third square from the River; bounded on the E by William **WHITE**, W by Indian St, W by an unsold lot, and N by Independence St; also as many logs as are needed to build a house 25 ft by 17 ft and 17 ft high, delivered to the lot. Signed L. **LORIMIER**. Test B **COUSIN**, John **BYRD** (JCCP). Rec 8 Jun 1808.

305. Page 220. State of Missouri, Co. of Cape Girardeau. I, Nathan C. **HARRISON**, Clerk of the Circuit Court and Ex-officio Recr. within and for the Co. aforesaid, after having carefully examined and compared the above and foregoing, hereby certify that the same is a full, true, and perfect copy of the original Books A & B as fully as the same appears in this office. Signed Nathan C. **HARRISON**, Clerk, 30 Apr 1870.

[End of Deed Book AB]

[Deed Book C]

306. Page 1. 20 Aug 1807. Frederick **BATES**, Secretary of La. Terr., to Christopher **HAYS**. Appointment as First Judge of the CCP and Quarter Sessions of the Peace for Cape Girardeau Dist. Signed Frederick **BATES**. Christopher **HAYS** is sworn in by Th. C. **SCOTT**. Rec 16 Jun 1808.

307. Page 1. 31 Mar 1807. Joseph **BROWN**, Secretary and Ex-officio Governor of La. Terr., to George **HENDERSON**. Appointment as Judge of Probate for the Cape Girardeau Dist. Signed Joseph **BROWNE**. George **HENDERSON** is sworn in by Joseph **McFERRON**. Rec 16 Jun 1808.

308. Page 2. 24 Aug 1807. Frederick **BATES**, Secretary of La. Terr, to Enoch **EVANS**. Appointment as JP for Cape Girardeau Twp. Signed Frederick **BATES**. Enoch **EVANS** is sworn in by Th. C. **SCOTT**. Rec 16 Jun 1808.

309. Page 2. 20 Aug 1807. Same to George **HENDERSON**. Appointment as Recorder for the Cape Girardeau Dist. Signed Frederick **BATES**. George **HENDERSON** is sworn in by Th. C. **SCOTT**. Rec 16 Jun 1808.

310. Page 3. 20 Aug 1807. Same to same. Appointment as Judge of Probate for the Cape Girardeau Dist. Signed Frederick **BATES**. George **HENDERSON** is sworn in by Th. C. **SCOTT**. Rec 16 Jun 1808.

311. Page 3. 20 Aug 1807. Same to same. Appointment as Treasurer for the Cape Girardeau Dist. Signed Frederick **BATES**. George **HENDERSON** is sworn in by Th. C. **SCOTT**. Rec 16 Jun 1808.

312. Page 4. 1 Jan 1805. William Henry **HARRISON**, Governor and Commander-in-chief of Ind. Terr and the Dist. of La., to William

DOUGHERTY. Appointment as Coroner of the Cape Girardeau Dist. Signed Willm. Henry **HARRISON**. Wit Jno. **GIBSON**, Secretary. William **DOUGHERTY** is sworn in by Joseph **McFERRON**. Rec 16 Jun 1808.

313. Page 4. 3 May 1808. Daniel **BRANT** to Charles **SAXTON**. For valuable consideration, one bay horse about 12 years old, one sorel mare about eight years old, one yoak of oxen about six years old, and all his cattel & hoges and household furniture. Signed Daniel **BRANT**. Test Jeremiah **CONAWAY**, Elijah (x) **WELCH**, Robert **BLAIR** (JP). Rec 16 Jun 1808.

314. Page 5. 5 Oct 1805. John **SUMMERS** to Alexander **SUMMERS**. For the sum of $500, 300 acres on Hubble's Creek as described in the grant, being the tract where he now lives and adjoining John **SUMMERS** Senr and Mr. **ABEL**. John **SUMMERS** also posts bond of $1000 to assign the same to Alexr. **SUMMERS** when a more proper right may be obtained. Signed John **SUMMERS**. Wit Hugh **FULTON**, John **SUMMERS** Senr. Test Christr. **HAYS** (JCCP). Rec 23 Jun 1808.

315. Page 5. 20 Aug 1807. Frederick **BATES**, Secretary of La. Terr, to John **BYRD**, Esq. Appointment as Judge of the CCP and Quarter Sessions of the Peace for Cape Girardeau Dist, beginning on 1 Sep next for a term of four years. Signed Frederick **BATES**. John **BYRD** is sworn in by Th. C. **SCOTT**. Rec 25 Jun 1808.

316. Page 6. 31 Aug 1803. Daniel **BRANT** to Norris **MONDAY**. For ___, a certain tract of land and the improvements thereon, being where he now lives. Signed Daniel **BRANT**. Test Sam. S. **KENNEDY**, Jacob **SHURDEN**, William **MATHEWS**, Esq. Norris **MONDAY** assigns title to George **CAVENDAR** for value received on 26 Sep [illegible]. Signed Norris (x) **MONDAY**. Test Jacob **KELLEY**, William **JACKSON**, Christr. **HAYS** (JCCP). Rec 27 Jun 1808.

317. Page 7. 28 Jun 1808. Andrew **SUMMERS** to Alexander **SUMMERS**. Quit claim to ___ acres, originally granted to John **SUMMERS** Junior, confirmed to Andrew **SUMMERS** by the Land Commission, and now owned by Alexander **SUMMERS**. Signed Andrew **SUMMERS**. Test Geo. **HENDERSON**, Christr. **HAYS** (JCCP). Rec 28 Jun 1808.

318. Page 7. 24 Aug 1807. Frederick **BATES**, Secretary of La. Terr., to John **DAVIS**, Esq.

Appointment as JP for Byrd Twp, beginning on 1 Sep next. Signed Frederick **BATES**. John **DAVIS** is sworn in by Th. C. **SCOTT**. Rec 30 Jun 1808.

319. Page 8. 16 Mar 1807. Benjamin **TENNILLE** to John **DAVIS**. For the sum of $300, 300 arpens, bounded on the E by Gilbert **HECTOR**, S by Henry **HAND**, W by David **PATTERSON**, and N by George **HAYS**; beginning at a stake near the mill at sd **PATTERSON's** SE corner; being the same bought by sd **TENNILLE** from Jonathan **FOREMAN**. Signed Benjn. **TENNELLE**. Wit John **MARTIN**, Margret T. **MARTIN**, Robt. **HALL** (JCCP). Rec 30 Jun 1808.

320. Page 8. 23 Nov 1805. Simon **BRUNDAGE** to Lemuel **CHENEY**. For the sum of $30, the land he obtained as a Spanish subject in 1803. Sd **CHENEY** is to bear expense of obtaining sd claim, and is to have no recourse against sd **BRUNDAGE**. Signed Simon ( ) **BRUNDAGE**. Test Thos. **BALLEW**, James **COX** Junr, Wm. **MATHEWS**, Esq. Rec 30 Jun 1808.

321. Page 9. 8 Jul 1808. Poly **BOYD** to Equila **WATHEN**. For value received, assignment of right and interest to a tract on Cane Creek, bounded on the W by John **McCAREY** and E by James **BOYD**. Signed Poly (x) **BOYD**. Test John **BOYD**, Js. **BOYD**, Robt. **GREEN** (JCCP). Rec 11 Jul 1808.

322. Page 9. 15 Aug 1806. James **WILKINSON**, Governor and Commander in chief of La. Terr., to Christopher **HAYES**. Appointment as Commissioner of Rates and Levies for the Cape Girardeau Dist for three years. Signed Jas. **WILKINSON**. Rec 16 Jul 1808.

323. Page 9. 1 Oct 1804. William Henry **HARRISON**, Governor of Ind. Terr., to same. Appointment as a Justice of the General Quarter Sessions of the Peace in the Cape Girardeau Dist. Signed Willm. Henry **HARRISON**. Wit Jno. **GIBSON**, Secretary. Christopher **HAYS** is administered the oath of office on 24 Nov 1804 by Joseph **McFERRON**. Signed Joseph **McFERRON**. Rec 16 Jul 1808.

324. Page 10. 1 Oct 1804. Same to same. Appointment as a Judge of the CCP in the Cape Girardeau Dist. Signed Willm. Henry **HARRISON**. Wit Jno. **GIBSON**, Secretary. Christopher **HAYS** is administered the oath of office on 24 Nov 1804 by Joseph **McFERRON**. Signed Joseph **McFERRON**. Rec 16 Jul 1808.

325. Page 11. 6 Jan 1800. Pierre **DUMAY**, resident of the province since childhood, requests a grant of 1000 arpents of unoccupied land in the Cape Girardeau District in Old Cape next to land belonging to Don Louis **LORIMIER**. Signed Pierre **DUMAY**. Cape Girardeau, 9 Jan 1800. We recommend Pierre **DUMAY** be granted land in the Cape Girardeau District. Signed Louis **LORIMIER**. [preceding IN FRENCH]. By virtue of the report from Cape Girardeau Post, Don L. **LORIMIER** informs me the plantiff has more than sufficient means to obtain the requested grant for himself and his heirs. The surveyor, Don Antonio **SOULARD**, confirms the grant requested by royal decree on 23 Jan 1800. Signed Carlos Dehault **DELASSUS**. Title is assigned to Don Pierre **MENARD** for $1000 (250 piastres) on 20 Feb 1806 at New Madrid. Signed Pierre **DUMAY**. Wit Peyroud ne **RODREYAS**, [preceding IN SPANISH], B. **COUSIN**, Robt. **GREEN** (JCCP). Rec 21 Jul 1808.

326. Page 13. 4 Nov 1798. Louis **LORIMIER**, commandant, to Barthelemy **RICHARD**, of Kaskaskias, currently of Cape Girardeau. For the sum of 250 piastres, land in old Cape granted to him on 4 Jan 1793 by Monsigneur le Baron de **CARONDELET**, including houses, fences and cleared land. Signed L. **LORIMIER**. Wit Bmy. **COUSIN**, Edward (ER) **ROBINSON**. 18 Feb 1800. B. **RICHARD** to Pierre **DUMAIST**. For __, receipt of the amount for the sale of the property that sd **DUMAIST** obtained at the entrance of the Ohio on the Spanish side at Fort Massac. Signed B. **RICHARD**. 5 Jun 1803. Pierre **DUMAIST** to Pierre **MENARD**. For the sum of 400 piastres paid me at Kaskaskia, sale of the property. Signed Pierre **DUMAY**. Wit Robt. **GREEN** (JCCP). Rec 21 Jul 1808. [IN FRENCH]

327. Page 15. 21 Jul 1808. James **RANDOL** to Christopher **EDINGER**. For the sum of $125, mortgage on 240 acres on the waters of Hubble's Creek, being where sd **RANDOL** now lives. The debt due within three months of this date. Signed James **RANDAL**. Wit John **DAVIS** (JP). Rec 21 Jul 1808. [Marginal note: Full satisfaction received on 11 Sep 1809. Signed Christopher ( ) **EDINGER**. Test Geo. **HENDERSON**, Recorder.]

328. Page 15. 25 Mar 1808. John C. **HARBISON** to **REINEKE & STEINBECK**, merchants of Cape Girardeau. For the sum of $250, 250 arpens about two and a half miles above Cape Girardeau, being the whole of sd **HARBISON**'s claim of old Louis **LASUER**, and being the same sd **HARBISON** had of William **LORIMIER** under the claimant Louis **LASUER**. Signed John C. **HARBISON**. Wit Levi **WOLVERTON**, Frederick **GIBLER**, Robt. **GREEN** (JCCP). Rec 22 Jul 1808.

329. Page 16. 9 Jan 1807. Joseph **WALLER**, and Richard **WALLER** and Medad **RANDELL**. Articles of agreement, in which Joseph **WALLER** agrees to give Richard **WALLER** and Medad **RANDEL** ½ of the claim where he now lives, the claim on the other side of the river, and the ferry. Sd claim is to be divided by Richard **WALLER** and **RANDELL**, then Joseph **WALLER** to have choice. Both parties to pay ½ of the costs of obtaining the right to sd lands. Signed Joseph ( ) **WALLER**, Richard **WALLER**, Medad **RANDLE**. Test Stephen **BYRD**, Isaac **WILLIAMS**, Christr. **HAYS** (JCCP), Stephen **BYRD**, John **DAVIS** (JP). Rec 3 Aug 1808.

330. Page 17. 5 Aug 1808. James **EVANS** to Thomas **GRAYHAM** of Fayette Co., Pa. For the sum of $1 paid out as an agent for sd **GRAYHAM**, 500 arpens, being the same purchased by sd **EVANS**, agent for sd **GRAYHAM**, at Sheriff's sale. Signed James **EVANS**. Wit Enoch **EVANS** (JP). Rec 5 Aug 1808.

331. Page 17. 7 Apr 1808. Elijah **WHITTAKER** of the Orleans Dist, Terr. of La., to Joseph **SEAWELL**. For a valuable consideration, 320 arpens about eight or ten miles from Cape Girardeau where he formerly lived and that was granted to him by the Spanish Government, joining William **WILLIAMS**. Signed Elijah (x) **WHITTAKER**. Test Wm. **KELSO**, Abner **HARRIS**, Edwd. **HOGAN** (JP). Rec 11 Aug 1808.

332. Page 18. 14 Mar 1808. John C. **HARBISON** to Dr. Jaben **SEELY**. Quit claim deed to Lot No. 8, Range F in Cape Girardeau; and bill of sale from Louis **LORIMIER** to sd **HARBISON** is declared null and void. Signed John C. **HARBISON**. Wit Ezekiel **ABLE**, B. **COUSIN**, Robert **BLAIR** (JP). Rec 20 Aug 1808.

333. Page 18. [marked through; same as C:25].

334. Page 19. 18 Aug 1808. Danniel **MULLINS** of Ind. Terr. to Dr. Jaben **SEELY**. For the sum of $650, 640 acres, more or less, about three miles from Charles **FRIEND**, including the gravelly springs. Signed Daniel (x) **MULLINS**. Wit Moses **HURLEY**, James **MONTGOMERY**, John **DAVIS** (JP). Rec 29 Aug 1808.

335. Page 19. 20 Aug 1807. Frederick **BATES**, Secretary of La. Terr., to Robert **GREEN**, Esq. Appointment as JCCP for the Cape Girardeau Dist, beginning on 1 Sep next for a term of four years. Signed Frederick **BATES**. Robert **GREEN** is sworn in by Th. C. **SCOTT**. Rec 7 Sep 1808.

336. Page 20. [no date] ___. Mary **RANDOL** to James **RANDOL**. Power of attorney to collect a legacy, money, and other things left to her as daughter and heir of Francis **PIERPONT**, late of Hardin Co., Ky., by sd **PIERPONT**'s last will and testament. Signed Mary (x) **RANDOL**. Wit John **BYRD** (JCCP), Joseph **McFERRON**, Clerk, CCP (as to John **BYRD**). Rec 12 Sep 1808.

337. Page 21. 5 Aug 1808. Meriwether **LEWIS**, Governor and Commander in chief of La. Terr., to Stephen **BYRD**. Appointment as JCCP for the Cape Girardeau Dist. Signed Meriwether **LEWIS**. Stephen **BYRD** is sworn in by Joseph **McFERRON**. Rec 12 Sep 1808.

338. Page 22. 15 Sep 1808. Joseph **WORTHINGTON** of Randolph Co., Ind. Terr. [now Ill.], to John **SIMPSON**. For the sum of $200, 200 acres, more or less, known as Shield's Improvement, adjoining **MORRISON**, etc. Signed Jos. **WORTHINGTON**. Wit James **EVANS**, Js. **BOYD**, Stephen **BYRD** (JCCP). Rec 16 Sep 1808.

339. Page 23. 29 Jan 1807. Daniel **GRETER** to Frederic **LIMBAUGH**, Esq. For the sum of $100, 300 acres in the Dutch Settlement on a certain creek about a mile upwards from sd **LIMBAUGH**, father of Michael **LIMBAUGH**. Michael **LIMBAUGH** (alias **LIMBACK**) received the land as a grant under the hand of the Spanish or French Commander Lewis **LORIMIER** and his Secretary **COUSANTS**, and deeded it to sd **GRETER** in late 1805. Signed Daniel **GRETER**. Wit [both signed in German] ___, Frederick **LIMBAUGH**, Stephen **BYRD** (JCCP). Rec 26 Sep 1808.

340. Page 24. 26 Sep 1808. John **BALLINGER** to Frederic **BULLINGER**. For the sum of $111, mortgage on a negro man named **George**, 22 years old last Jul. Sd **BULLINGER** is serving as security for a debt sd **BALLINGER** owes to Charles **DAUGHERTY**'s admininistrators. Signed John **BALLINGER**. Wit Stephen **BYRD** (JCCP). Rec 26 Sep 1808.

341. Page 25. 19 Aug 1808. Robert **QUIMBY** and Rebecca, his wife, to Edward **ROBERTSON** of the New Madrid Dist. For the sum of 950, 950 arpents, more or less, being the head right of sd **QUIMBY**; beginning at an ironwood and sassafras on Jacob **FRIEND**'s line. Signed Robert (x) **QUIMBY**, Rebecca (x) **QUIMBY**. Wit Elisha **WINSOR**, Wm. **COX**, Stephen **ROSS** (JP), John **DAVIS** (JP). Rec 3 Oct 1808.

342. Page 26. 28 Dec 1807. Thomas **WELLBORN** and John **WELLBORN** to John **ORDWAY**. For the sum of $340, 200 arpens, beginning at the lower end of Thomas **WELLBORN**'s head right of land on the W bank of the Mississippi, where sd **WELLBORN** now lives. Signed Thos. **WELLBORN**, John **WELLBORN**. Wit Willm. **KELSO**, James **WELBORN**, William **GRIFFIN**, Edmd. **HOGAN** (JP). Rec 15 Oct 1808.

343. Page 27. 24 Aug 1807. Frederick **BATES**, Secretary of La. Terr., to Jacob **KELLY**, Esq. Appointment as JP for Saint Francois Twp, Cape Girardeau Dist, beginning on 1 Sep next. Signed Frederick **BATES**. Jacob **KELLY** is sworn in by A. **HADEN**. Rec 28 Oct 1808.

344. Page 28. 3 Oct 1808. Meriwether **LEWIS**, Governor and Commander in chief of La. Terr., to George **HENDERSON**. Appointment as JP for Byrd Twp, Cape Girardeau Dist. Signed Meriwether **LEWIS**. Wit Frederick **BATES**, Secretary. George **HENDERSON** is sworn in by Joseph **McFERRON**. Rec 31 Oct 1808.

345. Page 29. 23 Sep 1808. William **WHITE** of Cape Girardeau to Frederick **REINEKIE** and Daniel F. **STEINBECK**, trading as Reineike & Steinbeck. For the sum of $225, Lot No. 3, Range D in Cape Girardeau, being the same Louis **LORIMIER** sold to sd **WHITE**; bounded on the N by a lot sold to John **BULLINGER** by Jos. **BUAT**(?), S by Themis St, E by another street, and W by the public square. Signed Wm. **WHITE**. Wit Isaac M. **BLEDSOE**, Levi **WOLVERTON**, Robert **GIBONEY**, Geo. **HENDERSON** (JP). Rec 31 Oct 1808.

346. Page 30. 17 Nov 1807. John **GUETHING** [and Andrew **RAMSEY**] to John **DUNN**. For the sum of $1100, bond to make a deed for 240 arpents; bounded by Wm. **DAUGHERTY** on the S and Wm. **DICKINS** on the N; as soon as land claims are established in the district. Signed John **GUETHING**, Andrew **RAMSEY**. Test Wm. **GARNER**, John **McCLEMURY**(?), Geo. **HENDERSON** (JP). Rec 7 Nov 1808.

347. Page 31. 5 Jan 1808. John **ORDWAY** [of Tywappity Twp] to John **BROOKS**. For the sum of $170, 50 arpents, beginning at the lower end of the grant sd **ORDWAY** purchased of Alexander **MILLIKIN** on the W bank of the Mississippi River in Tiwapaty Twp, and being where sd **ORDWAY** and William **GRIFFIN** now live. Signed John **ORDWAY**. Test William **GRIFFIN**, Elizabeth **GRIFFIN**, Edmond **HOGAN** (JP). Rec 21 Nov 1808.

348. Page 33. 13 Aug 1808. Same to Arthur **PITTMAN**. For the sum of $300, 100 arpents; bounded on the E by Alexander **MILLIKIN**, S by Jesse **BOWDEN**, W by vacant land, and N by John **LOYD** or Charles **FENLEY**. Signed John **ORDWAY**. Wit Edmd. **HOGAN** (JP). Rec 22 Nov 1808.

349. Page 34. 13 Aug 1808. Charles **FENLEY** of Tywappity Twp to William **GRIFFIN**. For the sum of $60, 6 acres in Tywappity Bottom, beginning at George **ROBERTSON**'s upper corner on the bank of the Mississippi. Signed Charles **FENLEY**. Test Wm. **KELSO**, James **CURRIN**, Edmd. **HOGAN** (JP). Rec 22 Nov 1808.

350. Page 35. 14 Nov 1808. James **MONTGOMERY** to Edward **ROBERTSON** of New Madrid Dist. For the sum of $2000, 450 arpents in Tywappity Bottom that formerly belonged to Robert **LAIN**, adjoining Stephen **QUIMBY** on the lower side and Danl. **MULLINS** on the upper side. Signed James **MONTGOMERY**. Wit Moses **HURLEY**, Jesse **BLANKS**, Geo. **HENDERSON** (JP for Byrd Twp). Rec 22 Nov 1808.

351. Page 36. 27 Oct 1808. Solomon **ELLIS** Senr and Elisha **ELLIS** to Erasmus **ELLIS**. This deed is to correct an error in the amount of the debt written in a deed dated 26 May 1808 (see AB:175). Signed Elisha **ELLIS**, Solomon **ELLIS**. Test Benj. **ELLIOTT**, G. W. **TRAT**, Frederick **GIBLER**, Jaben **SEELYE**, James **AUSTIN** (JP of Briton(?) Twp, Ste. Genevieve

Dist), Geo. **HENDERSON** (JP). Rec 22 Nov 1808.

352. Page 39. 23 Nov 1808. Edward **ROBISON**, Charles **FRIEND**, and Moses **HURLEY** to Andrew **RAMSEY** Jur. For the sum of $1200, bond make a deed on 300 arpens near Charles **FRIEND**, known as Danl. **MULLINS'** head right of 700 arpens. Should more than 300 arpens be confirmed, then sd **ROBISON** should let sd **RAMSEY** have the whole. Signed Edward (ER) **ROBERTSON**, Moses **HURLEY**, Charles **FRIEND**. Test Wm. **SHAW**, John **RANDAL**, Geo. **HENDERSON** (JP in Byrd Twp). Title is assigned to John **RAMSEY** Seign for value received on 24 Nov 1808. Signed Andrew **RAMSEY** Jur. Wit Geo. **HENDERSON** (JP). Rec 24 Nov 1808.

353. Page 40. 23 Nov 1808. John C. **HARBISON** by Sheriff John **HAYS** to Daniel F. **STEINBECK**. For the sum of $30.50, __ acres, part of 250 arpents on or near the Mississippi above the old Cape, being part of L. **LAGEAU**'s claim. Sold on 23 Jul 1808 in execution of four writs issued by CCP; to wit, Louis **LORIMIER** against sd **HARBISON** for $7.50 costs in an action of debt since discontinued (16 Jun 1808), **McLANAHAN** and **HARRY** against sd **HARBISON** for $87.17 and five mills damages for non-performance of a promise (6 Apr 1808), Louis **LORIMIER** against sd **HARBISON** for $8.45 costs in an action of debt since discontinued (16 Jun 1808), and Waters & Hall against sd **HARBISON** for $64.55 debt and $50 damages as adjudged by Robert **HALL** for detaining the debt (16 Jun 1808). Signed John **HAYS**, Sheriff. Wit Joseph **McFERRON**, Clerk, CCP. Rec 25 Nov 1808.

354. Page 45. 26 Nov 1808. John **RANDOL** and Margaret, his wife, to David **SHAW**, all of Cape Girardeau. For the sum of $120, Lot No. 6, Range D where sd **RANDOL** now lives, formerly occupied by Anthony **HADEN** Esq; bounded by Charles G. **ELLIS**, on the E by the public square, N by Harmony St, and S by Themis St. Signed John **RANDOL**, Margaret **RANDOL**. Wit Geo. **HENDERSON** (JP, Byrd Twp). Rec 26 Nov 1808.

355. Page 47. 24 Nov 1808. James **RANDOL** to Abraham **DAUGHHITT**. For the sum of $150, mortgage on 240 arpens where sd **RANDOL** now lives. The sum is due with interest within three months from date. Signed James **RANDOL**. Test John **DUNN**, Wm. (x)

DURKINS, Geo. HENDERSON (JP). Rec 5 Dec 1808.

356. Page 48. 28 Nov 1808. Andrew RAMSEY Senr and Andrew RAMSEY Junr to John RAMSEY of Monongalia Co., Va. For the sum of $2000, bond to make a deed for 550 arpens known as the Thorn and Bradley Improvements, adjoining the Big Swamp and the FITZ GIBBONS place. Signed Andrew RAMSEY, Andrew RAMSEY Junr. Wit Enoch EVANS, Geo. HENDERSON (JP). Rec 7 Dec 1808.

357. Page 49. 28 Nov 1808. Andrew RAMSEY Junr to same. For the sum of $800, bond to make a deed on 240 arpens known as John RAMSEY's head right, adjoining Abraham BIRD, John GIBONEY, and others. Sd deed to be make as soon as sd Andrew RAMSEY can obtain a patent from the government. Signed Andrew RAMSEY. Wit Enoch EVANS, Geo. HENDERSON (JP). Rec 7 Dec 1808.

358. Page 50. 24 Aug 1807. Frederick BATES, Secretary of La. Terr., to Edmund HOGAN, Esq. Appointment as JP for Tywappity Twp, Cape Girardeau Dist, beginning on 1 Sep next. Signed Frederick BATES. Edmund HOGAN is sworn in by Th. Ch. SCOTT. Rec 7 Dec 1808.

359. Page 51. 16 Jan 1808. Daniel MULLINS to John SHEPPARD. For the sum of $450, one negro woman named Kezia about 26 years old and black complected; sold to secure a bond sd MULLINS made on 16 Jan 1808 for title to land on the bank of the Mississippi River surveyed for and granted to Malaciah JONES. The woman is to remain in the possession of sd MULLINS, but not to be moved more than 50 miles, until the U. S. A. confirms title to sd land. John DAVIS and Robert GREEN swear before William MATHEWS that they saw the bill of sale executed at the house of Henry HAND. Signed John DAVIS, Robert GREEN. Wit William MATHEWS (JP). John SHEPPARD swears before sd MATHEWS that he has lost the bill of sale, and this deed confirms it. Signed John SHEPPARD. Rec 8 Dec 1808.

360. Page 53. 24 Aug 1807. Frederick BATES, Secretary of La. Terr., to John ABERNATHER, Esq. Appointment as JP for Cape Girardeau Twp, Cape Girardeau Dist, beginning on 1 Sep next. Signed Frederick BATES. John ABERNATHER is sworn in by Th. Ch. SCOTT on 19 Sep 1807. Rec 14 Dec 1808.

361. Page 54. 20 Oct 1808. Samuel BALDWIN to Eliza McCARTY. For the sum of $150, one sorrel mare about 14 ½ hands high, eight years old, with a small star in the forehead. Signed Saml. BALDWIN. Wit Geo. CAVANER, Davd. WALL, Geo. HENDERSON (JP). Rec 17 Dec 1808.

362. Page 55. 14 Nov 1808. Henry WAITE of Edgefield Co., S. Car. to William SHAW. Power of attorney to collect property and moneys from Fanny WATERS, adminr of Thomas W. WATERS, decd, that is due to him as one of the legal heirs of sd WATERS. Signed Henry WAITE. Test James COTTLE, R. WORTHINGTON, Enoch EVANS (JP). Rec 1 Feb 1809.

363. Page 56. 2 Feb 1809. James EARLS to David S. JENKINS. Articles of agreement for sd EARLS to rent to sd JENKINS the plantation where he now lives for five years for $100 annually, beginning on the ninth of the present month, together with the buildings and land fit for cultivation, with the exception of 1 acres where John WALL lives on sd premises. JENKINS also has access to timber for firewood, profits of fruit trees, half of the present growing wheat crop. Sd JENKINS is to keep the plantation in good repair; and EARLS is to provide a hand or hands within 6 days on request, is not to sell or cause to be sold any spirits, and is to retain the house and another known as the school house. Signed James EARLS, David S. JENKINS. Test Robt. GREEN, Jonathan BUIS, Geo. HENDERSON (JP). Rec 6 Feb 1809.

364. Page 58. 14 Mar 1809. John BYRD to Jeremiah SIMPSON. For the sum of $200, __ acres, being the same sd BYRD purchased of Joseph WORTHINGTON, assignee of William SMITH, on 22 Jul 1805, and which sd WORTHINGTON purchased of sd SMITH on 2 Nov 1803. Sd SIMPSON is to have no further demand of sd BYRD if title cannot be obtained from the U. S. A. Signed John BYRD. Test Geo. HENDERSON (JP). Rec 14 Mar 1809.

365. Page 59. 5 Nov 1807. John DAVIS to Andrew BURNS of the New Madrid Dist. For the sum of $1200, two tracts originally granted to Jonathan FOREMAN on Hubble's Creek; 240 acres, more or less, and 300 acres, more or less; bounded on the S by Jeremiah W. STILL, W by Edward HAIL and David PATTERSON, N by George HAYS, and E by Gilbert HECKTOR and Henry HANDS. Sd DAVIS holds the land as assignee of Benjamin **TENNILLE**, who is assignee of sd **FOREMAN**. Signed John **DAVIS**. Wit Elisha **WINSOR** (JCCP of New Madrid Dist), Geo. **HENDERSON** (JP). Rec 15 Mar 1809.

366. Page 61. 2 Jan 1809. Ezekiel **ABLE** to William **BONAR**. For the sum of $200, bond to make a deed for 50 acres on the Mississippi River, being the lower end of a tract claimed by Joseph **DENNIS**. If the claim cannot be confirmed, then this bond is void. Signed Ezekiel **ABLE**. Wit R. **BLAIR**, Geo. **HENDERSON** (JP). Rec 20 Mar 1809.

367. Page 62. 20 Dec 1808. William **LORIMIER** to Reinecke & Steinbeck (Frederick **REINECKE** and Daniel F. **STEINBECK**). For the sum of $300, 300 arpens, part of a tract of 1000 arpens four miles NW of Cape Girardeau granted to sd **LORIMIER** by the King of Spain. Signed Gm. **LORIMIER**. Test J. **MORRISON** Junr, William T. G. **DEW**, Geo. **HENDERSON** (JP). Rec 21 Mar 1809.

368. Page 63. 28 Nov 1805. John **SAVERS** to John C. **HARBISON**. For the sum of $1000, __ acres, being his head right and improvement granted by Louis **LORIMIER**, Commandant; joining sd **LORIMIER**'s land and Andrew **RAMSEY** senr. Signed John **SEAVERS**. Wit Gm. **LORIMIER**, A. **HADEN**, Charles **BRADLEY**, Geo. **HENDERSON** (JP). Rec 21 Mar 1809.

369. Page 64. 15 Mar 1808. David **HARRIS** to John C. **HARBISON**, agent for George C. C. **HARBISON** of Washington Co, Ky. For the sum of $334.75, 207 arpens; adjoining Andrew **RAMSEY** Senr and Joseph **THOMPSON**, and being part of the 250-arpen head right of sd **HARRIS** that he purchased of Andrew **RAMSEY** Senr, on which the house of John C. **HARBISON** stands; beginning at a marked hickory on sd **RAMSEY**'s line. Signed David (D) **HARRISS**. Wit Enoch **EVANS**, Geo. **HENDERSON** (JP). Rec 21 Mar 1809.

370. Page 66. 18 Nov 1808. Fanny **WATERS** and James **CURRIN** of Tywappity Bottom to Richard **DAVIS**. For the sum of $620, bond to make a deed on 200 acres in Tywappity Bottom about ten miles below Mrs. **WATERS** and near Charles **FINLEY**, the SE boundary of sd tract extending within one and a half miles of the Mississippi River. Sd **CURRIN** has sold the tract to sd **DAVIS** for $310. The deed is to be

executed derived from a patent from the Board of Commissioners by 25 Dec next. Signed Fanny **WATERS**, James **CURRIN**. Wit James **BRADY**, John **WATERS**, Geo. **HENDERSON** (JP). Title is assigned to Doctor Jaben **SEELYE** for value received on 17 Dec 1808. Signed Richd. **DAVIS**. Test R. **WORTHINGTON**, Geo. **HENDERSON** (JP). Rec 21 Mar 1809.

371. Page 68. 15 Nov 1808. James **RAMSEY** to Andrew **RAMSEY** Junr. For a consideration of ___, 400 arpens on White Water River at the Shewaney Trace Crossing, adjoining Thos. **MORGAN**; and he binds himself to make a title when the U. S. Commissioners make a title to him. Signed James **RAMSEY**. Wit Elihu **HORTON**, P. **CRAIG**, Geo. **HENDERSON** (JP). Rec 22 Mar 1809.

372. Page 69. 21 Mar 1809. Ezekiel **ABLE** to Charles **LUCUS**. For value received, agreement to pay sd **LUCUS** $32. Also bond to pay sd **LUCUS** $40, being the amount of a note given to Mr. **TAYLOR**, and if not paid to General James **ROBERTSON**; and $26, which the sd **LUCUS** promises to eat and drink out if sd **ABLE** should live so long. Signed Ezekiel **ABLE**. Test Jn. **SEELYE**, R. **WORTHINGTON**, Geo. **HENDERSON** (JP). Rec 22 Mar 1809.

373. Page 70. 1 Jul 1806. Louis **LORIMIER** to Andrew **RAMSEY** Senr. For the sum of $200 to be paid within 12 months, mortgage on Lot Nos. 7 & 8, Range D in Cape Girardeau; bounded on the N by Harmony St, S by Themis St, E by A. **HADEN**, and W by Indian St. Signed L. **LORIMIER**. Test B. **COUSIN**, Geo. **HENDERSON** (JP). Rec 24 Mar 1809.

374. Page 71. 22 Dec 1808. Andrew **RAMSEY** Senior to Enoch **EVANS**. For the sum of $1, Lot No. 7, Range D in Cape Girardeau, as described in the previous deed (C:70). Signed Andrew **RAMSEY**. Wit Geo. **HENDERSON** (JP). Rec 24 Mar 1809.

375. Page 72. 25 Mar 1809. Ezekiel **ABLE** by Sheriff John **HAYS** to Morgan **BYRNE**. For the sum of $32, 790 acres on the W side of White Water, adjoining Reason **BAILY** and being where James L. **FORTENBERRY** now resides. Sold on 24 Mar 1809 on a writ of execution issued on 13 Dec 1808 by CCP on judgment in favor of Edward F. **BOND** against sd **ABLE** for $93.12 and 5 mills for damages by reason of nonperformance of certain promises. Signed John **HAYS**, Sheriff. Test John **SCOTT**, F. M.

HENRY, Joseph W. McFERRON, Clerk, CCP. Rec 26 Mar 1809.

376. Page 74. 25 Mar 1809. James **RAMSEY** by same to Andrew **RAMSEY** Junr. For the sum of $17.75, 400 arpens on White Water Creek, adjoining John P. **ADUNAR**. Sold on 22 Mar 1809 on a writ of execution issued on 14 Dec 1808 by CCP on a judgment in favor of James **BRADY**; surviving partner of Thos. W. **WATERS** & Co. and assignee of Robert **HALL**, surviving partner of **WATERS & HALL**; and against James **RAMSEY** for $128.66 2/3 debt, and $39.12 damages and costs. Signed John **HAYS**, Sheriff. Test John **SCOTT**, Nat. **POPE**, Joseph W. **McFERRON**, Clerk, CCP. Rec 26 Mar 1809.

377. Page 77. 16 Jun 1808. Robert **CRUMP** to Job **THROCKMORTON**. Agreement to bind his son Robert from 1 May 1805 until sd Robert **CRUMP** is age 21, and sd **THROCKMORTON** agrees to teach the sd Robert to "reed, rite, and sipher as far as the Rules of three" and also the saddler's trade. As soon as sd Robert is free, sd **THROCKMORTON** agrees to give him two suits of country clothes and one suit of store clothes and one horse saddle and bridle to be worth $100. Signed Robert **CRUMP** Senr, Job **THROCKMORTON**. Test James **BURNS**, Geo. **HENDERSON** (JP). Rec 3 May 1809.

378. Page 78. 15 Jun 1808. Louis **LORIMIER** to Joseph **McFERRON**. For the sum of $200, Lot Nos. 6 & 7, Range C in Cape Girardeau; Lot No. 6 bounded on the S by Independence St, N by the public square, E by Thos. **MORGAN**, and W by Lorimier St; Lot No. 7 bounded on the E by Lorimier St, S by Independence St, N and W by Lot Nos. 8 & 10, Range C. Signed L. **LORIMIER** (also for money received). Wit B. **COUSIN**, Robert **BLAIR** (JP). Rec 5 May 1809.

379. Page 79. 29 Dec 1807. John **McCARTY** to John **BYRD**. For the sum of $240, 240 acres, more or less, on the main road leading from William **DOHERTY's** to sd **BYRD's**; adjoined on the E by Jonathan **FOREMAN**, N by John **BOYD**, and W by Bartholomew **COUSIN**. Signed John **McCARTY**. Wit Dens. O. **SULLIVAN**, Joseph **YOUNG**, Geo. **HENDERSON** (JP). Rec 18 May 1809.

380. Page 80. 22 Apr 1809. Richard **DAVIS** to Thomas **BALLEW**. For the sum of $250, two negro girls, **Franny** aged about six, and **Mary** aged about five. Signed Rich. **DAVIS**. Test R.

WORTHINGTON, David SHAW, Robert BLAIR (JP). Rec 22 May 1809.

381. Page 80. 25 Apr 1809. Same to William **SHAW**. For the sum of $650, a negro man named **Dick** about 45 years old, and a negro woman named **Philis** aged about 35 years. Signed Rich. **DAVIS**. Wit R. **WORTHINGTON**, Robert **BLAIR** (JP). Rec 22 May 1809.

382. Page 81. 30 Apr 1808. Th. C. **SCOTT** to Majr. Anthony **HADEN**. Power of attorney to collect $140 odd dollars from the Sheriff of the Cape Girardeau Dist, part of which may be due him as late Clerk of sd District, and to apply the same to payment of his debts. Signed Th. C. **SCOTT**. Wit James **BRADY**, Robert **BLAIR** (JP). Rec 9 Jun 1809.

383. Page 82. 16 May 1809. Frederick **GIBLER** to Frederick **REINECKE** of the New Madrid Dist. For securing payment of a debt and the sum of 5 shillings, Lot Nos. 5 & 8 and ½ of an adjoining lot in Cape Girardeau. Sd **GIBLER** is indebted to **REINECKE & STEINBECK** for $273.4 in a bond dated 20 Mar 1809, and due in one year. Signed Frederick **GIBLER**, Fredr. **REINECKE**. Test Geo. C. C. **HARBISON**, Levi **WOLVERTON**, Geo **HENDERSON** (JP). Rec 19 Jun 1809.

384. Page 84. 25 Oct 1808. Saml. **BALDWIN** to Moses **CARLOCK**. For the sum of $700, 250 arpens on the waters of Byrd Creek; originally granted to Josiah **LEE** Junr, and transferred to Anderson **NUNNELLY**, and from sd **NUNNELLY** to sd **BALDWIN**. Ten acres off the NW corner heretofore transferred to sd **LEE** are exempted. Signed Saml. **BALDWIN**. Wit Dennis O. **SULLIVAN**, Hugh **CRESWELL**, John **BYRD** (JCCP). Rec 22 Jun 1809.

385. Page 85. 25 Mar 1809. Robert **QUIMBY** by Sheriff John **HAYS** to George **HENDERSON** and A. **HADEN**. For the sum of $15.50, 700 arpens on the head waters of Lake St. Mary; adjoining Jacob **FRIEND**. Sold on 24 Mar 1809 on a writ of execution issued by CCP on 14 Dec 1808 in a judgment for James **MONTGOMERY** against sd **QUIMBY** for $482.38 damages for refusing to deliver a certain bond. Signed John **HAYS**, Sheriff. Wit John **BYRD**, Joseph **McFERRON**, Clerk, CCP. Rec 26 Jun 1809.

386. Page 86. 25 Mar 1809. William **SMITH** by same to same and same. For the sum of $12, 400 arpens, more or less, near the Paroqete Hill directly on the road leading from Mrs. WATERS' to Charles FRIEND's. Sold on 24 Mar 1809 on four writs of fieri facias; one in case of Joseph WORTHINGTON, assignee of Samuel STROTHER for $11.21 for costs in a case of trespass brought by sd SMITH, issued 27 Jan 1809; Jesse BOWDEN for $8.66 for costs in a case of trespass brought by sd SMITH and discontinued, issued 11 Jan 1809; Robert LANE for $31.03 for costs in a case of trespass brought by sd SMITH and discontinued, issued 27 Jan 1809; and James DUNCAN against sd SMITH for $76.18 damages by reason of non-performance of certain promises and undertakings, issued 27 Jan 1809. Signed John HAYS, Sheriff. Wit Robert BLAIR, Joseph W. McFERRON, Clerk, CCP. Rec 26 Jun 1809.

387. Page 94. 29 Apr 1809. Andrew LITTLE to John HAYS. For the sum of $90, a black mare which he purchased of Absolam MUCKLEMURY. Signed And. LITTLE. Wit Jas. GAINES, Geo. HENDERSON (JP). Rec 14 Jul 1809.

388. Page 95. 3 Feb 1807. William WHITE to Stephen BIRD. For the sum of $1200, bond to make a deed on a tract lately in possession of Hugh CRESSWELL and adjoining Charles G. ELLIS, Thos. BELEW's old place, Anthony RANDALL, James MORRISON, and others; to be make as soon as sd WHITE can obtain a right from the government. Signed Wm. WHITE. Wit Wm. OGLE, Solomon ELLIS, Geo. HENDERSON (JP). Rec 17 Jul 1809.

389. Page 96. 4 Jun 1809. Louis LORIMIER Senr and John C. HARBISON to John RAMSEY Senr. For the sum of $50 and interest from 1 May 1807, E moiety of Lot No. 8, Range C in Cape Girardeau; bounded on the E by Lorimier St which fronts on the public square, S by John McFERRON, N by Themis St., and W by the other half of Lot No. 8. Sd LORIMIER sold the lot to John C. HARBISON on 1 Jul 1806, which sd HARBISON gave in mortgage to sd LORIMIER. No part of the consideration money has been paid, and the deed from LORIMIER to HARBISON is canceled by mutual consent. Signed L. LORIMIER, John C. HARBISON. Test Ezekiel ABLE, B. COUSIN, Geo. HENDERSON (JP). Rec 19 Jul 1809.

390. Page 99. 4 Jul 1809. Meriwether LEWIS, Governor and Commander in chief of La. Terr., to George HENDERSON, Esq. Appointment as Auditor of Public Accounts for the Cape Girardeau Dist. Signed Meriwether LEWIS. Wit Frederick BATES, Secretary of La. Terr. George HENDERSON is sworn in by Robert BLAIR (JP) on 20 Jul 1809. Rec 20 Jul 1809.

391. Page 100. 21 Mar 1808. Joseph McFERRON, John HAYS, William DAUGHERTY, and John BYRD to Meriwether LEWIS, Governor of La. Terr. For the sum of $1500, bond to guarantee that sd McFERRON will faithfully discharge the office of Clerk of the Courts of Common Pleas and Quarter Sessions for the Cape Girardeau Dist. Signed Joseph McFERRON, John HAYS, Wm. DAUGHERTY, John BYRD. Wit George TENNILLE, Robt. GREEN (JCCP), Christr. HAYS (JCCP). Rec 27 Jul 1809.

392. Page 101. 17 Jul 1809. George HENDERSON, Andrew RAMSEY Jur, William MATTHEWS, and Lewis LATHAM to same. For the sum of $1000, bond to guarantee that sd HENDERSON will faithfully discharge the office of Auditor of Public Accounts for the Cape Girardeau Dist. Signed George HENDERSON, Andrew RAMSEY, William MATTHEWS, Lewis LATHAM. Wit Wm. DAUGHERTY, Wm. GARNER, John BYRD (JCCP), Robt. GREEN (JCCP), Stephen BYRD (JCCP). Rec 27 Jul 1809.

393. Page 103. 15 May 1809. Anthony HAYDEN to John SCOTT of the Ste. Genevieve Dist and Geo. C. C. HARBISON. For diverse and good causes, power of attorney to transact business, collect money, and make titles to real property. Signed A. HADEN. Wit Frek. REINEIKE, Isaac M. BLEDSOE, Geo. HENDERSON (JP). Rec 28 Jul 1809.

394. Page 104. 5 Sep 1809. Samuel BRADLEY of Cape Girardeau to John CROMWELL of Pittsburgh, Pa. Power of attorney to receive title to a tract of land from Isaac MASON of Pa., which sd MASON is obligated to convey because of noncompliance, and to sue to recover sums of money. Signed Saml. BRADLEY. Wit James EVANS, Robert BLAIR (JP). Rec 9 Sep 1809.

395. Page 105. 1 Jan 1807. John McCARTY to his son Nathan McCARTY. For diverse good causes and considerations, power of attorney to conduct business and sell or buy property within this Dist. Signed John McCARTY. Test John HAYS, Dens. SULLIVAN, Geo. HENDERSON (JP). Rec 16 Sep 1809.

396. Page 106. 2 Jan 1807. Nathan **McCARTY** to Dennis **SULLIVAN**. For the sum of $230, 200 acres, more or less, on the W side of White Water; known as Jonathan **HUBBELL's** improvement, and transferred by sd **HUBBLE** to John **McCARTY**, from sd **McCARTY** to Josiah **LEE**, and from sd **LEE** to Nathan **McCARTY**. Signed Nathan **McCARTY**. Wit John **HAYS**, Cynthia **HAYS**, Geo. **HENDERSON** (JP). Rec 16 Sep 1809.

397. Page 108. 24 Aug 1807. Frederick **BATES**, Secretary of La. Terr., to Benj. **SHELL**, Esq. Appointment as JP of German Twp. Signed Frederick **BATES**. Benjamin **SHELL** is sworn in by Th. C. **SCOTT**. Rec 21 Sep 1809.

398. Page 108. 7 Aug 1808. John **McCARTY** resigns all right, title, and claim to land on the W side of White Water known as Jonathan **HUBBEL's** improvement (C:106). Signed John **McCARTY**. Wit Henry **HAND**, Sarah (x) **HAND**, Geo. **HENDERSON** (JP). Rec 23 Sep 1809.

399. Page 109. 1 Feb 1808. Jacob **SKEAN** to George **HAYS**. For the sum of $2/acre and more for the improvement, $215 on this date and the balance when the improvement is valued; 100 acres improved by sd **SKEAN** where he now lives, excepting the house, which he is to have nothing for. Sd **SKEAN** has leave to live on the land until 1 Jan next. The improvement is to be valued by two disinterested men when sd **SKEAN** moves, and sd **SKEAN** is also to allow sd **HAYS** to have 130 apple trees now on the land for nothing. Signed Jacob **SKEAN**. Wit Charles **DEMOSS**, Geo. **HENDERSON**, Christr. **HAYS** (JCCP). Rec 28 Sep 1809.

400. Page 111. 20 Feb 1809. Edward **ROBERTSON** to John **SIMPSON**. For security on a bond, one negro man named **Sam**, one negro woman named **Diner** about 20 years old, and her child about 1 year old; given as security for a bond to make title to a tract of land to sd **SIMPSON**. Signed Edward (ER) **ROBERTSON**. Wit James **EVANS**, Geo. **HENDERSON** (JP). Rec 24 Oct 1809.

401. Page 112. 10 Nov 1809. Joseph **WALLER**, William **WILLIAMS**, and Isaac **WILLIAMS** to John and Henry **EARTHMAN**. For the sum of $1900, bond to make a title to 380 arpens where Isaac **LEE** now lives, as described in a deed of conveyance from sd **WALLER** and Susanah, his wife, to John and Henry **EARTHMAN**. Signed Joseph ( ) **WALLER**, William **WILLIAMS**, Isaac (x) **WILLIAMS**. Wit Geo. **HENDERSON** (JP). Rec 10 Nov 1809.

402. Page 113. 1 Jul 1809. Richard **DAVIS** of Cape Girardeau to Enoch **EVANS**. For the sum of $650, 240 arpens, more or less, on Ramsey's Creek; adjoined on the N by Samuel **TIPTON**, S by Enoch **EVANS** (formerly Peter **GODAR**), E by Andrew **RAMSEY** Senr, and W by land formerly granted to John **DITCH**. Signed Richd. **DAVIS**. Wit James **EVANS**, David **SHAW**, Geo. **HENDERSON** (JP). Rec 20 Nov 1809.

403. Page 115. 5 Nov 1809. Thomas **BURROWS** to John **BURROWS**. Power of attorney to collect and receive all moneys and property. Signed Thomas **BURROWS**, Edmond **HOGAN** (JP). Rec 20 Nov 1809.

404. Page 116. 5 Nov 1809. Thomas **BURROWS** and Pernelia, his wife, to John **BURROWS**. For the sum of $140, 53 1/3 acres, being all their right to land granted to Waters **BURROWS**. Signed Thomas **BURROWS**, Permilia (x) **BURROWS**. Test Edmond **HOGAN** (JP). Rec 20 Nov 1809.

405. Page 117. 18 Nov 1808. David **HARRIS** to George C. C. **HARBISON** of Washington Co., Ky. For the sum of $200 in the form of a horse and $75, 50 arpents; the land to be delivered by 8 Dec next, or as soon as John C. **HARBISON**, agent for George C. C. **HARBISON**, can pay. Sd **HARRIS** and John C. **HARBISON** bind themselves for $500 to make title to the land as soon as the government confirms it. Signed David (D) **HARRIS** (also for receipt of one horse creature at $125, and $75 cash), John C. **HARBISON**, agent for George C. C. **HARBISON**. Wit David **SHAW**, Jah. **ABLE**, Geo. **HENDERSON** (JP). Rec 21 Nov 1809.

406. Page 119. 14 May 1808. Edward **ROBERTSON** to James **MONTGOMERY**. For the sum of $750, 750 arpens known as the Lime Kiln Tract, the head right of Andrew **ROBERTSON**. Edward **ROBERTSON** binds himself for $1500 to make a deed by 1 Aug next. Signed Edward (ER) **ROBERTSON**. Test James **CURRIN**, Thos. **FLETCHER**, Geo. **HENDERSON** (JP). Bond is assigned to Joseph **SEAWELL** for value received on 8 Aug 1808. Signed James **MONTGOMERY**. Test A. **HADEN**, James **CURRIN**, Geo. **HENDERSON** (JP). Rec 20 Nov 1809.

407. Page 121. 13 Jun 1808. Louis **LORIMIER** to Robert **BLAIR**. For the sum of $100 payable by 1 May next, Lot No. 10, Range C in Cape Girardeau; bounded on the E by Joseph **McFERRON**, W by Indian St, S by Independence St, and N by Lot No. 9. Signed L. **LORIMIER** (also for receipt of $103). Wit B. **COUSIN**, Enoch **EVANS** (JP). Rec 28 Dec 1809.

408. Page 122. 1 Nov 1809. James **BRADY** and Fanny **WATERS** to John H. **MIFFLIN**. For the sum of $1400, bond to make a title on 240 arpens in Tywappity Bottom; bounded by the Mississippi River, Henry **COCKERHAM**, land that was late the property of Lemuel **CHENEY**, decd, and vacant land. The land was claimed by sd **BRADY** as assignee of William **SMITH**, who was assignee of Daniel **SAXON**, who was assignee of Benjamin **ROSE**, who first settled the same by permission of the Spanish government. Signed James **BRADY**, Fanny **WATERS**. Test James **CURRIN**, W. **GARNER**, Edmond **HOGAN** (JP). Rec 29 Dec 1809.

409. Page 123. 16 Jan 1809. John P. **EDDINGER** and James **ARREL** to Jacob **SHEPPARD**. For the sum of $2000, bond to make a deed to 300 acres on the waters of Whight Water; known as the Round Pond Tract, in the vicinity of **TAYLOR** and **BRANT**, and improved by Jeremiah **CONAWAY**. The deed to be made by 25 Dec 1812 or when the commissioners have decided on claims. Test Samuel **PEW**, John **SHEPPARD**, Geo. **HENDERSON** (JP). Rec 9 Dec 1809.

410. Page 125. 1 Jan 1810. James **ARREL** and Mary, his wife, to John **HAYS**. For the sum of $800, 240 arpens, being where David S. **JENKINS** now lives; adjoining lands formerly granted by the Spanish government to Jonathan **FOREMAN**, Henry **SHERIDAN**, Charles **FALINGASH**, and others. Signed James **ARREL**, Mary (x) **AREL** (also for receipt of $800). Wit Geo. **HENDERSON** (JP), W. **GARNER**. Rec 1 Jan 1810.

411. Page 127. 1 Jan 1810. James **AREL** to same. For a negroe boy named **Zack**, two bay mares, one rifle gun, and three cows; mortgage to secure title on the tract described in the previous deed (C:125). Signed James **ARREL**. Test Elizabeth **NEELY**, Geo. **HENDERSON** (JP). Rec 2 Jan 1810.

412. Page 128. 12 Jan 1810. James **DOWTY** to William **GARNER**. For the sum of $90.25, mortgage on 240 arpents, more or less, being where sd **DOWTY** now lives. Sd **DOWTY** owes sd **GARNER** a debt in a note due in six months from this date with interest. Signed James **DOWTY**. Wit Geo. **HENDERSON** (JP), John **HAYS**. Rec 12 Jan 1810.

413. Page 129. 8 Jan 1810. Isaac **LEE** to Andrew **MILLER** and Robert **MILLER**, his trusty and loving friends. Power of attorney to demand, sue for, levy, recover and receive money, etc. from Thomas **FULLWOOD**, late of Clark Co., Ga. Signed Isaac **LEE**. Wit Jno. **ABERNETHIE** (JP). Rec 15 Jan 1810.

414. Page 131. 25 Feb 1809. Jonathan **BUIS** to John **BYRD**, Esq. For the sum of $500, bond to make a deed to 150 arpens, more or less, on Hubble's Creek whereon Jeremiah W. **STILL** now lives; bounded on the S by land formerly owned by Henry **SHERADON**, E by Samuel **PEW**, N by Edward **HALE**. Should any land over the amount be granted to sd **BUIS** by the U. S. A., then that is land also to be included in the deed. Signed Jonathan **BUIS**. Test Jaben **SEELYE**, Jeremiah W. **STILL**, Robert **BLAIR** (JP). Title is assigned to James **ERRLES** for $500 on 10 Apr 1809. Signed John **BYRD**. Test John ( ) **BOYD**, James **CRAWFORD**. Title is assigned to John **DUNN** for value received on 28 Nov 1809. Signed James **EARL**. Test John **RANDOL**, Geo. **HENDERSON** (JP). Rec 25 Jan 1810.

415. Page 134. 18 Jan 1810. William **ROSS** and Elisabeth , his wife, to Stephen **STILLEY**. For diverse good causes, __ acres in Tywappity Twp; beginning at William **ROSS'** upper corner on the bank of the Mississippi River, and bounded by the river. Signed William **ROSS**, Elisabeth (x) **ROSS**. Wit Joseph **MOSBY**, John **MERIT**, Edmond **HOGAN** (JP). Rec 25 Jan 1810.

416. Page 135. 2 Jan 1910. Daniel **HARKLEROAD** and John **HALL** of Cape Girardeau. Exchange of land by 1 Mar next. Sd **HARKLEROAD** conveys to sd **HALL** 79 acres, more or less, on Franks Creek; being the same where sd **HARKLEROAD** now lives and that he purchased of Samuel **STROTHER**. Sd **HARKLEROAD** to reserve one pair of mill stones & irons now in the mill, and is to take good care of sd place. Sd **HARKLEROAD** binds himself to make a deed for sd land, as soon as he can receive title to the same. Sd **HALL** conveys to sd **HARKLEROAD** ½ acre, more or less, in Cape Girardeau, where John C. **HARBISON** formerly lived and which he sold to Thos. **GRAYHAM**, and sold by sd **HARBISON** to John **RAMSEY**, and from sd **RAMSEY** to sd **HALL**, and being where sd **HALL** now lives. The exchange is void if the commissioners fail to grant title to sd **HARKLEROAD**. Signed Dannal **HARKLEROAD**, John **HALL**. Wit John **RANDOL**, James **EVANS**, Geo. **HENDERSON** (JP). Rec 25 Jan 1810.

417. Page 137. 17 Feb 1809. James **RANDOLL** and Thomas **MORGAN** to Abram **DAUGHERTY**. For the sum of $1200, bond to make a deed on 240 arpens, French measure, more or less, where sd **RANDOLL** has resided with his family for several years; adjoined by Lewis **LAYTHOM**, John **PATTERSON**, Thomas **BULL**, and Lewis **TASH**. Signed James **RANDOL**, Thos **MORGAN**. Wit John **DAUGHERTY**, Jno. **ABERNETHIE**, Geo. **HENDERSON** (JP). Rec 3 Feb 1810.

418. Page 139. 4 Sep 1809. Enos **RANDOL** to Allen **McKINZY**. For the sum of $900, bond to make title on 100 acres, including the improvement where sd **McKINZEY** now lives, as quick as the commissioners adjust and settle land claims. Signed Enos **RANDOL**. Wit Wm. **GARNER**, John **RANDOL**, Robert **BLAIR** (JP). Rec 5 Feb 1810.

419. Page 140. 6 Jul 1809. William **BONNER** and Catherine, his wife, of Ill. Terr to Erasmus **ELLIS** of Ste. Genevieve Dist. For the sum of $750, 240 arpens on Ramsey's Creek, being where sd **BONNER** formerly lived; bounded on the N by heirs of Samuel **TIPTON**, decd, S by Peter **GODAIR**, E by Andrew **RAMSEY**, and W by land granted to John **DITCH** and owned by sd **RAMSEY**. Signed William ( ) **BONER**, Catherine ( ) **BONER** (RD). Wit Robert **BLAIR** (JP). Rec 5 Feb 1810.

420. Page 142. Elisha **JACKSON** of the New Madrid Dist to Benjamin **PATTERSON**. For the sum of $1000, 1150 arpens on Cape la Cruse Creek on the S side and adjoining the survey of Louis **LORIMIER**, to include an old mill seat and the improvement of James **RAINES**. Sd **JACKSON** also posts bond of $2000 to guarantee performance of the obligation. Signed E. **JACKSON**. Test Joseph **LEWIS**, Thomas Y. **HORSLEY**, John C. **HARBISON**, Geo. **HENDERSON** (JP). Rec 8 Feb 1810.

421. Page 144. 4 Jan 1810. John **FARTHMAN** to John **HAYS**. For the sum of $300, one negro boy named **Zack** about 9 or 10 years of age, and he warrants the boy to be sound, healthy, and clear of all impediments except that of one of his hands. Signed Jno. **EARTHMAN**. Wit Nathan G. **HAILE**, Geo. **HENDERSON** (JP). Rec 8 Feb 1810.

422. Page 145. 23 Feb 1810. John **RANDALL** and Margaret, his wife, Samuel **RANDALL** and Mary, his wife, all of Cape Girardeau, to Robert **DESHA** of Tenn. For the sum of $400, 300 acres, Spanish measure, on the waters of Hubble's Creek, adjoining Joseph **THOMPSON** on the W; more particularly known as Clingingsmith's Improvement. Signed John **RANDAL**, Samuel (x) **RANDAL**, Margaret **RANDAL**, Mary ( ) **RANDAL**. Wit William **CRACRAFT**, James M. **WILSON**, James **EVANS**, Geo. **HENDERSON** (JP). Rec 26 Feb 1810.

423. Page 147. 20 Dec 1810. Frederick **BATES**, Secretary of La. Terr., to Robert **BLAIR**, Esq. Appointment as Judge of the Courts of Pleas and Quarter Sessions for the Cape Girardeau Dist. Signed Frederick **BATES**. Robert **BLAIR** takes the oath of office. Signed Robert **BLAIR**. Wit J. M. **McFERRON**. Rec 10 Mar 1810.

424. Page 148. 12 Feb 1810. Frederick **BATES**, Secretary of La. Terr., to Richard **MILLS**, Esq. Appointment as JP for Tywappity Township. Signed Frederick **BATES**. Richard **MILLS** takes the oath of office. Signed Richard **MILLS**. Wit J. M. **McFERRON**. Rec 12 Mar 1810.

425. Page 149. 26 Nov 1809. John **BULLINGER** and Henry **BULLINGER** to William **CRAYCRAFT** and Andrew **RAMSEY**, son of Jno. For the sum of $200, bond to make a deed on the lower corner of a lot on the bank of the Mississippi in Cape Girardeau, as soon as John **BOLLINGER** receives title of Louis **LORIMIER**. Signed Johannes **BOLLINGER**, Heinrich **BOLLINGER** [both in German]. Wit James **EVANS**, Allen **ELLIS**, Enoch **ELLIS** (JP). Rec 19 Mar 1810.

426. Page 151. 12 Feb 1810. Frederick **BATES**, Secretary of La. Terr., to William **KELSO**, Esq. Appointment as JP for Tywappity Township. Signed Frederick **BATES**. William **KELSO** takes the oath of office. Signed William **KELSO**. Wit J. M. **McFERRON**. Rec 20 Mar 1810.

427. Page 152. 20 Mar 1810. Jeremiah **SIMPSON** by Sheriff John **HAYS** to Samuel G. **DUNN**. For the sum of $77.25, a negro girl named **Harriett**. Sold on 3 Mar 1810 in execution of a writ issued by the CCP in a judgment against sd **SIMPSON** and for Morgan **BYRNE**, assignee of Luke **BYRNE**. Signed John **HAYS**, Sheriff. Wit David S. **JENKINS**, Geo. **HENDERSON** (JP). Rec 20 Mar 1810.

428. Page 153. 23 Jan 1810. John **HENTHORN** of the Ste. Genevieve Dist to William **JENKINS**. For the sum of $480, 240 arpens on the road leading to New Madrid and known as Henthorn's Improvement; bounded on the E by Charles **FREIND**, S by Edward **ROBINSON**, W by Jonas **FREIND**'s heirs, and N by the hills. Signed John **HENTHORN**. Wit Enoch **EVANS** (JP). Rec 21 Mar 1810.

429. Page 154. 4 Sep 1809. Zellah **DICKSON** of the Cape Girardeau Dist and Frederick **DICKSON** of the St. Charles Dist to John **RANDOLL**. For the sum of $1000, bond to make a deed (with the claim that Wm. **LUNCEFORD** holds by lease excepted) to 240 acres, French measure, on Randoll's Mill Creek where Zillah **DICKSON** and sd **LUNCEFORD** now live; adjoined by where Wm. **WILLIAMS** & family live on Whitaker's old tract, and vacant land. The deed to be made within 10 months of when Zillah **DICKSON** receives a grant from the U. S. A. Signed Zillah (x) **DICKSON**, Frederick (x) **DICKSON**. Wit Jno. **ABERNETHIE**, William **WILLIAMS**, Robert **BLAIR** (JP). Rec 22 Mar 1810.

430. Page 156. 26 Feb 1810. James **CURRIN** to James **WELBURN**. For the sum of $750, bond to make a deed on 75 arpents in Tywappity Twp, adjoining the Mississippi River, and adjoined below by land recently purchased by Timothy **HARRIS** from sd **CURRIN**. Signed James **CURRIN**. Wit Richd. **MILLS**, Josiah **CHAMBERS**, Geo. **HENDERSON** (JP). Rec 23 Mar 1810.

431. Page 157. 12 Jan 1809. Thomas **FOSTER** to William **WILLIAMS**. For the sum of $100, 240 arpens on Turky Creek adjoining James **CARUTHERS**, decd, on the W. Signed Thomas (x) **FOSTER**. Wit Thos. S. **RODNEY**, Geo. **HENDERSON** (JP). Rec 23 Mar 1810.

432. Page 158. 25 Dec 1807. Ephraim **BILDERBACK** and John **BILDERBACK** of Kaskaskia, Ind. Terr [now Ill.], to Rufus **EASTON** of St. Louis, La. For the sum of $500,

undivided moeity of three tracts; an improvement, head right, and concession right of Philix **HOOVER** about 12 miles W of the Mississippi River near Enos **RANDOL**; other lands claimed by sd **HOOVER** and which they claim as assignee of sd **HOOVER**; an improvement, head donation, and concession right of John **DYE** in Tywappity Bottom at the E end of a sand prairie; rights and claims to land of sd **DYE** in the Cape Girardeau Dist; an improvement, head donation, and concession right made by Aaron **GRAHAM** in the New Madrid Dist about two miles N of New Madrid and adjoining John **DRYBREAD** and John **MURPHY** at Lake St. Maries; all lands of sd **GRAHAM** they claim as his assignee; also ¼ part of a concession, improvement right, and claim made to James **CALDWELL** on the St. Francois River in Kelly's Settlement; and ¼ part of the rights and claims of land of sd **CALDWELL** which they claim as assignee of Francis **GUTHRIE**, assignee of sd **CALDWELL**. Signed Ephrimm **BILDERBACK**, John **BELDERBACK**. Wit Nat. **POPE**, Robert **MORRISON**, Otho **SHRADER**, Judge of General Court of La. Rec 2 Apr 1810.

433. Page 160. 3 Apr 1810. Martin **RODNEY** and Hannah, his wife, to Thomas S. **RODNEY**. For the sum of $2500, 680 arpens, more or less, on the waters of Hubble's Creek, being the same whereon Martin & Hannah **RODNEY** now live; beginning at a sycamore; adjoined on the N by William **MATHEWS**, E by Stephen **BYRD**, S by vacant lands, and W by Thomas S. **RODNEY**. Signed Martin **RODNEY**, Hannah (x) **RODNEY**. Wit John **THOMPSON**, Wm. **DUNN**, Geo. **HENDERSON** (JP). Rec 4 Apr 1810.

434. Page 163. 21 Jul 1809. Isaac M. **BLEDSOE** and William **WHITE** by Sheriff John **HAYS** to David **SHAW**. For the sum of $33, Lot Nos. 9 & 13, Range B in Cape Girardeau. Sold on 18 Jul 1809 on a writ of execution in a judgment in CCP against sd **BLEDSOE** and sd **WHITE** and for McNutt Finley & Co. for $189.87 debt, $50 damages and costs. Signed John **HAYS**, Sheriff. Wit Geo. **HENDERSON** (JP), Joseph **McFERRON**, Clerk, CCP, Cape Girardeau Dist. Rec 10 Apr 1810.

435. Page 166. 24 Mar 1810. Louis **LORIMIER** Senr. to John **GUETHING**. For the sum of $100, Lot No. 13, Range B in Cape Girardeau; bonded on the N by Independence St, S by Geo. C. C. **HARBISON**, E by Indian St, and W by

Lot No. 16, unsold. Signed L. **LORIMIER**. Wit B. **COUSIN**, Geo. **HENDERSON** (JP). Rec 11 Apr 1810.

436. Page 168. 16 Nov 1809. Joseph **WALLER** and Susanah, his wife, to John and Henry **EARTHMAN**. For the sum of $950, 380 arpens on Randol's Creek whereon sd **WALLER** formerly lived and Isaac **LEE** now lives; adjoined on the W by John **ABERNETHIE**, Esq., S by John **HITT**, N by a dividing line designated in a title bond from Richard **WALLER** and Medad **RANDOL** to William **WILLIAMS** for 100 arpens of Joseph **WALLER**'s old survey dated 4 Jan 1808. Signed Joseph ( ) **WALLER**, Susannah ( ) **WALLER**. Wit William **WILLIAMS**, Geo. **HENDERSON** (JP), Nathan G. **HAILE** & Joshua **HAILE** (as to Susannah **WALLER**). Rec 21 Apr 1810.

437. Page 170. 6 Oct 1806. Louis **LORIMIER** to Pierre **MENARD** of Kaskaskia, Ind. Terr. For the sum of $13,600, 3600 arpens, more or less, where he usually resides, bounded on the E by the Mississippi River, S by the S boundary of his claim (including his purchase of Hippt. **MAROT**), W by a N-S line and N by an E-W line to the river, both lines to be drawn so as to take in the plantations formerly improved and occupied by Jona. **FORMAN**; excepting such lots in Cape Girardeau that have already been sold. Sd **LORIMIER** to retain use of the tract for three years. Also 90 head of horses or mares of his choice out of those branded with sd **LORIMIER**'s mark, including the stud Diamond and the mare named Dorsey Filly; sd **LORIMIER** to retain use and possession of as many horses as he needs for three years. Signed L. **LORIMIER**. Wit Pierre **MARRASSE**, Gme. **LORIMIER**, Robert **BLAIR**, Justice of Cape Girardeau Dist. Rec 9 May 1810.

438. Page 173. 12 Sep 1809. Charles **FRIEND** to James **JEFFERY**. For the sum of $1000, bond to make title to 200 arpens lying on the road to New Madrid and adjoining Isrial **FRIEND** near the Tywappity Hills, 1 ½ miles from his plantation. Charles **FRIEND** has sold the land to sd **JEFFERY** for $500, and this bond guarantees he will execute a deed in 12 months. Signed Charles **FRIEND** (also for receipt of $500). Wit William **SOWLE**, Hugh **CRESWELL**, Geo. **HENDERSON** (JP). Bond is assigned to Peter **CRAIG** for value received on 14 Nov 1809. Signed James ( ) **JEFFREY**. Wit James **RAVENSCROFT**, Andrew **RAMSEY**, Ann S.

RAMSEY, Geo. **HENDERSON** (JP). Rec 24 Nov 1809.

439. Page 175. 20 Mar 1810. Peter **CRAIG** to Andrew **RAMSEY**, son of John. For the sum of $400, the land described in the preceding deed (C:173). Sd **RAMSEY** is to have no recourse against sd **CRAIG** should title not prove to be good. Signed Peter **CRAIG**. Test Geo. **HENDERSON** (JP), John **SIMPSON**. Rec 16 May 1810.

440. Page 176. 10 Nov 1809. William **LORRIMIER** to George C. C. **HARBISON**. For the sum of $57 debt and $93 in property, bond to make a deed on 100 acres on Cape La Cruche Creek, on both sides of the creek and centered on Dodson's Improvement. Sd **LORRIMIER** is indebted to John **CROMWELL**, late of the Cape Girardeau Dist, for $57, to be collected by sd **HARBISON** as agent of sd **CROMWELL**, for which sd **LORRIMIER** has confessed a judgment before Robert **BLAIR**, Esq. Should sd **LORRIMIER** not pay the sum by 1 May next, then he binds himself to convey the land to sd **HARBISON**. Signed Gm. **LORRIMIER**, Geo. C. C. **HARBISON**. Wit Robert **BLAIR**, Geo. **HENDERSON** (JP). Rec 19 May 1810.

441. Page 178. 15 May 1810. John **ORDWAY** of the New Madrid Dist to Mary **ORDWAY**. For the sum of $600, 300 arpens in Tywappity Twp; beginning on the bank of the Mississippi River at a stake where a fence divides the improvement of John **ORDWAY** from William **KELSO**; being the same sd **ORDWAY** bought of Alexander **MILLIKIN**. Signed John **ORDWAY**. Wit John **HALCOMBE**, David J. **POOR**, Wm. **KELSO** (JP). Rec 22 May 1810.

442. Page 179. 21 Nov 1809. Elijah **WELSH** swears before John **DAVIS** (JP) that he was not present at any contract between Ezekiel **ABLE** and William **CRAWFORD** wherein lands or negroes were mentioned or conveyed. Signed Elijah **WELSH**. Wit John **DAVIS** (JP). Rec 22 May 1810.

443. Page 180. 12 Jan 1810. John **BYRD** to Ann **BYRD**, alias Ann **CRAWFORD**. Deed of gift to his beloved daughter for 200 acres beginning at Joseph **YOUNG**'s SW corner. Signed John **BYRD**. Test Jas. **MORRISON** Junr, Saml. **McILROY**, Geo **HENDERSON** (JP). Rec 22 May 1810.

444. Page 181. 5 Jun 1809. Robert **McCAY** to Edward **ROBERTSON**, both of the New Madrid Dist. Assignment of title papers to 320 arpens; sd papers now are in the office of the Recorder of the U. S. Land Commissioners to ascertain the claims to land in sd Terr; and consist of a petition by sd **McCAY** to the Spanish Government, confirmed by Don Juan **MORALES**, Intendant General, and Don Manuel ___no at New Orleans. Signed Robert **McCAY**. Test M. J. **AMOUREUX**, JCCP, New Madrid Dist. Bond is assigned to Samuel **RAVENSCRAFT** for $500 on 12 Mar 1810. Signed Edward (ER) **ROBERTSON**. Test Joseph **CAMPBELL**, John **SIMPSON**, Geo. **HENDERSON** (JP). Rec 8 Jun 1810.

445. Page 184. 31 May 1810. Alexander St. **SCOTT** and Elizabeth, his wife, to Frederick **REINEIKE** and Daniel F. **STEINBECK**, trading as Reineike & Steinbeck. For the sum of $250, improvements made by them on Lot No. 12, Range C in Cape Girardeau. Title in fee to sd lot is to be made by Louis **LORIMIER** on payment to him by Reineike & Steinbeck of $100. Signed Alex. St. **SCOTT**, Elizabeth (x) **SCOTT**. Wit Isaac M. **BLEDSOE**, Frederick **GIBLER**, Geo. **HENDERSON** (JP). Rec 22 Jun 1810.

446. Page 185. 24 Mar 1810. Joseph **WALLER** by Sheriff John **HAYS** to Isaac **WILLIAMS**. For the sum of $26, 240 arpens, more or less, being the head right of Jonathan **BUIS** in the Big Bend of the Mississippi. Sold on 20 Mar 1810 on writ of execution issued 16 Jan 1810 by the General Court of the U. S. in St. Louis on a judgment for Louis **LORIMIER** and against Daniel **MULLINS** and Joseph **WALLER** for $19.48 in costs. Signed John **HAYS**, Sheriff. Wit Joseph **McFERRON**, Clerk, CCP. Rec 28 Jun 1810.

447. Page 188. 9 Jul 1809. Israll **FRIEND** to Charles **FRIEND**. For a debt that Charles **FRIEND** paid for Israll **FRIEND** in 1796, all the land where he now lives, all his horses and cattel, hogs, farming tools, and house furniture. Signed Israll ( ) **FRIEND**. Wit James (x) **TILLER**, Joseph (x) **TILLER**, Enoch **EVANS** (JP). Rec 4 Jul 1810.

448. Page 189. 12 Jun 1808. Nathan **McCARTY** to William **McCARTY**. For the sum of $120, a certain sorrel horse about 5 foot and a inch high, two years old, that he purchased of Dennis O. **SULLIVAN** and known by the name of Shake Spear. Signed Nathan **McCARTY**. Wit Geo. **HENDERSON** (JP). Rec 6 Jul 1810.

449. Page 190. 3 May 1810. Frederick **BATES**, Secretary of La. Terr., to Frederick **LIMBAUGH** Senr, Esq. Appointment as JP for German Twp. Signed Frederick **BATES**. Frederick **LIMBAUGH** Senr. takes the oath of office. Signed Fredk. **LIMBAUGH** Senr. Wit Joseph **McFERRON**, Clerk, CCP. Rec 6 Jul 1810.

450. Page 191. 20 Apr 1809. Fanny **WATERS**, adminr of Thomas W. **WATERS**, decd, to William **SHAW**. For the sum of $140, to be deducted from his share of the estate of sd **WATERS**, one negro girl named **Anne** about 6 years old. The girl was the property of the estate of sd **WATERS**. Signed Fanny **WATERS**, adminr of Thos. W. **WATERS**, decd. Test James **BRADY**, Geo. **HENDERSON** (JP). Rec 13 Jul 1810.

451. Page 191. 3 Jan 1810. James **CURRIN** to Timothy **HARRIS**, now of Ill. Terr. For the sum of $3500, bond to make lawful title for 350 arpens on the bank of the Mississippi, being the plantation where he now lives; by 1 Jan next. Signed James **CURRIN**. Wit Richd. **MILLS**, Hy. **COCKERHAM**, Geo. **HENDERSON** (JP). Rec 15 Jul 1810.

452. Page 192. 18 Feb 1804. Louis **LORIMIER** to Hippolyte **MAROT**. In exchange for a grant of about 500 arpents bordering the low lands (swamp area) which sd **MAROT** sells to him today, 3/4 arpent in Cape Girardeau; bordered on the W by a street, N by Barthelemi **COUSIN**, S by the stream which marks the southern limit of the village, and E by a common green area. The land was surveyed 20 Jan last in the presence of sd **LORIMIER** and sd **MAROT**. Sd **LORIMIER**, at his expense, also has built a cabin for sd **MAROT**. When sd **LORIMIER** receives title to the land, he will cancel the balance of sd **MAROT**'s account. Signed L. **LORIMIER**. Wit B. **COUSINS**, Pierre **MENARD**, Otho **SHRADER**, Judge of General Court. Rec 17 Jul 1810. [IN FRENCH]

453. Page 194. 8 Jan 1805. Hippolite **MAROTE** to Barthelemi **COUSIN**. For the sum of 150 piastres, 3/4 arpent in Cape Girardeau, which he acquired from Louis **LORIMIER** [C:192]. Signed Hipolite **MAROTE**. Wit Valth(?) **FOELKEL**, John **GUETHING**, Robt. **GREEN** (JCCP). Rec 17 Jul 1810. [IN FRENCH]

454. Page 195. 31 Jan 1804. Louis **LORIMIER** to same. For the sum of 100 piastres, 1 arpent in Cape Girardeau; bordered on the S by Hippolyte **MAROT**, and E, N, & W by 3 streets; with the express stipulation that the land on the E side up to the Mississippi River be a common ground from the street on the N to the creek which makes the S border of the village. Signed L. **LORIMIER**. Test Wm. **LOWREY**, Benja. **GOODIN**, Otho **SHRADER**, Judge of General Court. Rec 17 Jul 1810. [IN FRENCH]

455. Page 197. [no date]. Same to same. In consideration and exchange for a site on the river acquired from Waters & Hall by sd **COUSIN**, about 2 arpents in the village of Cape Girardeau, E of and adjoining other properties previously sold to sd **COUSIN** and Hippolite **MAROTE**. This property was to have been left a common ground, but by mutual agreement is now sold to sd **COUSIN**, the only interested person, as the sole owner of the two sites; bordered to the N by a street, E by the Mississippi River, S by the creek which is the southern border of the village of Cape Girardeau, and W by the two sites mentioned above. Sd **COUSIN** will make sufficient passage to the river when needed. Signed L. **LORIMIER**. Wit Hipolite **MAROTE**, Thos. S. **RODNEY**, John **GUETHING** (JP), Otho **SHRADER**, Judge of General Court. Rec 17 Jul 1810. [IN FRENCH]

456. Page 199. 23 Aug 1806. Same to same. For the sum of __, Lot No. 2, Range C in Cape Girardeau; bordered on the NW by a creek which separates sd land from that currently occupied by sd **COUSIN**, S by street of Independence, and E by the Mississippi River. Sd **COUSIN** must furnish a passage of 50 feet along the river side for public use. Signed L. **LORIMIER**. Test Thos. S. **RODNEY**, John **GUETHING** (JP), Otho **SHRADER**, Judge of General Court. Rec 17 Jul 1810. [IN FRENCH]

457. Page 200. 20 Mar 1810. Ezekiel **ABLE** swears before John **ABERNETHIE** (JP) that he had two notes, one for $100, and one for $275, and both are mislaid. This is a sufficient bar against sd notes. All notes due to **ABLE** from Wm. **ROBERTS** are paid except one of $95. Signed Ezekiel **ABLE**, Jeremiah **ABLE**. Wit Jno. **ABERNETHIE** (JP). Rec 17 Jul 1810.

458. Page 201. 9 Jun 1809. Ezekiel **ABLE** and Jeremiah **ABLE** to William **ROBERTS**. For the sum of $2000, bond to make a deed on 320 acres on the waters of White Water, known as Morgan's Improvement, beginning about three

rods from the upper corner, as soon as sd **ABLE**s get a right to sd tract. Signed Ezekiel **ABLE**, Jeremiah **ABLE**. Wit Js. **BOYD**, William ( ) **TAILOR**, Geo. **HENDERSON** (JP). Rec 17 Jul 1810.

459. Page 202. 9 Jun 1809. Ezekiel **ABLE** to John **SHIELDS**. For the sum of $240, bond to make a deed for 120 arpens on the E side of Whitewater where sd **SHIELDS** now lives, as soon as a right can be obtained from the U. S. A. Signed Ezekiel **ABLE**. Wit Js. **BOYD**, William (x) **ROBERTS**, Geo. **HENDERSON** (JP). Rec 17 Jul 1810.

460. Page 203. 16 Aug 1809. James **HANNA** to John **GIBONEY**. For the sum of $100, bond to make title to 100 arpens on the S side of a certain gut between **HANNA**'s house and **GIBONEY**'s, being the place where sd **GIBONEY** now lives; if sd **HANNA** can obtain a title from the government. If title is not obtained, sd **HANNA** is to return the money he receives of sd **GIBONEY**. Signed James **HANNAH**. Test Dens. O. **SULLIVAN**, Geo. **HENDERSON** (JP). Rec 18 Jul 1810.

461. Page 203. 1 May 1809. Jerimiah **ABLE** and Ezekiel **ABLE** to James Leath **FORTENBERRY**. For the sum of $1800, bond to obtain right to 300 acres, including Wm. **SMITH**'s Improvement, beginning at a sugar tree near the fish trap, on a line between Wm. **MURFEY** and Wm. **SMITH**, till it crosses the Little Bayou to **BOYD**'s corner. Sd right is to be made as soon as rights can be obtained from the U. S. A., and excludes 1 acre at the fish trap. Signed Jeah. **ABLE**, Ezekiel **ABLE**. Test. David **FARRIL**, Js. **BOYD**, Geo. **HENDERSON** (JP). Rec 20 Jul 1810.

462. Page 204. 1 Jan 1810. Same and same to Samuel **RANEY**. For the sum of $500, bond to make a right to 100 acres on or near White Water, joining William **COX**. Sd **RANEY** has his choice on either side or end of sd line, and sd right is to be made as soon as the commissioners decide on land titles. Signed Jah. **ABLE**, Ezekiel **ABLE**, Wit John **SHIELDS**, Js. **BOYD**, Geo. **HENDERSON** (JP). Rec 20 Jul 1810.

463. Page 205. 24 Oct 1808. James **DOWTY** and Jane, his wife, to Martin **RODNEY**. For the sum of $40, 300 arpens, more or less, on the waters of Hubble's Creek, being the same that sd **DOWTY** bought of John **LATHAM** as sd **LATHAM**'s head right, and being known as Latham's Improvement whereon Aaron **DAVIS**

now lives; bounded on the S by John **GOZA**, E by John **BAILEY**(?) and Joshua **GOZA**, N by Elijah **DAUGHERTY**, and W by vacant land. Signed James **DOWTY**, Jane (x) **DOWTY**. Wit Thos. S. **RODNEY**, Jno. **RODNEY**, Jno. **ABERNETHIE** (JP). Rec 24 Aug 1810.

464. Page 207. 24 Oct 1808. James **DOWTY** to Martin **RODNEY**. For the sum of $25; two bay mares, one of them blind of an eye; one young sorrel horse two years old with a white mane and tail, one bay horse colt one year old come spring; one yoke of oxen; five milk cows and calves; two year-old heifers; one two year old steer; a two year old bull; six head of sheep; 30 head of hogs; three feather beds and bedding; and all his household furniture and farming utensils, crops, and rents. Signed James **DOWTY**. Wit Thos. S. **RODNEY**, John **RODNEY**, Jno. **ABERNETHIE** (JP). Rec 25 Aug 1810.

465. Page 208. 21 Mar 1810. Ezekiel **ABLE** and Jeremiah **ABLE** to James **DOWTY**. For the sum of $500, bond to make a deed for 100 acres on the waters of White Water River on the E end of the tract where James **BOYD** and his family now live. The deed to be made within 12 months after the U. S. A. shall make sufficient grants unto the claimants. Signed Ezekiel **ABLE**, Jeremiah **ABLE**. Wit Jno. **ABERNETHIE** (JP). Bond is assigned to Martin **RODNEY** on 15 Apr 1810. Signed James **DOWTY**. Test Jno. **RODNEY**, Michael **RODNEY**, Jno. **ABERNETHIE** (JP), Geo. **HENDERSON** (JP). Rec 5 Sep 1810.

466. Page 209. 26 Jun 1810. James **DOWTY** to William **GARNER**. For the sum of $800, bond to make title to 240 arpens, more or less, bounded on the N by William **WILLIAMS**, S by John **EARTHMAN**, and adjoining John **ABERNETHIE** and vacant lands; which sd **GARNER** has purchased from sd **DOWTY** for $240. Title to be made as soon as a complete title is made by the Board of Commissioners. Signed James **DOWTY**. Wit J. **McFERRON**, John **SCRIPPS**, Geo. **HENDERSON** (JP). Rec 5 Sep 1810.

467. Page 210. 10 Nov 1809. William **LORIMIER** to John **RANDALL**. For the sum of $400, bond to make a deed on 100 acres known as Stricklin's Improvement which was granted to sd **LORIMIER** by the Spanish Government; the deed to be made as soon as the U. S. A. sanctions his claim. Signed Gm. **LORIMIER**. Wit James **EVANS**, Enoch **EVANS** (JP). Rec 21 Sep 1810.

468. Page 211. 3 Feb 1806. Survey of plat for Lavina **MILLS** by B. **COUSIN**, No. 11 for 197 acres, 108 perches. The plat represents 231 arpens, 25 perches, French measure, on the dividing ridge between the waters of Hubble's and Randoll's Creeks about eight miles NW of Cape Girardeau. Signed B. **COUSIN**. Recorded on Page 10, Book B of Survey Book in St. Louis. Signed Antoine **SOULARD**, Surveyor General. Right and claim is assigned to Samuel D. **STROTHER** on 2 Oct 1810. Signed Levina (x) **MILLS**. Wit William **MATTHEWS** (JP). Rec 4 Oct 1810.

469. Page 211. 20 Jul 1810. Medad **RANDOL** by Sheriff John **HAYS** to Christian **GATES**. For the sum of $80, 300 acres, more or less, adjoining James **MORRISON** Senr, and Lewis **LATHAM** where Levina **MILLS** formerly lived. Sold on 17 Jul 1810 on a writ of execution issued 14 Apr 1810 on a judgment by CCP, in which Daniel **BULLINGER** and Peter **GRUNT** recovered $128.24 for debt and $50 damages and costs against sd **RANDOL**. Signed John **HAYS**, Sheriff. Wit Joseph **McFERRON**, Clerk, CCP. Rec 18 Oct 1810.

470. Page 214. 10 Nov 1809. Samuel D. **STROTHER** to William **MATTHEWS**. For the sum of $1000, 240 arpens, more or less, beginning at Ithamore **HUBBELL**'s SW corner, and also adjoining Thomas **RODNEY**. Signed S. D. **STROTHER**. Wit Js. **BOYD**, Henry **HENDRICK**, Geo. **HENDERSON** (JP). Rec 2 Nov 1810.

471. Page 215. 14 Jul 1806. Joseph **WALLER** to Richard **WALLER**, yeoman. For the sum of $400, bond to make a deed for 100 arpens, more or less, French measure, on both sides of Randle's Mill Creek and the left fork of sd creek; adjoining John **ABNATHA** and James **DOWTY**; being the upper end of Joseph **WALLER**'s old survey; beginning at a white walnut. Signed Joseph ( ) **WALLER**. Wit Thos. **NEWBERRY**, Jno. **ABERNETHIE**, Wa. **ABERNETHIE**, Geo. **HENDERSON** (JP). Rec 19 Nov 1810.

472. Page 216. 10 Nov 1810. Jesse **SCRUGGS** to his children. For the love, good will, and affection which he bears toward them; his negros as follows: to Matthew **SCRUGGS**, one negro girl named **Alesey** and one fellow named **Joseph**; to James **SCRUGGS** and his wife, one negro boy named **Peter**; to Sarah **TILMAN** of Edgefield Co., S. Car., one negro boy named **Joshua**; to his son-in-law Charles **WALL**, one negro girl named **Maria**. Signed Jesse (x) **SCRUGGS**. Wit Jacob **WOLF**, Andrew **RAMSEY**, William **JENKINS**, Enoch **EVANS** (JP). Rec 19 Nov 1810.

473. Page 218. 24 Nov 1809. Jeremiah **SIMPSON** by Sheriff John **HAYS** to James **RAVENSCROFT**. For the sum of $33, 300 arpents originally granted to Daniel **SEXTON**. Sold on 21 Nov 1809 on a writ of execution issued 21 Aug 1809 on a judgment by CCP, in which Morgan **BYRNE**, assignee of Luke **BYRNE**, recovered $106.50 for debt and $200 damages and costs against sd **SIMPSON**. Signed John **HAYS**, Sheriff. Wit Joseph **McFERRON**, Clerk, CCP. Rec 20 Nov 1810.

474. Page 220. 19 Sep 1810. John **GUETHING** of Randolph Co., Ill. Terr, to Geo. C. C. **HARBISON**. For the sum of $110, Lot No. 13, Range B in Cape Girardeau; bounded on the N by Independence St, S by Geo. C. C. **HARBISON**, E by Indian St, and W by Lot No. 16. Signed John **GUETHING**. Wit Isaac M. **BLEDSOE**, John **CROSS**, Geo. **HENDERSON** (JP). Rec 20 Nov 1810.

475. Page 221. 11 Nov 1810. Benjamin **HOWARD**, Governor of La. Terr., to David **WADE**, Esq. Appointment as JP for Cape Girardeau Twp. Signed Benja. **HOWARD**. Wit Frederick **BATES**, Secretary. David **WADE** takes the oath of office. Signed David **WADE**. Wit J. **McFERRON**. Rec 21 Nov 1810.

476. Page 222. 3 Apr 1810. Rachel **THOMPSON**, adminr of the estate of Joseph **THOMPSON** Senr, decd; and her sons Joseph **THOMPSON**, Isaac **THOMPSON**, and William **THOMPSON** to Pierre **GODAR**, John C. **HARBISON**, and Andrew **RAMSEY**. For serving as security for her administration of the estate of Joseph **THOMPSON**, decd, mortgage on two tracts; 200 arpens, more or less, being the plantation where she now lives; also 240 arpens, being the plantation where Josiah **HUNTER** now lives. Signed Rachel (R) **THOMPSON**, Joseph **THOMPSON**, Isaac **THOMPSON**, William **THOMPSON**. Wit Ezekiel **ABLE**, John **RAMSEY**, Wm. **SCRIPPS**, Geo. **HENDERSON** (JP). Rec 23 Nov 1810.

477. Page 223. 24 Nov 1810. Jeremiah **ABLE** to John **SCOTT**. For the sum of $500, to be paid as $200 in eight months, $100 every four months thereafter; mortgage on 250 arpens, more or less, adjoining David **GREEN**, Robert **GREEN**, William **DAUGHERTY**, **CROUSE**, and the

Widow **MARTIN**. The tract was deeded on this date to sd **ABLE** by sd **SCOTT** acting as atty of **CHANDLER** & **PRICE**, being the same claimed by Jesse **CAIN** as his head right, and sold by him to White **MATTACK**, and by sd **MATTACK** to **CHANDLER** & **PRICE**. Signed Jeremiah **ABLE**. Test Geo. C. C. **HARBISON**, J. **McFERRON**, Geo. **HENDERSON** (JP). Rec 24 Nov 1810. [Marginal notes: Acknowledge receipt of $300 on 23 Jul 1811. Signed John **SCOTT**. Test G. **HENDERSON**, Recorder. Full satisfaction received on 18 Mar 1812. Signed John **SCOTT**. Test G. **HENDERSON**, Recorder.]

478. Page 224. 24 Nov 1810. John **SCOTT**, atty for **CHANDLER** & **PRICE**, assignees of White **MATTOCK**, to Jeremiah **ABLE**. For the sum of $500, the tract described in the previous deed; bounded on the W by Robert **GREEN**, N by the Widow **MARTIN** and William **DAUGHERTY**, E by **CROUSE**, late Galys ___(?), and S by William **DAUGHERTY** and David **GREEN**. Signed John **SCOTT**, Atty for **CHANDLER** & **PRICE**. Test J. **McFERRON**, Geo. C. C. **HARBISON**, Geo. **HENDERSON** (JP). Rec 24 Nov 1810.

479. Page 225. 24 Nov 1810. Israel **FRIEND** by Sheriff John **HAYS** to John **SCOTT** and Nathaniel **POPE**. For the sum of $20, 480 acres, more or less, on the road to New Madrid, where sd **FRIEND** now lives. Sold on 20 Nov 1810 on a writ of execution issued by CCP on 2 Aug 1810 in favor of Edward **ROBERTSON**, assignee of James **MONTGOMERY**, and against sd **FRIEND**, for $1000 debt and the same $1000 damages and costs. Signed John **HAYS**, Sheriff. Wit Wm. **KELSO**, J. **McFERRON**, Clerk, CCP. Rec 26 Nov 1810.

480. Page 228. 24 Nov 1810. Jaben **SEELYE** by same to George C. C. **HARBISON**. For the sum of $102.75, Lot No. 8, Range F and a house in Cape Girardeau, being where John **LEE** now lives; bounded on the E by Charles G. **ELLIS** representing Garah **DAVIS**, S by Belleview St, N by Lorimier St, and W by a vacant lot. Sold on 20 Nov 1810 on a writ of execution issued by CCP on 27 Aug 1810 in favor of Medad **RANDOL** and John **RANDOL** and against sd **SEELYE**, for $65.51 for costs in a certain action. Signed John **HAYS**, Sheriff. Wit Wm. **KELSO**, J. **McFERRON**, Clerk, CCP. Rec 26 Nov 1810.

481. Page 230. 25 Oct 1809. Jacob **CAMPBELL** to George **HENDERSON**. For the sum of $300, a negro girl named **Darcus** about 12 years old. Signed Jacob **CAMPBELL**. Wit Jno. **EARTHMAN**, Joshua **HAILE**, George **HAYS**, Robt. **GREEN** (JCCP). Rec 4 Dec 1810.

482. Page 231. 5 Dec 1810. Ezekiel **ABLE** and Jeremiah **ABLE** to Chittenden **LYON**. For $340, mortgage on one negro girl named **Rose** about 12 years old. Sd **ABLE**s owe sd **LYON** several notes; one for $175.15 dated 13 Apr 1810 and payable with legal interest; one for $42.06 in a judgment for sd **LYON** against Jeremiah **ABLE** before George **HENDERSON** for debt, interest, and costs, due with interest by 1 Mar next; and $104.48 with interest from 22 Oct last and due by 1 Jul next. Signed Ezekiel **ABLE**, Jeremiah **ABLE**. Wit W. J. **STEPHENSON**, W. **GARNER**, Geo. **HENDERSON** (JP). Chittenden **LYON** binds himself to take a flat boat, completely finished as per verbal contact, 50 feet long, by 20 Feb next at $125, in part payment. Signed Chittn. **LYON**. Wit W. J. **STEPHENSON**, Geo. **HENDERSON** (JP). Rec 8 Dec 1810.

483. Page 233. 5 Sep 1810. Louis **LORIMIER** Senr and Marie, his wife, to John **RISHER**. For the sum of $455, 45 ½ acres, more or less, on the W bank of the Mississippi at the mouth of a spring branch about half a mile below Cape Girardeau, beginning at a stake below the mouth of sd branch. Signed L. **LORIMIER**, Marie (x) **LORIMIER** (RD). Wit B. **COUSIN**, Enoch **EVANS** (JP). Rec 13 Dec 1810.

484. Page 234. 29 Dec 1810. Same and same to William **GARNER**. For the sum of $100, Lot No. 9, Range C in Cape Girardeau; bounded on the N by Themis St, S by a lot belonging to the estate of Robert **BLAIR**, decd, E by Ezekiel **ABLE**, and W by Indian St. Signed L. **LORIMIER**, Marie **LORIMIER** (RD). Wit B. **COUSIN**, John C. **HARBISON**, Geo. **HENDERSON** (JP). Rec 3 Jan 1811.

485. Page 236. 23 May 1810. Fanny **WATERS** to James **BRADY**. For the sum of $1055, mortgage on all the goods and chattel stock she purchased at the sale of Thomas **WATERS**, decd; also all her property which she has bought since the death of Thomas **WATERS**. Fanny **WATERS** owes sd **BRADY** a note with interest, and this secures that debt. Signed Fanny **WATERS** (also promissory note). Test Igns. **WATHEN**, Richd. **MILLS** (JP). Rec 1 Feb 1811.

486. Page 238. 10 Nov 1809. John **DRYBREAD** to Samuel D. **STROTHER**. For the sum of $1000, 240 arpens, more or less, beginning at Ithenmore **HUBELL**'s SW corner and also bounded by Thomas **RODNEY**'s S line. Signed John (x) **DRYBREAD**. Wit Js. **BOYD**, Henry **HENDRICK**, William **MATTHEWS** (JP). Rec 9 Feb 1811.

487. Page 239. 20 Feb 1810. Nathan **McCARTY** to John **HAYS**. For the sum of $600, three tracts on the waters of Byrd's Creek; 285 arpens, more or less, being half of the tract where Sophia **McCARTY**, widow of John **McCARTY**, now lives; 137 ½ arpens, being part of the claim purchased by his father John **McCARTY**, decd, from Jacob **KELLEY**; and 120 arpens, being part of a claim purchased by John **McCARTY** of Samuel **DORSEY**, assignee of John **HAYS**, who was assignee of Joseph **CRUTCHLOW**, decd, adjoining the plantation where Sophia **McCARTY** now lives. Signed Nathan **McCARTY**. Wit Geo. **HENDERSON** (JP). Rec 15 Feb 1811.

488. Page 240. 5 Jan 1810. Alexander **WILLARD** to Chittenden **LYON**. For the sum of $100, an acre lot in Cape Girardeau near Major **LORIMIER**'s spring, including one hewed log house with a lap shingle roof, and the post and pail enclosure of the sd lot. Signed Alexander **WILLARD**. Wit James **DAVIS**, W. J. **STEPHENSON**, Geo. **HENDERSON** (JP). Title is assigned to Ignatius **WATHEN** as soon as $60 in cash is paid. Signed Chittn. **LYON**. Wit James **BRADY**, Richard **MILLS** (JP), Rec 23 Feb 1811.

489. Page 242. 26 Feb 1811. John **STRONG** to John **RODNEY**. For the sum of $19, 8 ½ arpents, more or less, on the waters of Hubble's Creek, beginning at a stake and stone black gum; bounded on the S by Martin **RODNEY**, E and N by John **STRONG**, and W by William **MATHEWS**. Signed John **STRONG**. Wit Thos. S. **RODNEY**, Michl. **RODNEY**, David **WADE** (JP). Rec 15 Mar 1811.

490. Page 244. 16 Mar 1811. James **CURRIN** of Tywappity Twp to John **CONYERS**. For the sum of $1200, 400 arpents in Tywappity Twp, beginning at a conditional line between John **ORDWAY** and sd **CURRIN** on the Mississippi River at three cottonwood trees and a sycamore; including an improvement made by Isaac **DEVORE**. Signed James **CURRIN**. Wit Zenas **PRIEST**, Andrew **STEWART**, Richard **MILLS** (JP). Rec 18 Mar 1811.

491. Page 245. 28 Feb 1811. James **CONYERS**, William **STEPHENSON**, John **LANE**, and John **CONNYERS** to James H. **STEPHENSON**; all of Tywappity Twp. For the sum of $300, 100 arpents in Tywappity Twp, beginning on the bank of the Mississippi River at a conditional line between John **ORDWAY** and James **CURREN** at a sycamore and three cottonwood trees and running down the river bank as to take in part of 400 arpents purchased by John **CONYERS** of James **CURREN** (C:244). Signed James **CONNYERS**, Wm. **STEPHENSON**, John **LANE**, John **CONYERS**. Wit Arthur **OWENS**, Martin **LAWRENCE**, Ilsey **HEW**, Wm. **KELSO** (JP). Rec 19 Mar 1811.

492. Page 246. 13 Apr 1810. William **GRIFFIN** to James **RITCHEY**, both of Livingston Co., Ky. For the sum of $200, 6 acres in Tywappity Bottom, beginning at George **ROBERTSON**'s upper corner on the bank of the Mississippi River. Signed William **GRIFFIN**. Wit Jno. L. **TINDALL**, John **RITCHEY**, Wm. **KELSO** (JP). Rec 20 Mar 1811.

493. Page 248. 7 Apr 1810. John **LOYD** of the New Madrid Dist to James **RICHIE**. For the sum of $400, 150 arpents in Tywappity Twp, being part of 300 arpents surveyed for sd **LOYD**, beginning on the bank of the Mississippi River at the lower corner of 6 acres that William **GRIFFIN** bought of Charles **FENLEY**; bounded on the W by Arthur **PITMAN**. Signed John **LOYD**. Wit Wm. **KELSO** (JP). Rec 20 Mar 1811.

494. Page 249. 16 Jan 1811. Samuel **STROTHER** to Thomas **ENGLISH** Junr. For the sum of $1200, bond to make a deed for 231 arpens, French measure, whereon **DRUMMOND** lived last year and known as the widow **MILLS** old place; adjoining Lewis **LAYTHAM** and **BYRD**'s land where Medad **RANDALL** formerly lived. Sd deed to be made when patent shall be obtained from the Commissioners. Signed S. D. **STROTHER**. Wit Jno. **ABERNETHIE**, Geo. **HENDERSON** (JP). Rec 20 Mar 1811.

495. Page 251. 23 Jan 1811. Thos. S. **RODNEY** and Louise, his wife, to Martin **RODNEY**. For the sum of $1600, 680 arpents, more or less, on the waters of Hubble's Creek, being the same where Martin **RODNEY** now lives, beginning at a sycamore; adjoined on the N by William **MATHEWS**, E by Stephen **BYRD**, S by vacant lands, and W by John **FARRAR**. Signed Thos.

S. **RODNEY**, Louise **RODNEY**. Wit James **DOWTY**, John **STRONG**, David **WADE** (JP). Rec 21 Mar 1811.

496. Page 253. 20 Nov 1810. John C. **HARBISON** to James **SCRUGGS**. Sd **HARBISON** swears that he has never had any past cause except hearsay for asserting or reporting anything which might injure the feelings or lessen the good opinion the neighbors of sd **SCRUGGS** might have of him. Sd **SCRUGGS** has instituted a slander suit against sd **HARBISON** in CCP. Signed John C. **HARBISON**. Test Enoch **EVANS**, Geo. **HENDERSON** (JP). Rec 21 Mar 1811.

497. Page 253. 20 Mar 1811. John **STRONG** to Louis **LORIMIER** Junr. For the sum of $2100, 640 arpens, more or less, on both sides of Hubble's Creek about eight and a half miles W of Cape Girardeau; bounded on the N by the heirs of W. **BURROWS**, decd, E by Matthew **HUBBLE** and public land, S by Abraham **BYRD** and John **RODNEY**, and W by William **MATTHEWS** and others; agreeable to a survey made by James **BOYD** on 26 Feb 1811. Signed John **STRONG**. Wit Thos. S. **RODNEY**, B. **COUSIN**, David **WADE** (JP). Survey is attached, beginning at an ash, and with the chain carried by John & Thos. S. **RODNEY**. Rec 9 Apr 1811.

498. Page 256. 23 Jun 1806. Frederick **GIBLER** to Louis **LORIMIER**. For the sum of $200 in silver dollars, mortgage on two lots in Cape Girardeau. Signed Frederick **GIBLER**. Wit B. **COUSIN**, Jn. **LAVALLEE**. Received $100 in part payment on 19 Feb 1807. Signed L. **LORIMIER**. Wit Geo. **HENDERSON** (JP). Rec 9 Apr 1811.

499. Page 256. 12 Mar 1808. Same to same. For the sum of $50, ½ acre S of and adjoining Lot Nos. 5 & 8, Range B in Cape Girardeau. Signed Frederick **GIBLER**. Test B. **COUSIN**, Geo. **HENDERSON** (JP). Rec 9 Apr 1811.

500. Page 257. 19 Jun 1810. Robert **GREEN** to David **GREEN**. For the sum of $400, 200 acres adjoined on the E by William **DAUGHERTY**, being part of the tract where Robert **GREEN** now lives. Signed Robt. **GREEN**. Wit G. W. **COCHRAN**, Henry **EARTHMAN**, Jane **GREEN**, G. **HENDERSON** (JP). Rec 31 May 1811.

501. Page 258. 3 Jun 1811. Samuel D. **STROTHER** to Alexander **WILSON**, merchant of Cape Girardeau. For the sum of $600, __ acres in Tywappity Twp, being the same that was Edmond **HOGAN**'s head right, and sold by sd **HOGAN** and Patsy, his wife, to sd **STROTHER** on 2 Jun 1811; beginning at a Spanish oak and hickory on the bank of the Mississippi River a short distance below the mouth of a creek at which John **BALDWIN** now lives. Signed S. D. **STROTHER**. Wit James **EVANS**, David **WADE** (JP). Rec 8 Jun 1811.

502. Page 260. 8 Apr 1811. James **CONYERS** and Mary, his wife, of Tywappity Twp to Alexander **WILSON** of Botetourt Co., Vir. For the sum of $500, 100 arpens beginning on the bank of the Mississippi River at the conditional line between John **ORDWAY** and James **CURREN** at a sycamore and three cottonwood trees (C:244). Signed James **CONNYERS**, Polley ( ) **CONYERS** (RD). Wit R. F. **HUGHES**, Jas. H. **STEPHENSON**, Isaac **HILL**, Samuel **WARE**, Wm. (x) **TAYLOR**, Wm. **KELSO** (JP). Rec 16 Jul 1811.

503. Page 262. 8 Jun 1811. Robert **ENGLISH** to Asa B. **LINCECUM** for Hermon **LINSECUM**, a minor under age. For the sum of $400, 640 acres, more or less, on the E side of White Water, being the head right of Jonathan **HUBBLE**, son of Jonathan **HUBBLE**; bounded on the N by Jonathan **HUBBLE** Senr and on the W by the main branch of White Water; beginning where a branch enters White Water and running up the branch (formerly the boundary between Jonathan **HUBBLE** Junr and his father Jonathan **HUBBLE** Senr. If no title can be obtained from the U. S. A., then sd **ENGLISH** binds himself to repay the money. Signed Robert **ENGLISH**. Wit John **DAVIS** (JP). Rec 8 Jun 1811.

504. Page 263. 27 Feb 1810. Louis **LORIMIER** Senr to George **HENDERSON**. For the sum of $100, Lot No. 13, Range C in Cape Girardeau; bounded on the E by a lot where Alex. **SCOTT** resides, W by Back St, the present W boundary of the town, N by Themis St, and S by an unsold lot. Signed L. **LORIMIER**. Test B. **COUSIN**. Received $104 in full payment with principal and interest from George **HENDERSON** on 27 Jul 1811. Signed L. **LORIMIER** Senr. Test B. **COUSIN**, David **WADE** (JP). Rec 27 Jul 1811.

505. Page 265. 24 Jun 1811. William **DAUGHERTY** and Elizabeth, his wife, to William **NEELY**. For the sum of $700, 240 arpens on the waters of Hubble's Creek; bounded on the E by Henry **SHERIDAN**'s concession, now Mr. **ASHLEY**'s, W by Jonathan

FORMAN's concession, now owned by the heirs of John **MARTIN**, S by William **CROWTZ** and Jeremiah **ABEL**, and N by James **ARRELL**'s concession, now claimed by Joseph **SEAWELL**, and by sd **FORMAN**'s concession. Signed Wm. **DAUGHERTY**, Elizabeth (o) **DAUGHERTY**. Wit John **HAYS**, Job **THROCKMORTON**, John **DAVIS** (JP). Rec 12 Aug 1811.

506. Page 266. 12 Aug 1811. John **HAYS** and Cynthia, his wife, to Joseph **SEAWELL**. For the sum of $1000, 240 arpens where sd **SEAWELL** now lives, being the same purchased by sd **HAYS** of James **ARREL** on 1 Jan 1810 and being the same granted by the Spanish government to Jonathan **FORMAN**, Henry **SHERIDAN**, Charles **FALINGASH**, and others. Signed John **HAYS**, Cynthia (x) **HAYS**. Wit G. **HENDERSON** (JP). Rec 12 Aug 1811.

507. Page 268. 17 Aug 1810. James **BOYD** and Sally, his wife, to Jonathan **STOUT**. For the sum of $1200, 370 acres beginning at a stake and stone on Isaac **SHEPPARD**'s W line, and bounded by Edward F. **BOND** and B. **COUSIN**. Signed Js. **BOYD**, Saly **BOYD**. Wit Bazel **BORAN**, Isaac **SHEPPARD**, G. **HENDERSON** (JP). Rec 16 Aug 1811.

508. Page 269. 23 Jul 1811. James **WILSON** to Matthew **SCRUGGS**. For the sum of $44.36, mortgage on one mare and colt, two cows and calves, two two-year-old heiffers, one yearlin heiffer, one yearlin steer, 36 hogs, two beds and furniture, and a parcel of dresser furniture. Sd **WILSON** owes sd **SCRUGGS** a debt by 23 Jul next. Signed James **WILSON**. Wit William **ALLEN**, Enoch **EVANS** (JP). Rec 24 Aug 1811.

509. Page 270. 16 Jul 1811. John C. **HARBISON** to Morgan **BYRNE**. For the sum of $125, 250 arpens on the E side of the Big Swamp; joining Louis **LORIMIER**, Andrew **RAMSEY**, and others. Signed John C. **HARBISON**. Test Geo. C. C. **HARBISON**, John **HAYS**, Robert **GREEN** (JCCP). Rec 28 Aug 1811.

510. Page 271. 18 Jul 1811. Danial **HARKLEROAD** to **REINECKE** & **STEINBECK**. For securing a debt of $150.25, mortgage on the lot and buildings where he now lives. Signed Danial **HARKELROAD**. Test Henry **ECKHART**, Allin **ELLIS**, G. **HENDERSON** (JP). Rec 4 Sep 1811.

511. Page 271. 9 Sep 1811. Louis **LORIMIER** senior and Mary, his wife, to Thomas S. **RODNEY** as trustee for Lewis (nearly four years old), Thomas Jefferson (about two years old), and Polly (12 months old) **RODNEY**, children of Louis **LORIMIER**'s daughter Louisa **RODNEY** and her husband Thomas S. **RODNEY**. For good reasons, and for the love they bear unto the grandchildren of sd Louis **LORIMIER**, 400 arpens, French measure, on the W bank of Cape La Cruche Creek about two miles W of Cape Girardeau, beginning at a hickory sapling on the W bank of the creek. Sd **LORIMIER** is to have the right to cut timber on the tract, and no mill is to be erected on the creek. Thomas S. **RODNEY** is not to sell or alien or dispose of the property, but is to hold it in trust until the children reach the years of majority. Signed L. **LORIMIER** sen, Marie **LORIMIER**. Wit B. **COUSIN**, David **WADE** (JP). Rec 9 Sep 1811.

512. Page 273. 8 & 9 Mar 1811. Survey for the children of Thomas S. **RODNEY** and Louisa, his wife, at the request of Louis **LORIMIER** senior (C:271). Signed B. **COUSIN**. Chain Carriers Thomas S. **RODNEY**, John **RODNEY**, Victor **LORIMIER**. Rec 9 Sep 1811. [see Figure 2]

513. Page 274. 13 Sep 1811. Louis **LORIMIER** and Marie, his wife, to Chittendan **LYON**. For the sum of $108.60, Lot No. 13, Range A in Cape Girardeau; bounded on the E by Indian St, N by Merywether St, and S & W by Lot Nos. 14 & 16. Signed L. **LORIMIER** senr, Marie **LORIMIER** (RD). Wit B. **COUSIN**, Enoch **EVANS** (JP). Rec 23 Sep 1811.

514. Page 276. 19 Sep 1811. Jeremiah **CONAWAY**, adminr of the estate of James **CAROTHERS**, decd, to Rachel **WORTH**. For the sum of $158, 580 arpents, 62 perches (496 acres, 96 poles) on Hubble's Creek, beginning at Abraham **BYRD**'s SW corner; bounded by James **HANNAH**, John **GUETHING**, and sd **BYRD**. Sold on 16 Jul 1811 on an order of General Court held at Ste. Genevieve in May 1811, to sell sd land. Signed Jeremiah **CONAWAY**, adminr of the estate of James **CAROTHERS**, decd. Wit James **EVANS**, David **WADE** (JP). Rec 25 Sep 1811.

515. Page 278. 20 Sep 1811. Rachel **WORTH** and John **BAKER** to Thomas S. **RODNEY**. For the sum of $600, 496 acres, 96 poles on Hubble's and Randol's Creeks, as described in the preceding deed (C:276). Signed Rachell (x)

WORTH, John **BAKER**. Wit Jno. **RODNEY**, Mich. **RODNEY**, Jno. **ABERNETHIE** (JP). Rec 25 Sep 1811.

516. Page 279. 30 Aug 1811. William **HILL** Senr and Mary, his wife, to Elisha **WHITE**. For the sum of $800, 300 arpens, more or less, on the Cow Creek where sd **WHITE** now lives, bounded on the N by John **BYRD**'s land, now occupied by Zedekiah **HOWARD**, S by John **MARTIN** decd, E by Stephen **BYRD**'s land, now occupied by Fielding **STUBBLEFIELD**, and W by Isaac **SHEPPARD**. Signed William ( ) **HILL**, Mary (x) **HILL**. Wit John **DAVIS** (JP). Rec 1 Oct 1811.

517. Page 280. 27 Feb 1809. John **BOYD** to Isaac **SHEPPARD**. For the sum of $800, 250 arpens, more or less, where sd **SHEPPARD** now lives, beginning at a hickory and a stone at the SW corner; bounded by Stephen **BYRD**, James **BOYD**, and B. **COUSIN**. Signed John ( ) **BOYD**. Wit John **SHEPPARD**, Elish. (x) **WHITE**, John **DAVIS** (JP). Elizabeth **BOYD** RD. Signed Elizabeth ( ) **BOYD**. Rec 1 Oct 1811.

518. Page 282. 7 Aug 1810. James **BOYD** and Sarah, his wife, to same. For the sum of $90, 30 acres, bounded on the E by the survey where sd **SHEPPARD** now lives, N by Stephen **BYRD**, W by Jonathan **STOUT**, and S by B. **COUSINS**. Signed Js. **BOYD**. Wit Bazil **BORAN**, Jonathan **STOUT**, John **DAVIS** (JP). Rec 1 Oct 1811.

519. Page 283. 9 Sep 1811. Jesse **SCRUGGS** to Charles **WALL**. For the love and affection sd **SCRUGGS** has for sd **WALLS**, one negro girl named **Silva** and her increase, and the land where sd **WALLS** now lives, being the same sd **SCRUGGS** purchased of Terrence **DOYLE**; bounded on the E by the heirs of Alexander **GIBONEY**, S by John **RAMSEY**, W by Matthew **SCRUGGS**, and N by John **SIMPSON**. Signed Jesse (x) **SCRUGGS**. Wit Enoch **EVANS** (JP), Jas. **RAVENSCROFT**. Rec 7 Oct 1811.

520. Page 284. 9 Sep 1811. Same to Matthew **SCRUGGS**, James **SCRUGGS**, and Charles **WALLS**, and Daniel **TILLMAN** of Edgefield Co., S. Car. For the love and affection he feels toward the grantees; negro slaves **James**, **Edward**, **John**, **Mary** and her increase, and **Ame**. The negroes to be equally divided between them after the decease of Jesse **SCRUGGS**, except **Ame** is to be the property of Daniel **TILLMAN** from this day. Signed Jesse (x)

SCRUGGS. Wit Enoch **EVANS** (JP), Jas. **RAVENSCROFT**. Rec 7 Oct 1811.

521. Page 285. 30 Sep 1811. Caty **BLEDSOE** to William Lytle **BLEDSOE**, both of Sumner Co., Tenn. Power of attorney to recover a negro girl named **Nice**, now in the possession of the heirs, executors, and adminrs of Isaac M. **BLEDSOE**, decd, of the Cape Girardeau Dist. Signed Caty **BLEDSOE**. Wit J[ames] **WINCHESTER**, M[athew] **ALEXANDER** (both JP in Sumner Co., Tenn.), David **SHELBY**, Clerk of Sumner Co., Tenn. Court of Pleas and Quarter Sessions, Edw. **DOUGLAS**, Presiding Justice, Sumner Co, Tenn. Rec 14 Oct 1811.

522. Page 286. 21 May 1811. Elijah **WHITEAKER** of West Floredy to William **NEELY** and Joseph **SEAWELL**. For the sum of $250, 370 arpens, more or less, on the waters of Randall's Creek, beginning at James **DOTY**'s NE corner, a rock and white oak on William **WILLIAMS'** W boundary. Signed Elijah (x) **WHITACRE**. Wit Jesse **HAM**(?), Samuel **BARKER**, John **WILSON**, G. **HENDERSON** (JP). Rec 15 Oct 1811.

523. Page 288. 9 Sep 1811. Jesse **SCRUGGS** to James **SCRUGGS**. For the love and affection that he bears toward James **SCRUGGS**, one negro man named **Edmund** and the land where James **SCRUGGS** now lives, that Jesse **SCRUGGS** purchased of Andrew **RAMSEY** senr; bounded on the E by the heirs of Samuel **TIPTON**, S by Enoch **EVANS**, W by Robert **GIBONEY**, and N by vacant lands or John C. **HARBISON**. Signed Jesse (x) **SCRUGGS**. Wit Enoch **EVANS** (JP), Jas. **RAVENSCROFT**. Rec 18 Oct 1811.

524. Page 288. 28 Sep 1811 (at Ste. Genevieve, Mo.). Chittenden **LYON** of Eddyville, Ken. to Ignatius **WATHEN**. For the sum of $200, Lot No. 13, Range A in Cape Girardeau; bounded on the E by Indian St, N by Meriwether St, S & W by Lot Nos. 14 & 16; being the same he purchased of Alexr. **WILLARD**, and which was conveyed to him by Louis **LORIMIER** and Marie, his wife, on 13 Sep 1811. Signed Chittn. **LYON**. Wit Jno. **WATERS**, G. **HENDERSON** (JP). Rec 18 Oct 1811.

525. Page 289. 1 Nov 1809. Nathan **McCARTY** and William **McCARTY** to Sophia **McCARTY**. For the sum of $3000, bond to make title for a tract of land and personal property. John **McCARTY**, decd, gave Nathan and William **McCARTY** all his real and personal property by deed of gift on 1 Jan 1807; including four tracts, one of 570 arpens, one of 550 arpens, one of 240 arpens, and one of 200 arpens; one negro girl named **Violet**; one yoke of oxen; 14 head of cattle; one mare and gelding; one crib of corn; 64 head of hogs; three feather beds and furniture; and all his household furniture. Sophia **McCARTY** is to have the plantation where she now lives and the personal property, and shall dispose of the same as she thinks for the benefit of the family. At her marriage or death, the personal property is to be divided equally between Nathan **McCARTY**, William **McCARTY**, John **HAYS**, John **THOMSON**, Eliza **McCARTY**, Lucy **McCARTY**, and Matilda **McCARTY**. Signed Nathan **McCARTY**, William **McCARTY**. Wit G. **HENDERSON** (JP). Rec 22 Oct 1811.

526. Page 291. 18 Oct 1811. Joshua **GOZA** to Belemus **HAYDEN**. For the sum of $600, 246 arpens on Hubble's Creek where sd **GOZA** now lives, beginning at the NW corner of Belemus **HAYDEN**'s land known as **LUSLEY**'s claim; bounded by Alexander **SUMMERS**, _____ **BOUNES**, and James **DOTY**. Signed Joshua **GOZA**. Test John R. **HAYDEN**, Wm. W. **COX**, Joh. **BOYD**, G. **HENDERSON** (JP). Rec 12 Nov 1811.

527. Page 292. 9 Feb 1811. Semmen **KENON** and James **COX** Jr. For the sum of $62, 36 acres and 4 poles, more or less, beginning at a gum on sd **COX**'s N corner. Signed Simmen (R) **KENON**. Wit Benjamin **HITT**, Js. **BOYD**, G. **HENDERSON** (JP). Rec 18 Nov 1811.

528. Page 293. 14 Nov 1811. John **CONYERS** to William **STEPHENSON**, both of Tywappity Twp. For the sum of $300, 100 arpens beginning on the bank of the Mississippi River on the lower side of a 400-arpen tract sd **CONYERS** bought of James **CURRIN**, so as to take in a fourth of the tract. Signed John **CONYERS**. Test Thos. **FLETCHER**, Laban (x) **TAYLOR**, R. F. **HUGHES**, G. **HENDERSON** (JP). Rec 18 Nov 1811.

529. Page 294. 3 Jul 1811. Louis **LORIMIER** Senr and Marie, his wife, to Joseph **ANDREWS**. For the sum of $50, the W moiety of Lot No. 14, Range E in Cape Girardeau; bounded on the S by Harmony St and W by Indian St. Signed L. **LORIMIER** Senr, Marie **LORIMIER**. Wit B. **COUSIN**, David **WADE** (JP). Rec 21 Nov 1811.

530. Page 295. 20 Mar 1811. John **STRONG** to Martin **RODNEY**. For the sum of $300, a negro man named **Isaac** about 21 years old, with a scar just above his right eye; a negro woman named **Rachel** about 17 years old, with her first child; a man child named **Jefferson** about 6 months old. The woman is of a very heavy countenance and the man stutters when he talks fast. Signed John **STRONG**. Test Thos. S. **RODNEY**. Bill of sale is assigned to Samuel D. **STROTHER** and Mary, his wife, on 22 Nov 1811 for the amount or for the recovery of the whole or any part of the same property. Signed Martin **RODNEY**, S. D. **STROTHER**, Mary (x) **STROTHER**. Test Thos. S. **RODNEY**, Jno. **RODNEY**, David **WADE** (JP). Rec 13 Dec 1811.

531. Page 296. 3 Jan 1811. William **HILL** senior to John **HITT**. For the sum of $100, a negro girl named **Vicy**, 2 years old. Signed William (x) **HILL**. Wit Wm. **McCLESKEY**, Ezekiel **SEELY**, Jno. **ABERNETHIE** (JP). Rec 13 Dec 1811.

532. Page 297. 12 Dec 1811. Thos. S. **RODNEY** to Saml. D. **STROTHER**. For the sum of $250, a lot in Cape Girardeau, adjoined by sd **RODNEY** on the N, and being the same he purchased of the estate of William **LOWREY**, decd. Signed Thos. S. **RODNEY**. Wit Mich. **RODNEY**, Jno. **RODNEY**, G. **HENDERSON** (JP). Rec 13 Dec 1811.

533. Page 298. 21 Nov 1811. Martin **RODNEY** to Michael **RODNEY**. For the love and affection he bears unto his beloved son, a negro boy named **Jerry**, about 4 years old. Signed Martin **RODNEY**. Wit Robert **BRADLEY**, Jno. **RODNEY**, Charlotte **RODNEY**, Jno. **ABERNETHIE** (JP). Rec 14 Dec 1811.

534. Page 299. 21 Nov 1811. Same to John **RODNEY**. For the love and affection he bears unto his beloved son, a negro boy named **Isaac**, about 8 years old. Signed Martin **RODNEY**. Wit Robert **BRADLEY**, Mich. **RODNEY**, Charlotte **RODNEY**, Jno. **ABERNETHIE** (JP). Rec 14 Dec 1811.

535. Page 299. 22 Nov 1811. Same and Hannah, his wife, to same. For the love and affection they bear unto their son, 358 acres and 149 poles, more or less, on Hubble's Creek, being part of Martin **RODNEY**'s head right, beginning at a sycamore on the creek; bounded on the N by sd John **RODNEY** and William **MATHEWS**, W by Michael **RODNEY**, S by vacant land, and E by Abraham **BYRD** and Thos. S. **RODNEY**.

The grantors delivered a handful of soil of the land in the name of the whole. Signed Martin **RODNEY**, Hannah (x) **RODNEY**. Wit Thos. S. **RODNEY**, Robert **BRADLEY**, Mich. **RODNEY**, Jno. **ABERNETHIE** (JP), G. **HENDERSON** (JP). Rec 21 Dec 1811.

536. Page 301. 22 Nov 1811. Same and same to Michael **RODNEY**. For the love and affection they bear unto their son, 266 acres, 71 poles, more or less, on Foster's Creek, being part of Martin **RODNEY**'s head right, beginning at an oak on the NW corner of the head right; bounded on the N by William **MATHEWS**, W by Robert **BRADLEY**, S by vacant lands, and E by John **RODNEY**. Should the entire tract not be confirmed to Martin **RODNEY**, then so much of the same as may ultimately be confirmed is to be conveyed. Signed Martin **RODNEY**, Hannah (x) **RODNEY**. The grantors delivered a handful of soil of the land in the name of the whole. Wit Robert **BRADLEY**, Thos. S. **RODNEY**, Jno. **RODNEY**, Jno. **ABERNETHIE** (JP), G. **HENDERSON** (JP). Rec 24 Dec 1811.

537. Page 304. 31 Dec 1811. Thomas **ENGLISH** senior and Jane, his wife, to Robert **CRAWFORD**. For the sum of $1600, 580 arpens, French measure, being the entire plantation where sd **ENGLISH** and his family now live, and the same granted to Jeremiah **THOMSON** in Apr 1798 and confirmed by the U. S. A., then conveyed by him to sd **ENGLISH** on 6 May 1806; adjoining John **SHEPPARD**, William **VIRGIN**, and Semon **KENON**. Signed Thomas (T) **ENGLISH**, Jane (x) **ENGLISH**. Wit Robert **ENGLISH**, Jno. **ABERNETHIE** (JP). Rec 7 Jan 1812.

538. Page 305. 31 Dec 1811. Lewis **LAYTHAM** and Lavina, his wife, to same. For the sum of $900, 300 arpens, French measure, where they formerly lived; adjoining John **SUMMERS** senr, Thos. **ENGLISH** Junr (formerly Lavina **MILLS**), Abram **DAUGHERTY** (formerly James **RANDOLL**), and Andrew **SUMMERS**. Signed Lewis **LATHAM**, Lavina (x) **LAYTHAM**. Wit Giles **THOMAS**, Jno. **ABERNETHIE** (JP). Rec 7 Jan 1812.

539. Page 307. 29 Jan 1812. Benjamin **HOWARD**, Esq, Governor of La., to George **HENDERSON**. Appointment as JP for Cape Girardeau Twp. Signed Benja. **HOWARD**. Wit Frederick **BATES**, Sec. of La. George **HENDERSON** takes the oath of office. Signed G. **HENDERSON**. Wit J. **McFERRON**. Rec 12 Feb 1812.

540. Page 308. 27 Jan 1812. John **SIMPSON** to William **CRACRAFT**. For the sum of $150, 150 acres adjoining Jacob **JACOBS** and Matthew **SCRUGGS**, being part of sd **SIMPSON**'s head right. Signed John **SIMPSON**. Wit G. **HENDERSON** (JP). Rec 21 Feb 1812.

541. Page 309. 17 Feb 1812. Martin **RODNEY** to John **RODNEY**. For the sum of $121, one negro man named **Dan**, 40 years of age, with a crooked left thigh which proceeded from its being broke. Signed Martin **RODNEY**. Wit Robt. **BRADLEY**, Mich. **RODNEY**, G. **HENDERSON** (JP). Rec 24 Feb 1812.

542. Page 310. 15 Sep 1808. Joseph **WORTHINGTON** of Randolph Co., Ind. [now Ill.] to John **SIMPSON**. For the sum of $200, 200 acres, more or less, adjoining **MORRISON** and others, known as Shield's Improvement. Signed Jos. **WORTHINGTON**. Wit James **EVANS**, Jas. **BOYD**, Stephen **BYRD** (JCCP). Rec 16 Sep 1808 [see C:22].

543. Page 311. 25 Feb 1811. John **SIMPSON** to James **RAVENSCROFT**. For the sum of $200, 200 acres as described in the preceding deed (C:310). Should the land not be confirmed to Joseph **WORTHINGTON**, the original grantor, then sd **RAVENSCROFT** has no recourse against sd **SIMPSON**. Signed John **SIMPSON**, James **RAVENSCROFT**. Wit James **EVANS**, G. **HENDERSON** (JP). Rec 24 Feb 1812.

544. Page 312. 16 Mar 1812. Jonathan **STOUT** and Agga, his wife, to Leonard **WILSON**. For the sum of $1000, 370 arpens that sd **STOUT** purchased of James **BOYD** and Sallay, his wife, on 17 Aug 1810, beginning at a stake and stone on Isaac **SHEPPARD**'s W line; also adjoining Edward F. **BOND**, James **BOYD**, and B. **COUSIN**. Signed Jonathan **STOUT**, Agga (x) **STOUT**. Wit G. **HENDERSON** (JP). Rec 16 Mar 1812.

545. Page 314. 6 Mar 1812. Benjamin **HOWARD**, Esq, Governor of La., to Robert **GREEN**. Appointment as Justice of the CCP and Quarter Sessions for four years. Signed Benja. **HOWARD**. Wit Frederick **BATES**, Sec. of La. Robert **GREEN** takes the oath of office. Signed Rob. **GREEN**. Wit J. **McFERRON**. Rec 16 Mar 1812.

546. Page 315. 17 Feb 1807. Edmond **HOGAN** to John **BALDWIN**. For the sum of $300, 200 arpens, more or less, bounded on the N by William **ROSS**, E by the Mississippi River, and S by Alex. Andrew **MILLIKIN**'s old line. Should title not be confirmed to sd **HOGAN**, then he is to pay sd **BALDWIN** for any improvements made to the land. Signed Edmond **HOGAN**. Test James **CURRIN**, G. **HENDERSON** (JP). Rec 17 Mar 1812.

547. Page 316. 19 Nov 1811. Benajah **LAUGHERTY** and Rachell, his wife, to William **WILLIAMS**. For the sum of $400, 200 acres on the waters of Randoll's Mill Creek, adjoining Allen **McKENZIE**, being the same sd **LAUGHERTY** purchased from Edward F. **BOND** on 26 Dec 1806, and by sd **BOND** from Enos **RANDALL** Junr on 22 Nov 1805. Signed Benijah **LAUGHERTY**. Wit John **RANDOL**, Jno. **ABERNETHIE** (JP). Rec 17 Mar 1812.

548. Page 317. 19 Aug 1811. Joseph **WALLER** senr and Susanah, his wife, of Randolph Co., Ill. to same. For the sum of $400, 100 arpens, French measure, on Randoll's Mill Creek and on both sides of the left fork of sd creek; adjoining Henry & John **EARTHMAN**, formerly sd **WALLER**'s land, Wm. **GARNER**, formerly James **DOWTY** and John **ABERNETHIE**, **EVANS**, and sd **WILLIAMS**; being the upper part of sd **WALLER**'s old survey where Richard **WALLER** formerly lived; beginning at a white walnut on the bank of the Pole Branch and including the field Adam **BINKLEY** now cultivates. Signed Joseph ( ) **WALLER**, Susannah ( ) **WALLER**. Wit Jno. **LANDERS**, Isaac (x) **WILLIAMS**, G. **HENDERSON** (JP). Rec 17 Mar 1812.

549. Page 320. 22 Mar 1811. Jeremiah **ABLE** to John **SCOTT** and Nathaniel **POPE**, attys at law. For the sum of $500, a lot in Cape Girardeau, being the same house and lot where Ezekiel **ABLE** now resides; bounded on the E by Daniel **HARKLEROAD**, S by Joseph **McFERRON**, N by the main street, and W by William **GARNER**. Signed Jeremiah **ABLE**. Wit Ezekiel **ABLE**, Geo. C. C. **HARBISON**, G. **HENDERSON** (JP). Rec 18 Mar 1812.

550. Page 321. 23 Apr 1812. William **CARR**, atty in fact for Chandler **PRICE** and Isaac **SMITH**, assignees of White **MATLOCK** and John **CAMPBELL** by his atty White **MATLOCK**, to John **SCOTT** of the Ste. Genevieve Dist. Power of attorney to dispose of property. Signed Will. C. **CARR**, atty in fact for Chandler **PRICE** and Isaac **SMITH**. Wit Nathaniel **POPE**, G. **HENDERSON** (JP). Rec 18 Mar 1812.

551. Page 322. 18 Mar 1812. John **SCOTT**, atty in fact for Chandler **PRICE** and Isaac **SMITH**, assignees of John **CAMPBELL** and White **MATTACK**, to Jeremiah **ABLE**. For the sum of $500, 250 arpents, more or less, being the head right of Jesse **CAIN** and transferred by him to sd **MATTACK** and sd **CAMPBELL**, and by them to sd **PRICE** and sd **SMITH**; adjoined on the W by Robert **GREEN**, N by widow **MARTIN** and William **DAUGHERTY**, E by **CROUSE** and sd **DAUGHERTY**, and S by David **GREEN**. Signed John **SCOTT**, atty in fact for Chandler **PRICE** and Isaac **SMITH**. Wit G. **HENDERSON** (JP). Rec 18 Mar 1812.

552. Page 323. 6 Mar 1812. Benjamin **HOWARD**, Esq, Governor of La., to George **HENDERSON**. Appointment as Notary Public for Cape Girardeau Dist. Signed Benja. **HOWARD**. Wit Frederick **BATES**, Sec. of La. George **HENDERSON** takes the oath of office. Signed G. **HENDERSON**. Wit J. **McFERRON**. Rec 25 Mar 1812.

553. Page 324. 25 Mar 1812. George **HENDERSON**, Morgan **BYRNE**, and William **KELSO** to Benjamin **HOWARD**, Governor of La. For the sum of $500 (**HENDERSON**) and $250 each (**BYRNE** and **KELSO**), bond for sd **HENDERSON** to perform the duties of Notary Public of the Cape Girardeau Dist. Signed G. **HENDERSON**, Morgan **BYRNE**, William **KELSO**. Wit Joseph **McFERRON**. Rec 25 Mar 1812.

554. Page 325. 27 Mar 1806. Louis **LORIMIER** to Henry **HAND**. For the sum of $100 received in a note with mortgage of this date, a lot in Cape Girardeau fronting on the Mississippi, being the SE corner of a 4 acre square where boats have been formerly built and launched. Signed L. **LORIMIER**. Wit B. **COUSIN**. Title is assigned to Daniel **HARKELRODE** on 12 Dec 1809. Signed Henry **HAND**. Test Bazel **BORAN**, John **RANDOL**. Sarah **HAND**, wife of Henry **HAND**, RD. Signed Sarah (   ) **HAND**. Test. G. **HENDERSON** (JP). Rec 31 Mar 1812.

555. Page 327. 26 Mar 1812. Samuel D. **STROTHER** and Mary, his wife, to George **HENDERSON**. For the sum of $200, lot in Cape Girardeau, adjoining Thomas S. **RODNEY** on the N, and being the same sd **STROTHER** purchased from sd **RODNEY** on 12 Dec 1811. Signed S. D. **STROTHER**, Mary (x) **STROTHER**. Wit William J. **STEPHENSON**, Wm. **KELSO** (JP). Rec 31 Mar 1812.

556. Page 329. 25 May 1811. James **CURRIN** and Essa, his wife, to Timothy **HARRIS**, all of Tywappity Twp. For the sum of $1750, 350 arpents in Tywappity Twp, beginning on the bank of the Mississippi River at a hackberry tree and bounded on the N by Barthomew **COUSINS**; being the same granted by the Spanish Government to Jacob **MYERS** and granted by sd **MYERS** to sd **CURRIN**. Signed James **CURRIN**, Essa (x) **CURRIN** (RD). Wit Wm. **KELSO** (JP). Rec 17 Apr 1812.

557. Page 331. 7 Jun 1811. Jeremiah **CONAWAY** to Samuel G. **DUNN**. For the sum of $700, 150 arpents on the waters of Welches Creek where sd **CONAWAY** now lives, beginning on the NE side of the farm on a white oak in **WELCH**es line marked SGD. Signed Jeremiah **CONAWAY**. Test John **DUNN**, John **GRAVES**, G. **HENDERSON** (JP). Rec 30 Apr 1812.

558. Page 332. 12 May 1812. Joseph **ANDREWS** of the Ste. Genevieve Dist to David **BRYANT**. For the sum of $350, lot in Cape Girardeau; bounded on the S by Harmony St, W by Indian St, N by Charles G. **ELLIS**, and E by sd **BRYANT**; being the W moiety of Lot No. 14, Range E, sold by Louis **LORIMIER** senr. and Marie, his wife, to sd **ANDREWS** on 3 Jul 1811 (C:294). The same is mortgaged to secure payment. Signed Joseph **ANDREWS**. Wit G. **HENDERSON** (JP). Rec 12 May 1812.

559. Page 334. 25 Apr 1812. John **RODNEY** to Samuel D. **STROTHER**. For the sum of $1200, 320 arpents on Hubble's Creek, beginning at an elm on Abraham **BYRD**'s W line; also bounded by Michael **RODNEY** and Thomas S. **RODNEY**. Signed Jno. **RODNEY**. Wit Robert **BRADLEY**, Thos. S. **RODNEY**, Mich. **RODNEY**, G. **HENDERSON** (JP). Rec 13 May 1812.

560. Page 336. 27 Apr 1812. James **CURRIN** to James **WELLBORN**. For the sum of $250, bond to make a deed by 1 May next to 25 arpents in Tywappity Twp, adjoining the Mississippi River and adjoined below by a tract purchased by sd **WELLBORN** from sd **CURRIN**. Signed James **CURRIN**. Wit Jesse **JEFFERY**, R. F. **HUGHES**, G. **HENDERSON** (JP). Rec 19 May 1812.

561. Page 337. 20 May 1812. Amos **BYRD** senr to Moses **BYRD**. For natural love and affection and for consideration that Moses **BYRD** shall maintain Amos **BYRD** during his natural life in conformity to a bond issued by Moses to Amos **BYRD**, and for the sum of $1, 650 arpents on Byrd's Creek, a fork of White Water, where Amos **BYRD** now resides; bounded on the S by Abraham **BYRD**, W by James **WILKERSON**, N by Austin **YOUNG** and Moses **BYRD**, and E by vacant land. Signed Amos **BYRD**. Wit Jacob **CAMPBELL**, John **DAVIS** (JP). Rec 21 May 1812.

562. Page 339. 9 May 1812. Benjamin **HOWARD**, Governor of La., to William **KELSO**. Appointment as JCCP for Cape Girardeau Dist for four years. Signed Benja. **HOWARD**. Wit Frederick **BATES**, Sec. of La. William **KELSO** takes the oath of office. Signed Wm. **KELSO**. Wit J. **McFERRON**. Rec 27 May 1812.

563. Page 340. 1 Jun 1811. Jeremiah **CONAWAY** and George **MORGAN** to John **GIBONEY**. For the sum of $400, 100 arpens on the waters of Welches Creek whereon sd **MORGAN** now lives; beginning at a white oak [at] **DUNN**'s beginning corner in **WELCH**es line. Signed George (x) **MORGAN**, Jeremiah **CONAWAY**. Test Samuel G. **DUNN**, Nancy (x) **CUMMINS**, G. **HENDERSON** (JP). Rec 30 May 1812.

564. Page 341. 18 May 1811. Elijah **WELCH** and Levinah **MILLS** to John **BOYD**. For the sum of $600, bond to make a deed to 100 acres on the waters of White Water where sd **MILLS** now lives; beginning on Ezekiel **ABLE**'s W line. Signed Elijah (x) **WELCH**, Levinah (x) **MILLS**. Wit Js. **BOYD**, William **JOHNSON**, G. **HENDERSON** (JP). Rec 30 May 1812.

565. Page 342. 30 Jan 1812. John **FARRAR** and Rebekah **FARRAR** to Thos. S. **RODNEY**. For the sum of $500, a negro boy named **Jim**, about 13 years of age. Signed Jno. **FARRAR**, Rebecah **FARRAR**. Wit John **MATHEWS**, Patsey **SMITH**, G. **HENDERSON** (JP). Rec 9 Jun 1812.

566. Page 344. 19 May 1812. John **LOYD** to Arthur **PITMAN**, both of Tywappity Twp. For the sum of $125, 50 arpens; bounded on the B by the heirs of Charles **FENLEY**, E by land conveyed by sd **LOYD** to James **RITCHEY**, S by sd **PITMAN**, and W by vacant land. Signed John **LOYD**. Wit James **RITCHEY**, Arthur (x) **PITMAN** Jr, G. **HENDERSON** (JP). Rec 9 Jun 1812.

567. Page 345. 2 Jun 1812. Benjamin **HOWARD**, Governor of La., to Thomas **BYRNE**. Appointment as JCCP for Cape Girardeau Dist for four years. Signed Benja. **HOWARD**. Wit Frederick **BATES**, Sec. of La. Thomas **BYRNE** takes the oath of office. Signed Thomas **BYRNE**. Wit J. **McFERRON**. Rec 15 Jun 1812.

568. Page 346. 3 Jul 1811. Louis **LORIMIER** Senr and Marie, his wife, to David **BRYANT**. For the sum of $50, the E moiety of Lot No. 14, Range E in Cape Girardeau; bounded on the E by Charles G. **ELLIS**, W by the other moiety, and S by Harmony St. Signed L. **LORIMIER**, Marie **LORIMIER**. Wit B. **COUSIN**, David **WADE** (JP). Rec 19 Jun 1812.

568A. Page 347. 14 Sep 1811. Amos **BYRD** to George **HAYS**. For the sum of $600, two negro girls, one 20 years of age named **Milley**, and the other 7 years old named **Sally**. Signed Amos (A) **BYRD**. Test Leonard **WILSON**, Moses **BYRD**, John **DAVIS** (JP). Rec 29 Jun 1812.

569. Page 348. 1 Jul 1811. Charles **McCONNEL** and Jean, his wife, to John **RAMSEY** senr and John **SIMPSON**. For the sum of $200, __ acres on the waters of Hubble's Creek, being the third part of a grant to John **LOGAN**'s heirs by the Spanish Government. Signed Charles **McCONNELL**, Jean (x) **McCONNEL** (RD). Wit Enoch **EVANS** (JP), James **RAVENSCROFT**, G. **HENDERSON** (JP). Rec 29 Jun 1812.

570. Page 349. 29 Jun 1812. Asa B. **LINCECUM**, in behalf of Herman **LINCECUM**, to Robert **ENGLISH**. For the sum of $400, 640 acres, more or less, which he purchased as agent for Herman **LINCECUM** from Robert **ENGLISH** on 8 Jun 1811. The U. S. Land Commission has rejected the claim of sd **ENGLISH** to the land, and Asa B. **LINCECUM** and sd **ENGLISH** have mutually agreed to dissolve sd land. Sd **LINCECUM** also posts bond of $2000 to defend title and claim to sd land from him. Signed Asa ( ) B. **LINCECUM**. Wit G. **HENDERSON** (JP). Rec 29 Jun 1812.

571. Page 350. 27 Nov 1811. James **CURRIN** of Tywappity Twp to Laban **TAYLOR**. For the sum of $780, bond to make a deed for 130 arpens in Tywappity Bottom on the W bank of the Mississippi; adjoining William **STEPHENS'** lower line, and being part of sd **CURRIN**'s Spanish Grant. Signed James **CURRIN**. Test Thos. **FLETCHER**, Jesse I. **RUSSELL**, James

H. **STEPHENSON**, G. **HENDERSON** (JP). Rec 20 Jul 1812.

572. Page 352. 24 Jul 1812. Jaben **SEELYE** by Sheriff John **HAYS** to Joseph **McFERRON**. For the sum of $32, 200 acres in Tywappity Bottom about 10 miles below Mr. **WATERS** and near Charles **FENLEY**, the SE boundary entering within one and one-half miles of the Mississippi. Sold on 21 Jul 1812 on a writ of execution from the CCP issued 23 Mar 1812 in favor of Peter **GODAR**, assignee of David **SHAW**, who was assignee of Richard **DAVIS**, and against Jaben **SEELYE** for $150 debt, $200 damages and costs. Signed John **HAYS**, Sheriff. Wit Joseph **McFERRON**, Clerk, CCP. Rec 24 Jul 1812.

573. Page 354. 22 Aug 1812. Andrew **RAMSEY** senior and Eve, his wife, to Jesse **SCRUGGS**. For the sum of $300, 240 arpens on Ramsey's Creek, being the same tract granted to Jonathan **DITCH** by the Spanish Government, excepting 8 arpens sold to David **HARRIS**; bounded on the N by sd **HARRIS**, W by Robert **GIBONEY** and vacant land, S by Morgan **BYRNE**, and E by Enoch **EVANS** and the heirs of Samuel **TIPTON**. Signed Andrew **RAMSEY**, Eve (cursive E) **RAMSEY** (RD). Wit Enoch **EVANS** (JP). Rec 24 Aug 1812.

574. Page 355. 3 Feb 1812. William **MATTHEWS** to George **EAKIN**. For the sum of $1000, 240 arpens, beginning at Ithermore **HUBELL**'s SW corner, and also bounded by Thomas **RODNEY**. Signed William **MATTHEWS**, Charity (x) **MATTHEWS**. Wit Geo. **HOOKER**, Robert **CRAWFORD**, Robert **ENGLISH**, Jno. **ABERNETHIE** (JP). Rec 24 Aug 1812.

575. Page 357. 22 Aug 1812. Jesse **SCRUGGS** to Andrew **RAMSEY** Junior. For causes mentioned, quit claim to any claim he may have on sd **RAMSEY**. Sd **RAMSEY** conveyed a tract known as the Ditch Place, bounded by the heirs of Samuel **TIPTON**, Enoch **EVANS**, and others, to sd **SCRUGGS**. It appears that the conveyance was not made by the proper person, Andrew **RAMSEY** Senior, who has since conveyed sd tract unto sd **SCRUGGS**. Signed Jesse (x) **SCRUGGS**. Wit Enoch **EVANS**, James **RAVENSCROFT**, G. **HENDERSON** (JP). Rec 3 Sep 1812.

576. Page 358. 20 Sep 1811. Thomas **FOSTER** and Mary, his wife, to John **GIBONEY**. For the sum of $200, quit claim to 1/3 part of 300 acres, more or less, owned by John **LOGAN**, decd, or

his heirs; bounded on the E by Jacob **JACOBS** and Mathew **SCRUGGS**, W by Abraham **BURD**'s mill seat tract, and N by James **HANNAH**. Signed Thomas (x) **FOSTER**, Mary (x) **FOSTER** (RD). Wit John C. **HARBISON**, John **SEAVERS**, Robert **McCALLISTER**, Enoch **EVANS** (JP). Rec 16 Sep 1812.

577. Page 359. 26 Sep 1812. B. **COUSIN** to Andrew **RAMSEY** Senior. Receipt for payment of mortgage given to sd **RAMSEY** by Louis **LORIMIER** senr, now decd, on 1 Jul 1806, for Lot Nos. 7 & 8, Range D, in the sum of $200. Signed B. **COUSIN**. Wit G. **HENDERSON** (JP). Rec 26 Sep 1812.

578. Page 359. 22 Oct 1812. James Hamilton **STEPHENSON** and Sally, his wife, "of the District of Cape Girardeau and Terr. of Louisianna, in future the Territory of Missouri" to James **RITCHEY**. For the sum of $200, 50 arpens, beginning at the lower corner of John **LOYD**'s claim and fronting on the bank of the Mississippi, and being part of 200 arpens formerly owned by sd **LOYD**. Signed Ja. H. **STEPHENSON**, Sally **STEPHENSON**. Wit Arthur **PITMAN**, Rosanna **ORDWAY**, Arthur (x) **PITMAN** Juner, G. **HENDERSON** (JP). Rec 24 Oct 1812.

579. Page 361. 12 May 1812. David **BRYANT** to Joseph **ANDREWS**. For the sum of $350, mortgage on W part of Lot No. 14, Range E in Cape Girardeau; bounded on the S by Harmony St, W by Indian St, N by Charles G. **ELLIS**, and E by sd **ANDREWS**; being the same deeded by sd **ANDREWS** to sd **BRYANT** on this date, and which sd **ANDREWS** purchased from Louis **LORIMIER** senr and Marie, his wife, on 3 Jul 1811. Signed David **BRYANT**. Wit G. **HENDERSON**. Received $39, Herculaneum, 16 Jul 1812. Signed Joseph **ANDREWS**. Test Ch. A. **AUSTIN**, G. **HENDERSON** (JP). Rec 29 Oct 1812.

580. Page 362. 25 Apr 1812. Samuel D. **STROTHER** to John **RODNEY**. For the sum of $600, a negro man named **Isaac** about 22 years of age, with a scar across above his right eye, and stutters when he talks fast. Signed S. D. **STROTHER**. Test Thos. S. **RODNEY**, Robt. **BRADLEY**, G. **HENDERSON** (JP). Rec 3 Nov 1812.

581. Page 363. 26 Sep 1812. James **HANNAH** to John **GIBONEY**, both of Cape Girardeau Twp. For the sum of $300, __ acres about nine miles from Cape Girardeau, being where sd

HANNAH now lives; bounded on the N by Abraham **BIRD**, E by Jacob **JACOBS**, W by Thomas **RODNEY**, and S by the widow **LOGAN**. Signed James (IH) **HANNAH**. Wit John **BEARDSLEY**, John **MORRISSON**, G. **HENDERSON** (JP). Rec 5 Nov 1812.

582. Page 364. 26 Sep 1812. Same to same. For the sum of $200, one mare and colt, two cows and yearlings, eight head of hogs, one plow and irons, one ax, one mattock, two hoes, one large iron kettle, one pot, one Dutch oven and skillet, one iron wedge, two feather beds and furniture, four chairs, one saddle, and all household furniture such as cooper ware, knives, and forks, etc., one hackle, the crop that is now growing on his plantation. Any articles omitted from the list are to be included. Signed James (IH) **HANNAH**. Wit John **BEARDSLEY**, John **MORRISSON**, G. **HENDERSON** (JP). Rec 5 Nov 1812.

583. Page 365. 6 Sep 1812. Jacob **FRIEND** to Gilbert **HECTOR**. In order to indemnify sd **HECTOR** of any damages or loss he may sustain for serving as security to the adminrs of the estate of Louis **LORIMIER**, decd, in a note for $134 and for the sum of $1, mortgage on 200 arpens where sd **FRIEND** now lives. Signed Jacob ( ) **FRIEND**. Wit G. **HENDERSON** (JP), W. **GARNER**. Rec 7 Nov 1812.

584. Page 366. 16 Nov 1811. John **FINDLEY** to James **BRADY**. Power of attorney to ask, demand, sue for, and receive all manner of property from the adminr of the estate of Charles **FINDLEY**, late of this dist, that is due to him as a lawful legatee of sd estate. Sd **BRADY** has paid to sd **FINDLEY** a valuable consideration for same. Signed Jno. **FENLEY**. Test Andrew **RAMSEY**, James **WELBORN**, William **KELSO** (JP). Rec 9 Nov 1812.

585. Page 367. 16 Nov 1811. Same to same. For the sum of $250, __ acres in the Tywappity Dist due to him from the estate of Charles **FINDLEY**, late of the Cape Girardeau Dist, decd; bounded on the E by James **RITCHEY**, N by John **RITCHEY**, and fronting on the Mississippi River; also all the real and personal property due to him from sd estate. Signed Jno. **FINDLEY**. Test Andrew **RAMSEY**, James **WELBORN**, G. **HENDERSON** (JP). Rec 9 Nov 1812.

586. Page 369. 18 Sep 1812. Benjamin **HOWARD**, Governor of La., to Benjamin **SHELL**. Appointment as JP for German Twp in

the Cape Girardeau Dist. Signed Benja. **HOWARD**. Wit Frederick **BATES**, Sec. of La. Benjamin **SHELL** takes the oath of office. Signed Benja. **SHELL**. Wit J. **McFERRON**. Rec 9 Nov 1812.

587. Page 369. 10 Dec 1811. James **CURRIN** and Essa, his wife, to Henry **COCKERHAM**, all of Tywappity Twp. For the sum of $600, 200 arpents, beginning on the bank of the Mississippi River at a walnut tree; bounded on the N by Benjamin **ROSE** and S by Bartholomew **COUSINS**; being the same granted by the Spanish Government to William **BYRD**, and conveyed by sd **BYRD** to sd **CURRIN**. Signed James **CURRIN**, Esse ( ) **CURRIN**. Test William **SMYTH**, John Y. **COCKERHAM**, Wm. **KELSO** (JP). Rec 16 Nov 1812.

588. Page 371. 18 Sep 1812. Benjamin **HOWARD**, Governor of La. Terr., to John **DUNN**. Appointment as JP for Byrd Twp in the Cape Girardeau Dist. Signed Benja. **HOWARD**. Wit Frederick **BATES**, Sec. of La. Terr. John **DUNN** takes the oath of office. Signed John **DUNN**. Wit J. **McFERRON**. Rec 17 Nov 1812.

589. Page 372. 26 Oct 1805. Thomas W. **WATERS** to James **CURRIN**. Deed of gift for half of two tracts that Danl. **SEXTON** sold to Jos. **MAGEE**; one being Joshua **SEXTON's** head right, and the other being Jno. **SHORTER's** head right. Both parties are to be at equal expense of clearing the tracts, and also the same of the widow **SMITH's** that was sold before. Sd **WATERS** engages to pay half of whatever the land sells for to sd **CURRIN**, and if the land is not recovered, then both parties are to lose equally. Signed Thos. W. **WATERS**. Test R. **WORTHINGTON**, Edmond **HAGAN** (JP). Rec 20 Nov. 1812.

590. Page 373. 12 Jun 1811. James **CURRIN** to James **BRADY**. For the sum of $280, bond to make a deed for 125 arpents in Tywappity Bottom adjoining Big Cypress about eleven miles from the head of Tywappity, about five miles from the Mississippi River, and about one mile from Chas. **LUCAS'** old plantation; being part of the settlement right of John **SHORTER**, which is in partnership with Thomas W. **WATERS**, decd, and sd **CURRIN**. Sd **BRADY** has purchased the land from sd **CURRIN** for $140, and sd **CURRIN** shall make a deed as soon as the commissioners of land claims decides on the claim. Signed James **CURRIN**. Test Igns. **WATHEN**. John C. **HARBISON** verifies the signatures. Wit G. **HENDERSON**

(JP). Rec 20 Nov 1812. [This is the first deed indicating Missouri Terr.]

591. Page 374. 12 Jun 1811. James **BRADY** to James **CURRIN**. Agreement that if title to the land in the previous deed (C:373) is not confirmed by the commissioners, then sd **CURRIN** shall not be bound to pay more than $140 with 6% interest, but does agree to pay for as much property as he receives in payment in good property at its value and also for as much cash as sd **CURRIN** received in payment for sd land. Sd **BRADY** agrees to give to sd **CURRIN** a good claim on Majr. A. **HADEN** for $80, also $20 on Wm. **HICKMAN**, which sd **BRADY** doth engage to make good to sd **CURRIN** if they should prove insolvent after just trial. Sd **BRADY** also agrees to furnish sd **CURRIN** with necessary papers at any time before sd **CURRIN** goes to Arkinsas. Signed James **BRADY**, James **CURRIN**. Test Igns. **WATHEN**, G. **HENDERSON** (JP), John C. **HARBISON**. Rec 20 Nov 1812.

592. Page 376. 5 Apr 1806. Thomas W. **WATERS** to William **EDWARDS** of Sumner Co., Tenn. For the sum of $625, 250 acres, French measure, in Tywappity Bottom, on the Mississippi River known as Moses **BURNET**'s head right; bounded on the N by Reese **BOWIE**'s head right and on all other parts by vacant land. Signed Tho. W. **WATERS**. Wit William **EDWARDS** Jur, John **EDWARDS**, Polly **WATERS**, James **BRADY** & John **WATERS** (as to signatures of Thomas W. & Polly **WATERS**), G. **HENDERSON** (JP). Rec 27 Nov 1812.

593. Page 377. 1 Feb 1805. Jesse **BOWDEN** to Daniel **MULLINS**. For the sum of $1200, bond to make title to 100 acres on the Mississippi River originally granted to Reece **BOOY** in 1799, bounded on the lower line by the land where sd **BOWDEN** now lives, and on the upper line by the land where sd **MULLINS** now lives. Signed Jesse **BOWDEN**, Cah. [Catherine] **BOWDEN**. Wit T. L. **NORRIS**, ___ **WELLBORN**. Title is assigned to William **EDWARDS** for value received on 20 Nov 1807. Signed Daniel (x) **MULLINS**. Test A. **HADEN**, James **BRADY**, G. **HENDERSON** (JP). Rec 27 Nov 1812.

594. Page 378. 9 Nov 1812. 9 Nov 1812. Samuel D. **STROTHER** and Mary, his wife, to John **RODNEY**. For the sum of $1400, 320 arpents on Hubble's Creek, beginning at an elm on Abraham **BIRD**'s W line; also bounded by

Michael **RODNEY** and Thomas S. **RODNEY**. Signed S. D. **STROTHER**, Mary (x) **STROTHER**. Wit John C. **HARBISON**, G. **HENDERSON**, Thos. S. **RODNEY**, Michael **RODNEY**, John **ABERNETHIE** (JP). Rec 1 Dec 1812. [This is the first deed to list the grantor and grantee as being from "County of Cape Girardeau and Terr. of Missouri".]

595. Page 380. 10 Dec 1812. Frederick **BATES**, Secretary of Missouri Terr, to Joseph **McFERRON**. Appointment to administer oaths of office to all persons who may be commissioned under Territorial authority. Signed Frederick **BATES**, Secretary of Missouri Terr. Rec 22 Dec 1812.

596. Page 380. 10 Dec 1812. Same to William **KELSO**. Appointment as JCCP for Cape Girardeau Co. for four years. Signed Frederick **BATES**, Secretary of Missouri Terr. William **KELSO** is administered the oath of office. Signed William **KELSO**. Wit J. **McFERRON**. Rec 22 Dec 1812.

597. Page 381. 10 Dec 1812. Same to Thomas **BYRNE**. Appointment as JCCP for Cape Girardeau Co. for four years. Signed Frederick **BATES**, Secretary of Missouri Terr. Thomas **BYRNE** is administered the oath of office. Signed Thomas **BYRNE**. Wit J. **McFERRON**. Rec 22 Dec 1812.

598. Page 382. 10 Dec 1812. Same to George **HENDERSON**. Appointment as Recorder for Cape Girardeau Co. Signed Frederick **BATES**, Secretary of Missouri Terr. George **HENDERSON** is administered the oath of office. Signed George **HENDERSON**. Wit J. **McFERRON**. Rec 24 Dec 1812.

599. Page 383. 10 Dec 1812. Same to John **HAYS**. Appointment as Sheriff of Cape Girardeau Co. Signed Frederick **BATES**, Secretary of Missouri Terr. John **HAYS** is administered the oath of office. Signed John **HAYS**. Wit J. **McFERRON**. Rec 27 Dec 1812.

600. Page 384. 31 Dec 1812. Same to William **KELSO**. Appointment as JP for Tywappity Twp for four years. Signed Frederick **BATES**, Secretary of Missouri Terr. William **KELSO** is administered the oath of office. Signed William **KELSO**. Wit J. **McFERRON**. Rec 8 Jan 1813.

601. Page 385. 1 Jan 1813. Same to John **RAMSEY** senr. Appointment as JCCP for Cape Girardeau Co. for four years. Signed Frederick

BATES, Secretary of Missouri Terr. John **RAMSEY** senior is administered the oath of office. Signed John **RAMSEY**. Wit J. **McFERRON**. Rec 9 Jan 1813.

602. Page 386. 31 Dec 1812. Same to George **HENDERSON**. Appointment as Judge of Probate for Cape Girardeau Co. Signed Frederick **BATES**, Secretary of Missouri Terr. George **HENDERSON** is administered the oath of office. Signed George **HENDERSON**. Wit J. **McFERRON**. Rec 9 Jan 1813.

603. Page 386. 31 Dec 1812. Same to same. Appointment as JP for Cape Girardeau Twp in Cape Girardeau Co for four years. Signed Frederick **BATES**, Secretary of Missouri Terr. George **HENDERSON** is administered the oath of office. Signed George **HENDERSON**. Wit J. **McFERRON**. Rec 9 Jan 1813.

604. Page 387. 31 Dec 1812. Same to John **ABERNATHIE**. Appointment as JP for Cape Girardeau Twp in Cape Girardeau Co for four years. Signed Frederick **BATES**, Secretary of Missouri Terr. John **ABERNETHIE** is administered the oath of office. Signed Jno. **ABERNETHIE**. Wit J. **McFERRON**. Rec 14 Jan 1813.

605. Page 388. 31 Dec 1812. Same to Enoch **EVANS**. Appointment as JP for Cape Girardeau Twp in Cape Girardeau Co for four years. Signed Frederick **BATES**, Secretary of Missouri Terr. Enoch **EVANS** is administered the oath of office. Signed Enoch **EVANS**. Wit J. **McFERRON**. Rec 14 Jan 1813.

606. Page 389. 31 Dec 1812. Same to David **GREEN**. Appointment as Coroner for Cape Girardeau Co. Signed Frederick **BATES**, Secretary of Missouri Terr. David **GREEN** is administered the oath of office. Signed David **GREEN**. Wit J. **McFERRON**. Rec 22 Jan 1813.

607. Page 390. 31 Dec 1812. Same to James **RITCHEY**. Appointment as JP for Tywappity Twp for four years. Signed Frederick **BATES**, Secretary of Missouri Terr. James **RITCHEY** is administered the oath of office. Signed James **RITCHEY**. Wit William **KELSO**. Rec 4 Feb 1813.

608. Page 391. 7 Feb 1812. James **WILSON**, husband of Sarah **WILSON**, late Sarah **THOMPSON**, and Martha **THOMPSON** to Joseph **THOMPSON** Junr. For the sum of $39, their share of the estate of Joseph **THOMPSON**

senr, decd. The grantors also agree to never molest in the future in their possession of all the late estate of Joseph **THOMPSON** senr; Rachel **THOMPSON** the elder, adminr of the estate of Joseph **THOMPSON** senr, decd; Joseph **THOMPSON** Junr, Isaac **THOMPSON**, William **THOMPSON**, and Rachel **THOMPSON** the younger. The grantors are now living on a plantation of the late Joseph **THOMPSON** senr, have given peaceable possession to Joseph **THOMPSON** Junr, agree to quit sd place whenever called, and bind themselves for $500 to do so. Signed James **WILSON**, Marther (x) **THOMPSON**, Sarah **WILSON**. Wit John C. **HARBISON**, Enos **HANNAH**, John (x) **HANNAH**, G. **HENDERSON** (JP), Enoch **EVANS** (JP). Rec 12 Feb 1813.

609. Page 392. 24 Jun 1811. Jonathan **BUIS** to John **WILSON** and George W. **COCHRAN**, two of the legatees of the estate of Amos **BYRD**, decd, and Abraham **BYRD**, guardian of John **BYRD**, another legatee of sd decd. For the sum of $491.82 ½, being the amount he owes sd estate, mortgage on two tracts; 600 arpens on the waters of Byrd's Creek, being the dower of Anna, widow of sd decd and now the wife of sd **BUIS**, originally granted to sd decd, bounded on the S by **COOPER**'s claim, W by John **BYRD**, and N & E by vacant land; and 250 arpens on the waters of Byrd's Creek granted to Elijah **EVERET**, decd, late of the Cape Girardeau Dist, and descending to Anna, widow of sd **EVERET**, now the wife of sd **BUIS**, bounded on the N by the first tract granted to sd Amos **BYRD**, decd, W & S by unknown, and E by **COOPER**'s claim. The debt is due by 1 Mar next. Signed Jonathan **BUIS**. Wit John **DAVIS** (JP). Received of the within, $120 on 4 Mar 1812. Signed Geo. W. **COCHRAN**, Abraham **BYRD**. Wit G. **HENDERSON** (JP). Rec 6 Mar 1813.

610. Page 394. 26 Oct 1812. Thomas S. **RODNEY** to John **AKIN**. For the sum of $350, 200 arpents, more or less, on Foster's Creek, that sd **RODNEY** bought from Jacob **FOSTER** Junr. and which was sd **FOSTER**'s head right, beginning at the NE corner at a white oak; adjoined on the E by Michael **RODNEY**, N & S by vacant lands, and W by Jacob **FOSTER** senr and vacant lands. Signed Thos. S. **RODNEY**. Wit Michael **RODNEY**, John **REYNOLDS**, Robt. **BRADLEY**, Enoch **EVANS** (JP). Rec 15 Mar 1813.

611. Page 395. 10 Dec 1812. Frederick **BATES**, Secretary of Missouri Terr, to George

HENDERSON. Appointment as Auditor for Cape Girardeau Co. Signed Frederick BATES, Secretary of Missouri Terr. George HENDERSON is administered the oath of office. Signed George HENDERSON. Wit J. McFERRON. Rec 15 Mar 1813.

612. Page 396. 30 Apr 1812. John EARTHMAN and Polly, his wife, and Henry EARTHMAN to Richard WALLER. For the sum of $950, 380 arpens on Randol's Creek, being the plantation where Joseph WALLER formerly lived and where John EARTHMAN now lives; adjoined on the W by John ABERNETHIE, Esq., S by John HITT, and N by a dividing line designated in a title bond from Richard WALLER and Medad RANDOL to William WILLIAMS dated 4 Jan 1808. Signed John EARTHMAN, Polley EARTHMAN, Henry EARTHMAN. Wit O. DAVIS, James DOWTY, Isaac (x) WILLIAMS, G. HENDERSON (JP). Rec 17 Apr 1813.

613. Page 398. 14 Apr 1813. Benjamin HOWARD, Governor of Missouri Terr, to Robert GREEN. Appointment as JCCP for Cape Girardeau Co for four years. Signed Benja. Howard. Wit Frederick BATES, Sec. of Mo. Terr. Robert GREEN takes the oath of office. Signed Robt. GREEN. Wit J. McFERRON. Rec 27 Apr 1813.

614. Page 399. 12 Feb 1813. Andrew RAMSEY senr. and Eve, his wife, and Andrew RAMSEY Junr to Thomas ENGLISH. For the sum of $800, 240 arpens, more or less (20 arpents N to S, and 12 arpents E to W); bounded on the N by Enoch EVANS, S by Andrew RAMSEY Junior, E by a tract formerly surveyed for Peter GODAIR, decd, and vacant lands, and W by Charles BRADLEY. Sd tract has been occupied and improved by their son Andrew RAMSEY Junior, and is where he still resides. [Survey No. 176 was written later in the margin.] Signed Andrew RAMSEY, Eve (x) RAMSEY (RD), Andrew RAMSEY. Wit William MATTHEWS, William RAMSEY, Enoch EVANS (JP). Rec 14 May 1813.

615. Page 401. 20 Apr 1813. Frederick BATES, Secretary of Missouri Terr, to Joseph McFERRON. Commission as Clerk of Cape Girardeau Co, his having been appointed by the Courts of Common Pleas and Quarter Sessions of the Peace. Signed Frederick BATES, Secretary of Missouri Terr. Joseph McFERRON is administered the oath of office.

Signed George HENDERSON. Wit William KELSO. Rec 31 May 1813.

616. Page 402. 14 & 24 Oct 1811. Stephen JARBER and Margaret, his wife, to Rebecca HARBISON, widow of George C. C. HARBISON, decd. Agreement to quit claim to their share of the estate of George C. C. HARBISON as heirs of sd decd, including real estate, personal property, slaves, and credits; excepting a tract of land on Cape a la Cruche purchased by sd decd of William LORIMIER. Signed Rebecca HARBISON, Stephen JARBOE, Margret JARBOE. Wit Joseph McFERRON, John CROSS, G. HENDERSON (JP). Rec 10 Jun 1813.

617. Page 403. 5 Jun 1809. Board of Land Commissioners met, with Jno. B. C. LUCAS, Clement B. PENROSE, and Frederick BATES, Commissioners, present. John B. HARBISON claims 1000 arpens as assignee of John HAYS, Sheriff of Cape Girardeau Dist, who sold the same as the property of Louis LARGEAU. Sd HARBISON produces a concession from Zenon TRUDEAU, Lt. Governor, to Louis LARGEAU for the same, dated 26 Aug 1797, and a conveyance from sd Sheriff HAYS dated 7 Dec 1805. Sd HARBISON appeared before the Board on 7 Jun 1808 and acknowledged transfer of 250 arpens to Anthony HAYDEN and 250 arpens to RHANEKER & STEINBECK. Laid over for decision (Minutes of the Board, Book 4:180). Signed Frederick BATES, Recr. L. Titles. Rec 11 Jun 1813.

618. Page 404. 25 Jun 1808. John C. HARBISON to Anthony HADEN. For a valuable consideration, 250 arpens, part of Louis LARJURE tract of 1000 arpens, when sd tract is confirmed by the commissioners. Signed John C. HARBISON. Wit Peter (x) GODAR, Robert BLAIR (JP). Rec 11 Jun 1813.

619. Page 404. 18 Apr 1812. Louis LORIMIER Junior to Louis LORIMIER Senior. For the sum of $3000, two tracts; 640 arpens, more or less, on Hubbell's Creek conveyed to him by John STRONG, and whereon a grist mill and saw mill are erected, bounded on the E by Mathew HUBBELL and a vacant lot, N by the heirs of Waters BURROWS, decd, S by Abraham BYRD and Martin RODNEY, and W by the assignees of John DRYBREAD, Joseph FYHT, and John LOSLA; and 1000 acres, more or less, on a small creek above the old cape, including an old Indian field and a lick or glaize, being granted to him by the Spanish Government; also all his horses in the Dist. Signed Louis **LORIMIER** Junr. Wit B. **COUSIN**, Henry **ECKHART**, G. **HENDERSON** (JP). 28 Jun 1813.

620. Page 406. 20 Jun 1813. Robert **CRAWFORD** and Elizabeth, his wife, to Thomas **ENGLISH** senr. For the sum of $256, 100 acres on the waters of Randell's Creek, being part of a survey granted to Jeremiah **THOMPSON** by the Spanish Government and sold by sd **ENGLISH** to sd **CRAWFORD**; bounded on the S by Semion **KENYON**, W by sd **THOMPSON**'s grant, N by Joseph **LEWIS**, and E by vacant lands. Signed Robert **CRAWFORD**, Elizabeth **CRAWFORD** (RD). Wit Enoch **EVANS** (JP). Rec 6 Jul 1813.

621. Page 408. 28 Sep 1812. William **VIRGIN** and Sophia, his wife, to Joseph **LEWIS**. For the sum of $550, 200 French acres on the waters of Randall's Creek, being the same sold to sd **VIRGIN** by Jerimiah **THOMPSON** and John **THOMPSON**, beginning at a hickory on the side of a ridge. Signed William (x) **VIRGIN**, Sophia ( ) **VIRGIN** (RD). Wit Enoch **EVANS** (JP). Rec 19 Jul 1813.

622. Page 409. 22 Dec 1812. Jacob **FOSTER** senr to Benjamin **THOMPSON**. For the sum of $200, 200 arpens, French measure, on both sides of Foster's Creek, a fork of Hubbell's Creek; being ½ of 400 arpens and the W end of sd tract where sd **FOSTER** formerly lived; bounded on the S, W, & N by vacant land and E by the other ½ of sd tract now belonging to William **WILLIAMS**. Signed Jacob **FOSTER**. Wit Richard **WALLER**, Jno. **ABERNETHIE** (JP). Rec 19 Jul 1813.

623. Page 410. 22 Jul 1813. James **CURRIN** by Sheriff John **HAYS** to Morgan **BYRNE**. For the sum of $126, 213 2/3 acres in Tywappity Bottom on the Mississippi River; adjoined by William **REED** and Robert **LANE**'s head right. Sold on 16 Mar 1813 on a writ of execution issued by CCP on 22 Feb 1813 in favor of Joseph **MICHEL** against James **CURRIN**, for $200 damages and costs for non-payment of a note and several promises. Signed John **HAYS**, Sheriff. Wit Joseph **McFERRON**, Clerk. Rec 26 Jul 1813.

624. Page 413. 6 Nov 1812. James **SCRUGGS** to his beloved father Jesse **SCRUGGS**. For diverse good causes, power of attorney to collect debts and sell real estate. Signed James **SCRUGGS**. Wit Abraham **BYRD**, Adam

MURRAY, G. **HENDERSON** (JP). Rec 9 Aug 1813.

625. Page 414. 26 Nov 1811. Stephen **JARBOE** to Joseph **McFERRON**. For the sum of $150, release of all claims against the estate of George C. C. **HARBISON** (C:402). This is a receipt for $25 of the amount, with the rest to be paid to him in trade in the spring, deducting the costs of a suit against him by James **LOGAN**. Signed Stephen **JARBOE**. Wit John **CROSS**, Wm. J. **STEPHENSON**, G. **HENDERSON** (JP). Rec 9 Aug 1813.

626. Page 415. 9 Aug 1813. Edward **ROBERTSON** Sr of New Madrid Co., Mo. to Lewis Buckingham **NEAL** of Madison Co., Miss. For the sum of $1000, 450 arpens in Tywappity Bottom, adjoining Stephen **QUIMBY** on the lower side and Daniel **MULLINS** on the upper side, being the same formerly belonging to Robert **LAIN**. Sd **ROBERTSON** agrees to obtain a patent from the government. Signed Edward (ER) **ROBERTSON**. Test Wm. **WOOD**, John **LOGAN**, G. **HENDERSON** (JP). Caterine **ROBERTSON**, wife of Edward **ROBERTSON** Sr, RD. Signed Caterine (x) **ROBERTSON**. Wit John B. **WHEELER** (JP). Rec 10 Aug 1813.

627. Page 417. 9 Oct 1804. Estate of William **LOWRY** by Commandant Louis **LORIMIER** to Thomas **RODNEY**. For the sum of $183, lot in the village of Cape Girardeau, joined on the N by unoccupied land and streets on the other sides, including a house of hewed logs, a kitchen, stable, fences, and improvements; being the same sold by Peter **GODAIR** to sd **LOWRY**, decd. Sd **RODNEY** is to have possession on 1 May next, because Andrew **BURT**, execr to the will of Wm. **LOWRY**, decd, has rented it for $3 per month to Joseph **BURT** until that date. Any excess over rental price is to be paid to the purchaser conformably to the decision of Samuel **BRADLEY**, John **GUETHING**, James **ARRELE**, and Robert **HALL**. Sold on 6 Oct 1804 and seized on 18 Sep 1804 to pay Peter **GODAIR**, a creditor to sd estate, as per agreement made on 8 Mar last between sd **LOWRY** and sd **GODAIR**. Sd **GODAIR** received payment as 300 gallons of whiskey from sd **LOWRY**, and the balance from sd **RODNEY**, and warrants the lot to sd **RODNEY**. [Indicated as a translation copy.] Signed Pierre (x) **GODAIR**. Wit B. **COUSIN**, Benn. **MORGAN**, L. **LORIMIER**, Commandant, G. **HENDERSON** (JP). Rec 31 Aug 1813.

628. Page 420. 2 Mar 1812. John **ABERNETHIE** and Havens Clary, his wife, to John **HITT**. For the sum of $200, 50 acres, more or less, being part of the tract whereon sd **ABERNETHIE** lives, and being whereon Parish **GREEN** and his family live, beginning at a sugar tree at sd **HITT**'s corner on sd **GREEN**'s spring branch (formerly called the Slab Branch) that runs into Randoll's Mill Creek, being the second branch that lies W from sd **ABERNETHIE**'s plantation; also bounded by [Solomon] **ELLIS**, ___ **BYRD**, and Anthony **RANDOLL**. Signed Jno. **ABERNETHIE**, Havens Clary (x) **ABERNETHIE**. Wit James **COX** Junr, Benjamin **HITT**, Solomon **ELLIS**, G. **HENDERSON** (JP). Rec 31 Aug 1813.

629. Page 422. 22 Jul 1813. Frederick **GIBLER** by Sheriff John **HAYS** to Daniel F. **STEINBECK**. For the sum of $151, Lot Nos. 5 & 8, ¼ of Lot No. 6, and ¼ of Lot No. 7 in Cape Girardeau. Sold on 16 Mar 1813 a on a writ of execution issued by CCP on 23 Mar 1809 in Case No. 561 in favor of Frederick **REINECKE** against sd **GIBLER**, for $273.04 debt in a mortgage foreclosure. Signed John **HAYS**, Sheriff. Wit Joseph **McFERRON**, Clerk. Rec 31 Aug 1813.

630. Page 424. 6 Aug 1813. Hugh **DOWLING** and Polly, his wife, of Johnson Co., Ill. to John **BURROWS**. For the sum of $140, 53 1/3 acres on Hubble's Creek, being part of Waters **BURROWS**' head right. Signed Hugh **DOLING**, Polly (x) **DOWLING** (RD). Wit William **KELSO** (JP). Rec 18 Oct 1813.

631. Page 426. 6 Aug 1813. William **BURROWS** to John **BURROWS**. For the sum of $160.75, 53 1/3 acres on Hubble's Creek, being part of Waters **BURROWS**' head right. Signed William **BURROWS**. Wit William **KELSO** (JP). Rec 18 Oct 1813.

[Joseph **McFERRON** began the duties of Clerk and Recorder with the next deed.]

632. Page 427. 1 Sep 1813. William **CLARK**, Governor of Missouri Terr, to Robert **GREEN**. Appointment as Judge of the CCP for Cape Girardeau Co. for four years. Signed William **CLARK**, Governor. Wit Frederick **BATES**, Secretary. Robert **GREEN** takes the oath of Office. Signed Robt. **GREEN**. Wit Joseph **McFERRON**. Rec 18 Oct 1813.

633. Page 427. 1 Sep 1813. William **CLARK**, Governor of Missouri Terr, to Isaac **SHEPPARD**. Appointment as Judge of the CCP for Cape Girardeau Co. for four years. Signed William **CLARK**, Governor. Wit Frederick **BATES**, Secretary. Isaac **SHEPPARD** takes the oath of Office. Signed Isaac **SHEPPARD**. Wit Joseph **McFERRON**. Rec 18 Oct 1813.

634. Page 427. 1 Sep 1813. William **CLARK**, Governor of Missouri Terr, to William **KELSO**. Appointment as Judge of the CCP for Cape Girardeau Co. for four years. Signed William **CLARK**, Governor. Wit Frederick **BATES**, Secretary. William **KELSO** takes the oath of Office. Signed William **KELSO**. Wit Joseph **McFERRON**. Rec 18 Oct 1813.

635. Page 428. 1 Sep 1813. William **CLARK**, Governor of Missouri Terr, to John **HAYS**. Appointment as Sheriff of Cape Girardeau Co. for two years. Signed William **CLARK**, Governor. Wit Frederick **BATES**, Secretary. John **HAYS** takes the oath of Office. Signed John **HAYS**. Wit Joseph **McFERRON**. Rec 18 Oct 1813.

636. Page 428. 16 Oct 1813. John **HAYS**, Morgan **BYRNE**, Daniel F. **STEINBECK**, and Levi **WOLVERTON** to William **CLARK**, Governor of Missouri Terr. For the sum of $5000, bond to guarantee that sd **HAYS** will faithfully discharge the duties of Sheriff of Cape Girardeau Co. Signed John **HAYS**, Morgan **BYRNE**, D. F. **STEINBECK**, Levi **WOLVERTON**. Wit Robt. **GREEN** (JCCP), William **KELSO** (JCCP). Rec 18 Oct 1813.

637. Page 428. 16 Oct 1813. Joseph **McFERRON**, John **HAYS**, and William **DAUGHERTY** to same. For the sum of $5000, bond to guarantee that sd **McFERRON** shall faithfully discharge the duties of the office of Clerk of the CCP. Signed Joseph **McFERRON**, John **HAYS**, Wm. **DAUGHERTY**. Wit William J. **STEPHENSON**, Zenas **PRIEST**, Robt. **GREEN** (JCCP), William **KELSO** (JCCP). Joseph **McFERRON** takes the oath of office. Signed Joseph **McFERRON**. Wit William **KELSO** (JCCP). Rec 18 Oct 1813.

638. Page 429. 24 Oct 1813. Frederick **BATES**, Secretary of Missouri Terr, to Joseph **McFERRON**. Commission as Clerk of the CCP for Cape Girardeau Co., his having been appointed by sd court. Signed Frederick **BATES**, Secretary of Missouri Terr. Joseph **McFERRON** takes the oath of office. Signed Joseph **McFERRON**. Wit William **KELSO** (JCCP). Rec 29 Oct 1813.

639. Page 429. 12 Mar 1813. Frederick **REINECKE** and Rebecca, his wife, to Daniel F. **STEINBECK**. For the sum of $700, quit claim to their moiety of Lot No. 3, Range D in Cape Girardeau now occupied by sd **STEINBECK**. A partnership was formed between the two parties in Aug 1803 in the city of Baltimore under the firm of **REINECKE & STEINBECKE**, and sd partnership was dissolved by mutual consent on 6 Dec 1811. Signed Fredk. **REINECKE**, Rebecca **REINECKE**. Test Zenas **PRIEST**, B. **COUSIN**, George **HENDERSON** (JP). Rec 3 Nov 1813.

640. Page 429. 13 Sep 1813. William **CLARK**, Governor of Missouri Terr, to John H. **MADISON**. Appointment as JP for Cape Girardeau and Byrd Twps for four years. Signed William **CLARK**, Governor. Wit Frederick **BATES**, Secretary. John H. **MADISON** takes the oath of Office. Signed John H. **MADISON**. Wit Joseph **McFERRON**. Rec 13 Nov 1813.

641. Page 430. 21 Aug 1813. William **CLARK**, Governor of Missouri Terr, to Jacob **KELLEY**. Appointment as JP for St. Francis Twp for four years. Signed William **CLARK**, Governor. Wit Frederick **BATES**, Secretary. Jacob **KELLEY** takes the oath of Office. Signed Jacob **KELLEY**. Wit Joseph **McFERRON**. Rec 15 Nov 1813.

642. Page 430. 3 Jun 1813. Mary **MATTHEWS** to Edward **KEW**, both of Tywappity Twp. For the sum of $200, 100 arpents in Tywappity Twp; beginning on the bank of the Mississippi River below James **RITCHEY**'s corner and to include 1/3 of a tract sold by Alexander **MILLIKIN** to John **ORDWAY** in 1807, except the front of 50 arpents on the lower side; then conveyed from sd **ORDWAY** to William **ORDWAY**; and since the death of William **ORDWAY**, John **ORDWAY** conveyed the 300 arpents to Mary **ORDWAY**, widow of William **ORDWAY**, now Mary **MATTHEWS**. Signed Mary **MATTHEWS**. Wit William **KELSO** (JP). Rec 16 Nov 1813.

643. Page 431. 21 Aug 1813. William **CLARK**, Governor of Missouri Terr, to John **DAVIS**. Appointment as JP for Byrd Twp for four years. Signed William **CLARK**, Governor. Wit Frederick **BATES**, Secretary. John **DAVIS** takes the oath of Office. Signed & wit John H. **MADISON**. Wit Joseph **McFERRON**. Rec 16 Nov 1813.

644. Page 431. 17 Nov 1813. Mary **MATTHEWS** and Thomas **FLETCHER**, adminrs of Edward **MATTHEWS**, decd, by Sheriff John **HAYS** to Edward W. **MATTHEWS**. For the sum of $31, 300 arpens on the Mississippi River whereon Edward **MATTHEWS**, decd, formerly lived. Sold on 16 Nov 1813 on a writ of execution issued by CCP on 17 Aug 1813 in favor of Alexander **WILSON** against Mary **MATTHEWS**, adminr, and Thomas **FLETCHER**, adminr of Edward **MATTHEWS**, decd, for $90 debt, $10 damages, and $25.47 and five mills costs. Signed John **HAYS**, Sheriff. Wit Joseph **McFERRON**, Clerk. Title is assigned to the heirs of William **ORDWAY**, decd; Grace **KEW**, Rosannah **ORDWAY**, Abigail S. **ORDWAY**, Mary **ORDWAY**, and Zelinda **ORDWAY**; for the sum of $35 on 17 Nov 1813. Signed Edwd. **MATTHEWS**. Wit J. **McFERRON**, James **BRADY**, Edward **KEW**, Robt. **GREEN** (JCCP). Rec 17 Nov 1813.

645. Page 432. 21 Aug 1813. William **CLARK**, Governor of Missouri Terr, to William **TINNIN**. Appointment as JP for German Twp for four years. Signed William **CLARK**, Governor. Wit Frederick **BATES**, Secretary. William **TINNIN** takes the oath of Office. Signed Wm. **TINNIN**. Wit J. **McFERRON**. Rec 23 Nov 1813.

646. Page 432. 1 Nov 1813. Andrew **RAMSEY** senior and Eve, his wife, to Rebecca **HARBISON**. For the sum of $400, 162 arpents near Cape Girardeau known as Cox'es Improvement; bounded on the W by sd Andrew **RAMSEY**, N & E by L. **LORIMIER**, and S by James **RAMSEY**. Signed Andrew **RAMSEY**, Eve ( ) **RAMSEY**. Wit Peter **CRAIG**, W. **GARNER**, George **HENDERSON** (JP). Rec 23 Nov 1813.

647. Page 433. 13 Nov 1813. Frederick **REINECKE** and Rebecca, his wife, late of Cape Girardeau Co., to Daniel F. **STEINBECK**. For the sum of $1200; $300 now, the remainder in four payments to be made yearly, the first of $100, second and third of $200 each, and the fourth of $400, all in four promissory notes dated this date; all land, debts due to, and obligations due by the former firm of **REINECKE & STEINBECK**. Sd **REINECKE** and sd **STEINBECK** become joint proprietors of diverse tracts in Cape Girardeau and New Madrid Cos., and diverse debts have become due to them, and they have become indebted to others. All of sd lands and obligations shall be assigned to sd **STEINBECK** by mutual agreement and the consideration paid. Sd **REINECKE** is to be held harmless for any actions, judgments, damages, and demands which may be brought against him arising from sd partnership. Signed Fredr. **REINECKE**, Rebecca **REINECKE**, D. F. **STEINBECK**. Wit Robert **McCAY**, W. **GARNER**, John **LAVALEE** (JCCP in New Madrid Co.). Rec 1 Dec 1813.

648. Page 434. 6 Dec 1813. Ezekiel **ABLE** and Sarah, his wife, to John **HAYS** and William J. **STEPHENSON**. For the sum of $250, 300 acres or upwards on the waters of White Water adjoining the Big Swamp, being part of the head right of Andrew **FRANKS**, beginning above the cabins formerly occupied by John **BOYD**, leaving about 100 acres adjoined on the W by the tract where the widow **MILLS** formerly lived. Sd **ABLE** gave bond to James **BOYD** to make him a title to the land. Sd **BOYD** still owes $250 to sd **ABLE**, and the tract was taken by John **HAYS**, Sheriff, in execution of a writ issued by CCP on 31 Jul 1813 at the suit of Antoine **SOULARD** and sold 17 Nov last for $16 to George **HENDERSON**. Signed Ezekiel **ABLE**, Sarah **ABLE**. Wit George **HENDERSON** (JP). Rec 6 Dec 1813.

649. Page 435. 4 Oct 1812. Isaac G. **KELLY** to William **RUSSELL**. For the sum of $5, ½ of 500 arpens, more or less, on the waters of the St. Francois River. The Board of Commissioners confirmed 300 arpens of an 800 arpen claim to sd **KELLY**, which he sold to Elijah **BETTIS**. This is ½ of the unconfirmed remainder of the claim. Should sd 500 arpens not be confirmed to sd **KELLY**, then sd **RUSSELL** is to have no recourse. Signed Isaac G. **KELLY**, Wm. **RUSSELL**. Wit Rufus **EASTON** (JP), John **ROUZER**, George **TOMPKINS** (JCCP, St. Louis Co.). Rec 8 Dec 1813.

650. Page 435. 1 Sep 1813. Edmond **HOGAN** and Patsey, his wife, of Stuart Co., Tenn. to John **BALDWIN**. For the sum of $300, 200 arpens, beginning on the bank of the Mississippi River at the SE corner of William **ROSS'es** Spanish Grant and also bounded by Alexander **MILLIKIN**'s head right. Signed Edmond **HOGAN**, Patsey (x) **HOGAN**. Wit Henry **ATKINS**, James H **RANDLE**, David **HOGAN** (JP in Stewart Co., Tenn.), Robert **COOPER**, Clerk of the CCP and Quarter Sessions for Stewart Co., Tenn., Joshua **WILLIAMS**, Presiding Judge of Stewart Co., Tenn. Rec 18 Dec 1813.

651. Page 436. 1 Dec 1813. Belemus **HAYDEN** to John **RAMSEY**. For the sum of $600, 246 arpens on the waters of Hubble's Creek, being the same deeded to sd **HAYDEN** by Joshua **GOZA** on 18 Oct 1811; adjoining Allaxander **SUMMERS**, James **DOUTY**, and B. **HAYDEN**. Signed Belemus **HAYDEN**. Wit John **AKIN**, Thomas W. **GRAVES**, John R. **HAYDEN**, William **KELSO** (JCCP). Rec 20 Dec 1813.

652. Page 436. 1 Dec 1813. Same to John **SIMPSON**. For the sum of $650, 240 arpens on the waters of Hubble's Creek, being the same deeded to sd **HAYDEN** by Edward **ROBERTSON** on 8 Oct 1806; adjoining Ithamer **HUBBLE**'s mill seat and Joseph **FITE**. Signed Belemus **HAYDEN**. Wit William **KELSO** (JCCP). Rec 20 Dec 1813.

653. Page 437. 20 Dec 1813. Matthew **HUBBLE** to Webb **HAYDEN**. For the sum of $900, 375 arpens on the waters of Hubble's Creek, being part of the land granted to sd **HUBBLE** by the Spanish Government; bounded on the E by Nicholas **SAVERS**, S by Abraham **BYRD**, W by **HUBBLE**'s old mill tract, and N & NE by land sold by ___ **HUBBLE** to Wilson **McCLENDON**, Joel **RENFROE**, and Webb **HAYDEN**. Signed Matthew **HUBBLE**. Test William W. **COX** (?), Solomon **HAYDEN**, Enos (x) **MASTERSON**, Enoch **EVANS** (JP). Rec 20 Dec 1813.

654. Page 437. 4 Sep 1813. Henry **HAND** to William **HAND** of Livingston Co., Ky. For natural love and affection to his only son and for the sum of $1, 308 arpens on the waters of Hubble's Creek; also one negro girl named **Sinah** 24 years old, ten head of horses, 38 head of cattle, ten head of sheep, 158 head of hogs, all the household and kitchen furniture, and all his farming tools. Signed Henry **HAND**. Wit Enoch **PRINCE**, Circuit Clerk of Livingston Co., Ky., G. **HENDERSON** (JP). Rec 3 Jan 1814.

655. Page 437. 2 Jan 1813. Jesse **SCRUGGS**, atty in fact for James **SCRUGGS**, to John **WHITTENBURGH**. For the sum of $600, 240 arpents, except 8 arpens, on Ramsey's Creek, being the same granted to Jonathan **DITCH** by the Spanish Government, and conveyed to Jesse **SCRUGGS** by Andrew **RAMSEY** senior and Eve, his wife, and conveyed by Jesse **SCRUGGS** to James **SCRUGGS**; bounded on the N by John C. **HARBISON**, W by Robert **GIBONEY** and vacant land, S by Morgan **BYRNE**, and E by Enoch **EVANS** and the heirs

of Samuel **TIPTON**. Signed Jesse ( )
SCRUGGS, atty in fact for James **SCRUGGS**.
Wit Enoch **EVANS** (JP), Thomas **FINCH**. Rec
17 Jan 1814.

656. Page 438. 27 Aug 1813. Robert
CRAWFORD and Elizabeth, his wife, to same.
For the sum of $1200, 472 arpens and 77 ½ poles
on Randellses Creek, being part of a tract granted
to Jeremiah **THOMPSON** by the Spanish
Government and conveyed by sd **THOMPSON**
to Thomas **ENGLISH** senior and by sd
ENGLISH to sd **CRAWFORD**; bounded on the
N by John **SHEPARD**, E by Joseph **LEWIS** and
Thomas **ENGLISH** senr, S by Simeon
KENYON, and W by vacant land. Signed
Robert **CRAWFORD**, Elizabeth **CRAWFORD**
(RD). Wit Enoch **EVANS** (JP). Rec 17 Jan 1814.

657. Page 439. 9 Apr 1813. Morgan **BYRNE** to
Mary **DAVIS**, late Mary **SCRUGGS**, adminr of
Matthew **SCRUGGS**, decd. For the sum of
$600, mortgage on 240 arpens on the waters of
Giboney's Creek where he now resides; being a
concession made to Timothy **CONNOLY**, and
adjoining Alexander **GIBONEY**'s heirs. The
debt is due with 6% interest per annum in one
year from date. Signed Morgan **BYRNE**. Wit G.
HENDERSON (JP), J. **McFERRON**. Rec 22
Jan 1814. [Marginal note: Full satisfaction of
$646.65 received on 28 Jul 1814. Signed Mary (
) **DAVIS**, late Mary **SCRUGGS**, adminr of
Matthew **SCRUGGS**, decd.]

658. Page 439. 11 Sep 1813. Lewis B. **NEAL** to
John **LOGAN**, both of New Madrid Co., Mo.
For the sum of $1000, 450 arpens in Tywappity
Bottom, adjoining Stephen **QUIMBY** on the
lower side and Daniel **MULLINS** on the upper
side, and being the same formerly belonging to
Rober **LANE**. Sd **NEAL** agrees to obtain a
patent for the tract from the government. Signed
Lewis B. **NEAL**, Elizabeth (x) **NEAL** [wife of
Lewis B. **NEAL**]. Wit Javan **McCAY** (JP in
Madison Co., Miss.), Rhoday **McCAY**, W. H.
WINSTON, Clerk of Madison Co, Miss. Court,
Thomas **BIBB**, Justice of Madison Co., Miss.
County Court. [By 11 Oct 1813, **NEAL** had
moved to Madison Co., Miss.] Rec 1 Feb 1814.

659. Page 440. 24 Aug 1805. John **LOSLA** to
Louis **LORIMIER**. For the sum of $70, all the
works and improvement for a place opposite the
Cypress Island. Signed John **LOSLA**. Test B.
COUSIN, G. **HENDERSON** (JP). Rec 9 Feb
1814.

660. Page 440. 28 Mar 1806. Jonathan
FORMAN to same. For ___, an improvement on
the land of sd **LORIMIER**. Signed Jona.
FORMAN, B. **COUSIN**. Wit G.
HENDERSON (JP). Rec 9 Feb 1814.

661. Page 440. 29 Nov 1806. Edward
ROBERSON to same. For the sum of $300, land
on the edge of the cypress swamps where he
formerly lived. Signed Edward (ER)
ROBERTSON. Test B. **COUSIN**, Gme.
LORIMIER, G. **HENDERSON** (JP). Rec 9
Feb 1814.

662. Page 441. 21 Aug 1813. William **CLARK**,
Governor of Missouri Terr, to Ezekiel
RUBOTTOM. Appointment as JP for St.
Francis Twp in Cape Girardeau Co. for four
years. Signed William **CLARK**, Governor. Wit
Frederick **BATES**, Secretary. Ezekiel
RUBOTTOM takes the oath of Office. Signed
Ezekiel **RUBOTTOM**. Wit J. **McFERRON**.
Rec 15 Mar 1814.

663. Page 441. 25 Mar 1814. Joseph **SEAWELL**
and Prudence, his wife, to John **DAVIS**, John
SHEPPARD, Samuel G. **DUNN**, Abraham
BYRD, and Benjamin **SHELL**, Commissioners
of the Courthouse and Jail of Cape Girardeau Co,
for the use of sd County. For the sum of $1 and
for the good causes, 55 acres on the waters of
Hubble's Creek, beginning at the creek; bounded
on the W & N by sd **SEAWELL**, E by Samuel
PUGH, and S by land purchased by the
commissioners of Wm. H. **ASHLEY**. Signed
Jos. **SEAWELL**, Prudence **SEAWELL**. Wit A.
BURNS, Will. **PENNY**, Isaac **SHEPPARD**
(JCCP). Rec 25 Mar 1814.

664. Page 441. 25 Mar 1814. Jesse
KRUTCHELOE by Sheriff John **HAYS** to
Peter **CRAIG**. For the sum of $51.50, 270 acres,
being the moiety of a tract where Eli **SHELBY**
now lives; bounded on the W by Peter Widow
WEAVER, E by John **WEAVER** and Joseph
THOMPSON, S by David **HARRISS**. Sold on
7 Nov 1813 on a writ of execution issued by CCP
on 14 Aug 1813 on a judgment in favor of
Erasmus **ELLIS** and against sd
KRUTCHELOE for $80 damages for
nonperformance of a covenant, and $17.47 and 5
mills costs. Signed John **HAYS**, Sheriff. Wit
Joseph **McFERRON**, Clerk. Rec 25 Mar 1814.

665. Page 442. 26 Mar 1814. Robert **GREEN**,
Isaac **SHEPPARD**, and William **KELSO**, all
Judges of the CCP of Cape Girardeau Co., to the
heirs of Louis **LORIMIER**, decd. Quit claim to

4 acres in Cape Girardeau, bounded on the E by Spanish St, W by Lorimier St, and divided in half by Themis St. Sd land was deeded by sd **LORIMIER** on 29 Jul 1804 to the Cape Girardeau Dist so long as Cape Girardeau remained the seat of justice for the district. The seat of justice was removed [to Jackson] on 17 Nov 1813 by the present commissioners, so this deed returns the land to sd heirs. Signed Robt. **GREEN**, Isaac **SHEPPARD**, William **KELSO**. Wit David **GREEN**, Morgan **BYRNE**, B. **COUSIN**, George **HENDERSON** (JP). Rec 26 Mar 1814.

666. Page 443. 12 Jul 1809. John **McCARTY** and Nathan, his son, to John **HAYS**. For the sum of $50, 275 arpens on Byrd's Creek adjoining Bartholomew **COUSIN** and others, being ½ of a tract purchased by John **McCARTY** from Jacob **KELLEY**. If title is not confirmed, sd **HAYS** is only to receive half of any settlement from sd **KELLEY** and agrees to pay half of the costs of any suit related to the land. Signed John **McCARTY**, Nathan W. **McCARTY**. Wit Robt. **GREEN** (JCCP), Geo. **HENDERSON** (JP). Rec 29 Mar 1814.

667. Page 443. 2 Jun 1812. Malinda **WADE** of Lincoln Co., Ky. to George **HENDERSON**, Esq. Power of attorney to settle her business, late the business of her decd husband David **WADE**. Signed Malinda **WADE**. Test Jordan G. **JOHNS**, John D. **THURMOND**, Thomas **HELM** (Clerk of Lincoln Co., Ky.), James **HICKMAN** (Presiding Justice in the Commission of the Peace in Lincoln Co., Ky.). Rec 5 Apr 1814.

668. Page 444. 9 Mar 1814. Same to John D. **THURMOND**, her brother. Power of attorney to make a settlement with George **HENDERSON** for her business, collect any money that has been collected for her, and to sue and force settlement if needed. Signed Malinda **WADE**. Test Bennett **THURMOND**, George **BIBB**, Thomas **HELM** (Clerk of Lincoln Co., Ky.), James **HICKMAN** (Presiding Justice in the Commission of the Peace in Lincoln Co., Ky.). Rec 5 Apr 1814.

669. Page 444. 5 Oct 1813. John **PATTERSON** and Eleanor, his wife, to Abraham **DAUGHERTY**. For the sum of $500, 135 acres, more or less, on the waters of Hubble's Creek; bounded on the E by sd **DAUGHERTY**, W by Elijah **DAUGHERTY**, N by William **DAUGHERTY**, and S by Andrew **SUMMERS**. Signed John **PATTERSON**, Eleanor (*) **PATTERSON**. Wit Havens C. (x)

ABERNETHIE, John K. (x) **ABERNETHIE**, Jno. **ABERNETHIE** (JP). Rec 5 Apr 1814.

670. Page 445. 30 Aug 1813. Enoch **EVANS** and Amelia, his wife, to Thomas **ENGLISH**. For the sum of $300, 100 acres on Ramsey Creek, beginning at a Spanish oak and stone, being part of a tract granted to Peter **GODAIR** by the Spanish Government and conveyed by sd **GODAIR** to sd **EVANS**. Signed Enoch **EVANS**, Amelia **EVANS**. Wit John **RAMSEY** (JCCP). Rec 6 Apr 1814.

671. Page 445. 24 Dec 1811. George W. **COCHRAN** and Betcy, his wife, to Joseph **YOUNG**. For the sum of $125, 50 acres off the S end of their part of a 600 arpen tract granted to Amos **BYRD**, now decd, and confirmed to his heirs, of which they represent one heir; bounded on the S by John **BYRD**'s tract originally granted to James **COOPER**, E by same, and W by Jonathan **BUICE**. Signed Geo. W. **COCHRAN**, Betsey **COCHRAN**. Wit John **WILSON**, Jonathan **BUIS**, John **DAVIS** (JP). Rec 8 Apr 1814.

672. Page 446. 25 Nov 1813. Wilson **McCLENDON** to Joel **RENFROE**. For the sum of $550, 170 arpens adjoining Thomas **MORGAN**. Signed Wilson (x) **McCLENDON**, Sarah (x) **McCLENDON** (RD). Test Robert **ENGLISH**, Thos. **ENGLISH** junr, Enoch **EVANS** (JP). Rec 8 Apr 1814.

673. Page 446. 26 Feb 1813. John **BYRD** to Joseph **YOUNG**. For the sum of $1600, bond to make a deed on 300 arpents, French measure, confirmed by the Board of Commissioners to sd **BYRD**, being the same where sd **YOUNG** now lives, and to be taken out of the W end of the survey made for James **COOPER**; the original survey bounded on the N by Amos **BYRD**, decd, now Joseph **YOUNG**, W by Elijah **EVERET**, decd, S by Edward F. **BOND**, and E by Stephen **BYRD**. The deed is to be made as soon as the survey can be completed on sd land. Signed John **BYRD**. Wit Nathan **McCARTY**, Robert **PATTERSON**, G. **HENDERSON** (JP). Rec 13 Apr 1814.

674. Page 447. 30 Aug 1813. Thomas **ENGLISH** and Jane, his wife, to Joseph **LEWIS**. For the sum of $300, 100 acres on the waters of Randell's Creek near Kenyon's Spring, being part of a tract granted to Jeremiah **THOMPSON**, and sold by sd **THOMPSON** to sd **ENGLISH**, beginning at a black oak at sd **LEWIS**' corner. Signed Thomas ( ) **ENGLISH**,

Jane (x) **ENGLISH** (RD). Wit John **RAMSEY** (JCCP). Rec 30 May 1814.

675. Page 447. 1 Jun 1814. Frederick **BATES**, Secretary of Missouri Terr, to Bartholomew **COUSIN**. Appointment as Surveyor for Cape Girardeau Co. Bartholomew **COUSIN** takes the oath of office. Signed B. **COUSIN**. Wit J. **McFERRON**, Clerk, CCP. Rec 14 Jun 1814.

676. Page 448. 21 Jun 1814. Bartholomew **COUSIN** and Daniel F. **STEINBECK** to the Governor of Missouri Terr. For the sum of $2000, bond to guarantee that sd **COUSIN** will perform the duties of Surveyor of Cape Girardeau Co. Signed B. **COUSIN**, D. F. **STEINBECK**. Test Robt. **GREEN** (JCCP), Isaac **SHEPPARD** (JCCP), Wm. **KELSO** (JCCP), J. **McFERRON**, Clerk. Rec 22 Jun 1814.

677. Page 448. 22 Jun 1814. John **HAYS**, Daniel F. **STEINBECK**, and Levi **WOLVERTON** to same. For the sum of $5000, bond to guarantee that sd **HAYS** will collect and pay all taxes for Cape Girardeau Co. for which he may be chargeable. Signed John **HAYS**, D. F. **STEINBECK**, Levi **WOLVERTON**. Wit William J. **STEPHENSON**. Test Robt. **GREEN** (JCCP), Isaac **SHEPPARD** (JCCP), Wm. **KELSO** (JCCP), J. **McFERRON**, Clerk. Rec 22 Jun 1814.

678. Page 448. 5 Feb 1805. Zebulon **REED** to Lewis **DICKSON**. For the sum of $105 in a note for salt @ $3/bushel, all his claim that he is entitled to as an inhabitant of the Cape Girardeau Dist. Signed Zebulon **REED**. Wit Charles **DEMOSS**, Martha **DEMOSS**, Wm. **KELSO** (JCCP). Rec 25 Jul 1814.

679. Page 448. 1 Aug 1814. George **RUDDLE** of New Madrid Co., Mo. to Jonas **MENEFEE**, agent for Jarrot **MENEFEE** of Fayette Co., Ky. For the sum of $200, 100 arpents on the waters of Hubble's Creek, adjoining James **FARRIS** and Isaac **RUDDELL** on the W and Raney **BRUMMET** on the S. Signed George **RUDDLE**. Wit John **MASSEY**, David **HOLLEY**, John **ABERNETHIE** (JP). Rec 1 Aug 1814.

680. Page 449. 30 Jul 1814. Raney **BRUMMET** to George **RUDDLE**, both of New Madrid Co., Mo. For the sum of $450, 433 1/3 arpens on the waters of Hubble's Creek, adjoining Joseph **FITE** and John **LUSLAY**, and being part of a tract granted to sd **BRUMMET** by the Spanish Government. Signed Raney (x) **BRUMMET**. Wit Enoch **EVANS** (JP). Rec 6 Aug 1814.

681. Page 449. 19 Nov 1813. David **BRYANT** by Sheriff John **HAYS** to Daniel F. **STEINBECK**. For the sum of $100, the E moiety of Lot No. 14, Range E in Cape Girardeau; bounded on the E by Charles G. **ELLIS**, W by the other half of the lot, and S by Harmony St. Sold on 20 Jul 1813 on seven writs of execution issued against sd **BRYANT** by CCP on 9 Jun 1813; three in favor of Daniel **HARCKELRODE** and against sd **BRYANT**-- for $40 debt and interest from 1 Jun 1812, $1.18 costs when the case was heard before George **HENDERSON**, JP, and $4.30 costs when the case was heard by CCP; for $36.80 debt and interest from 15 Jun 1812, $1.18 and $4.27 costs; and in favor of Daniel **HARCKELRODE** as assignee of Isaac **WORLEY**, who was assignee of John C. **HARBISON**, for $10 debt and interest from 5 May 1812, $1.03 and $4.12 costs- -; one in favor of James **PHILLIPS** for $39.50 debt and interest from 13 Jul 1812, $0.63 and $4.20 costs; and three in favor of William J. **STEPHENSON**, agent for Danl. F. **STEINBECK**--for $23.96 debt and interest from 22 Jun 1812, $1.03 and $4.22 and five mills costs; against sd **PHILLIPS** and sd **BRYANT** for $10.54 debt and interest from 20 Dec 1811, $1.73 and $4.22 costs; and against sd **PHILLIPS** and sd **BRYANT** for $13.50 debt and interest from 17 Feb 1812, $1.73 and $4.22 and five mills costs. Signed John **HAYS**, Sheriff. Wit J. **McFERRON**, Clerk. Rec 28 Oct 1814.

682. Page 453. 25 Mar 1814. Daniel F. **STEINBECK** and Levi **WOLVERTON**, adminrs of Peter **GODAIR**, decd, by same to same. For the sum of $20, lot in Cape Girardeau; bounded on the N & S by John **RANDOL**, W by Enoch **EVANS**, and E fronted by the public square. Sold on 13 Nov 1813 on two writs of execution issued by CCP on 17 Aug 1813 against sd **STEINBECK** and sd **WOLVERTON**, adminrs of sd **GODIER**, decd; one in favor of James **CARICO** for the use of Ephraim **HUBBARD** for $115 damages for nonpayment of a receipt made to sd **CARRICO** by sd **GODAIR** in his lifetime, and for $20.56 costs of sd **CARRICO** for the use of sd **HUBBARD**; the other in favor of William **HOLMES** by James **RAVENSCROFT**, his agent, for $25 debt, and $5.37 damages, and $24.36 costs. Signed John **HAYS**, Sheriff. Wit Joseph **McFERRON**, Clerk. Rec 28 Oct 1814.

683. Page 454. 7 Nov 1814. Andrew **RAMSEY** senior and Eve, his wife, to same. For the sum of $1000, 480 arpens, more or less, on the E side of Ramsey's Creek; bounded on the N by the heirs of Louis **LORIMIER**, decd, widow George C. C. **HARBISON**, and the tract where sd **RAMSEY** now resides, S by Peter **GODAIR**, decd, and vacant lands in the Big Swamp, E by vacant lands, and W by sd **RAMSEY**'s home tract and Peter **GODAIR**, decd. Sd tract is conveyed agreeable to the original survey made for Edward **ROBERTSON**, from whom sd **RAMSEY** purchased the same, and includes any additional land that may be granted by the U. S. government by virtue of a settlement of the tract being continued by their son James. Signed Andrew **RAMSEY** senr, Eve (x) **RAMSEY**. Wit James **RAMSEY**, Charles **BRADLEY**, G. **HENDERSON** (JP). Rec 8 Nov 1814.

684. Page 455. 25 Oct 1814. John **MILLER** and Nancy **WILSON**. Marriage contract. Sd Nancy owns one bed and bedding and five head of horse creatures, and she shall hold sd property free and independent of sd **MILLER**, and any property she acquires by trade or commerce shall be hers alone. Upon their marriage, sd **WILSON** also agrees to convey 4 tracts which he purchased of John **McLAUGHLIN** to her; 4 arpents front and 40 back in Point Coupe Parish on the Mississippi; 320 acres in the Concordia Parish, La. on Black River, adjoining Reuben **WHITE**; 320 acres in Catahoula Parish, La., adjoining James **WRITE**; and 400 acres in Catahoula Parish, La., adjoining Nicholas **SEVERS**. After the marriage is consummated, sd **MILLER** is to convey to sd **WILSON** 10,000 acres in Missouri. Sd land is then to be sold and the sales to be laid out by her in either negros or stock for her use. One-half of the land is to be vested in Nancy **WILSON** for her free and absolute disposal. Sd **MILLER** also agrees to will her $1200 of personal property as soon as the marriage is consummated. Should either party die, then the other is to hold all the personal property for their natural life. Signed John **MILLER**, Nancy **WILSON**. Wit John **WILSON** junr, John **LOGAN**, John **WILSON**, John **DAVIS** (JP). Rec 10 Nov 1814.

685. Page 456. 31 Jan 1814. Thomas **ENGLISH** senr to Samuel G. **DUNN**. For the sum of $250, one negro girl named **Easter** about 10 years of age. Signed Thomas (T) **ENGLISH**. Wit John **BEARDSLEY** (JP), Margaret (x) **McCLUSKEY**. Rec 22 Nov 1814.

686. Page 456. 13 Dec 1814. John **LOGAN** and Mary, his wife and widow of Louis **LORIMIER**, decd, to Daniel F. **STEINBECK**, one of the heirs and for the heirs of sd **LORIMIER**. For the sum of $8000, quit claim to all their interest in the estate of sd **LORIMIER**, arising from the marriage of sd Mary **LOGAN** to sd **LORIMIER**. Signed John **LOGAN**, Mary **LOGAN**. Wit B. **COUSIN**, Zenas **PRIEST**, G. **HENDERSON** (JP). Rec 14 Dec 1814.

687. Page 456. 4 Jan 1815. Andrew **RAMSEY** junior and Patsy, his wife, to James **RAMSEY**. For the sum of $30, 400 arpens on White Water Creek; adjoining Jacob **SHEPPARD**, late John P. **ADUNAR**; and being the tract Andrew **RAMSEY** junior bought of John **HAYS**, Sheriff, on 25 Mar 1809. Signed Andw. **RAMSEY**, Patsey ( ) **RAMSEY**. Wit Enoch **EVANS** (JP). Rec 6 Jan 1815.

688. Page 457. 21 Sep 1812. James **COTTLE** and Susana, his wife, to Jesse **KINCHELOE** and Eli **SHELBY**. For the sum of $405, 270 acres on the left hand fork of Ramsey's Creek; bounded on the S by the heirs of Joseph **THOMPSON** and vacant land, W by Ann Eva **WEAVER**, widow of Peter **WEAVER**, N by vacant land, and E by John **WEAVER**. Signed James **COTTLE**, Susanah (x) **COTTLE** (RD). Wit Enoch **EVANS** (JP). Rec 18 Jan 1815.

689. Page 457. 3 Feb 1815. Martin **RODNEY** and John **RODNEY** to Silvenus **CASTLEMAN** of Tenn. For the sum of $1200, 359 acres on Hubble's Creek, being part of Martin **RODNEY**'s head right and being where Martin **RODNEY** now lives except for 1 acre in the NW corner; beginning at an ash at Michael **RODNEY**'s and John **AKIN**'s lines, and also bounded by Wm. **MATHEWS**. Signed Martin **RODNEY**, Jno. **RODNEY**. Wit G. **HENDERSON** (JP). Rec 4 Feb 1815.

690. Page 458. 28 Sep 1814. William **CLARK**, Governor of Missouri Terr, to Joseph **McFERRON**. Appointment as Clerk of the Cape Girardeau Co. Court. Signed William **CLARK**, Governor. Wit Frederick **BATES**, Secretary. Joseph **McFERRON** takes the oath of Office. Signed Joseph **McFERRON**. Wit William **KELSO**. Rec 4 Feb 1815.

691. Page 458. 1 Mar 1815. Same to same. Appointment as Clerk of the Circuit Court of Cape Girardeau Co. Signed William **CLARK**, Governor. Rec 3 Apr 1815.

692. Page 458. 4 Oct 1811. David **DOWNARD** of Campbell Co., Ky., formerly of Cape Girardeau, to Obadiah **SCOT**. Assignment of all his right to any lands in Upper La., with the agreement that he is not liable to refund any price or payment made as the consideration of this conveyance. Signed David **DOWNARD**. Wit Richd. **SOUTHGATE**, Geo. **GORDON**, Deputy Clerk of Campbell Co., Ky. Acknowledged by **DOWNARD** 24 Jan 1812, recorded in Book D, page 81. Rec 3 Apr 1815.

693. Page 459. 14 Jan 1815. Daniel **HARKLEROAD** and Elizabeth, his wife, to Samuel **ALLEN**. For the sum of $600, lot in Cape Girardeau where sd **HARKLEROAD** now lives, fronting on the Mississippi, assigned to sd **HARKLEROAD** by Henry **HAND** on 12 Dec 1809 and by relinquishment of the dower rights of Sarah **HAND**, wife of Henry **HAND**, on 3 Mar 1812; originally purchased of Louis **LORIMIER**, decd, on 27 Mar 1806. The assignments appear on the back of the deed. Signed Dannal **HARKKLEROAD**, Elizabeth (x) **HARKKLEROAD**. Wit G. **HENDERSON** (JP), Wm. **MARTIN**, Abraham **ALLEN**. Rec 30 Apr 1815.

694. Page 460. 8 Feb 1814. Wm. H. **ASHLEY** and Mary, his wife, of Washington Co., Mo. to John **DAVIS**, John **SHEPPARD**, Saml. G. **DUNN**, Abriham **BYRD**, and Benjn. **SHELL**, Commissioners of the Courthouse and Jail of Cape Girardeau Co. For the sum of $500, 50 acres on the waters of Hubble's Creek, beginning at a stone on the NW corner of sd **ASHLEY's** survey; bounded on the W by Wm. **NEALY**, S by Wm. H. **ASHLEY**, E by sd **ASHLEY**, and N by Joseph **SEAWELL**. Signed William H. **ASHLEY**, Mary **ASHLEY** (RD). Wit John **THOMPSON**, Wm. **NEELY**, John **BRICKEY** (JP in Washington Co., Mo.), W. **CHRISTY** (JCCP, St. Louis Co.). Rec 9 May 1815. [This is the deed for the site of the town of Jackson.]

695. Page 461. 29 Apr 1815. William **CLARK**, Governor of Missouri Terr, to Joseph **McFERRON**. Appointment as Clerk of the Cape Girardeau Co. Court. Signed William **CLARK**, Governor. Wit Frederick **BATES**, Secretary. Rec 12 May 1815.

696. Page 461. 21 Mar 1815. John **RAMSEY** to Andrew **RAMSEY**, son of John, William **CRACRAFT**, and Thomas W. **GRAVES**. For the sum of $600, 246 arpens on Hubble's Creek, known as Sheridan's mill place; sold by Sheridan to Ezekiel **ABLE**, by sd **ABLE** to Joshua

GOZA, by sd **GOZA** to Blemus **HAYDEN**, and by sd **HAYDEN** to John **RAMSEY**; and bounded on the E by John **BURROWS**, N by Alexander **SUMERS** and John **SUMMERS**, Thomas W. **GRAVES**, and James **DOWTY**. Signed John **RAMSEY**. Wit Enoch **EVANS** (JP). Rec 14 May 1815.

[End of Deed Book C]

[Deed Book D]

697. Page 1. 15 Dec 1813. Francis **CLARK** of St. Francis Twp to William **RUSSELL** of St. Louis, Mo. For the sum of $50, 640 acres, more or less, about four miles W of St. Francis River on Logan's Creek, in St. Francis Twp; being the same that sd **CLARK** cultivated in 1804 and ever since, and where sd **CLARK** now lives. Sd **RUSSELL** to have no recourse if title is not confirmed. Signed Francis (x) **CLARK**. Wit J. O. **LOGAN**, Charles **LUCAS**, George **TOMPKINS**, Judge, St. Louis Co. CCP. Rec 19 May 1815.

698. Page 1. 21 Jun 1814. Belemus **HAYDEN** to Thomas W. **GRAVES**. For the sum of $500, one negro man named **Ause**(?) or **Roger**. Signed Belemus **HAYDEN**. Wit Samuel **RAVENSCROFT**, John R. **HAYDEN**, G. **HENDERSON** (JP). Wit 24 May 1815.

699. Page 1. 31 Jul 1812. James **COX** senr and Elizabeth, his wife, to James **COX** junr. For the sum of $400, 238 arpens, French measure, adjoining Simon **KEYNON**, Robert **CRAWFORD** formerly Thos. **ENGLISH** senr, Joel **RENFROE**, Web **HADEN** formerly S. **STROTHERS**, and James **FLIN**; beginning on the line that joins **FLIN**; and being where Jas. **COX** jur and his family now live. Signed James (x) **COX** senr, Elizabeth (x) **COX**. Wit William **HITT**, Benjamin **HITT**, Jno. **ABERNETHIE** (JP). Rec 3 Jun 1815.

700. Page 2. 16 Dec 1813. Simmons **KENON** and Elizabeth, his wife, to same. For the sum of $18, 6 acres, more or less, adjoining sd **KENON**, sd **COX**, and James **COX** senr. Signed Simmons ( ) **KENON**, Elizabeth (x) **KENON**. Wit James **SMITH**, Benjamin **HITT**, Jno. **ABERNETHIE** (JP). Rec 3 Jun 1815.

701. Page 3. 17 Dec 1814. Commissioners of the Courthouse and Jail to Anthony **NEELY**. For the sum of $51, Lot No. 27 in Jackson; bounded on the S and fronted by Main St, E and fronted by first east street, N by Lot No. 26, and W by Lot

No. 3. Signed John **DAVIS**, John **SHEPPARD**, Samuel G. **DUNN**, Abraham **BYRD**, Benja. **SHELL**. Wit Thos. **NEALE**, A. P. **PATTERSON**, Jno. **ABERNETHIE** (JP). Rec 15 Jun 1815.

702. Page 4. 25 Feb 1815. William **CLARK**, Governor of Mo. Terr, to Robert **GREEN**. Appointment as JP for Byrd Twp for four years. Signed Wm. **CLARK**, Governor. Wit Frederick **BATES**, Sec. of Mo. Terr. Robert **GREEN** takes the oath of office. Signed Robt. **GREEN**. Wit J. **McFERRON**. Rec 30 Jun 1815.

703. Page 4. 12 Mar 1815. Elijah **BETTIS** and Elisabeth **ROBERSON**. Marriage contract, with both to retain all the property they now possess, with the right to dispose of the same and its increase. Signed Elijah **BETTIS**, Elizabeth (x) **ROBERSON**. Wit Jacob **KELLEY** (JP), Overton **BETTIS**. Rec 4 Jul 1815.

704. Page 5. 30 Jul 1814. Radford **ELLIS** to John **DUNN**. For the sum of $1700, five negroes, one man named **Samabso**, his wife **Caty**, **Mary**, **Jessee**, and **Isabella**. Signed Radford **ELLIS**. Test Samuel G. **DUNN**, Wm. (x) **TOLOR**(?). John **DAVIS** (JP). Rec 9 Jul 1815.

705. Page 5. 12 Jun 1815. William **CLARK**, Governor of Mo. Terr, to Thomas **NUBERRY**. Appointment as JP for German Twp for four years. Signed Wm. **CLARK**, Governor. Wit Frederick **BATES**, Sec. of Mo. Terr. Thomas **NEWBERRY** takes the oath of office. Signed Thos. **NEWBERRY**. Wit J. **McFERRON**. Rec 4 Aug 1815.

706. Page 5. 12 Jun 1815. William **CLARK**, Governor of Mo. Terr, to James **RUSSELL**. Appointment as JP for Byrd Twp for four years. Signed Wm. **CLARK**, Governor. Wit Frederick **BATES**, Sec. of Mo. Terr. James **RUSSELL** takes the oath of office. Signed James **RUSSELL**. Wit J. **McFERRON**. Rec 29 Aug 1815.

707. Page 6. 10 Sep 1815. George **HENDERSON** to John **HAYS**. For the sum of $1, ¼ part of a tract sold to sd **HENDERSON** and Anthony **HADEN** by sheriff's deed as the property of William **SMITH**. Sd **HAYS** is to have no recourse should title not be confirmed. Signed George **HENDERSON**. Wit Joseph **McFERRON**, Robt. **GREEN** (JP). Rec 13 Sep 1815.

708. Page 6. 10 Sep 1815. Same to same. For the sum of $1, 200 arpens adjoining John **McCARTY**, James **BOYD**, and others; being the same sd **HENDERSON** bought by sheriff's deed on two executions against sd **McCARTY** in suits by **BRYAN & MORRISSON** and Charles **LUCAS**. Sd **HAYS** is to have no recourse should title not be confirmed. Signed George **HENDERSON**. Wit Joseph **McFERRON**, Robt. **GREEN** (JP). Rec 13 Sep 1815.

709. Page 6. 10 Sep 1815. Same to same and William J. **STEPHENSON**. For the sum of $1, 300 acres that was the head right of Andrew **FRANKS** adjoining the Big Swamp; being the same sold to sd **HENDERSON** by sheriff's deed on an execution against James **BOYD** and for Antoine **SOULARD**. Sd **HAYS** and **STEPHENSON** are to have no recourse should title not be confirmed. Signed George **HENDERSON**. Wit Joseph **McFERRON**, Robt. **GREEN** (JP). Rec 13 Sep 1815.

710. Page 7. 24 Jun 1815. Gilbert **HECKTOR** and Anna, his wife, to John **THOMPSON**. For the sum of $200, 100 acres on the waters of Hubble's Creek, being part of a survey on which sd **HECKTOR** now lives, originally granted to him; beginning at the SW corner of the original survey; bounded on the S by Henry **HAND** and other lands of John **HAND**, decd, NE by sd **HECKTOR**, and W by Andrew **BURNS**. Signed Gilbert (x) **HECKTOR**, Anna (x) **HECKTOR**. Wit John **DAVIS** (JP). Rec 30 Sep 1815.

711. Page 8. 30 Sep 1815. William **CLARK**, Governor of Mo. Terr, to John **HAYS**. Appointment as Sheriff of Cape Girardeau Co. for two years. Signed Wm. **CLARK**, Governor. Wit Frederick **BATES**, Sec. of Mo. Terr. John **HAYS** takes the oath of office. Signed John **HAYS**. Wit J. **McFERRON**. Rec 20 Oct 1815.

712. Page 8. 20 Oct 1815. John **HAYS**, William **NEELY**, Joseph **SEAWELL**, and Samul **PEW** to William **CLARK**, Governor of Mo. Terr. For the sum of $5000, bond to guarantee that sd **HAYS** will perform the duties of the office of Sheriff of Cape Girardeau Co. Signed John **HAYS**, Wm. **NEELY**, Jos. **SEAWELL**, Samuel **PEW**. Wit William **KELSO**, Joseph **McFERRON**, John **DAVIS** (JP). Rec 20 Oct 1815.

713. Page 8. 20 Oct 1815. Same, same, same, and same to same. For the sum of $2000, bond to guarantee that sd **HAYS** will collect and pay to the Territorial Treasury, all taxes and other money collected by him. Signed John **HAYS**, Wm. **NEELY**, Jos. **SEAWELL**, Samuel **PEW**. Wit William **KELSO**, Joseph **McFERRON**, John **DAVIS** (JP). Also attested to by William **KELSO**, John **DAVIS**, and Robt. **GREEN**, County Court Justices. Rec 20 Oct 1815.

714. Page 9. 29 Apr 1815. William H. **ASHLEY** and Mary, his wife, of Washington Co., Mo. to Richard S. **THOMAS**. For the sum of $1790, part in hand and the remainder to be paid, 478 arpens and 60 perches, more or less, nine or ten miles W of Cape Girardeau, except for 50 acres in the NW corner previously sold to the Commissioners of the Courthouse and Jail, whereon Jackson is laid off; beginning at a stone; being the same originally granted by the Spanish Government to Henry **SHARADIN**, a German, and surveyed by order of Zenon **TRUDEAU**, Lt. Gov., by Antoine **SOULARD**, Surveyor Gen., on 2 Oct 1799. Sd tract was assigned by sd **SHARADIN** to Ezekiel **ABLE**, and by him to sd **ASHLEY**, and was confirmed to sd **ASHLEY** by the Commissioners on 26 Nov 1810. Signed William H. **ASHLEY**, Mary **ASHLEY**. Wit L. **BROWNE**, D. **BARTON**, Judge of Northern Circuit. Rec 23 Oct 1815.

715. Page 10. 18 Oct 1815. David **STRICKLAND** senr to Daniel F. **STEINBECK**. For the sum of $200, 800 arpens, more or less, on the forks of Cape la Cruche Creek; being the same sd **STRICKLAND** settled, inhabited, and cultivated during the Spanish Government. Signed D. **STRICKLAND**. Wit Wm. J. **STEPHENSON**, Enoch **EVANS** (JP). Rec 24 Oct 1815.

716. Page 10. 10 July 1815. John **RODNEY** to Solvenus **CASTLEMAN**. For the sum of $16, 8 ½ arpens on the waters of Hubbel's Creek; beginning at a stake and stone and black gum; adjoined by John **AKIN** on the S & W, sd **CASTLEMAN** on the S, and Louis **LOROMIER** on the E. Signed John **RODNEY**. Wit Martin **RODNEY**, Enoch **EVANS** (JP). Rec 15 Nov 1815.

717. Page 11. 19 Sep 1815. John **BYRD** to Martin **COTNER**. For the sum of $500, one negro girl named **Win**. Signed John **BYRD**. Wit Hugh **CRESWELL**, Leonard **WELCKER**, John **DAVIS** (JP). Rec 17 Nov 1815.

718. Page 11. 10 Jul 1815. Eve **HAYS**, now of Cape Girardeau Co. and formerly of Westmoreland Co., Pa., swears that on about 3 Apr 1788 she was present in her own house in Westmoreland Co., Pa., and saw Elizabeth **HENDERSON**, widow of Capt. John **HENDERSON**, decd, lawfully married to Thomas **NEELY** by John **MILLER**, Esq. Sd Thomas and Elizabeth **NEELY** continued to live together until the end of Dec 1799, during which time they had five children, two of which are living, a daughter named Eve and a son named Jacob **HAYS**. Signed Eve (x) **HAYS**. Wit George **HENDERSON** (JP), George **HAYS**. Rec 20 Nov 1815.

719. Page 11. 10 Dec 1814. Lewis **TASH** and Mary, his wife, of Johnson Co., Ill. to John **BURNS**. For the sum of $600, 200 arpens, French measure, being part of a survey on which sd **TASH** formerly lived; to be taken off the E end of sd survey to include the plantation; bounded on the N by Abraham **RANDOL**, E by Anthony **RANDOL**, and S by Abraham **BYRD**; beginning at a stone and stake near a pond, being the SE corner of sd survey. Signed Lewis **TASH**, Mary (x) **TASH** (RD). Wit John **DAVIS** (JP), George **BOYCE**, William **KELSO** (JCCP). Rec 21 Nov 1815.

720. Page 12. 1 Sep 1815. William **CLARK**, Governor of Mo. Terr, to John **LANDERS**. Appointment as JP in St. Francis Twp for four years. Signed Wm. **CLARK**, Governor. Wit Frederick **BATES**, Sec. of Mo. Terr. John **LANDERS** takes the oath of office. Signed John **LANDERS**. Wit J. **McFERRON**. Rec 28 Nov 1815.

721. Page 13. 30 Nov 1815. George **RUDDELL** of Lawrence Co., Mo. Terr. [now Ark.] to James **FARRIS**. For the sum of $700, 300 arpens on the waters of Hubbell's Creek where sd **FARRIS** and family now live; being part of the land granted to Rainey **BRUMMETT** by the Spanish Government, and conveyed by sd **BRUMMITT** to sd **RUDDELL** on 30 Jul 1814; beginning on the **LOSLEA**'s line; adjoining Blemus **HADEN**, formerly **LOSLEA**'s, the heirs of Joseph **FITE**, decd, heirs of **McCRACKEN** that was formerly Rainey **BRUMMITT**'s, and land formerly belonging to John **LAYTHAM** and now James **DOWTY**'s. Signed George **RUDDELL**. Wit William **WILLIAMS**, Ch. S. **HEMPSTEAD**, Jno. **ABERNETHIE** (JP). Rec 30 Nov 1815.

722. Page 13. 7 Sep 1814. John C. **HARBISON** and Sarah, his wife, to Rebecca **HARBISON**. For the sum of $500, all of the rights and credits to real and personal property of George C. C.

HARBISON, decd, in either Mo. or Ken. Signed John C. **HARBISON**, Sarah (x) **HARBISON**. Wit W. **GARNER**, Wm. **KELSO** (JP). Rec 8 Dec 1815.

723. Page 14. 24 Nov 1814. Benjamin **ANTHONY** by Sheriff John **HAYS** to Richard S. **THOMAS** of Ste. Genevieve Co., Mo. For the sum of $200, 450 arpens on the waters of White Water where sd **ANTHONY** now lives; adjoining Daniel **BOLLINGER** and others, and being the head right grant of Jeremiah **BENIGH**, decd. Sold on 24 Nov 1814 on an execution issued by the Court of Common Pleas on 26 Jul 1814, in a session held at the meeting house on the plantation of Thomas **BULL**, against sd **ANTHONY** and Cyrus **LITTLE** and for Matthew **HUBBLE** for $65 damages and $74.48 and 5 mills costs in consequence of their disposing of a certain gelding that was sd **HUBBLE**'s property. Signed John **HAYS**, Shff. Wit Joseph **McFERRON**, Clerk. Rec 22 Dec 1815.

724. Page 15. 28 Dec 1815. William **WILLIAMS** to William **RUSSELL** of St. Louis, Mo. For the sum of $100, 460 arpens, more or less, on the waters of Hubbel's Creek, being part of Thomas **FOSTER**'s settlement right claim of 800 arpens. The claim depended on the testimony of Robert **CRUMP** taken on 20 Dec 1813 before the Recorder of Land Titles; which tract was then claimed by William **RUSSELL** in notice No. 63(?). Sd **FOSTER** has conveyed the whole of the tract to sd **WILLIAMS**. If only 340 arpens or less shall be held on the claim, then sd **RUSSELL** is to have no part thereof, but is to have any of it over 340 arpens. Signed William **WILLIAMS**, Wm. **RUSSELL**. Wit Thos. **STEWART**, Jesse **HAIL**, John **DAVIS** (JP). Rec 29 Dec 1815.

725. Page 16. 26 Mar 1808. John C. **HARBISON** to **REINECKE & STEINBECK**. For the sum of $250, 250 arpens, part of 1000 arpens that sd **HARBISON** purchased at sheriff's sale as the property of Louis F. **LARGUAU** in 1805. Signed John C. **HARBISON**. Wit Saml. **BRADLEY**, G. **HENDERSON** (JP). Rec 30 Dec 1815.

726. Page 16. 10 Mar 1812. John **BYRD** and Betsy, his wife, to John **WILSON**. For the sum of $1200, 336 acres, 2 roods, and 39 poles, English measure, on the E side of Stephen **BYRD**'s; beginning on sd **BYRD**'s twenty at a stone; being part of a survey granted by the King of Spain to Hugh **CONELY**, and confirmed by

the Commissioners. Signed John **BYRD**, Betsey **BYRD**. Test John **COCHRAN**, Robert M. **WILLIAMS**, John **DAVIS** (JP). Rec 14 Jan 1816.

727. Page 17. 5 Jan 1816. William **CLARK**, Governor of Mo. Terr, to John **BYRD**. Appointment as JP in Byrd Twp for four years. Signed Wm. **CLARK**, Governor. Wit Frederick **BATES**, Sec. of Mo. Terr. John **BYRD** takes the oath of office. Signed John **BYRD**. Wit J. **McFERRON**. Rec 5 Feb 1816.

728. Page 17. 1 Mar 1814. Antony **RANDOLL** and Mary, his wife, to James **MORRISON** and John **WILSON**. For the sum of $500, 199 acres on the waters of Randoll's Mill Creek, a fork of Hubbell's Creek; adjoining Charles **ELLIS**, formerly Enos **RANDOL** senr, Robert **ENGLISH**, Thomas **ENGLISH** jun, a tract formerly belonging to **CRESWELL** and land whereon sd **MORRISON** and sd **WILSON** now reside with their families; beginning at a gum in **ELLIS**' line; being a grant from the King of Spain to Antony **RANDOLL**. Signed Antony (x) **RANDOLL**, Mary (x) **RANDOLL**. Wit Jeremiah **MASTERSON**, Samuel P. **BARKER**, Jno. **ABERNETHIE** (JP). Rec 8 Feb 1816.

729. Page 18. 5 Jan 1816. William **CLARK**, Governor of Mo. Terr, to Thomas **STEWART**. Appointment as JP in Byrd Twp for four years. Signed Wm. **CLARK**, Governor. Wit Frederick **BATES**, Sec. of Mo. Terr. Thomas **STEWART** takes the oath of office. Signed Thomas **STEWART**. Wit J. **McFERRON**. Rec 9 Feb 1816.

730. Page 18. 20 Apr 1815. Amos **BYRD** seignor to James **WILKINSON**. For the sum of $400, two tracts; 350 arpens on the waters of Byrd's Creek, being the W part of a tract of 1000 arpens granted to sd **BYRD**, beginning at a stone and sugar tree, bounded on the W by Michel **O'HOGAN**, N by Austin **YOUNG**, E by the balance of the survey, and S by lands purchased by Amos **BYRD** of sd **O'HOGAN**; and 50 acres beginning at a stone and sugar tree, bounded on the E, S, & W by sd **O'HOGAN** and N by the first tract. Signed Amos (o) **BYRD**. Wit Abraham **BYRD**, Moses **BYRD**, Michel **O'HOGAN**, James **RUSSELL** (JP). Rec 12 Feb 1816.

731. Page 20. 18 Dec 1815.. William **CLARK**, Governor of Mo. Terr, to George H. **SCRIPPS**. Appointment as JP in Cape Girardeau Twp for four years. Signed Wm. **CLARK**, Governor. Wit

Frederick **BATES**, Sec. of Mo. Terr. George H. **SCRIPPS** takes the oath of office. Signed G. H. **SCRIPPS**. Wit J. **McFERRON**. Rec 17 Feb 1816.

732. Page 20. 5 Jan 1816. Same to John **AKIN**. Appointment as JP in Byrd Twp for four years. Signed Wm. **CLARK**, Governor. Wit Frederick **BATES**, Sec. of Mo. Terr. John **AKIN** takes the oath of office. Signed John **AKIN**. Wit J. **McFERRON**. Rec 24 Feb 1816.

733. Page 20. 9 Oct 1815. John **WEAVER** and Mary, his wife, to Moses **BYRNE**. For the sum of $300, 300 arpens, being the concession of Peter **WEAVER** now in the hands of sd **BYRNE**; bounded on the S by Eli **SHELBY**, and public lands on the other sides. Signed John **WEAVER**, Mary (x) **WEAVER**. Wit Enoch **EVANS** (JP). Rec 29 Feb 1816.

734. Page 21. 9 Feb 1816. William **CLARK**, Governor of Mo. Terr, to Joseph **McFERRON**. Appointment as Clerk of the Superior Court for the Southern Circuit. Signed Wm. **CLARK**, Governor. Rec 2 Mar 1816.

735. Page 21. 20 Mar 1816. Jeremiah **ABLE** and Martha, his wife, to Edward **CRIDDLE**. For the sum of $700, 250 arpens on the waters of Hubble's Creek in Byrd Twp; bounded on the N by the heirs of John **MARTIN**, decd, and William **NEELY**, W by Robert and David **GREEN**, S by David **GREEN** and William **DAUGHERTY**, and E by John **SHEPHERD**. Signed Jeremiah **ABLE**, Martha **ABLE**. Wit James **EVANS**, John **SHAW**, Thos. **STEWART** (JP). Rec 22 Mar 1816.

736. Page 22. 15 Mar 1816. Peter **CRITES** and Mary, his wife, to Joseph **FRIZEL** & Co. of St. Louis, Mo. For the sum of $100, Lot No. 64 in Jackson; bounded on the N and fronted by Main St, E and fronted by west street, S by Lot No. 65, and W by Lot No. 76. Signed Peter (x) **CRITES**, Mary (x) **CRITES**. Wit Thos. **STEWART** (JP), Elizabeth (x) **CRITES**. Rec 22 Mar 1816.

737. Page 23. 17 Dec 1814. Commissioners of the Courthouse and Jail to Robert **WASH** of St. Louis Co. For the sum of $75, Lot No. 51 in Jackson; bounded on the S and fronted by Main St, W and fronted by first west street, N by Lot No. 50, and E by Lot No. 15 appropriated for public use. Signed John **DAVIS**, John **SHEPPARD**, Samuel G. **DUNN**, Abraham **BYRD**, Benja. **SHELL**. Wit Tho. **NEALE**, A.

P. **PATTERSON**, Jno. **ABERNETHIE** (JP). Rec 10 Apr 1816.

738. Page 24. 20 Feb 1816. Robert **WASH** to Moses **SCOTT**, both of St. Louis, Mo. For the sum of $150, Lot No. 51 as described in the preceding deed (D:23). Signed R. **WASH**. Wit Thos. **STEWART** (JP). Rec 16 Apr 1816.

739. Page 25. 24 May 1815. Abraham **HUGHES** to William **RUSSELL** of St. Louis, Mo. For the sum of $100, the 1/3 part of __ acres on the waters of and about five miles S of Apple Creek, being the settlement and improvement right of sd **HUGHS**; to be taken off the end or side of the survey so as not to include any part of sd **HUGHES'** plantation. Signed Abraham **HUGHES**. Wit Ephraim (E) **JACKSON**, Joseph (x) **NATIONS**, Wm. **RECTOR**, Stephen **RECTOR**, Silas **BENT**, JP in St. Louis Co., Mo. Rec 17 Apr 1816.

740. Page 26. 15 Mar 1814. James **MORRISON** to Samuel **MORRISON**. For the sum of $600, moiety of 95 acres and 96 poles on Randol's Mill Creek, except for 1/8 acre in the NW corner reserved as a burial ground; beginning at a gum tree on C. G. **ELLIS'** line; adjoining land sd **ELLIS** and Robert **ENGLISH** bought of Anthony **RANDOL**, James **MORRISON**, and John **WILSON**, and bounded in part by John **WILSON**. Signed James **MORRISON**. Test J. **MORRISON** jur, John **WILSON**, Joshua **MORRISON**, Thos. **STEWART** (JP). Rec 23 Apr 1816.

741. Page 26. 15 Mar 1814. Same to same. For the sum of $100, 16 acres, being part of a tract formerly the property of Thomas **BALLEW**, now of C. G. **ELLIS**; beginning on the W boundary of sd **ELLIS'** line S of James **MORRISON's** improvement. Signed James **MORISON**. Test J. **MORRISON** jur, John **WILSON**, Joshua **MORRISON**, Thomas **STEWART** (JP). Rec 23 Apr 1816.

742. Page 27. 28 Mar 1816. Samuel **MORRISON** and Isabella, his wife, to William **NEELY** of Cape Girardeau Co. and Isaac **BLEDSOE** of Sumner Co., Tenn.; for the sold use and benefit of Susannah **PENNEY** during her lifetime, and for her children after her decease. For the sum of $550, two tracts; 95 acres on the waters of Randol's Mill Creek, adjoining C. G. **ELLIS** and Robert **ENGLISH**, being the same purchased by James **MORRISON** and John **WILSON** of Anthony **RANDOL**, except for 1/8 acre in the NW corner of the improvement that is reserved for a burial ground, beginning at a gum tree on C. G. **ELLIS'** line; and 16 acres, being part of a tract formerly the property of Thomas **BALLEW**, but now the property of C. G. **ELLIS**, beginning at the W boundary of sd **ELLIS**. Signed Saml. **MORRISON**, Isabella **MORRISON**. Wit J. **RANNEY**, Thos. **STEWART** (JP). Rec 23 Apr 1816.

743. Page 28. 17 Dec 1814. Commissioners of the Courthouse and Jail to John **SHEPHERD**. For the sum of $40, Lot No. 7 in Jackson; bounded on the W and fronted by High St, S and fronted by second south street, E by Lot No. 31, and N by Lot No. 6. Signed John **DAVIS**, John **SHEPPARD**, Samuel G. **DUNN**, Abraham **BYRD**, Benja. **SHELL**. Wit Tho. **NEALE**, A. P. **PATTERSON**, Jno. **ABERNETHIE** (JP). Rec 24 Apr 1816.

744. Page 29. 17 Dec 1814. Same to same. For the sum of $40, Lot No. 8 in Jackson; bounded on the W and fronted by High St, N and fronted by second south street, E by Lot No. 32, and S by Lot No. 9. Signed John **DAVIS**, John **SHEPPARD**, Samuel G. **DUNN**, Abraham **BYRD**, Benja. **SHELL**. Wit Tho. **NEALE**, A. P. **PATTERSON**, Jno. **ABERNETHIE** (JP). Rec 24 Apr 1816.

745. Page 30. 17 Dec 1814. Same to John **BYRD**. For the sum of $70, Lot No. 76 in Jackson; bounded on the N and fronted by Main St, W and fronted by second west street, S by Lot No. 77, and E by Lot No. 64. Signed John **DAVIS**, John **SHEPPARD**, Samuel G. **DUNN**, Abraham **BYRD**, Benja. **SHELL**. Wit Tho. **NEALE**, A. P. **PATTERSON**, Jno. **ABERNETHIE** (JP). Rec 27 Apr 1816.

746. Page 31. 27 Apr 1816. John **BYRD** to William **NEELY**. For the sum of $400, Lot No. 76 in Jackson, as described in the preceding deed (D:30). Signed John **BYRD**. Wit James **EVANS**, Thomas **STEWART** (JP). Rec 27 Apr 1816.

747. Page 32. 18 May 1816. Commissioners of the Courthouse and Jail to George **BULLITT** of Arkansas Co., Mo. and Jesse B. **THOMAS** of Ill. Terr. For the sum of $74, Lot No. 14 in Jackson; bounded on the E and fronted by High St, N and fronted by first north street, W by Lot No. 50, and S by Lot No. 15 appropriated to public use. Signed John **DAVIS**, John **SHEPPARD**, Samuel G. **DUNN**, Abraham **BYRD**. Wit J. **RANNEY**, Jos. **SEAWELL**,

Richard S. **THOMAS**, Judge of Southern Circuit. Rec 22 May 1816.

748. Page 33. 14 May 1816. Jesse **HAIL** to James P. **EDWARDS**. For the sum of $550, Lot No. 87 in Jackson; bounded on the E by second west street, S by Main St, W by Lot No. 99, and N by Lot No. 86. Signed Jesse **HAIL**. Wit J. **RANNEY**, Andw. **MARTIN**, Thomas **STEWART** (JP). Rec 28 May 1816.

749. Page 33. 28 May 1816. Commissioners of the Courthouse and Jail to Edley **EWING** and Jacob **CASTLEMAN**. For the sum of $46, Lot No. 63 in Jackson; bounded on the S and fronted by Main St, E and fronted by first west street, N by Lot No. 62, and W by Lot No. 75. Signed John **DAVIS**, John **SHEPPARD**, Samuel G. **DUNN**, Abraham **BYRD**, Benja. **SHELL**. Wit Thomas **STEWART** (JP). Rec 28 May 1816.

750. Page 34. 30 Mar 1816. Benjamin **PATTERSON** to Isaac **PATTERSON**, both of Breckenridge Co., Ken. Power of attorney to act for Dr. Elisha **JACKSON** of New Madrid Co., Mo. to sell 4000 arpents on Cape Lecruise in the Cape Girardeau Dist. Sd **JACKSON** had constituted Benjamin **PATTERSON** as his attorney in fact to do the same on 10 Mar 1810. Signed Benjn. **PATTERSON**. Wit Jo **ALLEN**, Clerk of Breckenridge Co., Ken. Court, Joseph **MASON**, JP in Breckenridge Co., Ken. Rec 30 May 1816.

751. Page 35. 28 Mar 1816. 28 Mar 1816. Same to same. For the sum of $500, 4000 arpents, more or less, on Cape Lecruise adjoining the Mississippi River and land granted to Capt **LARIMY** that Benjamin **PATTERSON** purchased of Dr. Elisha **JACKSON**; being the same granted to sd **JACKSON** by Baronade **CONDELET**, Governor of La., under direction of Col. de **LASUSE**, Commandant of the New Madrid Dist. Signed Benjn. **PATTERSON**. Wit Jo **ALLEN**, Clerk of Breckenridge Co., Ken. Court, Joseph **MASON**, JP in Breckenridge Co., Ken. Rec 30 May 1816.

752. Page 36. 29 May 1816. Ezekiel **FENWICK** to John **SCOTT**, both of Ste. Genevieve Co., Mo., and Nathaniel **POPE** of Randolph Co., Ill. For the sum of $600, mortgage on a lot in Cape Girardeau; bounded on the E by a lot formerly owned by Daniel **HARKLERODE**, S by Joseph **McFERRON**, N by Main St, and W by William **GARNER**; being the same conveyed to sd **SCOTT & POPE** by Jeremiah **ABLE** on 8 Mar 1816. Sd **FENWICK** owes the debt with interest as $200 by 1 Jan 1817, $200 on 1 Jan 1818, and $200 by 1 Jan 1819. Signed E. **FENWICK**. Wit D. **BARTON**, Richd. S. **THOMAS**, Judge of Southern Circuit. Rec 7 Jun 1816. [Marginal note: Full satisfaction received on 18 Oct 1817. Signed John **SCOTT**, John **SCOTT** for Nathl. **POPE**. Wit Joseph **McFERRON**, Clerk.]

753. Page 37. 5 Jan 1816. William **CLARK**, Governor of Mo. Terr, to Thomas **NEAL**. Appointment as JP for Byrd Twp for four years. Signed Wm. **CLARK**, Governor. Wit Frederick **BATES**, Sec. of Mo. Terr. Thomas **NEAL** takes the oath of office. Signed Thos. **NEAL**. Wit J. **McFERRON**. Rec 10 Jun 1816.

754. Page 37. 4 Dec 1811. Jane **HARBISON**, mother of George C. C. **HARBISON**, decd; Elisha **ADAMS** and Jane, his wife, and Stephen **JARBOE** and Margaret, his wife (sd Jane and sd Margaret are sisters and heirs of sd decd) to Rebecca **HARBISON**, widow of George C. C. **HARBISON**, decd. For the consideration that sd Rebecca has paid all the debts of sd decd and for the premises described, quit claim four tracts; 300 acres, more or less, near Hartford, Ken., claimed by purchase from William **DUVAL** by bond to sd decd on 6 Sep 1802; 50 arpents, more or less, purchased by sd decd of David **HARRIS** on 8 Nov 1808, where John **HARBISON**, father of sd decd, lived in his lifetime; 207 arpens, more or less, adjoining Andrew **RAMSEY** senr and Joseph **THOMPSON**, purchased by sd decd of David **RAMSEY** on 15 Mar 1808, and being where John **HARBISON**, brother of sd decd, now lives; and __ acres on the waters of Cape La Cruche Creek, purchased by the decd of William **LORIMIER** on 9 Nov 1809. Rebecca **HARBISON** conveys to sd heirs, for the sum of $1 and the above premises, quit claim to 162 arpents, more or less, purchased by sd decd of Andrew **RAMSEY** and known as Cox's Improvement; Lot No. 13, Range B in Cape Girardeau, purchased by sd decd of John **GUETHING**; a house and Lot No. 8, Range F, purchased at sheriff's sale as the property of Jaben **SEELYE** on 24 Nov 1810; and all the slaves and personal property. George C. C. **HARBISON** died in Sep last. This agreement has no operation on that part of the estate due to John **HARBISON**, the other heir. Signed Rebecca **HARBISON**, Jane C. **HARBISON**, Elisha **ADAMS**, Jane **ADAMS**. Wit R. **COCKE**, Mary **COCKE**, John **REED**, Clerk of Washington Co., Ken. Court, A. E. **GIBBINS**, acting presiding JP in Washington Co., Ken. (as to John **REED**, decd). Rec 24 Jun 1816.

755. Page 40. 17 Dec 1814. Commissioners of the Courthouse and Jail to Stephen **BYRD**. For the sum of $57, Lot No. 18 in Jackson; bounded on the N and fronted by first south street, E and fronted by High St, S by Lot No. 19, W by Lot No. 54. Signed John **DAVIS**, John **SHEPPARD**, Samuel G. **DUNN**, Abraham **BYRD**, Benja. **SHELL**. Wit Tho. **NEALE**, A. P. **PATTERSON**, Jno. **ABERNETHIE** (JP). Rec 3 Jul 1816.

756. Page 41. 25 Jun 1816. Stephen **BYRD** to Zenus **PRIEST** and Jonas N. **MENEFEE**. For the sum of $75, Lot No. 18 as described in the preceding deed (D:40). Signed Stephen (+) **BYRD**. Wit Joel **BLUNT**, John S. **MILLER**, Jno. **MASSEY**, Thos. **STEWART** (JP). Rec 2 Jul 1816.

757. Page 41. 4 Jul 1816. Samuel **PEW** and Eleanor, his wife, to Joseph **McFERRON**. For the sum of $50, 10 acres, more or less, between the branches of Hubble's Creek; beginning at a stake at the intersection of the W line of sd **PEW**'s land with the N boundary of Jackson; being part of a parcel originally granted by the Spanish Government to sd **PEW** and since confirmed to him by the American Government. Signed Samuel **PEW**, Eleanor (x) **PEW**. Test Robt. **GREEN** (JP). Rec 4 Jul 1816.

758. Page 43. 13 May 1816. Augustus B. **LORIMIER** to Daniel F. **STEINBECK**. For the sum of $1000, 1000 arpens, more or less, on the waters of Flora Creek; adjoining a tract of Louis **LORIMIER**'s on one side and public lands on the other; being the same granted to Augustus B. **LORIMIER** by the Spanish Government as his head right, and confirmed to him by the commissioners. Signed A. B. **LORIMIER**. Wit Wm. J. **STEPHENSON**, Raphael V. **LORIMIER**, William **KELSO** (JP). Rec 22 Jul 1816.

759. Page 44. 13 May 1816. Same to same. For the sum of $2000, his share of the lands, tenements, hereditaments, and appurtenances of his deceased father Louis **LORIMIER**, by virtue of the last will and testament of sd Louis. Signed A. B. **LORIMIER**. Wit Wm. J. **STEPHENSON**, Raphael V. **LORIMIER**, William **KELSO** (JP). Rec 22 Jul 1816.

760. Page 45. 21 Apr 1816. Abraham **HUGHS** to Marcus **HUGHS**. For the sum of $50, mortgage on __ acres, being the land and improvement where he now lives. The debt is due by 1 Mar next. Signed Abraham **HUGHES**.

Wit Joseph **MEDLEY**, John **DAVIS** (JP). Rec 16 Aug 1816. [Marginal note: Full satisfaction received on 22 Nov 1817. Signed Marcus **HUGHES**. Wit J. **McFERRON**, Clerk.]

761. Page 46. 22 Aug 1816. William **RUSSELL** of St. Louis, Mo. to Isaac E. **KELLY**. For the sum of $110, 225 arpens on the waters of St. Francis; being part of the settlement right of sd **KELLY**, which sd **RUSSELL** purchased of him on 4 Oct 1812; being part of a tract of 750 arpens confirmed to sd **KELLY**. Signed Wm. **RUSSELL**. Wit Jacob **KELLEY** (JP), James **KELLEY**. Rec 31 Aug 1816.

762. Page 47. 17 Jul 1816. John **THOMPSON** seiner to Samuel G. **DUNN**. For the sum of $450, a negro girl named **Eady** about 5 years of age. Signed John **THOMPSON** Sr. Wit John **RODNEY**, Peter **MASSIE**, Thos. **STEWART** (JP). Rec 2 Sep 1816.

763. Page 47. [no date.] John **BLACK** siner to Peter **CRAIG**. For a valuable consideration, ___ acres, being his improvement on the S side of the Big Swamp on the waters of John Ramsey's Creek; and his corn and blades on sd premises. Signed John (x) **BLACK**. Test Caleb **HALCOMB**, William **RAMSEY**, Enoch **EVANS** (JP). Rec 4 Sep 1816.

764. Page 48. 4 Sep 1816. John **HAYS**, Morgan **BYRNE**, and Levi **WOLVERTON** to the Governor of Mo. For the sum of $1832.72, bond to guarantee that sd **HAYS** as Sheriff will collect and pay over all taxes and monies to the Territorial Treasury. Signed John **HAYS**, Morgan **BYRNE**, Levi **WOLVERTON**. Wit J. **McFERRON**, Clerk. Rec 4 Sep 1816.

765. Page 48. 8 Mar 1816. John **SCOTT** of Ste. Genevieve, Mo. and Nathaniel **POPE** and Lucretia, his wife, of Kaskaskia, Ill. to Ezekiel **FENWICK** of Ste. Genevieve Co., Mo. For the sum of $600, house and lot in Cape Girardeau; bounded on the E by a lot formerly owned by Daniel **HARKLEROAD**, S by Joseph **McFERRON**, N by Main St, and W by William **GARNER**; being the same purchased by sd **SCOTT** and sd **POPE** of Jeremiah **ABLE** on 22 Mar 1811. Signed John **SCOTT**, Nat. **POPE**, Lucretia **POPE**. Test Matthew **DUNCAN**, acting JP in Randolph Co., Ill., Hugh H. **MAXWELL**, Richard S. **THOMAS**, Judge of Southern Circuit in Mo. Terr., Vivian **EDWARDS**, Governor of Ill. Terr. Rec 27 Sep 1816.

766. Page 49. 17 Dec 1814. Commissioners of the Courthouse and Jail to Frederick G. **BULLINGER**. For the sum of $50, Lot No. 17 in Jackson; bounded on the E and fronted by High St, S and fronted by first south street, W by Lot No. 53, and N by Lot No. 16. Signed Benja. **SHELL**, John **DAVIS**, John **SHEPPARD**, Samuel G. **DUNN**, Abraham **BYRD**. Wit Thos. **NEALE**, A. P. **PATTERSON**, Jno. **ABERNETHIE** (JP). Rec 17 Oct 1816.

767. Page 50. 17 Aug 1816. Robert **CRAWFORD** and Elizabeth, his wife, to George F. **BOLINGER**. For the sum of $300, 100 arpens on the waters of Hubble's Creek; bounded on the N by Abraham **DAUGHERTY** and W by the representatives of Andrew **SUMMERS**; being part of 300 arpens bought by sd **CRAWFORD** of Lewis **LATHUM**, the original owner. Signed Robert **CRAWFORD**, Elizabeth **CRAWFORD**. Wit Thompson **CRAWFORD**, Thomas **COOPER**, James **RUSSELL** (JP). Rec 17 Oct 1816.

768. Page 51. 16 Oct 1816. Andrew P. **PATTERSON** and Rachael, his wife, to William **NEELY**. For the sum of $100, 1/9 part of 300 acres, amounting to nearly 34 acres, on Byrd's Creek; formerly owned by David **PATTERSON**, decd, and now owned by his heirs; and being the share of Andrew P. **PATTERSON**. Signed Andrew P. **PATTERSON**, Rachel (x) **PATTERSON**. Wit J. **RANNEY**, Thos. **STEWART** (JP). Rec 21 Oct 1816.

769. Page 52. ___ Sep 1814. Rufus **EASTON** to William **RUSSELL**, both of St. Louis, Mo. For the sum of $500, six tracts; ½ of 800 arpens, more or less, on the Marrameek in St. Louis Co., being the settlement and head right of Asher **BAGLEY**; 800 arpens, more or less, about five miles from the Saline in Ste. Genevieve Co., being his interest in the settlement right of Christopher **BARNHART**; his interest in 750 arpens, more or less, on the waters of Woolf Creek in Ste. Genevieve Co., being the settlement and head right of Joab **LINE**; 800 arpens, more or less, as founded on an agreement between sd **EASTON** and Joseph **WALLER** dated 8 Oct 1808, being the settlement right of sd **WALLER** on the W bank of the Mississippi River at Waller's Ferry or Double Springs; 800 arpens, more or less on the waters of Hubble's Creek, being the settlement and head right of Peter **BELLEW**; and 30 arpens in St. Louis Co. that sd **EASTON** claimed as assignee of Louis **BOVEY**, assignee of John Baptiste **DUFOUR**, who had a Spanish Grant for sd land, with a notice to the recorder dated 20 Oct 1812. Should title to any of the tracts not be confirmed, then sd **RUSSELL** is to have no recourse against sd **EASTON**. Signed Rufus **EASTON**. Wit Joseph **CORNELIUS**, Richd. S. **THOMAS**, John B. C. **LUCAS**, Judge of Superior Court of Mo. Terr. Rec 30 Oct 1816.

770. Page 53. 2 Nov 1816. John **NEWBOULT** of Washington Co., Ken. to Joseph **McFERRON** in trust. For love and affection he bears toward John Hamilton Rowan **HARBISON**, minor son of John C. **HARBISON** and Sally, his wife and sister of sd **NEWBOULT**; a negro boy named **Isaac** about 11 years of age. Should sd John Hamilton Rowan **HARBISON** die before reaching the age of majority, then the slave to go to his surviving brothers and sisters. Signed John **NEWBOULT**. Wit Wm. F. **HALLEY**, Thos. **STEWART** (JP). Rec 2 Nov 1816.

771. Page 53. 28 Oct 1816. William **GARNER** to Jonas N. **MENEFEE**. For the sum of $160, Lot No. 9, Range C in Cape Girardeau; bounded on the N by Themis St, S by a lot belonging to the estate of Robert **BLAIR**, decd, E by Ezekiel **FENWICK**, and W by Indian St; being the same purchased by sd **GARNER** of Lewis **LORIMIER** senr. and Marie, his wife, on 9 Dec 1810. Signed W. **GARNER**. Wit George **HENDERSON** (JP). Rec 3 Nov 1816.

772. Page 54. 23 Oct 1811. Elijah **WELCH** and Jane, his wife, to Thomas S. **RODNEY** and Michael **RODNEY**. For the sum of $370, 200 acres on Welch's Creek; beginning at a white oak, Samuel G. **DUNN**'s NE corner; also bounded in part by John **BOYD** and John **GIBONEY**. Signed Elijah (x) **WELCH**, Jane (8) **WELCH** (RD). Wit Js. **BOYD**, Jeremiah **CONAWAY**, John **BOYD**, Jno. **ABERNETHIE** (JP). Rec 25 Nov 1816.

773. Page 56. 3 Dec 1816. Robert **RAVENSCROFT** to Zenis **PRIEST**. For the sum of $1200, one bay horse; one gray horse; one small bay horse; one sorrel mare; one sorrel stud horse; ten head of cattle; two beds and beding; the balance of his household and kitchen furniture and farming utensils; $200 worth of store goods; one woman's saddle and briddle; and one man's saddle, bridle, and martingill. Signed Robt. **RAVENSCROFT**. Wit Enoch **EVANS** (JP). Rec 3 Dec 1816.

774. Page 56. 20 Sep 1816. Elizabeth **NEELY** of Cape Girardeau to George **HENDERSON**, Eve **NEELY**, and Jacob Hays **NEELY**, her three children and heirs apparent. For natural love and affection and for her better maintenance, support, livelihood, and preferment; all her real and personal property; to Eve **NEELY**: all her clothes and wearing apparel, bed, bedstead, furniture, and her share of the property; to George **HENDERSON**: all her share of the estate of Capt. John **HENDERSON**, decd, her first husband; to Jacob Hays **NEELY**: all her share in the estate of her last husband Thomas **NEELY**, decd; to her two sons: all her share of the estate of her father, Col. Christopher **HAYS**, decd. She also appoints George **HENDERSON** as her true and lawful agent to receive from Eve **HAYS** and John **HAYS**, adminrs of Col. Christopher **HAYS**, decd, all her portion of sd estate; and to deliver the share of Jacob H. **NEELY** to him when he reaches the age of majority, except what shall pay for his schooling and maintenance, clothing, and support. Sd George and sd Jacob are to pay out of the estate an equal share to her "unfortunate" daughter Eve, on account of her not having her right reason. Signed Elizabeth (&) **NEELY**. Wit John **WATERS**, Enoch **EVANS** (JP). Rec 3 Dec 1816.

775. Page 58. 7 Feb 1816. James **WORTHINGTON** and Phebe, his wife, of Johnston Co., Ill. to Daniel **HARKELRODE**. For the sum of $12, 80 acres, being part of a tract granted by the Spanish Government to Samuel **STROTHER** as his head right; and being where sd **HARKELRODE** formerly lived and the same that sd **HARKELRODE** purchased of sd **STROTHER**, and which has since been confirmed to sd **STROTHER** for the use of sd **WORTHINGTON**. Signed James **WORTHINGTON**, Phebe **WORTHINGTON**. Wit James **EVANS**, Nathan **VANHORN**, George **HENDERSON** (JP). Rec 4 Dec 1816.

776. Page 59. 19 Oct 1816. John **RAMSEY** of New Madrid Co., Mo. to same. For the sum of $300, ½ of Lot No. 8, Range C in Cape Girardeau; bounded on the E by part of **LORIMIER**'s tract that fronts on the public square, S by Joseph **McFERRON** (Lot No. 7), N by Themis St, and W by the other ½ of the lot. Signed James **RAMSEY**. Wit Enoch **EVANS** (JP). Rec 4 Dec 1816.

777. Page 60. 4 Oct 1816. William **CLARK**, Governor of Mo. Terr, to William **GARNER**. Appointment as County Surveyor for four years, his having been appointed by Circuit Court. Signed Wm. **CLARK**, Governor. Wit Frederick **BATES**, Sec. of Mo. Terr. William **GARNER** takes the oath of office. Signed W. **GARNER**. Wit J. **McFERRON**. Rec 7 Dec 1816.

778. Page 61. 6 Dec 1816. William **GARNER** and George **HENDERSON** to the Governor of Mo. Terr. For the sum of $2000, bond to guarantee that sd **GARNER** will perform the duties of Surveyor for Cape Girardeau Co. Signed W. **GARNER**, George **HENDERSON**. Wit J. **McFERRON**. Rec 7 Dec 1816.

779. Page 61. 5 Jun 1816. Commissioners of the Courthouse and Jail to Daniel M. **STOUT**. For the sum of $62, Lot No. 5 in Jackson. Signed John **DAVIS**, John **SHEPPARD**, Samuel G. **DUNN**, Abraham **BYRD**, Benja. **SHELL**. Wit Thomas **STEWART** (JP). Rec 10 Dec 1816.

780. Page 62. 22 Jul 1816. James **THOMPSON** to John **THOMPSON** senr. Quit claim to three negroes who appear on a bill of sale from the sd John to him; known by the names of **Daniel**, **Tina**, and **Ezbal**. Signed James **THOMPSON**. Wit John B. (x) **GODARE**. Test John **THOMPSON** junr., Thomas **STEWART** (JP). Rec 21 Dec 1816.

781. Page 63. 28 Nov 1816. Daniel **HARKKLEROAD** and Elizabeth, his wife, to Charles **SEAVERS** and Samuel **RAVENSCROFT**. For the sum of $330, ½ of Lot No. 8, Range C in Cape Girardeau, as described in D:59. Signed Dannul **HARKKLEROD**, Elizabeth (x) **HARKKLEROAD**. Wit Enoch **EVANS** (JP). Rec 23 Dec 1816.

782. Page 64. 10 Dec 1816. William **CLARK**, Governor of Mo. Terr, to George **HENDERSON**. Appointment as JP for Cape Girardeau Twp for four years. Signed Wm. **CLARK**, Governor. Wit Frederick **BATES**, Sec. of Mo. Terr. George **HENDERSON** takes the oath of office. Signed George **HENDERSON**. Wit J. **McFERRON**. Rec 31 Dec 1816.

783. Page 64. 3 Jan 1816. Michael **RODNEY** and Matilda, his wife, to Edley **EWING** of Tenn. For the sum of $650, 153 acres on the waters of Hubble's Creek; beginning at an ash. Signed Michl. **RODNEY**. Wit John **AKIN** (JP). Rec 6 Jan 1817.

784. Page 66. 10 Dec 1816. William **CLARK**, Governor of Mo. Terr, to John **ABERNETHIE**. Appointment as JP for Cape Girardeau Twp for four years. Signed Wm. **CLARK**, Governor. Wit Frederick **BATES**, Sec. of Mo. Terr. John **ABERNETHIE** takes the oath of office. Signed Jno. **ABERNETHIE**. Wit J. **McFERRON**. Rec 7 Jan 1817.

785. Page 66. 10 Dec 1816. Same to William **KELSO**. Appointment as JP for Tywappity Twp for four years. Signed Wm. **CLARK**, Governor. Wit Frederick **BATES**, Sec. of Mo. Terr. William **KELSO** takes the oath of office. Signed William **KELSO**. Wit J. **McFERRON**. Rec 13 Jan 1817.

786. Page 67. 24 Jun 1805. Felex **HOOVER** of Ohio to John **BILDERBACK**. For the sum of $20, __ acres W of **RANDLE**'s about 12 miles from the Mississippi; being a settlement and improvement made by sd **HOOVER**. Signed Phelix (2) **HOOVER**. Test Daniel **McMILLIN**, Harry **MARTIN**, Benjn. **WHITEMAN**, JCCP in Green Co., Ohio, John **PAUL**, Clerk of CCP, Green Co., Ohio. Rec 3 Feb 1817.

787. Page 68. 7 Aug 1815. Rufus **EASTON** to William **RUSSELL**, both of St. Louis, Mo. For the sum of $1000, four tracts; ½ part of 800 arpens, more or less, being the settlement right of Felix **HOOVER**, near the farm lately Enos **RANDLE**'s; ½ of 800 arpens, more or less, in New Madrid Co. in Tywappity Bottom at the E edge of a sand prairie, being the settlement right of John **DYE**; ½ of 800 arpens in New Madrid Co., about two miles N of New Madrid, being the settlement right of Aaron **GRAHAM**; and ¼ of 800 arpens on the River St. Francis in Cape Girardeau Co., in Kelley's Settlement, being the settlement right of James **CALDWELL**. Sd **EASTON** purchased the tracts from Ephraim **BILDERBACK** and John **BILDERBACK** on 5 Dec 1807 (C:158). Sd **RUSSELL** to have no recourse against sd **EASTON** should title to any of the tracts not be confirmed. Signed Rufus **EASTON**, Wm. **RUSSELL**. Wit Edw. **BATES**, Charles **LUCAS**, John B. C. **LUCAS**, Judge of Superior Court for Mo. Terr. Rec 3 Feb 1817.

788. Page 69. 29 Dec 1815. Abraham **RANDOL** to same. For the sum of $450, 778.29 arpens, more or less, being the settlement of sd **RANDOL**, which claim was rejected by the Commissioners on 22 Dec 1809, and is the same that sd **RANDOL** settled by permission of Charles D. **de LASSUS** in about Jan 1803, and was surveyed in Feb 1806. Signed Abraham (x)

RANDOL. Wit C. N. **BLACKMORE**, Jesse **HAIL**, Thos. **BULL**, Thomas **STEWART** (JP). Rec 3 Feb 1817.

789. Page 70. 11 Feb 1817. Joseph **SEAWELL** and Prudence, his wife, to same. For the sum of $480, 5 acres adjoining Jackson; bounded on the S by town lots of Jackson, E by Joseph **McFERRON**, and N & W by sd **SEAWELL**; beginning at the NE corner of a lot in Jackson just E of Lot No. 37. Signed Jos. **SEAWELL**, Prudence **SEAWELL**. Wit Thomas **STEWART** (JP), Jesse **HAIL**. Rec 13 Feb 1817.

790. Page 72. 15 Feb 1817. Joseph **WALLER** and Susannah, his wife, to Parish **GREEN**. For the sum of $400 and diverse causes and valuable considerations, quit claim to 640 acres, more or less, on the W shore of the Mississippi River at Waller's Ferry; being the settlement right of sd **WALLER** that he settled in about 1804, and being where sd **GREEN** now resides. Sd **GREEN** is to have no recourse if no title can be completed. Signed Joseph (   ) **WALLER**, Susannah (x) **WALLER**. Wit Wm. **RUSSELL**, Leonard **WALLER**, Jno. **ABERNETHIE** (JP). Rec 20 Feb 1817.

791. Page 73. 20 Feb 1817. Commissioners of the Courthouse and Jail to Anthony B. **NEELY**. For the sum of $80, Lot No. 13 in Jackson; bounded on the E and fronted by High St, S and fronted by first north street, W by Lot No. 49, and N by a surplus of town land or Joseph **SEAWELL**. Signed John **DAVIS**, John **SHEPPARD**, Samuel G. **DUNN**, Abraham **BYRD**. Wit R. S. **THOMAS**, Judge of Southern Circuit, Thos. **BULL**. Rec 24 Feb 1817.

792. Page 74. 27 Feb 1817. John **DUNN** to Joseph **SEAWELL**. For the sum of $100, quit claim to 150 acres, more or less, which he holds by virtue of a sheriff's deed executed on 23 Nov 1811; bounded on the S by William H. **ASHLEY**, E by Samuel **PUGH**, N by John **DAVIS**, and W by sd **SEAWELL**. Signed John **DUNN**. Wit John **DAVIS**, acting County Justice, Edward (x) **HAILE**. Rec 24 Feb 1817.

793. Page 75. 26 Aug 1815. John **DAVIS** and Nancy, his wife, to same. For the sum of $400, 20 acres near Jackson, on the N side of the tract where sd **SEAWELL** now resides; beginning at a stake and stone on the SW corner of the tract where sd **DAVIS** now resides, and also bounded by Henry **HAND**'s lot. Signed John **DAVIS**, Nancy **DAVIS**. Wit William **FUGATE**, David

BARTON, Judge of Northern Circuit. Rec 24 Feb 1817.

794. Page 76. 26 Feb 1817. John **WILSON** to his grandson Junius Brutus **MILLER** and to his son Berry **WILSON**, and also to Thomas **WILSON** of Logan Co., Ken. (in trust for sd Junius Brutus **MILLER**). For natural love and affection; one negro girl named **Cynthia**, aged 10 years; one negro man named **Sam**, aged 21; two beds and beding; two ovens; one skillet; two buckets; one pewter bason; six pewter plats; one set of knives and forks; one spinning wheel; one pair of plane irons; one bay mare six years old; one sorrel filly rising two years old, with a white spot on the flank; three breeding sows and three shoats marked with an underbit and half crop in each ear. Sd Thomas **WILSON** is to hold the property in trust for sd **MILLER** until he reaches age 21; and should sd **MILLER** not live to age 21, then the trustee is to convey the property to Berry **WILSON**. Signed John **WILSON**. Wit Jason **CHAMBERLAIN**, Elijah **RANDOL**, Joseph **McFERRON**, Clerk. Rec 26 Feb 1817.

795. Page 76. 14 Sep 1816. Edward H. **MATTHEWS** to Jacob **GARRETT**. For the sum of $850, __ acres on both sides of Outer [Otter?] Creek, a branch of the River St. Francis, on the main road leading from Doctor **PETTIS**'s to Laurance Courthouse; being the same where sd **MATTHEWS** now lives, and which he claims as his improvement under the preemption acts; also all the corn now standing in sd fields, and turnips and all kitchen vegetables growing thereon. Signed Edw. H. **MATTHEWS**. Wit Jos. **MOORE**, C. G. **GAING**(?), Jacob **KELLER** (JP). Rec 1 Mar 1817.

796. Page 77. 15 Feb 1817. Medad **RANDALL** to Parish **GREEN**. For the sum of $5 and other good causes and valuable considerations, quit claim to his interest in __ acres on the W shore of the Mississippi River known as Waller's Ferry, acquired from Joseph **WALLER**; and where sd **WALLER** formerly lived and kept a ferry; being the same where sd **GREEN** now resides. Sd **GREEN** is to have no recourse if title cannot be obtained. Signed Medad **RANDOL**. Wit Wm. **RUSSELL**, Daniel **STOUT**, Thomas **STEWART** (JP). Rec 11 Mar 1817.

797. Page 78. 17 Jul 1809. David S. **JENKINS** to Joseph **BAKER**. For the sum of $500, a negro woman named **Win** aged 17 or 18 years, dark complected, and a female negro child aged 8 months named **Sullah**. Signed David S.

JENKINS. Test John **DAVIS** (JP), J. **BOYD**. Rec 22 Mar 1817.

798. Page 79. 29 Mar 1817. Elisha **WHITE** and Martha, his wife, to Andrew **RAMSEY**, son of John **RAMSEY**, and William **CRACROFT**. For the sum of $76 from sd **RAMSEY** and $38 from sd **CRACROFT**, 2/3 and 1/3 of 38 arpens, more or less, on the waters of the River Zenon, vulgarly called Hubble's Creek; beginning at a pawpaw stake on the E line of the late Andrew **SUMMERS**, decd, and also bounded by John **SUMMERS**; being part of a tract originally claimed by Louis **LATHAM**, and surveyed by sd **LATHAM** to Robert **CRAWFORD**, and from sd **CRAWFORD** to sd **WHITE**. Signed Elisha (x) **WHITE**, Martha (x) **WHITE**. Wit Joel **BLUNT**, Jason **CHAMBERLAIN**, Thos. **STEWART** (JP). Rec 29 Mar 1817.

799. Page 80. 10 Dec 1816. William **CLARK**, Governor of Mo. Terr., to Enoch **EVANS**. Appointment as JP for Tywappity Twp for four years. Signed Wm. **CLARK**, Governor. Wit Frederick **BATES**, Sec. of Mo. Terr. Enoch **EVANS** takes the oath of office. Signed Enoch **EVANS**. Wit J. **McFERRON**. Rec 1 Apr 1817.

800. Page 81. 7 Apr 1817. Daniel M. **STOUT** to Polly **MOTHERSHEAD**. For the sum of $500, Lot No. 5 in Jackson. Signed Daniel M. **STOUT**. Wit Joseph **McFERRON**, Clerk. Rec 7 Apr 1817.

801. Page 81. 17 Jun 1814. Richard **WALLER** and Susanah, his wife, to Isaac **WILLIAMS**. For the sum of $405, 90 acres on both sides of Randoll's Mill Creek adjoining sd **WALLER**, John **ABERNETHIE**, William **WILLIAMS**, Enos **RANDOLL** junr, and Thomas **MORGAN**; beginning at a white walnut in sd **ABERNETHIE**'s line; being part of the tract where sd **WALLER** and his family now live; formerly part of Joseph **WALLER**'s old concession. Signed Richard **WALLER**, Susany ( ) **WALLER**. Wit Parish **GREEN**, Jno. **ABERNETHIE** (JP). Rec 26 Apr 1817.

802. Page 83. 1 Mar 1817. Jonas N. **MENEFEE** to Zenas **PRIEST**. For the sum of $40, quit claim to Lot No. 18 in Jackson; bounded on the W by Lot No. 54, S by Lot No. 19, E by High St, and N by first south street. Signed J. N. **MENEFEE**. Wit Thos. **STEWART** (JP). Rec 28 Apr 1817.

803. Page 83. 9 Nov 1816. Edley **EWING** and Elizabeth, his wife, to Thos. **SULLINGER**. For the sum of $419.50, 151 acres on the waters of Hubble's Creek; beginning at an ash. Signed Edley **EWING**, Betsy **EWING**. Wit L. **LORIMIER**, Peggy (x) **LOURIMER**, John **AKIN** (JP). Rec 29 Apr 1817.

804. Page 85. 25 Dec 1816. Webb **HAYDON** and Elizabeth, his wife, to same. For the sum of $300, 100 acres on the waters of Hubble's Creek; beginning at a stake on Louis **LORIMIER**'s line, and also bounded by Joel **RENFROE**. Signed Web **HAYDEN**, Elizabeth **HAYDEN**. Wit William **HAYDEN**, Solomon **HAYDEN**, Hiram **HAYDEN**, John **AKIN** (JP). Rec 29 Apr 1817.

805. Page 86. 25 Aug 1815. Joseph **SEAWELL** and Prudence, his wife, to Thomas **NEALE**. For the sum of $100, 144 perches adjoining Jackson; fronted on the E by third west street, S & N and fronted by sd **SEAWELL**, and W by sd **SEAWELL** and a branch of Hubble's Creek; being the same where sd **NEALE** now lives. Signed Jos. **SEAWELL**, Prudence **SEAWELL**. Test D. **BARTON**, Judge of North Judicial Circuit. Rec 5 May 1817.

806. Page 87. 17 Dec 1814. Commissioners of the Courthouse and Jail to Jesse **HAIL**. For the sum of $53, Lot No. 87 in Jackson; bounded on the E and fronted by second west street, S and fronted by Main St, W by Lot No. 99, and N by Lot No. 86. Signed John **DAVIS**, John **SHEPPARD**, Samuel G. **DUNN**, Abraham **BYRD**, Benja. **SHELL**. Wit Tho. **NEALE**, A. P. **PATTERSON**, Jno. **ABERNETHIE** (JP). Rec 7 May 1817.

807. Page 88. 11 Feb 1817. James P. **EDWARDS** and Hannah, his wife, and Elijah **RANDOL** and Nelley, his wife, to same. For the sum of $600, Lot No. 87 in Jackson; bounded on the E and fronted by second west street, S and fronted by Main St, W by Lot No. 99, and N by Lot No. 86. Signed James P. **EDWARDS**, Hannah (x) **EDWARDS**, Elijah **RANDOL**, Nelly **RANDOL**. Wit J. **RANNEY**, William **NEELY**, Thomas **STEWART** (JP). Rec 7 May 1817.

808. Page 89. 3 Nov 1813. Charles **BRADLEY** to Morgan **BYRNE**. For the sum of $500, ___ acres, being the residue of 400 arpens granted to him by the Commissioners of the U. S. as his settlement right; bounded on the N by the assignees of William **BONER**, S by vacant land, W by sd **BYRNE**, and E by Thomas **ENGLISH**. The other part of the tract has been sold to sd

BYRNE on 28 Dec 1805. Signed Charles BRADLEY. Wit B. COUSIN, John C. HARBISON, George HENDERSON (JP). Rec 15 May 1817.

809. Page 90. 17 Jun 1814. John ABERNETHIE to Isaac WILLIAMS. For the sum of $80, bond to make a deed for 10 acres adjoining sd WILLIAMS that he got of Rd. WALLER, between the big road and branch that makes into Randoll's Mill Creek, and including part of the plantation where sd ABERNETHIE now lives. The deed to be executed within six months of his receiving a deed from the U. S. Signed Jno. ABERNETHIE. Test Richard WALLER, Parish GREEN, Joseph McFERRON, Clerk. Rec 24 May 1817.

810. Page 91. 21 Sep 1815. Thomas FOSTER to William WILLIAMS. For the sum of $100, __ acres, being his settlement right on Turkey Creek, a branch of Hubble's Creek. Signed Thomas (x) FOSTER. Wit Richard WRIGHT, Jacob FOSTER, Joseph McFERRON, Clerk. Rec 24 May 1817.

811. Page 92. 10 Apr 1817. Edley EWING and Elisabeth, his wife, to Joseph THORN. For the sum of $60, part of Lot No. 63 in Jackson, fronting on Main St. Signed Edley EWING, Elizabeth EWING. Wit Thos. STEWART (JP). Rec 30 May 1817.

812. Page 92. 10 Mar 1817. Samuel PUGH and Elenor, his wife, to the Commissioners of the Courthouse and Jail, for the use and benefit of the county. For the sum of $60, 19 acres, 13 ½ perches on the River Zenon, now called Hubble's Creek, being part of the tract where sd PUGH now lives; bounded on the S by land originally claimed by Henry SHEREDAN and now conveyed to sd commissioners, W by lands originally owned by Joseph SOWEL and now conveyed to sd commissioners, and other sides by sd PUGH; beginning at a stake at the intersection of the W line of sd SOWELL with the N line of sd SHEREDEN. Signed Samuel PEW, Elenor (x) PEW. Wit Thomas STEWART (JP). Rec 31 May 1817.

813. Page 94. 24 Feb 1814. Thomas S. RODNEY and Polly, his wife, to William MATTHEWS. For the sum of $400, 300 arpens on Hubble's Creek, being the S end of a tract purchased by sd RODNEY of Rachel WORTH, including all the buildings and improvements. Signed Thos. S. RODNEY, Polly RODNEY. Wit Enoch EVANS (JP). Rec 2 Jun 1817.

814. Page 94. 14 Sep 1816. Edward H. MATTHEWS to Jacob GARRETT of St. Genevieve Co., Mo. Power of attorney to enter his claim and receive patents to preemption land claims in Mo., specifically on Outer (Otter?) Creek, a branch of the River St. Francis; being the same conveyed by sd MATTHEWS to sd GARRETT. Signed Edw. H. MATTHEWS. Wit Jos. MOORE, C. S. GOINGS, Jacob KELLEY (JP). Rec 3 Jun 1817.

815. Page 95. 5 Oct 1816. Daniel HARKKLEROAD to Samuel G. DUNN. For the sum of $600, a negro man named Isaac. Signed Dannal HARKKLEROAD. Test C. G. ELLIS, John MARTIN, Thos. STEWART (JP). Rec 3 Jun 1817.

816. Page 95. [No date given] Charles DEMOSS to John HAYS. For the sum of $20, any land in excess of 500 acres that may be part of his head right. Sd HAYS is also to pay one two-year-old steer and ½ of the surveying costs of the 500 acres. Signed Charles DEMOSS, John HAYS. Test John SCOTT, Aquila WATHEN, George HENDERSON (JP). Rec 3 Jun 1817.

817. Page 96. 5 Jun 1817. Commissioners of the Courthouse and Jail to John McKENZIE. For the sum of $67.50, Lot No. 22 in Jackson; bounded on the E and fronted by High St, S and fronted by Lot No. 23, W and fronted by Lot No. 58, and N by third south street. Signed John DAVIS, John SHEPPARD, Samuel G. DUNN, Abraham BYRD, Benja. SHELL. Test J. RAVENSCROFT, Solomon R. BOLIN, Thos. STEWART (JP). Rec 4 Jun 1817.

818. Page 97. 20 Jan 1814. John HITT and Frances, his wife, to Washington ABERNETHIE. For the sum of $200, 50 acres, more or less, being where sd ABERNETHIE and his family now live; adjoining sd HITT, Charles G. ELLIS, where CRESWELL formerly lived, Anthony RANDOLL, and John ABERNETHIE; beginning at a sugar tree at sd HITT's corner on a spring branch running into Randoll's Mill Creek; being part of a tract where John ABERNETHIE now lives, that was conveyed to sd HITT on 2 Mar 1812. Signed John (x) HITT, Frances (x) HITT. Wit Elizabeth (x) STOUT, John HITT, John MURPHEY, Jno. ABERNETHIE (JP). Rec 7 Jun 1817.

819. Page 99. 3 Jun 1817. Commissioners of the Courthouse and Jail to Henry ECKHART. For the sum of $75 received of George F.

BOLLINGER, Lot No. 16 in Jackson; bounded on the E and fronted by High St, W by Lot No. 52, S by Lot No. 17, and N by Main St. Signed John **DAVIS**, John **SHEPPARD**, Samuel G. **DUNN**, Abraham **BYRD**. Wit Jesse **HAIL**, Robert **GIBONEY**, Thomas **STEWART** (JP). Rec 10 Jun 1817.

820. Page 100. 24 Dec 1813. Thomas **McCABE** to Peter **CRAIG**. For the sum of $15, his head right. Signed Thomas (   ) **McCABE**. Wit J. **RAVENSCROFT**, John **LANDERS**, Thos. **STEWART** (JP). Rec 6 Jun 1817.

821. Page 100. 20 Jun 1817. Louis **LORIMIER** and Peggy, his wife, to Daniel F. **STEINBECK**. For the sum of $4000, 640 arpens, more or less, on Hubble's Creek, about eight and a half miles W of Cape Girardeau; bounded by Webb **HAYDEN**, Sylvenus **CASTLEMAN**, Abraham **BYRD**, and vacant land; being the same purchased in two tracts from Ithamar **HUBBLE**, the original owner, by John **STRONG**, who conveyed the same to Louis **LORIMIER** junior, who conveyed it to Louis **LORIMIER** senior, and which came to sd Louis **LORIMIER** by common consent of the heirs of Louis **LORIMIER** senior; together with the mills and plantation. Signed Ls. **LORIMIER**, Peggy (x) **LORIMIER**. Test Robert **CRUMP**, John (   ) **PATTERSON**, John **AKIN** (JP). Rec 23 Jun 1817.

822. Page 102. 25 Jun 1817. Jeremiah **CONAWAY** and Rachel, his wife, of Lawrence Co., Mo. [now Ark.] to Charles S. **HEMPSTEAD** of Ste. Genevieve, Ste. Genevieve Co., Mo. For the sum of $300, 470 arpens, more or less, on White Water; adjoining lands sold by sd **CONAWAY** to Samuel G. **DUNN**; being the settlement right of Peter **BELLEW** sold to sd **CONAWAY**, and confirmed to him as assignee of sd **BELLEW**, except for the tract sold to sd **DUNN** and 100 arpens sold to John **GIBBONEY** by George **MORGAN**. Signed Jeremiah **CONAWAY**, Rachel (x) **CONAWAY**. Wit Richd. **SEARCY**, Clerk of Lawrence Co., Mo. Rec 3 Jul 1817. [Executed at Davidsonville, Mo. Terr.]

823. Page 103. 24 Aug 1816. Antony **RANDOLL** and Mary, his wife, to John **BURNS**. For the sum of $39, 13 acres, more or less, on a branch of Frank's Creek, being part of a tract whereon sd **RANDOLL** and family now live; adjoining where sd **BURNS** and family now live and Abram **BYRD** (**CRESWELL**'s old place); beginning at the SE corner of sd **BURNS**

land. Signed Antony (x) **RANDOLL**, Mary (x) **RANDOLL**. Wit Wa. **ABERNETHIE**, William (x) **MURPHY**, Jno. **ABERNETHIE** (JP). Rec 7 Jul 1817.

824. Page 104. 8 Mar 1817. Commissioners of the Courthouse and Jail to Jason **CHAMBERLAIN**. For the sum of $62, Lot No. 9 in Jackson; bounded on the N by Lot No. 8 owned by John **SHEPHERD**, E by Lot No. 33, S and fronted by third south street, and W and fronted by High St. Signed John **DAVIS**, John **SHEPPARD**, Samuel G. **DUNN**, Abraham **BYRD**. Wit Samuel S. **HALL**, Nathan **McCARTY**, William **HAND**, Jane (x) **HOWARD**, Thomas **STEWART** (JP). Rec 7 Jul 1817.

825. Page 105. 20 July 1816. Same to James **BRADY** of New Madrid Co., Mo. For the sum of $50, Lot No. 88 in Jackson; bounded on the E and fronted by second west street, S By Lot No. 89, and W by Lot No. 100. Signed John **DAVIS**, John **SHEPPARD**, Samuel G. **DUNN**, Abraham **BYRD**. Wit Stephen **BYRD**, Susanna R. **BOYCE**, Thomas **STEWART** (JP). Rec 7 Jul 1817.

826. Page 106. 17 Jul 1817. Same to John **SHEPPARD**. For the sum of $52(?), Lot No. 29 in Jackson; bounded on the E and fronted by first east street, S and fronted by first south street, W by Lot No. 5, and N by Lot No. 28. Signed John **DAVIS**, Samuel G. **DUNN**, Abraham **BYRD**, Benja. **SHELL**. Wit William **CRACRAFT**, James **RUSSELL** (JP). Rec 17 Jul 1817.

827. Page 107. 15 Feb 1816. Same to William **HAND**. For the sum of $80, Lot Nos. 109 & 110 in Jackson. Signed John **DAVIS**, John **SHEPPARD**, Samuel G. **DUNN**, Abraham **BYRD**, Benja. **SHELL**. Wit James **RUSSELL** (JP). Rec 19 Jul 1817.

828. Page 108. 19 May 1817. John **MAY** and Mary Ann, his wife, of Ste. Genevieve Co., Mo. to George **TENNILL** of New Madrid Co., Mo. For the sum of $600, two tracts; 300 arpens, more or less, on the waters of Whitewater, being the same which was granted and confirmed to sd **MAY** as his settlement or head right; and 250 arpens, more or less, being granted and confirmed to John **MAY** under Cornelius **AVERET** as the settlement or head right of sd **AVERET**. Signed John **MAY**, Mary Ann (x) **MAY**. Wit Jesse **HAIL**, Barnabas **BURNS**, JP in Ste. Genevieve Co., Mo. Rec 23 Jul 1817.

829. Page 110. 6 Jun 1817. Commissioners of the Courthouse and Jail to George Frederick **BOLLINGER**. For the sum of $70, Lot No. 4 in Jackson; bounded on the W and fronted by High St, N and fronted by Main St, E by Lot No. 28, and S by Lot No. 5. Signed John **DAVIS**, John **SHEPPARD**, Samuel G. **DUNN**, Abraham **BYRD**, Benjamin **SHELL**. Wit James **EVANS**; James **BRADY** as to John **DAVIS**, John **SHEPHERD**, Saml. G. **DUNN** & Benjn. **SHELL**; Thos. **STEWART** (JP); Richd. S. **THOMAS**, Judge of Southern Circuit. Rec 23 Jul 1817.

830. Page 111. 6 Jun 1817. Same to same. For the same of $50, Lot No. Lot No. 17 in Jackson; bounded on the E and fronted by High St, S and fronted by first south street, and W by Lot No. 16. This deed corrects the previous deed, which described the incorrect lot. Signed John **DAVIS**, John **SHEPPARD**, Samuel G. **DUNN**, Abraham **BYRD**, Benjamin **SHELL**. Wit James **EVANS**; James **BRADY** as to John **DAVIS**, John **SHEPHERD**, Saml. G. **DUNN** & Benjn. **SHELL**; Thos. **STEWART** (JP); Richd. S. **THOMAS**, Judge of Southern Circuit. Rec 23 Jul 1817.

831. Page 112. 13 Jul 1817. John **EDWARDS** to Preceller **JOHNSON** and her children. For value received in notes and cash, his negro man **Bob**. Signed John **EDWARDS**. Wit A. **BRAVAIS**, John **CORMAN**(?), Joseph **McFERRON**, Clerk. Rec 25 Jul 1817.

832. Page 113. 4 Aug 1817. Ezekiel **ABLE** and Sarah, his wife, and Jeremiah **ABLE** and Patsey, his wife, to John **DUNN**. For the sum of $1000, 320 acres on the waters of Whitewater, being part of Francis **MURPHY**'s head right, and known as George **MORGAN**'s Improvement, where sd **DUNN** now lives; beginning at a stone near a white hickory three poles from the upper corner of sd improvement; bounded in part by William **ROBERTS**. Signed Ezekiel **ABLE**, Sarah (x) **ABLE** (RD), Jeremiah **ABLE**, Patsey **ABLE**. Wit Enoch **EVANS** (JP), James **RUSSELL** (JP). Rec 5 Aug 1817.

833. Page 114. 27 Feb 1817. William **FUGATE** and Mirlinda, his wife, to Thomas **BULL**. For the sum of $93, Lot No. 26 in Jackson; bounded on the E and fronted by first east street, N and fronted by first north street, W by Lot No. 2, and S by Lot No. 27. Signed Wm. **FUGATE**, Merlinda **FUGATE**. Wit John **DAVIS**, William **HAND**, Thomas **STEWART** (JP). Rec 6 Aug 1817.

834. Page 115. 4 Aug 1817. Ezekiel **ABLE** and Sarah, his wife, and Jeremiah **ABLE** and Martha, his wife, to Phillip **BOLLINGER**, son of Daniel. For the sum of $1380, 640 acres on the E side of Castor River, being the head right of Joseph **WATKINS** and whereon Phillip **BOLLINGER** now lives. Signed Ezekiel **ABLE**, Sarah (x) **ABLE** (RD), Jeremiah **ABLE**, Martha **ABLE**. Test Thos. **STEWART** (JP), George **HENDERSON** (JP). Rec 7 Aug 1817.

835. Page 116. 1 Jun 1817. Ezekiel **ABLE** and Sarah, his wife, to Wilson **ABLE**. For the sum of $320, 160 acres in the Big Bend of the Mississippi River, to be surveyed in a square off the upper part of the back of the head right of Jabez **FISHER**. Signed Ezekiel **ABLE**, Saray ( ) **ABLE**. Wit George **HENDERSON** (JP). Rec 12 Aug 1817.

836. Page 117. 21 Jul 1817. William **CLARK**, Governor of Mo. Terr, to John B. **WHEELER**. Appointment as JP for German Twp for four years. Signed Wm. **CLARK**, Governor. Wit Frederick **BATES**, Sec. of Mo. Terr. John B. **WHEELER** takes the oath of office. Signed John B. **WHEELER**. Wit J. **McFERRON**. Rec 12 Aug 1817.

837. Page 118. 20 Jun 1815. Henry **HAND**, father and heir of John **HAND**, decd, to Catharine **HAND**, widow and adminr of sd John **HAND**. For the sums of $171.14 (his share of the sales and cash in hand of sd decd) and $125 (his share of a negro boy named **Charles**, who belonged to sd John). Henry **HAND** also obligates himself to pay his share of any debt or demand against sd estate. Signed Henry **HAND**. Wit Jos. **SEAWELL**, J. **McFERRON**, Clerk. Rec 13 Aug 1817.

838. Page 119. 19 Oct 1816. Daniel **HARKKLEROAD** and Elizabeth, his wife, to John **HALL** of New Madrid Co., Mo. For the sum of $350, 80 acres, more or less, being part of a tract granted by the Spanish Government to Samuel D. **STROTHER** as his head right; being where sd **HARKKLEROAD** formerly lived, and which he purchased of sd **STROTHER**; and which has since been confirmed to sd **STROTHER** for the use of James **WORTHINGTON**. Signed Dannal **HARKKLEROAD**, Elizabeth (x) **HARKKLEROAD**. Wit 18 Aug 1817.

839. Page 120. 3 Sep 1817. John Batiste **GODAIR** to James **EVANS**. For the sum of $50, 240 arpens, more or less, on the waters of

Ramsey's Creek, granted to sd **GODAIR** as his head right under the Spanish Government. Signed John Batiste (x) **GODAIR**. Wit George **HENDERSON** (JP). Rec 4 Sep 1817.

840. Page 121. 10 Nov 1806. John **BULLINGER** senr to William **TINNIN**. For the sum of $5000, bond to convey 200 acres where sd **TINNIN** is now settling, or 200 acres out of his survey on Boiling Spring Creek, including the Boiling Spring. Sd **TINNIN** is to pay $300 by 1 Jan next or this bond is void. Signed Johannes **BOLLINGER**. Test John (x) **PURKINS**, Sollomon ( ) **BULLINGER**. Title is assigned to Henary **BOLLINGER** for value received on 6 Sep 1817. Signed William **TINNIN**. Wit Henry **SLAGLE**, John (x) **BOLLINGER**. Wit James **RUSSELL** (JP). Rec 11 Sep 1817.

841. Page 121. 6 Sep 1817. William **TINNIN** to Henary **BOLLINGER**. For the sum of $600, bond to make a deed on 200 arpens, a balance of a tract granted to sd **TINNIN** by the King of Spain, where Jacob **YOUNT** senr now lives. Signed William **TINNIN**. Wit Henry **SLAGLE**, John (x) **BULLINGER**, James **RUSSELL** (JP). Rec 11 Sep 1817.

842. Page 122. 22 Nov 1811. Jacob **KELLEY** to Elijah **BETTIS** juner. For the sum of $230, __ acres on the E side of the River St. Francis, being whereon sd **KELLEY** now lives. Signed Jacob **KELLEY**. Test Ezekiel **RUBOTTOM** (JP). Rec 15 Sep 1817.

843. Page 122. 23 Dec 1816. Isaac E. **KELLY** and Agness, his wife, to Elijah **BETTIS**. For the sum of $330, 300 arpens, more or less, on the waters of the River St. Francis; beginning on a double hickory; being the same on which sd **BETTIS** now resides, and part of a grant to sd **KELLEY** by the late Board of Commissioners, No. 727 dated 31 May 1811. Signed Isaac E. **KELLEY**, Agness (x) **KELLEY**. Test Ro. A. **LOGAN**, Ezekiel **RUBOTTOM** (JP). Rec 15 Sep 1817.

844. Page 124. 25 Dec 1816. Isaac E. **KELLEY** to same. For the sum of $__, __ acres, beginning at a pappaw corner, the SE corner of a tract conveyed to sd **BETTIS** by sd **KELLEY** and wife. Signed Isaac E. **KELLEY**. Test Ezek. **RUBOTTOM** (JP), Jacob **KELLEY**. Rec 15 Sep 1817.

845. Page 124. 12 Sep 1817. James **EVANS** to Jonas N. **MENEFEE**. For the sum of $500, 1

acre and a brick building in Cape Girardeau. Signed James **EVANS**. Wit George **HENDERSON** (JP). Rec 17 Sep 1817.

846. Page 125. 25 Jun 1817. John **SHIELDS** and Jane, his wife, of Lawrence Co., Mo. [now Ark.] to Charles S. **HEMPSTEAD** of Ste. Genevieve, Mo. For the sum of $100, __ acres on the waters of Hubble's Creek, being his settlement right. Should title be defective, then sd **HEMPSTEAD** is to have no recourse. Signed John **SHIELDS**, Jane ( ) **SHIELDS**. Wit Fergus S. **MORRISON**, Esq., JP in Lawrence Co., Mo. Rec 17 Sep 1817.

847. Page 126. 3 Oct 1816. Edley **EWING** and Elizabeth, his wife, to Sylvanus **CASTLEMAN**. For the sum of $4, 1 3/4 acre on the waters of Hubble's Creek; beginning at a hickory sapling. Signed Edley **EWING**, Elizabeth (x) **EWING**. Wit R. S. **THOMAS**, Judge of Southern Circuit. Rec 22 Sep 1817.

848. Page 127. 17 Sep 1817. James **DRYBREAD** to Samuel **LOVE**. For the sum of $200, 640 acres, more or less, on the waters of Indian Creek; being his Spanish claim, head, or settlement right. Signed James ( ) **DRYBREAD**. Wit Thomas **HAIL**, James (x) **BEASLY**, R. S. **THOMAS**, Judge of Southern Circuit. Rec 26 Sep 1817.

849. Page 128. 2 Oct 1817. John **PATTERSON** and Eleanor, his wife, to Samuel **PEW**. For the sum of $80, 61 arpens, more or less, on the waters of Byrd's Creek, being the 1/9 part of the land of David **PATTERSON**, decd, father of John **PATTERSON**, confirmed by the U. S.; bounded by Edward **HAIL**, John **DAVIS**, Robert **PATTERSON**, and John **WILSON**. Signed John (x) **PATTERSON**, Eleanor ( ) **PATTERSON**. Wit Joseph **McFERRON**, Clerk. Rec 2 Oct 1817.

850. Page 129. 4 Oct [1817]. Charles **DEMOSS** and Martha, his wife, to George **HAYS**. For the sum of $100, 100 acres, more or less, on the waters of Hubble's Creek; bounded on the N by the heirs of Col. Christopher **HAYS**, decd, E by sd **DEMOSS**, S by Lewis **DICKSON**, and W by George **HAYS**; beginning at a white oak corner. Signed Charles **DEMOSS**, Martha (x) **DEMOSS**. Wit Joseph **McFERRON**, Clerk, W. **GARNER**. Rec 4 Oct 1817.

851. Page 130. 13 Feb 1815. Robert **CRAWFORD** and Elizabeth, his wife, of Ste. Genevieve Co., Mo. to Samuel **McCLAIRY** of

Garrard County, Ken. For the sum of $650, 200 arpens, being the S end of a tract that sd **CRAWFORD** purchased of Lewis **LAYTHAM**; adjoined on the S by John **SUMMERS** and E by Thomas **ENGLISH**. Signed Robert **CRAWFORD**, Elizabeth **CRAWFORD**. Wit Peter **BURNS** (JP), Jos. **MOORE**. Rec 10 Oct 1817.

852. Page 132. 20 Feb 1815. Same and same and Samuel **McCLAIRY** of Garrard County, Ken. to Elisha **WHITE**. For the sum of $650, 200 arpens on the waters of Hubble's Creek, being the S end of a tract originally claimed and occupied by Louis **LATHAM**, and conveyed by him to sd **CRAWFORD**; bounded on the S by John **SUMMERS** and E by Thomas **ENGLISH**. Signed Samuel **McCLARY**. Wit John **SHEPPARD**, John **DAVIS** (JP). Rec 10 Oct 1817.

853. Page 133. 31 Sep [sic] 1817. Stephen **STILLEY**, late of Cape Girardeau Co., and William **ROSS**. For the sum of $400, bond to abide by the judgment of a committee to settle a difference between them for __ acres joining sd **ROSS** on the Mississippi River, which sd **STILLEY** claims by virtue of a bargain from sd **ROSS**. If the committee decides, then sd **ROSS** is to make a deed to sd **STILLEY** and will forfeit the bond; or sd **STILLEY** to relinquish his claim on pain of paying the sum. Signed Steaphen **STILLEY**, William **ROSS**. Test James P. **EDWARDS**, Joseph **McFERRON**, Clerk. Rec 10 Oct 1817.

854. Page 134. 8 Oct 1817. William **ROSS** swears he signed the above bond (D:133). Signed William **ROSS**. Test James P. **EDWARDS**, Joseph **McFERRON**, Clerk. Rec 10 Oct 1817.

855. Page 134. 20 Sep 1817. John **BURROWS** and Bethina, his wife, to Joseph **WHITNEY**. For the sum of $150, 50 acres on the waters of Hubble's Creek; beginning at the NE corner of sd tract at a stake and stone, being Thomas **MORGAN**'s corner on John **SUMMERS**' line; also adjoining sd **BURROWS**. Signed John **BURROWS**, Bethena (x) **BURROWS**. Wit John **RODNEY**, James **DOWTY**, William **CRACRAFT**, John **AKIN** (JP). Rec 11 Oct 1817.

856. Page 136. 7 Oct 1817. Robert **CRAWFORD** and Elizabeth, his wife, of Ste. Genevieve Co., Mo. to James **CRAWFORD**. For the sum of $700, 200 arpens on a branch of

Hubble's Creek; being a part of 300 arpens granted by the Spanish Government to Lewis **LATHAM**, and sold by sd **LATHAM** to Robert **CRAWFORD**; including the improvement where Elisha **WHITE** now lives; adjoined on the N by a part of sd tract belonging to George F. **BOLINGER**, W by the representatives of Andrew **SUMMERS**, and E by lands formerly owned by the widow **MILLS**. Signed Robert **CRAWFORD**, Elizabeth **CRAWFORD**. Wit Jos. **MOORE**, James **BURNS**, James **RUSSELL** (JP). Rec 14 Oct 1817.

857. Page 137. 25 Sep 1817. William **CLARK**, Governor of Mo. Terr, to John **HAYS**. Appointment as Sheriff of Cape Girardeau Co. for two years. Signed Wm. **CLARK**, Governor. Wit Frederick **BATES**, Sec. of Mo. Terr. **HAYS** takes the oath of office. Signed John **HAYS**. Wit J. **McFERRON**. Rec 15 Oct 1817.

858. Page 138. 15 Oct 1817. John **HAYS**, Wm. **NEELY**, William **KELSO**, Thomas W. **GRAVES**, and Levi **WOLVERTON** to William **CLARK**, Governor of Mo. For the sum of $10,000, bond to guarantee that sd **HAYS** shall perform the duties of the office of Sheriff of Cape Girardeau Co. Signed John **HAYS**, Wm. **NEELY**, William **KELSO**, Thos. W. **GRAVES**, Levi **WOLVERTON**. Wit Joseph **McFERRON**, Clerk. Rec 15 Oct 1817.

859. Page 139. 9 Jun 1817. James **FARIS** and Clarissa, his wife, to John **RODNEY**. For the sum of $690, 300 arpens on the waters of Hubble's Creek, including the plantation where sd **FARIS** now lives; bounded on the E by Thomas W. **GRAVES** and the heirs of Joseph **FIGHT**, decd, S by the heirs of John **McCRAKEN**, decd, W by Jonas N. **MENNEFEE**, and N by James **DOWTY**; being part of the land granted to Raney **BRUMMITT**; beginning at a stake and stone near a hickory sapling on sd **GRAVES**' line at sd **DOWTY**'s SE corner. Signed James **FARIS**, Clarissa **FARIS**. Wit John **AKIN** (JP), Thos. S. **RODNEY**, Peter **MASSIE**. Rec 20 Oct 1817.

860. Page 140. 2 Aug 1817. Leonard **WILSON** and Polly, his wife, to Benjamin **WILSON**. For the sum of $400, 100 acres, more or less, on the waters of Byrd's Creek in Byrd Twp; being part of a tract granted to James **BOYD**, transferred by sd **BOYD** to Ezekiel **ABLE**, and by sd **ABLE** to Johnathan **STOUT**, and from sd **STOUT** to Leonard **WILSON**; beginning at the SW corner of sd tract. Signed Leonard **WILSON**, Polly (x)

WILSON. Test Abraham **BYRD**, James **RUSSELL** (JP). Rec 25 Oct 1817.

861. Page 141. 26 Jul 1817. Ezekiel **ABLE** to William **WILLIAMS**. For the sum of $400, 160 acres in Byrd Twp, being part of the head right of John **SHIELDS**; to commence toward the W end of sd tract, at the SE corner of a piece reserved by sd **ABLE**. Signed Ezekiel **ABLE**. Wit Johnson **RANNEY**, John **GILES**, Thos. **NEALE**, Esq. (JP), R. S. **THOMAS**, Judge of Southern Circuit. Rec 1 Nov 1817.

862. Page 142. [no date] William **HAND** to his parents and sisters. For the sum of $2000, bond to guarantee that he will not disinherit his father nor his mother of their land where they now live during their lifetimes in consequence of a bill of sale to him dated in 1813. He also agrees to let his sisters Paty **DOURITY** and Poly **GOZY**, after his father's and mother's deaths, to have 100 arpens so as to not infringe on the plantation where he now lives; Pats **DAURITY** is to have 100 arpens on the SE side of the creek, and Polly **GOZY** to have 100 arpens on the NW side of sd tract; and to include their equal part of other property after their deaths. Signed Wm. **HAND**. Wit Joseph (x) **SIMONS**, Joseph **McFERRON**, Clerk. Rec 4 Nov 1817.

863. Page 143. 26 Nov 1817. Martin **MILLER** to David **GREEN** and Sophia, his wife. For natural love and affection for his son-in-law and daughter and the sum of $450, a negro woman named **Mill**. Signed Martin (x) **MILLER**. Wit Edward **CRIDDLE**, Samuel H. **REED**, Joseph **McFERRON**, Clerk. Rec 29 Nov 1817.

864. Page 144. 8 Sep 1817. Silvanus **CASSELMAN** and Elizabeth, his wife, to John **RODNEY**. For the sum of $50, two tracts; 359 acres on Hubble's Creek, being part of Martin **RODNEY**'s head right and where sd **CASSELMAN** now lives, including the improvement except for 1 acre on the NW corner, beginning at an ash on Michael **RODNEY**'s and John **AKIN**'s lines; and 8 ½ arpens of the SW corner of Daniel F. **STEINBECK**'s Mill Tract on Hubble Creek, which was conveyed to sd **CASSELMAN** by John **RODNEY** on 10 Jul 1815, beginning at a stake and stone and black gum. Signed Sylvanus **CASSELMAN**, Elizabeth (x) **CASSELMAN**. Test Thos. S. **RODNEY**, Thomas **SULLENGER**, James **DOWTY**, John **AKIN** (JP). Rec 2 Dec 1817.

865. Page 145. 2 Oct 1817. William **CLARK**, Governor of Mo. Terr, to Zenas **PRIEST**. Appointment as JP for Byrd Twp for four years. Signed Wm. **CLARK**, Governor. Wit Frederick **BATES**, Sec. of Mo. Terr. Zenas **PRIEST** takes the oath of office. Signed Zenas **PRIEST**. Wit J. **McFERRON**. Rec 10 Dec 1817.

866. Page 146. 11 Dec 1817. Ezekiel **ABLE** senior and Sally **HANNA**, both of Cape Girardeau. Marriage contract. Sally **HANNA**, or her heirs if she should die first, is to receive $1000 and all the property she may possess in lieu of her right of dower, out of the estate of sd **ABLE** at his death; and is to have no other claim on sd estate. Signed Ezekiel **ABLE**, Sally **HANNAH**. Wit C. G. **ELLIS**, Levi **WOLVERTON**, George **HENDERSON** (JP). Rec 15 Dec 1817.

867. Page 146. 9 Jun 1806. Joseph **WALLER** and Richard **WALLER** to Nicholas **SEVERS** of Hampshire Co., Vir. For the sum of $1000, bond to make a deed on 500 acres or arpens, French measure, on Randoll Creek, where Benjamin **HARGROVE** and his first wife and family formerly lived; which was granted by the Spanish Government to sd **HARGROVE**; adjoining Math. **HUBBELL**, Jos. **WORTHINGTON** formerly Saml. **STROTHER**, Abram **BYRD**, and John **RAMSEY**. Sd deed to be made when title is obtained from the U. S. A. Signed Joseph ( ) **WALLER**, Richard **WALLER** (also for receipt of $600 from sd **SEAVERS**). Wit Jno. **ABERNETHIE**, Andrew **RAMSEY**, Wa. **ABERNETHIE**, Joseph **McFERRON**, Clerk. Rec 29 Dec 1817.

868. Page 147. 31 May 1802. Louis **LORIMIER**, Commandant, and Daniel **MEREDITH** and Rolland **MEREDITH**, brothers, of Ste. Genevieve. Agreement to release Daniel **MEREDITH** of all responsibilities in the estate of their brother Rees **MEREDITH**, decd. Daniel **MEREDITH** gave his brother Rolland all his part of sd estate, and Rolland **MEREDITH** will take charge of all business affairs and debts of sd estate. Signed Daniel **MEREDITH**, Louis **LORIMIER**, Roland **MEREDITH**. Wit James **ARREL**, Henry **SHARADIN**. On application of Johnson **RANNEY** and/or Joseph **SEAWELL**. Rec 31 Dec 1817.

869. Page 148. 24 Aug 1816. Thomas **STEWART** and Elizabeth, his wife, to Johnson **RANNEY**. For the sum of $10, part of Lot No.

52 on Main St in Jackson. Signed Thos. STEWART, Elizabeth STEWART. Wit Andw. MARTIN, John DUNN, John DAVIS (JP). Rec 6 Jan 1818.

870. Page 148. 27 Nov 1817. James WORTHINGTON and Phebe, his wife, to Web HAYDEN. For the sum of $501, 167 acres on the waters of Randol's Creek; bounded on the S by Nicholas SAVERS, W by Mathew HUBBLE's old claim, N by Joel RENFROE, and E by James COX. Signed James WORTHINGTON, Phebe ( ) WORTHINGTON (RD). Wit Enoch EVANS (JP). Rec 6 Jan 1818.

871. Page 149. 6 Dec 1817. James RAMSEY and Rebecca his wife, to same. For the sum of $1, quit claim to 167 acres as described in the preceding deed (D:148). Signed James RAMSEY. Wit Enoch EVANS (JP). Rec 6 Jan 1818.

872. Page 150. 18 Oct 1817. Henry BULLINGER, son of John BULLINGER senior, decd, to Joseph ROGERS. For the sum of $400, 200 acres on the W fork of Whitewater Creek in German Twp; being part of a survey of 640 acres granted to John BULLINGER senior by the King of Spain; beginning at the NE corner of sd survey at a stake; being the same where sd ROGERS now lives; adjoining Jacob BULLINGER, William TINNIN, and Henry BULLINGER. Signed Henry BOLLINGER. Wit Azariah TINNIN, Jacob (x) YOUNT, William TINNIN (JP). Rec 9 Jan 1818.

873. Page 151. 19 Dec 1817. Ezekiel ABLE senior to John HANNA of Ste. Genevieve, Mo., a minor. In consideration of the love and affection he bears to his step-son and the sum of $1, 200 acres on the waters of Whitewater in Byrd Twp; being 5/16 of 640 acres, the settlement right of Jesse HARGROVE; being the same confirmed to sd HARGROVE and conveyed by him to sd ABLE. Signed Ezekiel ABLE. Wit George HENDERSON (JP). Rec 15 Jan 1818.

874. Page 152. 30 Oct 1817. William CLARK, Governor of Mo. Terr, to Ezekiel RUBOTTOM. Appointment as JP for St. Francis Twp for four years. Signed Wm. CLARK, Governor. Wit Frederick BATES, Sec. of Mo. Terr. Ezekiel RUBOTTOM takes the oath of office. Signed Ezekiel RUBOTTOM. Wit J. McFERRON. Rec 16 Jan 1818.

875. Page 153. 20 Oct 1817. Henrey HAND to Marey GOSEY. For the sum of $5, 100 acres on Hubble's Creek, being part of the tract whereon he now lives, and which was confirmed to him; beginning at the NE corner at a stone. Marey GOSEY is not to sell or barter the land in the lifetime of sd HAND. Signed Henry HAND. Wit Joseph McFERRON, Clerk. Rec 16 Jan 1818.

876. Page 154. 26 Apr 1817. Thomas NEALE and Ellen, his wife, to Joseph HAWKS. For the sum of $300, a lot just outside Jackson, fronting on the E on third west street, N & S by Joseph SEAWELL, and W by sd SEAWELL and a branch of Hubble's Creek; being where sd HAWKS now lives. Signed Tho. NEALE, Ellen NEALE. Wit Thomas STEWART (JP). Rec 19 Jan 1818.

877. Page 155. 8 Mar 1816. Hugh CRESWELL and Nancy, his wife, to Samuel PEW. For the sum of $105, undivided 1/10 share of 350 arpens on the waters of Byrd's Creek, whereon David PATTERSON, decd, formerly lived; bounded by Edward HAIL, John DAVIS, Robert PATTERSON, and John WILSON. Signed Hugh CRESWELL, Nancy (x) CRESWELL. Wit John BYRD, David HILER, Joseph McFERRON, Clerk. Rec 21 Jan 1818.

878. Page 156. 11 Jun 1817. Ephraim STOUT and Jane, his wife, of Washington Co., Mo. to Sammuel MONTGUMRY. For the sum of $500, 340 acres, more or less, on the St. Francis River; being part of a tract confirmed to him by the Commissioners; beginning on a rock and sugar tree on the bank of the St. Francis River. Signed Ephraim STOUT, Jane ( ) STOUT. Wit Jacob KELLEY (JP). Rec 21 Jan 1818.

879. Page 156. 1 Jan 1813. Allen McKENZIE and Magdelana, his wife, to Thomas MORGAN. For the sum of $500, 240 arpens, French measure, on the waters of Franks' Creek, a fork of Randoll's Mill Creek, being where sd MORGAN now lives, and where sd McKENZIE formerly lived; adjoining Robert ENGLISH (formerly FRANKS'), John SUMMERS senr, Walters BORRAUGHS, Mathew HUBBELL, and William HADEN (formerly Jos. THOMSON); being the same granted to sd McKENZIE by the Spanish Government. Signed Allen McKINZE, Magdalana (x) McKENZIE. Wit Rebecca ( ) RANDOLL, Thankful RANDOLL, John ABERNETHIE (JP). Rec 23 Jan 1818.

880. Page 158. 5 Nov 1817. Ezekiel **ABLE** to George **HENDERSON**, both of Cape Girardeau. For the sum of $73.22, ½ acre of a lot in Cape Girardeau, being the N end of the lot, and a brick house in which sd **ABLE** now lives. Signed Ezekiel **ABLE**. Wit John **HAYS**, John S. **MILLER**, Joseph **McFERRON**, Clerk. Rec 29 Jan 1818.

881. Page 158. 1 Jan 1814. Elisha **WHITE** and Martha, his wife, to Robert **BUCKNER**. For the sum of $565.25, 161 acres and 72 perches where sd **WHITE** now lives; bounded on the S by heirs of John **MARTIN**, decd, W by Isaac **SHEPPERD**, NE by William **RUSSELL**; beginning at a stone at the SW corner of the original survey; also bounded by Wright **DANIEL**'s improvement. Signed Elisha (x) **WHITE**, Martha (x) **WHITE**. Wit A. **BURNS**, William **RUSSELL**, John **DAVIS** (JP). Rec 2 Feb 1818.

882. Page 160. 5 Jan 1818. Frederick **BATES**, Sec of Mo. Terr., exercising the government thereof, to Jacob **GARRETT**. Appointment as JP for St. Francis Twp for four years. Signed Frederick **BATES**. Jacob **GARRETT** takes the oath of office. Signed Jacob **GARRETT**. Wit Jno. **LANDERS** (JP). Rec 9 Feb 1818.

883. Page 161. 24 Nov 1817. Francis **MURPHY** and Elizabeth, his wife, to Samuel **PERRY**, all of Washington Co., Mo. For the sum of $800, 640 acres on White Water about seven or eight miles SW of Jackson; adjoining Gerry **CONAWAY** on the E, **FRANKS** on the SW; being the same that was confirmed to sd **MURPHY** by the Commissioners. Signed Francis (K) **MURPHY**, Elizabeth **MURPHY**. Wit James **YOUNG**, James **SCOTT**, John **BRICKEY**, Clerk of Washington Co., Mo. Circuit Court. Rec 9 Feb 1818.

884. Page 162. 11 Feb 1818. Ezekiel **ABLE** to William **MILBURN** of St. Louis Co., Mo., and William **GORDON** of Howard Co., Mo. For the sum of $2000, bond to make a deed on 320 acres on White Water, being the improvement where Alexander **McDANIEL** now lives; adjoining William **COX** and William **BOLIN** on the N, or upper, side; and to be surveyed so as to be not more than double as long as broad. Sd **MILBURN** and sd **GORDON** obligate themselves to pay $2.50 per acre, ½ paid within three years, and the other within four years; the deed to be made upon the final payment. Signed Ezekiel **ABLE**, Wm. **MILBURN**, Wm. **GORDON**. Wit Jno. **RODNEY**, Alex.

McDONALD, George **HENDERSON** (JP). Rec 11 Feb 1818.

885. Page 164. 11 Feb 1818. Same to same and same. For the sum of $250, 330 acres on White Water, being part of two tracts; one originally owned by William **SMITH**, the other by Jacob **SHARIDAN**; beginning at the lower corner of Ruth **DUNN**'s survey on White Water; bounded in part by sd **ABLE** in right of William **MURPHY**. Signed Ezekiel **ABLE**. Wit Jno. **RODNEY**, George **HENDERSON** (JP). Rec 11 Feb 1818.

886. Page 166. 31 Jan 1818. Thomas **BULL** to Isaac **SHEPPARD** and Thomas **ENGLISH**, Deacons of Bethel Church. For the sum of $1, __ acres, beginning at a stone on the line between William **DAUGHERTY** and sd **BULL**; including Bethel Meeting House, graveyard, and spring. Sd land to be for the benefit of the Baptist Church as long as it continues. Should it dissolve, then the land to revolve back as it formerly was. Signed Thomas **BULL**. Wit John **SHEPPARD**, Robert **ENGLISH**, Zenas **PRIEST** (JP). Rec 11 Feb 1818.

887. Page 167. 9 Feb 1818. Jeremiah **ABLE** to Ezekiel **ABLE**. For the sum of $2000, quit claim to all bonds and deeds assigned to him by Ezekiel **ABLE**. Signed Jeremiah **ABLE**. Wit Johnson **RANNEY**, Joseph **McFERRON**, Clerk. Rec 11 Feb 1818.

888. Page 168. 25 Apr 1817. David **DOWNARD** and Sally, his wife, late of Cape Girardeau Co. and now of Campbell Co., Ken., to Obadiah **SCOTT** of Ste. Genevieve Co., Mo. For the sum of $1, 300 arpents, being an improvement to which he was entitled in consequence of formerly being a resident and for military service at that time. Signed D. **DOWNARD**. Wit James **TAYLOR**, Clerk of Campbell Co., Ken. Court, James **KENNEDY**, Presiding Magistrate of Campbell Co., Ken. Court. Rec 14 Feb 1818.

889. Page 169. 28 Jul 1817. John **HAYS**, Joseph **SEAWELL**, and William **GARNER** to William **CLARK**, Governor of Mo. Terr. For the sum of $2000, bond to assure that sd **HAYS** will collect and pay out all money due for county purposes for the present year. Signed John **HAYS**, Jos. **SEAWELL**, W. **GARNER**. Wit Nathan **McCARTY**, Joseph **McFERRON**, Clerk. Rec 14 Feb 1818.

890. Page 170. 26 Jul 1817. John **HAYS**, Levi **WOLVERTON**, and Daniel F. **STEINBECK** to same. For the sum of $2500, bond to guarantee that sd **HAYS** will collect and pay over into the Territorial Treasury all taxes or other monies collectable within the present year. Signed John **HAYS**, Levi **WOLVERTON**, D. F. **STEINBECK**. Wit Robt. **GREEN**, Joseph **McFERRON**, Clerk. Rec 14 Feb 1818.

891. Page 171. 16 Feb 1818. Ezekiel **ABLE** of Cape Girardeau to Samuel **SMILEY** of St. Charles Co., Mo. For the sum of $600, 216 acres in the Big Bend of the Mississippi River about six miles above Cape Girardeau; being part of a head right confirmed to Jabez **FISHER**; beginning at the end of the E line of sd head right at a white oak 15 inches in diameter. Signed Ezekiel **ABLE**. Wit George **HENDERSON** (JP). Rec 16 Feb 1818.

892. Page 172. 15 Feb 1817. Anthony B. **NEELY** and Margaret, his wife, to Jonas **WHITTENBURG**. For the sum of $125, Lot No. 27 in Jackson; bounded on the S by Main St, E by first east street, N by Lot No. 26, and W by Lot No. 3. Signed A. B. **NEELY**, M. D. **NEELY**. Wit Thos. **STEWART** (JP), C. W. **BLACKMORE**. Rec 20 Feb 1818.

893. Page 174. 30 Jun 1817. William **NEELY** and Rachel, his wife, to same. For the sum of $150, Lot No. 28 in Jackson; bounded on the E and fronted by first east street, S by Lot No. 29, W by Lot No. 4, and N and fronted by Main St; being the same that sd **NEELY** purchased of the Commissioners of the Courthouse and Jail. Signed William **NEELY**, Rachel **NEELY**. Wit Thos. **STEWART** (JP). Rec 20 Feb 1818.

894. Page 175. 20 Jul 1816. Commissioners of the Courthouse and Jail to William **NEELY**. For the sum of $52, Lot No. 28 in Jackson as described in the preceding deed (D:174). Signed John **DAVIS**, John **SHEPPARD**, Samuel G. **DUNN**, Abraham **BYRD**. Wit Stephen **BYRD**, Susanna R. **BOYCE**, Zenas **PRIEST** (JP). Rec 20 Feb 1818.

895. Page 176. 20 Feb 1818. Jonas **WHITTENBURGH** to Clifton **MOTHERSHEAD**. For the sum of $200, part of Lot No. 28 in Jackson; bounded and fronted by Main St, and adjoining George F. **BOLLINGER**'s Lot No. 4 and Polly **MOTHERSHEAD**. Signed Jonas **WHITTENBERG**. Wit Thos. **NEWBERRY**, Zenas **PRIEST** (JP). Rec 20 Feb 1818.

896. Page 177. 2 Mar 1809. John **HAYS** and Jeremiah **STILL** to George **ANTHONY**. For the sum of $36.25, ___ acres that they purchased of Cornelus **EVERIT** on 30 Mar 1805. Sd **ANTHONY** to have no recourse if the head right cannot be recovered from the U. S. A. Signed Jeremiah **STILL**, John **HAYS**. Test John **DUNN**, Robert R. **NIXON**, Thos. **STEWART** (JP). Title is assigned to John **HAYS** for the sum of $1 on 3 Mar 1809. Signed George **ANTHONY**. Test David **WALL**, John **McCARTY**, George **HENDERSON** (JP). Rec 20 Feb 1818.

897. Page 179. 16 Dec 1811. Anthony **RANDOL**, James **RANDOL**, Medad **RANDOL**, Abram **RANDOL**, Alen **McKINZIE**, William **MASTERSON**, and Thomas **MORGAN** with Eligah **RANDOL**, all lawful heirs of Enos **RANDOL**, sen., to John **DOWTY**. In consideration of the esteem and regard which they have and bear unto their brother-in-law, 50 arpens, French measure, on the waters of Ramsey's Creek in Cape Girardeau Twp, it being a gift of Enos **RANDOL** seanor, decd, and the W end of the tract where Enos **RANDOL** sen. lately lived and where his widow now lives. Signed Antony (x) **RANDOLL**, Allen (x) **McKENZIE**, Medad **RANDOL**, James **RANDOL**, Abaham (x) **RANDOL**, Elijah **RANDOL**. Wit Jno. **EARTHMAN**, James **DOWTY**, Zenas **PRIEST** (JP). Rec 23 Feb 1818.

898. Page 180. 24 Jan 1818. John **DOWTY** to Thomas **MORGAN**. For the sum of $10, 50 arpents on the waters of Ramsey's Creek as described in the preceding deed (D:179). Signed John **DOWTY**, Thos. **MORGAN**. Wit J. **RANNEY**, Zenas **PRIEST** (JP). Rec 23 Feb 1818.

899. Page 182. 10 Feb 1818. Commissioners of the Courthouse and Jail to James **WILKINSON**. For the sum of $90, Lot No. 147 in Jackson; bounded on the S and fronted by Main St, E and fronted by third east street, N by Lot No. 146, and W by Lot No. 135. Signed John **DAVIS**, John **SHEPPARD**, Samuel G. **DUNN**, Abraham **BYRD**. Wit J. **FRIZEL**, Thos. **NEWBERRY**, Zenas **PRIEST** (JP). Rec 23 Feb 1818.

900. Page 183. 13 Jul 1817. John **EDWARDS** to Preceller **JOHNSON**. For diverse good causes and considerations, all his property in Cape Girardeau; a bay horse; bed and furniture with one small table; and all other household and movable property in her possession which she possessed when sd **EDWARDS** first lived with her as per receipt and listed when she first took him to board with her or became his housekeeper; also one cow and calf she bought with her own money; and 50 acres she purchased of him. She also authorized him as guardian for her children and to act in her defense in case of any unlawful attacks upon her or her property, sd property being listed in the contract, and which she held in Ohio and which she moved to Ken. Signed John **EDWARDS**. Wit A. **BRAVAIS**, John **CAMRON**, Henry **HAND**, William **WILLIAMS**, Joseph **McFERRON**, Clerk. Rec 24 Feb 1818.

901. Page 184. 9 Feb 1818. Commissioners of the Courthouse and Jail to Rufes **EASTON**. For the sum of $51, Lot No. 2 in Jackson; bounded on the W and fronted by High St, N and fronted by first north street, E by Lot No. 26, and S by Lot No. 3. Signed John **DAVIS**, John **SHEPPARD**, Samuel G. **DUNN**, Abraham **BYRD**. Wit Wm. **NEELY**, Zenas **PRIEST** (JP). Rec 24 Feb 1818.

902. Page 185. 26 Feb 1818. William **DAUGHERTY**, authorized and appointed by the last will and testament of Andrew **RAMSEY**, decd, to John **RAMSEY** of New Madrid Co., brother of sd Andrew. As specified in sd will and by title bonds, title to two tracts sold to sd John; 240 arpens on Randol's Creek, known as John **RAMSEY**'s head right, adjoining Abraham **BYRD**, John **GIBONEY**, and others; and 540 arpens adjoining the Big Swamp, known as **THORN** and **BRADLEY**'s improvements; and __ acres known as **FITZGIBBONS**' place. Signed William **DAUGHERTY**. Wit Joseph **McFERRON**, Clerk, William **ALLEN**. Rec 26 Feb 1818.

903. Page 187. 26 Feb 1818. John **RAMSEY** to his son Andrew **RAMSEY**. For the sum of $1, 540 arpens, more or less, in Cape Girardeau Twp adjoining the Big Swamp and known as **THORN** and **BRADLEY**'s improvements; also adjoining **FITZGIBONS**' claim. Signed John **RAMSEY**. Wit Joseph **McFERRON**, Clerk, William **DAUGHERTY**. Rec 26 Feb 1818.

904. Page 188. 26 Feb 1818. Same to James **FLYNN**. For the sum of $400, 240 arpents, being the head right of John **RAMSEY** in Cape Girardeau Twp. Signed John **RAMSEY**. Wit Joseph **McFERRON**, Clerk, Wm. **DAUGHERTY**. Rec 26 Feb 1818.

905. Page 189. 7 Mar 1817. Richard S. **THOMAS** and Francis, his wife, to the Commissioners of the Courthouse and Jail. For 12 acres and 82 perches to be taken off the S side of 50 acres purchased by sd Commissioners from William H. **ASHLEY**, including the frame house where sd **THOMAS** now lives; 12 acres, more or less, beginning at **PUGH**'s and **SEAWELL**'s corner; for the use and benefit of Cape Girardeau Co. Signed Richard S. **THOMAS**, Frances **THOMAS**. Wit Thomas **STEWART** (JP). Rec 26 Feb 1818.

906. Page 190. 10 May 1817. Commissioners of the Courthouse and Jail to William **NEELY**. For the sum of $50, Lot No. 40 in Jackson; bounded on the N and fronted by Main St, E by Lot No. 124, S by Lot No. 41, and W and fronted by first east street. Signed John **DAVIS**, John **SHEPPARD**, Samuel G. **DUNN**, Abraham **BYRD**. Wit Thos. **NEWBERRY**, Jesse **HAIL**, Zenas **PRIEST** (JP). Rec 27 Feb 1818.

907. Page 192. 22 Feb 1818. John **SIMPSON** and Mary, his wife, to James **COX** seinior. For the sum of $600, 300 arpents, being the same tract granted by the Spanish Government to sd **SIMPSON**; bounded on the E by Andrew **RAMSEY** of John, N & S by vacant land, and W by Matthew **SCRUGGS**. Signed John **SIMPSON** by William **CRACROFT**, his attorney in fact, Mary **SIMPSON**. Wit Enoch **EVANS** (JP). Rec 28 Feb 1818.

908. Page 193. 3 Feb 1816. James **RANDOLL** and Nancy, his wife, to Antony **RANDOL**. For the sum of $600, 240 French arpens, more or less, on both sides of Franks' Creek, a fork of Randoll's Creek, including the plantation where Antony **RANDOLL** and his family now live and have lived for several years; adjoining Washington **ABERNETHIE**, **CRESWELL**'s old place, John **BURNS** formerly **TASH**'s, Abram **RANDOL**, and John **ABERNETHIE**; beginning at a white oak, a corner tree near the old Ridge Road in Washington **ABERNETHIE** and **CRESWELL**'s old place lines. Signed James **RANDOL**, Nancy (x) **RANDOL**. Wit Samuel K. **PARKER**, John **BURROWS**, Jno. **ABERNETHIE** (JP). Rec 28 Feb 1818.

909. Page 195. 25 Feb 1818. James **RAMSEY** to Jonas N. **MENEFEE**. For the sum of $60, __ acres lying about ¼ mile W from where John **SIMPSON** now lives. Signed James **RAMSEY**. Wit Thos. **MILLIS**, George **HENDERSON** (JP). Rec 2 Mar 1818.

910. Page 196. 2 Mar 1818. Samuel **PEW** and Eleanor, his wife, to Jason **CHAMBERLAIN**. For the sum of $200, 12 acres in Byrd Twp; beginning at a post on the SE corner of Mount Labedoyene, the seat of Joseph **McFERRON**, Esq.; also bounded by the town of Jackson, Richard S. **THOMAS**, and sd **PEW**; part of a tract confirmed to sd **PEW** as his settlement right, and which is hereinafter to be called Mount Loucas in memory of the late Charles **LUCAS**, Esq. Signed Samuel **PEW**, Eleanor (x) **PEW**. Wit Joseph **McFERRON**, Clerk, Margaret (x) **BERRY**. Rec 2 Mar 1818.

911. Page 197. 3 Mar 1818. Enoch **EVANS** to Benjamin **HITT**. For the sum of $1000, bond to make a title by deed to 204 arpents (173.54 acres) on a fork of Ramsey's Creek by 1 Jul next; being the same conveyed by Batist **GODAIR** to James **EVANS**, and that was granted to sd **GODAIR** by the Spanish Government and confirmed by the Commissioners. Signed Enoch **EVANS**. Wit Chas. **HUTCHINGS**, Joseph **McFERRON**, Clerk. Rec 4 Mar 1818.

912. Page 198. 31 Jul 1812. James **COX** Junr. and Anna, his wife, to James **COX** Senr., all of Cape Girardeau Twp. For the sum of $200, 150 arpens, French measure, in Cape Girardeau Twp, being the head right of James **COX** Junr confirmed by the Commissioners; adjoining Simon **KEYNON**, John **COX**, and James **COX** senr.; beginning at sd **KEYNON**, James **COX** senr, and John **COX**'s corner. Signed James **COX** jur., Anna **COX**. Wit William **HITT**, Benjamin **HITT**, Jno. **ABERNETHIE** (JP). Rec 4 Mar 1818.

913. Page 200. 7 Oct 1817. James **COX** senior and Elizabeth, his wife, to John **HITT** senr. For the sum of $600, 240 French arpens, more or less, on the waters of Randol's Creek; being part of sd **COX**'s head right, part of Simon **KENON**, and 158 arpens of the head right of James **COX** Junr; adjoining James **COX** Junr, sd **KENON**, John **GIBBONY**, etc.; beginning at sd **KENON**'s corner. Signed James (x) **COX** senr, Elizabeth (x) **COX**. Wit Richard **WALLER**, James **SMITH**, John **SHEPPARD**, Jno. **ABERNETHIE** (JP). Rec 4 Mar 1818.

914. Page 202. 14 Dec 1817. Martin **MILLER** to his son and daughter-in-law George C. **MILLER** and Caty, his wife. For natural love and affection and the sum of $500, one negro man named **Mark**. Signed Martin (x) **MILLER**. Wit Robt. R. **GREEN**, Robt. **GREEN**, Joseph **McFERRON**, Clerk. Rec 5 Mar 1818.

915. Page 203. 17 Feb 1818. Ezekiel **ABLE** and Sarah, his wife, to John **DUNN**. For the sum of $160, 80 acres on the waters of White Water; beginning at a post at the NE corner of sd **DUNN**'s survey. Signed Ezekiel **ABLE**, Sally **ABLE**. Test Samuel G. **DUNN**, George **HENDERSON** (JP). Rec 5 Mar 1818.

916. Page 204. 19 Jun 1816. Benijah **LAUGHARTY** and Rachel, his wife, to Jacob **CAMPBELL**. For the sum of $450, 150 acres on the head waters of Randol's Creek, being where sd **CAMPBELL** now lives, and part of a tract originally granted to sd **LAUGHERTY** as his head right; beginning at a stake, white oak, and black oak on the E line of sd survey, directly E of the southernmost part of sd **CAMPBELL**'s plantation. Signed Benijah **LAUGHERTY**, Rachel **LAUGHERTY**. Wit David **McCLUSKEY**, Thomas (x) **NEWEL**, John **DAVIS** (JP). Rec 6 Mar 1818.

917. Page 205. 24 Aug 1816. Joseph **SEAWELL** and Prudence, his wife, to Thomas **STEWART**. For the sum of $85, Lot No. 52 in Jackson; bounded on the N by Main St, W by first west street, S by Lot No. 53, and E by Lot No. 16. Signed Jos. **SEAWELL**, Prudence **SEAWELL**. Wit Tho. **NEALE** (JP). Rec 9 Mar 1818.

918. Page 206. 20 Feb 1817. Commissioners of the Courthouse and Jail to same. For the sum of $35, Lot No. 53 in Jackson; bounded on the W and fronted by first west street, N by Lot No. 22, E by Lot No. 17, and S and fronted by first south street. Signed John **DAVIS**, John **SHEPPARD**, Samuel G. **DUNN**, Abraham **BYRD**. Wit R. S. **THOMAS**, Judge of Southern Circuit, Thos. **BULL**. Rec 9 Mar 1818.

919. Page 207. 1 Apr 1817. Thomas **STEWART** and Elisabeth, his wife, to James **TANNER**. For the sum of $1600, Lot Nos. 52 & 53 in Jackson; bounded on the N by Main St, W by first west street, S by first south street, and E by Lot No. 16 & 17; excepting the part of Lot No. 52 heretofore sold to Johnson **RANNEY**; the same being their tavern stand. Signed Thomas **STEWART**, Elizabeth **STEWART**. Wit John **DAVIS** (JP), John **HOWARD**. Rec 9 Mar 1818.

920. Page 209. 25 Dec 1817. Thomas **SLOAN** and Catherine, his wife, to Anthony **BRAVAIS**. For the sum of $100, ½ of Lot No. 112 in Jackson, being the same that sd **SLOAN** purchased of the Commissioners; beginning at the NW corner of sd lot; bounded on the W and fronted by the River Zenon, S by Lot No. 113, and N by Main St. Signed Thomas **SLOAN**, Catherine **SLOAN**. Wit Josiah **VINCENT**, John **HERBERT**, Joseph **McFERRON**, Clerk. Rec 9 Mar 1818.

921. Page 210. 15 Jan 1818. Joseph **HAWKS** and Phineas **COBURN** to Joseph **FRIZLE**. For the sum of $352.95 ½, mortgage on a large horse waggon, geers, and harness, the same that was purchased of John G. **LOVE**; one chesnut sorrel gelding purchased of Robert **BUCKNER**; one rhoane gelding purchased of Elisha **SHEPHERD**; one sorrel gelding purchased of S. **PARKER**; one bay mare purchased of S. **HALL**; and one brown mare purchased of one **LACY**. The amount is due from one or both grantors within six months. Signed Joseph **HAWKS**, Phineas **COBURN**. Wit _ **RANNEY**, Zenas **PRIEST** (JP). Rec 12 Mar 1818.

922. Page 211. 11 Dec 1817. Frances **MURPHY** and Elizabeth, his wife, to Ruben **SMITH**, all of Washington Co., Mo. For the sum of $960, 640 acres on White Water River about eight miles SE of Jackson; being the same confirmed to sd **MURPHY** by the Commissioners as his settlement right; adjoining Andrew **FRANKS** and **SHIELDS**. Signed Fras. **MURPHY**, Elizabeth (x) **MURPHY**. Wit D. N. **DEADERICK**, J. **McCLANAHAN**, B. J. **THOMPSON**, JP in Washington Co., Mo. Rec 12 Mar 1818.

923. Page 212. 4 Nov 1817. Lemuel **HARGROVES** of St. Louis Co., Mo. to Burwell J. **THOMPSON** of Washington Co., Mo. For the sum of $1000, 640 acres on White Water, being the same granted to sd **HARGROVES** by the General Government. Signed Lamuel **HARGROVES**. Wit W. W. **THOMPSON**, Cazuel **McELROY**, Saml. **THOMPSON**, Zenas **PRIEST** (JP), Joseph **McFERRON**, Clerk. Elizabeth **HARGROVE**, consort of Lemuel, RD. Rec 13 Mar 1818.

924. Page 213. 5 Mar 1818. Ezekiel **ABLE** to Jenifer T. **SPRIGG**. For the sum of $300, 139 acres, more or less, being the same conveyed to sd **ABLE** by Andrew **FRANKS** and confirmed to sd **FRANKS** by the U.S.; beginning at a post near the house of Dr. **ELLIS**, being a corner of Jno. **HAYS** and the heirs of Wm. J. **STEVENSON**. Signed Ezekiel **ABLE**. Wit Jonas N. **MENEFEE**, Alfred P. **ELLIS**, George **HENDERSON** (JP). Rec 14 Mar 1818.

925. Page 214. 11 Aug 1817. Jonas **WHITTENBURG** to George **FRICKE**. For the sum of $120, part of Lot No. 28 in Jackson; bounded on the E and fronted by first east street, S by Lot No. 29, W by the remainder of the lot, and N and fronted by Main St; being the same sd **WHITTENBURG** purchased of William **NEELY** and wife on 30 Jun 1817. Signed Jonas **WHITTENBERG**. Wit John **BROWN**, Burrel S. **COSTILLO**, Zenas **PRIEST** (JP). Rec 16 Mar 1818.

926. Page 216. 30 Sep 1815. George **HAYS**, John **HAYS**, and Elizabeth **NEELY**. Articles of agreement. They are joint owners with Polly **JOHNSTON** of 400 arpents on the Mississippi River, 100 arpents apiece. George **HAYS** wishes to move on the land before it can be divided, and agrees to settle so it will not hinder division into four equal parts, with dividing lines beginning at the river. John **HAYS** and Elizabeth **NEELY** agree to let George **HAYS** have choice of his part, and each posts bond of $500 for observance of the agreement. Signed George **HAYS**, John **HAYS**, Elisabeth **NEELY**. Wit J. **McFERRON**, Zenas **PRIEST** (JP). Rec 18 Mar 1818.

927. Page 217. 10 May 1817. Commissioners of the Courthouse and Jail to Berry A. **WILSON**. For the sum of $51, Lot No. 19 in Jackson; bounded on the E and fronted by High St, S and fronted by second south street, W by Lot No. 55, and N by Lot No. 18. Signed John **DAVIS**, John **SHEPPARD**, Samuel G. **DUNN**, Abraham **BYRD**. Wit Thos. **NEWBERRY**, Jesse **HAIL**, R. S. **THOMAS**, Judge of Southern Circuit. Rec 21 Mar 1818.

928. Page 218. 11 Jun 1817. Ephraim **STOUT** and Jane, his wife, of Washington Co., Mo. to Bartlet **ZACHERY** of Ste. Genevieve Co., Mo. For the sum of $__, 300 acres, more or less, on the waters of St. Francois River; beginning at a white oak; to include a plantation where sd **STOUT** formerly lived, and being the same confirmed to him by the Commissioners. Signed Ephraim **STOUT**, Jane ( ) **STOUT**. Wit Jacob **KELLEY** (JP). Rec 24 Mar 1818.

929. Page 219. 27 Feb 1818. James **TANNER** to William **BACON**, both of New Madrid Co., Mo. For the sum of $1200, two lots in Jackson, being the same purchased by sd **TANNER** of Thomas **STEWART** and wife, now occupied by John **BROWN** as a tavern. Signed Jas. **TANNER**. Wit Richd. H. **WATERS**, Clerk of Southern Circuit, New Madrid Co., Mo. Rec 24 Mar 1818.

930. Page 220. 23 Mar 1818. Joseph **THORN** and Phinette, his wife, to Phineas **COBURN**. For the sum of $72, ½ of Lot No. 61 in Jackson, beginning on the SE corner of sd lot in the angle of first north and west streets. Signed Joseph **THORN**, Phinetta **THORN**. Wit Zenas **PRIEST** (JP). Rec 24 Mar 1818.

931. Page 221. 12 Aug 1817. Edley **EWING** and Jacob **CASTLEMAN** to Samuel S. **HALL**. For the sum of $200, two parts of Lot No. 63 in Jackson; ¼ of sd lot, beginning at the SE corner of sd lot, fronting on first west street and Main St, being the same conveyed to sd **EWING** and sd **CASTLEMAN** by the Commissioners on 28 May 1816; and ¼ of sd lot, beginning at the NW corner of Lot No. 63, bounded by Lot No. 62. Signed Edley **EWING**, Jacob **CASTLEMAN**. Wit Elijah **RANDOL**, Joel **BLUNT**, R. S. **THOMAS**, Judge of Southern Circuit. Rec 25 Mar 1818.

932. Page 222. 26 Aug 1817. Samuel S. **HALL** to Joseph **THORN**. For the sum of $100, ¼ of Lot No. 63 in Jackson, beginning at the NW corner of sd lot, and bounded in part by Lot No. 62. Signed Samuel S. **HALL**. Test Jos. **SEAWELL**, Wm. **SHEPPARD**, R. S. **THOMAS**, Judge of Southern Circuit. Rec 25 Mar 1818.

933. Page 223. 28 Oct 1817. Same to William **SHEPPARD**. For the sum of $200, part of Lot No. 63 in Jackson, beginning at the SE corner of sd lot; fronting on first west street and Main St. Signed Samuel S. **HALL**. Test Thomas W. **CROSBY**, Elisha **SHEPPARD**, R. S. **THOMAS**, Judge of Southern Circuit. Rec 25 Mar 1818.

934. Page 224. 5 Mar 1818. Berry **WILSON** to same. For the sum of $150, part of Lot No. 19 in Jackson on High St; bounded on the S by second south street, W by Lot No. 55, and N by Lot No. 18; beginning on the SE corner of sd lot. Signed Berry A. **WILSON**. Wit R. S. **THOMAS**, Judge of Southern Circuit. Rec 25 Mar 1818.

935. Page 225. 5 May 1803. Jabuz **FISHER** to Ezekiel **ABLE**. For the sum of $200, __ arpens on the bank of the Mississippi River in the Big Bend; being the head right of sd **FISHER**. Signed Jabus (x) **FISHER**. Wit James **CHEEK**, Jeremiah **ABLE**, George **HENDERSON** (JP). Rec 26 Mar 1818.

936. Page 226. 22 Jun 1803. Stephen **CAVENDER** to Ezekiel **ABLE** senr. For the sum of $200, __ arpens on the bank of the Mississippi River in the Big Bend. Signed Stephen (^) **CAVENDER**. Wit James **CHEEK**, Jeremiah **ABLE**, George **HENDERSON** (JP). Rec 26 Mar 1818.

937. Page 227. 24 Mar 1818. Daniel **BRANT** and Patience, his wife, to Ezekiel **ABLE**. For the sum of $100, 640 acres on Crooked Creek in German Twp, being his head settlement Spanish right; adjoining **HARTGROVE** and Rezin **BAILEY**. Signed Daniel **BRANT**, Patience (x) **BRANT**. Wit John B. **WHEELER** (JP). Rec 27 Mar 1818.

938. Page 228. 27 Mar 1818. Ezekiel **ABLE** to Joseph **FRIZLE** and Johnson **RANNEY**. For the sum of $1600, 640 acres as described in the preceding deed (D:227), including the improvement where Radford **ELLIS** lately resided. Signed Ezekiel **ABLE**. Wit Zenas **PRIEST** (JP), Rebecca (x) **GIBONY**. Rec 27 Mar 1818.

939. Page 229. 21 Jun 1817. John **WHITTENBURGH** and Rachel, his wife, to Eli **SHELBY**. For the sum of $800, 240 arpens on Ramsey Creek, being the same granted to Jonathan **DITCH** by the Spanish Government; bounded on the N by David **HARRIS**, W by Robert **GIBONEY**, S by Morgan **BYRNE**, and E by Enoch **EVANS** and the heirs of Samuel **TIPTON**; excepting 8 arpens sold to sd **HARRIS**. Signed Johannes **WITTENBERG**, Rachel **WHITTENBURGH** acknowledges her right of dower. Wit Enoch **EVANS** (JP). Rec 28 Mar 1818.

940. Page 230. 18 Oct 1817. Joseph **TAYLOR** and Elenor, his wife and formerly Elenor **TIPTON**, to William **RAMSEY**. For the sum of $200, 60 acres, more or less, adjoining survey of Samuel **TIPTON**, decd; being part of the survey of Andrew **RAMSEY**, decd, and the same bequeathed to sd Elenor by the last will and testament of Andrew **RAMSEY**. Signed Joseph **TAYLOR**, Elenor (x) **TAYLOR**. Test Wilson **ABLE** (as to Elenor **TAYLOR**), George **HENDERSON** (JP). Rec 30 Mar 1818.

941. Page 231. 18 Oct 1817. Same and same to same. For the sum of $100, quit claim to their interest in the head right of Samuel **TIPTON**, decd. Also, for the sum of $100, their 1/3 part of the head right of Nicholas **SAVAGE** in New Madrid Co., Mo. Signed Joseph **TAYLOR**, Elenor (x) **TAYLOR**. Test Wilson **ABLE**, George **HENDERSON** (JP). Rec 30 Mar 1818.

942. Page 232. 31 Oct 1817. Eli **SHELBY** and Mary, his wife, to James **RAVENSCROFT**. For the sum of $1200, a certificate of 640 acres (W. 206), granted by Frederick **BATES**, Recorder of Land Titles, dated 7 Aug 1816, in the name of Henry **MASTERS** or his legal representatives. Signed Eli **SHELBY**, Mary **SHELBY**. Wit Enoch **EVANS** (JP). Rec 31 Mar 1818.

943. Page 233. 20 Nov 1814. Joseph **WALLER** to Stephen **OWINS**. For two horse creatures and his obligation for one more valued at $80 and payable on 20 Nov next, 300 arpens in the Big Bend of the Mississippi River; being the improvement of sd **WALLER** and head right of Jonathan **BUIS**. Sd **WALLER** posts bond of $200 to defend against a Sheriff's title made by John **HAISE**, High Sheriff of the Cape Girardeau Dist, to Isack **WILLIAMS** for 240 arpens on sd claim. Signed Joseph (   ) **WALLER**. Test Jno. **THOMPSON**, Thomas **ROGERS**. Nero **THOMPSON**, son of John **THOMPSON**, decd, testifies to his father's signature. James **WILLIAMS** testifies that he saw John **THOMPSON** write the deed at the request of sd **WALLER**, and sign his name. Wit Jno. **ABERNETHIE** (JP). Rec 3 Apr 1818.

944. Page 234. 8 Jan 1818. Elijah **RANDOL** to Hiram C. **DAVIS**. For the sum of $300, __ acres on the waters of Flora in Cape Girardeau Twp, being his improvement and preemption right made before 1814; and sd **DAVIS** is given power of attorney to obtain a patent from the U.S. Signed Elijah **RANDOL**. Wit J. **RANNEY**, Zenas **PRIEST** (JP). Rec 4 Apr 1818.

945. Page 235. 1 Oct 1817. Medad **RANDOL** to Elijah **RANDOL**. For the sum of $300, __ acres on the waters of Flora in Cape Girardeau Twp, being an improvement and preemption right; and Elijah **RANDOL** is given power of attorney to obtain a patent from the U.S. Signed Medad **RANDOL**. Wit Johnson **RANNEY**, Zenas **PRIEST** (JP). Rec 6 Apr 1818.

946. Page 236. 1 Mar 1818. Johnson **STRONG** to Elijah **STRONG** and Polley, his wife. For natural love and affection which he bears to his son and daughter-in-law and for diverse other good causes and considerations, three negroes: **Will**, **Robbin**, and **Martin**; and all his blacksmith tools. Johnson **STRONG** delivers the property to Isaac **BREWER**, agent for Elijah and Polley **STRONG**. Signed Johnson **STRONG**. Wit Edward **KEW**, Charles **KEW**, Wm. **KELSO** (JP). Rec 7 Apr 1818.

947. Page 237. 1 Mar 1818. Same to William **BROOM** and Patsey, his wife. For natural love and affection which he bears to his son-in-law and daughter and for diverse other good causes and considerations, two negroes: **Stephen** and **Abram**. Signed Johnson **STRONG**. Wit Edward **KEW**, Charles **KEW**, Wm. **KELSO** (JP). Rec 7 Apr 1818.

948. Page 238. 1 Mar 1818. Same to Samuel **CROWLEY** and Fanny, his wife. For natural love and affection which he bears to his son-in-law and daughter and for diverse other good causes and considerations, two negroes: **Jack** and **Rodey**. Johnson **STRONG** delivers the negroes to Isaac **BREWER**, agent for Samuel and Fanny **CROWLEY**. Signed Johnson **STRONG**. Wit Edward **KEW**, Charles **KEW**, Wm. **KELSO** (JP). Rec 7 Apr 1818.

949. Page 239. 1 Apr 1818. Same to Isaac **BREWER** and Betsey, his wife. For natural love and affection which he bears to his son-in-law and daughter and for diverse other good causes and considerations, three negroes: a woman named **Poll** and her two children **Gabriel** and **Hannah**. Signed Johnson **STRONG**. Wit Edward **KEW**, Charles **KEW**, Wm. **KELSO** (JP). Rec 7 Apr 1818.

950. Page 240. 17 Feb 1818. Ezekiel **ABLE** and Sarah, his wife, to Alexander **McDONALD**. For the sum of $312.50, two tracts on the W side of White Water, part of Jacob **SEARDEN**'s head right; 100 acres, beginning at the NE corner; and 50 acres, beginning at the SE corner of the 100-acre survey. Signed Ezekiel **ABLE**, Sally **ABLE**. Test Samuel G. **DUNN**, George **HENDERSON** (JP). Rec 14 Apr 1818.

951. Page 241. 31 Mar 1818. William **RAMSEY** and Elizabeth, his wife, to Rebecca **HARBISON**. For the sum of $2000, 352 acres and 128 perches on Ramsey's Creek; beginning on Louis **LORIMIER**'s third line at the NW corner of a tract confirmed to James **COX** at a post. Sd **RAMSEY** owns the tract as heir by will of his deceased father Andrew **RAMSEY**, the original grantee. Signed William **RAMSEY**, Elizabeth **RAMSEY**. Wit George **HENDERSON** (JP), L. **LORIMIER**. Rec 14 Apr 1818.

952. Page 243. 13 Sep 1817. Joseph **HAWKS** and Electua, his wife, to Daniel F. **STEINBECK**. For the sum of $200, mortgage on a lot adjoining Jackson where sd **HAWKS**

now lives; continued N beyond the limits of and fronting on the west street of the town, and bounded on the S by Joseph **SEAWELL** and W by sd **SEAWELL** and Hubble's Creek. The obligation is due by 1 Jan next with 10% interest per annum. Signed Joseph **HAWKS**. Wit J. **CHAMBERLAIN**, Henry **ECKHART**, Joseph **McFERRON**, Clerk. Rec 14 Apr 1818. [Full satisfaction received of Charles G. **ELLIS** and William **NEELY** on 21 Aug 1819. Signed D. F. **STEINBECK**. Wit Joseph **McFERRON**, Clerk.]

953. Page 244. 24 Mar 1818. Rufus **EASTON** and Abial, his wife, of St. Louis Co., Mo. to Jason **CHAMBERLAIN**. For the sum of $372, Lot No. 2 in Jackson; bounded on the W and fronted by High St, N and fronted by first north street, E by Lot No. 26, and S by Lot No. 23; being the same that sd **EASTON** purchased of the Commissioners on 9 Feb 1818. Signed Rufus **EASTON**, Abial **EASTON**. Wit P. **QUARLES**, J. A. **QUARLES**, N. B. **TUCKER**, Judge of Northern Circuit. Rec 16 Apr 1818.

954. Page 246. 19 Feb 1818. Jonas **WHITTENBERG** to Jason **CHAMBERLAIN**, both of Jackson. For the sum of $20, part of Lot No. 27 in Jackson, beginning at a stake on the E side of the public square; being the same conveyed by the Commissioners to Anthony B. **NEELY**, and by sd **NEELY** and Margaret, his wife, to sd **WHITTENBERG**. Signed Jonas **WHITTENBERG**.   Wit   Chrs. **MOTHERSHEAD**, Solomon R. **BOLIN**, Joseph **McFERRON**, Clerk. Rec 16 Apr 1818.

955. Page 247. 31 Mar 1818. Ezekiel **ABLE** to Ruth **DUNN**. For the sum of $125, 50 acres on the E side of White Water; beginning at a post on the bank of White Water. Signed Ezekiel **ABLE**. Wit George **HENDERSON** (JP), Robert **GIBONEY**. Rec 21 Apr 1818.

956. Page 248. 31 Jan 1818. John P. **AIDENER** of Ste. Genevieve Co., Mo. to Jacob **SHEPPERD**. For __, 255.90 acres; beginning at an elm 10 inches in diameter, and crossing the line between Secs 29 & 30, Secs 31 & 32, and Secs 29 & 32, Twp 30 N, Rng 12 E. Signed John P. (P) **AIDENAR**, Betsey (x) **ADUNER**. Wit Joel **BLUNT**, Clifton **MOTHERSHEAD**, Richard **WRIGHT**, A. **BIRD**, JP in Ste. Genevieve Co., Mo. Rec 27 Apr 1818.

957. Page 249. 25 Dec 1808. Joseph **DENNIS** to Jeremiah **ABLE**. For the sum of $200, __ acres on the banks of the Mississippi in the Big Bend,

being the same where sd **DENNIS** now lives. Signed Joseph ( ) **DENNIS**. Wit W. **GARNER**, Wm. H. **ASHLEY**, Joseph **McFERRON**, Clerk. Rec 28 Apr 1818.

958. Page 250. 16 Apr 1818. Jos. **WALLER** to Jenifer T. **SPRIGG**. For services rendered to him by sd **SPRIGG**, quit claim to 640 acres on the waters of White Water, adjoining Doctor **ELLIS**; being the same claimed by Andrew **FRANKS**, confirmed to sd **FRANKS'** representatives, and conveyed by sd **FRANKS** to sd **WALLER**. Signed Joseph (x) **WALLER**. Test Chas. **HUTCHINGS**, John **HILL**, George **HENDERSON** (JP). Rec 29 Apr 1818.

959. Page 251. 2 May 1818. James **HOWARD** to John **BROWN**. For the sum of $70, Lot No. 73 in Jackson; bounded on the S and fronted by first north street, W and fronted by second west street, N by Joseph **SUEL** or surplus town lands, and E by Lot No. 61. Signed James (x) **HOWARD**. Wit George **FRICKE**, Tho. **NEALE** (JP). Rec 4 May 1818.

960. Page 252. 10 Feb 1818. Commissioners of the Courthouse and Jail to James **HOWARD**. For the sum of $40, Lot No. 73 in Jackson as described in the preceding deed. Signed John **DAVIS**, John **SHEPPARD**, Samuel G. **DUNN**, Abraham **BYRD**. Wit Thos. **NEWBERRY**, J. **FRIZEL**, Tho. **NEALE** (JP). Rec 4 May 1818.

961. Page 253. 14 Feb 1818. Adam **BEATY**, John **BEATY**, and Joseph **BEATY**, brothers, and sons of Francis **BEATY**, decd, of St. Francis Twp to Jeremiah **CRAVENS**, son of W. **CRAVENS**. For the sum of $450 cash and $675 in horses, 548 arpents, more or less, that is or may be granted by the U. S.; bounded on the E by the river and opposite W. **JOHNSON**'s; and which was willed to them on 8 May 1816. Also power of attorney to secure the right to sd land. Signed Adam **BEATY**, John **BEATY**, Joseph (x) **BEATY**, Mary ( ) **BEATY**. Test John **KIMDREL**(?), William **JOHNSON**, Ezek. **RUBOTTOM** (JP). Rec 6 May 1818.

962. Page 254. 10 Feb 1818. Commissioners of the Courthouse and Jail to James **HOWARD**. For the sum of $40, Lot No. 61 in Jackson; bounded on the E and fronted by first west street, S and fronted by first north street, W by Lot No. 73, and N by Joseph **SOWEL** and surplus town lands. Signed John **DAVIS**, John **SHEPPARD**, Samuel G. **DUNN**, Abraham **BYRD**. Wit Thos. **NEWBERRY**, J. **FRIZEL**, Tho. **NEALE** (JP). Rec 7 May 1818.

963. Page 255. 8 May 1818. John **THOMPSON** and Jane, his wife, to John **DANIEL**. For the sum of $800, 100 acres on the waters of Hubble's Creek, being part of the original grant and survey of Gilbert **HECTOR**; beginning at the SW corner of the original survey; bounded on the S by Henry **HAND** and the lands of John **HAND**, decd, NE by sd **HECTOR**, and W by Andrew **BURNS**. Signed John **THOMPSON**, Jane **THOMPSON**. Test John **JOHNSON**, Wm. **McGUIRE**, Joseph **McFERRON**, Clerk. Rec 8 May 1818.

964. Page 257. 21 Mar 1818. Michael **O'HOGAN** and Elezebeth, his wife, to James **WILKENSON**. For the sum of $150, 100 acres on the waters of Byrd's Creek, bounded on all sides by sd **O'HOGAN**; beginning at Philip **YOUNG's** NE corner at three white oaks about six feet apart. Signed Michl. **O'HOGAN**, Elizebeth (x) **O'HOGAN**. Wit James **RUSSELL** (JP), John **HOUK**. Rec 9 May 1818.

965. Page 258. 27 Apr 1818. Francois **BERTHIAUME** to John **HAYS**. For the sum of $55, 640 acres, more or less, on the waters of Apple Creek, being the settlement or preemption right of sd **BERTHIAUME**. Signed Francois ( ) **BERTHIAUME**. Wit W. **GARNER**, George **HENDERSON** (JP). Rec 11 May 1818.

966. Page 259. 8 Sep 1817. Silvanus **CASSELMAN** and Elizabeth, his wife, to Thomas S. **RODNEY**. For the sum of $4, 1 3/4 acre on the waters of Hubble's Creek, on the W side or corner of sd **CASSELMAN's** improvement; beginning on Thomas **SULLINGER's** E line at a hickory sapling. Signed Silvanus **CASSELMAN**, Elizabeth (x) **CASSELMAN**. Test Jno. **RODNEY**, James **DOWTY**, Michl. **RODNEY**, John **AKIN** (JP). Rec 12 May 1818.

967. Page 260. 30 Mar 1818. Andrew **RAMSEY** of New Madrid Co., Mo. to Thomas **ENGLISH** senr. For the sum of $2000, bond to make a deed on 250 acres or more on Ramsey Creek at the edge of the Big Swamp where sd **RAMSEY** lately lived; adjoined on the W by Morgan **BYRNE**, N by sd **ENGLISH**, and S & E by vacant land; to be made if the claim is confirmed by the U.S. Sd **RAMSEY** has sold the land to sd **ENGLISH** for the sum of $225, and has a Spanish claim to sd land. Signed Andrew **RAMSEY**. Wit George **HENDERSON** (JP), Jacob **SHEPHERD**. Rec 12 May 1818.

968. Page 262. 13 May 1818. John **RISHER** to the public. The space in front Lot No. 1 to Lot No. 11 in the town of Decatur; bounded on the N by Cape Girardeau, E by the Mississippi River, S by a line parallel to the N boundary from the SE corner of sd Lot No. 11, and W by sd town lots; to be for the common use of sd town. Sd **RISHER** had surveyed the town lots and outlots, and designated it the town Decatur after "that distinguished officer, Commodore Stephen **DECATUR**". Signed John **RISHER**. Wit Robt. **GREEN**, W. **GARNER**, Joseph **McFERRON**, Clerk. Rec 13 May 1818.

969. Page 263. 9 Feb 1818. Thomas **WALL** to Samuel **RAVENSCROFT**. For the sum of $15, __ acres, being his preemption right on the E side of the E fork of Cape Lacruse Creek, on the N side of the road leading to George F. **BOLLINGER's** mill to Cape Girardeau. Signed Thomas (x) **WALL**. Wit William **KELSO** (JP). Rec 13 May 1818.

970. Page 263. 11 May 1818. John **RISHER** and Mary, his wife, to Jenifer T. **SPRIGG**. For the sum of $100, Lot Nos. 4 & 5 in Decatur, on the Mississippi River, being part of 45 acres or more sold by Louis **LORIMIER** senr to sd **RISHER**. Signed John **RISHER**, Mary (x) **RISHER**. Wit Jonas N. **MENEFEE**, Victor **LORIMIER**, George **HENDERSON** (JP). Rec 15 May 1818.

971. Page 264. 2 Jun 1817. Commissioners of the Courthouse and Jail to George **MORROW** of Ste. Genevieve Co., Mo. For the sum of $58, Lot No. 41 in Jackson; bounded on the S and fronted by first south street, W and fronted by first east street, N by Lot No. 40, and E by Lot No. 125. Signed John **DAVIS**, John **SHEPPARD**, Samuel G. **DUNN**, Abraham **BYRD**, Benja. **SHELL**. Wit Thos. **STEWART** (JP), Robert **ENGLISH**. Rec 16 May 1818.

972. Page 266. 16 May 1818. Jones **WHITENBURG** to George **MORROW**, both of Jackson. For the sum of $50, part of Lot No. 27 in Jackson; beginning at a stake at the E side of the public square, 30 feet S of the NE corner of sd square; being the same conveyed by the Commissioners to Anthony B. **NEELY**, and by sd **NEELY** and Margrat, his wife, to sd **WHITTENBURG**. Signed Jonas **WHITTENBERG**. Wit Tho. **NEALE** (JP). Rec 16 May 1818.

973. Page 267. 19 May 1818. George F. **BOLINGER** to David **DAVIS** of Bracken Co., Ken. For the sum of $375, Lot No. 17 in Jackson;

bounded on the E and fronted by High St, S and fronted by first south street, W by Lot No. 53, and N by Lot No. 16. Signed G. F. **BOLLINGER**. Wit Alexndr. **BUCKNER**, Chrs. **MOTHERSHEAD**, Zenas **PRIEST** (JP). Rec 19 May 1818.

974. Page 268. 19 May 1818. James **COX** senior to Rebecca **HARBISON**. Quit claim to 162 ½ arpents on the waters of Cape Lacruch, adjoining the heirs of Louis **LORIMIER**, decd, and land sold by William **RAMSEY** to sd **HARBISON**. Sd **COX** transferred the tract to Andrew **RAMSEY** some years back, who then transferred it to sd **HARBISON**; this deed confirms that transaction. Signed James (x) **COX**. Wit Enoch **EVANS** (JP). Rec 20 May 1818.

975. Page 269. 16 Feb 1818. James **PATTERSON** to David **PATTERSON**, both of Greene Co., Ga. Power of attorney to receive money and property that he is entitled to as a legatee of his father, and conduct business relative to the estate of David **PATTERSON**. Signed James **PATTERSON**. Wit Geo. W. **MOORE**, B. **PORTER**, Presiding Justice of Superior Court of Wilkes Co., Ga. Charles **SMITH**, Clerk of Inferior Court of Wilkes Co., Ga. Rec 25 May 1818.

976. Page 270. 7 Mar 1818. John **GIBONEY** to John **LANGDON**. For the sum of $5000, bond to make a deed for 239 arpens and some additional poles on the waters of Randol's Creek, being the head right of sd **GIBONEY** granted by the Spanish Government; adjoined on the W by James **FLIN**, N by James **COX**, E by Robert **GIBONEY**, and S by ___ **THOMPSON**. Sd **GIBONEY** has sold the tract for $900 to sd **LANGDON**. Signed John **GIBONEY**. Elizabeth, wife of John **GIBONEY**, RD. Wit W. **GARNER**, George **HENDERSON** (JP). Rec 25 May 1818.

977. Page 271. 12 May 1818. John **RISHER** and Mary, his wife, to Charles **HUTCHINGS**. For the sum of $86, Lot Nos. 6, 21, & 44 in Decatur. Signed John **RISHER**, Mary (x) **RISHER**. Wit Jonas N. **MENEFEE**, Victor **LORIMIER**, George **HENDERSON** (JP). Rec 27 May 1818.

978. Page 272. 11 Feb 1814. Heirs of Louis **LORIMIER**, decd. Agreement that the mills and plantations on Hubbell's Creek, together with the adjoining tract, purchased of John **STRONG**, shall be put in the possession of Louis **LORIMIER**, son of Louis **LORIMIER**,

decd, as the whole of his inheritance. The value is to be determined by John **RAMSEY** senr, Nicholas **SEAVERS**, and John **WHITTENBURGH**. Should the value of the tract exceed his share, then he is to pay the excess to the other legatees the value of the tract. The tract is liable and subject to any demands on the estate, and sd **LORIMIER** is to give security to that effect. Signed Mary **LORIMIER**, Louis **LORIMIER**, D. F. **STEINBECK** for himself and as guardian of Victor **LORIMIER**, A. **LORIMIER**, Gme. **LORIMIER** as guardian to Verneuil R. **LORIMIER**, Thos. S. **RODNEY** as guardian for his three children. Wit George **HENDERSON** (JP), B. **COUSIN**. Rec 27 May 1818.

979. Page 274. 26 May 1818. Daniel F. **STEINBECK** to David **DAVIS** of Bracken Co., Ken. For the sum of $12,000, bond to make a deed for 640 arpents, more or less, as described in a deed from John **STRONG** to Louis **LORIMIER**; bounded on the N by the heirs of W. **BURROWS**, decd, E by Matthew **HUBLE** and a public lot, S by Abraham **BYRD** and John **RODNEY**, and W by William **MATTHEWS**. Sd **DAVIS** purchased the tract from sd **STEINBECK** for $6000, $2000· down, $2000 due in one year, and $2000 due in two years from 7 Jun next; and the deed is to be made after the last payment. Mrs. **STEINBECK** RD to the tract. Signed D. F. **STEINBECK**. Test Timothy **DAVIS**, Jason **CHAMBERLAIN**, R. S. **THOMAS**, Circuit Judge. Rec 30 May 1818.

980. Page 275. 1 Jun 1818. Josiah **LEE** and Polly, his wife, to William **WILKINSON**. For the sum of $150, two tracts on Byrd's Creek; their moiety of 240 arpens, formerly the property of Josiah **LEE** senior, decd, bounded on the N by the other half of sd tract, E by John **BYRD**'s heirs and George **CAVANER**, and S by the heirs of George W. **COCHRAN**; and 10 acres off the NW corner of the survey of Josiah **LEE** [junior], where sd **WILKINSON** now lives. Signed Josiah **LEE**, Polly (x) **LEE** (RD). Wit Tho. **NEALE** (JP), Jno. **ABERNETHIE**. Rec 1 Jun 1818.

981. Page 276. 2 Apr 1818. John **RAMSEY** to James **FLINN**. For the sum of $5, quit claim to 240 arpents on Charles Creek, known by Randell's Creek, which was granted to sd **RAMSEY** by the Spanish Government as his head right, and was confirmed by the commissioners; being conveyed by him to his father Andrew **RAMSEY**, then to sd John **RAMSEY**'s uncle John **RAMSEY** by the will of sd Andrew, and then to sd **FLINN**. Signed John (x) **RAMSEY**. Wit Enoch **EVANS** (JP). Rec 4 Jun 1818.

982. Page 276. 10 May 1817. Commissioners of the Courthouse and Jail to James **EVANS**. For the sum of $60.50, Lot No. 77 in Jackson; bounded on the S and fronted by first south street, W and fronted by second west street, N by Lot No. 76, and E by Lot No. 65. Signed John **DAVIS**, John **SHEPPARD**, Samuel G. **DUNN**, Abraham **BYRD**. Wit Jesse **HAIL**, Joseph **McFERRON**, Clerk. Rec 8 Jun 1818.

983. Page 277. 12 May 1818. John **RISHER** and Mary, his wife, to Jonas N. **MANEFEE**. For the sum of $80, Lot Nos. 10 & 23 in Decatur. Signed John **RISHER**, Mary (x) **RISHER**. Wit Jenifer T. **SPRIGG**, Victor **LORIMIER**, George **HENDERSON** (JP). Rec 9 Jun 1818.

984. Page 278. 18 Apr 1818. Joseph **WALLER** and Susanah, his wife, to Charles **SEAVERS** and Nicholas **SEAVERS**. For the sum of $500, 500 arpents on Randall Creek, being the same sold to him by Benjamin **HARGROVE**; bounded on the S by Abraham **BYRD**, E by John **RAMSEY**, N by Samuel G. **STROTHER**'s grant now owned by Web **HAYDEN**, and W by Matthew **HUBLE**. Signed Joseph ( ) **WALLER**, Susanah ( ) **WALLER**. Enoch **EVANS** (JP). Rec 9 Jun 1818.

985. Page 279. 7 May 1818. William **CLARK**, Governor of Mo. Terr, to Barnard **SNIDER**. Appointment as JP for German Twp for four years. Signed Wm. **CLARK**, Governor. Wit Frederick **BATES**, Sec. of Mo. Terr. Barnet **SNIDER** takes the oath of office. Signed Barnet **SNIDER**. Wit J. **McFERRON**. Rec 9 Jun 1818.

986. Page 280. 7 May 1818. Same to William **JOHNSON**. Appointment as JP for German Twp for four years. Signed Wm. **CLARK**, Governor. Wit Frederick **BATES**, Sec. of Mo. Terr. William **JOHNSON** takes the oath of office. Signed William **JOHNSON**. Wit J. **McFERRON**. Rec 9 Jun 1818.

987. Page 281. 17 Mar 1818. Bartholomew **COUSIN** for Jonathan **STOKER** to John **GUIBONY**. For the sum of $350 as provided in a deed of trust, 350 arpents, more or less, about six miles W of Cape Girardeau; bounded on the E by Morgan **BYRNE** and others, W by James **RAVENSCROFT** and Ch. **WALLS**, N by Robert **GUIBONY** and sd **BYRNE**, and S by Alexander **GUIBONY** and vacant land. Sd

STOKER mortgaged the tract to sd **GUIBONY** on 30 Dec 1801; and if the debt was not paid within one year, was to be conveyed by Louis **LORIMIER** senr and sd **COUSIN** to sd **GUIBONY**. Signed B. **COUSIN** for Jonathan **STOKER**. Wit Ulysses **MUNN**, Enoch **EVANS** (JP). Rec 9 Jun 1818.

988. Page 282. 22 Aug 1817. Thomas **FOSTER** and Mary, his wife, to John **GIBONEY**. In consideration of 100 acres, more or less, being the 1/3 part of a grant to John **LOGAN** on the waters of Hubble's Creek; quit claim to 240 arpens on Hubble's Creek, being a confirmation granted to sd **FOSTER** as his head right. Signed Thomas (x) **FOSTER**, Mary (x) **FOSTER**. Test David ( ) **LOGAN**, Hutson (x) **FARMER**(?), Samuel G. **DUNN**, John **AKIN** (JP). Rec 9 Jun 1818.

989. Page 283. 10 Jun 1818. Jeremiah **ABLE** to Ezekiel **ABLE**. For the sum of $60, one rone stud horse with a meely face three years old, and one sorrel mare six years old. Signed Jeremiah **ABLE**. Wit James **EVANS**, U. **MUNN**, Joseph **McFERRON**, Clerk. Rec 10 Jun 1818.

990. Page 283. 23 May 1818. John **RISHER** and Mary, his wife, to Ulysses **MUNN**. For the sum of $42, two lots in Decatur; Lot No. 8, bounded on the N by Lot No. 7, S by Lot No. 9, W by Water St, and E by vacant space between it and the Mississippi River; and Lot No. 19, bounded on the N by Lot No. 20, S by Lot No. 18, E by Water St, and W by an alley. Signed John **RISHER**, Mary (x) **RISHER**. Wit James **PARRISH**, B. **COUSIN**, George **HENDERSON** (JP). Rec 10 Jun 1818.

991. Page 284. 11 Apr 1818. Ezekiel **FENWICK** and Isabella, his wife, of Ste. Genevieve Co., Mo. to Daniel F. **STEINBECK**. For the sum of $800, house and lot in Cape Girardeau; bounded on the E by a lot formerly owned by Daniel **HARKLEROAD**, S by Joseph **McFERRON**, N by Main St, and W by a lot formerly owned by William **GARNER** and now owned by Jonas N. **MENEFEE**; being the same conveyed by Jeremiah **ABLE** to Nathaniel **POPE** and John **SCOTT** on 22 Mar 1811, and by sd **POPE** and Lucretia, his wife, and sd **SCOTT** to sd **FENWICK** on 8 Mar 1816. Signed E. **FENWICK**, Isabel **FENWICK**. Wit Enoch **EVANS** (JP). Rec 10 Jun 1818.

992. Page 286. 16 Apr 1818. Ezekiel **ABLE** to his daughter Elizabeth **STEPHENSON**. For natural love and affection and diverse other good causes, a negro girl named **Matilda** aged about 13 years and 10 months. Signed Ezekiel **ABLE**. Wit George **HENDERSON** (JP). Rec 11 Jun 1818.

993. Page 287. 8 Jun 1818. Jeremiah **ABLE** to his sister Elizabeth **STEPHENSON**. For natural love and affection and the sum of $400, four head of horses, two head of horned cattle, 11 head of sheep, 20 head of hogs, and all his household and kitchen furniture. Signed Jeremiah **ABLE**. Wit James **EVANS**, Ezekiel **ABLE**, George **HENDERSON** (JP). Rec 11 Jun 1818.

994. Page 288. 21 Apr 1809. Henry **HOWARD** to his son Zedekiah **HOWARD**. For natural love and affection and for the better maintenance of his son, 80 acres on a branch of Byrd's Creek; being the N corner of a tract where sd Henry now lives, on the W side of the creek. This deed to be null and void if Henry **HOWARD** should not obtain a complete title. Signed Henry **HOWARD**. Wit Geo. **HENDERSON** (JP). Rec 11 Jun 1818.

995. Page 289. 4 Sep 1816. John **DAVIS** by Sheriff John **HAYS** to William **KELSO**. For the sum of $100, 300 arpens, beginning on the bank of the Mississippi a short distance below the mouth of a creek at which John **BALDWIN** now lives. Sold on 3 Sep 1816 on a writ of execution issued 9 Aug 1816 by Circuit Court in favor of Medad **RANDOL** and against sd **DAVIS**, surviving partner of Alexander **WILSON** and John **DAVIS**, for $115 damages for non-performance of certain promises, and $33.93 costs. Signed John **HAYS**, Shff. Wit Joseph **McFERRON**, Clerk. Rec 12 Jun 1818.

996. Page 291. 30 Oct 1815. Fergus S. **MORISON** to Samuel **RAVENSCROFT**. For the sum of $200, ___ acres on Cape la Cruche Creek about three and a half miles from Cape Girardeau, on the Mine la Motte Road, on Congress land; being his improvement where he now lives. Signed Fergus S. **MORISON**. Wit W. J. **STEPHENSON**, D. F. **STEINBECK**, George **HENDERSON** (JP). Rec 12 Jun 1818.

997. Page 292. 24 Apr 1818. William **CLARK**, Governor of Mo. Terr, to William **TINNIN**. Appointment as JP for German Twp for four years. Signed Wm. **CLARK**, Governor. Wit Frederick **BATES**, Sec. of Mo. Terr. William **TINNIN** takes the oath of office. Signed William **TINNIN**. Wit J. **McFERRON**. Rec 12 Jun 1818.

998. Page 293. 22 Nov 1797. Don Louis **LORIMIER** to Andrew **RAMSEY** Jr. of Ken. Concession for 240 arpens on the Zenon River about 10 miles W of Cape Girardeau, and the improvements thereon. Sd **RAMSEY** wants to settle on this side of the river, and requests of sd **LORIMIER** a grant of 12 arpents of land; bordered on the N by Willm **DEAKINS**, and S & W by Wm **DAUGHERTY**. He will agree to follow the rules prescribed by the law. Signed Andrew **RAMSEY**, Jr. Cape Girardeau, 29 Nov 1797. To Lt. Governor from L. **LORIMIER**: I will allow a provisional grant until surveyor can officially survey this grant. St. Louis of Illinois. Jan 1798. The land requested by Don L. **LORIMIER** is open/vacant. Antonio **SOULARD** allows the grant to be given. Signed Zenon **TRUDEAU**. [IN FRENCH] Title is assigned to John **GUETHING** on 29 Apr 1805. Signed Andrew **RAMSEY**. Wit B. **COUSIN**, James **RUSSELL** (JP). Rec 12 Jun 1818.

999. Page 294. 26 Feb 1818. Moses **SCOTT** and Magdalen, his wife, of St. Louis Co., Mo. to Rene LeMULLEUR of Ste. Genevieve, Mo. For the sum of $1200, Lot No. 51 in Jackson, bounded on the S and fronted by Main St, W and fronted by first west street, N by Lot No. 50, and E by Lot No. 15; being the same that Robert **WASH**, Esq., purchased of the Commissioners Signed Moses **SCOTT**, Magdalen **SCOTT**. Wit J. V. **TAMIEZ**(?), Clerk of Superior Court, Northern Circuit, M. P. **LEDUE**, Clerk of St. Louis Co. Court. Rec 13 Jun 1818.

1000. Page 296. 14 Feb 1818. Benjamin **PATTERSON** by Sheriff John **HAYS** to Morgan **BYRNE** and Joseph **SEWEL**. For the sum of $40.50, 1150 arpents on Cape La Cruse, on the S side and adjoining the survey of Louis **LORIMIER**, to include an old mill seat and the improvement of James **RAINES**. Sold on 14 Oct 1817 on a writ of execution from New Madrid Co. Court of Common Pleas issued at Nov 1812 court in favor of John C. **HARBISON** and against sd **PATTERSON** for $50 debt, $6.75 damages, and $7.49 costs. Signed John **HAYS**, Shff. Wit Joseph **McFERRON**, Clerk. Rec 13 Jun 1818.

1001. Page 298. 30 Apr 1818. John **HAYS** to William **NEELY** and Joseph **SEWALL**. For the sum of $1, 100 arpens on the waters of Randal's Creek that he purchased of Elijah **WHITAKER**; being part of the head right of sd **WHITAKER**. Signed John **HAYS**. Test John D. **COOK**, J. **RAINEY**, Joseph **McFERRON**, Clerk. Rec 13 Jun 1818.

1002. Page 298. 13 Jun 1818. Charles **DEMOSS** by Sheriff John **HAYS** to James **RAVENSCROFT**. For the sum of $187, 100 acres, being the NW corner of a tract whereon sd **DEMOSS** formerly lived. Sold on 9 Jun 1818 on a writ of execution issued on 9 May 1818 by Circuit Court on a case heard before John **AKIN**, JP in Byrd Twp, in favor of William **CRACROFT**, agent for Charles **CRACROFT**, and against Joseph **THROCKMORTON** and sd **DEMOSS** (as bail), for $45 debt, $5.62 and 5 mills interest, $4.50 costs, and $2.70 court costs. Signed John **HAYS**, Shff. Wit Joseph **McFERRON**, Clerk. Rec 13 Jun 1818.

1003. Page 300. 13 Jun 1818. John **HAYS**, Joseph **SEAWELL**, and Levi **WOLVERTON** to William **CLARK**, Governor of Mo. Terr. For the sum of $2500, bond to guarantee that sd **HAYS** will perform the duties of Sheriff of Cape Girardeau Co.. Signed John **HAYS**, Jos. **SEAWELL**, Levi **WOLVERTON**. Wit Joseph **McFERRON**, Clerk. Rec 13 Jun 1818.

1004. Page 301. 13 Jun 1818. Same, same, and same to same. For the sum of $2500, bond to guarantee that sd **HAYS** will collect and pay all taxes and other monies over to the territorial treasury. Signed John **HAYS**, Jos. **SEAWELL**, Levi **WOLVERTON**. Wit Joseph **McFERRON**, Clerk. Rec 13 Jun 1818.

1005. Page 302. 16 May 1818. Rene **LeMELLIEUR** and Agatha, his wife, of Ste. Genevieve Co., Mo. to David **DAVIS** of Bracken Co., Ken. and now in Jackson, Mo. For the sum of $400, nearly ¼ of Lot No. 51 in Jackson, except for 6 feet of the N end for use as a public lane; beginning at the E corner of the lot on Main St, adjoining the public square; being the same conveyed by the Commissioners to Robert **WASH** of St. Louis Co. Signed Rene **LeMEILLEUR**, Bolduc **LeMEILLEUR**. Wit R. S. **THOMAS**, Judge of Southern Circuit. Rec 15 Jun 1818.

1006. Page 304. 28 May 1818. Ezekiel **ABLE** to John **DRYBREAD**. For the sum of $400, 120 acres on the Big Swamp, being part of the head right of Andrew **FRANKS**; beginning at the SW corner of sd tract at a stake and stone near a sugar tree and white oak; and adjoining Isaac **DEVORE** on the W and sd **ABLE** on the E. Signed Ezekiel **ABLE**. Wit George **HENDERSON** (JP), Alexander **McDONALD**. Rec 16 Jun 1818.

1007. Page 305. 18 Jun 1818. Andrew **BURNS** and Jane, his wife, to James B. **WILSON**. For the sum of $500, two tracts on the waters of Hubble's Creek granted to Johnathan **FIRMAN**; 240 __ whereon John **DAVIS** now lives; and 100 acres whereon Thomas **BOYCE** lives; bounded on the S by Joseph **SEAWELL**, W by Edward **HAIL** and David **PATTERSON**, N by sd **BURNS** and George **HAYS**, and E by Gilbert **HECTOR**. Signed A. **BURNS**, Jane **BURNS**. Wit Zenas **PRIEST** (JP), James(?) **BURNS**. Rec 18 Jun 1818.

1008. Page 306. 23 May 1818. John **RISHER** and Mary, his wife, to Bartholomew **COUSIN**. For the sum of $60, two lots in Decatur; Lot No. 7, bounded on the N by a street, S by Lot No. 8 sold to Ulysses **MUNN**, E by a public lot on the Mississippi, and W by a street; and Lot No. 14, bounded on the N by Lot No. 15 sold to Henry H. **SNIDER**, S by Lot No. 13, E by a street, and W by an alley. Signed John **RISHER**, Mary (x) **RISHER**. Wit James **PARRISH**, U. **MUNN**, George **HENDERSON** (JP). Rec 20 Jun 1818.

1009. Page 307. 12 Jun 1818. John **CANNON** to Robert **BROOKS**. For the sum of $30, __ acres on Old Cape Creek about two and a half miles above Cape Girardeau, being a preemption right between the surveys of Louis **LORIMORE**, decd, and Louis **LARGEAU**, decd. Signed John **CANNON**. Wit Daniel (x) **HARKKLEROAD**, George **HENDERSON** (JP). Rec 23 Jun 1818.

1010. Page 308. 17 Dec 1814. Commissioners of the Courthouse and Jail to Christian **GATES**. For the sum of $42, Lot No. __ in Jackson; bounded on the S and fronted by Main St, E and fronted by third west street, N by Lot No. 110, and W by Lot No. 123. Signed John **DAVIS**, John **SHEPPARD**, Samuel G. **DUNN**, Abraham **BYRD**, Benja. **SHELL**. Wit Tho. **NEALE**, A. P. **PATTERSON**, Jno. **ABERNETHIE** (JP). Rec 26 Jun 1818.

1011. Page 309. 28 Mar 1818. Elijah **RANDOL** and Nelly, his wife, to Simon **POE** Jur. For the sum of $428 ½, 200 acres, more or less, on the waters of Randol's Creek, being part of 640 acres confirmed to Enos **RANDOL** Jur.; beginning at a white oak, the SE corner of the original survey. Signed Elijah **RANDOL**, Penelope **RANDOL**. Wit Zenas **PRIEST** (JP), Alexander **SUMMERS**. Rec 26 Jun 1818.

1012. Page 310. 12 Jun 1818. John **BYRNES** to William **CRACROFT**. For ___, 82 acres, more or less. that was transferred to him by quit claim from William **WHITE**, who purchased of Hugh **CRISWELL**; bounded by the widow **MILLS** and James **RANDELL** on one side, and lands purchased of Hugh **CRISSWILL** by sd **WHITE** on the other. Signed John **BURNS**. Wit Enoch **EVANS**, John **DAVIS**, Zenas **PRIEST** (JP). Rec 27 Jun 1818.

1013. Page 311. 10 May 1817. Commissioners of the Courthouse and Jail to Thomas **SLONE**. For the sum of $50, Lot No. 112 in Jackson; bounded on the N and fronted by Main St, E and fronted by third west street, S by Lot No. 113, and W by surplus lands of the town. Signed John **DAVIS**, Samuel G. **DUNN**, Abraham **BYRD**. Wit Thos. **NEWBERRY**, Jesse **HAIL**, Zenas **PRIEST** (JP). Rec 4 Jul 1818.

1014. Page 312. 29 Jul 1817. Verneuil R. **LORIMIER** to Daniel F. **STEINBECK**. For the sum of $3000, a 1/6 undivided part of the lands and tenements sold to Pierre **MENARD** of Kaskaskia, Ill. Terr. by his father Louis **LORIMIER** senior, decd, on 6 Oct 1806, and conveyed by sd **MENARD** to Louis **LORIMIER**, sd **STEINBECK** and Agathe, his wife, Augustus Bogainville **LOURIMIER**, the heirs of Mary Louisa **RODNEY**, decd, sd Verneuil, and Victor **LORIMIER** on 26 Aug 1812. Also power of attorney to obtain a sufficient deed from sd **MENARD** should the earlier deed prove insufficient. Signed Verneuil R. **LORIMIER**. Wit B. **COUSIN**, J. **CHAMBERLAIN**, George **HENDERSON** (JP). Rec 6 Jul 1818.

1015. Page 313. 29 Jul 1817. Verneuil Raphael **LORIMIER** to same. For the sum of $5010, his full share and undivided part of all the lands and hereditaments belonging to his father Louis **LORIMIER**, decd, as devised to him by the last will and testament of his father dated 12 Mar 1808. Signed Verneuil R. **LORIMIER**. Wit B. **COUSIN**, J. **CHAMBERLAIN**, George **HENDERSON** (JP). Rec 6 Jul 1818.

1016. Page 314. 1 Jan 1818. Augustus B. **LORIMIER** to same. For the sum of $3000, a 1/6 undivided part of the lands and tenements sold to Pierre **MENARD** of Kaskaskia, Ill. Terr. by his father Louis **LORIMIER** senior, decd, on 6 Oct 1806, and conveyed by sd **MENARD** to Louis **LORIMIER**, sd **STEINBECK** and Agathe, his wife, Augustus Bogainville **LOURIMIER**, the heirs of Mary Louisa **RODNEY**, decd, Verneuil R. **LORIMIER**, and Victor **LORIMIER** on 26 Aug 1812. Also power of attorney to obtain a sufficient deed

from sd **MENARD** should the earlier deed prove insufficient. Signed A. B. **LORIMIER**. Wit Jenifer T. **SPRIGG**, B. **COUSIN**, George **HENDERSON** (JP). Rec 6 Jul 1818.

1017. Page 315. 21 Jan 1818. Augustus Bougainville **LORIMIER** to same. For the sum of $3800, his full share and undivided part of all the lands and hereditaments belonging to his father Louis **LORIMIER**, decd, as devised to him by the last will and testament of his father dated 12 Mar 1808. Signed A. B. **LORIMIER**. Wit Jenifer T. **SPRIGG**, B. **COUSIN**, George **HENDERSON** (JP). Rec 6 Jul 1818.

1018. Page 316. 2 Jul 1818. Abijah **O'NEAL** to William **TIPTON**, late of Cape Girardeau Co., and now of Lawrence Co., Mo. [now Ark.]. For the sum of $400, a moiety of 300 arpents coming to him from the estate of Samuel **TIPTON**, decd; adjoined on the N by **LARRYMEY**(?), E by **RAMSEY**, and S & SE by Enoch **EVANS**. Signed Abijah (x) **O'NEAL**. Peggy (|) **O'NEAL** RD. Wit Absolom **TIDWELL**, Morgan **MAGNESS**, James **GARNER**, JP in Laurance Co., Mo. Rec 11 Jul 1818.

1019. Page 317. 8 May 1818. John **WILSON** and Sarah, his wife, to William **McGUIRE** of Clark Co., Ken. For diverse good considerations and the sum of $2450, 400 arpens (or 336 acres, 2 roods, and 39 poles), beginning on the E side of Stephen **BYRD**'s. Signed John **WILSON**, Sarah **WILSON**. Test John **JOHNSON**, Charles **WOOD**, Joseph **McFERRON**, Clerk. Rec 11 Jul 1818.

1020. Page 319. 6 Mar 1813. Andrew **BURNS** and Jane, his wife, to John **DAVIS**. For the sum of $600, quit claim to three tracts; 240 arpents, more or less, on a fork of Hubble's Creek, bounded on the N by David **PATTERSON** and the tract where sd **BURNS** now lives, E by sd **BURNS** and Henry **HAND**, S by Samuel **PUGH** and Joseph **SEAWELL**, and W by Edward **HAILE**; being originally granted to Jonathan **FOREMAN**, conveyed by him to Benjamin **TENNILL**, by him to John **DAVIS**, and by him to sd **BURNS**, and being the same where John **DAVIS** now lives; 10 acres, more or less, adjoining the NE corner of the first tract, beginning at a gum on the W line of the survey on which sd **BURNS** now lives; 100 acres, more or less, beginning at the NE corner of the survey where sd **BURNS** now lives, and bounded in part by David G. L. **CALDWELL**. Signed A. **BURNS**, Jane (x) **BURNS**. Wit D. G. L.

CALDWELL, John H. **MADISON** (JP). Rec 15 Jul 1818.

1021. Page 320. 3 Jun 1818. Rene **LeMEILLEUR** and Agathe, his wife, of Ste. Genevieve, Mo. to Edmund **RUTTER** of Washington Co., Ken., Christopher G. **HOUTS** of Jackson, Mo., and Mark H. **STALLCUP** of New Madrid Co., Mo. For the sum of $500, ¼ of Lot No. 51 in Jackson, less 6 feet on the N side for a public lane; beginning at a stake on Main St 37 feet E of the SW corner of sd lot; being the same conveyed by the Commissioners to Robert **WASH** on 17 Dec 1814, by him to Moses **SCOTT** on 20 Feb 1816, and by him to sd **LeMEILLEUR** on 26 Feb 1818. Signed Rene **LeMEILLEUR**, Bolduc **LeMEILLEUR**. Wit R. S. **THOMAS**, Judge of Southern Circuit. Rec 21 Jul 1818.

1022. Page 322. 20 Jan 1812. Moses **CARLOCK** and Margaret, his wife, to Geo. W. **COCHRAN**. For the sum of $1000, 250 arpens on Byrd's Creek; being the same granted to Josiah **LEE** Junr, transferred by him to Anderson **NUNNELLY**, by him to Samuel **BALDWIN**, and by sd **BALDWIN** to sd **CARLOCK**; less 10 acres that sd **BALDWIN** transferred to sd **LEE**. Signed Moses **CARLOCK**, Margrat **CARLOCK**. Wit John **MILLER**, William (x) **CHRISTY**, James **RUSSEL** (JP). Rec 23 Jul 1818.

1023. Page 322. 1 Sep 1817. Hugh **CURSWELL** to Abraham **BYRD**. For the sum of $80, 295 arpents on the waters of Randle's Creek; bounded on the E by Antony **RANDOL**, S by Charles **ELLIS** and William **PENNY**, W by lands formerly owned by Leviney **MILLS**, and N by John **BURNS**. Signed Hugh **CRESWELL**. Wit J. **RANNEY**, R. S. **THOMAS**, Judge of Southern Circuit. Rec 23 Jul 1818.

1024. Page 323. 24 Jul 1818. Rene **LeMEILLEUR** and Bolduc, his wife, of Ste. Genevieve, Co., Mo. to Edward **McGUIRE**. For the sum of $800, ½ of Lot No. 51 in Jackson; beginning at a stake 37 feet E of the SW corner of sd lot; bounded by Main St, and the parts of the lot previously conveyed to David **DAVIS**, and **RUTTER, HOUTS, & STALLCUP**; being the same conveyed by the Commissioners to Robert **WASH** on 17 Dec 1814, by him to Moses **SCOTT** on 20 Feb 1816, and by him to sd **LeMEILLEUR** on 26 Feb 1818. Signed Rene **LeMEILLEUR**, Bolduc **LeMEILLEUR**. Wit

Tho. **OLIVER**, Clerk of Ste. Genevieve Co. Circuit Court. Rec 30 Jul 1818.

1025. Page 325. 10 Mar 1818. Mathew **HUBBEL** to David **STRICKLAND**. For the sum of $100, __ acres, being an improvement on Cedar Creek that sd **HUBBLE** improved and lived on. Signed Matthew (x) **HUBBLE**. Wit John **AKIN** (JP). Rec 4 Aug 1818.

1026. Page 325. 29 Jan 1818. Lavina **MILLS** of Lawrence Co., Mo. [now Ark.] to the heirs and legal representatives of Thomas **ENGLISH** Juniour, late of Cape Girardeau Co. For the sum of $350, 231 arpents and 25 perches, French measure, between the River Zenon and Randall's Creek, about 8 miles WNW of Cape Girardeau; bounded by the original claims of Louis **LATHAM** on the W, S by John **SOMERS** senior, E by Anthony **RANDALL** and Hugh **CHRISWELL**, and N by sd **CHRISWELL**; and being the same confirmed to her the by the late Board of Commissioners. Signed Levina (x) **MILLS**. Wit James **MILLS**, Manul(?) **MILLS**, William **RUSSEL**, JP in Lawrence Co., Mo. Rec 5 Aug 1818.

1027. Page 327. 27 Jun 1812. John **BYRD** and Betsy, his wife, to David **PATERSON**. For the sum of $148.50, 41 ½ acres and 1 pole, more or less (49 arpens), lying W of sd **PATERSON's** old survey, being part of a tract granted by the King of Spain to Hugh **CONELY** senior, and confirmed to sd **BYRD** by the Commissioners; beginning at a stake and stone at the NE corner of the original survey. Signed John **BYRD**, Betsey **BYRD**. Wit John **DAVIS** (JP). Rec 7 Aug 1818.

1028. Page 328. 6 Aug 1818. Jonas **WHITTENBURG** to Anthony B. **NEELY** and John G. **LOVE**. For the sum of $900, Lot No. 27 in Jackson; bounded on the S by Main St, E by first east street, N by Lot No. 26, and W by the public square; except for the part previously sold to Jason **CHAMBERLAIN** and George **MORROW**; and including the house where sd **WHITTENBURG** now lives, his shop, all the furniture, cabinet work, and window sashes, finished and unfinished, all his cabinet maker's tools, and all the plank in his kiln. Signed Jonas **WHITTENBERG**. Wit __ **WHITTENBERG**, David **HOLLEY**, Jno. **ABERNETHIE** (JP). Rec 8 Aug 1818.

1029. Page 329. 27 Jul 1818. William **NEELY** and Rachel, his wife, and Joseph **SEWALL** and Prudence, his wife, to Daniel **HOUSER**. For the sum of $1200, 443 arpens, on or near the boundary line of Byrd Twp, being Elisha **WHITTAKER**'s head right; adjoining William **WILLIAMS**, Drusilla **DIXEN**, and William **HAND**. Signed Wm. **NEELY**, Rachel **NEELY**, Jos. **SEAWELL**, Prudence **SEAWELL**. Wit Tho. **NEALE** (JP), J. **RANNEY**. Rec 10 Aug 1818.

1030. Page 330. 31 Mar 1818. Jeremiah **ABLE** and Patsey, his wife, and Ezekiel **ABLE** to the heirs of William **DUNN** Seiner, decd [not named]. For the sum of $625, 250 acres on White Water where the widow **DUNN** now lives; beginning at a post on the bank of White Water above the mouth of a small brook. Signed Ezekiel **ABLE**, Jeremiah **ABLE**, Patsey **ABLE**. Wit George **HENDERSON** (JP). Rec 11 Aug 1818.

1031. Page 332. 29 Nov 1806. Louis **LORIMIER** to James **ELLIS**, represented by his father Solomon **ELLIS**. For the sum of $100 to be paid by 1 Jul 1808 with interest from 1 Jul 1807, Lot No. 9, Range E in Cape Girardeau; bounded on the N by St Belleview, S by Erasmus & Allen **ELLIS**, E by Elisha **ELLIS**, and W by Lorimier St. Signed L. **LORIMIER**. Test B. **COUSIN**, Wm. **OGLE**. Full amount received on 21 Jun 1811. Signed L. **LORIMIER** senr. Test B. **COUSIN**, G. **HENDERSON** (JP). Rec 12 Aug 1818.

1032. Page 333. 21 Jan 1818. Heirs of Louis **LORIMIER**, decd, to Louis **LORIMIER**. For the sum of $1, their shares of 1000 acres, more or less, on a small creek above the old Cape, including an old Indian field and a lick or glaize on sd stream, granted to sd Louis **LORIMIER**, son of Louis, on 28 Dec 1799, and confirmed by the U.S. The tract was conveyed to his father on 18 Apr 1812. Signed A. B. **LORIMIER**, D. F. **STEINBECK**, Agathe **STEINBECK**, Raphl. V. **LORIMIER**. Wit Jenifer T. **SPRIGG**, B. **COUSIN**, George **HENDERSON** (JP). Rec 21 Aug 1818.

1033. Page 334. 30 May 1818. Jonathan **LAMB** of Logan Co., Ken. to David **EVANS**. Quit claim to all property and legal actions he may have or hold against sd **EVANS**. Signed Jonathan **LAMB**. Wit Isidore **MOORE**, James **RUSSELL** (JP). Rec 22 Aug 1818.

1034. Page 335. 25 Jul 1818. John **SHERADAN** of Natchitoches Parish, La. to John L. **LAFFERTY** of Lawrance Co., Mo. [now Ark.]. For the sum of $200, 640 acres, more or less,

being a settlement right. Signed John (   ) **SHAREDEN**. Wit Eliza ( ) **FRANKS**, William (   ) **COMMANS**, P. D. Cailleau LaFONTAINE, Judge of Natchitoches Parish, La. Rec 27 Aug 1818.

1035. Page 336. 5 Sep 1818. Jermiah **CRAVENS** to William **CRAVENS**. For the sum of $1000, 468 acres lying on the River St. Francis, on the W side opposite William **JOHNSON**, formerly occupied by Francis **BEATY**, then by **BEATY**'s sons, and then by Jeremiah **CRAVENS**. Signed Jeremiah **CRAVENS**. Wit Joseph **McFERRON**, Clerk, L. **STINSON**. Rec 5 Sep 1818.

1036. Page 337. 15 Sep 1818. William **CLARK**, Governor of Mo. Terr, to Solomon R. **BOLEN**. Appointment as JP for Byrd Twp for four years. Signed Wm. **CLARK**, Governor. Wit Frederick **BATES**, Sec. of Mo. Terr. Solomon R. **BOLEN** takes the oath of office. Signed Solomon R. **BOLEN**. Wit J. **McFERRON**. Rec 22 Sep 1818.

1037. Page 338. 8 Sep 1818. Andrew **MARTIN** and Sally, his wife, to George **HENDERSON**. For the sum of $90, Lot No. 37 in Jackson. Signed Andrew **MARTIN**, Sally **MARTIN**. Wit Zenas **PRIEST** (JP), S. **McNEEL**. Rec 23 Sep 1818.

1038. Page 338. 6 Jul 1818. John **SHIELDS** of Lawrence Co., Mo. [now Ark.] to Richard **SEARCY**. For the sum of $250, 640 acres, more or less, on White Water, being the settlement right of William **PAGE**, and confirmed in his name; also his right to any other lands in Cape Girardeau Co. Signed John **SHIELDS**. Wit Samuel S. **HALL**, Richard S. **THOMAS**, Judge of Southern Circuit. Rec 24 Sep 1818.

1039. Page 339. 24 Sep 1818. Richard **SEARCY** of Lawrence Co., Mo. [now Ark.] to James **RAVENSCROFT**. For the sum of $125, quit claim to 500 arpens, more or less, originally confirmed to John **SHIELDS**, and conveyed by him to sd **SEARCY**; bounded on the N by Robert **GIBONY**, E by Jonathan **STOKER**, S by Matthew **SCRUGGS**, and W by Jacob **JACOBS**. Signed Richd. **SEARCY**. Wit Solomon R. **BOLIN** (JP). Rec 25 Sep 1818.

1040. Page 340. 24 Sep 1818. Ezekiel **ABLE** to Charles S. **HEMPSTEAD** of St. Louis, Mo. For the sum of $10, quit claim to 640 acres, more or less, on Hubble's Creek in Twp 30 N, Rng 12 E, being the settlement and improvement right of

John **SHIELDS**, and confirmed to his representatives. Signed Ezekiel **ABLE**. Wit Zenas **PRIEST** (JP), William **JAMES**. Rec 25 Sep 1818.

1041. Page 341. 16 Jul 1818. Henery **BULLINGER** of Laurence Co., Mo. [now Ark.] to Wm. **POLK**. For the sum of $640, 640 acres on the main stream of Whitewater, joining to Danil **BULLINGOR** above; beginning near Daniel **BOLLINGER**'s corner on a stake; and being the same confirmed to sd Henery, son of Danil **BOLLINGER** ser, and where sd Henery formerly lived and had a mill. Signed Henruh **BLLINGER**. Test Daniel **BOLLINGER**, James **SMITH**, John **POLK**, Solomon R. **BOLIN** (JP). Rec 30 Sep 1818.

1042. Page 342. 2 Oct 1818. George **MORROW** and Susannah, his wife, to Saml. H. **REID**. For the sum of $50, ½ of Lot No. 42 in Jackson, to be taken off the E square of sd lot and to include the house where Robert **MILLICAN** now lives, adjoining Thos. **NEWBERRY**. Signed Geo. **MORROW**, Susannah **MORROW**. Wit Zenas **PRIEST** (JP), E. **CRIDDLE**. Rec 6 Oct 1818.

1043. Page 343. 8 Sep 1818. Abraham **CRADER** to Jacob **CRADER** and Samuel **CRADER**. For the sum of $2000, 640 acres on the waters of White Water. Signed Abraham **GREDER**. Wit James **RUSSELL** (JP), Clair **RUSSELL**. Rec 6 Oct 1818.

1044. Page 344. 29 Sep 1818. Same to same and same. For the sum of $50, two horse creatures, one cow, and all his hogs; which property is remaining in a certain farm or tenement in the late occupation of sd Abraham **CRADER**. Signed Abraham **GREDER**. Wit James **RUSSELL** (JP), Clair **RUSSELL**. Rec 6 Oct 1818.

1045. Page 345. 26 Sep 1818. James **PATTERSON** to John B. **WHEELER**. For the sum of $450, 156 acres, more or less, in German Twp, being part of a tract granted and confirmed to William **PATTERSON**, decd, and on the NE corner thereof; bounded on the E by Whitewater, N by public land and Daniel **CLINGINGSMITH**. Sd **PATTERSON** acknowledges $3 for every acre should the tract not total 156 acres. Signed James **PATTERSON**. Betsy **PATTERSON**, wife of James, acknowledges the deed as her act. Wit Barnet **SNIDER** (JP), Caty (x) **COLWELL**. Rec 7 Oct 1818.

1046. Page 347. 10 Jul 1818. William **CLARK**, Governor of Mo. Terr, to Alexander **BUCKNER**. Appointment as Circuit Attorney for the Southern Circuit. Signed Wm. **CLARK**, Governor. Wit Frederick **BATES**, Sec. of Mo. Terr. Alexander **BUCKNER** takes the oath of office. Wit Solomon R. **BOLIN** (JP). Rec 12 Oct 1818.

1047. Page 347. 5 Oct 1818. Benjn. **HARGRAVE** of Washington Co., Mo. to Robt. T. **BROWN** of Washington Co., Mo. and George **BULLITT** of Arkansas Co., Mo. Quit claim to 640 acres on the waters of White Water, acquired by settlement. Signed Benjamin **HARGRAVE**. Test Jno. **DAVIS**, Reubn. H. **BOWER**, W. B. **TUCKER**, Judge of Northern Circuit. Rec 13 Oct 1818.

1048. Page 349. 24 Oct 1817. Thomas J. **WATHERS** of Ind., and Thos. **NEALE** and Jno. **SHEPHERD** of Mo. to Stephen **BYRD** and Isaac **SHEPHERD**. For the sum of $2000, bond to guarantee that Elizabeth **MOUNT**, execr of Jasper **MOUNT**, shall discharge her duties as execr of the last will and testament of Jasper **MOUNT**, decd. Signed Thos. J. **WATHERS**, Tho. **NEALE**, John **SHEPPARD**. Wit Abraham **BYRD**, Wm. **SHEPPARD**, B. S. **COSTILLO**, John **SHEPPARD**, Zenas **PRIEST** (JP). Rec 14 Oct 1818.

1049. Page 349. 12 Oct 1818. Sieges **HALL**, adminr of the estate of Thomas **RING**, decd, to Jacob **KELLEY**. For the sum of $200, 94 ½ acres, more or less, being the same tract where sd **KELLEY** now lives; beginning at an ironwood. Signed Seges (x) **RING**. Test Ezekiel **RUBOTTOM** (JP), Levi **HAGH**. Rec 15 Oct 1818.

1050. Page 351. 28 Apr 1818. Elijah **RANDOL** to William **MONTGOMERY** of New Madrid Co., Mo. For the sum of $2700, bond to make a deed for Lot No. 6 in Jackson. Sd **RANDOL** sold the lot to sd **MONTGOMERY** for the sum of $1350--$100 in hand, $575 payable on 22 Jul next, and the balance payable on 22 Apr next; sd deed to be made on 22 Jul next if payments are made. Signed Elijah **RANDOL**. Wit J. **RANNEY**, James **RAVENSCROFT**, Solomon R. **BOLIN** (JP). Rec 19 Oct 1818.

1051. Page 352. 17 Oct 1818. John **BURROWS** and Bethena, his wife, to Isaiah **POE** and Sarah, his wife and daughter of Waters **BURROWS**, decd. For the sum of $.01, quit claim to 118 ½ acres on the waters of Hubble's Creek in Cape

Girardeau Twp, being the head right of Waters **BURROWS**, decd; beginning 25 chains S of the NE corner of sd tract on the E line. Isaiah **POE** and Sarah, his wife, to John **BURROWS**. For the sum of $.01, quit claim to 222 acres, being their interest in the head right of Waters **BURROWS**; beginning on the NW corner of sd tract, and bounded in part by sd **POE**. None of the parties are to be held responsible for any defect of title, which John **BURROWS** and Sarah **POE** have as heirs of Waters **BURROWS**. Signed John **BURROWS**, Bethena (x) **BURROWS**, Isaiah **POE**, Sarah **POE**. Test John **AKIN** (JP), Joseph (x) **WHITNEY**. Rec 23 Oct 1818.

1052. Page 354. 12 Dec 1813. John **BYRD** to his daughter Polley **BYRD**, alias Poll **TYNER**. For ___, 200 arpens; beginning at Josiah **LEE** Junr's NW corner, and also bounded by George W. **COCHRAN**. Signed John **BYRD**. Test Joseph **YOUNG**, Job **THROCKMORTON**, John **DAVIS** (JP). Rec 29 Oct 1818.

1053. Page 355. 4 Jun 1818. Daniel F. **STEINBECK** to John **SIMPSON**. For the sum of $200, a negro man named **Isaac** about 48 years old, being the same man he purchased of Verneuil **LORIMIER**. Signed D. F. **STEINBECK**. Wit B. **COUSIN**, Raphael V. **LORIMIER**, George **HENDERSON** (JP). Rec 29 Oct 1818.

1054. Page 355. 15 Sep 1818. William **CRACROFT** to same. For the sum of $300, quit claim to 150 acres on the waters of the Big Swamp, being part of sd **SIMPSON**'s head right. Signed William **CRACRAFT**. Wit John **RODNEY**, Zenas **PRIEST** (JP). Test John B. **GUSEMAN**. Rec 29 Oct 1818.

1055. Page 356. 30 May 1818. Peter **GROUNDS** to Henery **YUNT**. For the sum of $240, 242 ½ acres, more or less, on the main stream of White Water; beginning on a Spanish oak. Signed Peter **GROUND**. Test William **POLK**, Aaron **BOLLINGER**, Charity (   ) **YUNT**, William **TINNIN** (JP). Rec 3 Nov 1818.

1056. Page 358. 19 Oct 1818. Henry **BURNLEY** to Shared G. **SWAIN**. For the sum of $200, 160 acres on the River St. Francis in St. Francis Twp, being where he now lives, and improved by him in 1812. Signed Henry **BURNLEY**. Wit Ezekiel **RUBOTTOM** (JP). Rec 3 Nov 1818.

1057. Page 358. 19 Oct 1818. Samuel **STREET** to Chesley **PEYTON**. For the sum of $100, __

acres on the River St. Francis in St. Francis Twp, being improved by him in 1810. Signed Samuel **STREET**. Wit Ezek. **RUBOTTOM** (JP). Rec 3 Nov 1818.

1058. Page 359. 19 Sep 1818. Rene **LeMEILLEUR** and Agathe, his wife, late Agathe **BOLDUC**, to Edmund **RUTTER** of Washington Co., Ken., Christopher G. **HOUTS** of Jackson, Mo., and Mark H. **STALLCUP** of New Madrid Co., Mo.; merchants trading as Rutter, Houts, & Stallcup. For the sum of $500, part of Lot No. 51 as described in a deed made on 3 Jun 1818 (D:320) The name of Agathe **LeMEILLEUR** is written in the body of the earlier deed, and she signed Bolduc **LeMEILLEUR**. She RD to the lot, and this deed confirms the earlier deed. Signed Rene **LeMEILLEUR**, Agathe **LeMEILLEUR**. Wit Tho. **OLIVER**, Clerk of Ste. Genevieve Co. Circuit Court. Rec 3 Nov 1818.

1059. Page 361. 3 Sep 1818. John **BROWN** and Rachel, his wife, to John **HERBERT** & Co. For the sum of $80, ½ of Lot No. 73 in Jackson; bounded on the S and fronted by first north street, W by the other half of the lot, N by Joseph **SEAWELL** or surplus town land, and E by Lot No. 61. Signed John **BROWN**, Rachel **BROWN**. Wit Tho. **NEALE** (JP), G. **FRICKE**. Rec 4 Nov 1818.

1060. Page 363. 10 Sep 1818. Joseph **THORN** and Phinelle, his wife, to same. For the sum of $350, ½ of Lot No. 61 in Jackson; bounded on the S and fronted by first north street, W by Lot No. 73, N by Joseph **SEWELL** or surplus town land, and E by the other half of sd lot. Signed Joseph **THORN**, Phinette **THORN**. Wit Josiah **VINCENT**, Tho. **NEALE** (JP). Rec 4 Nov 1818.

1061. Page 365. 9 Sep 1818. Burrel S. **COSTILLO** to same. For the sum of $150, Lot No. 66 in Jackson; bounded on the N and fronted by first south street, E and fronted by first west street, S by Lot No. 67, and W by Lot No. 78. Signed Burrel S. **COSTILLO**. Wit Nathan **McCARTY**, Tho. **NEALE** (JP). Rec 10 Nov 1818.

1062. Page 366. 24 Dec 1817. Robert **PATTERSON** and Sarah, his wife, to William **NEELY**. For the sum of $100, 33 acres in Byrd Twp, being the 1/9 part of the plantation of their father David **PATTERSON** (sd Robert being son of David **PATTERSON**). Signed Robert

PATTERSON. Wit J. **RANNEY**, Zenas **PRIEST** (JP). Rec 11 Nov 1818.

1063. Page 367. 25 May 1818. David **PATTERSON**, by virtue of power of attorney granted to him by James **PATTERSON** of Ga. on 6 Feb 1818, to same. For the sum of $200, 51 acres, more or less, being all the right James **PATTERSON** has to the plantation of his father in Byrd Twp as one of nine heirs of David **PATTERSON**, decd. Signed David **PATTERSON**. Wit Tho. **NEALE** (JP), Samuel **PEW**. Rec 11 Nov 1818.

1064. Page 369. 25 Jun 1818. Hugh **CRESWELL** and Nancy, his wife and one of the daughters of David **PATTERSON**, decd, to same. For the sum of $62, __ acres, being the 1/9 part of a plantation in Byrd Twp, and the same that descended from David **PATTERSON**, decd, to sd Nancy; and where David **PATTERSON** lived in his lifetime (except 35 acres formerly sold to Samuel **PEW**). Signed Hugh **CRESWELL**, Nancy **CRESWELL**. Wit J. **RANNEY**, Zenas **PRIEST** (JP). Rec 11 Nov 1818.

1065. Page 370. 14 Oct 1818. John **PEW** and Jane, his wife and formerly Jane **PATTERSON**, granddaughter and heir of David **PATTERSON**, decd, to same. For the sum of $28, 7 3/4 acres in Byrd Twp, being their interest in the head right of David **PATTERSON**, decd. Signed John **PEW**, Jane (|) **PEW**. Wit Zenas **PRIEST** (JP), William **CRACRAFT**. Rec 11 Nov 1818.

1066. Page 371. __ Jun 1818. Commissioners of the Courthouse and Jail to Christopher G. **HOUTS**. For the sum of $72, Lot No. 49 in Jackson; bounded on the E by Lot No. 13, S and fronted by first north street, W and fronted by first west street, and N by surplus lands of the town or Joseph **SEWEL**. Signed John **DAVIS**, John **SHEPPARD**, Samuel G. **DUNN**, Abraham **BYRD**. Wit George **FRICKE**, Phinehas **COBURN**, Jason **CHAMBERLAIN**, Joseph **McFERRON**, Clerk. Rec 12 Nov 1818.

1067. Page 373. 11 Mar 1818. Christian **SEABAUGH** to Mathias **BOLLINGER**. For the sum of $805, 640 acres, more or less, on Whitewater; joined on the E by sd **BOLLINGER**, and W by Frederick **SLINKER**; being the whole of the head right and confirmation of George **GROUND**. Signed Christian (o) **SEABAUGH**. Wit John B.

WHEELER, George F. **BOLLINGER**, Tho. **NEALE** (JP). Rec 13 Oct 1818.

1068. Page 374. 12 Nov 1818. Jesse **HAIL** to Nathan **VANHORN**. For the sum of $800, Lot No. 87 in Jackson, being where sd **HAIL** now resides; bounded on the E and fronted by second west street, S and fronted by Main St, W by Lot No. 99, and N by Lot No. 86. Signed Jesse **HAIL**. Wit A. B. **NEELY**, Wm. **NEELY**, Zenas **PRIEST** (JP). Rec 16 Nov 1818.

1069. Page 375. 16 Nov 1818. Gilbert **HECTOR** and Ann, his wife, to Lewis **DICKSON**. For the sum of $100, 1/8 part of 400 acres, being Ann **HECTOR**'s dower right to Zilla **DICKSON**'s head settlement right and a Spanish claim, less 240 acres sold to John **RANDOL** in the lifetime of sd Zilla; bounded on the S by the part sold to sd **RANDOL**, W by the widow **TAYLOR**, N by Benijah **LAUGHERTY**'s head right now owned by Jacob **CAMPBELL**, and E by unknown. Signed Gilb. **HECTOR**, Ann (x) **HECTOR**. Wit Solomon R. **BOLIN** (JP). Rec 16 Nov 1818.

1070. Page 376. 3 Nov 1818. Samuel **PERRY** and Ann M., his wife, to William M. **PERRY**, all of Washington Co., Mo. For the sum of $800, 640 acres on the waters of Whitewater about seven or eight miles SW of Jackson, being the same that Samuel **PERRY** purchased from Francois **MURPHEY** on 4 Nov 1817, and that was confirmed to sd **MURPHEY** by the Commissioners; adjoined on the E by Gerry **CONAWAY** and SW by Andrew **FRANKS**. Signed Samuel **PERRY**, Ann M. **PERRY**. Wit Jas. F. **PERRY**, Holly **JOHNSON**. Wit John **BRICKERY**, Clerk of Washington Co. Circuit Court. Rec 18 Nov 1818.

1071. Page 378. 17 Nov 1818. Ezekiel **ABLE** and Sally, his wife, to same. For the sum of $100, 320 acres on the waters of White Water about 10 miles SW of Jackson, being ½ of a tract confirmed to Francis **MURPHY**, so divided as to give sd **PERRY** an equal portion of the good and bad land of the tract; adjoined on one side by Samuel **DUNN**, formerly Garry **CONWAY**, and on the other by John **DUNN**. Signed Ezekiel **ABLE**, Sally **ABLE**. Wit Chas. **HUTCHINGS**, Alfred P. **ELLIS**, Enoch **EVANS** (JP). Rec 18 Nov 1818.

1072. Page 379. 18 Nov 1818. James **RANDOL** to same. For the sum of $20, quit claim to the head and settlement right of Francis **MURPHY**, and to 640 acres confirmed to sd **MURPHY** on the waters of White Water about seven or eight miles SW of Jackson; adjoining Jerry **CONAWAY** on the E and Andrew **FRANKS** on the SW. Signed James **RANDOL**. Wit Solomon R. **BOLIN**, Joseph **McFERRON**, Clerk. Rec 18 Nov 1818.

1073. Page 380. 10 May 1817. Commissioners of the Courthouse and Jail to Andrew **MARTIN**. For the sum of $76, Lot No. 37 in Jackson; bounded on the E by Lot No. 121, S and fronted by first north street, W and fronted by first east street, and N by surplus town lands. Signed John **DAVIS**, John **SHEPPARD**, Samuel G. **DUNN**, Abraham **BYRD**. Wit Thos. **NEWBERRY**, Jesse **HAIL**, Solomon R. **BOLIN** (JP). Rec 19 Nov 1818.

1074. Page 382. 26 Oct 1818. William **BACON** of New Madrid Co., Mo. to John **BROWN**. For the sum of $1500, two lots in Jackson, being the same that James **TANNER** purchased of Thomas **STEWART** and wife, and sold to sd **BACON**, and being the same occupied by sd **BROWN** as a tavern, with the exception of 20 feet square occupied by Johnson **RANNEY**. Sd **BROWN** is to have no recourse against sd **BACON**. Signed William **BACON**. Wit Jason **CHAMBERLAIN**, Solomon R. **BOLIN** (JP). Rec 23 Nov 1818.

1075. Page 383. 14 Nov 1818. John **DAVIS** and Nancy, his wife. For the sum of $180.83 1/3, quit claim to two tracts on the waters of Hubble's Creek; 10 acres, bounded on the S by Joseph **SEAWELL**, E by Henry **HAND**, and N & W by sd **DAVIS**, beginning at a stake near a gum and two dogwood saplings; and 5 acres and 33 perches, bounded on the W by Edward **HAIL**, N & E by sd **DAVIS**, and S by sd **SEAWELL**, beginning at a stake, two sycamores, and a walnut. Should the Spanish concession not be confirmed, then sd **BROWN** is granted right of preemption to sd tracts. Signed John **DAVIS**, Nancy **DAVIS**. Test George **FRICKE**, Solomon R. **BOLIN** (JP). Rec 23 Nov 1818.

1076. Page 385. 4 Oct 1803. Robert **HARPER** to Samuel **CAMPBELL**. For the sum of $200, 750 arpens, more or less, on the W side of Castor Creek; being all his Spanish, head, settlement, and improvement rights. Signed Robert **HARPER**. Wit Ezekiel **ABLE**, James **CAMPBELL**, George **HENDERSON** (JP). Rec 25 Nov 1818.

1077. Page 386. 27 Oct 1818. Ezekiel **ABLE** to same. For the sum of $1, quit claim to __ acres

on Caster River, being the head right and survey of Robert **HARPER**. Signed Ezekiel **ABLE**. Wit George **HENDERSON** (JP). Rec 25 Nov 1818.

1078. Page 387. 16 Nov 1818. Samuel **CAMPBELL** of Ste. Genevieve Co., Mo. to Henry **WHITENER**. For the sum of $1200, bond make a deed for 640 acres on the River Castor, including the improvement where the widow **WHITENER** now lives; being the same confirmed to Robert **HARPER**. The deed to be made immediately after a patent is received. Signed Samuel **CAMPBELL**. Wit William **TINNIN** (JP). Rec 25 Nov 1818.

1079. Page 388. 2 Mar 1803. William **CAMPBELL** to Samuel **CAMPBELL**. For the sum of $200, 750 arpens, more or less, on Caster Creek, being all his Spanish, head, and settlement rights. Signed William **CAMPBELL**. Wit Ezekiel **ABLE**, James **CAMPBELL**, George **HENDERSON** (JP). Rec 25 Nov 1818.

1080. Page 389. 28 Oct 1818. Ezekiel **ABLE** to same, of Ste. Genevieve Co. For the sum of $1, quit claim to 750 arpens, more or less, on Castor River, being the head right of William **CAMPBELL**. Signed Ezekiel **ABLE**. Wit George **HENDERSON** (JP). Rec 25 Nov 1818.

1081. Page 389. 16 Nov 1818. Samuel **CAMPBELL** to Michael **MOWSER**. For the sum of $640, 640 acres on Castor Creek, confirmed in the name of William **CAMPBELL**, and settled by sd **MOWSER** in 1804. Sd deed is to be made when patents are issued. Signed Samuel **CAMPBELL**. Wit William **TINNIN** (JP). Rec 25 Nov 1818.

1082. Page 390. 30 Nov 1818. Robert **GREEN** senior and Elizabeth, his wife, to David **GREEN**. For the sum of $400, 209 acres on the waters of Hubble's Creek; beginning at the beginning of sd **GREEN**'s survey. Signed Robt. **GREEN**, Elizabeth **GREEN**. Wit Charles **DEMOSS**, Joseph **McFERRON**, Clerk. Rec 30 Nov 1818.

1083. Page 392. 21 Nov 1818. Andrew **BURNS** and Jane, his wife, to John **DAVIS**. For the sum of $92, quit claim to 75 acres, more or less, being the same heretofore conveyed by sd **DAVIS** to sd **BURNS**; to be taken off the E part of sd tract, so as to not interfere with 125 acres sold by sd **DAVIS** to sd **BURNS**, nor to 100 acres in the NE corner upon which sd **BURNS** now lives. Signed

A. **BURNS**, Jane **BURNS** (RD). Wit Tho. **NEALE** (JP). Rec 1 Dec 1818.

1084. Page 394. 23 Nov 1818. Same and same to same. For diverse good causes and considerations, power of attorney to claim or receive all their preemption right to 125 acres from the U.S., being the tract where sd **BURNS** now lives. Signed A. **BURNS**, Jane **BURNS**. Wit Tho. **NEALE** (JP). Rec 1 Dec 1818.

1085. Page 394. 21 Nov 1818. Andrew **BURNS** as principal, and Robert **MORRISON** and Robert **PATTERSON** as securities, to John **DAVIS**. For the sum of $5000, bond to guarantee that sd **BURNS** will cause James B. **WILSON** or his representatives to make title for 100 arpens, more or less, to sd **DAVIS**; being where sd **DAVIS** now lives. Signed A. **BURNS**, Robt. **PATTERSON**, Robert **MORRISON**. Wit Tho. **NEALE** (JP). Rec 1 Dec 1818.

1086. Page 395. 31 Jul 1818. James B. **WILSON** to James **BURNS**. For the sum of $700, two tracts on the waters of Hubble's Creek granted to Jonathan **FIRMAN**, bounded on the S by Joseph **SEAWELL**, W by Edward **HAILE** and David **PATTERSON**, N by Andrew **BURNS** and George **HAYS**, and E by Hanry **HAND** and Gilbert **HECTOR**; one of 240 arpents whereon John **DAVIS** now lives; and one of 100 arpents, more or less, whereon Thomas **BOYCE** and Andrew **BURNS** now live; sd land is held by James B. **WILSON**, assignee of sd **BURNS**, assignee of sd **DAVIS**, assignee of Benjamin **TENNEL**, assignee of sd **FIRMAN**. Signed James B. **WILSON**. Test Zenas **PRIEST** (JP), A. **BURNS**. Rec 1 Dec 1818.

1087. Page 396. 21 Nov 1818. John **DAVIS**, principal, and Stephen **BYRD** and John **BURNS**, securities, to Andrew **BURNS**. For the sum of $5000, bond to make a deed for 125 acres; bounded on the N by George **HAYS**, W by David **PATTERSON**, W & SW by sd **DAVIS**, S by Henry **HAND**, E by sd **DAVIS**, and N & NW by D. E. L. **CALDWELL**; and beginning at a black oak. Signed John **DAVIS**, Stephen **BYRD**, John **BURNS**. Wit H. **SANFORD**, Wm. **NEELY**, Z. **PRIEST** (JP). Rec 2 Dec 1818.

1088. Page 397. 23 Nov 1818. Same as principal, and same and same, securities, to same. For the sum of $2000, bond to indemnify against the claim of Elisha **WINSOR** and the U. S. to all damage that may arise in consequence of a power of attorney given to George **TENNILE** to

convey __ acres in New Madrid Co. back to the U.S. The tract is at Bresh Prairie, adjoined on the N by John **ROBERTS** and E by a swamp called Bayou St. John, including sd **BURNS'** first improvement. Signed John **DAVIS**, Stephen **BYRD**, John **BURNS**. Wit Tho. **NEALE** (JP), Josiah **VINCENT**. Rec 2 Dec 1818.

1089. Page 398. 2 Jul 1818. William **BLACK** to Solomon **BOLLINGER**. For the sum of $5, __ acres, being a preemption right on the E side of Big Black in St. Francis Twp; being his improvement made in 1811. Also power of attorney to obtain a patent from the U.S. Signed William (x) **BLACK**. Wit John **BOLLINGER**, Johnson **RANNEY**, R. S. **THOMAS**, Judge of Southern Circuit. Rec 3 Dec 1818.

1090. Page 400. 12 Nov 1818. Solomon **CARTER** of Arkansas Co., Mo. [now Ark.] to same. For the sum of $500, quit claim to __ acres on the N side of Big Black River at the crossing on the main road from Jackson to Davidsonville in Laurance Co.; being an improvement and preemption right settled by him in Oct 1811. Signed Solomon **CARTER**. Fanny (x) **CARTER** RD in the presence of Perly **WALLIS**. Wit James C. **NEWELL**, JP in Arkansas Co., Mo. Rec 3 Dec 1818.

1091. Page 401. 30 Nov 1818. Jamime **SWIFFT** of Larrance Co., Mo. [now Ark.] to same. For the sum of $150, __ acres in Larrance Co., on the S side of Big Black River at the crossing of the main road from Jackson to Davissonville, Larrance Co.; being an improvement and preemption right settled by her in Jan 1813. Signed Jamime (   ) **SWIFFT**. Test George C. **MILLER**, Joseph **MILLER**, Jacob **GARRETT** (JP). Rec 3 Dec 1818.

1092. Page 402. 30 Nov 1818. Sarah **CASH** to same. For the sum of $100, __ acres on the E side of Big Black River about ½ mile below his ferry landing, being an improvement settled in 1814 and cultivated. Signed Sarah (x) **CASH**. Test George C. **MILLER**, Joseph **MILLER**, Jacob **GARRETT** (JP). Rec 3 Dec 1818.

1093. Page 402. 30 [Nov] 1818. Same to same. For the sum of $200, __ acres on the S side of Big Black River about 1 mile below sd **BOLLINGER'S** ferry landing on the main road from Jackson to Davisonville in Larrance Co., Mo.; being an improvement and preemption right settled, improved, and occupied by her in May 1812. Signed Sarah (x) **CASH**. Test George

C. **MILLER**, Joseph **MILLER**, Jacob **GARRETT** (JP). Rec 3 Dec 1818.

1094. Page 403. 2 Jun 1818. Ezekiel **HILL** to John **MORRISSON**. For the sum of $150, __ acres on the waters of White Water, being an improvement and preemption right settled by him in summer 1812; being between Ebenezer **HUBELL** and the improvement of Peter **FRANKS** where A. **LITTON** now lives. Sd **HILL** also grants power of attorney to sd **MORRISSON** to secure the preemption right. Signed Ezekiel **HILL**. Wit Joseph **LEWIS**, William **SHEPPARD**, Zenas **PRIEST** (JP). Rec 5 Dec 1818.

1095. Page 404. 8 Sep 1813. Elijah **WELCH** to Isaac **DEVORE**. For the sum of $300, __ acres on the waters of White Water, known as Welch's Creek; beginning on a water beech marked with a "W"; bounded in part by Ezekiel **ABLE**'s W line. Signed Elijah (x) **WELCH**. Wit Js. **BOYD** (JP), Jon **BOYD**. Rec 7 Dec 1818.

1096. Page 406. 26 Nov 1818. John **RISHER** and Mary, his wife, to Jonas N. **MENEFEE**. For the sum of $150, two lots in Decatur; Lot No. 9, bounded on the N by Lot No. 8 sold to Ulysses **MUNN**, S by Lot No. 10 belonging to sd **MENEFEE**, E by a vacant space on the Mississippi River, and W by a street; and Lot No. 11, bounded on the N by Lot No. 10, S by sd **RISHER**, and E & W as was the other lot. Signed John **RISHER**, Mary (x) **RISHER**. Wit George **HENDERSON** (JP), Henry H. **SNIDER**. Rec 12 Dec 1818.

1097. Page 407. 29 Nov 1817. John **DAUGHERTY** to Bartholomew **COUSIN**. For the sum of $5, quit claim to __ acres on the waters of Byrd's Creek whereon Jas. **BROWLEY** now lives; being an improvement he made some years since. Sd **COUSIN** is to consider sd **BROWLEY** as his tenant, and receive any rent he may owe. Signed John **DAUGHERTY**. Test Ulysses **MUNN**, George **HENDERSON** (JP). Rec 18 Dec 1818.

1098. Page 408. 1 Aug 1818. Charnal **HIGHTOWER** of New Madrid Co., Mo. to Joshua **HAIL**. For the sum of $60, __ acres on Cany Creek in Byrd Twp, being all his improvement and preemption right, where he formerly lived. Signed Charnel (x) **HIGHTOWER**. Wit Elias **WHEAT**, James **HAIL**, Enoch **LEGGET**, JP in New Madrid Co., Mo. Rec 22 Dec 1818.

1099. Page 409. 11 Aug 1818. Joshua **HAIL** to Daniel **HOOSER**. For the sum of $300, __ acres, being all his improvement and preemption right in the NW ¼, Sec 19 and the SW ¼, Sec 18, Twp 32 N, Rng 13 E. Signed Joshua (x) **HAIL**. Wit William (x) **HAIL**, John G. **LOVE**, Tho. **NEALE** (JP). Rec 22 Dec 1818.

1100. Page 410. 11 May 1818. John **RISHER** and Mary, his wife, to Ebenezer **HUNTINGTON** of Frankfort, Ken. For the sum of $64.50, Lot Nos. 2, 3, & 18 in Decatur, lying on the bank of the Mississippi River; being part of a purchase made by sd **RISHER** of Louis **LORIMIER**. Signed John **RISHER**, Mary (x) **RISHER**. Wit Jonas N. **MENEFEE**, Victor **LORIMIER**, George **HENDERSON** (JP). Rec 23 Dec 1818.

1101. Page 411. 26 Dec 1818. Henry **HAND** and William **HAND** swear that Peter **BELLEW** told them in 1804 that he had conveyed to Jacob **ISOM** a certain improvement right made by him; bounded by Lewis **TASH**, Richard S. **THOMAS** formerly Henry **SHERIDAN**, Anthony **RANDOL**, Samuel **PEW**, and U.S. lands; and that Henry **HAND** would be safe in purchasing sd improvement. Signed Henry **HAND**, Wm. **HAND**. Wit Joseph **McFERRON**, Clerk. Jason **CHAMBERLAIN** swears that a diligent search has failed to locate the deed, and it is lost or mislaid. Signed Jason **CHAMBERLAIN**. Wit Joseph **McFERRON**, Clerk. Rec 26 Dec 1818.

1102. Page 412. 8 Oct 1818. Rebeca **PATTERSON** to Benjamin **MABRY**. For the sum of $250, 20 acres in Byrd Twp, being her improvement and preemption right. She also grants power of attorney to sd **MABRY** to obtain a title to sd preemption right. Signed Rebeca **PATTERSON**. Wit James **RUSSELL** (JP), Ezekiel **SEELY**. Rec 28 Dec 1818.

1103. Page 413. 23 Nov 1818. Benjamin **MAYBERRY** to John **THOMPSON**. For the sum of $300, __ acres on the waters of Cane Creek, on which David **CAMPBELL** now resides, and known as the widow **PATTERSON**'s place, adjoining Robert **PATTERSON**; being sd **MAYBERRY**'s preemption right purchased from Rebecca **PATTERSON**. Also power of attorney to enter the land in the U.S. Land Office and obtain title. Signed Benjn. **MABRY**. Wit Tho. **NEALE** (JP). Rec 28 Dec 1818.

1104. Page 414. 6 Oct 1818. John **HAHN** jr. to David **KINDER**. For the sum of $55, __ acres on Whitewater in German Twp, being the same granted and confirmed to Jacob **SLINKARD**, decd; joined on the N by the heirs of Phillip **BOLLINGER**, decd. Signed John **HAHN**, Elisabeth **HAHN** [his wife]. Wit John B. **WHEELER** (JP), Daniel **HAHN** snr, John (x) **PERKINS**. Rec 29 Dec 1818.

1105. Page 416. 17 Dec 1818. Commissioners of the Courthouse and Jail to David **ARMOUR** and John **JUDEN**. For the sum of $43, Lot No. 6 in Jackson; bounded on the W and fronted by High St, N and fronted by first south street, E by Lot No. 30, and S by Lot No. 7. Signed John **DAVIS**, John **SHEPPARD**, Samuel G. **DUNN**. Wit S. R. **BOLIN** (JP). Rec 5 Jan 1819.

1106. Page 417. 12 Oct 1818. Leonard **WILLSON** and Mary, his wife, to Maximilian **HORRELL**. For the sum of $1253, 224 acres, more or less, on which he now resides, being the same granted to James **BOYD** as 400 arpens; beginning at a stake and sugar tree on Isaac **SHEPHERD's** W line; bounded in part by Edward F. **BOND**, Benjamin **WILSON**, and B. **COUSIN**. Signed Leonard **WILSON**, Mary (x) **WILSON**. Wit Zenas **PRIEST** (JP), Josiah **VINCENT**. Rec 5 Jan 1819.

1107. Page 419. 12 Jun 1818. Ezekiel **ABLE**, and Jeremaiah **ABLE** and Patsy, his wife, to William **BOLIN**. For the sum of $1787.20, 300 acres in German Twp; being the same on which sd **BOLIN** now lives; and beginning at a water beech. Signed Ezekiel **ABLE**, Jeremiah **ABLE**, Patsy **ABLE**. Wit Wm. **KELSO**, John **DUNN**, Solomon R. **BOLIN** (JP). Rec 12 Jan 1819.

1108. Page 420. 18 Jul 1818. William **WILLIAMS** and Elisabeth, his wife, to Joseph **ENGLISH**. For the sum of $300, 100 arpens, more or less, on the waters of Turkey Creek, part of a tract confirmed to sd **WILLIAMS**, assignees of Thomas **FOSTER**; beginning at a stake on William **MATTHEWS'** line. Signed William **WILLIAMS**, Elisabeth (x) **WILLIAMS**. Wit John **RANDOL**, Isaiah **POE**, John **AKIN** (JP). Rec 15 Jan 1819.

1109. Page 421. 20 Oct 1818. Abraham **HUGHS** and Peggy, his wife, to John **JOHNSON**. For the sum of $700, 100 acres on the waters of Apple Creek, including the plantation where sd **HUGHS** now lives; being the head right of sd **HUGHS**; beginning at the NW corner of sd tract; and bounded in part by Abraham **BYRD**. Signed Abraham **HUGHS**, Peggy (x) **HUGHES**. Wit Greer W. **DAVIS**, Joel **BLUNT**, Tho. **NEALE** (JP). Rec 16 Jan 1819.

1110. Page 422. 21 Oct 1805. John **HAYS** to Edward F. **BOND**. For the sum of $1, two tracts ; 240 acres, being a grant from the Spanish Government to Alexander **ANDREW**, and being purchased of sd **ANDREW** by John McGEE, who assigned the same to Michael **QUINN**, who conveyed the same to sd **HAYS** on 5 Oct 1804; and __ acres, which was conveyed to sd **HAYS** by Elijah **WHITAKER** on 1 Oct 1804. Signed John **HAYS**. Wit Geo. **HENDERSON**, John **SCOTT**, Christr. **HAYS**, JCCP. Rec 21 Jan 1819.

1111. Page 424. 16 Oct 1818. Jacob **SLINKARD** to Daniel **CLIPPERD**. For the sum of $125, Lot No. 102 in Jackson; bounded on the W and fronted by third west street, N and fronted by first south street, E by Lot No. 90, and S by Lot No. 103. Signed Jacob **SLINKARD**. Wit John B. **WHEELER** (JP), Thomas J. **WHEELER**. Rec 26 Jan 1819.

1112. Page 425. 8 Aug 1811. Maurice **WILLIAMS** of New Orleans, La., mariner, to Daniel Frederick **STEINBECK**. Power of attorney to obtain title to any tract or tracts of land in the Cape Girardeau Dist, that he obtained under the Spanish Government. Signed Maurice **WILLIAMS**. Wit David V. **WILLIAMS**, David **WRIGHT**, Stephen de **QUINONES**, Notary Public in New Orleans, La. Rec 26 Jan 1819.

1113. Page 425. 28 Jan 1819. Parish **GREEN** and Clary, his wife, to William **RUSSELL** of St. Louis Co., Mo. For the sum of $500, 640 acres as surveyed by Charles **HUTCHINGS**, on the W side of the Mississippi River; being the settlement and improvement right of Joseph **WALLER** at Waller's Ferry, now called Green's Ferry; with the exception of 100 acres reserved to sd **GREEN**, which shall be 1/3 of a mile along the river and at right angles to the river. Signed Parish **GREEN**, Clary ( ) **GREEN**. Wit Jno. **ABERNETHIE** (JP), Jason **CHAMBERLAIN**. Rec 28 Jan 1819.

1114. Page 427. 23 Jul 1818. William **GORDON** of Howard Co., Mo. to Thomas W. **THURSTON** of St. Louis, Mo. For the sum of $200, undivided moiety of 330 acres on White Water River; being the same purchased by William **MILBURN** and sd **GORDON** from Ezekiel **ABEL** on 11 Feb 1818. Signed William

GORDON. Test Jno. A. **SANDERSON**, John D. **POTEET**, Jas. S. **CONWAY**, Frn. **GUYAL**, JP in St. Louis Co., Mo., A. **GAMBLE**, Clerk of St. Louis Co. Circuit Court. Rec 1 Feb 1819.

1115. Page 427. 30 Jan 1819. Joseph **SEAWELL** and Rene LeMEILLEUR. Articles of agreement. For the sum of $9000 payable in six years, sd **LeMEILLEUR** will purchase 240 arpens, more or less, owned by sd **SEAWELL**, being part of the head right of James **EARLES**; bounded on the N by Edward **HALE**, W by ___ **MARTIN**, S by William **NEELY**, and E by Hubble's Creek. Sd **SEAWELL** will give sd **LeMEILLEUR** possession of the land in one year, but shall repossess the land if the cost is not paid by the due date, six years from this date. Signed Jos. **SEAWELL**, Rene **LeMEILLEUR**. Wit J. **RANNEY**, Zenas **PRIEST**, David **ARMOUR**, Solomon R. **BOLIN** (JP). Rec 2 Feb 1819.

1116. Page 429. 30 Jan 1819. Joseph **SEAWELL** to Rene **LeMEILLEUR**. Permission to lay off one range of lots on each side of the road leading from Jackson to Bolllinger's Mill on the tract where sd **SEAWELL** now resides; except the lots in the meadow on the right hand side of the road leading from Jackson are to remain in the possession of sd **SEAWELL** for one year. Sd **LeMEILLEUR** also has permission to lay off a road through the south field of sd **SEAWELL**, running direct from the head of the lane passing the house south to the W road leading from Jackson. Signed Jos. **SEAWELL**. Wit Solomon R. **BOLIN** (JP). Rec 2 Feb 1819.

1117. Page 430. 26 Jan 1819. Levi **BENNETTE** to Nathan **VANHORN** and Jesse **HAIL**. For the sum of $300, ___ acres, being an improvement and preemption in Sec 25, Twp 32, Rng 12 E, made by sd **BENNETTE** in 1810. Signed Levi **BENNETT**. Wit David **ARMOUR**, Tho. **NEALE** (JP). Rec 2 Feb 1819.

1118. Page 431. 30 Sep 1817. Enos **RANDOL** to Elijah **RANDOL**. For the sum of $500, 640 acres, more or less, excepting 200 acres heretofore sold to Edward F. **BOND**; being his head and settlement right, granted by the Spanish Government, and confirmed by the U.S. Signed Enos **RANDOL**. Wit J. **RANNEY**, Zenas **PRIEST** (JP). Rec 3 Feb 1819.

1119. Page 432. 3 Sep 1818. John **BROWN** and Rachael, his wife, to George H. **SCRIPPS**. For the sum of $80, ½ of Lot No. 73 in Jackson;

bounded on the S and fronted by first north street, W and fronted by second west street, N by Joseph **SEAWELL** or surplus town lands, and E by the other half of sd lot. Signed John **BROWN**, Rachel **BROWN**. Wit G. **FRICKE**, Tho. **NEALE** (JP). Rec 3 Feb 1819.

1120. Page 433. 20 Nov 1818. Joshua **HALE** to same. For the sum of $145, 20 acres on Cane Creek, Byrd Twp, being his improvement and preemption right; also power of attorney to complete a title to the land. Signed Joshua (x) **HALE**. Wit Ezekiel **SEELY**, James **RUSSELL** (JP). Rec 3 Feb 1819.

1121. Page 435. 21 Nov 1818. David **HILER** to same. For the sum of $100, 20 acres in Byrd Twp, being his improvement and preemption right; also power of attorney to complete title to the land. Signed David **HILER**. Wit James **RUSSELL** (JP), Ezekiel **SEELY**. Rec 3 Feb 1819.

1122. Page 436. 1 Nov 1813. Erasmus **ELLIS** to his mother Margret **ELLIS**, widow. For natural love and affection, a negro girl named **Lydia** about 18 years old, a sorrel horse, a bay mare, 10 head of neat cattle, and all the household and kitchen furniture. Signed Erasmus **ELLIS**. Test Samuel M. **PHILLIPS**, Perly **WALLIS**, George **HENDERSON** (JP). Rec 8 Feb 1819.

1123. Page 437. 4 Feb 1819. Margaret **ELLIS** to her son James **ELLIS**. For natural love and affection and 1 silver dollar, and for the care and affection he has shown to her since the death of his father; one negro woman named **Liddy** about 24 years old, one negro boy named **George** (**Liddy**'s son) about 5 years old, one female negro child named **Milly** (daughter of sd **Liddy**) about 2 years and 5 months old, one sorrel horse, one bay mare & iron gray colt, one bay colt about 3 years old, one gig & harness, 10 head of cattle, and all her household furniture, beds and bedding (all of which has been in the possession of sd James for some time). Signed Margaret (x) **ELLIS**. Wit James **EVANS**, Alfred P. **ELLIS**, George **HENDERSON** (JP). Rec 8 Feb 1819.

1124. Page 438. 8 Jan 1818. Commissioners of the Courthouse and Jail to John G. **LOVE**. For the sum of $50, Lot No. 62 in Jackson; bounded on the E by first west street, S by Lot No. 63, W by Lot No. 74, and N by first north street. Signed John **DAVIS**, Samuel G. **DUNN**, Abraham **BYRD**. Wit J. **RANNEY**, David **CAMPBELL**, Richd. S. **THOMAS**, Judge of Southern Circuit. Rec 9 Feb 1819.

1125. Page 439. 30 May 1818. John **WILSON** to Fieldin **GLASCOCK**. For the sum of $100, quit claim to __ acres, being an improvement made by him in Secs 19 & 20, Twp 32 N, Rng 13 E. Signed John **WILSON**. Wit J. **CHAMBERLAIN**, Zenas **PRIEST** (JP). Rec 9 Feb 1819.

1126. Page 440. 30 May 1818. Fieldin **GLASCOCK** to John G. **LOVE**. For the sum of $450, __ acres, being an improvement and preemption right in Twp 32 N, Rng 13 E; including NE ¼, Sec 19; SE fractional ¼, Sec 19; NW ¼ Sec 20; and SW fractional ¼, Sec 20. Signed Fieldin **GLASSCOCK**. Wit J. **CHAMBERLAIN**, Zenas **PRIEST** (JP). Rec 9 Feb 1819.

1127. Page 441. 12 Jun 1818. Commissioners of the Courthouse and Jail to same. For the sum of $47, Lot No. 114 in Jackson; bounded on the N and fronted by first south street, E and fronted by third west street, S by Lot No. 115, and W by Lot No. 195. Signed John **SHEPPARD**, Samuel G. **DUNN**, Abraham **BYRD**. Wit S. R. **BOLIN**, Richard **WALLER**, James **RUSSELL** (JP). Rec 9 Feb 1819.

1128. Page 442. 24 Feb 1797. Henry **SHERADAN**, a German national, to Louis **LORIMIER**. Request for grant of 480 arpents on the Zenon River nine miles W of Cape Girardeau; joined on the E by the grant of Moses **HURLEY**. Sd **SHERADAN** wishes to settle on this side of the river with his family. Signed Henry **SHARADIN**. Cape Girardeau, 24 Feb 1797. Lt Governor requests provisory grant be given to Henry **SHARADIN**. St. Louis of Illinois, 5 Jan 1798. Informed **LORIMIER** the requested grant is vacant and doesn't infringe upon the adjacent properties. The surveyor Don Antonio **SOULARD** gives the grant requested. Signed Zenon **TRUDEAU**. [IN FRENCH] Title is assigned to Ezekiel **ABLE** for value received on 30 Apr 1805. Signed Henry **SHARADEN**. Test Jona. **FORMAN**, Js. **BOYD**. Title is assigned to Wm. H. **ASHLEY** for value received on 8 Mar 1808. Signed Ezekiel **ABLE**. Test A. **HADEN**, James **EVANS**, John **BYRD**, JCCP. Originally recorded in B:84. Rec 13 Feb 1819.

1129. Page 443. 16 Dec 1818. 16 Dec 1818. Commissioners of the Courthouse and Jail to David **ARMOUR**. For the sum of $72, Lot No. 98 in Jackson; bounded on the E by Lot No. 86, S by Lot No. 99, W and fronted by third west street, and N and fronted by first north street. Signed John **DAVIS**, John **SHEPPARD**,

Samuel G. **DUNN**, Abraham **BYRD**, Benja. **SHELL**. Wit Andw. **MARTIN**, John **DUNN**, Zenas **PRIEST** (JP). Rec 15 Feb 1819.

1130. Page 445. 9 Feb 1819. Commissioners of the Courthouse and Jail to David **ARMOUR** and John **JUDEN** Jr. For the sum of $73, Lot No. 21 in Jackson; bounded on the E and fronted by High St, S and fronted by third south street, W by Lot No. 57, and N by Lot No. 20. Signed John **SHEPPARD**, Samuel G. **DUNN**, Abraham **BYRD**, Benja. **SHELL**. Wit Samuel **PUTNAM**, William **JOHNSON**, Zenas **PRIEST** (JP). Rec 15 Feb 1819.

1131. Page 446. 17 Nov 1818. Charles **DEMOSS** to George **HAYS**. For the sum of $100, 100 acres, more or less, on the waters of Hubble's Creek, being part of a tract originally granted to sd **DEMOSS** as his settlement right; bounded on the N by the heirs of Christopher **HAYS**, decd, E by sd **DEMOSS**, S by Levi **DICKSON** and George **HAYS**, and W by George **HAYS**; beginning at the NW of the tract surveyed for sd **DEMOSS** at a stake near a black gum. The tract is the same to be conveyed by title bond dated 1 Feb 1808, and was conveyed by deed on 4 Oct 1817 (by mistake 1818). Signed Charles **DEMOSS**. Wit Richard **MENEFEE**, Joseph **McFERRON**, Clerk. Rec 16 Feb 1819.

1132. Page 448. 7 Jan 1818. Commissioners of the Courthouse and Jail to Joseph **FRIZLE** and Henry **VONPHUL**. For the sum of $50, Lot No. 65 in Jackson; bounded on the S and fronted by first south street, E and fronted by first west street, N by Lot No. 64, and W by Lot No. 77. Signed John **DAVIS**, John **SHEPPARD**, Samuel G. **DUNN**, Abraham **BYRD**, Benja. **SHELL**. Wit Thos. **NEWBERRY**, J. **RANNEY**, Zenas **PRIEST** (JP). Rec 19 Feb 1819.

1133. Page 449. 9 Jun 1818. John **THOMSON** to John **HAYS**. For diverse good causes and considerations, power of attorney to ask, demand, sue for, recover, and take possession of an improvement granted by the U.S., and convey the same. Sd improvement, lying between **GIBBONEE** and Turrence **DYAL**, was purchased by sd **THOMSON** of John **SHIELDS** on 9 May 1805, and was made in Sep 1802. Signed John **THOMSON**. Wit Nathan W. **McCARTY**, Joseph **McFERRON**, Clerk. Rec 20 Feb 1819.

1134. Page 450. 15 Apr 1817. Commissioners of the Courthouse and Jail to Charles **LUCAS**. For the sum of $57.50, Lot No. 90 in Jackson; bounded on the E and fronted by second west street, S by Lot No. 91, W by Lot No. 102, and N and fronted by first south street. Signed John **DAVIS**, John **SHEPPARD**, Samuel G. **DUNN**, Abraham **BYRD**. Wit Thos. **NEWBERRY**, Jesse **HAIL**, Tho. **NEALE** (JP). Rec 22 Feb 1819.

1135. Page 452. 5 Sep 1818. John **BURROW** and Bethena, his wife, to Isaiah **POE**. For the sum of $150, 49 acres, more or less, on Hubble's Creek, being where sd **POE** now lives; beginning at the SE corner of the head right of Waters **BURROWS**; and adjoined on the E by U. S. lands, N & W by sd **POE**, and S by David **DAVIS**. Signed John **BURROWS**, Bethena (x) **BURROWS**. Wit John **RODNEY**, John **AKIN** (JP). Rec 4 Mar 1818.

1136. Page 454. 12 Dec 1818. Lewis **DICKSON** of Ste. Genevieve Co., Mo. to Nicholas **WHITLOW**. For the sum of $1600, 400 arpens on the waters of Hubble's Creek, being the same granted to sd **DIXON** by the Spanish Government; bounded on the S by the widow **TAYLOR** and Gilbert **HECTOR**, and N by Charles **DEMOSS**; beginning at a hickory marked "L. D." on sd **HECTOR**'s N & S line. Sd **DICKSON** also agrees to execute any further actions so that sd **WHITLOW** can secure title to the tract. Signed Lewis **DICKSON**. Wit Tho. **NEALE** (JP), John **DANIEL**. Elisabeth **DICKSON**, wife of Lewis, RD before B. **BURNS**, JP in Ste. Genevieve Co. Rec 8 Mar 1819.

1137. Page 456. 23 Feb 1819. Alexander **MILLIKIN** of Union Co., Ill. to James **BRADY** of New Madrid Co., Mo. For the sum of $180, quit claim to 240 arpens and 20 poles granted to him by the Spanish Government; bounded on the E by the Mississippi River, N by John **BALDWIN** originally granted to Edmond **HOGAN**, and S & W by public land; also power of attorney to secure confirmation of title from the U. S. Signed Alexander **MILLIKIN**. Wit Thos. **FLETCHER**, John **WATHEN**, Joseph **McFERRON**, Clerk. Rec 13 Mar 1819.

1138. Page 458. 18 Mar 1819. John **HAYS** to George **HAYS**. For the sum of $600, bond to make a deed for 100 arpens from a tract above and adjoining the mouth of Indian Creek, otherwise called Table River. John **HAYS** has sold the tract to George **HAYS** for the sum of $300, and the deed is to be made within three years. Signed John **HAYS**. Wit Joseph

McFERRON, Clerk, Richard **MENEFEE**. Rec 18 Mar 1819.

1139. Page 459. 25 Mar 1819. John **BROWN** to James **TANNER** of New Madrid Co., Mo. For the sum of $10, quit claim to 640 acres on White Water, being the same that he purchased of James **SMITH** and Rachel, his wife. Signed John **BROWN**. Wit Richd. **PHILLIPS**, James **EVANS**, Joseph **McFERRON**, Clerk. Rec 25 Mar 1819.

1140. Page 460. 28 Jan 1819. James **ELLIS** swears that he had a bill of sale given to him by Erasmus **ELLIS** for a negro fellow named **Ralph**; which bill of sale was made to him in 1813, and is now lost or mislaid. Signed James **ELLIS**. Wit G. **HENDERSON** (JP). Samuel M. **PHILLIPS** also swears that he witnessed the bill of sale. Signed Samuel M. **PHILLIPS**. Wit George **HENDERSON** (JP). Rec 25 Mar 1819.

1141. Page 461. 25 Mar 1819. Ezekiel **ABLE** to John **CROSS** and William **GARNER**. For the sum of $3200, bond to make a title for 640 acres adjoining Gilbert **HECTOR** and whereon the widow **TAYLOR** now lives; being the same originally granted to William **HAND**. Sd **ABLE** has sold the tract for $1600 to sd **CROSS** and sd **GARNER**, and title is to be made within two years, or as soon as a dispute between sd **ABLE** and the heirs of John **TAYLOR**, decd, shall be decided. Signed Ezekiel **ABLE**. Wit George **HENDERSON** (JP). Rec 25 Mar 1819.

1142. Page 463. 26 Jan 1819. James **BOYD** and Sarah, his wife, of Lawrance Co., Mo. [now Ark.] to Phillip **ROSS** of New Madrid Co., Mo. For the sum of $60, quit claim to 640 acres on White Water, being the settlement and improvement right of William **PAGE**. Signed James **BOYD**, Sarah (x) **BOYD**. Wit James **TANNER**, James **CAMPBELL**, Joseph **McFERRON**, Clerk. Rec 26 Mar 1819.

1143. Page 464. 27 Jan 1819. James **SMITH** and Rachel, his wife, to John **BROWN**. For the sum of $100, 640 acres on White Water, being the settlement and improvement right of sd **SMITH**. Signed James ( ) **SMITH**, Rachel (x) **SMITH**. Wit James **TANNER**, William **ROBERTSON**, Sarah (x) **ROBERTSON**, Joseph **McFERRON**, Clerk. Rec 26 Mar 1819.

County of Cape Girardeau, in the Southern Circuit of the Territory of Missouri of the United States of America. J. L. M.

[End of Deed Book D]

[Deed Book E]

1144. Page 1. 15 Mar 1819. Washington **ABERNETHIE** and Martha, his wife, to James **SMITH**. For the sum of $200, 50 acres, more or less, on the waters of Randall's Creek, beginning at a sugar tree on John **HITT**'s corner, being part of John **ABERNETHIE**'s settlement right and confirmation; where sd **SMITH** and his family now live and where sd **ABERNETHIE** and family formerly lived, and where Parish **GREEN** and David **GREEN** formerly lived; also bounded by ____ **ELLIS**, **BYRD**, and **RANDALL**. Signed Wa. **ABERNETHIE**, Martha (x) **ABERNETHIE**. Wit James **RANDOL**, Medad **RANDOL**, Jno. **ABERNETHIE** (JP). Rec 27 Mar 1819.

1145. Page 2. 10 Feb 1819. Commissioners of the Courthouse and Jail to Thomas **NEALE**. For the sum of $57.50, Lot No. 75 in Jackson; bounded on the S and fronted by Main St, W by second west street, N by Lot No. 74, and E by Lot No. 63. Signed John **SHEPPARD**, Samuel G. **DUNN**, Abraham **BYRD**, Benja. **SHELL**. Wit Zenas **PRIEST** (JP). Rec 29 Mar 1819.

1146. Page 3. 6 Mar 1819. John L. **LAFFERTY** to John **MILLER**, both of Lawrence Co., Mo. Terr [now Ark.]. For the sum of $100, being ½ of the purchase money, 640 acres on the waters of White water which he purchased of John **SHERIDAN**; being confirmed to sd **SHERIDAN** as his settlement right. Signed John L. **LAFFERTY**. Wit Jason **CHAMBERLAIN**, Richd. **SEARCY**, Circuit Court Clerk of Lawrence Co., Mo. Terr. Rec 1 Apr 1819.

1147. Page 3. 30 Mar 1819. James Huchinson **MARTIN** to John **MARTIN**, both of Hempstead Co., Mo. Terr [now Ark.]. For the sum of $1800, 190 arpens and 20 poles, being the ¼ part of a tract of 760 arpens and 80 poles confirmed to Jonithan **FOURMAN** and conveyed by him to Benjamin **TENNEL**, by sd **TENNEL** to John **MARTIN** senior, and by the last will and testament of sd **MARTIN** to his four eldest sons John **MARTIN**, Andrew **MARTIN**, James Hutshinson **MARTIN**, and Allen **MARTIN**; bounded on the W by Stephen **BYRD** senior, N by Isaac **SHEPHERD** and **ARRIL**, E by Andrew **MARTIN**, and S by Allen **MARTIN** and John **MARTIN**. Signed James H. **MARTIN**. Test Enoch **STEEN** (JP), Samuel **COLLINS**. Rec 8 Apr 1819.

1148. Page 4. 17 Jun 1809. David **FARRIL** to John and Robert **GIBONEY**. Receipt for $75 paid for a claim of land. Signed David **FARRIL**. Test Ezekiel **ABLE**, George **HENDERSON** (JP), John **AKIN** (JP). Rec 10 Apr 1819.

1149. Page 5. 23 Mar 1819. Peter **BELLEW** and Polly, his wife, of Perry Co., Ohio to Rucker **TANNER** of New Madrid Co., Mo. For the sum of $1000, 640 acres, more or less, on the waters of Hubble's Creek between Jackson and **LARAMORE**'s new mill, being the settlement and improvement of sd **BELEW**. Signed Peter **BELLEW**, Polly (x) **BELLEW**. Wit Roswell **MILLS** (JP in Perry Co., Ohio), Peter **BUGLE** senr. Rec 14 Apr 1819.

1150. Page 6. 17 Apr 1819. Deposition of Charles **BRADLY** of Ill. regarding land transaction of John **SEAVERS** to John C. **HARBISON**, before George **HENDERSON** (JP). Given on order of Circuit Court, Southern Circuit, in case of Adenirum **SEAVERS**, an infant, by Charles **SEAVERS**, next of kin. Adenirum **SEAVERS**' father John **SEAVERS** died when he was but a few months old, and has 240 acres of land confirmed to him adjoining the Big Swamp. Morgan **BYRNE** claims the same land as assignee of John C. **HARBISON**, who claims as assignee of John **SEAVERS**. The tract was the head right of John **SEAVERS**, and he agreed to give sd **HARBISON** ½ of the land, and sd **HARBISON** was to pay all expenses. **BRADLEY** testifies that sd **SEAVERS** was groggy at the time, and may not have signed the deed; also he did not see any consideration paid. Signed George **HENDERSON** (JP). Wit Joseph **McFERRON**, Clerk. Rec 19 Apr 1819.

1151. Page 8. 19 Apr 1819. Daniel **HICKMAN** to Robert and Austin **HICKMAN**. For love and affection to his two sons and the sum of $1, all his estate and property except 39 hogs. Signed Daniel (x) **HICKMAN**. Wit Morgan **BYRNE**, Jno. **ABERNETHIE**, Joseph **McFERRON**, Clerk. Rec 19 Apr 1819.

1152. Page 8. 6 Mar 1819. William **RAMSEY** and Elizabeth, his wife, of Lawrence Co., Mo. [now Ark.] to William **TIPTON**. For the sum of $75, 54 ½ acres, more or less, being part of a grant from the Spanish Government to Andrew **RAMSEY** senar, the balance of which is now owned by Rebecka **HARBISON**. Signed William **RAMSEY**, Elizabeth **RAMSEY**. Wit George **RUDDELL** (JP in Lawrence Co., Mo.). Rec 20 Apr 1819.

1153. Page 9. 28 Jul 1818. Ezekiel **ABLE** to John **DUNN**. For the sum of $450, a negro girl named **Frances** about 12 years old. Signed Ezkil **ABLE**. Wit George **HENDERSON**, Jno. **ABERNETHIE** (JP). Rec 20 Apr 1819.

1154. Page 10. 11 Jun 1818. Same to William P. **LACEY**. For the sum of $450, bond to make a deed by 1 Aug next to part of a tract on the Mississippi River opposite Devil's Island, being the same confirmed to Jabez **FISHER**. The entire tract is to be divided into three equal parts, as nearly as can be made at right angles with the river, with the deed to be to the middle third. Signed Ezekiel **ABLE**. Test Timothy **DAVIS**, A. **BUCKNER**, Jno. **ABERNETHIE** (JP). Rec 20 Apr 1819.

1155. Page 11. 20 Oct 1818. William **WILLIAMS** and Elizabeth, his wife, to Uriah **BROCK**. For the sum of $300, 180 acres on Randol's Creek, being part of a 640 acre tract granted to Enos **RANDOL** by the Spanish Government, conveyed by sd **RANDOL** to Edward F. **BOND**, from sd **RANDOL**[sic] to Benajah **LAUGHERY**, and from sd Laugherty to sd **WILLIAMS**; beginning at a stone and bounded on the N by sd **WILLIAMS'** Spanish Grant where he now lives, W by John and James **MASSEY**, originally James **DOWTY**, S by sd **WILLIAMS** and vacant land, and E by Simon **POE** senior and Simon **POE** junr. Signed William **WILLIAMS**, Elizabeth (x) **WILLIAMS**. Wit Jacob **FOSTER**, John ( ) **WILLIAMS**, Jno. **ABERNETHIE** (JP). Rec 20 Apr 1819.

1156. Page 12. 1 Mar 1810. Louis **LORIMIER** senr. to John **SCRIPPS**. For the sum of $150 to be paid by 10 Feb next, 6 acres on the W side of Cape Girardeau, ¼ mile from the bank of the Mississippi, beginning at a stake 80 ft W of a spring. Signed L. **LORIMIER**. Wit B. **COUSIN**, Zenas **PRIEST** (JP). Rec 21 Apr 1819.

1157. Page 13. 19 Apr 1819. Pierre **MENARD** and Angelique, his wife, to Louis **LORIMIER**, Daniel F. **STEINBECK** in right of his wife Agatha and as assignee of Auguste Bougainville **LORIMIER** and of Raphael Verneuil **LORIMIER**, Victor **LORIMIER**, and the children of Thomas S. **RODNEY** by Marie **LORIMIER**, decd, his wife (Thomas Jefferson **RODNEY** and Polly **RODNEY**), all heirs of Louis **LORIMIER**, decd. For the sum of $13,600, 3600 arpens, more or less, including Cape Girardeau; bounded on the E by the river

Mississippi, S by the S boundary of sd **LORIMIER's** land that he purchased of Hippte. **MAROTE**, W by a N & S line, and N by an E & W line to the river; the two lines drawn to take in the plantation that Jonathan **FORMAN** improved and where he formerly lived. Any lots and outlots conveyed by L. **LORIMIER** during his lifetime are ratified and confirmed. The tract to be conveyed in three shares to sd **STEINBECK**, and one share each to Louis **LORIMIER**, Victor **LORIMIER**, and the heirs of Marie **RODNEY**, decd. Signed Pierre **MENARD**, Angelique **MENARD**. Wit Raphael **WIDEN** (JP in Randolph Co., Ill.), Shadrach **BOND**, Governor of Ill., by Elias K. **KANE**, Sec. of State. Rec 21 Apr 1819.

1158. Page 15. 22 Apr 1819. Robert **BUCKNER** and Eliza, his wife, to John **HORRELL**. For the sum of $1610, 161 acres and 72 perches where sd **HORRELL** now lives; bounded on the S by the heirs of John **MARTIN**, decd, W by Isaac **SHEPARD**, and SE by William **RUSSEL**; beginning at a stone at the SW corner of the original survey. Signed Robert **BUCKNER**, Eliza **BUCKNER**. Test Richard **MENEFEE**, Thomas **NEALE** (JP). Rec 22 Apr 1819.

1159. Page 16. 7 Apr 1819. John **BILDERBACK** and Ephraim **BILDERBACK** of Randolph Co., Ill. to Jason **CHAMBERLAIN**. For the sum of $1000, quit claim to two tracts; ½ of 640 acres, being the settlement and improvement right of Felix **HOOVER**, confirmed to John **BILDERBACK** as assignee of sd **HOOVER**, and being their share of sd tract; and ½ of 640 acres, being the settlement and improvement right of John **DYE** in Tywappity Bottom in New Madrid Co., Mo, confirmed to John **BILDERBACK** as assignee of sd **DYE**. Signed John **BILDERBACK**, Ephraim **BILDERBACK**. Wit Joseph **PHILIPS**, Chief Justice of Ill., Shadrach **BOND**, Governor of Ill., Elias K. **KANE**, Secretary of State. Rec 22 Apr 1819.

1160. Page 18. 7 Apr 1819. Robert **DESHAY** to Jonathan **MALONE**. For the sum of $20, his improvement and preemption right on the waters of Apple Creek in Byrd Twp. where sd **MALONE** now resides. Signed Robert (x) **DESWAY**. Test Isaac **JETTON**, Thos. **MALOAN**, William **LEGET**, Zenas **PRIEST** (JP). Rec 29 Apr 1819.

1161. Page 19. 7 May 1818. Jenifer T. **SPRIGG** to John **HAYS** for the use of the heirs of William J. **STEPHENSON** (Louisa Donaldson

STEPHENSON, Andrew Ashley STEPHENSON, and William Johnson STEPHENSON). For the sum of $1, quit claim to two tracts, part of the head right of Andrew FRANKS; 300 acres on the waters of White Water adjoining the Big Swamp, beginning at a post near the house of Dr. E. ELLIS; bounded on the E by sd SPRIGG, W by 120 acres belonging to DRYBREAD and formerly part of sd FRANKS' head right; and 100 acres on the E of the first tract. Signed Jenifer T. SPRIGG. Wit B. COUSIN, Chas. HUTCHINGS, Joseph McFERRON, Clerk. Rec 29 Apr 1819.

1162. Page 20. 30 Apr 1819. John HAYS, Daniel F. STEINBECK, and John ABERNETHIE to William CLARK, Governor of Mo. Terr. For the sum of $2000, bond to perform tax collection duties for Cape Girardeau Co. Signed John HAYS, D. F. STEINBECK, Jno. ABERNETHIE. Wit Joseph W. McFERRON, Clerk. Rec 30 Apr 1819.

1163. Page 20. 30 Apr 1819. Same, same, and same to same. For the sum of $2500, bond to guarantee he will collect and pay money collected to the Territorial Treasury. Signed John HAYS, D. F. STEINBECK, Jno. ABERNETHIE. Wit Joseph McFERRON, Clerk. Rec 30 Apr 1819.

1164. Page 21. 10 Feb 1819. John DAVIS and Nancy, his wife, to Benjamin BOYCE. For the sum of $150, 100 acres, more or less, on a fork of Hubble's Creek where Thomas BOYCE now lives and being first improved by David L. L. CALDWELL; bounded on the N by George HAYS, W and S by Andrew BURNS, and E by Gilbert HECTOR; being part of a tract of 300 acres originally granted to Jonathan FOREMAN, conveyed by him to Benjamin TENNILLE, and by sd TENNILLE to sd DAVIS; beginning on the NE corner of the original survey. Signed John DAVIS, Nancy DAVIS (RD). Wit Thomas BOYCE, J. B. DAVIS, Thos. NEALE (JP). Rec 10 May 1819.

1165. Page 22. 2 Oct 1818. Stephen CAVENDER and Elizabeth, his wife, of Davidson Co., Tenn. to James BRADY of New Madrid Co., Mo. For the sum of $550, 640 acres in the Big Bend above Cape Girardeau on the Mississippi; being the settlement and only improvement of sd CAVENDER; and also power of attorney to sue concerning the tract. Sd CAVENDER has heard that Zeacal [Ezekiel] ABLE has by some means procured a fictitious deed to sd tract, and this deed conveys to sd

BRADY all the power against sd ABLE. Signed Stephen ( ) CAVENDER, Elizabeth (x) CAVENDER. Wit James TANNER, J. L. McCORMICK, William (x) McCORMICK, Joseph McFERRON, Clerk. Rec 10 May 1819.

1166. Page 23. 9 Feb 1819. Leavin WADKINS to Thomas S. RODNEY. For the sum of $75, __ acres on the waters of Whitewater in the Great Swamp where he formerly lived, being his improvement he made prior to 1814 and his preemption right, joining Jacob SHEPHERD's land in Byrd Twp. Sd WADKINS also gives sd RODNEY power of attorney to gain title to sd tract. Signed Leavin (x) WADKINS. Wit John AKIN (JP). Rec 10 May 1819.

1167. Page 25. 24 May 1818. Abraham HUGHS and Marget, his wife, to Abraham BYRD. For the sum of $54, 75 acres, more or less, on the waters of Apple Creek, granted to sd HUGHS, beginning at the NW corner of sd tract; bounded on the W & N by public lands, and E & S by sd HUGHS. Signed Abraham HUGHS, Marget (x) HUGHS. Wit James RUSSELL (JP). Rec 11 May 1819.

1168. Page 26. 8 Feb 1819. Commissioners of the Courthouse and Jail to Scarlet GLASCOCK. For the sum of $70, Lot No. 196 in Jackson; bounded on the W and fronted by fourth west street, N and fronted by first south street, E by Lot No. 114, and S by Lot N. 197. Signed John SHEPPARD, Samuel E. DUNN, Abraham BYRD. Wit Morris YOUNG, John DUNN, Thos. NEALE (JP). Rec 12 May 1819.

1169. Page 27. 6 May 1819. Ezekiel ABLE to Charles HUTCHINGS of Madison Co., Mo. For the sum of $150, __ acres, being a preemption right of an improvement, made under the direction of sd ABLE, on the main road from Cape Girardeau to Jackson, adjoining the N boundary of Louis LORIMIER's survey and the S boundary of LARSURE's survey. Signed Ezekiel ABLE. Wit George HENDERSON (JP). Rec 14 May 1819.

1170. Page 28. 21 Apr 1819. Charles DEMOSS and Martha, his wife, to George HAYS. For the sum of $100, 100 acres, more or less, on the waters of Hubble's Creek, originally confirmed to sd DEMOSS as his settlement right, beginning at a stake near a black gum at the W of the tract surveyed for sd DEMOSS; bounded on the N by the heirs of Christopher HAYS, decd, E by sd DEMOSS, S by lands late of Lewis DICKSON and by George HAYS, and W by George **HAYS**. The same tract was to be conveyed to sd **HAYS** by title bond dated 1 Feb 1808, and a deed dated 4 Oct 1817 (by mistake 1818). Signed Charles **DEMOSS**, Martha (x) **DEMOSS**. Wit Robert P. **CLARK**, Circuit Court Clerk, Cooper Co., Mo. Rec 20 May 1819.

1171. Page 29. 21 May 1819. John **DAVIS** to John **DELAP**. For the sum of $120 paid now and $173 when the land office is opened, 24 acres and 75 poles on the waters of Hubble's Creek, beginning at a stake, a hickory, and two dogwood saplings. For his entire preemption right, sd **DAVIS** binds himself to make a deed as soon as it is known whether his Spanish grant is established or disallowed. Signed John **DAVIS**, John **DELAP**. Wit J. A. **MOFFETT**, Joseph **McFERRON**, Clerk. Rec 24 May 1819.

1172. Page 30. 16 Mar 1819. Samuel **DORSEY** of Claiborne Co., Miss. to James **TANNER** of New Madrid Co., Mo. For the sum of $600, 300 arpens agreeable to the confirmation of the Commissioners and known as Harris **AUSTIN's** tract. Signed Saml. **DORSEY**. Wit Andrew P. **GILLASPIE**, Stephen D. **CARSON**, Joseph **McFERRON**, Clerk. Rec 27 May 1819.

1173. Page 31. 20 Apr 1819. Anderson **FISHER**, Benjamin **FISHER**, William **FISHER**, William **BURK** and Rebecca [**BURK**], formerly Rebecca **FISHER**; all of Tenn. and heirs and legal representatives of Jabez **FISHER**, decd; to same. For the sum of $150, 640 acres in the Big Bend of the Mississippi about six miles above Cape Girardeau, granted by the Spanish government to Jabez **FISHER** and confirmed to him by the Commissioners. Signed Benjamin **FISHER**, William **FISHER**, William (B) **BURK**, Rebeckah (x) **BURKE**. Wit John **DARL**, Joseph **ESSERY**, Joseph **McFERRON**, Clerk. Rec 27 May 1819.

1174. Page 32. 29 May 1819. Ezekiel **ABLE** and Margaret, his wife, to John **SCOTT** of Washington Co., Mo. Division of 640 acres confirmed to Jesse **HARTGROVE** near the Big Swamp; adjoining John **GIBONEY** and **FRANKS'** headright; pursuant to a conditional bond dated 8 May 1818 by which they were each entitled to a proportion of sd tract. Signed Ezekiel **ABLE**, Margaret (x) **ABLE**. Wit James **EVANS**, David **BRYANT**, George **HENDERSON** (JP). Rec 29 May 1819.

1175. Page 33. 2 Jun 1819. John **EDWARDS** and Preceller **JOHNSON** to William **MARTAIN**. For the sum of $29, 12 acres, being part of a tract purchased by sd **EDWARDS** from Elijah **RANDOL** out of a confirmed claim first granted to Enas **RANDOL** and sold to sd Elijah; beginning at a stake at the SE corner of Simon **POE** near the big road leading to Jackson. Signed John **EDWARDS**, Preceller (x) **JOHNSON**. Wit Eleanor **EDWARDS**, Jno. **ABERNETHIE** (JP). Rec 4 Jun 1819.

1176. Page 34. 2 Jun 1819. Elijah **RANDOL** and Nelley, his wife, to Preceller **JOHNSON**, a free woman of colour. For the sum of $500, 125 acres, more or less, being the remaining part of land granted to Enas **RANDOL** who sold to sd Elijah **RANDOL**, including the old improvement; beginning at a stake and two white oaks, and bounded by Simon **POE** and Scarlet **GLASCOCK**. Signed Elijah **RANDOL**, Penelope **RANDOL**. Wit James **RANDOL**, John **RANDOL**, Jno. **ABERNETHIE** (JP). Rec 5 Jun 1819.

1177. Page 36. 31 Jul 1818. John **EDWARDS** to same. For the sum of $340, all the crop that is his part, 2/3 thereof that he has raised, and all his real, personal, and moveable property in Mo.; reserving to himself the value of a common horse of middling value out of the sale of his improvement, called a preemption, near Feeling **GLASCOCK's**; also reserving all debts due or owing to him. Signed John **EDWARDS**. Test Tho. P. **GREEN**, James **RANDOL**, Joseph **McFERRON**, Clerk. Rec 5 Jun 1819.

1178. Page 37. 26 Apr 1819. Commissioners of the Courthouse and Jail to Elizabeth **PHILLIPS** and Richard **PHILLIPS** of New Madrid Co., Mo. For the sum of $46, Lot No. 86 in Jackson; bounded on the E and fronted by second west street and S by Lot No. 87. Signed Samuel G. **DUNN**, Abraham **BYRD**, Benjn. **SHELL**. Wit Christr. G. **HAUTZ**, Stephen **BACON**, Joseph **McFERRON**, Clerk. Rec 5 Jun 1819.

1179. Page 38. 2 Oct 1818. Catherine **BYRD**, widow and relict of Amos **BYRD**, decd, to William **RUSSELL**. For the sum of $55, quit claim to all her rights to any real and personal property of her late husband. Signed Catherine (x) **BYRD**. Wit Ezekiel **SEELY**, John **HAUK**, James **RUSSELL** (JP). Rec 5 Jun 1819.

1180. Page 38. 11 May 1819. William **RUSSELL** of St. Louis Co., Mo. to Jason **CHAMBERLAIN**. For the sum of $1300, 640 acres near Jackson, being Peter **BELLEW's** settlement right, beginning at the SW corner of

Samuel **PEW**'s survey; also bounded by Richard S. **THOMAS** under William H. **ASHLEY**, Thomas **BULL**, Lewis **TASH**, and Anthony **RANDOL**. Sd tract was conveyed by sd **BELLEW** to Jacob **ISHAM**, by sd **ISHAM** to Rufus **EASTON**, and by sd **EASTON** to sd **RUSSELL**. Signed Wm. **RUSSELL**. Wit Geo. **BULLITT**, Judge of the General Court of Arkansas Co., Mo., Eli J. **LEWIS**. Rec 9 Jun 1819.

1181. Page 40. 5 Feb 1819. William **HAND** and Sarah, his wife, to Johnson **RANNEY**. For the sum of $400, Lot No. 109, adjoining the creek [Hubble Creek] on the W side of Jackson; bounded on the S by first north street, E by third west street, W by the creek, and N by sd **RANNEY**'s land. Signed Wm. **HAND**, Sarah **HAND**. Wit Robert **GORDON**, Wm. **MATHEWS**, Zenas **PRIEST**, Esq. (JP). Rec 12 Jun 1819.

1182. Page 41. 2 Feb 1819. Enoch **EVANS** of New Madrid Co., Mo. and James **EVANS** to Benjamin M. **HORRELL**. For the sum of $1855, bond to make a deed on 265 acres, more or less, where Enoch **EVANS** formerly lived and where sd **HORRELL** now lives. Signed Enoch **EVANS**, James **EVANS**. Wit Robert **GIBONEY**, Joseph **McFERRON**, Clerk. Rec 14 Jun 1819.

1183. Page 42. 20 Jul 1816. Commissioners of the Courthouse and Jail to Charnel **GLASCOCK**. For the sum of $40.01, Lot No. 100 in Jackson; bounded on the N and fronted by Main St, E by Lot No. 88, S by Lot No. 101, and W by third west street. Signed John **DAVIS**, John **SHEPPARD**, Samuel G. **DUNN**, Abraham **BYRD**. Wit Stephen **BYRD**, Susanna R. **BOYCE**, James **RUSSELL** (JP). Rec 14 Jun 1819.

1184. Page 43. 14 Oct 1818. James **LOGAN** and Mary, his wife, of Ste. Genevieve Co. to Alexander **BUCKNER**. For the sum of $125, Lot No. 123 in Jackson; bounded on the S and fronted by Main St, E and fronted by second east street, W by Lot No. 39. Signed James **LOGAN**, Mary **LOGAN**. Wit Samuel G. **DUNN**, Abraham **BYRD**, Cyrus **EDWARDS**, Thos. **NEALE** (JP). Rec 15 Jun 1819.

1185. Page 44. 14 Jun 1819. William **HAND** to David **ARMOUR** and John **JUDEN**, all of Jackson. For the sum of $248.61, mortgage on four beds and bed furniture, including three bedsteads, bureau, sugar chest, and small bureau;

tenplate stove; large dining table; smaller dining table; cardtable; rifle gun; candle stand; dressing glass; two looking glasses; cupboard and furniture; two horses; cow and calf; yearling; four bee stands; 1000 lbs. bacon; one barrel hogs' lard; two large kettles; two ovens; three spiders; one set dog irons; two sets patracks; kitchen crockery, etc.; four large iron pots now in Cape Girardeau. Sd **HAND** owes two notes to sd **ARMOUR** and sd **JUDEN** for the amount of mortgage. Signed William **HAND**. Wit Joseph **McFERRON**, Clerk. Rec 10 Jun 1819.

1186. Page 45. 15 Mar 1819. Medad **RANDOL** and Thankful, his wife, to Abraham **DAUGHERTY**. For the sum of $600, 240 arpens on a branch, the waters of Hubble's Creek, beginning at a sugar tree, ash, and gum; being the same confirmed to sd **RANDOL** by the U. S.; adjoining sd **DAUGHERTY**, Thomas **BULL**, Lewis **TASH**, heirs of **SUMMERS**, decd, and **WHITE**. Signed Medad **RANDOL**, Thankful **RANDOL**. Wit James **SMITH**, Jno. **ABERNETHIE** (JP). Rec 19 Jun 1819.

1187. Page 46. 10 Jun 1819. Thomas **SULLINGER** and Rutha, his wife, to Joel **RENFROE**. For the sum of $1000, 100 acres on the waters of Hubble's Creek, beginning at a stake on **DAVIS**'s line; also bounded by sd **RENFROE**. Signed Thomas **SULLENGER**, Rutha **SULLENGER**. Wit John **AKIN** (JP), John **PATTERSON**, Sally **AKIN**. Rec 19 Jun 1819.

1188. Page 48. 27 Apr 1819. Joseph **HAWKS** by Sheriff John **HAYS** to William **NEELY** and Charles G. **ELLIS**. For the sum of $207.50, two tracts on Hubble's Creek, 100 acres, more or less, being part of a tract originally granted to James **HANNAH**, where David **HOLLEY** now lives; the other of 240 arpens, granted to Thomas **FOSTER** and joining the first tract; also a lot adjoining Jackson and Joseph **SEAWELL**. Sold on 20 Apr 1819 on four writs of execution against sd **HAWKS** issued by Circuit Court in four judgments: for John S. **MILLER** before Zenas **PRIEST**, JP, for $52 debt and $1.50 costs, dated 13 Feb 1819; for Shadrach **BOND** for $143.80 debt and $10.97 and five mills costs, dated 4 Jan 1819; for James **LEMAN** before Zenas **PRIEST**, JP, for $43.75 debt and $1.25 costs, dated 13 Feb 1819; and for Joseph **HAGAN** against sd **HAWKS**, impleaded with Elisha **AXLEY**, for $98.58 debt and $10.30 costs, dated 14 Jan 1819. Signed John **HAYS**, Sheriff. Wit Joseph **McFERRON**, Clerk. Rec 21 Jun 1819.

1189. Page 51. 18 May 1818. James **LOGAN** and Alexander **BUCKNER**. Agreement for sd **LOGAN** to convey Lot No. 29 in Jackson to sd **BUCKNER** by 1 Oct next, if sd **BUCKNER** pays sd **LOGAN** $125. Should sd **LOGAN** not get the title completed, then sd **BUCKNER** pays no consideration. Signed James **LOGAN**, A. **BUCKNER**. Test John G. **LOVE**, Nathan **McCARTY**, Joseph **McFERRON**, Clerk. Rec 26 Jun 1819.

1190. Page 52. 24 Jun 1819. John **GILES** to John **HORRELL**. For the sum of $200, __ acres on Cape La Croix in Cape Girardeau Twp, between the improvements of Samuel **RAVENSCROFT** and John **RANDEL**, being an improvement and preemption right settled by sd **GILES** on or prior to 1814. Signed John **GILES**. Wit J. **RANNEY**, Tho. **NEALE** (JP, Byrd Twp). Rec 29 Jun 1819.

1191. Page 53. 1 Jul 1819. Johnson **RANNEY** to William **SHEPPARD**. For the sum of $144, ¼ part of Lot No. 63 in Jackson; beginning on the NE corner of sd lot. Signed J. **RANNEY**. Wit Isaac **SHEPPARD**, B. S. **COSTILLO**, Tho. **NEALE** (JP). Rec 2 Jul 1819.

1192. Page 53. 1 Jul 1819. William **SHEPPARD** to John **SHEPPARD**. For the sum of $200, part of Lot No. 63 in Jackson; beginning at the SE corner of sd lot. Signed William **SHEPPARD**. Test B. S. **COSTILLO**, John **GLASSCOCK**, Tho. **NEALE** (JP). Rec 2 Jul 1819.

1193. Page 54. 1 Jul 1819. Same to same. For the sum of $150, ¼ part of Lot No. 63 in Jackson; beginning on the NE corner of sd lot. Signed William **SHEPPARD**. Test B. S. **COSTILLO**, John **GLASSCOCK**, Tho. **NEALE** (JP). Rec 2 Jul 1819.

1194. Page 55. 2 Jul 1819. Same to same. For the sum of $200, part of Lot No. 19 in Jackson on High St; beginning at the SE corner of sd lot; bounded on the S by second south street, W by Lot No. 54, and N by Lot No. 18. Signed William **SHEPPARD**. Test B. S. **COSTILLO**, Tho. **NEALE** (JP). Rec 2 Jul 1819.

1195. Page 56. 2 Jul 1819. Burrell S. **COSTILLO** to Rene **LeMEILLIEUR** of Ste. Genevieve Co. For the sum of $425, part of Lot No. 19 in Jackson on High St; beginning at the NE corner of sd lot. Signed B. S. **COSTELLO**. Wit James **EVANS**, Tho. **NEALE** (JP). Rec 2 Jul 1819.

1196. Page 57. 8 Sep 1817. John **RODNEY** and Rachel, his wife, to Thomas S. **RODNEY**. For the sum of $1100, 247 acres on Hubble's Creek, being part of Martin **RODNEY**'s head right, the part that he first improved; excepting 1 acre on the NW corner; beginning at a sycamore at Abraham **BYRD**'s NW corner; also bounded by **AKIN**, Thomas **SULLINGER**, Foster's Creek, and Martin **RODNEY**. Signed John **RODNEY**, Rachel (x) **RODNEY**. Wit Thomas **SULLINGER**, Michl. **RODNEY**, James **DOWTY**, John **AKIN** (JP). Rec 2 Jul 1819.

1197. Page 58. 1 Jun 1819. Rucker **TANNER** and Sally, his wife, of New Madrid Co., Mo. to Morton A. **RUCKER** of Caldwell Co., Ken. For the sum of $173, 160 acres on the waters of Hubble's Creek, immediately on the road from Jackson to the mill built by **LARAMOR** now owned by **DAVIS**, being part of 640 acres, the settlement right of and confirmed to Peter **BELLEW**. Sd tract has been divided into four equal parts, sd **RUCKER** to have his choice. Signed Rucker **TANNER**, Sally **TANNER**. Wit Enoch **LEGGET** (JP in New Madrid Co.), Margarett **LEGGET**, Leml. H. **MAULSBY**, Deputy Clerk, New Madrid Co. Circuit Court. Rec 2 Jul 1819.

1198. Page 59. 29 Jun 1819. John **HITT** and Frances, his wife, to James **COX** Junr. For the sum of $.25, 5 acres, more or less, being part of the tract where sd **HITT** and his family now live, bought from James **COX** Senr, and adjoining James **COX** Junr; beginning at a branch between sd **HITT** and James **COX** Junr. Signed John (x) **HITT** Senr., Frances (x) **HITT**. Wit Benjamin **HITT**, Robert **BROOKS**, Jno. **ABERNETHIE** (JP). Rec 9 Jul 1819.

1199. Page 61. 24 Jun 1819. George **FRICKE** to John **BROWN**. For the sum of $1000, part of Lot No. 28 in Jackson; bounded on the E and fronted by first east street, S by Lot No. 29, W by Clifton **MOTHERSHEAD**, and N and fronted by Main St; being the same sd **FRICKE** purchased of Jonas **WHITTENBURG** on 30 Jun 1817. Signed George **FRICKE**. Wit T. E. **STRANGE**, Wm. **JONES**, Tho. **NEALE** (JP). Rec 13 Jul 1819.

1200. Page 61. 9 Jul 1819. John **BROWN** and Rachel [his wife] to George **FRICKE**. For the sum of $1800, part of Lot No. 42 in Jackson; bounded on the N by Main St, also bounded by first west street, sd **BROWN**, and Johnson **RANEY**; beginning at Johnson **RANEY**'s office. Signed John **BROWN**, Rachel (RD) **BROWN**. Wit Wm. **JONES**, Rachel **BROWN**, Tho. **NEALE** (JP). Rec 13 Jul 1819.

1201. Page 62. 19 Apr 1819. Robert **DASHE** to John **DEALWOOD**. For value received, assignment of an improvement where sd **DEALWOOD** now lives on the waters of Apple Creek. Signed Robert **DESHA**. Test Marget **MOSS**, William **REED**. Rec 15 Jul 1819.

1202. Page 63. 20 Apr 1815. Michael **O'HOGAN** to Amos **BYRD**. For the sum of $50, 50 acres on the waters of Byrd's Creek, being part of a tract where sd **HOGAN** now lives, beginning at a stone; bounded on the E, S, & W by sd **O'HOGAN** and N by land sold to James **WILKINSON** by sd **BYRD**. Signed Michel **O'HOGAN**. Wit Abraham **BYRD**, Moses **BYRD**, James **WILKINSON**, James **RUSSELL** (JP). Rec 17 Jul 1819.

1203. Page 64. 2 Sep 1815. Same and Elizabeth, his wife, to John **BYRD**. For the sum of $200, 105 arpens and 95 poles on the waters of Byrd's Creek granted to sd **O'HOGAN**; bounded on the N by Amos **BYRD** and James **WILKINSON**, E by Abraham **BYRD**, S by land granted to Joseph **YOUNG**, and W by sd **O'HOGAN**; beginning at a stake, white oak, dogwood, and Spanish oak. Signed Michel **O'HOGAN**, Elizabeth (x) **O'HOGAN**. Wit James **WILKINSON**, Job **THROCKMORTON**, James **RUSSELL** (JP). Rec Jul 1819.

1204. Page 65. 14 Oct 1818. John **PATTERSON** Junior to same. For the sum of $34, 7 acres, being part of a tract confirmed to David **PATTERSON** Senior, now decd. Signed John (x) **PATTERSON**. Wit James **RUSSELL** (JP), Ezekiel **SEELY**. Tract is assigned to Moses **BYRD** for value received on 18 Jun 1819. Signed John **BYRD**. Wit John **RUSSELL** (JP). Rec 21 Jul 1819.

1205. Page 66. 16 Jun 1819. James **PATTERSON** Senior to Moses **BYRD**. For the sum of $175, 35 acres on the waters of Byrd's Creek, being part of a tract confirmed to David **PATTERSON** Senior, now decd. Signed James **PATTERSON**. Wit James **RUSSELL** (JP), Susanah (x) **CRADER**. Rec 21 Jul 1819.

1206. Page 66. 20 Jun 1819. Frederick **BATES**, Secretary of Mo. Terr., to William **CREATH**. Appointment as JP for Byrd Twp. Signed Frederick **BATES**. William **CREATH** takes the

oath of office. Signed Wm. **CREATH**. Wit Joseph **McFERRON**, Clerk. Rec 21 Jul 1819.

1207. Page 67. 21 Jun 1819. James E. **HAWKINS** to John **MONTGOMERY** of Wayne Co., Ill. For the sum of $96, $5 now given in hand and $91 to be paid to the Commissioners of the Courthouse and Goal by Feb next, power of attorney to make a deed on Lot No. 128 in Jackson to sd **MONTGOMERY**. Signed J. E. **HAWKINS**. Test Saml. G. **HALL**, Andrw. **HAYNES**, Joseph **McFERRON**, Clerk. Rec 24 Jul 1819.

1208. Page 67. 21 Jun 1819. Same to Andrew **HAYNES**. For the sum of $86, $5 now given in hand and $81 to be paid to the Commissioners of the Courthouse and Goal by Feb next, power of attorney to make a deed on Lot No. 70 in Jackson to sd **HAYNES**. Signed J. E. **HAWKINS**. Test Saml. G. **HALL**, John **MONTGOMERY**, Joseph **McFERRON**, Clerk. Rec 24 Jul 1819.

1209. Page 68. 1 Apr 1819. Thomas **WILLBORN** of New Madrid Co., Mo. to James **BRADY**. For the sum of $50, 500 arpens, more or less, on the Mississippi River, being the same confirmed to sd **WILLBORN**. Survey of sd tract is to be completed under the direction of sd **BRADY**, and if sd tract is not confirmed, then sd **BRADY** is to have no recourse. Signed Thos. **WELLBORN**. Wit Charles S. **RAMSEY**, Andrew M. **RAMSEY**, Joseph **McFERRON**, Clerk. Rec 26 Jul 1819.

1210. Page 69. 26 Jul 1819. James **BRADY** of New Madrid Co., Mo. to James **EVANS**. For the sum of $500, 250 arpens, or the ½ part of Thomas **WELLBORN**'s claim. Sd claim, should it be confirmed, is to be divided evenly between sd **BRADY** and sd **EVANS**. Signed James **BRADY**. Wit Andrew M. **RAMSEY**, John **WATHEN**, Zenas **PRIEST** (JP). Rec 26 Jul 1819.

1211. Page 70. 2 Jan 1819. Edward **McGUIRE** and Frances W., his wife, of Winchester, Clarke Co., Ken. to Lyne **STARLING** and E. N. **DLASHMUTT** of Jackson. For the sum of $1000, ½ of Lot No. 51 in Jackson; beginning at a stake at the SW corner of sd lot, and bounded by Main St, the part of the lot conveyed by Rene **LeMEILLEUR** to David **DAVIS**, and the part of sd lot conveyed by sd **LeMEILLEUR** to Rutter **HOUTS** and **STALLCUP**. Sd lot was conveyed from the Commissioners of the Court House and Jail to Robert **WASH** on 17 Dec 1814, by sd **WASH** to Moses **SCOTT** on 20 Feb

1816, and by sd **SCOTT** and wife to sd **LeMEILLEUR** on 26 Feb 1818. Signed Edwd. **McGUIRE**, Frances W. (RD) **McGUIRE**. Wit James P. **BULLOCK**, Clerk of Clarke Co., Ken., Benjn. J. **SAUL**, Presiding Judge of Clarke Co., Ken. Rec 28 Jul 1819.

1212. Page 71. 17 Jul 1819. Richard **WALLER** and Susanna, his wife, to Van B. **DLASHMUTT** of Madison Co., Ohio. For the sum of $1155, 231 acres on Randall's Creek, being where sd **WALLER** formerly lived; adjoined on the W by John **ABERNETHIE**, Esq., S by John **HITT**, N by a line between Isaac **WILLIAMS** and sd **WALLER**, and E by vacant land. Signed Richard **WALLER**, Susanna **WALLER**. Wit Thos. **NEALE** (JP), Charles C. **JACKSON**. Rec 28 Jul 1819.

1213. Page 72. 31 Jul 1819. Andrew **RAMSEY** to William **CRACROFT**. For the sum of $76, undivided 2/3 of 38 arpents, more or less, which sd **RAMSEY** and sd **CRACRAFT** purchased of Elisha **WHITE**; being the SW corner of the head right of Lewis **LATHAM**; bounded on the W by the heirs of Andrew **SOMMERS**, decd, and S by John **SOMMERS**. Signed Andrew **RAMSEY**. Wit Jason **CHAMBERLAIN**, Matthew **McKINNEY**, Joseph **McFERRON**, Clerk. Rec 31 Jul 1819.

1214. Page 73. 31 Jul 1819. Same to Charles C. **JACKSON**. For the sum of $1666, undivided 1/3 of __ acres on the River Zenan, being the tract on which are Cracraft's Mills in Twp 31 N, Rng 12 E; beginning at a stake at the corner of Thomas W. **GRAVES** and James **DOWTY**; also bounded by **SOMMERS**, John **SOMMERS**, and the U. S. Signed Andrew **RAMSEY**. Wit Jason **CHAMBERLAIN**, William **CRACRAFT**, Joseph **McFERRON**, Clerk. Rec 31 Jul 1819.

1215. Page 74. 31 Jul 1819. Charles C. **JACKSON** to Andrew **RAMSEY**. For the sum of $1666, mortgage on two undivided 1/3 parts of the tract and mills described in the preceding deed (E:73). Sd **JACKSON** owes three notes to sd **RAMSEY**, dated 31 Jul 1819, two for $555.45, and one for $555.56. Signed Charles C. **JACKSON**. Wit J. **CHAMBERLAIN**, William **CRACRAFT**, Joseph **McFERRON**, Clerk. Rec 31 Jul 1819.

1216. Page 76. 17 Jul 1819. George **MORROW** and Susan, his wife, to Henry **CLINARD** and John **BINKLEY**, all of Jackson, Mo. For the sum of $110, part of Lot No. 27 in Jackson,

beginning at a stake at the E side of the public square; being the same conveyed by the Commissioners of the Court House and Jail to Anthony B. **NEELY**, and by sd **NEELY** and Margret, his wife to John **WHITTENBURG**, and by sd **WHITTENBURGH** to sd **MORROW**. Signed Geo. **MORROW**, Susannah **MORROW**. Wit Zenas **PRIEST** (JP), Stephen **BACON**. Rec 4 Aug 1819.

1217. Page 77. 7 Jun 1819. Prescilla **JOHNSON** and John **EDWARDS** to Simon **POE** Junr. For the sum of $20, 5 acres and 16 poles, being where sd **POE** now lives with his family, and being part of the tract where sd **JOHNSON** and sd **EDWARDS** now live and that was conveyed to sd **JOHNSON** by Elijah **RANDOLL**; adjoining land sd **POE** purchased from sd **RANDOLL**; beginning at a stake near sd **POE**'s spring. Signed Preceller (x) **JOHNSON**, John **EDWARDS**. Wit William **MARTIN**, Anna **MARTIN**, Jno. **ABERNETHIE** (JP). Rec 7 Aug 1819.

1218. Page 78. 3 Aug 1819. John G. **LOVE** and Rebecca, his wife, to Thomas **SLOAN**. For the sum of $600, Lot No. 62 in Jackson; bounded on the E by first west street, S by Lot No. 63, W by Lot No. 74, and N by first north street. Signed John G. **LOVE**, Rebecka (x) **LOVE**. Wit Zenas **PRIEST** (JP), Anthony (x) **RANDOL**. Rec 9 Aug 1819.

1219. Page 79. 2 Dec 1818. Arthur **BURNS** and Mary, his wife, of St. Charles Co., Mo. to Lewis **DICKSON** of Ste. Genevieve Co., Mo. For the sum of $100, their interest and right of dower to 50 acres, more or less, near Jackson; granted to Zillah **DICKSON**, decd, by the Spanish government; being the 1/8 part of 400 acres which was the legal inheritance of Zillah **DICKSON**; bounded on the S by 240 acres sold by Zillah **DICKSON** to John **RANDEL**, E unknown, N by Benijah **LAUGHERTY**, and W by the widow **TAYLOR**. Signed Arthur **BURNS**, Mary **BURNS**. Wit John **BRYSON**, JP in St. Charles Co. Rec 16 Aug 1819.

1220. Page 79. 17 Aug 1819. Commissioners of the Court House and Jail to Thomas **SULLINGER**. For the sum of $99, Lot No. 133 in Jackson; bounded on the S and fronted by first north street, W and fronted by second east street, N by lands formerly owned by Samuel **PEW**, and E by sd **PEW**. Signed John **DAVIS**, John **SHEPPARD**, Abraham **BYRD**. Wit E. N. **DLASHMUTT**, John B. **FENNIMORE**, James **RUSSELL** (JP). Rec 18 Aug 1819.

1221. Page 80. 15 May 1819. Margaret **McCLUSKEY** to Ezekiel **ABLE**. For the consideration of a marriage unto and shortly to be had between the parties and the sum of $1000 to be received as one negro girl and land, agreement that if sd marriage takes place and sd Margaret survives sd **ABLE**, then she is not to receive any dower out of the remaining estate. Signed Ezekiel **ABLE**, Margaret (x) **McCLUSKY**. Wit Erasmus **ELLIS**, Thos. **MILLS**, Joseph **McFERRON**, Clerk. Rec 20 Aug 1819.

1222. Page 81. 5 Jul 1819. James **TANNER** of New Madrid Co., Mo. to Danial F. **STEINBECK**, Louis **LORIMIER**, and Thomas **RODNEY**, guardian of the two minor heirs of Elizbeth **RODNEY**, late Elizbeth **LORRIMIER**. For the sum of $125, 1 acre on the N side of Cape Girardeau, sold by the grantees to sd **TANNER** in 1816. Signed James **TANNER**. Wit George **HENDERSON** (JP). Rec 20 Aug 1819.

1223. Page 82. 13 Jul 1819. John C. **HARBISON** and Sarah, his wife, to Daniel F. **STEINBECK**. For the sum of $1000, 1000 arpens, more or less, on the waters of Cape La Cruche Creek to the N of a 1 league square tract belonging to the heirs of Louis **LORIMIER**, being the original claim of Louis F. **LARGEAU** conveyed to sd **HARBISON** on 7 Dec 1805 by John **HAYS**, Sheriff. Signed John C. **HARBISON**, Sarah (x) **HARBISON**. Wit George **HENDERSON** (JP). Rec 20 Aug 1819.

1224. Page 83. 3 Jun 1819. Thomas S. **RODNEY** to William **HAND**. For the sum of $4000, bond to make a deed for Lot No. 110 in Jackson, sd **HAND** having paid $750 for the same. Signed Thoms. S. **RODNEY**. Test C. N. **BLACKMAN**, William **WATHEN**, Wm. **NEELY**, Thos. **SLOAN**, Thos. **NEALE** (JP). The obligation and power of attorney is assigned to C. G. **HAUTS** for $100 on 26 Jun 1819. Signed William **HAND**. Wit Scarlet **GLASSCOCK**, Presley **PHILLIPS**. Christr. G. **HAUTS** assigns power of attorney to Isaac **RODGERS** on 14 Aug 1819. Signed Christr. G. **HAUTS**, attorney for William **HAND**. Wit Thos **NEALE** (JP). Rec 21 Aug 1819.

1225. Page 84. 2 Jun 1819. William **HAND** and Sarah, his wife, to Thomas S. **RODNEY**. For the sum of $750, Lot No. 110 in Jackson, including the bark mill, stock of leather on hand, and all tools belonging to the tanning business; being the same lot where sd **HAND** now lives and the

tanyard is situated. Signed Wm. **HAND**, Sarah **HAND** (RD). Wit Wm. **NEELY**, C. N. **BLACKMAN**, Th. S. **SLOAN**, William **WATHEN**, Thos. **NEALE** (JP). Rec 23 Aug 1819.

1226. Page 85. 7 Oct 1816. Simon **KINEON** and Elizabeth, his wife, to Thomas **SULLINGER**. For the sum of $70, __ acres where sd **KINEON** now lives, part of a tract that he was granted from the Spanish Government; adjoining James **COX** Senior and Junior and Robert **CRAFORD**; beginning at a dogwood on the branch where Moses **BYRNE** now lives. Signed Simon (x) **KINEON**, Elizabeth (x) **KINON**. Wit William **THOMPSON**, William **MATTHEWS**, John **AKIN** (JP). Rec 23 Aug 1819.

1227. Page 86. 23 Aug 1819. Thomas **SULLINGER** and Rutha, his wife, to John **HITT**. For the sum of $70, the tract described in the preceding deed (E:85), so as to include a spring on the N side of the branch. Signed Thomas **SULLENGER**, Rutha (x) **SULLINGER**. Test John **AKIN** (JP), William **MATTHEWS**. Rec 23 Aug 1819.

1228. Page 87. 26 Feb 1813. Joseph **YOUNG** and Sally, his wife, to John **BYRD**. For the sum of $800, 200 arpents, French measure, more of less, on the waters of Byrd's Creek granted to sd **YOUNG**; bounded on the N by Michael **O'HOGAN**, W by Philip **YOUNG** and James **CRAWFORD**, S by John **BYRD**, and E by Abraham **BYRD**. Signed Joseph **YOUNG**, Sally (x) **YOUNG**. Wit Nathan **McCARTY**, Robert **PATTERSON**, James **RUSSELL** (JP). Rec 23 Aug 1819.

1229. Page 88. 22 Jul 1815. Stephen **OWANS** to Medad **RANDOL**. For the sum of $500, -- acres at the mouth of Boice's Creek on the Mississippi, first taken up by Jonathan **BOICE** as his head right. Signed Steph. **OWENS**. Test Parish **GREEN**, George (x) **JAMES**, Zenas **PRIEST** (JP). Rec 25 Aug 1819.

1230. Page 88. 27 Jan 1819. Joseph **THORN** and Rhinette, his wife, and Hyram C. **DAVIS** and Nancy, his wife, to John **ARMSTRONG**. For the sum of $400, 1/8 and ¼ part of Lot No. 63 in Jackson; beginning on Main St at the SW corner of sd lot. Signed Joseph **THORN**, Rhinette **THORN**, Hiram C. **DAVIS**, Nancy **DAVIS**. Wit J. **RANNEY**, Zenas **PRIEST** (JP). Rec 27 Aug 1819.

1231. Page 89. 30 Jun 1819. James **BRADY** to Thomas **FLETCHER**, both of New Madrid Co., Mo. For the sum of $100, 120 acres and 10 poles, being ½ of 240 arpens and 20 poles on the bank of the Mississippi River, part of a tract originally granted to Alexander **MILLIKIN** by Don Louis **LORIMIER**, Commandant of the Cape Girardeau Dist, and conveyed by sd **MILLIKIN** to sd **BRADY**. Sd **FLETCHER** is to have no recourse against sd **BRADY** concerning title to sd land. Signed James **BRADY**. Wit John **WATHEN**, Victor **LORIMIER**, Rich. **WATHEN**, Zenas **PRIEST** (JP). Rec 27 Aug 1819.

1232. Page 91. 13 Aug 1819. Medad **RANDOL** to Thomas **MOSELY** Jr. and James M. **CROPPER**. For the sum of $1000, to be paid as $500 within 12 months, and $500 to be paid within 9 months of the day the land is to be entered, bond to make a deed on equal moiety of sd **RANDOL**'s preemption claim whereon he now lives, supposed to contain at least 400 acres, which contains the unsold town lots in Bainbridge. Sd **RANDOL** binds himself to return the money with interest if he fails in his preemption right, and the price shall be adjusted if the quantity does not amount to 400 acres, using ½ of the government price for sd land. Signed Medad **RANDOL**, Tom **MOSELEY** Jr., Jm. **CROPPER**. Wit Thomas **STALEY**, Joseph **McFERRON**, Clerk. Rec 28 Aug 1819.

1233. Page 92. 31 Aug 1819. Simmons **KENYON** to Benjamin **HORRELL**. For the sum of $2000 to be paid before 1 May 1820, bond to make a deed on 200 arpens on the waters of Randel's Creek where sd **KENYON** now lives, for which sd **HORRELL** has paid $1000, $200 in hand and the balance by 1 May next. Should the tract not total 200 arpens by survey, then sd **KENYON** is to deduct the amount from the amount of the deposit paid, and if it is more than 200 arpens, then sd **HORRELL** is to pay the surplus at the same rate. Signed Simmons (R) **KENYON**. Test A. **BUCKNER**, Zenas **PRIEST** (JP). Rec 31 Aug 1819.

1234. Page 93. 28 Aug 1819. Isaac **RODGERS** of Jackson to Thomas S. **RODNEY**. For value received, bond given by sd **RODNEY** to William **HAND** for conveyance of Lot No. 110 in Jackson; which was assigned by sd **HAND** to Christopher L. **HAUTZ** for value received, and by sd **HAUTZ** to sd **RODGERS** on 14 Aug 1819 for value received. Signed Isaac **RODGERS**. Wit James **EVANS**, Wm. **CREATH** (JP). Rec 2 Sep 1819.

1235. Page 94. 2 Jan 1819. Elijah **RANDOL** and Neley, his wife, to Scarlet **GLASSCOCK**. For the sum of $230, 115 acres, being part of the head right of Enos **RANDOL**; beginning at Simon **POE**'s NW corner, and also bounded by W. **WILLIAMS** and **EDWARDS**. Signed Elijah **RANDOL**, Nelly **RANDOL** (RD). Wit Joel **BLUNT**, David **ARMOUR**, Tho. **NEALE** (JP). Rec 4 Sep 1819.

1236. Page 95. 14 Jun 1819. John **HERBERT** & Co. to same. For the sum of $250, Lot No. 66 in Jackson; bounded on the N and fronted by first south street, E and fronted by first west street, S by Lot No. 67, and W by Lot No. 78. Signed John **HERBERT** & Co. Wit Samuel S. **HALL**, Zenas **PRIEST** (JP). Rec 4 Sep 1819.

1237. Page 96. 4 Sep 1819. John **DELAP** to James **BURNS**. For the sum of $611.50, undivided ½ of 24 acres and 75 poles on the River Zenon in Byrd Twp; beginning at a stake, a hickory, and two dogwood saplings, and bounded in part by John **BROWN**; and subject to the conditions of the indenture in which sd **DELAP** purchased the tract from John **DAVIS**, and completion of the title by sd **DELAP**. Sd **DELAP**'s wife [not named] RD. Signed John **DELAP**. Wit Jason **CHAMBERLAIN**, Joseph **McFERRON**, Clerk. Rec 4 Sep 1819.

1238. Page 97. 11 Jun 1819. Conrad **STATLER** and Catherine, his wife, to Peter **STATLER**. For the sum of $2000, 500 arpents in German Twp, being his headright and confirmation, and being where sd Peter now lives. Signed Conrat **STATLER**, Catherine (x) **STATLER**. Wit J. **RANNEY**, Zenas **PRIEST** (JP). Rec 7 Sep 1819.

1239. Page 98. 17 Jul 1819. William **CRACROFT** and Elizabeth, his wife, to Charles C. **JACKSON**. For the sum of $1300, 1/3 part of 246 arpens, more or less, on Hubble's Creek, being the 1/3 part of a tract conveyed by John **RAMSEY** to Andrew **RAMSEY**, Thomas W. **GRAVES**, and sd **CRACROFT**, and being where sd **JACKSON** now lives and where Andrew **RAMSEY**, sd **GRAVES**, and sd **CRACROFT** built a saw and grist mill; adjoined on the E by John **BURROWS**, S by sd **GRAVES**, W by James **DOWTY**, and N by Alexander **SUMMERS**. Signed William **CRACROFT**, Elizabeth (x) **CRACROFT**. Wit John **RODNEY**, Thos. W. **GRAVES**, James **DOWTY**, John **AKIN** (JP). Rec 8 Sep 1819.

1240. Page 99. 30 Jul 1819. Thomas W. **GRAVES** and Mary, his wife, to same. For the sum of $1000, 1/3 part of the tract described in the preceding deed (E:98). Signed Thomas W. **GRAVES**, Mary **GRAVES**. Wit John **RODNEY**, James **DOWTY**, John **AKIN** (JP). Rec 8 Sep 1819.

1241. Page 101. 19 Aug 1819. William **JONES** and Catharine, his wife, to Michael **KNOX**. For the sum of $100, ½ of Lot No. 56 in Jackson; bounded on the N and fronted by second south street, W and fronted by first west street, S by Lot No. 57, and E by sd **JONES**. Signed William **JONES**, Catherine **JONES**. Test John **BROWN**, George **FRICKE**, William **CREATH** (JP). Rec 10 Sep 1819.

1242. Page 102. 10 Sep 1819. Robert **McCAY** of New Madrid Co., Mo. to Samuel **RAVENSCROFT**. Quit claim to 320 arpents which he conveyed to Edward **ROBERTSON** on 5 Jun 1809, being his Spanish grant. Signed Robert **McCAY**. Wit James **EVANS** (JP), James **RAVENSCROFT**. Rec 22 Sep 1819.

1243. Page 103. 23 Mar 1819. Peter **BELLEW** of Perry Co., Ohio to Rucker **TANNER** of New Madrid Co., Mo. For the sum of $1000, 640 acres, more or less, on the waters of Hubble's Creek between Jackson and Laramore's new mill, being his settlement right and improvement; also power to obtain the sole right to sd land. Signed Peter **BELLEW**, Polly (x) **BELLEW**. Wit Roswell **MILLS**, JP in Perry Co., Ohio, Peter **BUGH** Senr, Jacob D. **DIETRUB**(?), Notary Public in Lancaster Dist, Fairfield Co., Ohio. Rec 23 Sep 1819.

1244. Page 105. 30 Sep 1819. Stephen **BYRD** to Abraham **BYRD** of East Baton Rouge Parish, La. For the sum of $4000, three tracts he purchased of sd Abraham **BYRD** and which were the head right of Abraham **BYRD**; 560 acres on Hubble's Creek adjoining M. **RODNEY**'s head right; 200 acres adjoining Jacob **JACOBS**, the head right of Thompson **BYRD**; and 240 acres, the head right of Abraham **BYRD** Junr, adjoining the head right of Thompson **BYRD**. Signed Stephen **BYRD**. Wit Tho. **NEALE** (JP), John **BYRD**. Rec 30 Sep 1819.

1245. Page 106. 9 Jul 1819. Gilbert **HECTOR** and [Anna] his wife to Nicholas **WHITE**. For the sum of $92, 11 acres and 56 poles, beginning at a white oak and stake on a ridge. Signed Gilbert (x) **HECTOR**, Anna (x) **HECTOR**. Wit

T. E. **STRANGE**, Wm. **NEILL**, Zenas **PRIEST** (JP). Rec 3 Oct 1819.

1246. Page 107. 3 Jul 1819. Commissioners of the Court House and Jail to William **WATHIN**. For the sum of $60, Lot No. 85 in Jackson; bounded on the E and fronted by second west street, S and fronted by first north street, W by Lot No. 97, and N by lands formerly owned by Joseph **SEAWELL**. Signed John **DAVIS**, John **SHEPPARD**, Samuel G. **DUNN**, Abraham **BYRD**. Test Chas. **MOTHERSHEAD**, James **McARTEE**, Zenas **PRIEST** (JP). Rec 4 Oct 1819.

1247. Page 108. 17 Dec 1818. Same to Polly **MOTHERSHEAD** and William **MOTHERSHEAD**, he being of Ken. For the sum of $73.25, Lot No. 137 in Jackson; bounded on the S and fronted by first south street, W and fronted by second east street, N by Lot No. 136, and E by Lot No. 149. Signed John **DAVIS**, John **SHEPPARD**, Samuel G. **DUNN**, Abraham **BYRD**. Wit Thomas W. **McLAUGHLAN**, Chas. **MOTHERSHEAD**, William **CREATH** (JP). Rec 5 Oct 1819.

1248. Page 110. 10 Jun 1819. Thomas S. **RODNEY** and Polly, his wife, to Hiram C. **DAVIS**. For the sum of $1452, 240 acres, two chains, and ⅕ of a chain on Hubble's and Foster's Creeks, beginning at a sycamore at Abraham **BYRD**'s NW corner; also bounded by ___ **AIKIN** and Thomas **SULLINGER**. Signed Thos. S. **RODNEY**, Polly (x) **RODNEY**. Wit John **RODNEY**, Greer W. **DAVIS**, James **DOWTY**, John **AKIN** (JP). Rec 5 Oct 1819.

1249. Page 111. 10 Jun 1819. Same and same to same. For the sum of $1, 1 3/4 acre on the waters of Hubble's Creek on the W side or corner of sd **RODNEY**'s improvement, beginning on Thomas **SULLINGER**'s E line at a hickory sapling. Signed Thos. S. **RODNEY**, Polly (x) **RODNEY**. Wit John **RODNEY**, Greer W. **DAVIS**, James **DOWTY**, John **AKIN** (JP). Rec 5 Oct 1819.

1250. Page 113. 5 Oct 1819. John **HITT** Senr to John **HITT** Junior. For natural love and affection he has and bears unto his son, 300 arpens or 255 acres, more or less, where he and his family formerly lived, known as Daniel O **DUGGAN**'s concession; adjoining John **RANDOLL** Junr, Charles A. **ELLIS**, James **SMITH**, John **ABERNETHIE**, and **DELASHMUTT** (formerly Richard **WALLER**). Signed John (x) **HITT** Senr. Wit James **COX** Junr, Hiram

KINNISON, Jno. **ABERNETHIE** (JP). Rec 18 Oct 1819.

1251. Page 114. 24 Apr 1818. Medad **RANDOL** and Thankful, his wife, to Jenifer T. **SPRIGG**. For the sum of $50, Lot No. 9 in Bainbridge on the Mississippi River, beginning at the NW corner of Water St and Lawrence St. Signed Medad **RANDOL**, Thankful **RANDOL**. Wit Daniel **STOUT**, Lewis **RANDOL**, George **HENDERSON** (JP). Rec 21 Oct 1819.

1252. Page 115. 1 Apr 1809. Peter **GODAR** to **REINECKE & STEINBECK**. For the sum of $200, 100 acres fronting on the Mississippi, for which he promises to make a deed. Signed Peter (x) **GODAR**. Test Levi **WOLVERTON**, John **ROCKE**, George **HENDERSON** (JP). Rec 21 Oct 1819.

1253. Page 115. 1 Apr 1809. William **BONER** to same and same. For the sum of $70, the improvement on the land Peter **GODAR** sold them. Signed William ( ) **BONER**. Test Levi **WOLVERTON**, John **ROCKE**, George **HENDERSON** (JP). Rec 21 Oct 1819.

1254. Page 116. 4 Jun 1818. John **SIMPSON** to Daniel F. **STEINBECK**. For the sum of $450, 200 acres, more or less, in two tracts; one on the N edge of the Big Swamp that he settled in 1811, on which there are about 40 acres in cultivation, and where he now resides; the other of 40 acres, adjoining the first and being the SE corner of a tract originally granted to Edward **ROBERTSON**, purchased by sd **SIMPSON** of John **RAMSEY**. Signed John **SIMPSON**. Wit B. **COUSIN**, Raphl. V. **LORIMIER**, George **HENDERSON** (JP). Rec 21 Oct 1819.

1255. Page 117. 15 Sep 1819. John **RISHER** and Mary, his wife, to Charles S. **HEMPSTEAD** of St. Louis. For the sum of $2000 ($666.66 2/3 in nine months, the same in 18 months, and the same in 24 months), 45 acres and 84 poles adjoining Cape Girardeau, which he purchased of Louis **LORIMIER**, as surveyed in Sep 1809 by Bartholomew **COUSIN**; beginning on the bank of the Mississippi at Simon **WOODROW**'s lower line; including Lot Nos. 2, 3, 4, 5, 6, 7, 8, 9, 10, 11, 14, 15, 16, 17, 18, 19, 21, 23, & 44 [in the town of Decatur]. Sd **HEMPSTEAD** also mortgages the property to sd **RISHER** for the purchase price. Signed John **RISHER**, Mary (x) **RISHER**, Chs. S. **HEMPSTEAD**. Wit B **COUSIN**, D. F. **STEINBECK**, George **HENDERSON** (JP). Rec 21 Oct 1819.

1256. Page 119. 1 Oct 1819. Ezekiel **ABLE** and Margaret, his wife, to George **HENDERSON** and Daniel F. **STEINBECK**. For the sum of $1750, S ½ of Lot No. 8, Range D in Cape Girardeau; bounded on the S by Themis St, N by the other half of the lot belonging to sd **HENDERSON**, E by Lot No. 7, and W by Indian St; being purchased by sd **ABLE** of Andrew **RAMSEY**, now decd. Signed Ezekiel **ABLE**, Margaret (x) **ABLE**. Wit Thos. **MILLIS**, A. **LORIMIER**, William **KELSO** (JP). Rec 21 Oct 1819.

1257. Page 120. 25 Oct 1819. William **HAND** and Sally, his wife, to Henry **HAND**. For the sum of $1500, 380 arpents on the waters of Hubble's Creek in Byrd Twp; also one negro girl named **Sinah**, ten head of horses, 38 head of cattle, ten head of sheep, 158 head of hogs, all the household and kitchen furniture, and farming tools. Sd property was conveyed by Henry **HAND** to William **HAND** on 4 Sep 1813 (C:437). Signed William **HAND**, Sarah **HAND**. Wit Jason **CHAMBERLAIN**, Joseph **McFERRON**, Clerk. Rec 25 Oct 1819.

1258. Page 121. 6 Oct 1819. William **HAND** and Sarah, his wife, and Henry **HAND** and Sarah, his wife, to Thomas S. **RODNEY**. For the sum of $1000, 100 acres, American measure, being the W part of a tract where Henery **HAND** now lives, beginning at the SW corner of sd tract at a stake and stone near a hickory and elm; bounded on the W by John **BROWN** and John **DAVIS**, E by James **GOZA** and Henery **HAND**, and S by Samuel **PEW**. Signed William **HAND**, Sarah **HAND**, Henry **HAND**, Sarah **HAND**. Wit J. **RODNEY**, Joseph **McFERRON**, Clerk. Rec 26 Oct 1819.

1259. Page 123. 27 Oct 1819. James **EVANS** to Jenifer T. **SPRIGG** of St. Louis. For the sum of $200, 20 acres, being part of a claim confirmed to Thomas **WELLBURN** near Bainbridge, beginning at the upper or NE corner at a post standing on the Mississippi River. Signed James **EVANS**. Wit Victor **LORIMIER**, Medad **RANDOL**, George **HENDERSON** (JP). Rec 27 Oct 1819.

1260. Page 124. 16 Oct 1819. Frederick **BATES**, Secretary of Missouri Terr, to John C. **HARBISON**. Appointment as JP for Cape Girardeau Twp. Signed Frederick **BATES**. John C. **HARBISON** takes the oath of office. Signed John C. **HARBISON**. Wit Joseph **McFERRON**. Rec 27 Oct 1819.

1261. Page. 124. 26 Oct 1819. Thomas S. **RODNEY** and Polly, his wife, to William **HAND**. For the sum of $750, quit claim to Lot No. 110, being the same where the tanyard is situated, as well as the bark mill, stock of leather now on hand, and all tools belonging to the tanning business. Signed Thos. S. **RODNEY**, Polly **RODNEY**. Wit Elijah **DAUGHERTY**, Michl. **RODNEY**, John **AKIN** (JP). Rec 29 Oct 1819.

1262. Page 125. 29 Oct 1819. James **TANNER** of New Madrid Co., Mo. to Ithamar **HUBBEL**. For the sum of $400, 300 arpens on the waters of Whitewater, being the same granted by the U. S. Commissioners to Samuel **DORSEY** under Harris **AUSEN**. Signed James **TANNER**. Wit Stephen **BYRD**, Wm. P. **LACEY**, Wm. **CREATH** (JP). Rec 29 Oct 1819.

1263. Page 126. 22 Oct 1819. John **ARMSTRONG** and Eliza, his wife, to Erasmus **ELLIS**. For the sum of $1700, part of Lot No. 63 in Jackson on Main St; beginning at Main St on the S side of sd lot at the SW corner of their dwelling house; also bounded by land purchased by sd **ARMSTRONG** from J. **RANNEY**. Signed John **ARMSTRONG**, Hulale **ARMSTRONG**. Wit Phinehas **COBURN**, Zenas **PRIEST** (JP). Rec 2 Nov 1819.

1264. Page 127. 3 Nov 1819. Frederick **BATES**, Secretary of Missouri Terr, to John **HAYS**. Appointment as Sheriff of Cape Girardeau Co. Signed Frederick **BATES**. John **HAYS** takes the oath of office. Signed John **HAYS**. Wit Joseph **McFERRON**. Rec 8 Nov 1819.

1265. Page 128. 10 Nov 1819. William **TIPTON** and James **RAVENSCROFT** to John **CROSS**. For the sum of $3848, bond to make a deed on land by 1 Mar 1822. Sd **TIPTON**, for the sum of $1000 paid and of $924 to be paid, has sold two tracts; 232 arpens, more or less, on the waters of Ramsey's Creek, confirmed to the representatives of Samuel **TIPTON**, decd; also 54 ½ acres, more or less, adjoining the first tract and devised by the last will and testament of Andrew **RAMSEY**, decd, to his daughter Elenor; bounded by Rebecca **HARBISON**, Benjamin M. **HORRELL**, and others. Signed William **TIPTON**, James **RAVENSCROFT**. Wit Merritt **RANSOM**, Joseph **McFERRON**, Clerk. Rec 11 Nov 1819.

1266. Page 129. 11 Nov 1819. William **TIPTON**, grandson of Andrew **RAMSEY**, decd, and son of Elenor, daughter of sd

RAMSEY, to same. Power of attorney to take possession of the tracts described in the preceding deed (E:128) and to obtain a complete title to the same. Signed William **TIPTON**. Wit James **RAVENSCROFT**, Joseph **McFERRON**, Clerk. Rec 11 Nov 1819.

1267. Page 130. 8 Nov 1819. John **HAYS**, Robert **GREEN**, William **NEELY**, and John **BROWN** to William **CLARK**, Governor of Mo. Terr. For the sum of $10,000, bond to guarantee that sd **HAYS** shall perform the duties of Sheriff of Cape Girardeau Co. for two years. Signed John **HAYS**, Robert **GREEN**, Wm. **NEELY**, John **BROWN**. Wit W. **GARNER**, R. S. **THOMAS**, Judge of Southern Circuit. Rec 12 Nov 1819.

1268. Page 131. 7 Sep 1819. Ezekiel **ABLE** to John **JOHNSON**. For the sum of $2120, bond to make a deed for 212 acres in the Big Bend of the Mississippi River; the upper part confirmed to Jabez **FISHER**, and conveyed to sd **ABLE**, by 1 Aug next, and full possession to sd **JOHNSON** by 1 Nov next. Signed Ezekiel **ABLE**. Test J. **FRIZEL**, Wm. P. **LACEY**, Joseph **McFERRON**, Clerk. Rec 17 Nov 1819.

1269. Page 132. 17 Aug 1819. Daniel **CLIPPARD** to Franklin **CONON** & William **RANDLES**. For the sum of $200, Lot No. 102 in Jackson; bounded on the W and fronted by third west street, N and fronted by first south street, E by Lot No. 90, and S by Lot No. 103. Signed Daniel **CLIPARD**. Wit Saml. **HARRIS**, Lott **ABERNATHY**, Abraham **BYRD**, Wm. **CREATH** (JP). Rec 17 Nov 1819.

1270. Page 133. 13 Oct 1819. George **HAYS** and Sarah, his wife, to Alexander **BUCKNER**. For the sum of $400, 100 acres, more or less, on the waters of Hubble's Creek; beginning at a stake near a black gum at the NW of the tract surveyed for Charles **DEMOSS**, the original claimant; bounded on the N by the heirs of Christopher **HAYS**, decd, E by sd **DEMOSS**, S by lands late of Lewis **DICKSON** and George **HAYS**, and W by George **HAYS**; being the same confirmed to sd **DEMOSS** as his settlement right and conveyed by him to George **HAYS** on 21 Apr 1819. Signed George **HAYS**, Sarah **HAYS**. Wit James **EVANS**, Joseph **McFERRON**, Clerk. Rec 18 Nov 1819.

1271. Page 134. 8 Nov 1819. Christopher G. **HOUTS** and Lettitia, his wife, and Mark H. **STALLCUP** and Hannah, his wife to Edmund **RUTTER** of Jackson. For the sum of $1250, their undivided interest to nearly ¼ part of Lot No. 51 in Jackson; beginning at a stake on Main St and also bounded by first west street; being the same conveyed by the Commissioners of the Court House and Jail to Robert **WASH** on 7 Dec 1814, and by sd **WASH** to Moses **SCOTT** on 20 Feb 1816, and by sd **SCOTT** and wife to Rene **LeMEILEUR** on 26 Feb 1818. The parties are tenants in common of sd lot, it being where their storehouse now stands. Signed Christr. G. **HOUTS**, Letitia G. **HOUTS**, Mark H. **STALLCUP**, Hannah **STALLCUP**. Wit Lemuel H. **MAULSBY**, Deputy Clerk of South Circuit, Wm. **CREATH** (JP). Rec 19 Nov 1819.

1272. Page 137. 12 Nov 1819. Christopher G. **HOUTS** and Letitia, his wife, to same. For the sum of $2500, Lot No. 49 in Jackson; bounded on the E by Lot No. 13, S and fronted by first north street, W and fronted by first west street, and N by the surplus of Jackson on land of Joseph **SEWELL**; being where the dwelling house of sd **HOUTS** now stands, now occupied by sd **RUTTER**. Signed Christr. G. **HOUTS**, Letitia G. **HOUTS**. Wit Wm. **CREATH** (JP). Rec 19 Nov 1819.

1273. Page 138. 9 Feb 1819. Samuel S. **HALL** and Samuel **LOCKHART**. For the sum of $530, agreement to divide Lot No. 54 in Cape Girardeau, being where sd **HALL** now lives, including house, kitchen, and stable; to be divided in half by a line running N-S. Sd **HALL** posts bond of $1060 to execute a deed when title is settled between Joseph **SEAWELL** and the heirs of **MILLS**, decd, the original grantee of sd land. Signed Samuel S. **HALL**. Wit James **EVANS**, Wm. **CREATH** (JP). Rec 19 Nov 1819.

1274. Page 139. 10 Jun 1818. Commissioners of the Court House and Jail to William **WILLIAMS**. For the sum of $132, Lot No. 50 in Jackson; bounded on the E by Lot No. 14, S by Lot No. 51, W and fronted by first west street, and N and fronted by first north street. Signed John **SHEPPARD**, Samuel G. **DUNN**, Abraham **BYRD**, Benja. **SHELL**. Test Wm. **JOHNSON**, Samul **PUTNAM**, Zenas **PRIEST** (JP). Rec 20 Nov 1819.

1275. Page 140. 21 Nov 1818. Coleman **STUBBLEFIELD** to Ezekiel **SEALY**. For the sum of $180, 15 acres, being an improvement and preemption right on Congress land on the waters of Byrd's Creek, Byrd Twp; also the power to complete title by the sd preemption right. Signed Coleman **STUBBLEFIELD**. Wit

Geo. H. **SCRIPPS**, James **RUSSELL** (JP). Rec 27 Nov 1819.

1276. Page 141. 9 Nov 1819. William **LORIMIER** of Humphreys Co., Tenn. to Daniel F. **STEINBECK**. For the sum of $1000, 500 arpens on the forks of Cape la Cruche Creek where John **RANDOL** now resides, being the residue of 1000 arpens granted to him by the Spanish Government on 28 Dec 1799, as recorded in the Office of the Recorder of Land Titles E:25-26. Signed Wm. **LORIMIER**. Wit John **HAYS**, George **HENDERSON** (JP). Rec 29 Nov 1819.

1277. Page 142. 30 Nov 1819. Commissioners to Partition Lands of the heirs of Louis **LORIMIER**, decd, to Joseph **McFERRON**. For the sum of $590, 80 acres, more or less, being Outlot Nos. 35 & 36 near and N of Cape Girardeau; bounded on the N by heirs of Louis **LORIMIER**, S by Outlot Nos. 30 & 31, E by Outlot No. 34, and W by Outlot No. 37. Sold on order of Circuit Court issued Aug Term 1819, on petition for partition of sd lands. Signed B. **COUSIN**, Wm. **KELSO**, W. **GARNER**. Wit John C. **HARBISON** (JP). Rec 30 Nov 1819.

1278. Page 143. 15 Feb 1819. Jarrot **MENEFEE** of Fayette Co., Ken. to his son Richard **MENEFEE**. For divers good causes and considerations, power of attorney to convey a tract of land. Signed Jarrot **MENEFEE**. Wit J. C. **RODES**, Clerk of Fayette Co., Ken., Oliver **KEEN**, JP in Fayette Co., Ken. Rec 30 Nov 1819.

1279. Page 144. 13 Sep 1819. Jenifer T. **SPRIGG** to John S. **PORTERFIELD**, both of St. Louis Co., Mo. For the sum of $80, Lot No. 5 in Decatur, on the bank of the Mississippi River, being part of a tract sold by Louis **LORIMIER** Senr to John **RISHER**, and conveyed by sd **RISHER** to sd **SPRIGG**. Signed Jenifer T. **SPRIGG**. Wit John **O'FARRALL**, Nathan **SEYMOUR**, J. V. **GARNIER**, JP in St. Louis Co., Mo., Joseph **McFERRON**, Clerk. Rec 2 Dec 1819.

1280. Page 146. 4 Dec 1819. John **PROPST** to Josiah **LEE**. For the sum of $312, 200 acres, more or less, on Caney Fork, beginning at the mouth of Caney Fork of Whitewater on three sycamores; bounded in part by Joseph **NISWONGER**. Signed John **PROBST**. Wit Tho. **NEALE** (JP), Wm. **FISHBACK**. Rec 4 Dec 1819.

1281. Page 147. 6 Dec 1819. William **HAND** and Sarah, his wife, to Edward **McGUIRE**. For the sum of $1600, Lot No. 110 in Jackson, being the same where they now dwell, and where their tanyard is situated. Signed Wm. **HAND**, Sarah **HAND**. Wit Wm. **CREATH** (JP), Thos. S. **RODNEY**. Rec 6 Dec 1819.

1282. Page 148. 21 Sep 1819. John L. **LAFFERTY** of Lawrence Co., Ark. to Joseph **HARDIN**. For the sum of $320, undivided ½ of 640 acres, more or less, on White Water, being the settlement and improvement confirmed to John **SHAREDON**. Signed John L. **LAFFERTY**. Wit Townsend **DICKINSON**, B. S. **COSTILLO**, Homan **HEWITT**, Jason **CHAMBERLAIN**, R. S. **THOMAS**, Judge of Southern Circuit Court. Rec 7 Dec 1819.

1283. Page 149. 18 Nov 1819. Joseph **HARDIN** to John **MILLER**, both of Lawrence Co., Ark. For the sum of $160, equal and undivided ¼ part of 640 acres described in the preceding deed (E:148); being the same conveyed by John **SHERIDAN** to John **LAFFERTY**. Signed Joseph **HARDIN**. Wit Richd. **SEARCY**, Townsend **DICKINSON**, Jason **CHAMBERLAIN**, R. S. **THOMAS**, Judge of Southern Circuit Court. Rec 7 Dec 1819.

1284. Page 150. 2 Dec 1818. Moses **CRAWFORD** to Charles **WILLIAMS**. For the sum of $485, all his improvement where he now resides, purchased by him of Lewis **SHELHOUSE**, and lying on the great road leading to Green's Ferry, and to which he is entitled by the right of preemption; also power of attorney to obtain sd preemption. Signed Moses (x) **CRAWFORD**. Wit Tho. **NEALE** (JP), Josiah **VINCENT**. Rec 7 Dec 1819.

1285. Page 151. 15 Oct 1818. John **GIBBONEY** and Elizabeth, his wife, to David **HOLLEY**. For the sum of $600, 100 acres on the E side of Hubble's Creek, being part of the head right of James **HANNAH**; beginning at a sugar tree. Signed John **GIBONEY**, Elizabeth **GIBONEY**. Wit Isaac (x) **FOSTER**, James (H) **HANNAH**, John **AKIN** (JP). Rec 17 Dec 1819.

1286. Page 153. 15 Oct 1818. Same and same to same. For the sum of $450, 240 arpens on both sides of Hubble's Creek, being the head right of Thomas **FOSTER**; beginning at William **MATHEWS'** SE corner at a stake and stone, and also bounded in part by Jane **LOGAN**. Signed John **GIBONEY**, Elizabeth **GIBONEY**. Wit

Isaac (x) **FOSTER**, James (H) **HANNAH**, John **AKIN** (JP). Rec 17 Dec 1819.

1287. Page 154. 2 Nov 1819. Commissioners to Partition Lands of the heirs of Louis **LORIMIER**, decd, to Alexander **BUCKNER**. For the sum of $320, the S ½, Lot No. 1, Range A in Cape Girardeau; bounded on the E by Aquamsi or Front St, S by Lot No. 2, and W by Lot No. 3. Sold on order of Circuit Court issued Aug Term 1819, on petition for partition of sd lands. Signed B. **COUSIN**, C. G. **ELLIS**, W. **GARNER**, Wm. **KELSO**, Benjn. M. **HORRELL**. Wit John C. **HARBISON** (JP). Rec 17 Dec 1819.

1288. Page 155. 24 Nov 1819. Same to same. For the sum of $400, N ½ of Lot No. 10, Range B in Cape Girardeau; bounded on the E by Lorimier St, N by Lot No. 9, and W by Lot No. 11. Sold under the conditions described in the preceding deed (E:154). Signed B. **COUSIN**, Wm. **KELSO**, W. **GARNER**. Wit John C. **HARBISON** (JP). Rec 17 Dec 1819.

1289. Page 156. 26 Nov 1819. Same to same. For the sum of $745, two lots in Cape Girardeau; Lot No. 7, Range F, bounded on the N by North St and W by Lorimier St; and S ½, Lot No. 7, Range E, bounded on the S by Harmony St and E by Spanish St. Sold under the conditions described in E:154. Signed B. **COUSIN**, C. G. **ELLIS**, Wm. **KELSO**. Test John C. **HARBISON** (JP). Rec 17 Dec 1819.

1290. Page 157. 22 Nov 1819. James **EVANS** to the heirs of Louis **LORIMIER**, decd. For the sum of $1438, mortgage on four portions of lots in Range A in Cape Girardeau; the N ½, Lot No. 1 and N ½, Lot No. 2, both fronting on Aquamsi St; and N ½, Lot No. 3 and N ½, Lot No. 5, both fronting on Spanish St. The amount in three promissory notes of even date is due in three equal payments at nine, 18, and 24 months. Signed James **EVANS**. Wit William **KELSO** (JP). Rec 20 Dec 1819. [Marginal note: Full satisfaction received on 30 Nov 1821. Signed Victor **LORIMIER**. Wit John **JUDEN** Jr, Clerk.]

1291. Page 158. 22 Nov 1819. Alexander **BUCKNER** to same. For the sum of $320, mortgage on S ½, Lot No. 1, Range A in Cape Girardeau, as described in E:154. Terms as in E:157. Signed A. **BUCKNER**. Wit Wm. **KELSO** (JP). Rec 20 Dec 1819.

1292. Page 159. 22 Nov 1819. Augustus Bougainville **LORIMIER** to same. For the sum of $879, mortgage on the S ½, Lot No. 2, Range A and S ½, Lot No. 3, Range A in Cape Girardeau; bounded on the E by Front or Aquamsi St, and W by Spanish St. Terms as in E:157. Signed A. **LORIMIER**. Wit Wm. **KELSO** (JP). Rec 20 Dec 1819.

1293. Page 160. 22 Nov 1819. Louis **LAPORTE** of Ste. Genevieve Co. to same. For the sum of $887, mortgage on Lot No. 4, Range A in Cape Girardeau; bounded on the N by Merriwether St and W by Spanish St. Terms as in E:157. Signed L. **LAPORTE**. Wit Wm. **KELSO** (JP). Rec 20 Dec 1819. [Marginal note: Full satisfaction received on 7 Aug 1839. Signed Edwin **WHITE**, James P. **FULKERSON**, Reuben **DOWTY**, Thomas J. **RODNEY**.]

1294. Page 161. 23 Nov 1819. Abraham **NEWFIELD** to same. For the sum of $546, mortgage on the S ½ of Lot No. 5 and N ½ of Lot No. 7 in Range A in Cape Girardeau. Terms as in E:157. Signed Abraham **NEWFIELD**. Wit Wm. **KELSO** (JP). Rec 20 Dec 1819.

1295. Page 162. 23 Nov 1819. Louis **LAPORTE** to same. For the sum of $1767, mortgage on the S ½ of Lot No. 6, N ½ of Lot Nos. 8, 19, & 23, all in Range A in Cape Girardeau. Terms as in E:157. Signed L. **LAPORTE**. Wit Wm. **KELSO** (JP). Rec 20 Dec 1819. [Marginal note: Full satisfaction received on the S ½ of Lot No. 6 and N ½ of Lot No. 8, Range A, on 7 Aug 1839. Signed Reuben **DOWTY**, James P. **FULKERSON**, Thos. J. **RODNEY**. Wit Hy. **SANFORD**, Clerk.]

1296. Page 163. 23 Nov 1819. Jeremiah **ABEL** to same. For the sum of $198, mortgage on the S ½ of Lot No. 7, Range A in Cape Girardeau. Terms as in E:157. Signed Jeremiah **ABLE**. Wit Wm. **KELSO** (JP). Rec 20 Dec 1819.

1297. Page 164. 23 Nov 1819. John **MONTGOMERY** to same. For the sum of $255, mortgage on the S ½ of Lot No. 8, Range A in Cape Girardeau. Terms as in E:157. Signed John **MONTGOMERY**. Wit Wm. **KELSO** (JP). Rec 20 Dec 1819.

1298. Page 165. 23 Nov 1819. Victor **LORIMIER** to same. For the sum of $1426, mortgage on Lot Nos. 10 & 11, Range A in Cape Girardeau. Terms as in E:157. Signed Victor **LORIMIER**. Wit Wm. **KELSO** (JP). Rec 20 Dec 1819.

1299. Page 166. 23 Nov 1819. James **EVANS** to same. For the sum of $3000, mortgage on Lot No. 17, Range A in Cape Girardeau; bounded on the E by Aquamsi or Front St, W by Lot No. 18, and S by Williams St. Terms as in E:157. Signed James **EVANS**. Wit Wm. **KELSO** (JP). Rec 20 Dec 1819. [Marginal note: One third of the amount received on 23 Nov 1821. Signed Victor **LORIMIER**. Wit John **JUDEN**, Dep Clerk.]

1300. Page 167. 23 Nov 1819. Daniel F. **STEINBECK** to same. For the sum of $681, mortgage on Lot No. 18, Range A in Cape Girardeau. Terms as in E:157. Signed D. F. **STEINBECK**. Wit Wm. **KELSO** (JP). Rec 20 Dec 1819.

1301. Page 168. 23 Nov 1819. Samuel **WARDEN** to same. For the sum of $235, mortgage on Lot Nos. 21 & 22, Range A in Cape Girardeau. Terms as in E:157. Signed Saml **WARDEN**. Wit Wm. **KELSO** (JP). Rec 20 Dec 1819. [Marginal note: Full satisfaction received on 31 Jul 1823. Signed D. F. **STEINBECK**. Wit C. S. **THOMAS**.]

1302. Page 169. 24 Nov 1819. Louis **LAPORTE** of Ste. Genevieve Co. to same. For the sum of $1422, mortgage on Lot Nos. 15 & 24, Range A, and the N ½ of Lot No. 1 and all of Lot No. 6, Range B in Cape Girardeau. Terms as in E:157. Signed L. **LAPORTE**. Wit Wm. **KELSO** (JP). Rec 20 Dec 1819. [Marginal note: Full satisfaction received for Lot Nos. 15 & 24, Range A on 7 Aug 1839. Signed Reuben **DOWTY**, James P. **FULKERSON**, Thos. J. **RODNEY**. Wit Hy. **SANFORD**, Clerk.]

1303. Page 170. 24 Nov 1819. John **MONTGOMERY** to same. For the sum of $271, mortgage on Lot No. 16, Range A in Cape Girardeau; bounded on the N by Merriwether St and W by Middle St. Terms as in E:157. Signed John **MONTGOMERY**. Wit Wm. **KELSO** (JP). Rec 20 Dec 1819.

1304. Page 171. 24 Nov 1819. Louis **LAPORTE** of Ste. Genevieve Co. to same. For the sum of $200, mortgage on Lot No. 14, Range A in Cape Girardeau; bounded on the N by Lot No. 13, S by Lot No. 23, and E by Fountain St. Terms as in E:157. Signed L. **LAPORTE**. Wit Wm. **KELSO** (JP). Rec 20 Dec 1819. [Marginal note: Full satisfaction received on 7 Aug 1839. Signed R. **DOWTY**, Thos. J. **RODNEY**. Wit Hy. **SANFORD**, Clerk.]

1305. Page 172. 24 Nov 1819. **MENEFEE** and **ISOM** to same. For the sum of $157, mortgage on Lot No. 20, Range A in Cape Girardeau; bounded on the S by Williams St and W by Lorimier St. Terms as in E:157. Signed Jonas N. **MENEFEE**, Wm. **ISOM**. Wit Wm. **KELSO** (JP). Rec 20 Dec 1819.

1306. Page 173. 25 Nov 1819. Edmund B. W. **JONES** of Union Co., Ill. to same. For the sum of $520, mortgage on the S ½ of Lot No. 1, Range B in Cape Girardeau. Terms as in E:157. Signed E. B. W. **JONES**. Wit Wm. **KELSO** (JP). Rec 20 Dec 1819.

1307. Page 174. 25 Nov 1819. Richard **WATHEN** of New Madrid Co., Mo. to same. For the sum of $385, mortgage on the S ½ of Lot No. 10, Range B in Cape Girardeau; bounded on the E by Lorimier St and S by Merriweather St. Terms as in E:157. Signed Richd. **WATHEN**. Wit Wm. **KELSO** (JP). Rec 20 Dec 1819.

1308. Page 175. 25 Nov 1819. James **EVANS** to same. For the sum of $625, mortgage on the S ½ of Lot No. 2, Range B in Cape Girardeau; bounded on the E by Aquamsi or Front St, W by Lot No. 3, and S by Merriweather St. Terms as in E:157. Signed James **EVANS**. Wit Wm. **KELSO** (JP). Rec 20 Dec 1819. [Marginal note: Full satisfaction received on 30 Nov 1821. Signed Victor **LORIMIER**. Wit John **JUDEN** Jr., Clerk.]

1309. Page 176. 25 Nov 1819. Jenifer T. **SPRIGG** to same. For the sum of $785, mortgage on Lot No. 3, Range B in Cape Girardeau; bounded on the N by Lot No. 4, S by Merriwether St, E by Lot No. 2, and W by Spanish St. Terms as in E:157. Signed Jenifer T. **SPRIGG**. Wit Wm. **KELSO** (JP). Rec 20 Dec 1819.

1310. Page 177. 24 Nov 1819. Charles **SEAVERS** to same. For the sum of $785, mortgage on Lot No. 4, Range B in Cape Girardeau; bounded on the N by Independence St and W by Spanish St. Terms as in E:157. Signed Charles **SEAVERS**. Wit Wm. **KELSO** (JP). Rec 20 Dec 1819.

1311. Page 178. 24 Nov 1819. George **JASPERSEN** to same. For the sum of $440, mortgage on Lot No. 7, Range B in Cape Girardeau; bounded on the S by Merriwether St and W by Lorimier St. Terms as in E:157. Signed Geo. **JASPERSEN**. Wit Wm. **KELSO** (JP). Rec 20 Dec 1819.

1312. Page 179. 24 Nov 1819. Alexander **BUCKNER** to same. For the sum of $400, mortgage on the N ½ of Lot No. 10, Range B in Cape Girardeau; bounded on the E by Lorimier St and N by Lot No. 9. Terms as in E:157. Signed A. **BUCKNER**. Wit Wm. **KELSO** (JP). Rec 20 Dec 1819.

1313. Page 180. 24 Nov 1819. Samuel D. **DIXON** of Jackson Co., Ill. to same. For the sum of $615, mortgage on two lots in Cape Girardeau; the S ½ of Lot No. 11, Range B, bounded on the W by Fountain St and S by Merriwether St; and Lot No. 14, Range C; bounded on the W by Middle St and S by Independence St. Terms as in E:157. Signed Saml. D. **DIXON**. Wit Wm. **KELSO** (JP). Rec 20 Dec 1819.

1314. Page 181. 24 Nov 1819. Rebecca **HARBISON** to same. For the sum of $304, mortgage on Lot Nos. 15 & 16, Range B in Cape Girardeau; bounded on the N by Independence St, S by Merriwether St, and W by Middle St. Terms as in E:157. Signed Rebecca **HARBISON**. Wit John C. **HARBISON** (JP). Rec 20 Dec 1819.

1315. Page 182. 26 Nov 1819. Jacob **STAHL** to same. For the sum of $322, mortgage on the S ½ of Lot No. 10, Range D in Cape Girardeau, fronting on Themis St. Terms as in E:157. Signed J. **STAHLE**. Wit Wm. **KELSO** (JP). Rec 20 Dec 1819.

1316. Page 183. 25 Nov 1819. Michael **RODNEY**, Louis **LORIMIER**, and Thomas S. **RODNEY** to same. For the sum of $1055, mortgage on Lot No. 11, Range D in Cape Girardeau; bounded on the W by Middle St, E by Lot No. 10, N by Harmony St, and S by Themis St. Terms as in E:157. Signed Michl. **RODNEY**, Louis **LORIMIER**, Thos. S. **RODNEY**. Wit Wm. **KELSO** (JP). Rec 20 Dec 1819.

1317. Page 184. 25 Nov 1819. Van B. **DLASHMUTT** to same. For the sum of $300, mortgage on the N ½ of Lot No. 7, Range E in Cape Girardeau; bounded on the N by Lot No. 8, W by Lot No. 10, and E by Spanish St. Terms as in E:157. Signed Van B. **DLASHMUTT**. Wit Wm. **KELSO** (JP). Rec 20 Dec 1819.

1318. Page 185. 26 Nov 1819. Alexander **BUCKNER** to same. For the sum of $745, mortgage on the S ½ of Lot No. 7, Range E, and Lot No. 7, Range F in Cape Girardeau. Terms as in E:157. Signed A. **BUCKNER**. Wit Wm. **KELSO** (JP). Rec 20 Dec 1819.

1319. Page 186. 25 Nov 1819. Minor M. **WHITNEY** to same. For the sum of $430, mortgage on the N ½ of Lot No. 12, Range E in Cape Girardeau; bounded on the N by St Bellevue and E by Lorimier St. Terms as in E:157. Signed Minor M. **WHITNEY**. Wit Wm. **KELSO** (JP). Rec 20 Dec 1819.

1320. Page 187. 26 Nov 1819. Charles G. **ELLIS** to same. For the sum of $1248, mortgage on the N ½ of Lot No. 10 Range D, S ½ of Lot No. 12 Range E, and Lot No. 12, the N ½ of Lot No. 13, and Lot No. 16 in Range F in Cape Girardeau. Terms as in E:157. Signed C. G. **ELLIS**. Wit Wm. **KELSO** (JP). Rec 20 Dec 1819.

1321. Page 188. 26 Nov 1819. Levi L. **LIGHTNER** to same. For the sum of $720, mortgage on Lot No. 6, Range F in Cape Girardeau; bounded on the N by St Bellevue, E by German St, and W by Spanish St. Terms as in E:157. Signed Levi L. **LIGHTNER**. Wit Wm. **KELSO** (JP). Rec 20 Dec 1819.

1322. Page 189. 26 Nov 1819. Augustus Bougainville **LORIMIER** to same. For the sum of $670, mortgage on Lot Nos. 3 & 4, Range F in Cape Girardeau; fronting on North St, Spanish St, and St Bellevue. Terms as in E:157. Signed A. **LORIMIER**. Wit Wm. **KELSO** (JP). Rec 20 Dec 1819.

1323. Page 190. 26 Nov 1819. William **GARNER** to same. For the sum of $545, mortgage on two lots in Cape Girardeau; the N ½ of Lot No. 11, Range B, bounded on the W by Fountain St and N by Lot No. 12; and Lot Not 6, Range F, fronting on North St and Spanish St. Terms as in E:157. Signed W. **GARNER**. Wit Wm. **KELSO** (JP). Rec 20 Dec 1819.

1324. Page 191. 26 Nov 1819. Jonas N. **MENEFEE** to same. For the sum of $200, mortgage on Lot No. 10, Range F in Cape Girardeau, fronting on North St and Spanish St. Terms as in E:157. Signed Jonas N. **MENEFEE**. Wit Wm. **KELSO** (JP). Rec 20 Dec 1819.

1325. Page 192. 25 Nov 1819. John **MONTGOMERY** to same. For the sum of $445, mortgage on Lot Nos. 11 & 14, Range F in Cape Girardeau; bounded on the N by North St and divided by Fountain St. Terms as in E:157.

Signed John **MONTGOMERY**. Wit Wm. **KELSO** (JP). Rec 20 Dec 1819.

1326. Page 193. 26 Nov 1819. James **RAVENSCROFT** to same. For the sum of $145, mortgage on the S ½ of Lot No. 13, Range F in Cape Girardeau; fronting on St Bellevue and Fountain St. Terms as in E:157. Signed James **RAVENSCROFT**. Wit Wm. **KELSO** (JP). Rec 20 Dec 1819.

1327. Page 194. 25 Nov 1819. John **BURNS** to same. For the sum of $118, mortgage on the N ½ of Lot No. 15, Range F in Cape Girardeau; bounded on the N by North St and W by Middle St. Terms as in E:157. Signed John **BURNS**. Wit Wm. **KELSO** (JP). Rec 20 Dec 1819.

1328. Page 195. 25 Nov 1819. Richard **WATHEN** to same. For the sum of $545, mortgage on the N ½ of Lot No. 2, Range B in Cape Girardeau; bounded on the N by Lot No. 1 and E by Aquamsi or Front St. Terms as in E:157. Signed Richd. **WATHEN**. Wit Wm. **KELSO** (JP). Rec 20 Dec 1819. [Marginal note: Full satisfaction received on 30 Nov 1821. Signed Victor **LORIMIER**. Wit John **JUDEN** Jr., Clerk.]

1329. Page 196. 1 Dec 1819. John C. **HARBISON** to same. For the sum of $705, mortgage on Lot No. 2, Range G in Cape Girardeau; bounded on the N by Lot No. 1, S by Lot No. 3, E by Aquamsi or Front St, and W by Lot No. 11. Terms as in E:157. Signed John C. **HARBISON**. Wit Wm. **KELSO** (JP). Rec 20 Dec 1819.

1330. Page 197. 1 Dec 1819. Daniel F. **STEINBECK** to same. For the sum of $1070, mortgage on Lot Nos. 4 & 9, Range G in Cape Girardeau; bounded on the N by Lot Nos. 3 & 10, S by Lot Nos. 5 & 8, E by Aquamsi St, and W by Spanish St. Terms as in E:157. Signed D. F. **STEINBECK**. Wit Wm. **KELSO** (JP). Rec 20 Dec 1819.

1331. Page 198. 1 Dec 1819. Victor **LORIMIER** to same. For the sum of $1110, mortgage on Lot No. 6, Range G in Cape Girardeau; bounded on the N by Lot No. 5, S by St of Good Hope, E by Aquamsi St, and W by Lot No. 7. Terms as in E:157. Signed Victor **LORIMIER**. Wit Wm. **KELSO** (JP). Rec 20 Dec 1819.

1332. Page 199. 1 Dec 1819. Maria J. **CROSS** to same. For the sum of $700, mortgage on Lot No.

7, Range G in Cape Girardeau; bounded on the N by Lot No. 8, S by St of Good Hope, E by Lot No. 6, and W by Spanish St. Terms as in E:157. Signed M. J. **CROSS**. Wit John C. **HARBISON** (JP). Rec 20 Dec 1819. [Marginal note: Full satisfaction received on 19 Nov 1821. Signed Victor **LORIMIER**. Wit John **JUDEN** Jr., Clerk.]

1333. Page 200. 30 Nov 1819. Daniel **TISDALE** of Bristol Co., Rhode Is. to same. For the sum of $315, mortgage on Lot No. 11, Range G in Cape Girardeau; bounded on the N by Lot No. 12, S by Lot No. 10, E by Lot No. 2, and W by Spanish St. Terms as in E:157. Signed Daniel **TISDALE**. Wit Wm. **KELSO** (JP). Rec 20 Dec 1819.

1334. Page 201. 1 Dec 1819. George **HENDERSON** to same. For the sum of $415, mortgage on Lot No. 13, Range G in Cape Girardeau, bounded on the N by Williams St, S by Lot No. 14, E by Spanish St, and W by an alley. Terms as in E:157. Signed George **HENDERSON**. Wit Wm. **KELSO** (JP). Rec 20 Dec 1819.

1335. Page 202. 30 Nov 1819. Charles **SEAVERS** to same. For the sum of $310, mortgage on Lot No. 15, Range G in Cape Girardeau; bounded on the N by Lot No. 14, S by Lot No. 16, E by Spanish St, and W by an alley. Terms as in E:157. Signed Charles **SEAVERS**. Wit Wm. **KELSO** (JP). Rec 20 Dec 1819.

1336. Page 203. 1 Dec 1819. Enoch **PARKER** to same. For the sum of $322, mortgage on Lot No. 17, Range G in Cape Girardeau; bounded on the N by Lot No. 16, S by Lot No. 18, E by Spanish St, and W by an alley. Terms as in E:157. Signed Enoch **PARKER**. Wit Wm. **KELSO** (JP). Rec 20 Dec 1819.

1337. Page 204. 1 Dec 1819. Raphael Verneuil **LORIMIER** to same. For the sum of $510, mortgage on Lot No. 19, Range G in Cape Girardeau; bounded on the N by Lot No. 20, S by St of Good Hope, E by an alley, and W by Lorimier St. Terms as in E:157. Signed R. V. **LORIMIER**. Wit Wm. **KELSO** (JP). Rec 20 Dec 1819.

1338. Page 205. 1 Dec 1819. Augustus Bougainville **LORIMIER** to same. For the sum of $360, mortgage on Lot No. 21, Range G in Cape Girardeau; bounded on the N by Lot No. 22, S by Lot No. 20, E by an alley, and W by Lorimier St. Terms as in E:157. Signed A.

LORIMIER. Wit Wm. **KELSO** (JP). Rec 20 Dec 1819.

1339. Page 206. 1 Dec 1819. Daniel F. **STEINBECK** to same. For the sum of $545, mortgage on Lot No. 23, Range G in Cape Girardeau; bounded on the N by Lot No. 24, S by Lot No. 22, E by an alley, and W by Lorimier St. Terms as in E:157. Signed D. F. **STEINBECK**. Wit Wm. **KELSO** (JP). Rec 20 Dec 1819.

1340. Page 207. 1 Dec 1819. Same to same. For the sum of $625, mortgage on Lot Nos. 25, 29, 31, 33, & 37, Range G in Cape Girardeau. Terms as in E:157. Signed D. F. **STEINBECK**. Wit Wm. **KELSO** (JP). Rec 20 Dec 1819.

1341. Page 208. 1 Dec 1819. Victor **LORIMIER** to same. For the sum of $140, mortgage on Lot No. 27, Range G in Cape Girardeau; bounded on the N by Lot No. 26, S by Lot No. 28, E by Lorimier St, and W by an alley. Terms as in E:157. Signed Victor **LORIMIER**. Wit Wm. **KELSO** (JP). Rec 20 Dec 1819.

1342. Page 209. 1 Dec 1819. Erasmus **ELLIS** to same. For the sum of $141, mortgage on Lot No. 35, Range G in Cape Girardeau; bounded on the N by Lot No. 34, S by Lot No. 36, E by Fountain St, and W by an alley. Terms as in E:157. Signed Erasmus **ELLIS**. Wit Wm. **KELSO** (JP). Rec 20 Dec 1819.

1343. Page 210. 1 Dec 1819. Augustus Bougainville **LORIMIER** to same. For the sum of $110, mortgage on Lot No. 39, Range G in Cape Girardeau; bounded on the N by Lot No. 40, S by Lot No. 38, E by an alley, and W by Middle St. Terms as in E:157. Signed A. B. **LORIMIER**. Wit Wm. **KELSO** (JP). Rec 20 Dec 1819.

1344. Page 211. 27 Nov 1819. Daniel F. **STEINBECK** to same. For the sum of $7880, mortgage on two outlots near Cape Girardeau; 160 acres on Cape La Cruche Creek, being Outlot No. 63, including the mills and plantation; and 130 1/3 acres to the S of the first tract, being Outlot No. 66. Terms as in E:157. Signed D. F. **STEINBECK**. Wit Wm. **KELSO** (JP). Rec 20 Dec 1819.

1345. Page 212. 29 Nov 1819. Same to same. For the sum of $1015, mortgage on 260 2/3 acres in two outlots on Cape la Cruche Creek near Cape Girardeau, being Outlot Nos. 67 & 68; bounded on the N by Outlot No. 66, and on the other parts by vacant and other lands. Terms as in E:157. Signed D. F. **STEINBECK**. Wit John C. **HARBISON** (JP). Rec 20 Dec 1819.

1346. Page 213. 27 Nov 1819. Charles G. **ELLIS** and Jenifer T. **SPRIGG** to same. For the sum of $3510, mortgage on 10 acres in two outlots adjoining Cape Girardeau; Outlot No. 1, bounded on the N by Outlot No. 32, and S by North St; and Outlot No. 5, bounded on the N by Outlot No. 30, S by North St, E by Outlot No. 4, and W by Outlot No. 6. Terms as in E:157. Signed C. G. **ELLIS**, Jenifer T. **SPRIGG**. Wit Wm. **KELSO** (JP). Rec 20 Dec 1819.

1347. Page 215. 27 Nov 1819. John **HAYS** to same. For the sum of $2210, mortgage on 26 ½ acres, more or less, in three outlots above and adjoining Cape Girardeau; being Outlot Nos. 2, 3, & 4; bounded on the N by Outlot No. 31 and the grave yard, S by North St and the public square including the spring, E by Outlot No. 1, and W by Outlot No. 5. Terms as in E:157. Signed John **HAYS**. Wit Wm. **KELSO** (JP). Rec 20 Dec 1819.

1348. Page 216. 29 Nov 1819. Abraham **NEWFIELD** of Ste. Genevieve Co., Mo. to same. For the sum of $285, mortgage on 10 acres, more or less, adjoining Cape Girardeau to the NW, being Outlot No. 6; bounded on the N by Outlot No. 30, S by North St and Outlot A, E by Outlot No. 5, and W by Outlot No. 7. Terms as in E:157. Signed Abraham **NEWFIELD**. Wit John C. **HARBISON** (JP). Rec 20 Dec 1819.

1349. Page 217. 30 Nov 1819. Daniel F. **STEINBECK** to same. For the sum of $289, mortgage on 3 ¼ acres W of and adjoining Cape Girardeau, being Outlot G; bounded on the N by Outlot F, S by Outlot H (public), E by Pacific St, and W by Outlot No. 11 and six acres formerly sold to **SCRIPPS**. Terms as in E:157. Signed D. F. **STEINBECK**. Wit Wm. **KELSO** (JP). Rec 20 Dec 1819.

1350. Page 218. 29 Nov 1819. Thomas S. **RODNEY** to same. For the sum of $305, mortgage on 3 ¼ acres W of and adjoining Cape Girardeau, being Outlot E; bounded on the E by Pacific St, W by Outlot No. 10, N by Outlot D, and S by Outlot F. Terms as in E:157. Signed Thos. S. **RODNEY**. Wit Wm. **KELSO** (JP). Rec 20 Dec 1819. [Marginal note: Full satisfaction received on 30 Nov 1821. Signed Victor **LORIMIER**. Wit John **JUDEN** Jr., Clerk.]

1351. Page 219. 29 Nov 1819. Same to same. For the sum of $294, mortgage on 3 ¼ acres, more or less, W of and adjoining Cape Girardeau, being Outlot C; bounded on the E by Pacific St, W by Outlot No. 9, N by Outlot B, and S by Outlot D. Terms as in E:157. Signed Thos. S. **RODNEY**. Wit Wm. **KELSO** (JP). Rec 20 Dec 1819. [Marginal note: Full satisfaction received on 30 Nov 1821. Signed Victor **LORIMIER**. Wit John **JUDEN** Jr., Clerk.]

1352. Page 220. 29 Nov 1819. Abraham **NEWFIELD** of Ste. Genevieve Co., Mo. to same. For the sum of $125, mortgage on 3 ¼ acres, more or less, W of and adjoining Cape Girardeau, being Outlot A; bounded on the N by Outlot No. 6, S by Outlot B, E by Pacific St, and W by Outlot No. 8. Terms as in E:157. Signed Abraham **NEWFIELD**. Wit Wm. **KELSO** (JP). Rec 20 Dec 1819.

1353. Page 221. 29 Nov 1819. John Nicholas **ROOST** to same. For the sum of $255, mortgage on 20 acres, more or less, NW of Cape Girardeau, being Outlot No. 30; bounded on the N by Outlot No. 36, S by Outlot Nos. 5 & 6, E by Outlot No. 31, and W by Outlot No. 20. Terms as in E:157. Signed J. N. **RUST**. Wit Wm. **KELSO** (JP). Rec 20 Dec 1819. [Marginal note: Full satisfaction received on 13 Jan 1858. Signed J. R. **WATHEN**, adminr with the will annexed of D. F. **STEINBECK**, decd. Wit Hy. **SANFORD**, Clerk.]

1354. Page 222. 29 Nov 1819. Charles G. **ELLIS** to same. For the sum of $275, mortgage on 20 acres N of Cape Girardeau, being Outlot No. 31; bounded on the N by Outlot No. 35, S by Outlot Nos. 3 & 4, E by Outlot No. 32 and the church yard, and W by Outlot No. 30. Terms as in E:157. Signed C. G. **ELLIS**. Wit Wm. **KELSO** (JP). Rec 20 Dec 1819.

1355. Page 223. 30 Nov 1819. Daniel F. **STEINBECK** to same. For the sum of $7530, mortgage on 17 acres N of Cape Girardeau, being Outlot No. 32; bounded on the N by Outlot No. 34, S by Outlot No. 1 and the grave yard, E by space reserved for public use, and W by Outlot No. 31. The amount is due in three promissory notes of even date. Signed D. F. **STEINBECK**. Wit Wm. **KELSO** (JP). Rec 20 Dec 1819.

1356. Page 224. 1 Dec 1819. Same to same. For the sum of $2360, mortgage on 60 acres, more or less, above Cape Girardeau, being Outlot Nos. 33 & 34; bounded on the S by Outlot No. No. 32

and a vacant space designated for a boat yard or other public uses, E by the Mississippi River, and W by Outlot No. 35. Terms as in E:157. Signed D. F. **STEINBECK**. Wit Wm. **KELSO** (JP). Rec 20 Dec 1819.

1357. Page 225. 30 Nov 1819. Joseph **McFERRON** to same. For the sum of $590, mortgage on 80 acres, N of Cape Girardeau, being Outlot Nos. 35 & 36; bounded on the E by Outlot No. 34, W by Outlot No. 37, S by Outlot Nos. 30 & 31, and N by heirs of Louis **LORIMIER**, decd. Terms as in E:157. Signed Joseph **McFERRON**. Wit Wm. **KELSO** (JP). Rec 20 Dec 1819.

1358. Page 226. 23 Nov 1819. Commissioners to Partition Lands of the heirs of Louis **LORIMIER**, decd, to Daniel F. **STEINBECK**. For the sum of $681, Lot No. 18, Range A in Cape Girardeau; bounded on the N by Lot No. 3, S by Williams St, E by Lot No. 17, and W by Spanish St. Sold on order of Circuit Court issued Aug Term 1819, on petition for partition of sd lands. Signed B. **COUSIN**, Wm. **KELSO**, W. **GARNER**, C. G. **ELLIS**, Benjn. M. **HORRELL**. Test John C. **HARBISON** (JP). Rec 20 Dec 1819.

1359. Page 227. 27 Nov 1819. Same for same to same. For the sum of $7000, 160 acres, more or less, on Cape la Cruche Creek, including the mills and plantation; being Outlot No. 63, bounded on the N by Outlot Nos. 51 & 52, S by Hippolyte **MAROTE** and other lands, E by Outlot Nos. 64 & 65, and W by Outlot No. 62. Sold as in E:226. Signed B. **COUSIN**, Wm. **KELSO**, C. G. **ELLIS**. Wit John C. **HARBISON** (JP). Rec 20 Dec 1819.

1360. Page 228. 27 Nov 1819. Same for same to same. For the sum of $880, 130 1/3 acres, more or less, on Cape la Cruche Creek; being Outlot No. 66, bounded on the N by Outlot No. 63 and S by a line parallel to the S boundary of Outlot No. 63. Sold as in E:226. Signed B. **COUSIN**, Wm. **KELSO**, C. G. **ELLIS**. Test John C. **HARBISON** (JP). Rec 20 Dec 1819.

1361. Page 230. 29 Nov 1819. Same for same to same. For the sum of $289, 3 ¼ acres adjoining and W of Cape Girardeau; bounded on the N by Outlot F, S by Outlot H (public), E by Pacific St, and W by Outlot No. 11 and a 6-acre tract formerly sold to **SCRIPPS**. Sold as in E:226. Signed W. **GARNER**, Wm. **KELSO**, B. **COUSIN**. Test John C. **HARBISON** (JP). Rec 20 Dec 1819.

1362. Page 231. 29 Nov 1819. Same for same to same. For the sum of $1015, 260 2/3 acres on or near Cape la Cruche Creek; being Outlot Nos. 67 & 68; bounded on the N by Outlot No. 66 and on the other parts by public or other lands. Sold as in E:226. Signed B. **COUSIN**, C. G. **ELLIS**, W. **GARNER**, Benjn. M. **HORRELL**. Test John C. **HARBISON** (JP). Rec 20 Dec 1819.

1363. Page 232. 30 Nov 1819. Same for same to same. For the sum of $7530, 17 acres near and N of Cape Girardeau, being Outlot No. 32; bounded on the N by Outlot No. 34, S by Outlot No. 1 and the grave yard, E by vacant space designated for a boat yard or other public uses, and W by Outlot No. 31. Sold as in E:226. Signed W. **GARNER**, Wm. **KELSO**, B. **COUSIN**. Test John C. **HARBISON** (JP). Rec 20 Dec 1819.

1364. Page 233. 1 Dec 1819. Same by same to same. For the sum of $1070, Lot Nos. 4 & 9, Range G in Cape Girardeau; bounded on the N by Lot Nos. 3 & 10, S by Lot Nos. 5 & 8, E by Aquamsi or Front St, and W by Spanish St. Sold as in E:226. Signed W. **GARNER**, B. **COUSIN**, Wm. **KELSO**. Test John C. **HARBISON** (JP). Rec 20 Dec 1819.

1365. Page 234. 1 Dec 1819. Same for same to same. For the sum of $545, Lot No. 23, Range G in Cape Girardeau; bounded on the N by Lot No. 24, S by Lot No. 22, E by an alley, and W by Lorimier St. Sold as in E:226. Signed W. **GARNER**, B. **COUSIN**, Wm. **KELSO**. Test John C. **HARBISON** (JP). Rec 20 Dec 1819.

1366. Page 235. 1 Dec 1819. Same for same to same. For the sum of $625, Lot Nos. 25, 29, 31, 33, & 37, Range G in Cape Girardeau. Sold as in E:226. Signed B. **COUSIN**, Wm. **KELSO**, W. **GARNER**, C. G. **ELLIS**. Test John C. **HARBISON** (JP). Rec 20 Dec 1819.

1367. Page 236. 1 Dec 1819. Same for same to same. For the sum of $2360, Outlot Nos. 33 & 34 near and above Cape Girardeau; bounded on the N by heirs of Louis **LORIMIER**, S by Outlot No. 32 and a vacant space reserved for public uses, E by the Mississippi River, and W by Outlot No. 35. Sold as in E:226. Signed W. **GARNER**, B. **COUSIN**, Wm. **KELSO**. Test John C. **HARBISON** (JP). Rec 20 Dec 1819.

1368. Page 238. 22 Nov 1819. Same for same to Augustus Bougainville **LORIMIER**. For the sum of $601, S ½ of Lot No. 2, Range A in Cape Girardeau; bounded on the E by Aquamsi or

Front St, W by Lot No. 3, and S by Lot No. 17. Sold as in E:226. Signed B. **COUSIN**, C. G. **ELLIS**, W. **GARNER**, William **KELSO**, Benjn. M. **HORRELL**. Test John C. **HARBISON** (JP). Rec 20 Dec 1819.

1369. Page 239. 22 Nov 1819. Same for same to same. For the sum of $278, S ½ of Lot No. 3, Range A in Cape Girardeau; bounded on the E by Lot No. 2, W by Spanish St, and S by Lot Nos. 17 & 18. Sold as in E:226. Signed William **KELSO**, Benj. M. **HORRELL**, B. **COUSIN**, C. G. **ELLIS**, W. **GARNER**. Test John C. **HARBISON** (JP). Rec 20 Dec 1819.

1370. Page 240. 26 Nov 1819. Same for same to same. For the sum of $670, Lot Nos. 3 & 4, Range F in Cape Girardeau; bounded on the N by North St, E by an alley, S by St Bellevue, and W by Spanish St. Sold as in E:226. Signed B. **COUSIN**, Wm. **KELSO**, C. G. **ELLIS**. Test John C. **HARBISON** (JP). Rec 20 Dec 1819.

1371. Page 241. 1 Dec 1819. Same for same to same. For the sum of $360, Lot No. 21, Range G in Cape Girardeau; bounded on the N by Lot No. 22, S by Lot No. 20, E by an alley, and W by Lorimier St. Sold as in E:226. Signed W. **GARNER**, B. **COUSIN**, Wm. **KELSO**. Test John C. **HARBISON** (JP). Rec 20 Dec 1819.

1372. Page 242. 1 Dec 1819. Same for same to same. For the sum of $110, Lot No. 39, Range G in Cape Girardeau; bounded on the N by Lot No. 40, S by Lot No. 38, E by an alley, and W by Middle St. Sold as in E:226. Signed B. **COUSIN**, Wm. **KELSO**, W. **GARNER**, C. G. **ELLIS**. Test John C. **HARBISON** (JP). Rec 20 Dec 1819.

1373. Page 243. 1 Dec 1819. Same for same to Raphael Verneuil **LORIMIER**. For the sum of $510, Lot No. 19, Range G in Cape Girardeau; bounded on the N by Lot No. 20, S by St of Good Hope, E by an alley, and W by Lorimier St. Sold as in E:226. Signed W. **GARNER**, B. **COUSIN**, Wm. **KELSO**. Test John C. **HARBISON** (JP). Rec 20 Dec 1819.

1374. Page 245. 23 Nov 1819. Same for same to Victor **LORIMIER**. For the sum of $865, Lot No. 10, Range A in Cape Girardeau; bounded on the E by Lorimier St, W by Lot No. 11, N by Lot No. 9, and S by Lot No. 21. Sold as in E:226. Signed B. **COUSIN**, Wm. **KELSO**, W. **GARNER**, C. G. **ELLIS**, Benj. M. **HORRELL**. Test John C. **HARBISON** (JP). Rec 20 Dec 1819.

1375. Page 246. 23 Nov 1819. Same for same to same. For the sum of $561, Lot No. 11, Range A in Cape Girardeau; bounded on the N by Lot No. 12, S by Lot No. 22, W by Fountain St, and E by Lot No. 10. Sold as in E:226. Signed B. **COUSIN**, Wm. **KELSO**, W. **GARNER**, C. G. **ELLIS**, Benjn. M. **HORRELL**. Test John C. **HARBISON** (JP). Rec 20 Dec 1819.

1376. Page 247. 1 Dec 1819. Same for same to same. For the sum of $1110, Lot No. 6, Range G in Cape Girardeau; bounded on the N by Lot No. 5, S by St of Good Hope, E by Aquamsi St, and W by Lot No. 7. Sold as in E:226. Signed W. **GARNER**, B. **COUSIN**, Wm. **KELSO**. Test John C. **HARBISON** (JP). Rec 20 Dec 1819.

1377. Page 248. 25 Jun 1817. Commissioners of the Courthouse and Jail to Elisha **SHEPHERD**. For the sum of $51, Lot No. 89 in Jackson; bounded on the E and fronted by second west street, S and fronted by first south street, W by Lot No. 101, and N by Lot No. 88. Signed John **DAVIS**, John **SHEPPARD**, Samuel G. **DUNN**, Abraham **BYRD**. Wit Thos. **STEWART**, Robert **ENGLISH**, Wm. **CREATH** (JP). Rec 20 Dec 1819.

1378. Page 249. 20 Dec 1819. Elisha **SHEPHERD** to Anderson **BULL**. For the sum of $56, part of Lot No. 89 in Jackson, beginning at the NE corner of sd lot. Signed Elisha **SHEPPARD**. Wit John **DANIEL**, Joel **RENFROW**, Wm. **CREATH** (JP). Rec 20 Dec 1819.

1379. Page 250. 26 Nov 1819. Commissioners to Partition Lands of the heirs of Louis **LORIMIER**, decd, to William **GARNER**. For the sum of $545, two lots in Cape Girardeau; Lot No. 6, Range F, bounded on the N by North St, E by Spanish St, and W by an alley; and the N ½ of Lot No. 11, Range B, bounded on the W by Fountain St and N by Lot No. 12. Sold as in E:226. Signed B. **COUSIN**, Wm. **KELSO**, C. G. **ELLIS**. Test John C. **HARBISON** (JP). Rec 21 Dec 1819.

1380. Page 251. 22 Nov 1819. Abraham **HUGHES** and Peggy, his wife, of Wayne Co., Mo. to Obadiah **MALONE**. For the sum of $400, 250 acres on the waters of Apple Creek; being part of a tract granted to sd **HUGHES**; beginning at the NE corner of John **JOHNSON**'s tract, deeded by sd **HUGHES**. Signed Abraham **HUGHES**, Peggy (x) **HUGHES** (RD). Wit Benjamin **WILSON**, Andrew **MARTIN**, Thos. **NEALE** (JP). Rec 21 Dec 1819.

1381. Page 252. 20 Oct 1819. Jacob **BULLINGER** to John **WILSON**. For the sum of $5, 1 acre on the waters of the W fork of White Water in German Twp; beginning at Joseph **ROGERS'** SE corner at a stake and being where sd **WILSON**'s stable and corn crib stand. Signed Jacob **BOLLINGER**. Wit Hugh **TINNIN**, Elizabeth **TINNIN**, William **TINNIN** (JP). Rec 21 Dec 1819.

1382. Page 253. 3 Apr 1819. James **PHILLIPS** to Richard **WALLER**. For the sum of $15, __ acres on Old Cape Creek, being where sd **WALLER** now lives, in the same section where John **CAMRON**'s Improvement is, and being an improvement made by sd **PHILLIPS** on Congress land, entitled to a preemption under the acts of Congress for settlers on public lands in Mo. Signed James **PHILLIPS**. Wit George **HENDERSON** (JP), William **ROBERTS**. Rec 21 Dec 1819.

1383. Page 254. 23 Oct 1815. Samuel **ALLEN** to Levi **WOLVERTON**. For the sum of $500, Lot No. 5, Range F, fronting on the Mississippi in Cape Girardeau; bounded on the N by Elisha **ELLIS**, W by Lot No. 4, S by St Belleview, and E by vacant public land on the river. Signed Samuel **ALLEN**, Elizabeth (x) **ALLEN** (RD). Rec 21 Dec 1819.

1384. Page 255. 1 Dec 1819. Commissioners to Partition Lands of the heirs of Louis **LORIMIER**, decd, to John C. **HARBISON**. For the sum of $705, Lot No. 2, Range G in Cape Girardeau; bounded on the N by Lot No. 1, S by Lot No. 3, E by Aquamsi or Front St, and W by Lot No. 11. Sold on order of Circuit Court issued Aug Term 1819, on petition for partition sd lands. Signed W. **GARNER**, Wm. **KELSO**, B. **COUSIN**. Test John C. **HARBISON** (JP). Rec 21 Dec 1819.

1385. Page 256. 1 Dec 1819. Same for same to George **HENDERSON**. For the sum of $415, Lot No. 13, Range G in Cape Girardeau; bounded on the N by Williams St, S by Lot No. 14, E by Spanish St, and W by an alley. Sold as in E:226. Signed B. **COUSIN**, Wm. **KELSO**, W. **GARNER**, C. G. **ELLIS**, Benjn. M. **HORRELL**. Test John C. **HARBISON** (JP). Rec 21 Dec 1819.

1386. Page 257. 22 Dec 1819. Medad **RANDOL** to Jeneifer T. **SPRIGG**. For the sum of $600, the 1/3 part of the town of Bainbridge and the preemption right of land on which the town is laid off, including his interest in all lots sold

since 13 Aug last except the lot where sd **RANDOL** now lives, the same being on Buis Creek on the bank of the Mississippi River. Signed Medad **RANDOL**. Wit James **EVANS**, Wm. **CREATH** (JP). Rec 24 Dec 1819.

1387. Page 258. 5 Dec 1819. John **BURNS** to Abraham **RANDOL**. For the sum of $200, __ acres on Dobson's Fork of Cape la Cruch Creek, on the SW corner of Sec 12, Twp 31 N, Rng 13 E; also his preemption right to the SW ¼ of sd Sec and to as much of sd Sec as he has a right to by his improvement; and authorization to secure the preemption right and to convey his wife's dower to sd land. Signed John **BURNS**. Wit Jason **CHAMBERLAIN**, William **CRACRAFT**, Joseph **McFERRON**, Clerk. Rec 25 Dec 1819.

1388. Page 259. 13 Nov 1819. George W. **BOYCE**, late of Cape Girardeau Co., but now of Pulaski Co., Ark., to William **CRACROFT**. For the sum of $322, __ acres on the waters of the River Zenon, being his improvement near a tract confirmed to Lavina **MILLS**; also his preemption to ¼ and fractional ¼ Secs on which sd improvement is located; and power of attorney to secure the preemption right and title. Signed Geo. W. (x) **BOYCE**. Wit Abraham (A) **RANDOL**, Wright **DANIEL**, Joseph **McFERRON**, Clerk. Rec 25 Dec 1819.

1389. Page 260. 25 Dec 1819. William **CRACRAFT** to Jesse **STORY**. For the sum of $320, assignment of the improvement and preemption right in the preceding deed (E:259). Signed William **CRACRAFT**. Wit Jason **CHAMBERLAIN**, Eliza **CHAMBERLAIN**, Joseph **McFERRON**, Clerk. Rec 25 Dec 1819.

1390. Page 261. 2 Jul 1819. David **ARMOUR** and John **JUDEN** Jr. to William **SURRELL**. For the sum of $90, ½ of Lot No. 21 in Jackson; bounded on the E and fronted by High St, S by a line drawn E-W through the middle of Lot No. 21, W by Lot No. 57, and N by Lot No. 20. Signed David **ARMOUR**, John **JUDEN** Jr. Wit Zenas **PRIEST** (JP). Rec 27 Dec 1819.

1391. Page 262. 5 Oct 1819. Enos **RANDOL** and Allen **McKINSEY** to Preciller **JOHNSON**, Scarlet **GLASSCOCK**, and Simon **POE**; all of Cape Girardeau Co. except sd **McKINSEY**, who is of Ill. For the sum of $100, being the balance claimed by Enos **RANDOL**, 440 acres, being a portion of sd **RANDOL**'s claim. Enos **RANDOL** executed a bond some years past to sd **McKINSEY**, to sell 100 acres on the road to

Jackson, including his improvement, adjoining William **WILLIAMS**. Sd **McKINSEY** later sold the tract to sd **RANDOL** and received full payment, but never relinquished the bond. Sd **RANDOL** also sold 440 acres, being his improvement, to Elijah **RANDOL** for $500, and Elijah **RANDOL** later sold the tract to John **EDWARDS** and Simon **POE** Junr (240 acres to sd **EDWARDS** and 200 acres to sd **POE**). The 240 acres has been deeded at the request of sd **EDWARDS** to Preciller **JOHNSON** and Scarlet **GLASSCOCK**. Signed Enos **RANDOL**. Allen **McKINZE**. Wit Jeremiah **RANDOL**, John **RANDOL**, James **RANDOL**, Zenas **PRIEST** (JP). Rec 27 Dec 1819.

1392. Page 263. 11 Jan 1817. George **OLLER** of Johnson Co., Ill. to James **PHILLIPS**. For the sum of $25, quit claim to ___ acres on the middle fork of Flora Creek, being an improvement he made in 1813, below **LORIMIER**'s line. Signed George (O) **OLLER**. Test Saml. M. **PHILLIPS**, Wm. **AB.**, George **HENDERSON** (JP). Rec 27 Dec 1819.

1393. Page 264. 17 Dec 1819. James **PHILLIPS** to Richard **WALLER**. For the sum of $50, quit claim to ___ acres on the middle or lower fork of Flora Creek, being an improvement he purchased of George **OLLER** Senr in 1817 (E:263). Signed James **PHILLIPS**. Wit S. M. **PHILLIPS**, Miles (x) **DOYAL**, George **HENDERSON** (JP). Rec 27 Dec 1819.

1394. Page 265. 17 Dec 1819. Samuel M. **PHILLIPS** to same. For the sum of $100, ___ acres, being an improvement on the lower fork of Flora which he made in 1811. Signed Saml. M. **PHILLIPS**. Wit James **PHILLIPS**, Miles (x) **DOYAL**, George **HENDERSON** (JP). Rec 27 Dec 1819.

1395. Page 265. 25 Nov 1819. Commissioners to Partition Lands of the heirs of Louis **LORIMIER**, decd, to John **BURNS**. For the sum of $118, N ½ of Lot No. 15, Range F in Cape Girardeau; bounded on the N by North St and W by Middle St. Sold on order of Circuit Court issued Aug Term 1819, on petition for partition sd lands. Signed Wm. **KELSO**, C. G. **ELLIS**, W. **GARNER**, B. **COUSIN**. Test John C. **HARBISON** (JP). Rec 29 Dec 1819.

1396. Page 266. 28 Dec 1819. Robert **PACKIE** to John **BURNS**. For the sum of $1280, mortgage on two tracts on Franks Creek where sd **BURNS** now lives and which sd **PACKIE** purchased of sd **BURNS** on 27 Dec 1819; 13

acres beginning at the SE corner of the tract which sd **BURNS** purchased of Lewis **TASH**, bounded by Abraham **BYRD**, Anthony **RANDOL**; and 200 arpents, French measure, being the E part of a tract confirmed to sd **TASH**. The debt is due in six obligations; $204 due by 1 May 1821, $208 due by 1 May 1822, $212 due by 1 May 1823, $216 due by 1 May 1824, $220 due by 1 May 1825, and $313.60 by 1 May 1826. Signed Robert **PACKIE**. Wit J. **RANNEY**, Zenas **PRIEST** (JP). Rec 29 Dec 1819. [Marginal note: Full satisfaction received on 12 Jul 1821. Signed John **BURNS**. Wit John **JUDEN** Jr, Clerk.]

1397. Page 268. 27 Dec 1819. John **BURNS** and Mary, his wife, to Robert **PACKIE**. For the sum of $2200, two tracts in Cape Girardeau Twp that sd **BURNS** purchased of Anthony **RANDOL** on 10 Dec 1814, and Lewis **TASH** on 24 Aug 1819; as described in the preceding deed (E:266). Signed John **BURNS**, Mary **BURNS**. Wit Zenas **PRIEST** (JP), J. **RANNEY**. Rec 29 Dec 1819.

1398. Page 269. 23 Nov 1819. Commissioners to Partition Lands of the heirs of Louis **LORIMIER**, decd, to Samuel **WARDEN**. For the sum of $235, Lot Nos. 21 & 22, Range A in Cape Girardeau; bounded on the S by Williams St, E by Spanish St, and W by Lorimier St. Sold on order of Circuit Court issued Aug Term 1819, on petition for partition sd lands. Signed W. **GARNER**, Benjn. M. **HORRELL**, B. **COUSIN**, C. G. **ELLIS**, Wm. **KELSO**. Test John C. **HARBISON** (JP). Rec 30 Dec 1819.

1399. Page 270. 24 Nov 1819. Same to Rebecca **HARBISON**. For the sum of $304, Lot Nos. 15 & 16, Range B in Cape Girardeau; bounded on the N by Independence St, W by Middle St, and S by Merriwether St. Sold as in E:226. Signed Benjn. M. **HORRELL**, B. **COUSIN**, Wm. **KELSO**, W. **GARNER**. Test John C. **HARBISON** (JP). Rec 12 Jan 1820.

1400. Page 271. 1 Dec 1819. Same to Maria J. **CROSS**. For the sum of $700, Lot No. 7, Range G in Cape Girardeau; bounded on the N by Lot No. 8, S by St of Good Hope, E by Lot No. 6, and W by Spanish St. Sold as in E:226. Signed Wm. **KELSO**, B. **COUSIN**, W. **GARNER**. Test John C. **HARBISON** (JP). Rec 12 Jan 1820.

1401. Page 272. 13 Oct 1819. Jesse **VAN** to Frank J. **ALLEN**. For the sum of $200, ___ acres on the waters of Flora Creek in Rng 14, Twp 31 N, being his preemption right made in 1811. Sd **ALLEN** is to pay the Congress price, for which sd **VAN** is not answerable. Signed Jesse **VAN**. Test Jm. **CROPPER**, James **EDMOND**, Zenas **PRIEST** (JP). Rec 17 Jan 1820.

1402. Page 273. 26 Apr 1819. Charnel **GLASSCOCK** and Polly, his wife, to Samuel **PUTNAM**. For the sum of $200, Lot No. 100 in Jackson; bounded on the N by Main St, E by Lot No. 88, S by Lot No. 101, and W and fronted by third west street. Signed Charnal **GLASSCOCK**, Polly (x) **GLASSCOCK**. Wit Zenas **PRIEST** (JP), Samuel S. **HALL**. Rec 25 Jan 1820.

1403. Page 274. 15 Nov 1819. Elijah **RANDOL** to same. For the sum of $600, __ acres on the waters of Cape a la Croix, being all that improvement made by Daniel **STOUT** Senior and conveyed to sd **RANDOL** in 1811, and to which sd **RANDOL** is entitled by right of preemption; bounded on the N by Isaac **WILLIAMS**. Sd **PUTNAM** is empowered to secure a competent title to the preemption. Signed Elijah **RANDOL**. Test Zenas **PRIEST** (JP), Elizabeth **GREEN**. Rec 25 Jan 1820.

1404. Page 276. 25 Jan 1820. Samuel **PUTNAM** and Mary, his wife, to William **McGUIRE** and Willis **McGUIRE**. For the sum of $713, Lot No. 100 in Jackson, as described in E:273. Signed Samul. **PUTNAM**, Mary **PUTNAM**. Wit Robert **MORRISON**, Wm. **CREATH** (JP). Rec 25 Jan 1820.

1405. Page 277. 7 Jun 1819. Scarlet **GLASSCOCK** to Robert **MORRISON**. For the sum of $250, Lot No. 196 in Jackson, lying on first south street. Signed Scarlet **GLASSCOCK**. Wit J. **RANNEY**, Tho. **NEALE** (JP). Rec 25 Jan 1830.

1406. Page 278. 23 Nov 1819. Peter **SLAGLE** of Ste. Genevieve Co., Mo. to the heirs of Louis **LORIMIER**, decd. For the sum of $341, mortgage on the N ½ of Lot No. 6, Range A in Cape Girardeau. Terms as in E:157. Signed Peter **SLAGLE**. Wit Wm. **KELSO** (JP). Rec 25 Jan 1820.

1407. Page 279. 26 Nov 1819. Jenifer T. **SPRIGG** to same. For the sum of $895, Lot No. 9, Range D in Cape Girardeau; bounded on the N by Harmony St, S by Themis St, E by Fountain St, and W by Lot No. 10. Terms as in E:157. Signed Jenifer T. **SPRIGG**. Wit Wm. **KELSO** (JP). Rec 25 Jan 1820.

1408. Page 280. 25 Nov 1819. Andrew **GIBONEY** to same. For the sum of $80, S ½ of Lot No. 15, Range F in Cape Girardeau; bounded on the S by Lot No. 10 and W by Middle St. Terms as in E:157. Signed Andrew **GIBONEY**. Wit Wm. **KELSO** (JP). Rec 25 Jan 1820. [Marginal note: Full satisfaction received on 12 Jul 1827. Signed L. **LORIMIER**.]

1409. Page 281. 26 Jan 1820. Rene **LAMILLIEUR** of Ste. Genevieve Co., Mo. to John **SHEPPARD**. For the sum of $250, ¼ of Lot No. __ in Jackson; bounded on the E by High St, W by a lot, N by Zenas **PRIEST**, and S by the remainder of the lot; being the same sd **LAMILLIEUR** purchased of Burrel S. **COSTILLO**. Signed Rene **LEMEILLEUR**. Wit James **EVANS**, Edward **CRIDDLE**, Wm. **CREATH** (JP). Rec 27 Jan 1820.

1410. Page 282. 1 Jan 1820. Johnson **RANNEY** to John **ARMSTRONG** and Andrew **HAYNES**. For the sum of $500, part of Lot No. 63 in Jackson; beginning at a stake on Main St on the S side of sd lot; bounded by Main St, land formerly owned by Joseph **HORN**, and William **SHEPPARD**. Signed John **RANNEY**. Wit Wm. **CREATH** (JP), Elias K. **DAVIS**. Rec 31 Jan 1820.

1411. Page 283. 11 Sep 1817. Berry A. **WILSON** to Burrell S. **COSTILLO**. For the sum of $100, part of Lot No. 19 in Jackson, granted to sd **WILSON** by deed on 12 May 1817; beginning at the NE corner of sd lot and fronting on High St. Signed Berry A. **WILSON**. Test Saml. S. **HALL**, Wm. **SHEPPARD**, R. S. **THOMAS**, Judge of Southern Circuit of Mo. Rec 7 Feb 1820.

1412. Page 284. 24 Nov 1819. Commissioners to Partition Lands of the heirs of Louis **LORIMIER**, decd, to Samuel D. **DIXON**. For the sum of $615, two tracts in Cape Girardeau; the S ½ of Lot No. 11, Range B, bounded on the S by Merriwether St and W by Fountain St; and Lot No. 14, Range C; bounded on the W by Middle St and S by Independence St. Sold on order of Circuit Court issued Aug Term 1819, on petition for partition sd lands. Signed B. **COUSIN**, Wm. **KELSO**, W. **GARNER**. Test John C. **HARBISON** (JP). Rec 9 Feb 1819.

1413. Page 285. 12 Jan 1820. Frederick **BATES**, Secretary of Mo. Terr., to Thomas **MOSELEY** Jr. Appointment as JP in Cape Girardeau Co. Signed Frederick **BATES**. Thomas **MOSELEY** Jr. takes the oath of office on 15 Feb 1820.

Signed Tom. **MOSELEY** Jr. Wit Zenas **PRIEST** (JP). Rec 15 Feb 1820.

1414. Page 286. 14 Sep 1819. James **COX** Seignor and Elizabeth, his wife, to William **COX**. For the sum of $100, 100 arpens, being the W 1/3 of a tract granted by the Spanish Government to John **SIMPSON** and conveyed to William **CRACRAFT**, and by sd **CRACRAFT** to James **COX** Seignor; bounded on the N by public land, W by heirs of Matthew **SCRUGGS**, decd, S by public land, and E by the balance of the survey. Signed James (x) **COX**, Elizabeth (x) **COX**. Wit George **HENDERSON** (JP). Rec 16 Feb 1820.

1415. Page 287. 26 Nov 1819. Commissioners to Partition Lands of the heirs of Louis **LORIMIER**, decd, to James **RAVENSCROFT**. For the sum of $155, the S ½ of Lot No. 13, Range F in Cape Girardeau; bounded on the S by St Bellevue, E by Fountain St, and W by an alley. Sold on order of Circuit Court issued Aug Term 1819, on petition for partition sd lands. Signed B. **COUSIN**, Wm. **KELSO**, W. **GARNER**. Test John C. **HARBISON** (JP). Rec 17 Feb 1819.

1416. Page 289. 1 Jan 1820. Jacob **SLINKERD** and Elizabeth, his wife, to Daniel **SLINKERD**, their brother. For the sum of $134, their interest in 550 arpents on White Water in German Twp, being a tract confirmed to the representatives of their father Jacob **SLINKERD**. Signed Jacob **SLINKERD**, Elsebeth **SLINKERD**. Test David (x) **SLINKERD**, Curtis **WELLBORN** (JP), Creed **TAYLOR**. Rec 17 Feb 1820.

1417. Page 290. 17 Feb 1820. David **SLINKERD** and Margaret, his wife, to their brother Daniel **SLINKERD**. For the sum of $120, their interest in the land described in the preceding deed (E:289). Signed David ( ) **SLINKERD**, Margaret (x) **SLINKERD**. Wit John **BERRY**, J. **RANNEY**, Wm. **CREATH** (JP). Rec 17 Feb. 1820.

1418. Page 291. 25 Nov 1819. Commissioners to Partition Lands of the heirs of Louis **LORIMIER**, decd, to Van B. **DELASHMUTT**. For the sum of $300, the N ½ of Lot No. 7, Range E in Cape Girardeau; bounded on the N by Lot No. 8, E by Spanish St, and W by Lot No. 8. Sold as in E:226. Signed W. **GARNER**, B. **COUSIN**, Wm. **KELSO**. Test John C. **HARBISON** (JP). Rec 18 Feb 1819.

1419. Page 292. 23 Nov 1819. Same to Abraham **NEWFIELD** of Ste. Genevieve Co., Mo. For the sum of $320, the S ½ of Lot No. 5, Range A in Cape Girardeau; bounded on the E by Spanish St and S by Lot No. 6. Sold as in E:226. Signed C. G. **ELLIS**, Benjn. W. **HORRELL**, B. **COUSIN**, Wm. **KELSO**, W. **GARNER**. Test John C. **HARBISON** (JP). Rec 23 Feb 1819.

1420. Page 293. 23 Nov 1819. Same to same. For the sum of $226, the N ½ of Lot No. 7, Range A in Cape Girardeau; bounded on the N by Lot No. 8 and W by Lorimier St. Sold as in E:226. Signed C. G. **ELLIS**, Benjn. W. **HORRELL**, B. **COUSIN**, Wm. **KELSO**, W. **GARNER**. Test John C. **HARBISON** (JP). Rec 23 Feb 1819.

1421. Page 294. 29 Nov 1819. Same to same. For the sum of $125, 3 ¼ acres, being Outlot No. A, adjoining Cape Girardeau to the W; bounded on the N by Outlot No. 6, S by Outlot B, E by Pacific St, and W by Outlot No. 8. Sold as in E:226. Signed B. **COUSIN**, Wm. **KELSO**, W. **GARNER**, Benjn. W. **HORRELL**. Test John C. **HARBISON** (JP). Rec 23 Feb 1819.

1422. Page 295. 29 Nov 1819. Same to same. For the sum of $285, 10 acres, more or less, being Outlot No. 6, adjoining Cape Girardeau to the NW; bounded on the N by Outlot No. 30, S by North St and Outlot A, E by Outlot No. 5, and W by Outlot No. 7. Sold as in E:226. Signed Benjn. W. **HORRELL**, B. **COUSIN**, W. **GARNER**, C. G. **ELLIS**. Test John C. **HARBISON** (JP). Rec 23 Feb 1819.

1423. Page 297. 25 Nov 1819. Same to Michl. **RODNEY**, Louis **LORIMIER**, and Thos. S. **RODNEY**. For the sum of $1055, Lot No. 11, Range D in Cape Girardeau; bounded on the W by Middle St, E by Lot No. 10, N by Harmony St, and S by Themis St. Sold as in E:226. Signed B. **COUSIN**, Wm. **KELSO**, W. **GARNER**. Test John C. **HARBISON** (JP). Rec 24 Feb 1819.

1424. Page 298. 29 Nov 1819. Same to Thomas S. **RODNEY**. For the sum of $294, 3 ¼ acres, more or less, being Outlot C, adjoining Cape Girardeau to the W; bounded on the N by Outlot B, S by Outlot D, E by Pacific St, and W by Outlot No. 9. Sold as in E:226. Signed C. G. **ELLIS**, W. **GARNER**, B. **COUSIN**, Wm. **KELSO**. Test John C. **HARBISON** (JP). Rec 24 Feb 1819.

1425. Page 299. 29 Nov 1819. Same to same. For the sum of $305, 3 ¼ acres, more or less, being Outlot E, adjoining Cape Girardeau to the W;

bounded on the N by Outlot D, S by Outlot F, E by Pacific St, and W by Outlot No. 10. Sold as in E:226. Signed W. **GARNER**, Wm. **KELSO**, B. **COUSIN**, C. G. **ELLIS**. Test John C. **HARBISON** (JP). Rec 24 Feb 1819.

1426. Page 300. 21 Sep 1819. John **THOMPSON** and James **THOMPSON**, adminrs of the estate of John **THOMPSON** Senr, decd, to James **THOMPSON**. For the sum of $742, __ acres on the waters of Flora Creek; being an improvement and preemption right belonging to the estate of John **THOMPSON** Senr, decd; the heirs being John and Sally **CLARK**, Samuel and Peggy **DUNN**, James and Narcissa **ELLIS**, Uriah and Polly **WILLIAMS**, and Nero, John, James, Betsy, Sally, and Elvira **THOMPSON**. Sold on 20 Sep 1819 on order of Circuit Court. Signed John **THOMPSON**, adminr, James **THOMPSON**, adminr. Wit J. **RANNEY**, William **CRAFT**, Wm. **CREATH** (JP). Rec 25 Feb 1820.

1427. Page 302. 5 Nov 1819. Peter **FRANKS** and Rachel, his wife, of the waters of Saline Creek in Natchitoches Parish, La. to William **RUSSELL** of St. Louis Co. For the sum of $40, quit claim to their interest in 400 acres, more or less, on the S margin of the Arkansas River at or near Little Rocks, Ark. Terr.; being the same they inhabited, cultivated, and improved in 1814. Sd **RUSSELL** is also empowered to enter and purchase sd land from the U. S., and sd **FRANKS** then has the right to make a regular quit claim deed to sd tract, and sd **RUSSELL** has no recourse for any costs or damages on account of this agreement. Signed Peter **FRANKS**, Rachel (x) **FRANKS**. Wit James ( ) **MURPHY**, Edmund **HOGAN**, Eli J. **LEWIS**, Clerk of Arkansas Co., Ark. Also recorded in Pulaski Co. Ark. Deed Book A:75-77. Rec 6 Mar 1820.

1428. Page 303. 27 Dec 1819. Wright **DANIEL** of Pulaski Co., Ark. swears that Peter **FRANKS** and his family settled the place now occupied by George W. **BOYCE**, joining the S margin and ½ miles above a point of rocks in the Arkansas River called Little Rocks, and occupied the same on 12 Apr 1814 and for some years after. Signed Wright **DANIEL**. Wit Edmund **HOGAN**, JP in Pulaski Co., Ark., Samuel **GATES**, JP in Pulaski Co., Ark. Also recorded in Pulaski Co., Ark. Deed Book A:78-79. Rec 6 Mar 1820.

1429. Page 304. 6 Dec 1819. Anthony **BRAVAIS** to Barnabas W. **ALLEN**. For the sum of $1000, ½ of Lot No. 112 in Jackson; bounded on the W by the western branch of the

River Zenon, N and fronted by Main St, E by the E ½ of Lot No. 112 owned by Thomas **SLOAN**, and S by Samuel **PUTNAM**'s Lot No. 113. Signed A. **BRAVAIS**. Wit James **EVANS**, Whiting **RICHARDS**, Wm. **CREATH** (JP). Rec 8 Mar 1820.

1430. Page 305. 22 Dec 1819. Jenifer T. **SPRIGG** to Medad **RANDOL**. For the sum of $1000, 139 acres, being the same conveyed by Ezekiel **ABLE** to sd **SPRIGG** on 5 Mar 1818; beginning at a post near the house at a corner of a tract owned by John **HAYS**' and the heirs of William J. **STEPHENSON**; also cornering at the corner of Secs 15 & 16, Twp 30 N, Rng 12 E. Signed Jenifer T. **SPRIGG**. Wit James **EVANS**, Wm. **CREATH** (JP). Rec 9 Mar 1820.

1431. Page 306. 15 Mar 1820. Daniel **DAVIS** to James **DAVIS**, Smith **DAVIS**, Elisabeth **DAVIS**, Patsy **DAVIS**, Dovey **DAVIS**, and Adaline **DAVIS**. For love and affection that he bears to his children and 1 cent; to James **DAVIS** an improvement and preemption right on the head waters of Byrd's Creek in Byrd Twp that he purchased of **HENDRICKS**, to Smith **DAVIS** an improvement and preemption right in Byrd Twp that he purchased of **HICKMAN**, and to Elisabeth, Patsey, Dovy, and Adaline all his personal estate except his stud colt named Clockfast. Signed Danel **DAVIS**. Wit Stephen **MALON**, J. **RANNEY**, Zenas **PRIEST** (JP). Rec 17 Mar 1820.

1432. Page 307. _____. Samuel **GIBBS** of Howard Co., Mo. to Elijah **RANDOL**. For the sum of $125, __ acres, being his improvement and preemption right on Flora Creek, and the same where he lived near John **CLARK**. Sd **RANDOL** is to secure the preemption and pay all expenses to the U. S. Also power of attorney to sd **RANDOL** to reduce sd preemption, enter sd land, and obtain a patent from the U. S. Signed Samuel **GIBBS**. Wit Luther **WHITING**, JP in Howard Co., Mo., Nero M. **THOMPSON**. Rec 21 Mar 1820.

1433. Page 308. 2 Jan 1820. Thos. **NEALE** to John **THOMPSON**. For the sum of $530, mortgage on part of Lot No. 75 on Main St in Jackson, including one frame house occupied by Peter **SLAGLE**, and one brick house occupied by Saml. **LOCKHART** as a sadler's shop. The obligation to be paid by 2 Jul next. Signed Thos. **NEALE**. Wit Jesse **HAIL**, Edward **CRIDDLE**, Joseph **McFERRON**, Clerk. Rec 22 Mar 1820.

1434. Page 309. 28 Jan 1820. Christian **GATES** to William **HAND**. For the sum of $84 paid by Josiah **VINCENT**, Lot No. 111 in Jackson; bounded on the S and fronted by Main St, N and fronted by Lot No. 110, E and fronted by third west street, and W and fronted by Lot No. 123. Signed Christian **GATES**. Wit William **McCLAIN**, Elizabeth **BYRD**, Wm. **CREATH** (JP). Rec 25 Mar 1820.

1435. Page 310. 15 Feb 1820. William **HAND** and Sally, his wife, to Thomas **MOOSLY**, James M. **CROOPER**, Medad **RANDOL**, and Jenifer T. **SPRIGG**. For the sum of $500, Lot No. 111 in Jackson as described in the preceding deed (E:309). Signed Wm. **HAND**, Sarah **HAND**. Wit Wm. **CREATH** (JP). Rec 25 Mar 1820.

1436. Page 312. 3 Jul 1819. Commissioners of the Courthouse and Jail to Thomas **MORGAN**. For the sum of $96, Lot No. 94 in Jackson; bounded on the N and fronted by third south street, E and fronted by second west street, S by part of Lot No. 95, and W by Lot No. 106. Signed John **DAVIS**, John **SHEPPARD**, Samuel G. **DUNN**, Abraham **BYRD**. Wit Chas. **MOTHERSHEAD**, James **McARTEE**, Joseph **McFERRON**, Clerk. Rec 25 Mar 1820.

1437. Page 313. 12 Dec 1819. Robert and Benjamin **DESHA** of Sumner Co., Tenn. to Charles N. **BLACKMORE**. For the sum of $1000, 300 acres, more or less, Spanish measure, on the waters of Hubble's Creek, adjoining Joseph **THOMPSON** on the W, known as Clingingsmith's Improvement. Signed Robert **DESHA**, Benjamin **DESHA**. Wit Anthony B. **SHELBY**, A. W. **REESE**. Telitha **DESHA** and Nelly **DESHA** RD before Sth. **BLYTHE**, JP in Sumner Co., Tenn., and W. **SMITH**, JP in Sumner Co., Tenn. Proved at Feb 1820 Session of Sumner Co., Tenn. Court of Pleas and Quarter Sessions. Signed David **SHELBY**, Clerk. Wit Edwd. **DOUGLAS**, Presiding Magistrate. Rec 27 Mar 1820.

1438. Page 314. 27 Mar 1820. Charles C. **JACKSON** to Samuel **WRIGHT** and John P. **WRIGHT**. For the sum of $4200, 208 3/4 acres on the River Zenon or Hubble's Creek, known as Ramsey and Cracroft's Mill Tract, in Twp 31 N, Rng 12 E; beginning at a stake at Thomas W. **GRAVES'** and James **DOWTY's** corner; also bounded by **SUMMERS**, John **SUMMERS**, and vacant land. Signed Charles C. **JACKSON**, Elizabeth M. **JACKSON**. Wit James **EVANS**,

Edward **CRIDDLE**, Zenas **PRIEST** (JP). Rec 28 Mar 1820.

1439. Page 316. 27 Mar 1820. Samuel **WRIGHT** and John P. **WRIGHT** to Andrew **RAMSEY**. For the sum of $2666, mortgage on 2/3 part of 208 3/4 acres on the River Zenon, alias Hubble's Creek, known as Ramsey and Cracroft's Mill Tract. The amount is due in four obligations bearing equal date with this deed. Signed Samuel **WRIGHT**, John P. **WRIGHT**. Wit Edward **CRIDDLE**, James **EVANS**, Zenas **PRIEST** (JP). Rec 28 Mar 1820.

1440. Page 317. 27 Mar 1820. Same and same to Charles C. **JACKSON**. For the sum of $1400, mortgage on 1/3 part of 208 3/4 acres as described in the preceding deed (E:316). The deed to be null and void if $933.33 1/3 in three obligations is paid to sd **JACKSON**. Signed Samuel **WRIGHT**, John P. **WRIGHT**. Wit Edward **CRIDDLE**, James **EVANS**, Zenas **PRIEST** (JP). Rec 28 Mar 1820.

1441. Page 318. 29 Mar 1820. Leo **FENWICK** of Ste. Genevieve Co., Mo. to John **HORRELL**. For the sum of $750, his interest in 500 arpens on both sides of Apple Creek, being the sixth lot on the plat of survey of 3000 arpens confirmed to the representatives of Joseph **FENWICK**, decd, which he holds as one of the joint heirs of sd **FENWICK**. Signed Leo **FENWICK**. Wit James **EVANS**, John **JUDEN** Jr., Joseph **McFERRON**, Clerk. Rec 29 Mar 1820.

1442. Page 319. 24 Jan 1820. Deposition of James **THOMPSON** before John **ABERNETHIE** and George **HENDERSON**, JP in Cape Girardeau Twp. William H. **MINTON** presented a petition for dedimus to Circuit Court on 26 Aug 1819; showing that James **WEEKLEY** purchased a preemption right on Flora Creek from David **McCLUSKY**, witnessed by James **THOMPSON**, and which was assigned to sd **MINTON**. Sd **MINTON** had since had his house broken open, and the transfer of preemption right was taken. Sd **THOMPSON** swears that about one year ago he was called to the house of sd **WEEKLEY** on Flora Creek to witness a trade of the preemption right from sd **WEEKLY** to sd **MINTON**, and that the wife of sd **McCLUSKEY** was also present and swore that the handwriting was that of her husband. Signed James **THOMPSON**. Wit Jno. **ABERNETHIE** (JP), George **HENDERSON** (JP). Rec 13 Apr 1820.

1443. Page 321. 1 Dec 1819. Commissioners to Partition Lands of the heirs of Louis **LORIMIER**, decd, to Enock **PARKER**. For the sum of $322, Lot No. 17, Range G in Cape Girardeau; bounded on the N by Lot No. 16, S by Lot No. 18, E by Spanish St, and W by an alley. Sold as in E:226. Signed W. **GARNER**, Wm. **KELSO**, B. **COUSIN**. Test John C. **HARBISON** (JP). Rec 17 Apr 1819.

1444. Page 322. 31 Aug 1819. Enos **RANDOL** to Sarah **BRANT**. For the sum of $125, __ acres on Cape La Croes, being his improvement and preemption right made on Congress land in and since 1811; bounded on the S by A. **RANDOL**. Also power of attorney to obtain a compete estate of sd improvement and to convey title if it is patented to sd **RANDOL**. Signed Enos **RANDOL**. Test Jm. **CROPPER**, John **RANDOL**, John C. **HARBISON** (JP). Rec 17 Apr 1820.

1445. Page 323. 25 Nov 1819. Commissioners to Partition Lands of the heirs of Louis **LORIMIER**, decd, to Edmund B. W. **JONES**. For the sum of $520, the S ½ of Lot No. 1, Range B in Cape Girardeau; bounded on the E by Front St, W by Lot No. 4, and S by Lot No. 2. Sold as in E:226. Signed B. **COUSIN**, C. G. **ELLIS**, Wm. **KELSO**, . Test John C. **HARBISON** (JP). Rec 17 Apr 1819.

1446. Page 325. 19 Feb 1820. John **PATTERSON** [and Peggy, his wife] to Samuel **McMIN**. For the sum of $350, 100 acres in German Twp, being the N part of a tract confirmed to William **PATTERSON**, decd, and known as the Gravelly Spring Place; bounded on the N by Daniel **CLINGINGSMITH**. Signed John **PATTERSON**. Wit John B. **WHEELER**, Peter **HAHN**, George **SNIDER**. Rec 18 Apr 1820.

1447. Page 326. 29 Dec 1819. Martin **MILLER** to John **PERKINS**. For the sum of $260, a negro boy named **Charles**, supposed to be about six years old. Signed Martin (x) **MILLER**. Wit Morris **YOUNG**, Christopher **EAKER**, Jno. **ABERNETHIE** (JP). Rec 18 Apr 1820.

1448. Page 327. 18 Apr 1820. Ezekiel **ABLE** to William **GARNER** and John **CROSS**. For the sum of $1100, 640 acres on the Mississippi River above the old Cape, which was confirmed as the settlement right of Stephen **CAVENDAR**. Signed Ezekiel **ABLE**. Wit John C. **HARBISON** (JP), John **JOHNSON**. Rec 18 Apr 1820.

1449. Page 328. 18 Apr 1820. Same to same and same. For the sum of $400, __ acres on the Mississippi River above the old Cape, joining the upper end of 640 acres confirmed as the settlement right of Stephen **CAVENDER**, being an improvement first made by Samuel **HINCK** and preemption right, where sd **ABLE** formerly lived. Signed Ezekiel **ABLE**. Wit John C. **HARBISON** (JP), John **JOHNSON**. Rec 18 Apr 1820.

1450. Page 329. 18 Apr 1820. John **JOHNSON** to same and same. For the sum of $1, quit claim to 640 acres as described in E:327, and conveyed to him as the right of Ezekiel **ABLE** at sheriff's sale. Signed John **JOHNSON**. Wit Sm. **WAUGH**, J. T. **ROSS**, John C. **HARBISON** (JP). Rec 18 Apr 1820.

1451. Page 330. 1 Feb 1820. Isaac **WILLIAMS** to Alexander **BUCKNER**. For diverse good causes and services rendered, power of attorney to settle a claim sd **WILLIAMS** made to __ acres on the Mississippi River at the mouth of Byse's Creek, known as the head right of Johnathan **BYSE**. Signed Isaac (x) **WILLIAMS**. Test John **MASSEY**, Joseph **McFERRON**, Clerk. Rec 18 Apr 1820.

1452. Page 331. 25 Mar 1820. Alexander **BUCKNER** and Isaac **WILLIAMS** to Thomas **MOSELY** Junr, James M. **CROPPER**, Medad **RANDLE**, and Jenifer T. **SPRIGG**. For the sum of $1000, quit claim to 80 acres above the mouth of Boyce's Creek, being part of a tract named **BOYCE**'s head right; beginning on the Mississippi River at a post immediately above the mouth of Boyce's Creek. Signed A. **BUCKNER**, Isaac **WILLIAMS** by A. **BUCKNER**, atty in fact. Wit Joseph **McFERRON**, Clerk. Rec 18 Apr 1820.

1453. Page 332. 23 Mar 1820. **MOSELEY & CROPPER** and Medad **RANDOL** to Jenifer T. **SPRIGG**. Power of attorney to execute a quit claim deed to Alexander **BUCKNER** and Isaac **WILLIAMS** for their interest in the head right of Johnathan **BOYCE** on the Mississippi River at Boyce's Creek. Signed **MOSELY & CROPPER**, Medad **RANDOL**. Wit Edward F. **EVANS**, Joseph **McFERRON**, Clerk. Rec 18 Apr 1820.

1454. Page 332. 25 Mar 1820. Thomas **MOSELY** Junr, James M. **CROPPER**, Medad **RANDOL**, and Jenifer T. **SPRIGG** to Alexander **BUCKNER** and Isaac **WILLIAMS**. For 80 acres of land granted to them by sd

BUCKNER and sd WILLIAMS (E:331), quit claim to __ acres, being the head right of Jonathan BOICE above the mouth of Boyce's Creek, except the 80 acres mentioned. Signed Thomas MOSELY Junr, James M. CROPPER, and Medad RANDOL by Jenifer T. SPRIGG, atty in fact. Wit Joseph McFERRON, Clerk. Rec 18 Apr 1820.

1455. Page 334. 10 Mar 1820. John ARMSTRONG and Elisa, his wife, to Edward CRIDDLE. For the sum of $73, part of Lot No. 63 on Main St and first west street in Jackson; beginning at the SW corner of sd lot. Signed John ARMSTRONG, Hulale ARMSTRONG. Wit Wm. CREATH (JP). Rec 19 Apr 1820.

1456. Page 334. 21 Jan 1820. William PENNY to Thomas S. RODNEY. For the sum of $25, __ acres on the waters of the Great Swamp in Byrd Twp, being an improvement and preemption settled and cultivated by sd PENNY, and being the same where sd RODNEY now lives. Also power of attorney to enter the preemption and obtain title. Signed Will. PENNEY. Wit Franklin CANNON, Wm. CREATH (JP). Rec 20 Apr 1820.

1457. Page 335. 18 Apr 1820. Ezekiel ABLE to William P. LACEY. For the sum of $1000, 213 1/3 acres in the Big Bend of the Mississippi River, being the middle part of a settlement right of 640 acres confirmed to Jabez FISHER; beginning at the bank of the Mississippi River at a post, and bounded on the S by Samuel SMILEY, N by John JOHNSON, E by the Mississippi River, and W by public land. Signed Ezekiel ABLE. Wit Robert BUCKNER, John C. HARBISON (JP). Rec 20 Apr 1820.

1458. Page 337. 3 Mar 1820. William NEELY, Anthony B. NEELY, Joseph FRISEL, and Johnson RANNEY, executors of the last will and testament of Joseph SEAWEL, decd, to Edmund RUTTER. For the sum of $200, Lot No. 2 adjoining Jackson; bounded on the N by Seawel St, E by Lot No. 1 owned by John DELAP, S by sd RUTTER where he now lives, and W by first west street. Signed A. B. NEELY, Wm. NEELY, J. FRIZEL, Johnson RANNEY. Wit James G. SEAY, R. DAUGHERTY, Zenas PRIEST (JP). Rec 21 Apr 1820.

1459. Page 338. 21 Apr 1820. Ezekiel ABLE by Sheriff John HAYS to William GARNER and John CROSS. For the sum of $310, four tracts; 640 acres on White Water confirmed to Jacob SHARADIN Junr's representatives, 640 acres on White Water confirmed to John SHARADIN's representatives, 640 acres on the waters of White Water confirmed to James SMITH's representatives, and 640 acres on the waters of White Water confirmed to Peter FRANKS' representatives. Sold on 19 Apr 1820 at order of Circuit Court on three writs of execution against sd ABLE obtained by judgments in sd court; one in favor of John SCOTT for $150 debt, $7.64 damages, and $17.82 and 5 mills costs; one in favor of Robert RAVENSCROFT for $120 debt, $8.75 damages, and $21.57 and 5 mills costs; and one in favor of John DICK, adminr of Abraham DICK, decd, against sd ABLE, William VIRGIN, and Richard WALLER for $96 debt, $5.49 damages, and $23.77 and 5 mills costs. Also sold on order of Superior Court, Southern Circuit on two writs of execution against sd ABLE obtained by judgments in sd court; one in favor of Daniel F. STEINBECK and George HENDERSON, adminr with the will annexed of Louis LORIMIER, decd, and against sd ABLE impleaded with Jeremiah ABLE for $145.59 debt, $54.90 damages, and 36.44 costs; and one in favor of Margaret TAYLOR for $40.53 and 2 ½ mills costs on a plea of trespass and ejectment against her by sd ABLE. Signed John HAYS, Sheriff. Wit Joseph McFERRON, Clerk. Rec 21 Apr 1820.

1460. Page 342. 1 Jul 1806. Louis LORIMIER to Andrew RAMSEY Senr. For the sum of $200 to be paid within 12 months, two lots in Cape Girardeau, being Lot Nos. 7 & 8, Range D; joining each other and bounded on the N by Harmony St, S by Themis St, E by A. HADEN, and W by Indian St. Signed L. LORIMIER. Test B. COUSIN, Geo. HENDERSON (JP). Recorded in Book C:70 on 24 Mar 1809. Signed Geo. HENDERSON, Recorder. Title is assigned to Ezekiel ABLE for value received on 4 Mar 1811. Signed Andrew RAMSEY [Senr]. Wit Samuel CAMPBELL, Wm. KELSO (JP). Rec 25 Apr 1820.

1461. Page 344. 1 Mar 1820. William CLARK, Governor of Mo. Terr, to John AKIN. Appointment as JP for Bird Twp for four years. Signed Wm. CLARK. John AKIN takes the oath of office. Signed John AKIN. Wit Joseph McFERRON. Rec 26 Apr 1820.

1462. Page 344. 19 Apr 1820. James MOONEY to John HAYS. For the sum of $150, 75 arpens, more or less, on Hubble's Creek, being the moiety of a tract originally improved by James MILLS. Sd MOONEY is entitled to the same by virtue of articles of agreement dated 9 Jun 1802 between him and Roland **MERIDETH**, brother and heir of Rees **MERIDETH**, decd, who purchased the same from sd **MILLS** in his lifetime. Signed James **MOONY**. Wit John **THOMARSON**, Henry (H) **BOYER**, Zenas **PRIEST** (JP). Rec 26 Apr 1820.

1463. Page 345. 9 Jun 1802. James **MOONAY**, tanner and currier, and Roland **MEREDITH**, both of Ste Genevieve. Agreement to establish a tannery on the land sold by James **MILLS** to Rees **MEREDITH**, and inherited by Rolland **MEREDITH**, his brother. Sd **MOONAY** and sd **MEREDITH** agree to the following: 1) Sd **MOONAY** will reimburse Rolland **MEREDITH** one half the sum paid by Rees **MEREDITH**, his brother, and **MILLS** for the land and one half of the expenses and work done on the land by the deceased Rees **MEREDITH** to establish the tannery. Sd sums are payable in tanned hides at the current price--one half due this fall, the other half due a year from this fall which in 1803. 2) Rolland **MEREDITH** promises to give to sd **MOONAY** one half of the above mentioned land and to give him a bill of sale as soon as he has the title for the land. Sd **MEREDITH** will also cede to sd **MOONAY** one half of the tools and tannery equipment used in tanning. 3) Sd **MOONAY** promises to teach Rolland **MEREDITH** all aspects of the profession of tanner and currier. 4) Each will provide one half the work needed to practice this profession and one half the costs and expenditures necessary for establishing and maintaining the tannery. Each will take an equal portion of the profits from the tannery. If one of the two gets sick and cannot contribute to the common work in the tannery, his account will not be charged with the loss of time occasioned by this accident, which will be supported by the partnership. 5) The parties agree furthermore that if one of them desires to withdraw from the agreement or to sell his part of the property and tools, this will be possible; however, this condition is formal and provided that he give his associate the preference before anyone else, and in case they cannot come to an agreement on the value of the half of the said property, they agree to bring the problem to the judgment of two judicious and honest men. 6) The above mentioned parties agree that the one of the two who does not meet the above stipulated rules will pay the other the sum of 1000 piastres. [IN FRENCH] Signed James **MOONEY**, Roland **MEREDITH**. Wit B. **COUSIN**, Surveyor, L. **LORIMIER**. Rec 26 Apr 1820.

1464. Page 347. 17 Mar 1820. Henry **LEGGET** to Obadiah **MALONE**. For the sum of $200, __ acres on the waters of Apple Creek in Byrd Twp, being an improvement and preemption right originally settled by James **HUGHS**. Signed Henry (x) **LEGGET**. Wit J. **RANNEY**, Stephen **MALON**, Zenas **PRIEST** (JP). Rec 1 May 1820.

1465. Page 348. 16 Feb 1820. Isaac **HODGE** of Allaghany Co., Pa. to Thomas **BYRNE** of Monongalia Co., Vir. For the sum of $100, __ acres at the mouth of Cape a la Cruche Creek on the Mississippi River, being the same confirmed to James **HODGES** and two others, believed to be **LEMMONS** and **WILLIAMS**, to which Isaac **HODGE** is entitled as farther and heir of James **HODGE**, decd, by his last will and testament. Signed Isaac **HODGE**. Wit Mathew B. **LOWRIE**, Notary Public in Pittsburgh, Pa., Adly **MONTOOTH**. Rec 5 May 1820.

1466. Page 349. 5 May 1820. Commissioners of the Courthouse and Jail to Richard S. **THOMAS**. For the sum of $1000, 12 ½ acres, more or less, S of fourth south street in Jackson, including the house where sd **THOMAS** now resides; being part of 50 acres purchased of William H. **ASHLEY** by sd commissioners. Signed John **DAVIS**, John **SHEPPARD**, Samuel G. **DUNN**, Abraham **BYRD**, Benjamin **SHELL**. Wit Joseph **McFERRON**, Zenas **PRIEST** (JP). Rec 6 May 1820.

1467. Page 350. 3 Jul 1819. Same to John **DAUGHERTY**. For the sum of $102, Lot No. 106 in Jackson; bounded on the N and fronted by third south street, W and fronted by third west street, S by part of Lot No. 107, and E by Lot No. 94. Signed John **DAVIS**, John **SHEPPARD**, Samuel G. **DUNN**, Abraham **BYRD**. Test Chas. **MOTHERSHEAD**, James **McCARTEE**, Joseph **McFERRON**, Clerk. Rec 9 May 1820.

1468. Page 351. 20 Apr 1819. Same to Jonathan **JOHNSON**. For the sum of $47, Lot No. 10 in Jackson; bounded on the N and fronted by third south street, W and fronted by High St, S by Lot No. 11, and E by Lot No. 34. Signed John **SHEPPARD**, Samuel G. **DUNN**, Abraham **BYRD**, Benjamin **SHELL**. Wit Alfred **WHEELER**, Andrew **BOLLINGER**, Joseph **McFERRON**, Clerk. Rec 9 May 1820.

1469. Page 352. 9 May 1820. Same to Lyne **STARLING** and Elias N. **DLASHMUTT** trading as **STARLING & DLASHMUTT**. For the sum of $379.50, Lot Nos. 30, 39, 69, & 81 in

Jackson; Lot No. 30 is bounded on the N and fronted by first south street, E and fronted by first east street, S by Lot No. 31, and W by Lot No. 6; Lot No. 39 is bounded on the S and fronted by Main St, W and fronted by first east street, N by Lot No. 38, and E by Lot No. 123; Lot No. 69 is bounded on the E and fronted by first west street, S and fronted by third south street, W by Lot No. 81, and N by Lot No. 68; and Lot No. 81 is bounded on the S and fronted by third south street, W and fronted by second west street, N by Lot No. 80, and E by Lot No. 69. Signed John **DAVIS**, John **SHEPPARD**, Samuel G. **DUNN**, Abraham **BYRD**, Benjamin **SHELL**. Wit Stephen **BYRD**, Wm. G. **BYRD**, John **DOUGHERTY**, Joseph **McFERRON**, Clerk. Rec 9 May 1820.

1470. Page 354. 31 Mar 1820. William **CLARK**, Governor of Mo. Terr, to William **POLK**. Appointment as JP for Byrd Twp for four years. Signed Wm. **CLARK**. William **POLK** takes the oath of office. Signed William **POLK**. Wit Joseph **McFERRON**. Rec 10 May 1820.

1471. Page 354. 10 May 1820. John **HAYS**, Daniel F. **STEINBECK**, and Nicholas **SEAVERS** to William **CLARK**, Governor of Mo. For the sum of $2500, bond to guarantee that sd **HAYS** will collect and pay over taxes as Sheriff of Cape Girardeau Co. Signed John **HAYS**, D. F. **STEINBECK**, N. **SEAVERS**. Wit Joseph **McFERRON**, Clerk. Rec 10 May 1820.

1472. Page 355. 10 May 1820. Same, same, and same to same. For the sum of $2000, bond to guarantee that sd **HAYS** will collect and pay out monies for county purposes. Signed John **HAYS**, D. F. **STEINBECK**, N. **SEAVERS**. Wit Joseph **McFERRON**, Clerk. Rec 10 May 1820.

1473. Page 355. 10 May 1820. Charles **MOTHERSHEAD** by Sheriff John **HAYS** to Alexander **BUCKNER**. For the sum of $200, lot in Jackson where Doctr Edward S. **GANTT** now lives. Sold on 20 Apr 1820 at order of Circuit Court on a writ of execution issued 5 Jan 1820 in favor of Nicholas **PEAY** against sd **MOTHERSHEAD** impleaded with Daniel M. **STOUT**, for $1047.09 debt, $128.22 damages, and $21.47 and 5 mills costs. Signed John **HAYS**, Sheriff. Wit Joseph **McFERRON**, Clerk. Rec 10 May 1820.

1474. Page 357. 19 Apr 1820. Barnabas W. **ALLEN** to Anthony **BRAVAIS**. For the sum of

$700, mortgage on the W ½ of Lot No. __ in Jackson; bounded on the N and fronted by Main St, W and fronted by the River Zenon, S by a lot, and E by the E ½ of sd lot. The debt is due in two obligations, one dated 6 Dec 1819 for $350 payable 12 months after date, and one dated 6 Dec 1819 for $350 payable 18 months after date. Signed Barnabas W. **ALLEN**. Wit Greer W. **DAVIS**, David **ARMOUR**, Zenas **PRIEST** (JP). Rec 13 May 1820.

1475. Page 359. 11 Feb 1818. Commissioners of the Courthouse and Jail to Samuel **PUTNAM**. For the sum of $42, Lot No. 113 in Jackson; bounded on the N and fronted by Lot No. 112, E and fronted by third west street, S and fronted by first south street, and W by fractions of the town. Signed John **DAVIS**, John **SHEPPARD**, Samuel G. **DUNN**, Abraham **BYRD**. Wit Thos. **NEWBERRY**, J. **FRIZEL**, Zenas **PRIEST** (JP). Rec 15 May 1820.

1476. Page 360. 11 Feb 1818. Same to same. For the sum of $45.50, Lot No. 101 in Jackson; bounded on the N by Lot No. 100, E by Lot No. 89, S and fronted by first south street, and W and fronted by third west street. Signed John **DAVIS**, John **SHEPPARD**, Samuel G. **DUNN**, Abraham **BYRD**, Benja. **SHELL**. Wit Thos. **NEWBERRY**, J. **FRIZEL**, Zenas **PRIEST** (JP). Rec 19 May 1820.

1477. Page 361. 31 Mar 1820. William **CLARK**, Governor of Mo., to James **RUSSELL**. Appointment as JP for Bird Twp for four years. Signed Wm. **CLARK**. James **RUSSELL** takes the oath of office. Signed James **RUSSELL**. Wit Joseph **McFERRON**, Clerk. Rec 22 May 1820.

1478. Page 362. 21 Feb 1820. William **NEELY**, Anthony B. **NEELY**, Joseph **FRISEL**, and Johnson **RANNEY**, executors of the last will and testament of Joseph **SEAWEL**, decd, to Henry **CLINARD** and John **BINKLEY**. For the sum of $200, Lot No. 3 adjoining Jackson; bounded on the N by Seawel St, E by first west street, S by James H, **JENKINS** and Phinehas **COBURN**, and W by Lot No. 4. Signed Wm. **NEELY**, A. B. **NEELY**, Johnson **RANNEY**, Joseph **FRIZEL**. Wit Alfred **WHEELER**, Scarlet **GLASSCOCK**, Wm. **CREATH** (JP). Rec 23 May 1820.

1479. Page 362. 28 Mar 1820. William A. **BULL** to Henry **CLINARD**. For the sum of $300, Lot No. 114 in Jackson; bounded on the N and fronted by first south street, E and fronted by third east street, N by Lot No. 115, and W by Lot

No. 195. Signed Wm. A. **BULL**. Wit Saml. **LOCKHART**, John **ARMSTRONG**, Wm. **CREATH** (JP). Rec 23 May 1820.

1480. Page 364. 20 May 1820. Samuel **PUTNAM** and Mary, his wife, to James **RUSSELL**. For the sum of $750, two lots in Jackson; Lot No. 101, bounded on the N by Lot No. 100, E by Lot No. 89, S and fronted by first south street, and W and fronted by third west street; and Lot No. 113, bounded on the N by Lot No. 112, E and fronted by third west street, S and fronted by first south street, and W by fractional parts of the town. Signed Samuel **PUTNAM**, Mary **PUTNAM**. Wit Wm. **CREATH** (JP), Sarah (x) **STOUT**. Rec 24 May 1820.

1481. Page 365. 5 May 1820. John **BILDERBACK** of Randolph Co., Ill. to Jason **CHAMBERLAIN**. For the sum of $1000, two tracts; undivided ½ of 640 acres, being the settlement and improvement right of Felix **HOOVER**, confirmed to sd **BILDERBACK** as assignee of sd **HOOVER**; and undivided ½ of 640 acres in Tywappity Bottom in New Madrid Co., being the settlement and improvement right of John **DYE**, confirmed to sd **BILDERBACK** as assignee of sd **DYE**. This deed confirms a conveyance of 7 Apr 1819, the other undivided ½ of the tracts have heretofore been conveyed to Rufus **EASTON** of St. Louis Co., Mo. Sd **BILDERBACK** will execute a quit claim deed to the tracts after they are surveyed. Signed John **BILDERBACK**. Wit Joseph **McFERRON**, Clerk, B. **COUSIN**. Rec 25 May 1820.

1482. Page 366. 20 Aug 1819. Franklin **CANNON** to William **RANDLES**. For the sum of $1, quit claim to part of Lot No. 102 on third west and first south streets in Jackson; beginning at the NE corner of sd lot on first south street. Sd **RANDLES** also conveys to sd **CANNON**, for the sum of $1, the part of sd lot beginning at the NW corner of sd lot. The parties also agree to a passway free from all hindrance from the NE corner of sd **CANNON**'s part to the SW corner of sd **RANDLES**' part. Signed Franklin **CANNON**, William **RANDLES**. Wit ____ **RANNEY**, William **CREATH** (JP). Rec 26 May 1820.

1483. Page 368. 28 Feb 1820. Joseph **NEWSWANGER** Senior to John **RISHER**. For the sum of $50, __ acres, being an improvement that he purchased of Jacob **MILLER** on Painter Crick [Panther Creek], cultivated in 1804, on which he has laid a residue of his own grant of 100 acres. Should the grant be confirmed, then sd **RISHER** has preemption right to sd improvement and the interest of both claims. Signed Joseph **NEYSWANGER** Sr. Wit Joseph **NEYSWANGER** Jur, Joseph **SEABOUCH**, John B. **WHEELER** (JP). Rec 26 May 1820.

1484. Page 368. 1 Apr 1820. Ezekiel **ABLE** and Margaret, his wife, and Jeremiah **ABLE** and Patsey, his wife, to Henry **FORTENBERRY** of Larrence Co., Ark. For the sum of $1048, 316 acres on White Water, part of a tract confirmed to Wm. **SMITH**; beginning at a stake between two white walnuts near an old fish trap. Signed Ezekiel **ABLE**. Wit Zenas **PRIEST** (JP), T. E. **STRANGE**. Rec 27 May 1820.

1485. Page 370. 31 Jan 1806. Jacob **MILLER** to Joseph **NISWEKER**. For the sum of ___, his improvement on Panter Crke joining Joseph **BAKAR** and Daniel **CLINKINGSMITH**. Signed Jacob **MILLER**. Wit Martin (M) **THOMAS**, Zenas **PRIEST** (JP). Rec 27 May 1820.

1486. Page 370. 28 Feb 1820. Martain **THOMAS** to John **RISHER**. For the sum of $1000, all his preemption right, improvements, and buildings where he now lives on Painter Creek, and also the confirmation if confirmed. Signed Martin (M) **THOMAS**. Wit Joseph **NEYSWANGER** Junior, Joseph **SEABACH**, Zenas **PRIEST** (JP). Rec 27 May 1820.

1487. Page 371. 30 May 1820. Robert B. **DAWSON** of New Madrid Co., Mo. to John **PRIM**. For the sum of $640, Certificate of New Location (#17) for 160 acres, issued by Frederick **BATES**, Recorder of Land Titles, issued in the name of Joseph **GENEREUX** under the Act of Congress of 17 Feb 1815. Signed Robert D. **DAWSON**. Wit James **EVANS**, Stephen **BYRD**, Zenas **PRIEST** (JP). Rec 30 May 1820.

1488. Page 372. 16 Mar 1820. Reuben **NORMAN** to Martin **THOMAS**. For the sum of $150, 250 arpents on Caney Fork of White Water; surveyed in the Spanish time for Allen **McKINSEY** and Jacob **FOSTER** by order of the commandant for services done in the expedition to New Madrid, conveyed by sd **McKINSEY** and sd **FOSTER** to sd **NORMAN**, and since improved and cultivated by him; adjoining the widow **WISE** and Michael **SHILL**. Signed Reuben **NORMAN**. Wit John **RISHER**, Alexr. **PORTER**, John **AKIN** (JP). Rec 2 Jun 1820.

1489. Page 372. 3 Feb 1819. Thomas **BOLING** to George F. **BOLLINGER**. For the sum of $300, __ acres, being an improvement and preemption right on Little White Water in German Twp, near **PATTERSON** and **COTNER**, and where he lately resided; also power to enter sd land in the proper land office. Signed Thomas (x) **BOLING**. Wit J. **RANNEY**, Wm. **NEELY**, John B. **WHEELER** (JP). Rec 7 Jun 1820.

1490. Page 373. 6 Jun 1820. Anthony B. **NEELY** and Margaret, his wife, to James **BURNS**. For the sum of $150, Lot No. 13 in Jackson; bounded on the E by High St, S by first north street, and W by Edmund **RUTTER**. Signed A. B. **NEELY**, Ma. **NEELY**. Wit Wm. **CREATH** (JP), John **DELAP**. Rec 7 Jun 1820.

1491. Page 374. 7 Jun 1820. James **BURNS** to Samuel W. **MITCHEL**. For the sum of $1, the S part of Lot No. 13 in Jackson; beginning at the SW corner of sd lot on first north street. Signed James **BURNS**. Wit A. B. **NEELY**, Wm. **CREATH** (JP). Rec 7 Jun 1820.

1492. Page 375. 9 May 1820. Joseph **McFERRON**, Clerk of Circuit Court, to Bartholomew **COUSIN**. Appointment as Deputy Clerk of the Circuit Court for Cape Girardeau Co., Southern Circuit. Signed Joseph **McFERRON**, Clerk. Bartholomew **COUSIN** takes the oath of office. Signed B. **COUSIN**. Wit Zenas **PRIEST** (JP). Rec 8 Jun 1820.

1493. Page 376. 20 Jun 1820. Hugh **WHITE** to John **RAMSEY**. By order of Circuit Court, 800 arpens adjoining the Big Swamp on the road leading to New Madrid, being the concession and confirmation of sd **WHITE**, where sd **RAMSEY** now resides. Conveyed on order of the court at Sep Term 1819, on motion arising from an original bill of John **RAMSEY**, complainant, against Hugh **WHITE**, defendant. Provided that if the defendant shall not appear within five years, bring his bill of review, and file an answer to the original bill, this decree shall become absolute. Signed B. **COUSIN**, Deputy Clerk. Rec 20 Jun 1820.

1494. Page 376. 27 Jun 1820. Nathan **McCARTY**, William **McCARTY**, and John **HAYS** and Cynthia, his wife, to Christian **GATES**. For the sum of $1293, 431 acres, more or less, on the waters of Byrd's Creek; beginning at a post in Bartholomew **COUSIN**'s line. Signed Nathan **McCARTY**, William **McCARTY**, John **HAYS**, Cynthia **HAYS**. Wit

W. **GARNER**, B. **COUSIN**, Wm. **CREATH** (JP. Rec 1 Jul 1820.

1495. Number not used.

1496. Page 378. 8 Nov 1805. Edward **HATHORNE** to Samuel **CAMPBELL**. For the sum of $100, 750 arpens, more or less, on Castor River, being a Spanish right and head right he improved. Signed Edward **HATHORNE**. Test Jeremiah **ABLE**, Ezekiel **ABLE**, Wm. **CREATH** (JP). Rec 7 Jul 1820.

1497. Page 378. 23 Sep 1819. John **HEBERT** & Co. of Jackson to Christopher G. **HOUTS**. Power of attorney to rent, sell, or both, ½ of Lot No. 61 in Jackson and a house, bounded on the S by first north street, W by Lot No. 73, N by Joseph **SEAWELL** or surplus town land, and E by the other ½ of the lot; also ½ of Lot No. 73 in Jackson, bounded on the S by first north street, W by the other ½ of No. 73, N by Joseph **SEAWELL** or surplus town land, and E by Lot No. 61. Signed John **HERBERT** & Co. Wit James **EVANS**, Wm. **CREATH** (JP). Rec 13 Jul 1820.

1498. Page 379. 23 Jun 1820. Richard **SEARCY** to Charles S. **HEMPSTEAD**, both of St. Louis Co. Statement that sd **HEMPSTEAD** is entitled to ½ of 640 acres they purchased of John **SHIELDS** on 6 Jul 1818; being the settlement and improvement right of William **PAGE**. Signed Richd. **SEARCY**. Wit Richd. S. **THOMAS**, Judge of Southern Circuit of Mo. Terr. Rec 21 Jul 1820.

1499. Page 380. 22 Jul 1820. Commissioners of the Courthouse and Jail to John **MASSEY**. For the sum of $65, Lot No. 138 in Jackson; bounded on the E by Lot No. 150, S by Lot No. 139, W and fronted by second east street, and N and fronted by first south street. Signed John **DAVIS**, John **SHEPPARD**, Samuel G. **DUNN**. Wit Richard **WALLER**, Zenas **PRIEST** (JP). Rec 22 Jul 1820.

1500. Page 381. 11 Apr 1820. Hiram C. **DAVIS** to David **DAVIS** of Bracken Co., Ken. For the sum of $1452, 240 acres, two chains, and ⅕, more or less, on Hubble's and Foster's Creeks; beginning at a sycamore at Abraham **BYRD**'s NW corner, also bounded by **AIKIN**, Thomas **SULLINGER**, and Martin **RODNEY**'s head right. Signed Hiram C. **DAVIS**. Wit John **DAVIS**, Augustus **DAVIS**, Zenas **PRIEST** (JP). Rec 24 Jul 1820.

1501. Page 382. 11 Apr 1820. Same to same. For the sum of $1, __ acre on the W side of Hubble's Creek of Thomas S. **RODNEY**'s improvement; beginning on Thomas **SULLINGER's** E line at a hickory sapling. Signed Hiram C. **DAVIS**. Wit John **DAVIS**, Augustus **DAVIS**, Zenas **PRIEST** (JP). Rec 24 Jul 1820.

1502. Page 383. 24 Jul 1820. Charles W. **BLACKMORE** to Robert **ENGLISH**. For the sum of $1200, 300 arpens, Spanish measure, on the waters of Randol's Creek, known as Clingingsmith's Improvement, being the same he purchased of Robert and Benjamin **DESHA** of Tenn on 12 Dec 1819. Signed Charles W. **BLACKMORE**. Wit Jesse **HAIL**, Erasmus **ELLIS**, Zenas **PRIEST** (JP). Rec 24 Jul 1820. [Marginal note: Acknowledgment of Mary **BLACKMORE**, wife of Charles, is recorded in F:308.]

1503. Page 384. 2 Dec 1819. Jesse **LANGSTON** to Peter **HINCLE**. For the sum of $150, in Byrd Twp in the Apple Creek settlement near the residence of Daniel **WELKER**, being a certain improvement and preemption right made by him on Congress land in Mar 1814. Signed Jesse **LANGSTON**. Wit Johnson **RANNEY**, Daniel **TISDALE**, Wm. **CREATH** (JP). Rec 25 Jul 1820.

1504. Page 384. 28 Jul 1820. Commissioners to Partition Lands of the heirs of Louis **LORIMIER**, decd, to William **GARNER**. For the sum of $84, two lots in Cape Girardeau; Lot No. 31, Range A, bounded on the W by a street and E by an alley; and Lot No. 3, Range H, bounded on the E and fronted by Front or Aquamsi St and W by Lot No. 10. Sold as in E:226. Signed B. **COUSIN**, Wm. **KELSO**, C. G. **ELLIS**. Test John C. **HARBISON** (JP). Rec 29 Jul 1820.

1505. Page 386. 27 Jul 1820. Same to Robert **GIBONEY**. For the sum of $11, Lot No. 33, Range H in Cape Girardeau; bounded on the N and fronted by St of Good Hope, E and fronted by Fountain St, and W by an alley. Sold as in E:226. Signed B. **COUSIN**, W. **GARNER**, Wm. **KELSO**, C. G. **ELLIS**. Test John C. **HARBISON** (JP). Rec 29 Jul 1820.

1506. Page 387. 28 Jul 1820. Same to same. For the sum of $73, three lots in Cape Girardeau; Lot No. 15, Range H, bounded on the E by Spanish St; Lot No. 23, Range H, bounded on the W by Lorimier St; and Lot No. 10, Range I, bounded on the W by Spanish St and E by Gravesend St.

Sold as in E:226. Signed B. **COUSIN**, W. **GARNER**, C. G. **ELLIS**. Test John C. **HARBISON** (JP). Rec 29 Jul 1820.

1507. Page 388. 8 Aug 1820. Robert **GIBONEY** to Christian **LINT**. For the sum of $31.25, Lot No. 33, Range H in Cape Girardeau, as described in E:386. Signed Robert **GIBONEY**. Wit Joseph **McFERRON**, Clerk. Rec 8 Aug 1820.

1508. Page 388. 25 Jul 1820. Commissioners to Partition Lands of the heirs of Louis **LORIMIER**, decd, to Van B. **DLASHMUTT**. For the sum of $34, two lots in Range F in Cape Girardeau; Lot No. 18, bounded on the E by Middle St; and Lot No. 22, bounded on the W by a street. Sold as in E:226. Signed B. **COUSIN**, W. **GARNER**, Wm. **KELSO**. Test John C. **HARBISON** (JP). Rec 11 Aug 1820.

1509. Page 390. 26 Jul 1820. Same to same. For the sum of $435, five contiguous outlots NW of Cape Girardeau on the road to Jackson; Outlot Nos. 7 & 8, each containing 10 acres; Outlot Nos. 28 & 29, each containing 20 acres, and Outlot No. 38 containing 40 acres. Sold as in E:226. Signed W. **GARNER**, B. **COUSIN**, Wm. **KELSO**, C. G. **ELLIS**. Test John C. **HARBISON** (JP). Rec 11 Aug 1820.

1510. Page 391. 26 Jul 1820. Same to same. For the sum of $10, Lot No. 27, Range A in Cape Girardeau; bounded on the E and fronted by Middle St, N by Lot No. 28 and S by Lot No. 26. Sold as in E:226. Signed W. **GARNER**, B. **COUSIN**, Wm. **KELSO**, C. G. **ELLIS**. Test John C. **HARBISON** (JP). Rec 11 Aug 1820.

1511. Page 392. 29 Jul 1820. Same to same. For the sum of $1480, six outlots S of Cape Girardeau; Outlot Nos. 15 & 17 adjoining Cape Girardeau and being 10 acres each; Outlot Nos. 24 & 26 SW of Cape Girardeau and being 20 acres each; and Outlot Nos. 50 & 52 containing 80 acres each. Sold as in E:226. Signed B. **COUSIN**, Wm. **KELSO**, C. G. **ELLIS**. Test John C. **HARBISON** (JP). Rec 11 Aug 1820.

1512. Page 393. 2 Jul 1819. William **NEELY** to Robert **MORRISON**. For the sum of $900, his interest in __ acres in Byrd Twp, being the plantation where David **PATTERSON** lived at the time of his death, being sd **PATTERSON's** Spanish claim and confirmation. Signed Wm. **NEELY**. Wit J. **RANNEY**, James B. **WILSON**, Wm. **CREATH** (JP). Rec 11 Aug 1820.

1513 Page 394. 25 Jul 1820. Commissioners to Partition Lands of the heirs of Louis **LORIMIER**, decd, to George **HENDERSON**. For the sum of $121, four lots in Cape Girardeau; Lot No. 22, Range E; the N ½ of Lot No. 12 and S ½ of Lot No. 14 in Range D; and Lot No. 18, Range C. Sold as in E:226. Signed B. **COUSIN**, C. G. **ELLIS**, Wm. **KELSO**, W. **GARNER**. Test John C. **HARBISON** (JP). Rec 14 Aug 1820.

1514. Page 395. 27 Jul 1820. Same to same. For the sum of $404, two outlots near Cape Girardeau; 10 acres, being Outlot No. 10 W of Cape Girardeau, bounded on the N by Outlot No. 9, S by Outlot No. 11, W by Outlot No. 27, and E by Outlot Nos. C & F; and 40 acres, more or less, being Outlot No. 41, bounded on the N by Outlot No. 40, S by Outlot No. 42, E by Outlot Nos. 26 & 27, and W by Outlot No. 58. Sold as in E:226. Signed W. **GARNER**, B. **COUSIN**, Wm. **KELSO**, C. G. **ELLIS**. Test John C. **HARBISON** (JP). Rec 14 Aug 1820.

1515. Page 396. 12 Apr 1819. Louis **LORIMIER** and Michael **RODNEY** to Polly **DUNHAM**. For the sum of $3000, bond to make a deed for 284 acres on the S fork of Flora Creek, to be struck off the NW part of a survey of sd **LORIMIER**, totaling 1006 arpens and 32 perches; for the sum of $1060, to be paid as $600 received on this date and $460 to be paid by sd **DUNHAM** and Richard **WALLER** by 15 Apr 1820. The deed to be executed on payment of the last installment. Signed Louis **LORIMIER**, Michl. **RODNEY**. Wit George **HENDERSON**, W. **GARNER**, John **AKIN** (JP). Rec 21 Aug 1820. [Marginal note: Full satisfaction as by the amended bond on 18 Mar 1822. Signed Polly (x) **DUNHAM**. Wit C. S. **THOMAS**, Clerk.]

1516. Page 397. 16 Jun 1820. William **RANDLES** and Jane, his wife, to James **RUSSELL**. For the sum of $225, the NE part of Lot No. 102 on third west and first south streets in Jackson, being where they now live. Signed William **RANDLES**, Jan **RANDLES**. Wit Saml. D. **HUSTON**, Wm. **CREATH** (JP). Rec 21 Aug 1820.

1517. Page 398. 10 Jul 1820. John **RODNEY** and Rachel, his wife, to Joseph **OBANNON**. For the sum of $2550, 300 arpents on the waters of Hubble's Creek, being part of the land granted to Rany **BRUMIT**; adjoined on the E by Joseph **FIGHT**'s heirs and vacant land, N by James **DOWTY**, W by Jonas N. **MENEFEE**, and S by John **McCRACKIN**; beginning at Joseph

FIGHT's NW corner. Signed John **RODNEY**, Rachel (x) **RODNEY**. Wit John **AKIN** (JP), John **DAVIS**, G. N. **OBANNON**. Rec 21 Aug 1820.

1518. Page 400. 14 Jul 1820. John **HALL** and Rebecca, his wife, James **TANNER**, and Andrew P. **GILASPIE**, all of New Madrid Co., Mo. to Jenifer T. **SPRIGG**. For the sum of $2000, New Madrid Certificate No. 373 dated 8 May 1818, in fractional Sec 6, Twp 31 N, Rng 15 E, issued by Frederick **BATES**, Recorder of Land Titles, to Jacob **BOGARD**; not to exceed 400 arpents on any unappropriated land belonging to the U. S. as per the act of 17 Feb 1815 for the relief of sufferers by earthquakes in New Madrid Co. Signed John **HALL**, Rebekah **HALL**, James **TANNER**, Andrew P. **GILLASPIE**. Wit James **RUSSELL**, Mark H. **STALLCUP** as to Rebecca **HALL**, Robert **RAVENSCROFT**, Zenas **PRIEST** (JP). Rec 21 Aug 1820.

1519. Page 401. 18 Jul 1820. Jenifer T. **SPRIGG** to James **RUSSELL**. For the sum of $3000, 400 arpens or 340 28/100 acres on the Mississippi River near Bainbridge, as described in the preceding deed (E:400); located by James **TANNER** and sd **SPRIGG** in the NW fractional ¼, E fractional ½, and part of the E side, SW ¼, Sec 6, Twp 31 N, Rng 15 E. Signed Jenifer T. **SPRIGG**. Wit Nathan **VANHORN**, Robert **ENGLISH**, Zenas **PRIEST** (JP). Rec 21 Aug 1820.

1520. Page 402. 25 Jul 1820. Commissioners to Partition Lands of the heirs of Louis **LORIMIER**, decd, to same. For the sum of $62, three lots in Cape Girardeau; Lot No. 24, Range F, bounded on the W by a street and S by St Belleview; Lot No. 20, Range C, bounded on the W by a street; and Lot No. 16, Range C, bounded on the E by Middle St. Sold as in E:226. Signed W. **GARNER**, B. **COUSIN**, Wm. **KELSO**, C. G. **ELLIS**. Test John C. **HARBISON** (JP). Rec 21 Aug 1820.

1521. Page 404. 26 Jul 1820. Same to Joseph **OBANNON** and James **RUSSELL**. For the sum of $82, four lots in Cape Girardeau; Lot No. 19, Range B; Lot No. 29, Range A; Lot No. 48, Range G; and Lot No. 46, Range H. Sold as in E:226. Signed B. **COUSIN**, Wm. **KELSO**, W. **GARNER**, C. G. **ELLIS**. Test John C. **HARBISON** (JP). Rec 21 Aug 1820.

1522. Page 405. 27 Jul 1820. Same to same and same. For the sum of $17, Lot No. 31, Range H in Cape Girardeau; bounded on the W and fronted by Fountain St, E by an alley, N by Lot No. 32, and S by Lot No. 30. Sold as in E:226. Signed C. G. **ELLIS**, B. **COUSIN**, W. **GARNER**, Wm. **KELSO**. Test John C. **HARBISON** (JP). Rec 21 Aug 1820.

1523. Page 406. 28 Jul 1820. Same to same and same. For the sum of $100, four lots in Cape Girardeau; Lot Nos. 2, Range I, bounded on the W by Gravesend St and E and fronted by the Mississippi River; Lot No. 21, Range I, bounded on the W by Lorimier St; Lot No. 25, Range I, bounded on the W by Fountain St and S by Chas. **HEMPSTEAD**; and Lot No. 11, Range H, bounded on the W by Spanish St. Sold as in E:226. Signed B. **COUSIN**, Wm. **KELSO**, C. G. **ELLIS**. Test John C. **HARBISON** (JP). Rec 21 Aug 1820.

1524. Page 407. 29 Jul 1820. Same to same and same. For the sum of $534, two outlots; __ acres, being Outlot No. I, W of and adjoining Cape Girardeau, bounded on the E and fronted by Pacific St; and 148 acres, more or less, being Outlot No. 54 SW of and adjoining Cape Girardeau, bounded on the E by Outlot No. 53, N by Outlot No. 55, and W by Cape La Cruche Creek. Sold as in E:226. Signed B. **COUSIN**, Wm. **KELSO**, C. G. **ELLIS**. Test George **HENDERSON** (JP). Rec 21 Aug 1820.

1525. Page 408. 24 Jun 1820. William **CLARK**, Governor of Mo. Terr., to Greer W. **DAVIS**. Appointment as Circuit Attorney for the Southern Circuit. Signed Wm. **CLARK**. Greer W. **DAVIS** takes the oath of office. Signed G. W. **DAVIS**. Wit Joseph **McFERRON**, Clerk. Rec 22 Aug 1820.

1526. Page 409. 8 Dec 1802. Daniel O **DUGGAN** to Edward **ROBERSON** of New Madrid. For the sum of 300 piastres due next Christmas in a note, 300 arpents about seven miles W of Cape Girardeau; bordered on the N by Joseph **WALLER** and John **ABERNATHY**, S by Samuel **RANDALL**, son of Enos, W by Enos **RANDALL**, and E by vacant lands of His Majesty; being the same granted to sd **DUGGAN** on 1 Apr 1798 by decree of Zenon **TRUDEAU** Commandant of the Province, and surveyed 20 Apr as recorded by the surveyor's certificate sent 5 May 1798. Sd **DUGGAN** has not yet obtained title, and will transfer it to sd **ROBERSON** or his representatives once it is received. Sd **ROBERSON** is responsible for the costs of dispatching the title and will take care of clearing the land to fulfill the conditions

prescribed in the decree. Daniel **DUGGAN** signed this document after hearing a reading for the seller and buyer in their mother tongue by the interpreter of this Post. Wit Phillippe **ROCHEBLANC**. Signed Daniel **DUGGAN**. Wit Phillippe **ROCHEBLANC**, Hippolite **MAROT**, L. **LORIMIER**. [IN FRENCH] Title is assigned to Medad **RANDOLL** for value received on 1 Jan 1804. Signed Edward (ER) **ROBERSON**. Wit B. **COUSIN**, Jeremiah **THOMSON**, Jno. **ABERNETHIE** (JP). Rec 22 Aug 1820.

1527. Page 411. 25 Jul 1820. Michael **TANEY** to the heirs of Louis **LORIMIER**, decd. For the sum of $17.50, mortgage on Lot No. 20, Range F in Cape Girardeau; bounded on the N and fronted by North St and E and fronted by Middle St. Terms as in E:157. Signed Michl. **TANEY**. Wit William **KELSO** (JP). Rec 23 Aug 1820.

1528. Page 412. 25 Jul 1820. Van B. **DLASHMUTT** to same. For the sum of $29.75, mortgage on two lots in Cape Girardeau; Lot No. 18, Range F, bounded on the E by Middle St; and Lot No. 22, Range F, bounded on the W by a street. Terms as in E:157. Signed Van B. **DLASHMUTT**. Wit William **KELSO** (JP). Rec 23 Aug 1820. [Marginal note: Full satisfaction received on 31 Jul 1823. Signed D. F. **STEINBECK**. Wit C. S. **THOMAS**, Clerk.]

1529. Page 413. 25 Jul 1820. James **RUSSELL** to same. For the sum of $54.25, mortgage on Lot No. 24, Range F; and Lot Nos. 16 & 20, Range C, all in Cape Girardeau. Terms as in E:157. Signed James **RUSSELL**. Wit William **KELSO** (JP). Rec 23 Aug 1820.

1530. Page 414. 25 Jul 1820. George **HENDERSON** to same. For the sum of $105.87 ½; mortgage on Lot No. 22, Range E; the N ½ of Lot No. 12 & S ½ of Lot No. 14, Range D; and Lot No. 18, Range C in Cape Girardeau. Terms as in E:157. Signed George **HENDERSON**. Wit William **KELSO** (JP). Rec 23 Aug 1820.

1531. Page 415. 15 Jul 1820. Alexander **POSEY** to same. For the sum of $28, mortgage on Lot Nos. 20 & 24, Range E in Cape Girardeau. Terms as in E:157. Signed A. **POSEY**. Wit William **KELSO** (JP). Rec 23 Aug 1820.

1532. Page 416. 25 Jul 1820. Nathan **McCARTY** to same. For the sum of $43.75, mortgage on Lot No. 26, Range E in Cape Girardeau; bounded on the N by Lot No. 25, W by a street, W by Harmony St, and E by an alley.

Terms as in E:157. Signed Nathan **McCARTY**. Wit William **KELSO** (JP). Rec 23 Aug 1820.

1533. Page 417. 26 Jul 1820. Thomas **ENGLISH** to same. For the sum of $15.75, mortgage on Lot No. 17, Range B in Cape Girardeau. Terms as in E:157. Signed Thomas (T) **ENGLISH**. Wit William **KELSO** (JP). Rec 23 Aug 1820.

1534. Page 418. 26 Jul 1820. Victor **LORIMIER** to same. For the sum of $49, mortgage on Lot No. 25, Range A; and Lot Nos. 21 & 23, Range B in Cape Girardeau. Terms as in E:157. Signed Victor **LORIMIER**. Wit John C. **HARBISON** (JP). Rec 23 Aug 1820.

1535. Page 419. 26 Jul 1820. Joseph **OBANNON** and James **RUSSELL** to same. For the sum of $71.75, mortgage on Lot No. 19, Range B; Lot No. 29, Range A; Lot No. 48, Range G, and Lot No. 46, Range H in Cape Girardeau. Terms as in E:157. Signed James **RUSSELL**, James **RUSSELL**, attorney in fact for Joseph **OBANNON**. Wit William **KELSO** (JP). Rec 23 Aug 1820.

1536. Page 420. 25 Jul 1820. Joseph **OBANNON** to James **RUSSELL**. Power of attorney to bid off and purchase lots in and near Cape Girardeau, and execute notes or mortgages, jointly with him. Signed Joseph **OBANNON**. Wit J. P. N. **OBANNON** (JP). Rec 23 Aug 1820.

1537. Page 420. 26 Jul 1820. Van B. **DLASHMUTT** to the heirs of Louis **LORIMIER**, decd. For the sum of $389.37 ½; mortgage on five outlots NW of Cape Girardeau, Outlot Nos. 7 & 8, 10 acres each; Outlot Nos. 28 & 29, 20 acres each; Outlot No. 38, of 40 acres; and Lot No. 27, Range A in Cape Girardeau. Terms as in E:157. Signed Van B. **DLASHMUTT**. Wit William **KELSO** (JP). Rec 23 Aug 1820. [Marginal note: Full satisfaction received on 31 Jul 1823. Signed D. F. **STEINBECK**. Wit C. S. **THOMAS**, Clerk.]

1538. Page 421. 26 Jul 1820. John **MAST** to same. For the sum of $10.50, mortgage on Lot No. 33, Range A in Cape Girardeau; bounded on the W and fronted by a street and E by an alley. Terms as in E:157. Signed John **MAST**. Wit William **KELSO** (JP). Rec 23 Aug 1820.

1539. Page 422. 26 Jul 1820. Joseph **ENGLISH** to same. For the sum of $12.25, mortgage on Lot No. 42, Range G in Cape Girardeau; bounded on the E and fronted by Middle St. Terms as in

E:157. Signed Joseph **ENGLISH**. Wit William **KELSO** (JP). Rec 23 Aug 1820.

1540. Page 423. 26 Jul 1820. Alexander **POSEY** to same. For the sum of $54.25, mortgage on two lots in Range G in Cape Girardeau; Lot No. 44, bounded on the E by Middle St; and Lot No. 46, bounded on the W by another street. Terms as in E:157. Signed A. **POSEY**. Wit William **KELSO** (JP). Rec 23 Aug 1820. [Marginal note: Full Satisfaction received of Patrick **CURRAN** on 30 Aug 1851. Signed William W. **GITT**, adminr de bonis non of D. F. **STEINBECK**. Wit Hy. **SANFORD**, Clerk.]

1541. Page 424. 26 Jul 1820. Michael **TANEY** to same. For the sum of $165.37 ½, mortgage on Lot No. 42, Range H in Cape Girardeau, fronting on Middle St; and 40 acres, being Outlot No. 37 NW of sd town. Terms as in E:157. Signed Michl. **TANEY**. Wit William **KELSO** (JP). Rec 23 Aug 1820.

1542. Page 425. 25 Jul 1820. George K. **COOK** to same. For the sum of $16.62 ½, mortgage on Lot No. 44, Range H in Cape Girardeau. Terms as in E:157. Signed Geo. K. **COOK**. Wit William **KELSO** (JP). Rec 23 Aug 1820.

1543. Page 426. 27 Jul 1820. Abner **KENNISON** to same. For the sum of $15.75, mortgage on Lot No. 37, Range H in Cape Girardeau; bounded on the W by Middle St, S by another street, and E by an alley. Terms as in E:157. Signed Abner **KENNISON**. Wit William **KELSO** (JP). Rec 23 Aug 1820.

1544. Page 427. 27 Jul 1820. Robert **GIBONEY** to same. For the sum of $9.62 ½, mortgage on Lot No. 33, Range H in Cape Girardeau; bounded on the N by St of Good Hope, E by Fountain St, and W by an alley. Terms as in E:157. Signed Robert **GIBONEY**. Wit William **KELSO** (JP). Rec 23 Aug 1820.

1545. Page 428. 27 Jul 1820. Joseph **OBANNON** and James **RUSSELL** to same. For the sum of $14.87 ½, mortgage on Lot No. 31, Range H in Cape Girardeau; bounded on the W by Fountain St and E by an alley. Terms as in E:157. Signed James **RUSSELL**. Wit William **KELSO** (JP). Rec 23 Aug 1820.

1546. Page 429. 27 Jul 1820. Simeon **ENGLISH** to same. For the sum of $16.62 ½, mortgage on Lot No. 29, Range H in Cape Girardeau; bounded on the W and fronted by Fountain St and S by another street. Terms as in E:157.

Signed Simeon **ENGLISH**. Wit William **KELSO** (JP). Rec 23 Aug 1820.

1547. Page 430. 27 Jul 1820. Bartholomew **COUSIN** to same. For the sum of $15.75, mortgage on Lot No. 27, Range H in Cape Girardeau; bounded on the E and fronted by Lorimier St. Terms as in E:157. Signed B. **COUSIN**. Wit William **KELSO** (JP). Rec 23 Aug 1820.

1548. Page 431. 27 Jul 1820. George **HENDERSON** to same. For the sum of $353.50, mortgage on two Outlots; 10 acres, being Outlot No. 10, bounded on the N by Lot No. 9, S by Outlot No. 11, W by Outlot No. 27, and E by Outlot Nos. C & F; and 40 acres, being Outlot No. 41, bounded on the N by Outlot No. 40, S by Outlot No. 42, E by Outlot Nos. 26 & 27, and W by Outlot No. 50. Terms as in E:157. Signed George **HENDERSON**. Wit William **KELSO** (JP). Rec 23 Aug 1820.

1549. Page 432. 27 Jul 1820. Jacob **WELSH** to same. For the sum of $74.37 ½, mortgage on 10 acres, being Outlot No. 13 SW of Cape Girardeau. Terms as in E:157. Signed Jacob **WELSH**. Wit William **KELSO** (JP). Rec 23 Aug 1820.

1550. Page 433. 27 Jul 1820. Nathan **McCARTY** to same. For the sum of $237.12 ½, mortgage on 40 acres, more or less, being Outlot No. 39, 3/4 mile NW of Cape Girardeau; bounded on the N by Outlot No. 38, S by Outlot No. 40, W by Outlot No. 60, and E by Outlot Nos. 28 & 29. Terms as in E:157. Signed Nathan **McCARTY**. Wit William **KELSO** (JP). Rec 23 Aug 1820.

1551. Page 434. 27 Jul 1820. Michael **TANEY** to same. For the sum of $446.25, mortgage on about 77 acres, being Outlot No. 59 a mile W of Cape Girardeau; bounded on the E, S, and N by Outlot Nos. 40, 58, & 60. Terms as in E:157. Signed Michl. **TANEY**. Wit William **KELSO** (JP). Rec 23 Aug 1820.

1552. Page 436. 28 Jul 1820. William **HUTCHINSON** to same. For the sum of $14.87 ½, mortgage on Lot No. 21, Range H in Cape Girardeau; bounded on the W and fronted by Lorimier St. Terms as in E:157. Signed Wm. **HUTCHINSON**. Wit William **KELSO** (JP). Rec 23 Aug 1820.

1553. Page 436. 28 Jul 1820. Robert **GIBONEY** to same. For the sum of $63.87 ½, mortgage on three lots in Cape Girardeau; Lot Nos. 15 & 23, Range H, one fronting E on Spanish St, the other fronting W on Lorimier St; and Lot No. 10, Range I, bounded E by Gravesend St and W by Spanish St. Terms as in E:157. Signed Robert **GIBONEY**. Wit William **KELSO** (JP). Rec 23 Aug 1820.

1554. Page 438. 28 Jul 1820. Alexander **POSEY** to same. For the sum of $22.75, mortgage on Lot No. 17, Range H in Cape Girardeau; bounded on the E by Spanish St. Terms as in E:157. Signed A. **POSEY**. Wit William **KELSO** (JP). Rec 23 Aug 1820.

1555. Page 439. 28 Jul 1820. Daniel F. **STEINBECK** to same. For the sum of $26.25, mortgage on Lot No. 14, Range I in Cape Girardeau; bounded on the E by Spanish St and N by another street. Terms as in E:157. Signed D. F. **STEINBECK**. Wit William **KELSO** (JP). Rec 23 Aug 1820.

1556. Page 440. 28 Jul 1820. Nathan **McCARTY** to same. For the sum of $31.40, mortgage on Lot No. 12, Range I in Cape Girardeau; bounded on the E by Gravesend St, W by Spanish St, N by Lot No. 13, and W by Lot No. 11. Terms as in E:157. Signed Nathan **McCARTY**. Wit William **KELSO** (JP). Rec 23 Aug 1820.

1557. Page 441. 28 Jul 1820. Abner **KENNISON** to same. For the sum of $13.12 ½, mortgage on Lot No. 16, Range I in Cape Girardeau, bounded on the E and fronted by Spanish St. Terms as in E:157. Signed Abner **KINNISON**. Wit William **KELSO** (JP). Rec 23 Aug 1820.

1558. Page 442. 28 Jul 1820. Charles G. **ELLIS** to same. For the sum of $67.37 ½, mortgage on three lots in Range I in Cape Girardeau; Lot No. 8, bounded on the E by Gravesend St and W by Spanish St; Lot No. 18, bounded on the E by Spanish St; and Lot No. 19, bounded on the W by Lorimier St. Terms as in E:157. Signed C. G. **ELLIS**. Wit William **KELSO** (JP). Rec 23 Aug 1820.

1559. Page 443. 28 Jul 1820. Joseph **OBANNON** and James **RUSSELL** to same. For the sum of $87.50, mortgage on Lot Nos 2, 21, & 25, Range I, and Lot No. 11, Range H; all in Cape Girardeau. Terms as in E:157. Signed James **RUSSELL**, James **RUSSELL**, attorney in fact for Joseph **OBANNON**. Wit William **KELSO** (JP). Rec 23 Aug 1820.

1560. Page 444. 28 Jul 1820. Thomas **MUNROW** to same. For the sum of $8.75, mortgage on Lot No. 23, Range I in Cape Girardeau; bounded on the N and fronted by a street and E by Lorimier St. Terms as in E:157. Signed Thomas (x) **MUNRAW**. Wit William **KELSO** (JP). Rec 23 Aug 1820.

1561. Page 445. 28 Jul 1820. John **EVANS** to same. For the sum of $9.62 ½, mortgage on Lot No. 27, Range I in Cape Girardeau; bounded on the E by Fountain St and N by another street. Terms as in E:157. Signed John **EVANS**. Wit William **KELSO** (JP). Rec 23 Aug 1820.

1562. Page 446. 28 Jul 1820. Joseph **ENGLISH** to same. For the sum of $44.62 ½, mortgage on Lot No. 7, Range H in Cape Girardeau; bounded on the W and fronted by Spanish St and S by another street. Terms as in E:157. Signed Joseph **ENGLISH**. Wit William **KELSO** (JP). Rec 23 Aug 1820.

1563. Page 447. 28 Jul 1820. Enoch **LARRABEE** to same. For the sum of $8.75, mortgage on Lot No. 29, Range I in Cape Girardeau; bounded on the W by Middle St, E by an alley, N by Lot No. 30, and S by lands formerly of John **RISHER**. Terms as in E:157. Signed Enoch **LARRABEE**. Wit William **KELSO** (JP). Rec 23 Aug 1820.

1564. Page 448. 28 Jul 1820. Samuel **CUTTER** to same. For the sum of $26.25, mortgage on Lot No. 9, Range H in Cape Girardeau; bounded on the W and fronted by Spanish St, E by Lot No. 4, N by Lot No. 10, and S by Lot No. 8. Terms as in E:157. Signed Samuel **CUTTER**. Wit William **KELSO** (JP). Rec 23 Aug 1820.

1565. Page 449. 28 Jul 1820. Thomas W. **GRAVES** to same. For the sum of $59.50, mortgage on Lot No. 5, Range H in Cape Girardeau; bounded on the E by Front or Aquamsi St, W by Lot No. 8, N by Lot No. 4, and S by Lot No. 6. Terms as in E:157. Signed Thomas W. **GRAVES**. Wit William **KELSO** (JP). Rec 23 Aug 1820.

1566. Page 450. 28 Jul 1820. William **GARNER** to same. For the sum of $73.50, mortgage on two lots in Cape Girardeau; Lot No. 31, Range A, bounded on the W by a street and E by an alley; and Lot No. 3, Range H, bounded on the E and fronted by St Aquamsi. Terms as in E:157. Signed W. **GARNER**. Wit William **KELSO** (JP). Rec 23 Aug 1820. [Marginal note: Full

satisfaction received on 31 Jul 1823. Signed D. F. **STEINBECK**. Wit C. S. **THOMAS**, Clerk.]

1567. Page 451. 28 Jul 1820. John **CROSS** to same. For the sum of $113.75, mortgage on Lot No. 1, Range H in Cape Girardeau; bounded on the N and fronted by St of Good Hope, and E by Aquamsi St. Terms as in E:157. Signed John **CROSS**. Wit William **KELSO** (JP). Rec 23 Aug 1820.

1568. Page 452. 29 Jul 1820. Joseph **OBANNON** and James **RUSSELL** to same. For the sum of $467.25, mortgage on two outlots; 3 ¼ acres, being Outlot No. I W of and adjoining Cape Girardeau, bounded on the E by Pacific St and W by a tract formerly owned by Jno. **SCRIPPS**; and 148 acres, being Outlot No. 54 a mile SW of sd town. Terms as in E:157. Signed James **RUSSELL**, James **RUSSELL**, attorney in fact for Joseph **OBANNON**. Wit William **KELSO** (JP). Rec 23 Aug 1820.

1569. Page 453. 29 Jul 1820. Robert **BATES** to same. For the sum of $23.62 ½, mortgage on 3 ¼ acres, being Outlot No. L, SW of Cape Girardeau; bounded on the E by Pacific St, W by Outlot No. 13, N by Outlot No. K, and S by Outlot No. M. Terms as in E:157. Signed Robert (x) **BATES**. Wit William **KELSO** (JP). Rec 23 Aug 1820. [Marginal note: Full satisfaction received of Henry R. **HYNSON** on 28 May 1829. Signed Greer W. **DAVIS**, attorney for Louis **LORIMIER** et al., mortgaged for the use of T. J. **BYRNE**, execr of D. F. **STEINBECK**. Wit Hy. **SANFORD**, Clerk.]

1570. Page 454. 29 Jul 1820. Van B. **DLASHMUTT** to same. For the sum of $1295, mortgage on six outlots S of Cape Girardeau; 10 acres each, being Outlot Nos. 15 & 17 adjoining sd town; 20 acres each, being Outlot Nos. 24 & 26 SW of sd town; and 80 acres each, being Outlot Nos. 50 & 52 S of sd town. Terms as in E:157. Signed Van B. **DLASHMUTT**. Wit William **KELSO** (JP). Rec 23 Aug 1820. [Marginal note: Full satisfaction received on 31 Jul 1823. Signed D. F. **STEINBECK**. Wit C. S. **THOMAS**, Clerk.]

1571. Page 455. 29 Jul 1820. Daniel F. **STEINBECK** to same. For the sum of $458.50, mortgage on three outlots; about 13 acres, being Outlot No. 22 S of Cape Girardeau, bounded on the N by Outlot Nos. 17 & 18, S by Outlot No. 47, E by lands formerly of John **RISHER**, and W by Outlot No. 23; 40 acres, being Outlot No. 46; and 18 acres, being Outlot No. 48, bounded on the N by lands formerly of **RISHER** and E by the Mississippi. Terms as in E:157. Signed D. F. **STEINBECK**. Wit William **KELSO** (JP). Rec 23 Aug 1820.

1572. Page 456. 29 Jul 1820. Thompson **BYRD** to same. For the sum of $212.62 ½, mortgage on 40 acres, being Outlot No. 44 about ½ mile SW of Cape Girardeau; bounded by Outlot Nos. 53, 55, 43, & 45. Terms as in E:157. Signed Thompson **BYRD**. Wit William **KELSO** (JP). Rec 23 Aug 1820. [Marginal note: Full satisfaction received on 31 Jul 1823. Signed D. F. **STEINBECK**. Wit C. S. **THOMAS**.]

1573. Page 457. 29 Jul 1820. John **RODNEY** to same. For the sum of $278.25, mortgage on 78 acres, more or less, being Outlot No. 56, 3/4 mile W of Cape Girardeau; bounded on the E by Outlot No. 43, N by Outlot No. 57, S by Outlot No. 55, and W by heirs of Louis **LORIMIER**, decd. Terms as in E:157. Signed John **RODNEY**. Wit William **KELSO** (JP). Rec 23 Aug 1820. [Marginal note: Full satisfaction received on 11 Sep 1821. Signed Thos. S. **RODNEY**, guardian of Thos. Jefferson **RODNEY** & Polly **RODNEY**, Victor **LORIMIER**. Wit John **JUDEN** Jr, Clerk.]

1574. Page 458. 29 Jul 1820. Enoch **LARRABEE** to same. For the sum of $14, mortgage on almost 2 acres, being Outlot No. 18, S of and adjoining Cape Girardeau; bounded on the N by a street, S by Outlot No. 22, W by Outlot No. 17, and E by Middle St and lands formerly of John **RISHER**. Terms as in E:157. Signed Enoch **LARRABEE**. Wit William **KELSO** (JP). Rec 23 Aug 1820.

1575. Page 459. 28 Jul 1820. Commissioners to Partition Lands of the heirs of Louis **LORIMIER**, decd, to Daniel F. **STEINBECK**. For the sum of $30, Lot No. 14, Range I in Cape Girardeau; bounded on the E and fronted by Spanish St, W by an alley, N by a street, and S by Lot No. 15. Sold as in E:226. Signed Wm. **KELSO**, B. **COUSIN**, C. G. **ELLIS**. Test John C. **HARBISON** (JP). Rec 23 Aug 1820.

1576. Page 462. 29 Jul 1820. Same to same. For the sum of $524, three outlots S of Cape Girardeau; 13 acres, being Outlot No. 22, bounded on the N by Outlot Nos. 17 & 18, S by Outlot No. 47, E by lands formerly of John **RISHER**, and W by Outlot No. 23; 40 acres, being Outlot No. 46, bounded on the E by Outlot No. 47, W by Outlot No. 45, N by Outlot No. 23, and S by Outlot No. 51; and 18 acres, being

Outlot No. 48, bounded on the N by lands formerly of John **RISHER**, S by Outlot No. 49, W by Outlot No. 47, and E by the Mississippi River. Sold as in E:226. Signed B. **COUSIN**, Wm. **KELSO**, C. G. **ELLIS**. Test John C. **HARBISON** (JP). Rec 23 Aug 1820.

1577. Page 463. 28 Jul 1820. Same to Thomas W. **GRAVES**. For the sum of $68, Lot No. 5, Range H in Cape Girardeau; bounded on the E by Front or Aquamsi St, W by Lot No. 8, N by Lot No. 4, and S by Lot No. 6. Sold as in E:226. Signed B. **COUSIN**, Wm. **KELSO**, C. G. **ELLIS**. Test John C. **HARBISON** (JP). Rec 23 Aug 1820.

1578. Page 464. 26 Nov 1819. Same to Jenifer T. **SPRIGG**. For the sum of $895, Lot No. 9, Range D in Cape Girardeau; bounded on the N by Harmony St, S by Themis St, E by Fountain St, and W by Lot No. 10. Sold as in E:226. Signed B. **COUSIN**, W. **GARNER**, Wm. **KELSO**, C. G. **ELLIS**. Test John C. **HARBISON** (JP). Rec 24 Aug 1820.

1579. Page 465. 10 Jan 1820. Charles **HUTCHINGS** to Daniel F. **STEINBECK** and George **JASPERSON**, trading under the firm of **STEINBECK & JASPERSON**. For the sum of $75, Lot No. 6 in Decatur on the bank of the Mississippi River. Signed Chas. **HUTCHINGS**. Wit C. E. **ZOELLER**, Levi L. **LIGHTNER**, George **HENDERSON** (JP). Rec 24 Aug 1820.

1580. Page 466. 13 Jan 1820. Jenifer T. **SPRIGG** to Victor **LORIMIER**. For the sum of $890, Lot No. 9, Range D in Cape Girardeau, as described in E:464. Signed Jenifer T. **SPRIGG**. Wit Nathan **VANHORN**, George **HENDERSON** (JP). Rec 24 Aug 1820.

1581. Page 467. 14 Jan 1820. Victor **LORIMIER** to George **JASPERSON**. For the sum of $60, S ½ of Lot No. 9, Range D in Cape Girardeau, as described in E:464. Signed Victor **LORIMIER**. Wit Jenifer T. **SPRIGG**, George **HENDERSON** (JP). Rec 24 Aug 1820.

1582. Page 468. 22 Nov 1819. Commissioners to Partition Lands of the heirs of Louis **LORIMIER**, decd, to Louis **LAPORTE** of Ste. Genevieve Co., Mo. For the sum of $887, Lot No. 4, Range A in Cape Girardeau; bounded on the N by Merriwether St and W by Spanish St. Sold as in E:226. Signed B. **COUSIN**, W. **GARNER**, C. G. **ELLIS**, Wm. **KELSO**, Benjn. M. **HORRELL**. Test John C. **HARBISON** (JP). Rec 24 Aug 1820.

1583. Page 469. 23 Nov 1819. Same to same. For the sum of $326, Lot No. 23, Range A in Cape Girardeau; bounded on the E by Fountain St and S by Williams St. Sold as in E:226. Signed B. **COUSIN**, Wm. **KELSO**, C. G. **ELLIS**, W. **GARNER**, Benjn. M. **HORRELL**. Test John C. **HARBISON** (JP). Rec 24 Aug 1820.

1584. Page 470. 23 Nov 1819. Same to same. For the sum of $365, the S ½ of Lot No. 6, Range A in Cape Girardeau; bounded on the E by Spanish St and S by Lot No. 19. Sold as in E:226. Signed B. **COUSIN**, W. **GARNER**, C. G. **ELLIS**, Wm. **KELSO**, Benjn. M. **HORRELL**. Test John C. **HARBISON** (JP). Rec 24 Aug 1820.

1585. Page 471. 23 Nov 1819. Same to same. For the sum of $431, the N ½ of Lot No. 8, Range A in Cape Girardeau; bounded on the N by Merriwether St and W by Lorimier St. Sold as in E:226. Signed B. **COUSIN**, Wm. **KELSO**, C. G. **ELLIS**, W. **GARNER**, Benjn. M. **HORRELL**. Test John C. **HARBISON** (JP). Rec 24 Aug 1820.

1586. Page 472. 23 Nov 1819. Same to same. For the sum of $645, Lot No. 19, Range A in Cape Girardeau; bounded on the N by Lot No. 6, S by Williams St, E by Spanish St, and W by an alley. Sold as in E:226. Signed B. **COUSIN**, C. G. **ELLIS**, Wm. **KELSO**, W. **GARNER**, Benjn. M. **HORRELL**. Test John C. **HARBISON** (JP). Rec 24 Aug 1820.

1587. Page 473. 24 Nov 1819. Same to same. For the sum of $295, Lot No. 6, Range B in Cape Girardeau; bounded on the N by Lot No. 5, S by Merriwether St, and E by Spanish St. Sold as in E:226. Signed B. **COUSIN**, W. **GARNER**, Wm. **KELSO**. Test John C. **HARBISON** (JP). Rec 24 Aug 1820.

1588. Page 474. 24 Nov 1819. Same to same. For the sum of $201, Lot No. 24, Range A in Cape Girardeau; bounded on the N by Lot No. 15, S by Williams St, and W by Middle St. Sold as in E:226. Signed Wm. **KELSO**, B. **COUSIN**, W. **GARNER**. Test John C. **HARBISON** (JP). Rec 24 Aug 1820.

1589. Page 476. 24 Nov 1819. Same to same. For the sum of $211, Lot No. 15, Range A in Cape Girardeau; bounded on the N by Lot No. 16, S by Lot No. 24, W by Middle St, and E by an alley. Sold as in E:226. Signed Wm. **KELSO**, B. **COUSIN**, W. **GARNER**, Benjn. M. **HORRELL**. Test John C. **HARBISON** (JP). Rec 24 Aug 1820.

1590. Page 477. 24 Nov 1819. Same to same. For the sum of $200, Lot No. 14, Range A in Cape Girardeau; bounded on the N by Lot No. 13, S by Lot No. 23, E by Fountain St, and W by an alley. Sold as in E:226. Signed B. **COUSIN**, W. **GARNER**, Wm. **KELSO**, C. G. **ELLIS**. Test John C. **HARBISON** (JP). Rec 24 Aug 1820.

1591. Page 478. 24 Nov 1819. Same to same. For the sum of $715, the N ½ of Lot No. 1, Range B in Cape Girardeau; bounded on the N by Independence St, E by Aquamsi or Front St, and W by Lot No. 4. Sold as in E:226. Signed B. **COUSIN**, Wm. **KELSO**, W. **GARNER**. Test John C. **HARBISON** (JP). Rec 24 Aug 1820.

1592. Page 479. 14 Aug 1820. Simeon **KENON** and Elizabeth, his wife, to Simmons **BLOCK** Junr. For the sum of $900, 180 arpens, more or less, including the plantation where sd **BLOCK** and his family now live, and where sd **KENON** formerly lived; adjoining John **HITT** Senr, James **COX** Junr, Joseph **LEWIS**, John **WHITTENBERG**, and Joel **RENFRO**; being the same granted to sd **KENON** by the Spanish Government. Signed Simons ( ) **KINYON**, Elizabeth (x) **KINYON**. Wit Benjn. M. **HORRELL**, Robert **ENGLISH**, Jno. **ABERNETHIE** (JP). Rec 28 Aug 1820.

1593. Page 480. 5 Jul 1820. Commissioners to Partition Lands of the heirs of Louis **LORIMIER**, decd, to Nathan **McCARTY**. For the sum of $50, Lot No. 26, Range E in Cape Girardeau; bounded on the W by a street, S by Harmony St, E by an alley, and N by Lot No. 25. Sold as in E:226. Signed B. **COUSIN**, Wm. **KELSO**, W. **GARNER**, C. G. **ELLIS**. Wit John C. **HARBISON** (JP). Rec 30 Aug 1820.

1594. Page 482. 27 Jul 1820. Same to same. For the sum of $271, 40 acres, being Outlot No. 39, about 3/4 mile NW of Cape Girardeau; bounded on the N by Outlot No. 38, S by Outlot No. 40, W by Outlot No. 60, and E by Outlot Nos. 28 & 29. Sold as in E:226. Signed B. **COUSIN**, W. **GARNER**, Wm. **KELSO**, C. G. **ELLIS**. Wit John C. **HARBISON** (JP). Rec 30 Aug 1820.

1595. Page 483. 28 Jul 1820. Same to same. For the sum of $36, Lot No. 12, Range I in Cape Girardeau; bounded on the E and fronted by Gravesend St, W and fronted by Spanish St, N by Lot No. 13, and S by Lot No. 11. Sold as in E:226. Signed W. **GARNER**, C. G. **ELLIS**, B. **COUSIN**, Wm. **KELSO**. Wit John C. **HARBISON** (JP). Rec 30 Aug 1820.

1596. Page 484. 19 Apr 1819. Matthew **SMITH** to Christian **SEAPOCH**. For the sum of $65, his undivided portion of 65 acres, more or less, on White Water, adjoining widow Elizabeth **BOLLINGER** and Christopher **EDDINNER**; being where Daniel **SLINKERD** now lives. Signed Matthew **SMITH**. Wit Thos. **NEALE** (JP), Jacob **SEETZ**. Polly **SMITH**, wife of Matthew **SMITH**, swears to the deed before John B. **WHEELER** (JP). Rec 30 Aug 1820.

1597. Page 485. 30 May 1820. Christian **SEABOUGH** Sr to David **KINDER**. For the sum of $100, one undivided part of 65 acres, more or less, being the tract belonging to the heirs of Jacob **SLINKARD**, decd; being part of sd tract which fell to Mary **SMITH**, daughter of sd **SLINKARD**, joined on the N by the heirs of Phillip **BOLLINGER**, decd. Signed Christian (C) **SEABOUGH**. Wit Frederick **REEP**, [German signature], John B. **WHEELER** (JP). Rec 30 Aug 1820.

1598. Page 486. 25 Jul 1820. Commissioners to Partition Lands of the heirs of Louis **LORIMIER**, decd, to Alexander **POSEY**. For the sum of $32, two lots in Range E in Cape Girardeau; Lot No. 20, bounded on the E and fronted by Middle St; and Lot No. 24, bounded on the W by a street. Sold as in E:226. Signed B. **COUSIN**, C. G. **ELLIS**, Wm. **KELSO**, W. **GARNER**. Wit John C. **HARBISON** (JP). Rec 1 Sep 1820.

1599. Page 487. 26 Jul 1820. Same to same. For the sum of $62, two lots in Range G in Cape Girardeau; Lot No. 44, bounded on the E and fronted by Middle St; and Lot No. 46, bounded on the W and fronted by a street. Sold as in E:226. Signed B. **COUSIN**, Wm. **KELSO**, W. **GARNER**, C. G. **ELLIS**. Wit John C. **HARBISON** (JP). Rec 1 Sep 1820.

1600. Page 488. 28 Jul 1820. Same to same. For the sum of $26, Lot No. 17, Range H in Cape Girardeau; bounded on the E and fronted by Spanish St, W by an alley, N by Lot No. 16, and S by Lot No. 18. Sold as in E:226. Signed B. **COUSIN**, Wm. **KELSO**, C. G. **ELLIS**, W. **GARNER**. Wit John C. **HARBISON** (JP). Rec 1 Sep 1820.

1601. Page 489. 25 Jul 1820. Same to Michael **TANEY**. For the sum of $20, Lot No. 20, Range F in Cape Girardeau; bounded on the N by North St, W by an alley, S by Lot No. 19, and E by Middle St. Sold as in E:226. Signed B. **COUSIN**, C. G. **ELLIS**, Wm. **KELSO**, W.

GARNER. Wit John C. **HARBISON** (JP). Rec 4 Sep 1820.

1602. Page 490. 26 Jul 1820. Same to same. For the sum of $18, Lot No. 42, Range H in Cape Girardeau; bounded on the N by Lot No. 41, S by Lot No. 43, E and fronted by Middle St, and W by an alley. Sold as in E:226. Signed B. **COUSIN**, W. **GARNER**, Wm. **KELSO**, C. G. **ELLIS**. Wit John C. **HARBISON** (JP). Rec 4 Sep 1820.

1603. Page 491. 26 Jul 1820. Same to same. For the sum of $171, 40 acres, more or less, being Outlot No. 37 NW of Cape Girardeau; bounded on the W by Outlot No. 38, S by Outlot No. 29, and E by Outlot No. 36. Sold as in E:226. Signed B. **COUSIN**, Wm. **KELSO**, W. **GARNER**, C. G. **ELLIS**. Wit John C. **HARBISON** (JP). Rec 4 Sep 1820.

1604. Page 492. 27 Jul 1820. Same to same. For the sum of $510, 77 acres, more or less, being Outlot No. 59 one mile W of Cape Girardeau; bounded on the E by Outlot No. 40, S by Outlot No. 48, N by Outlot No. 60, and W by heirs of Louis **LORIMIER**, decd. Sold as in E:226. Signed B. **COUSIN**, Wm. **KELSO**, W. **GARNER**, C. G. **ELLIS**. Wit John C. **HARBISON** (JP). Rec 4 Sep 1820.

1605. Page 494. 4 Sep 1820. William **GARNER** to Samuel G. **DUNN**. For the sum of $500, 255.90 acres, more or less, on the waters of White Water, being James **MURPHY**'s head right and Survey No. 2239; beginning on the W boundary of Jeremiah **CONAWAY**'s survey under Peter **BELLEW** at a post. Signed W. **GARNER**. Wit Joseph **McFERRON**, Clerk, John **DUNN**. Rec 4 Sept 1820.

1606. Page 495. 31 Aug 1820. Tubal E. **STRANGE** of Jackson to Zenas **PRIEST**. For the sum of $600, the Printing Office of the *Missouri Herald* in Jackson; including one printing press, four fonts of type, cases, stands, gallies, chases, and all the book accounts due to this date, and one walnut desk and table. Signed Tubal E. **STRANGE**. Wit Wm. **CREATH** (JP), Stephen **REMINGTON**. Rec 4 Sep 1820.

1607. Page 495. 8 Apr 1820. Samuel **PUTNAM** to Elijah **RANDOL**. For the sum of $500, mortgage on a preemption right in Cape Girardeau Twp, being the same originally improved by Daniel **STOUT** and sold by sd **RANDOL** to sd **PUTNAM**; bounded on the N by Isaac **WILLIAMS**, and E, W, & S by U. S.

lands. The mortgage is due by 15 Nov next. Signed Saml. **PUTNAM**. Wit S. A. **BIRD**, Wm. **McGUIRE**, Jno. **ABERNETHIE** (JP). Rec 9 Sep 1820.

1608. Page 496. 11 Sep 1820. Heirs of Louis **LORIMIER**, decd, to the inhabitants of Cape Girardeau. For the sum of $1 and diverse good considerations and for the convenience and encouragement of the town of Cape Girardeau, quit claim to several lots; about 4 acres in Ranges C & D, being the lots designated as the Public Square, bounded on the E by Spanish St and W by St of Independence; Lot No. 22, Range C, bounded on the W by a street and S by St of Independence, including a spring; Lot No. 22, Range A, bounded on the W by Fountain St and S by Williams St; all the vacant space between the river Mississippi and the front of Ranges A, B, G, and H, designated as Front St or Aquamsi; all the ground appropriated to streets and alleys in sd town; 100 feet square in Outlot No. 2 adjoining North St so as to afford access to a spring and to include sd spring; 6 acres, part in Outlot No. 2 and part in Outlot No. 32, now used as a graveyard, with the condition that the W ½ remain appropriated to the Roman Catholic Church; and 3 ¼ acres, being Outlot No. H, bounded on the E by Pacific St, W by John **SCRIPPS**, N by Outlot G, and S by Outlot I, including a spring, to be used for a public school. Provided that the land shall be appropriated for public uses, and none shall ever become private property. Signed Louis **LORIMIER**, D. F. **STEINBECK**, Victor **LORIMIER**, Thos. S. **RODNEY**. Wit B. **COUSIN**, William **KELSO** (JP). Rec 12 Sep 1820.

1609. Page 498. 8 Jul 1820. Rucker **TANNER** and Sally, his wife, to Jason **CHAMBERLAIN**. For the sum of $1200, 640 acres near Jackson; beginning at the SW corner of Samuel **PEW**'s survey, and also bounded by Richard S. **THOMAS**' survey under William H. **ASHLEY**, Lewis **TASH**, and Anthony **RANDOL**; being the settlement and improvement right confirmed to Peter **BELLEW** and Polly, his wife, and conveyed by them to sd **TANNER** on 23 Mar 1819. Signed Rucker **TANNER**, Sally **TANNER**. Wit John C. **GRAY**, Andrew P. **GILLASPIE**, Enoch **EVANS**, New Madrid Co. Clerk. Rec 12 Sep 1820.

1610. Page 500. 29 Jul 1820. Commissioners to Partition Lands of the heirs of Louis **LORIMIER**, decd, to John **RODNEY**. For the sum of $318, 78 acres, more or less, being Outlot No. 56 about 3/4 mile W of Cape Girardeau;

bounded on the E by Outlot No. 43, N by Outlot No. 57, S by Outlot No. 55, and W by land of sd heirs. Sold as in E:226. Signed Wm. **KELSO**, B. **COUSIN**, C. G. **ELLIS**. Wit John C. **HARBISON** (JP). Rec 15 Sep 1820.

1611. Page 501. 8 Sep 1817. Thomas S. **RODNEY** and Polly, his wife, to Michael **RODNEY**. For the sum of $210, quit claim to 200 acres on the waters of White Water, on Welches Creek; adjoining Samuel G. **DUNN**, Isaac **DEVORE**, and John **GIBONEY**; being the claim that Thomas S. and Michael **RODNEY** bought of Elijah **WELCH** as sd **WELCH**'s head right. Signed Thomas S. **RODNEY**, Polly (x) **RODNEY**. Wit James **DOWTY**, Isaac **DEVORE**, John **RODNEY**, Zenas **PRIEST** (JP). Rec 16 Sep 1820.

1612. Page 502. 8 Jul 1820. Jacob **WELKER** to Benjamin **WILSON**. For the sum of $200, __ acres, being his improvement and preemption right on the NW ¼, Sec 21, Twp 33 N, Rng 12 E, settled by him before 12 Apr 1814. Signed Jacob **WELKER**. Wit Jason **CHAMBERLAIN**, Eliza **CHAMBERLAIN**, Zenas **PRIEST** (JP). Rec 16 Sep 1820.

1613. Page 503. 5 Nov 1817. John **ROCHE** to Ezekiel **ABLE**. For the sum of $500, 100 acres, about 3 ½ miles above Cape Girardeau on the bank of the Mississippi on both sides of Old Cape Creek, being the same that sd **ROCHE** purchased of Daniel F. **STEINBECK**, and being where sd **ROCHE** now lives. Signed John **ROCHE**. Test George **HENDERSON** (JP). Rec 25 Sep 1820.

1614. Page 504. 2 Jul 1805. William **PAGE** to same. For the sum of $500, 750 arpens, more or less, on the waters of White Water, being his Spanish right, head right, settlement right, and improvement. Signed William (x) **PAGE**. Test Samuel **CAMPBELL**, Jeremiah **ABLE**, Wm. **CREATH** (JP). Rec 25 Sep 1820.

1615. Page 505. 11 Oct 1820. Commissioners to Partition Lands of the heirs of Louis **LORIMIER**, decd, to George **HENDERSON**. For the sum of $213, two outlots W of Cape Girardeau; 3 ¼ acres, being Outlot F, bounded on the W by Outlot No. 10, E by Pacific St; and 40 acres, more or less, being Outlot No. 40, bounded on the N by Outlot No. 39, S by Outlot No. 41, E by Outlot Nos. 27 & 28, and W by Outlot No. 59. Sold as in E:226. Signed B. **COUSIN**, Wm. **KELSO**, W. **GARNER**. Wit John C. **HARBISON** (JP). Rec 13 Oct 1820.

1616. Page 506. 10 Oct 1820. Same to Nathan **McCARTY**. For the sum of $32, Lot No. 11, Range I in Cape Girardeau; bounded on the E and fronted by Gravesend St, W by Spanish St, N by Lot No. 12, and S by Lot No. 10. Sold as in E:226. Signed B. **COUSIN**, W. **GARNER**, Wm. **KELSO**. Wit John C. **HARBISON** (JP). Rec 13 Oct 1820.

1617. Page 507. 11 Oct 1820. Same to William **SURRELL**. For the sum of $60, Square No. 8, Range C, in Cape Girardeau, including Lot Nos. 39, 40, 41, 42, 43, 44, 45, & 46; bounded on the W by Pacific St, E by another street, N by Themis St, and S by Independence St. Sold as in E:226. Signed B. **COUSIN**, Wm. **KELSO**, W. **GARNER**. Wit John C. **HARBISON** (JP). Rec 13 Oct 1820.

1618. Page 508. 11 Oct 1820. Same to same. For the sum of $26, Lot No. 14, Range H in Cape Girardeau; bounded on the E by Spanish St, W by an alley, N by Lot No. 13, and S by Lot No. 15. Sold as in E:226. Signed B. **COUSIN**, Wm. **KELSO**, W. **GARNER**. Wit John C. **HARBISON** (JP). Rec 13 Oct 1820.

1619. Page 509. 18 Jul 1820. Burwell J. **THOMPSON** to Reubin **SMITH**, both of Washington Co., Mo. For the sum of $1280, 640 acres on White Water, being the tract confirmed to Lamuel **HARGROVES**, and conveyed by sd **HARGROVES** to sd **THOMPSON** on 4 Nov 1817. Signed B. J. **THOMPSON**. Wit Danl. **DUNKLIN**, Wm. **FICKLIN**, A. **GRAY**, Judge of Northern Circuit. Rec 16 Oct 1820.

1620. Page 510. 4 Oct 1820. William **VIRGIN** of Tywappity Twp to John **McKAY** of Washington Co., Ky. For the sum of $400, __ acres, being the improvement where he now lives, 9 miles south of Cape Girardeau on the road from Cape Girardeau to New Madrid, together with the right of preemption. Signed William (o) **VIRGIN**. Wit William **KELSO** (JP). Rec 17 Oct 1820.

1621. Page 510. 13 Oct 1820. Commissioners to Partition Lands of the heirs of Louis **LORIMIER**, decd, to Samuel **CUPPLES**. For the sum of $42, 8 acres, more or less, being Outlot No. 12 W of Cape Girardeau; bounded on the N by Outlot No. 11 and land formerly of John **SCRIPPS**, S by Outlot No. 13, E by land formerly of sd **SCRIPPS** and Outlot K, and W by Outlot No. 26. Sold as in E:226. Signed B. **COUSIN**, Wm. **KELSO**, C. G. **ELLIS**. Wit John C. **HARBISON** (JP). Rec 17 Oct 1820.

1622. Page 512. 12 Jun 1820. Sandford **YANSEY** to Joshua **McDONALD** and James **McDONALD**. For the sum of $300, bond to make a deed on the W ½ of Lot No. 125 in Jackson, adjoining George **MORROW**'s lot, if sd grantees shall pay $74 three months from date. Signed Sandford **YANSEY**. Test Erasmus **ELLIS**, Wm. **CREATH** (JP). Rec 20 Oct 1820.

1623. Page 512. 10 Oct 1820. Commissioners to Partition Lands of the heirs of Louis **LORIMIER**, decd, to William **GARNER**. For the sum of $41, Lot No. 10, Range H in Cape Girardeau; bounded on the E by Lot No. 3, W and fronted by Spanish St, N by Lot No. 11, and S by Lot No. 9. Sold as in E:226. Signed B. **COUSIN**, Wm. **KELSO**, C. G. **ELLIS**. Wit John C. **HARBISON** (JP). Rec 21 Oct 1820.

1624. Page 513. 12 Oct 1820. Same to same. For the sum of $82, two blocks in Cape Girardeau; Block No. 8, Range F, bounded on the N by North St, S by St Belleview, E by a street, and W by Pacific St, and containing Lot Nos. 41, 42, 43, 44, 45, 46, 47, & 48 in Range F; and Block No. 8, Range G, bounded on the N by Williams St, S by St of Good Hope, E by a street, and W by Pacific St, and containing Lot Nos. 65, 66, 67, 68, 69, 70, 71, & 72 in Range G. Sold as in E:226. Signed B. **COUSIN**, C. G. **ELLIS**, Wm. **KELSO**, Benja. M. **HORRELL**. Wit John C. **HARBISON** (JP). Rec 21 Oct 1820.

1625. Page 514. 12 Oct 1820. Same to John P. **WRIGHT**. For the sum of $72, Lot Nos. 21, 22, 23, 24, 25, & 26 in Range D in Cape Girardeau, all in Block No. 7; bounded on the N by Harmony St, S by Themis St, and E & W by other streets. Sold as in E:226. Signed B. **COUSIN**, W. **GARNER**, Wm. **KELSO**, C. G. **ELLIS**. Wit John C. **HARBISON** (JP). Rec 21 Oct 1820.

1626. Page 515. 11 Oct 1820. Same to Andrew **GIBONEY**. For the sum of $21, fractional Block No. 8, Range H in Cape Girardeau; bounded on the N by St of Good Hope, S by an alley, W by Pacific St, and E by another street; including Lot Nos. 55, 56, 57, & 58 in Range H. Sold as in E:226. Signed Wm. **KELSO**, B. **COUSIN**, W. **GARNER**. Wit John C. **HARBISON** (JP). Rec 21 Oct 1820.

1627. Page 516. 12 Oct 1820. Same to Raphael V. **LORIMIER**. For the sum of $43, 3 ¼ acres, being Outlot K adjoining and W of Cape Girardeau; bounded on the E and fronted by Pacific St, W by Outlot No. 12, S by Outlot L,

Cape Girardeau Co., Mo. Deed Book E

and N by Outlot I. Sold as in E:226. Signed W. **GARNER**, B. **COUSIN**, Wm. **KELSO**. Wit John C. **HARBISON** (JP). Rec 21 Oct 1820.

1628. Page 518. 11 Oct 1820. Same to Louis **LORIMIER**. For the sum of $1410, 155 acres, more or less, being Outlot No. 60 about a mile NW of Cape Girardeau; bounded on the E by Outlot Nos. 38 & 39, S by Outlot No. 59, and otherwise by the heirs of Louis **LORIMIER**, decd. Sold as in E:226. Signed B. **COUSIN**, Wm. **KELSO**, W. **GARNER**. Wit John C. **HARBISON** (JP). Rec 21 Oct 1820.

1629. Page 519. 13 Oct 1820. Same to Barthelemi **COUSIN**. For the sum of $67, Lot Nos. 45, 46, 47, 48, 49, 50, 51, 52, 53, & 54 in Range A and Block No. 7 in Cape Girardeau; bounded on the N by Merriwether St, S by Williams St, E and W by other streets. Sold as in E:226. Signed W. **GARNER**, C. G. **ELLIS**, Wm. **KELSO**, . Wit John C. **HARBISON** (JP). Rec 21 Oct 1820.

1630. Page 520. 12 Oct 1820. Same to Daniel F. **STEINBECK**. For the sum of $134, two blocks in Cape Girardeau; Block No. 8, Range E, including Lot Nos. 43, 44, 45, 46, 47, 48, 49, & 50; and Block No. 8, Range B, including Lot Nos. 41, 42, 43, 44, 45, 46, 47, & 48; all bounded on the W by Pacific St and E by another street. Sold as in E:226. Signed Wm. **KELSO**, B. **COUSIN**, W. **GARNER**. Wit John C. **HARBISON** (JP). Rec 21 Oct 1820.

1631. Page 521. 13 Oct 1820. Same to same. For the sum of $291, Lot Nos. 33, 34, 35, 36, 37, 38, 39, & 40, Range B, Block No. 7 in Cape Girardeau; and 20 acres, more or less, being Outlot No. 27 W of sd town; bounded on the E by Outlot Nos. 9 & 10, and W by Outlot Nos. 40 & 41. Sold as in E:226. Signed Wm. **KELSO**, B. **COUSIN**, C. G. **ELLIS**. Wit John C. **HARBISON** (JP). Rec 21 Oct 1820.

1632. Page 522. 10 Oct 1820. Same to same. For the sum of $81, Lot No. 6, Range H in Cape Girardeau; bounded on the E by Aquamsi, S by St or Morgan's Oak, W by Lot No. 7, and N by Lot No. 5. Sold as in E:226. Signed B. **COUSIN**, W. **GARNER**, Wm. **KELSO**. Wit John C. **HARBISON** (JP). Rec 21 Oct 1820.

1633. Page 523. 12 Oct 1820. Same to same. For the sum of $653, two outlots S of Cape Girardeau; 20 acres, being Outlot No. 23, bounded on the N by Outlot Nos. 15 & 16, S by Outlot No. 46, W by Outlot No. 24, and E by

Outlot No. 22; and 38 acres, more or less, being Outlot No. 47, bounded on the N by Outlot No. 22 and lands formerly of John **RISHER**, S by Outlot No. 50, W by Outlot No. 46, and E by Outlot No. 48 and lands formerly of sd **RISHER**. Sold as in E:226. Signed B. **COUSIN**, Wm. **KELSO**, W. **GARNER**. Wit John C. **HARBISON** (JP). Rec 21 Oct 1820.

1634. Page 524. 29 Jul 1820. Same to Thompson **BYRD**. For the sum of $243, 40 acres, more or less, being Outlot No. 44, ½ mile SW of Cape Girardeau; bounded on the N by Outlot No. 43, S by Outlot No. 53, E by Outlot No. 45, and W by Outlot No. 55. Sold as in E:226. Signed B. **COUSIN**, Wm. **KELSO**, C. G. **ELLIS**. Wit John C. **HARBISON** (JP). Rec 27 Oct 1820.

1635. Page 525. 10 Oct 1820. Same to same. For the sum of $79, Lot No. 2, Range H in Cape Girardeau; bounded on the E and fronted by Aquamsi or Front St, W by Lot No. 11, S by Lot No. 3, and N by Lot No. 1. Sold as in E:226. Signed B. **COUSIN**, Wm. **KELSO**, W. **GARNER**, C. G. **ELLIS**. Wit John C. **HARBISON** (JP). Rec 27 Oct 1820.

1636. Page 526. 6 Jul 1820. Anthony **BRAVAIS** to Daniel F. **STEINBECK**, Joseph **McFERRON**, Bartholomew **COUSIN**, and John **CROSS**. For the sum of $1000, mortgage on personal property; three copper stills, 60 still tubs, 20 whiskey barrels now remaining in his distillery, one four-wheel waggon, one horse cart, two plows and all the farming utensils, the crop on the plantation where he now lives, all the household and kitchen furniture now in his house, 100 head of hogs, two yoke of oxen, and two horses. Sd **BRAVAIS** is indebted to sd **STEINBECK** for $336, to sd **CROSS** for $184, and sd **COUSIN** for $340; and sd **McFERRON** is his security to William **McGUIRE** for $115; all amounts due by 1 Jun next with interest. Signed A. **BRAVAIS**. Wit Jason **CHAMBERLAIN**, Eliza **CHAMBERLAIN**, Wm. **CREATH** (JP). Rec 30 Oct 1820.

1637. Page 527. 17 Jul 1820. Uriah **BROCK** and Sylva, his wife, to John **BURNS**. For the sum of $25, __ acres on Randoll's Creek; beginning at a stake on the original line, and so as to include the spring; being the same tract granted to Enos **RANDOL** Jur. Signed Uriah **BROCK**, Silvia **BROCK**. Wit John **MASSEY**, John **GILES**, Jno. **ABERNETHIE** (JP. Rec 31 Oct 1820.

1638. Page 528. 22 Jul 1820. John **MASSEY** to same. For the sum of $1200, bond to make a deed to 120 French arpens, being ½ and the N end of a tract granted by the Spanish Government to James **DOWTY** on Randol's Creek; beginning on the boundary of the original survey at a stake. Signed John **MASSEY**. Wit John **DAVIS**, John **GILES**, Wm. **CREATH** (JP). Rec 4 [Nov] 1820.

1639. Page 529. 28 Jul 1820. Commissioners to Partition Lands of the heirs of Louis **LORIMIER**, decd, to John **CROSS**. For the sum of $130, Lot No. 1, Range H in Cape Girardeau; bounded on the N and fronted by St of Good Hope and E and fronted by Front or Aquamsi St. Sold as in E:226. Signed B. **COUSIN**, Wm. **KELSO**, C. G. **ELLIS**. Test John C. **HARBISON** (JP). Rec 4 Nov 1820.

1640. Page 530. 10 Oct 1820. Same to same. For the sum of $70, Lot No. 12, Range H in Cape Girardeau; bounded on the N and fronted by St of Good Hope and W and fronted by Spanish St. Sold as in E:226. Signed B. **COUSIN**, W. **GARNER**, Wm. **KELSO**. Wit John C. **HARBISON** (JP). Rec 4 Nov 1820.

1641. Page 531. 14 Sep 1820. William P. **LACY** and Emily M., his wife, to Joseph **OBANNON**. For the sum of $1400, 213 1/3 acres, more or less, in the Big Bend of the Mississippi River where they now live; being the middle 1/3 of a settlement right of 640 acres confirmed by the U. S. to Jabez **FISHER**, and conveyed by him to Ezekiel **ABLE**, and by sd **ABLE** to sd **LACY** on 18 Apr 1820; beginning at a post on the bank of the Mississippi from which an ash 24 inches diameter; bounded on the S by Samuel **SMILEY**'s part of sd section, N by John **JOHNSTON**'s part, E by the Mississippi, and W by public lands. Signed Wm. P. **LACEY**, Emily M. **LACEY** (RD). Wit Wm. **CREATH** (JP), James **RUSSELL**. Rec 4 Nov 1820.

1642. Page 533. 12 Oct 1820. Commissioners to Partition Lands of the heirs of Louis **LORIMIER**, decd, to Ulysses **MUNN**. For the sum of $41, Block No. 8, Range D in Cape Girardeau; bounded on the W by Pacific St, E by another street, N by Harmony St, and S by Themis St; including Lot Nos. 27, 28, 29, 30, 31, & 32. Sold as in E:226. Signed B. **COUSIN**, Wm. **KELSO**, W. **GARNER**. Test John C. **HARBISON** (JP). Rec 6 Nov 1820.

1643. Page 534. 28 Jul 1820. Same to Enoch **LARRABEE**. For the sum of $10, Lot No. 29, Range I in Cape Girardeau; bounded on the W by Middle St, E by an alley, N by Lot No. 30,

and S by Charles **HEMPSTEAD**. Sold as in E:226. Signed B. **COUSIN**, Wm. **KELSO**, C. G. **ELLIS**. Wit John C. **HARBISON** (JP). Rec 11 Nov 1820.

1644. Page 535. 29 Jul 1820. Same to same. For the sum of $16, 2 acres, more or less, being fractional Outlot No. 18 adjoining and S of Cape Girardeau; bounded on the N by a street, S by Outlot No. 22, W by Outlot No. 17, and E by Middle St and lands formerly of John **RISHER**. Sold as in E:226. Signed B. **COUSIN**, Wm. **KELSO**, C. G. **ELLIS**. Wit John C. **HARBISON** (JP). Rec 11 Nov 1820.

1645. Page 536. 19 Nov 1820. Ignatius **WATHEN** of New Madrid Co., Mo. revokes power of attorney dated Oct 1818 to John **WATERS**, which was issued to sd **WATERS** to act for sd **WATHEN** as an heir of Thomas W. **WATERS**, decd. Signed Igs. **WATHEN**. Wit Greer W. **DAVIS**, Nathl. **CREATH**, Wm. **CREATH** (JP). Rec 13 Nov 1820.

1646. Page 536. 20 Nov 1819. Stephen **STILLEY** and Elezebeth, his wife, of Pope Co., Ill. to William **ROSS** and Jane, his wife. For the sum of $300, __ acres in Tywappity Twp on the Mississippi River; beginning at the NE corner of William **ROSS**'s survey. Signed Stephen **STILLEY**, Elizabeth (x) **STILLEY**. Wit Edward **KEW**, John **BALDWIN**, A. G. **YOUNG**, JP in Gallatin Co., Ill., Wm. **KELSO** (JP). Rec 17 Nov 1820.

1647. Page 537. 18 Apr 1820. Certification that the bearer, the negro **Singleton**, otherwise called Singleton **TYLER**, is free and was born free in Montgomery Co., Md. Sd **TYLER** is about 19 years of age, 5', 8 ¼" high, has three crooked fingers on the right hand, has two scars on the shin of the left leg, also a scar on the left foot just above the little toe, and a high forehead. Signed Upton **PEALE**, Clerk of Montgomery Co., Md. Rec 28 Nov 1820.

1648. Page 538. 17 Nov 1820. Charnel **GLASSCOCK** to Scarlet **GLASSCOCK**. For the sum of $375, mortgage on 75 acres on the waters of Hubble's Creek; bounded on the S by Isaac **WILLIAMS**, E by William **WILLIAMS**, and W and N by John **ABERNETHIE**; being a tract Charnell **GLASSCOCK** purchased of William **WILLIAMS**, and where sd Charnell now lives. The amount is due by 1 Sep 1821 with lawful interest. Signed Charnal **GLASSCOCK**. Test John **GLASSCOCK**, Wm. **CREATH** (JP). Rec 2 Dec 1820. [Marginal note: Full satisfaction received on 22 May 1821. Signed Scarlet **GLASSCOCK**. Wit Cnr. S. **THOMAS**, Deputy Clerk.]

[End of Deed Book E]

[Deed Book F]

1649. Page 1. 10 Oct 1820. John J. **DLASHMUTT** to the heirs of Louis **LORIMIER**, decd. For the sum of $41.12 ½, mortgage on Lot Nos. 27, 28, 31, & 32, Range F in Cape Girardeau. The amount in three promissory notes of even date is due in three equal payments at nine, 18, and 24 months. Signed John J. **DLASHMUTT**. Wit William **KELSO** (JP). Rec 5 Mar 1821. [Marginal note: Full satisfaction received on 29 Nov 1851. Signed W. **GITT**, adminr of D. F. **STEINBECK**. Wit Jacob **TOBLER**, Dep. Clerk.]

1650. Page 1. 10 Oct 1820. Joseph **DORFEVILLE** to same. For the sum of $19.25, mortgage on Lot No. 30, Range E in Cape Girardeau; bounded on the E by a street, W by an alley, N by St Belleview, and S by Lot No. 28. Terms as in F:1. Signed J. **DORFEVILLE**. Wit Wm. **KELSO** (JP). Rec 5 Mar 1821. [Marginal note: Full satisfaction received on 2 Dec 1851. Signed William W. **GITT**, adminr of D. F. **STEINBECK**. Wit Jacob **TOBLER**, Dep. Clerk.]

1651. Page 2. 10 Oct 1820. Andrew **GIBONEY** to same. For the sum of $30.62 ½, mortgage on Lot No. 8, Range H in Cape Girardeau; bounded on the W and fronted by Spanish St. Terms as in F:1. Signed Andrew **GIBONEY**. Wit John C. **HARBISON** (JP). Rec 5 Mar 1821.

1652. Page 2. 10 Oct 1820. Thompson **BIRD** to same. For the sum of $69.12 ½, mortgage on Lot No. 2, Range H in Cape Girardeau; bounded on the E and fronted by Front or Aquamsi St. Terms as in F:1. Signed Thompson **BIRD**. Wit John C. **HARBISON** (JP). Rec 5 Mar 1821.

1653. Page 3. 10 Oct 1820. John **CROSS** to same. For the sum of $61.25, mortgage on Lot No. 12, Range H in Cape Girardeau; bounded on the N and fronted by St of Good Hope, and W and fronted by Spanish St. Terms as in F:1. Signed John **CROSS**. Wit Wm. **KELSO** (JP). Rec 6 Mar 1821.

1654. Page 3. 10 Oct 1820. William **GARNER** to same. For the sum of $35.87 ½, mortgage on

Lot No. 10, Range H in Cape Girardeau; bounded on the E by Lot No. 3, and W and fronted by Spanish St. Terms as in F:1. Signed W. **GARNER**. Wit Wm. **KELSO** (JP). Rec 6 Mar 1821. [Marginal note: full satisfaction received on 31 Jul 1823. Signed D. F. **STEINBECK**. Wit C. S. **THOMAS**, Clerk.]

1655. Page 4. 10 Oct 1820. Robert **BATES** to same. For the sum of $34, mortgage on Lot No. 13, Range I in Cape Girardeau; fronted on the N by St of Morgan's Oak, W by Spanish St, and E by Gravesend St. Terms as in F:1. Signed Robert (x) **BATES**. Wit Wm. **KELSO** (JP). Rec 6 Mar 1821. [Marginal note: Full satisfaction received of Henry **SANFORD** for the mortgagor for $44.75 on 23 Jul 1820. Signed Greer W. **DAVIS**, attorney for the mortgagees.]

1656. Page 4. 10 Oct 1820. Nathan **McCARTY** to same. For the sum of $28, mortgage on Lot No. 11, Range I in Cape Girardeau; fronting on the E by Gravesend St and W by Spanish St. Terms as in F:1. Signed Nathan **McCARTY**. Wit William **KELSO** (JP). Rec 6 Mar 1821.

1657. Page 5. 12 Oct 1820. Robert **GIBONEY** to same. For the sum of $21, mortgage on Lot No. 9, Range I in Cape Girardeau; fronting on the E by Gravesend St and W by Spanish St. Terms as in F:1. Signed Robert **GIBONEY**. Wit Wm. **KELSO** (JP). Rec 6 Mar 1821.

1658. Page 6. 11 Oct 1820. Robert **BATES** to same. For the sum of $42, mortgage on 3 1/3 acres, being Outlot M, adjoining and SW of Cape Girardeau; bounded on the N by Outlot L, S by Outlot No. 15, W by Outlot No. 13, and E by Pacific St. Terms as in F:1. Signed Robert (x) **BATES**. Wit Wm. **KELSO** (JP). Rec 7 Mar 1821.

1659. Page 6. 12 Oct 1820. Raphael V. **LORIMIER** to same. For the sum of $37/62 ½, mortgage on 3 ¼ acres, being Outlot K, W of and adjoining Cape Girardeau; bounded on the E and fronted by Pacific St. Terms as in F:1. Signed R. V. **LORIMIER**. Wit Wm. **KELSO** (JP). Rec 7 Mar 1821.

1660. Page 7. 11 Oct 1820. George **HENDERSON** to same. For the sum of $186.37 ½, mortgage on two outlots W of Cape Girardeau; 3 ¼ acres, being Outlot F, bounded on the E by Pacific St; and 40 acres, being Outlot No. 40. Terms as in F:1. Signed George **HENDERSON**. Wit Wm. **KELSO** (JP). Rec 7 Mar 1821.

1661. Page 7. 11 Oct 1820. Samuel **RAVENSCROFT** to same. For the sum of $34, mortgage on 3 ¼ acres, being Outlot B, adjoining and NW of Cape Girardeau; bounded on the E by Pacific St and W by Outlot No. 8. Terms as in F:1. Signed Samuel **RAVENSCROFT**. Wit Wm. **KELSO** (JP). Rec 7 Mar 1821.

1662. Page 8. 11 Oct 1820. Samuel **CUPPLE** to same. For the sum of $52.50, mortgage on 10 acres, more or less, being Outlot No. 14 SW of Cape Girardeau; bounded on the N by Outlot No. 13 and S by Outlot No. 24. Terms as in F:1. Signed Samuel **CUPPLES**. Wit Wm. **KELSO** (JP). Rec 7 Mar 1821.

1663. Page 8. 12 Oct 1820. William **GARNER** to same. For the sum of $71.74, mortgage on two blocks in Cape Girardeau; Block No. 8, Range F, bounded on the N by North St and S by St Belleview and containing Lot Nos. 41, 42, 43, 44, 45, 46, 47, & 48; and Block No. 8, Range G, bounded on the N by William's St and S by St of Good Hope, containing Lot Nos. 65, 66, 67, 68, 69, 70, 71, & 72. Terms as in F:1. Signed W. **GARNER**. Wit Wm. **KELSO** (JP). Rec 8 Mar 1821. [Marginal note: Full satisfaction received on 31 Jul 1828. Signed D. F. **STEINBECK**. Wit C. S. **THOMAS**, Clerk.]

1664. Page 9. 12 Oct 1820. Ulysses **MUNN** to same. For the sum of $35.87 ½, mortgage on Block No. 8, Range D in Cape Girardeau; bounded on the W by Pacific St, E by another St, N by Harmony St, and S by Themis St; containing Lot Nos. 27, 28, 29, 30, 31, & 32. Terms as in F:1. Signed Ulysses **MUNN**. Wit Wm. **KELSO** (JP). Rec 9 Mar 1821.

1665 Page 10. 11 Oct 1820. William **SURRELL** to same. For the sum of $75.25, mortgage on two parcels in Cape Girardeau; Block No. 6, Range C, containing Lot Nos. 39, 40, 41, 42, 43, 44, 45, & 46; and Lot No. 14, Range H fronting on the E on Spanish St. Terms as in F:1. Signed William **SURRELL**. Wit John C. **HARBISON** (JP). Rec 9 Mar 1821.

1666. Page 10. 12 Oct 1820. Charles G. **ELLIS** to same. For the sum of $145.25, mortgage on Lot Nos. 55, 56, 57, 58, 59, 60, 61, 62, 63, & 64, Range A in Cape Girardeau; and 10 acres, being Outlot No. 16 adjoining Cape Girardeau. Terms as in F:1. Signed C. G. **ELLIS**. Wit Wm. **KELSO** (JP). Rec 9 Mar 1821.

1667. Page 11. 16 Oct 1820. Samuel **CUPPLES** to same. For the sum of $36.75, mortgage on about 8 acres W of Cape Girardeau, being Outlot No. 12; bounded on the N by Outlot No. 11, N & E by land formerly of John **SCRIPPS**, E by Outlot K, S by Outlot No. 13, and W by Outlot No. 26. Terms as in F:1. Signed Saml. **CUPPLES**. Wit John **HARBISON** (JP). Rec 9 Mar 1821.

1668. Page 11. 11 Oct 1820. Andrew **GIBONEY** to same. For the sum of $18.37 ½, mortgage on Lot Nos. 55, 56, 57, & 58, in Range H in Cape Girardeau; in a block bounded on the W by Pacific St, S by another street, N by St of Good Hope, and E by another street. Terms as in F:1. Signed Andrew **GIBONEY**. Wit John C. **HARBISON** (JP). Rec 12 Mar 1821.

1669. Page 12. 12 Oct 1820. William P. **LACEY** to same. For the sum of $56.87 ½, mortgage on part of Block No. 7, Range F in Cape Girardeau; bounded on the N by North St, S by St Belleview, and E & W by two other streets; including Lot Nos. 33, 34, 35, 36, 37, 38, 39 & 40. Terms as in F:1. Signed Wm. P. **LACEY**. Wit Wm. **KELSO** (JP). Rec 12 Mar 1821.

1670. Page 13. 13 Oct 1820. Charles G. **ELLIS** to same. For the sum of $127.75, mortgage on Lot Nos. 35, 36, 37, 38, 39, 40, 41, & 42, Block No. 7, Range E; and Lot Nos. 31, 32, 33, & 34, fractional Block No. 7, Range H; all in Cape Girardeau. Terms as in F:1. Signed C. G. **ELLIS**. Wit Wm. **KELSO** (JP). Rec 12 Mar 1821.

1671. Page 13. 12 Oct 1820. John P. **WRIGHT** to same. For the sum of $63, mortgage on Lot Nos. 21, 22, 23, 24, 25, & 26, Block No. 7, Range D in Cape Girardeau. Terms as in F:1. Signed John P. **WRIGHT**. Wit Wm. **KELSO** (JP). Rec 17 Mar 1821.

1672. Page 14. 13 Oct 1820. Levi L. **LIGHTNER** to same. For the sum of $72.62 ½, mortgage on two blocks in Cape Girardeau; Block No. 7, Range C, including Lot Nos. 31, 32, 33, 34, 35, 36, 37 & 38; and Block No. 7, Range G, including Lot Nos. 57, 58, 59, 60, 61, 62, 63, & 64. Terms as in F:1. Signed Levi L. **LIGHTNER**. Wit Wm. **KELSO** (JP). Rec 19 Mar 1821. [Marginal note: full satisfaction received on 3 May 1821. Signed D. F. **STEINBECK**. Wit John **JUDEN** Jr, Clerk.]

1673. Page 14. 13 Oct 1820. Van B. **DLASHMUTT** to same. For the sum of $175, mortgage on 40 acres, more or less, being Outlot No. 42 W of Cape Girardeau; bounded on the N by Outlot No. 41, S by Outlot No. 43, E by Outlot Nos. 25 & 26, and W by Outlot No. 57. Terms as in F:1. Signed Van B. **DLASHMUTT**. Wit Wm. **KELSO** (JP). Rec 20 Mar 1821.

1674. Page 15. 11 Oct 1820. Thomas S. **RODNEY** to same. For the sum of $41.12 ½, mortgage on 3 ¼ acres, being Outlot D adjoining and W of Cape Girardeau; bounded on the E by Pacific St and W by Outlot No. 9. Terms as in F:1. Signed Thos. S. **RODNEY**. Wit Wm. **KELSO** (JP). Rec 20 Mar 1821. [Marginal note: full satisfaction received on 30 Nov 1821. Signed Victor **LORIMIER**. Wit C. S. **THOMAS**, Dep Clerk.]

1675. Page 16. 11 Oct 1820. Thomas S. **RODNEY** and John **RODNEY** to same. For the sum of $850.50, mortgage on 153 acres in two outlots about a mile W of Cape Girardeau; being Outlot Nos. 57 & 58; bounded on the E by Outlot Nos. 41 & 42, N by Outlot No. 59, and S by Outlot No. 56. Terms as in F:1. Signed Thos. S. **RODNEY**, John **RODNEY**. Wit Wm. **KELSO** (JP). Rec 20 Mar 1821. [Marginal note: Full satisfaction received on 30 Nov 1821. Signed Victor **LORIMIER**. Wit C. S. **THOMAS**, Dep Clerk.]

1676. Page 16. 11 Oct 1820. Thomas S. **RODNEY** to same. For the sum of $62.12 ½, mortgage on about 6 acres, being Outlot No. 11 W of Cape Girardeau; bounded on the E by Outlot G and land formerly of John **SCRIPPS**, W by Outlot No. 26, N by Outlot No. 10, and S by Outlot No. 12. Terms as in F:1. Signed Thos. S. **RODNEY**. Wit Wm. **KELSO** (JP). Rec 20 Mar 1821. [Marginal note: Full satisfaction received on 30 Nov 1821. Signed Victor **LORIMIER**. Wit C. S. **THOMAS**, Dep Clerk.]

1677. Page 17. 13 Oct 1820. Same to same. For the sum of $131.25, mortgage on 10 acres, being Outlot No. 9 W of Cape Girardeau; bounded on the E by Outlot D and W by Outlot No. 27. Terms as in F:1. Signed Thos. S. **RODNEY**. Wit Wm. **KELSO** (JP). Rec 20 Mar 1821. [Marginal note: Full satisfaction received on 30 Nov 1821. Signed Victor **LORIMIER**. Wit C. S. **THOMAS**, Dep Clerk.]

1678. Page 17. 13 Dec 1820. Richard S. **THOMAS**, Judge of Fourth Judicial Circuit, to Joseph **McFERRON**. Appointment as Clerk of Circuit Court for Cape Girardeau Co. Signed R. S. **THOMAS**. Joseph **McFERRON** takes the oath of office. Signed Joseph **McFERRON**. Wit

R. S. **THOMAS**, Judge of Fourth Judicial Circuit. Rec 21 Mar 1821.

1679. Page 18. 14 Dec 1820. Joseph **McFERRON**, Samuel **PEW**, and John **AKIN** to Alexander **McNAIR**, Governor of Mo. For the sum of $3000, bond to discharge the duties of Clerk of the Cape Girardeau Co. Circuit Court. Signed Joseph **McFERRON**, John **AKIN**, Samuel **PEW**. Wit R. S. **THOMAS**, Judge of Fourth Judicial Circuit. Rec 21 Mar 1821.

1680. Page 18. 13 Dec 1820. Commissioners to Partition Lands of the heirs of Louis **LORIMIER**, decd, to John **JUDEN** Junr. For the sum of $190, 153 3/4 acres, more or less, being Outlot No. 74 a mile and a half NW of Cape Girardeau; bounded on the E by Outlot No. 73, S by Outlot No. 60, W by Outlot No. 75, and N by the N boundary of Louis **LORIMIER's** original survey. Sold on order of Circuit Court issued Aug Term 1819, on petition for partition of sd lands. Signed B. **COUSIN**, Wm. **KELSO**, C. G. **ELLIS**. Wit John C. **HARBISON** (JP). Rec 21 Mar 1821.

1681. Page 19. 5 Mar 1820. Christo. G. **HOUTS** of Jackson, attorney in fact for John **HERBERT** & Co., to William **CREATH**. For the sum of $600, ½ of Lot No. 61 in Jackson; bounded on the S and fronted by first north street, W by Lot No. 73, N by Joseph **SEWELL**, and E by the other half of sd lot. Signed Christo. G. **HOUTS**, Attorney in fact for John **HERBERT** & Co. Wit James G. **SEAY** (JP), Chs. **MOTHERSHEAD**. Rec 21 Mar 1821.

1682. Page 19. 16 Nov 1820. Alexander **McNAIR**, Governor of Mo., to George **HENDERSON**. Appointment as JP for Cape Girardeau Twp for four years. Signed A. **McNAIR**. Wit Joshua **BARTON**, Sec. of State. George **HENDERSON** takes the oath of office. Signed George **HENDERSON**. Wit R. S. **THOMAS**, Judge of Fourth Judicial Circuit. Rec 21 Mar 1821.

1683. Page 20. 16 Nov 1820. Alexander **McNAIR**, Governor of Mo., to Barnet **SNIDER**. Appointment as JP for German Twp for four years. Signed A. **McNAIR**. Wit Joshua **BARTON**, Sec. of State. Barnet **SNIDER** takes the oath of office. Signed Barnit **SNIDER**. Wit R. S. **THOMAS**, Judge of Fourth Judicial Circuit. Rec 22 Mar 1821.

1684. Page 20. 14 Dec 1820. Commissioners to Partition Lands of the heirs of Louis

LORIMIER, decd, to George HENDERSON. For the sum of $54, Lot No. 21, Range E; the N ½ of Lot No. 14, Range D; and Lot No. 17, Range C in Cape Girardeau. Sold on order of Circuit Court issued Aug Term 1819, on petition for partition of sd lands. Signed B. COUSIN, C. G. ELLIS, Wm. KELSO. Wit John C. HARBISON (JP). Rec 22 Mar 1821.

1685. Page 21. 16 Dec 1820. Same to same. For the sum of $171, Lot Nos. 22 & 24, Range I; and Lot Nos. 12, 14, 26, & 28, Range G in Cape Girardeau. Sold as in F:20. Signed B. COUSIN, W. GARNER, Wm. KELSO. Wit John C. HARBISON (JP). Rec 22 Mar 1821.

1686. Page 22. 16 Dec 1820. Same to Victor LORIMIER, George HENDERSON, and Nathan McCARTY. For the sum of $380, Lot No. 1, Range G in Cape Girardeau; bounded on the N and fronted by William's St, E and fronted by Aquamsi St, and W by Lot No. 12. Sold as in F:20. Signed B. COUSIN, W. GARNER, Wm. KELSO. Wit John C. HARBISON (JP). Rec 22 Mar 1821.

1687. Page 22. 12 Oct 1820. Same to William P. LACEY. For the sum of $65, Block No. 7, Range F in Cape Girardeau; bounded on the N by North St, S by St Belleview, and E & W by two other streets; including Lot Nos. 33, 34, 35, 36, 37, 38, 39, & 40. Sold as in F:20. Signed B. COUSIN, Wm. KELSO, C. G. ELLIS. Wit John C. HARBISON (JP). Rec 22 Mar 1821.

1688. Page 23. 22 Oct 1820. Samuel SMILEY of Lincoln Co., Mo. to James RUSSELL. For the sum of $450, quit claim to 216 acres, more or less, in the Big Bend of the Mississippi River; being the SW part of a tract of 640 acres confirmed to Jabez FISHER, and conveyed by sd FISHER to Ezekiel ABLE, who sold it to sd SMILEY. Signed Saml. SMILEY. Wit J. B. READ, Wm. CHRISTY Jr., Clerk of Lincoln Co., Mo. Circuit Court. Rec 22 Mar 1821.

1689. Page 24. 21 Jun 1820. Commissioners of the Courthouse and Jail to John SHEPPARD. For the sum of $102, Lot Nos. 31 & 32 in Jackson; bounded on the S by Lot No. 33, W by Lot Nos. 7 & 8, N by Lot No. 30, and E and fronted by first east street. Signed John DAVIS, Samuel G. DUNN, Abraham BYRD, Benja. SHELL. Wit Wm. S. GANTT, Edw. S. GANTT, Joseph McFERRON, Clerk. Rec 23 Mar 1821.

1690. Page 24. 21 Jun 1820. Same to Charles G. ELLIS. For the sum of $165, two lots in Jackson; Lot No. 34, bounded on the E and fronted by first east street, N and fronted by third south street, W by Lot No. 10, and S by a fraction of Lot No. 1; and Lot No. 142, bounded on the B and fronted by third south street, W and fronted by second east street, S by a fraction of Lot No. 143, and E by Lot No. 154. Signed John DAVIS, John SHEPPARD, Samuel G. DUNN, Abraham BYRD, Benja. SHELL. Wit Wm. S. GANTT, Edw. S. GANTT, Joseph McFERRON, Clerk. Rec 23 Mar 1821.

1691. Page 25. 17 Jun 1820. Same to Joel RENTFROE. For the sum of $81, Lot No. 54 in Jackson; bounded on the N and fronted by second south street, W and fronted by first east street, S by Lot No. 45, and E by another lot. Signed John DAVIS, John SHEPPARD, Samuel G. DUNN, Abraham BYRD. Wit N. BUCKNER, Greer W. DAVIS, Joseph McFERRON, Clerk. Rec 23 Mar 1821.

1692. Page 25. 10 Oct 1820. William CRACRAFT to William LITTLEJOHN. For the sum of $200, 38 arpens, more or less, which sd CRACRAFT and Andrew RAMSEY purchased of Elisha WHITE, and which sd RAMSEY conveyed to sd CRACRAFT; being the SW corner of the head right of Lewis LATHAM; bounded by the heirs of Andrew SUMMERS, decd, on the W and John SUMMERS on the S. Signed William CRACRAFT, Elizabeth CRACRAFT. Wit Zenas PRIEST (JP), Stephen REMINGTON. Rec 23 Mar 1821.

1693. Page 26. 14 Dec 1820. Commissioners to Partition Lands of the heirs of Louis LORIMIER, decd, to Nathan McCARTY. For the sum of $13, Lot No. 25, Range E in Cape Girardeau; bounded on the W and fronted by a street, E by an alley, N by Lot No. 24, and S by Lot No. 26. Sold as in F:20. Signed B. COUSIN, C. G. ELLIS, Wm. KELSO. Wit George HENDERSON (JP). Rec 23 Mar 1821.

1694. Page 27. 7 Jun 1820. Commissioners of the Courthouse and Jail to same. For the sum of $39, Lot No. 79 in Jackson; bounded on the S and fronted by second south street, W and fronted by second west street, N by Lot No. 78, and E by Lot No. 67. Signed John DAVIS, John SHEPPARD, Samuel G. DUNN, Abraham BYRD. Wit N. BUCKNER, Greer W. DAVIS, Zenas PRIEST (JP). Rec 24 Mar 1821.

1695. Page 27. 16 Nov 1820. Alexander **McNAIR**, Governor of Mo., to William **KELSO**. Appointment as JP for Tywappity Twp for four years. Signed A. **McNAIR**. Wit Joshua **BARTON**, Sec. of State. William **KELSO** takes the oath of office. Signed William **KELSO**. Wit George **HENDERSON** (JP). Rec 24 Mar 1821.

1696. Page 28. 21 Sep 1820. Medad **RANDOL** to James M. **CROPPER**. For the sum of $435, 139 acres, more or less, on White Water which he purchased of Jenifer T. **SPRIGG**; beginning at a post near the house. Signed Medad **RANDOL**. Wit Tom **MOSELEY** Jr. (JP), W. **GARNER**. Rec 24 Mar 1821.

1697. Page 28. 16 Nov 1820. Alexander **McNAIR**, Governor of Mo., to John **ABERNETHIE**. Appointment as JP for Cape Girardeau Twp for four years. Signed A. **McNAIR**. Wit Joshua **BARTON**, Sec. of State. John **ABERNETHIE** takes the oath of office. Signed Jno. **ABERNETHIE**. Wit George **HENDERSON** (JP). Rec 24 Mar 1821.

1698. Page 29. 18 Dec 1820. William **SUBLETT** to Isaac **BAILEY**, John **ALLOWAY**, and Nathiel **BAILEY**, merchants. For the sum of $3000, mortgage on **Milly**, **Saley**, **Tom**, **Daniel**, **Charles**, **Anthony**, **Moses**, and **George**, all negro slaves; also 12 feather beads & furniture, four beaurows, one side board, three dining tables, one breakfast table, 2 round tables, 4 sets of knives & forks, 1 dozen silver spoons, 2 dozen tea spoons, 4 dozen chenia plates, 5 dozen earthen plates & set of chenia, 2 dozen chenia cups & saucers, 1 press, 1 desk, 1 dozen split bottom chairs, 2 do winsor chairs, 10 common beadsteds, 2 castor beadsteds & furniture, 3 dozen tumblers, 6 pitchers, one dozen of dishes, 2 looking glasses, 2 trabords, three teapots, 6 pair of five irons, 3 coffe pots, 3 pots, one large kettle, 5 ovens & lids, 1 brass kettle, 1 baking oven, 1 tin roster, and one wagon & five horses & harness belonging to sd wagon. The debt is due by 1 Sep next, and the property is to stay in the possession of sd **SUBLETT** until then. Signed William **SUBLETT**. Wit A. **BUCKNER**, Thos. S. **SUBLETT**, Joseph **McFERRON**, Clerk. Rec 24 Mar 1821.

1699. Page 29. 15 Jul 1820. John **BEST** and Catharine, his wife, to Daniel **SLINKARD**. For the sum of $133.50, one undivided 1/7 part of __ acres on the waters of White Water, being a tract confirmed to Jacob **SLINKARD**; adjoining the heirs of Philip **BOLLINGER**, decd, and Christopher **EDINGER**. Signed John ( ) **BEST**,

Catharine (x) **BEST**. Wit Zenas **PRIEST** (JP), T. E. **STRANGE**. Rec 24 Mar 1821.

1700. Page 30. 16 Nov 1820. Alexander **McNAIR**, Governor of Mo., to David **ARMOUR**. Appointment as JP for Byrd Twp for four years. Signed A. **McNAIR**. Wit Joshua **BARTON**, Sec. of State. David **ARMOUR** takes the oath of office. Signed David **ARMOUR**. Wit George **HENDERSON** (JP). Rec 24 Mar 1821.

1701. Page 30. 13 Dec 1820. Commissioners to Partition Lands of the heirs of Louis **LORIMIER**, decd, to Maria J. **CROSS**. For the sum of $1226, 888 acres, more or less, in 9 outlots near Cape Girardeau; being Outlot Nos. 53 & 69, 80 acres each, Outlot Nos. 61, 71, 72, & 73, 157 acres each, Outlot Nos. 43 & 45, 50 acres each, and Outlot No. 25, 20 acres. Sold as in F:20. Signed B. **COUSIN**, C. G. **ELLIS**, Wm. **KELSO**. Test John C. **HARBISON** (JP). Rec 24 Mar 1821.

1702. Page 31. 16 Nov 1820. Alexander **McNAIR**, Governor of Mo., to Johnson **STRONG**. Appointment as JP for Tywappity Twp for four years. Signed A. **McNAIR**. Wit Joshua **BARTON**, Sec. of State. Johnson **STRONG** takes the oath of office. Signed Johnson **STRONG**. Wit David **ARMOUR** (JP). Rec 26 Mar 1821.

1703. Page 31. 16 Nov 1820. Alexander **McNAIR**, Governor of Mo., to William **JOHNSON**. Appointment as JP for German Twp for four years. Signed A. **McNAIR**. Wit Joshua **BARTON**, Sec. of State. William **JOHNSON** takes the oath of office. Signed William **JOHNSON**. Wit David **ARMOUR** (JP). Rec 26 Mar 1821.

1704. Page 32. 16 Nov 1820. Same to John **AKIN**. Appointment as JP for Byrd Twp for four years. Signed A. **McNAIR**. Wit Joshua **BARTON**, Sec. of State. John **AKIN** takes the oath of office. Signed John **AKIN**. Wit David **ARMOUR** (JP). Rec 26 Mar 1821.

1705. Page 32. 30 Dec 1820. Thomas **MORGAN**, Robert **ENGLISH**, John **RANDOL** junior, and Erasmus **ELLIS** to Alexander **McNAIR**, Governor of Mo. For the sum of $6000, bond to guarantee that sd **MORGAN** shall perform the duties of Coroner of Cape Girardeau Co. Signed Thos. **MORGAN**, John **RANDOL** Ju, Robert **ENGLISH**, Erasmus **ELLIS**. Wit R. S.

THOMAS, Judge of Fourth Judicial Circuit. Rec 26 Mar 1821.

1706. Page 32. 29 Dec 1820. Thomas W. **THRUSTON** to Charles S. **HEMPSTEAD**, both of St. Louis, St. Louis Co., Mo. For the sum of $400, mortgage on 330 acres on White water, being the same conveyed by Ezekiel **ABLE** to William **MILLBURN** and William **GORDON** on 11 Feb 1818 (D:164), and sold by sd **GORDON** to sd **THRUSTON**. Sd **THRUSTON** owes $350 plus interest to John **EWING**, merchant of Vincennes, assignee of John **MYERS**, who was assignee of James **NABB**, in a note dated 7 Nov 1818 and due by 7 Apr next; the amount is to be paid to sd **HEMPSTEAD** as attorney for sd **EWING**, or the land is to be sold to pay the debt. Signed Tho. W. **THRUSTON**. Wit Sam. P. **JONES**, William **HEMPSTEAD**, Archibald **GAMBLE**, Clerk of St. Louis Co. Court, by Ewel **BAKER**, Dep Clerk. Rec 26 Mar 1821.

1707. Page 33. 16 Nov 1820. Alexander **McNAIR**, Governor of Mo., to William **CREATH**. Appointment as JP for Byrd Twp for four years. Signed A. **McNAIR**. Wit Joshua **BARTON**, Sec. of State. William **CREATH** takes the oath of office. Signed Wm. **CREATH**. Wit David **ARMOUR** (JP). Rec 26 Mar 1821.

1708. Page 34. 16 Nov 1820. Same to John B. **WHEELER**. Appointment as JP for German Twp for four years. Signed A. **McNAIR**. Wit Joshua **BARTON**, Sec. of State. John B. **WHEELER** takes the oath of office. Signed John B. **WHEELER**. Wit David **ARMOUR** (JP). Rec 26 Mar 1821.

1709. Page 33. 17 Nov 1820. Same to John **HAYS**. Appointment as Sheriff of Cape Girardeau Co. for two years, his having been duly elected. Signed A. **McNAIR**. Wit Joshua **BARTON**, Sec. of State. John **HAYS** takes the oath of office. Signed John **HAYS**. Wit R. S. **THOMAS**, Judge of Fourth Judicial Circuit. Rec 27 Mar 1821.

1710. Page 35. 11 Jan 1821. John **HAYS**, John **BROWN**, and John **WHITTENBURG** to Alexander **McNAIR**, Governor of Mo. For the sum of $10,000, bond to guarantee that sd **HAYS** will perform the duties of Sheriff of Cape Girardeau Co. Signed John **HAYS**, John **BROWN**, John **WHITTENBURG**. Wit Wm. S. **GANTT**, R. S. **THOMAS**, Judge of Fourth Judicial Circuit. Rec 27 Mar 1821.

1711. Page 35. 13 Dec 1820. Alexander **McNAIR**, Governor of Mo., to Joseph **McFERRON**. Appointment as Clerk of the Supreme Court for the Fourth Judicial Circuit. Signed A. **McNAIR**. Wit Joshua **BARTON**, Sec. of State. Joseph **McFERRON** takes the oath of office. Signed Joseph **McFERRON**. Wit R. S. **THOMAS**, Judge of Fourth Judicial Circuit. Rec 27 Mar 1821.

1712. Page 35. 10 Oct 1820. Commissioners to Partition Lands of the heirs of Louis **LORIMIER**, decd, to John J. **DLASHMUTT**. For the sum of $47, four lots in Range F in Cape Girardeau; Lot Nos. 27 & 28, bounded on the E by a street and W by an alley, Lot No. 28 fronting on North St; and Lot Nos. 31 & 32, bounded on the W by a street and E by an alley, Lot No. 32 fronting on St Belleview on the S. Sold as in F:20. Signed B. **COUSIN**, W. **GARNER**, Wm. **KELSO**. Test John C. **HARBISON** (JP). Rec 27 Mar 1821.

1713. Page 36. 27 Jul 1820. Same to Jacob **WELSH**. For the sum of $85, 10 acres, more or less, SW of Cape Girardeau, being Outlot No. 13; bounded on the N by Outlot No. 12, W by Outlot No. 26, S by Outlot No. 14, and E by Outlot Nos. L & M. Sold as in F:20. Signed B. **COUSIN**, Wm. **KELSO**, C. G. **ELLIS**. Test John C. **HARBISON** (JP). Rec 27 Mar 1821.

1714. Page 37. 5 Aug 1820. Jacob **WELTCH** to John J. **DELASHMUTT**. For the sum of $90, 10 acres, more or less, being Outlot No. 13 as described in the preceding deed (F:36). Signed Jacob **WELCH**. Wit Zenas **PRIEST** (JP). Rec 27 Mar 1821.

1715. Page 37. 22 Jan 1821. John J. **DLASHMUTT** of Jackson to Lyne **STARLING** and Elias N. **DLASHMUTT**, trading as **STARLING & DLASHMUTT**. For the sum of $85, 10 acres, being Outlot No. 13 as described in F:36. Signed John J. **DLASHMUTT**. Wit David **ARMOUR** (JP). Rec 28 Mar 1821.

1716. Page 38. 13 Dec 1820. Alexander **McNAIR**, Governor of Mo., to William **TINNIN**. Appointment as JP for German Twp for four years. Signed A. **McNAIR**. Wit Joshua **BARTON**, Sec. of State. William **TINNIN** takes the oath of office. Signed William **TINNIN**. Wit R. S. **THOMAS**, Judge of Fourth Judicial Circuit. Rec 28 Mar 1821.

1717. Page 38. 23 Dec 1820. Commissioners to Partition Lands of the heirs of Louis **LORIMIER**, decd, to Victor **LORIMIER**. For the sum of $1640, 301 acres, more or less, being Outlot Nos. 76 & 77 about two miles NW of Cape Girardeau; bounded on the E by Outlot No. 75, W by Outlot No. 78a, S by Outlot Nos. 79 & 80, and N by the N boundary of Louis **LORIMIER**'s Spanish Grant. Sold as in F:20. Signed B. **COUSIN**, Wm. **KELSO**, W. **GARNER**. Test George **HENDERSON** (JP). Rec 28 Mar 1821.

1718. Page 39. 23 Dec 1820. Same to Louis **LORIMIER**. For the sum of $650, 160 acres, more or less, W of Cape Girardeau, being Outlot No. 80; bounded on the E by Outlot No. 60, S by Outlot No. 81, W by Outlot No. 79, N by Outlot Nos. 75 & 76. Sold as in F:20. Signed B. **COUSIN**, Wm. **KELSO**, W. **GARNER**. Test George **HENDERSON** (JP). Rec 28 Mar 1821.

1719. Page 40. 16 Dec 1820. Same to same, acting in behalf of William **LORIMIER** Junr. For the sum of $660, 146 acres, more or less, being Outlot No. 86; bounded on the E by Outlot No. 54, S by the S boundary of L. **LORIMIER**'s Spanish Grant, W by Outlot No. 85, and N by the heirs of M. Louisa **RODNEY**, decd. Sold as in F:20. Signed B. **COUSIN**, Wm. **KELSO**, W. **GARNER**. Wit George **HENDERSON** (JP). Rec 29 Mar 1821.

1720. Page 41. 14 Dec 1820. Same to Barthelemi **COUSIN**. For the sum of $145, Block Nos. 6 in Ranges A, B, G, & H in Cape Girardeau; containing Lot Nos. 35, 36, 37, 38, 39, 40, 41, 42, 43, & 44 in Range A, Lot Nos. 25, 26, 27, 28, 29, 30, 31, & 32 in Range B, Lot Nos. 49, 50, 51, 52, 53, 54, 55, & 56 in Range G, and Lot Nos. 47, 48, 49, & 50 in Range H. Sold as in F:20. Signed W. **GARNER**, C. G. **ELLIS**, Wm. **KELSO**. Wit John C. **HARBISON** (JP). Rec 29 Mar 1821.

1721. Page 41. 15 Dec 1820. Same to same. For the sum of $50, Lot No. 4, Range H in Cape Girardeau; bounded on the E and fronted by Front or Aquamsi St, W by Lot No. 9, N by Lot No. 3, and S by Lot No. 5. Sold as in F:20. Signed Wm. **KELSO**, C. G. **ELLIS**, W. **GARNER**. Wit John C. **HARBISON** (JP). Rec 29 Mar 1821.

1722. Page 42. 15 Dec 1820. Same to same. For the sum of $125, Lot No. 24, Range B; Lot Nos. 45, 41, 34, 30, 28, & 26, Range H; and Lot Nos. 16, 18, 20, 22, & 24, Range H; all in Cape Girardeau. Sold as in F:20. Signed Wm. **KELSO**, C. G. **ELLIS**, W. **GARNER**. Wit John C. **HARBISON** (JP). Rec 29 Mar 1821.

1723. Page 43. 13 Dec 1820. Same to Valentine **MILLER**. For the sum of $330, 80 acres, more or less, about 3/4 of a mile S of Cape Girardeau, being Outlot No. 51; bounded on the E by Outlot No. 50, S by Outlot No. 63, W by Outlot No. 52, and N by Outlot No. 46. Sold as in F:20. Signed B. **COUSIN**, Wm. **KELSO**, C. G. **ELLIS**. Wit John C. **HARBISON** (JP). Rec 30 Mar 1821.

1724. Page 43. 15 Dec 1820. Same to same. For the sum of $23, two lots in Cape Girardeau; Lot No. 18, Range B, fronting on the E by Middle St; and Lot No. 32, Range A, fronting on the W on a street. Sold as in F:20. Signed B. **COUSIN**, Wm. **KELSO**, C. G. **ELLIS**. Wit John C. **HARBISON** (JP). Rec 30 Mar 1821.

1725. Page 44. 16 Dec 1820. Same to William **GARNER**. For the sum of $130, Lot Nos. 5 & 8, Range G in Cape Girardeau; bounded on the E and fronted by Front or Aquamsi St, W by Spanish St, S by Lot No. 6 & 7, and N by Lot Nos. 4 & 9. Sold as in F:20. Signed B. **COUSIN**, Wm. **KELSO**, C. G. **ELLIS**. Wit John C. **HARBISON** (JP). Rec 30 Mar 1821.

1726. Page 45. 15 Dec 1820. Same to William **HUTCHINSON**. For the sum of $78, five lots in Cape Girardeau; Lot No. 30, Range A; Lot No. 22, Range B; Lot No. 41, Range G; and Lot Nos. 40 & 36, Range H. Sold as in F:20. Signed B. **COUSIN**, Wm. **KELSO**, Wm. **KELSO**. Wit John C. **HARBISON** (JP). Rec 31 Mar 1821.

1727. Page 45. 26 Nov 1819. Same to Levi L. **LIGHTNER**. For the sum of $720, Lot No. 6, Range E in Cape Girardeau; bounded on the N by St Bellevue, S by Lot No. 5, E by German St, and W by Spanish St. Sold as in F:20. Signed B. **COUSIN**, C. G. **ELLIS**, Wm. **KELSO**. Wit John C. **HARBISON** (JP). Rec 27 Apr 1821.

1728. Page 46. 16 Dec 1820. Same to same. For the sum of $36, Lot No. 18, Range G in Cape Girardeau; bounded on the E by Spanish St, W by an alley, S and fronted by St of Good Hope, and N by Lot No. 11. Sold as in F:20. Signed B. **COUSIN**, Wm. **KELSO**, W. **GARNER**, C. G. **ELLIS**. Wit John C. **HARBISON** (JP). Rec 27 Apr 1821.

1729. Page 46. 13 Oct 1820. Same to same. For the sum of $83, town lots in Cape Girardeau; being Lot Nos. 31, 32, 33, 34, 35, 36, 37, & 38 in Range C, Block No. 7; and Lot Nos. 57, 58, 59, 60, 61, 62, 63, & 64 in Range G, being Block No. 7. Sold as in F:20. Signed B. **COUSIN**, Wm. **KELSO**, C. G. **ELLIS**, . Wit John C. **HARBISON** (JP). Rec 27 Apr 1821.

1730. Page 47. 16 Dec 1820. Same to Barthelemi **COUSIN**. For the sum of $550, town lots in Cape Girardeau; Lot No. 28 in Range A; Lot Nos. 1, 3, 4, 5, 15, 26, 28, & 30 in Range I; and Lot Nos. 3, 10, 16, 20, 22, 24, 30, 32, 34, 36, 38, & 40 in Range G. Sold as in F:20. Signed W. **GARNER**, Benjn. M. **HORRELL**, Wm. **KELSO**, C. G. **ELLIS**. Wit John C. **HARBISON** (JP). Rec 27 Apr 1821.

1731. Page 48. 23 Dec 1820. Same to Daniel F. **STEINBECK**. For the sum of $36, 8 acres, more or less, N of Cape Girardeau, being Outlot No. 32; bounded on the E by the River Mississippi, S by public ground intended for a boat yard, W by Outlot No. 32, and N by Outlot No. 33. Sold as in F:20. Signed B. **COUSIN**, Wm. **KELSO**, W. **GARNER**. Wit George **HENDERSON** (JP). Rec 28 Apr 1821.

1732. Page 48. 23 Dec 1820. Same to same. For the sum of $2535, five outlots within 2 ½ miles W and NW of Cape Girardeau; about 152 acres, being Outlot No. 75; about 155 acres, being Outlot No. 78a; about 116 acres, being Outlot No. 78b; about 160 acres, being Outlot No. 82; and 116 acres, more or less, being Outlot No. 83. Sold as in F:20. Signed B. **COUSIN**, Wm. **KELSO**, W. **GARNER**. Wit George **HENDERSON** (JP). Rec 28 Apr 1821.

1733. Page 49. 6 Jan 1820. Charles **HUTCHINGS** of Madison Co., Mo. to Levi L. **LIGHTNER**. For the sum of $75, Lot No. 21 in Decatur on the bank of the Mississippi River. Signed Chas. **HUTCHINGS**. Wit Jenifer T. **SPRIGG**, Geo. **JASPERSEN**, George **HENDERSON** (JP). Rec 28 Apr 1821.

1734. Page 49. 16 Dec 1820. Commissioners to Partition Lands of the heirs of Louis **LORIMIER**, decd, to Daniel F. **STEINBECK**. For the sum of $14, Lot No. 21, Range C in Cape Girardeau; bounded on the W by a street and S by public Lot No. 22 (supposed to contain a spring, which is to remain accessible to the public if it is in Lot No. 21). Sold as in F:20. Signed B. **COUSIN**, Wm. **KELSO**, W. **GARNER**, C. G. **ELLIS**. Wit John C. **HARBISON** (JP). Rec 28 Apr 1821.

1735. Page 50. 13 Dec 1820. Same to same. For the sum of $780, 466 acres, more or less, in 5 outlots near Cape Girardeau; 68, 82, and 120 acres, respectively, being Outlot Nos. 49, 64, & 65, fronting on the Mississippi River; and 116 and 80 acres, respectively, being Outlot Nos. 62 & 55 on Cape la Cruche Creek. Sold as in F:20. Signed B. **COUSIN**, C. G. **ELLIS**, Wm. **KELSO**. Wit John C. **HARBISON** (JP). Rec 28 Apr 1821.

1736. Page 51. 15 Dec 1820. Same to same. For the sum of $77, seven lots in Cape Girardeau; Lot No. 34, Range A; Lot No. 20, Range B; Lot Nos. 17, 19, & 21, Range F; and Lot Nos. 32 & 43, Range H. Sold as in F:20. Signed B. **COUSIN**, Wm. **KELSO**, C. G. **ELLIS**. Wit John C. **HARBISON** (JP). Rec 30 Apr 1821.

1737. Page 51. 12 Dec 1820. Robert **SMITH** to the heirs of Louis **LORIMIER**. For the sum of $206.50, mortgage on town lots in Cape Girardeau; Lot Nos. 29 & 30, Range F; Lot Nos. 27, 28, 31, 32, 33, & 34, Range E; Lot Nos. 15, 16, 17, 18, 19 & 20, Range D. Terms as in F:1. Signed R. **SMITH** Senr. Wit Wm. **KELSO** (JP). Rec 30 Apr 1821. [Marginal note: Full satisfaction received on 19 May 1852. Signed William W. **GITT**, adminr of D. F. **STEINBECK**. Wit Hy. **SANFORD**, Clerk.]

1738. Page 52. 12 Dec 1820. Nathaniel W. **WATKINS** to same. For the sum of $18, mortgage on Lot Nos. 25 & 26, Range F in Cape Girardeau; bounded on the E by a street, W by an alley, and S by St Belleview. Terms as in F:1. Signed Nathl. W. **WATKINS**. Wit Wm. **KELSO** (JP). Rec 30 Apr 1821.

1739. Page 53. 13 Dec 1820. Maria J. **CROSS** to same. For the sum of $1072.75, mortgage on nine outlots near Cape Girardeau; Outlot No. 69 containing 80 acres; Outlot No. 71, 158 ¼ acres; Outlot No. 72, 156 3/4 acres; Outlot No. 73, 155 ¼ acres; Outlot No. 61, 157 ½ acres; Outlot No. 53, 80 acres; Outlot No. 43 & 45, 40 acres each; and Outlot No. 25, 20 acres. Terms as in F:1. Signed Maria J. **CROSS**. Wit John C. **HARBISON** (JP). Rec 30 Apr 1821.

1740. Page 53. 13 Dec 1820. Voluntine **MILLER** to same. For the sum of $288, mortgage on 80 acres S of Cape Girardeau, being Outlot No. 51. Terms as in F:1. Signed Vallnntin **MULLER**. Wit William **KELSO** (JP). Rec 30 Apr 1821.

1741. Page 54. 13 Dec 1820. John **JUDEN** Junior to same. For the sum of $166.25, mortgage on 153 3/4 acres a mile and a half NW of Cape Girardeau, being Outlot No. 74. Terms as in F:1. Signed John **JUDEN** Jr.. Wit William **KELSO** (JP). Rec 1 May 1821.

1742. Page 54. 14 Dec 1820. Thomas **MILLIS** to same. For the sum of $65.62 ½, mortgage on eight town lots in Cape Girardeau; being Block No. 6 in Range C, including Lot Nos. 23, 24, 25, 26, 27, 28, 29, & 30. Terms as in F:1. Signed Thos. **MILLES**. Wit William **KELSO** (JP). Rec 1 May 1821. [Marginal note: Full satisfaction received on 13 Jan 1858. Signed J. R. **WATHEN**, adminr of Daniel F. **STEINBECK**, decd. Wit Hy. **SANFORD**.]

1743. Page 55. 14 Dec 1820. George **JASPERSON** to same. For the sum of $7.87 ½, mortgage on Lot No. 23, Range F in Cape Girardeau. Terms as in F:1. Signed Geo. **JASPERSEN**. Wit William **KELSO** (JP). Rec 1 May 1821.

1744. Page 55. 14 Dec 1820. Thomas S. **RODNEY** to same. For the sum of $48.12 ½, mortgage on Lot Nos. 19 & 23, Range E in Cape Girardeau; being the SE and NW corners of Block No. 6. Terms as in F:1. Signed Thos. S. **RODNEY**. Wit William **KELSO** (JP). Rec 1 May 1821. [Marginal note: Full satisfaction received on 3 Nov 1821. Signed Victor **LORIMIER**. Wit C. S. **THOMAS**, Dep Clerk.]

1745. Page 56. 14 Dec 1820. George **HENDERSON** to same. For the sum of $47.25, mortgage on Lot No. 21, Range E; Lot No. 14, Range D; and Lot No. 17, Range C in Cape Girardeau. Terms as in F:1. Signed George **HENDERSON**. Wit William **KELSO** (JP). Rec 1 May 1821.

1746. Page 56. 14 Dec 1820. Nathan **McCARTY** to same. For the sum of $11.37 ½, mortgage on Lot No. 25, Range E in Cape Girardeau; bounded on the W and fronted by a street and E by an alley. Terms as in F:1. Signed Nathan **McCARTY**. Wit William **KELSO** (JP). Rec 2 May 1821.

1747. Page 57. 14 Dec 1820. James **RAVENSCROFT** to same. For the sum of $37.62 ½, mortgage on the S ½ of Lot No. 12, Range D in Cape Girardeau; bounded on the E by Middle St and S by Themis St. Terms as in F:1. Signed James **RAVENSCROFT**. Wit William **KELSO** (JP). Rec 2 May 1821.

1748. Page 58. 14 Dec 1820. Martin B. **LAWRENCE** to same. For the sum of $15.75, mortgage on two lots in Range C in Cape Girardeau; Lot No. 15, bounded on the S by Independence St and E by Middle St; and Lot No. 19, bounded on the N by Themis St and W by another street. Terms as in F:1. Signed Martin B. **LAWRENCE**. Wit William **KELSO** (JP). Rec 2 May 1821.

1749. Page 58. 15 Dec 1820. Valentine **MILLER** to same. For the sum of $20, mortgage on two lots in Cape Girardeau; Lot No. 18, Range B, fronting on the E on Middle St; and Lot No. 32, Range A, fronting on the W on a street. Terms as in F:1. Signed Vallnntin **MULLER**. Wit William **KELSO** (JP). Rec 2 May 1821.

1750. Page 59. 15 Dec 1820. William **HUTCHINSON** to same. For the sum of $68.25, mortgage on five town lots in Cape Girardeau; Lot No. 30, Range A; Lot No. 22, Range B; Lot No. 41, Range G; and Lot Nos. 40 & 36, Range H. Terms as in F:1. Signed William **HUTCHINSON**. Wit William **KELSO** (JP). Rec 2 May 1821.

1751. Page 59. 15 Dec 1820. Jacob **STAHL** to same. For the sum of $21.87 ½, mortgage on three town lots in Cape Girardeau; Lot No. 26, Range A; Lot No. 47, Range G; and Lot No. 38, Range H. Terms as in F:1. Signed Jacob **STAHL**. Wit William **KELSO** (JP). Rec 3 May 1821.

1752. Page 60. 15 Dec 1820. Samuel **CUTTER** to same. For the sum of $22.75, mortgage on Lot Nos. 43 & 45, Range G in Cape Girardeau. Terms as in F:1. Signed Samuel **CUTTER**. Wit William **KELSO** (JP). Rec 3 May 1821. [Marginal note: Full satisfaction received from Patrick **CURRIN** (Lot No. 43) and Ignatius R. **WATHEN** (Lot No. 45) on 30 Aug 1851. Signed William W. **GITT**, adminr with the will annexed of Daniel F. **STEINBECK**. Wit Jacob **TOBLER**, Dep Clerk.]

1753. Page 60. 16 Dec 1820. George **HENDERSON** to same. For the sum of $149.62 ½, mortgage on six lots in Cape Girardeau; Lot Nos. 22 & 24, Range I; and Lot Nos. 12, 14, 26, & 28, Range G. Terms as in F:1. Signed George **HENDERSON**. Wit William **KELSO** (JP). Rec 3 May 1821.

1754. Page 61. 16 Dec 1820. Levi L. **LIGHTNER** to same. For the sum of $31.50, mortgage on Lot No. 18, Range G in Cape

Girardeau; bounded on the E by Spanish St and S by St of Good Hope. Terms as in F:1. Signed L. L. **LIGHTNER**. Wit William **KELSO** (JP). Rec 3 May 1821.

1755. Page 61. 16 Dec 1820. Charles G. **ELLIS** to same. For the sum of $119, mortgage on Lot Nos. 6, 7, 17, & 20, Range I in Cape Girardeau; the first two bounded E by the Mississippi and W by Gravesend St. Terms as in F:1. Signed C. G. **ELLIS**. Wit William **KELSO** (JP). Rec 3 May 1821. [Marginal note: Full satisfaction received on 12 Jul 1827. Signed L. **LORIMIER**. Test Hy. **SANFORD**.]

1756. Page 62. 16 Dec 1820. William **GARNER** to same. For the sum of $114.62 ½, mortgage on Lot Nos. 5 & 8, Range G in Cape Girardeau; fronting on the E on Aquamsi or Front St and W on Spanish St. Terms as in F:1. Signed W. **GARNER**. Wit William **KELSO** (JP). Rec 4 May 1821.

1757. Page 63. 16 Dec 1820. Victor **LORIMIER**, George **HENDERSON**, and Nathan **McCARTY** to same. For the sum of $332.50, mortgage on Lot No. 1, Range G in Cape Girardeau; bounded on the E by St of Aquamsi, W by Lot No. 12, N by Williams St, and S by Lot No. 2. Terms as in F:1. Signed Victor **LORIMIER**, Nathan **McCARTY**, George **HENDERSON**. Wit William **KELSO** (JP). Rec 4 May 1821.

1758. Page 63. 23 Dec 1820. Thomas S. **RODNEY** to same. For the sum of $998.37 ½, mortgage on two outlots near Cape Girardeau; 160 acres, being Outlot No. 79; and about 70 acres, being Outlot No. 87 on both sides of Cape la Cruche Creek and adjoining the heirs of M. Louisa **RODNEY**. Terms as in F:1. Signed Thomas S. **RODNEY**. Wit William **KELSO** (JP). Rec 4 May 1821. [Marginal note: Full satisfaction received on 30 Nov 1821. Signed Victor **LORIMIER**. Wit C. S. **THOMAS**, Dep Clerk.]

1759. Page 64. 23 Dec 1820. Michael **TANEY** and Nathan **McCARTY** to same. For the sum of $459.37 ½, mortgage on 160 acres, more or less, being Outlot No. 81 a mile and three-fourths W of Cape Girardeau. Terms as in F:1. Signed Michl. **TANEY**, Nathan **McCARTY**. Wit William **KELSO** (JP). Rec 4 May 1821.

1760. Page 64. 26 Jul 1820. Commissioners to Partition Lands of the heirs of Louis **LORIMIER**, decd, to Thomas **ENGLISH**. For the sum of $18, Lot No. 17, Range B in Cape Girardeau; bounded on the N by Independence St , W by an alley, S by Lot No. 18, and E and fronted by Middle St. Sold as in F:20. Signed B. **COUSIN**, William **KELSO**, W. **GARNER**, C. G. **ELLIS**. Test John C. **HARBISON** (JP). Rec 4 May 1821.

1761. Page 65. 28 Jul 1820. Same to Joseph **ENGLISH**. For the sum of $51, Lot No. 7, Range H in Cape Girardeau; bounded on the W and fronted by Spanish St, and S and fronted by another street. Sold as in F:20. Signed W. **GARNER**, Wm. **KELSO**, C. G. **ELLIS**, B. **COUSIN**. Wit John C. **HARBISON** (JP). Rec 5 May 1821.

1762. Page 66. 26 Jul 1820. Same to same. For the sum of $14, Lot No. 42, Range G in Cape Girardeau; bounded on the E and fronted by Middle St and W by an alley. Sold as in F:20. Signed B. **COUSIN**, Wm. **KELSO**, W. **GARNER**, C. G. **ELLIS**. Wit John C. **HARBISON** (JP). Rec 5 May 1821.

1763. Page 66. 16 Oct 1820. Christian **SEABAUCH** to William **McMURTRY** of Madison Co. [no state given]. For the sum of $80, Lot No. 99 in Jackson; bounded on the W by third west street, N by Lot No. 98, and E by Lot No. 87. Signed Christian (o) **SEABOCK**. Wit William **TINNIN** (JP), John (x) **TINNIN**. Rec 5 May 1821.

1764. Page 67. 16 Feb 1820. William **JONES** to Elias **BARBER**. For the sum of $52, Lot No. 56 in Jackson; bounded on the N by second south street, W by first west street, S by Lot No. 57, and E by Lot No. 29. Signed Wm. **JONES**. Wit J. **RANNEY**, Henry **CLINARD**, Zenas **PRIEST** (JP). Rec 5 May 1821.

1765. Page 67. 16 Nov 1820. Alexander **McNAIR**, Governor of Mo., to James **RUSSELL**. Appointment as JP for Byrd Twp for four years. Signed A. **McNAIR**. Wit Joshua **BARTON**, Sec. of State. James **RUSSELL** takes the oath of office. Signed James **RUSSELL**. Wit William **CREATH** (JP). Rec 5 May 1821.

1766. Page 68. 15 Sep 1820. William P. **LACEY** to Joseph **OBANNON**. To secure the purchase price of a tract of land, mortgage on a negro man named **George** and a negro girl named **Jenny**, which girl sd **LACEY** had of sd **OBANNON** in part payment for sd land. Sd **LACEY** sold sd **OBANNON** 213 1/3 acres, more or less, in the

Big Bend of the Mississippi River for $1400
[E:531]. Because sd **LACEY** is sued by James
TANNER for the sd land, sd **LACEY** will grant
the slaves to sd **OBANNON** should the suit not
be settled in his favor or should he not obtain sd
TANNER's claim to the land. Signed Wm. P.
LACEY, Joseph **OBANNON**. Wit James
RUSSEL, Wm. **CREATH** (JP). Rec 5 May
1821. [Marginal note: Tax paid. J. **McF.**]

1767. Page 68. 9 Feb 1821. Richard S.
THOMAS, Judge of Fourth Judicial Circuit, to
John **JUDEN** Junr. Appointment as Clerk of the
Cape Girardeau Co. Circuit Court. Signed R. S.
THOMAS. Wit Cne. S. **THOMAS**, Dep Clerk.
Rec 9 Feb 1821.

1768. Page 68. 9 Feb 1821. John **JUDEN** Jr.,
David **ARMOUR**, and William **SURRELL** to
Alexander **McNAIR**, Governor of Mo. For the
sum of $3000, bond to guarantee that sd **JUDEN**
shall perform the duties of Clerk of the Cape
Girardeau Co. Circuit Court. Signed John
JUDEN Jr., David **ARMOUR**, William
SURRELL. Wit Claibrn. S. **THOMAS**, R. S.
THOMAS, Judge of Fourth Judicial Circuit. Rec
9 Feb 1821.

1769. Page 69. 13 Oct 1820. Commissioners to
Partition Lands of the heirs of Louis
LORIMIER, decd, to Van B. **DLASHMUTT**.
For the sum of $200, 40 acres, more or less,
being Outlot No. 42 W of Cape Girardeau;
bounded on the N by Outlot No. 41, S by Outlot
No. 43, E by Outlot Nos. 25 & 26, and W by
Outlot No. 57. Sold as in F:20. Signed B.
COUSIN, Wm. **KELSO**, C. G. **ELLIS**. Test
John C. **HARBISON** (JP). Rec 15 Feb 1821.

1770. Page 70. 15 Feb 1821. Van B.
DLASHMUTT and Margaret, his wife, to Lyne
STARLING and Elias N. **DLASHMUTT**,
trading as **STARLING & DLASHMUTT**. For
the sum of $2472, four lots in Cape Girardeau
and 12 outlots near sd town; ½ of Inn Lot No. 7
in Range E, Inn Lot No. 18 & 22 in Range F, and
Inn Lot No. 27 in Range A; and Outlot Nos. 7, 8,
15, & 17 containing 10 acres each; Outlot Nos.
24, 26, 28, & 29 containing 20 acres each; Outlot
Nos. 38 & 42 containing 40 acres each; and
Outlot Nos. 50 & 52, containing 80 acres each.
All are part of a tract granted by the Spanish
Government to Louis **LORIMIER** and
confirmed to him by the U. S. Signed Van B.
DLASHMUTT, Margarett **DLASHMUTT**
(RD). Wit John (x) **DUNLAP**, Jno.
ABERNETHIE (JP). Rec 15 Feb 1821.

1771. Page 70. 15 Feb 1821. Same and same to
Elias N. **DLASHMUTT**. For $577.50,
undivided ½ of 231 acres on Randall's Creek;
being where Van B. **DLASHMUTT** now lives
and adjoined on the W by John **ABERNETHIE**,
Esq, S by John **HITT**, N by Isaac **WILLIAMS**,
and E by vacant lands; and being the same
purchased by Van B. **DLASHMUTT** of Richard
WALLER. Signed Van B. **DLASHMUTT**,
Margarett **DLASHMUTT** (RD). Wit John (x)
DUNLAP, Jno. **ABERNETHIE** (JP). Rec 15
Feb 1821.

1772. Page 71. 2 Dec 1820. John **WEAVER** to
Samuel **RAVENSCROFT**. For the sum of $500,
250 arpens, more or less, on Ramsey's Creek,
being an unconfirmed Spanish Grant. Should the
tract not be confirmed, sd **WEAVER** warrants
the tract where he now lives as a preemption
right to sd **RAVENSCROFT**; SW ¼, Sec 34,
Twp 31 N, Rng 13 E and NW ¼, Sec 3, Twp 30
N, Rng 13 E. Signed John **WEAVER**, Mary (x)
WEAVER. Wit Solomon H. **ARMOUR**, David
ARMOUR, Zenas **PRIEST** (JP). Rec 15 Feb
1821.

1773. Page 72. 17 Jan 1820. Thomas S.
RODNEY and Polly, his wife, to James
RUSSELL. For the sum of $200, 20 acres near
Jackson on the waters of Hubble's Creek; being
part of a tract confirmed to Henry **HAND** and
sold to sd **RODNEY** by sd **HAND**; beginning at
the SW corner of the tract at a stake and stone
near an elm and hickory. Signed Thos. S.
RODNEY, Polley **RODNEY** (RD). Wit John
RODNEY, G. N. **O'BANNON**, Wm. **DOWTY**,
David **ARMOUR** (JP). Rec 20 Feb 1821.

1774. Page 72. 27 Jan 1821. John **MASSEY** to
John **JUDEN** Junr. For the sum of $150, __ acres
on Sandy Branch, waters of Bird Creek; being
his preemption right and the SW ¼, Sec 17, Twp
31 N, Rng 12 E. Signed John **MASSEY**. Wit
William **CREATH** (JP), Stephen
REMINGTON. Rec 20 Feb 1821.

1775. Page 73. 11 Dec 1820. John **JOHNSON**
and Mary, his wife, to Welton **OBANNON**. For
the sum of $2100, 212 acres, more or less, in the
Big Bend of the Mississippi River; being the
upper third part of a settlement right of 640 acres
granted to Jabez **FISHER**; beginning at the NE
corner of the land conveyed by Ezekiel **ABEL** to
William P. **LACEY** on the bank of the
Mississippi. Signed John **JOHNSON**, Mary
JOHNSON (RD). Wit James **RUSSELL**, Wm.
CREATH, David **ARMOUR** (JP). Rec 20 Feb
1821.

1776. Page 73. 17 Nov 1820. Alexander **McNAIR**, Governor of Mo., to Thomas **MORGAN**. Appointment as Coroner of Cape Girardeau Co. for two years, his having been elected on the fourth Monday of Aug last. Signed A. **McNAIR**. Wit Joshua **BARTON**, Sec. of State. Thomas **MORGAN** takes the oath of office. Signed Thos. **MORGAN**. Wit John **JUDEN** Jr. Rec 22 Feb 1821.

1777. Page 74. 24 Feb 1820. Commissioners of the Courthouse and Jail to John **SHEPPARD**. For the sum of $25, Lot No. 141 in Jackson, bounded on the S and fronted by third south street, W and fronted by second east street, N by Lot No. 140, and E by Lot No. 153. Signed John **DAVIS**, John **SHEPPARD**, Samuel G. **DUNN**, Benja. **SHELL**. Test John **JUDEN** Jr, Clerk, Cne. S. **THOMAS**. Rec 24 Feb 1821.

1778. Page 75. 30 Aug 1820. William **MILBURN** of St. Louis Co., Mo. and Ezekiel **ABLE**. Articles of agreement to make null and of no effect a contract on land dated 11 Feb 1818 between sd **MILBURN** and William **GORDON** of one part and sd **ABLE** of the other part; sd land on White Water to include an improvement where Alexander **McDONALD** then lived. Sd **MILBURN** for himself and sd **GORDON** relinquish all claim to the land, and sd **ABLE** relinquishes all claim on them for payment of the sum in the contract. Signed William **MILBURN**, Ezekio **ABLE**. Wit George **HENDERSON** (JP). Rec 28 Feb 1821.

1779. Page 75. 23 Feb 1821. Commissioners to Partition Lands of the heirs of Louis **LORIMIER**, decd, to Daniel F. **STEINBECK**. For the sum of $265, 160 acres, more or less, being Outlot No. 84 about two and 3/4 miles W of Cape Girardeau; bounded on the S by Outlot No. 85, W by an unconfirmed part of L. **LORIMIER**'s grant, and N by Outlot Nos. 82 & 83. Sold as in F:20. Signed B. **COUSIN**, Benjn. M. **HORRELL**, Wm. **KELSO**. Test George **HENDERSON** (JP). Rec 1 Mar 1821.

1780. Page 76. 12 Dec 1820. James **COX** Senr to Bartholomew **COUSIN**. Quit claim to all the improvements and work done by or for him since 1816 on sd **COUSIN**'s Spanish grant on the E side of Hubble's Creek at the edge of the Big Swamp, adjoining Jeremiah **SIMPSON**'s original survey; also acknowledgment that he has received $100 back from sd **COUSIN** paid in 1817 toward the piece of land. Signed James (x) **COX** sen. Test Geo. **JASPERSEN**, John C. **HARBISON** (JP). Rec 1 Mar 1821.

1781. Page 76. 20 Dec 1820. Louis **LORIMIER**, acting for William **LORIMIER** Junior, to the heirs of Louis **LORIMIER**. For the sum of $577.50, being the residue of the purchase price, mortgage on about 146 acres, about a mile and a half or two miles SW of Cape Girardeau, being Outlot No. 86; bounded on the E by Outlot No. 54, W by Outlot No. 85, S by the S boundary of L. **LORIMIER**'s Spanish Grant, and N by the S line of the heirs of M. Louisa **RODNEY**. Terms as in F:1. Signed Ls. **LORIMIER**. Wit William **KELSO** (JP). Rec 1 Mar 1821.

1782. Page 77. 2 Jan 1821. Charles G. **ELLIS** to same. For the sum of $882, mortgage on 147 acres, two and a half miles W of Cape Girardeau, being Outlot No. 85. Terms as in F:1. Signed C. G. **ELLIS**. Wit William **KELSO** (JP). Rec 1 Mar 1821. [Marginal note: Full satisfaction received on 12 Jul 1827. Signed Ls. **LORIMIER**.]

1783. Page 77. 1 Mar 1821. Willis **McGUIRE** to James **RUSSELL**. For the sum of $105, undivided ½ of Lot No. 100 in Jackson, that he holds in partnership with William **McGUIRE**; bounded on the N and fronted by Main St, E by Lot No. 88, S by Lot No. 101, and W and fronted by third west street. Signed Willis **McGUIRE**. Wit William **CREATH** (JP), Stephen **REMINGTON**. Rec 3 Mar 1821.

1784. Page 78. 11 Dec 1820. John **JOHNSON** to Welton **OBANNON**. For the sum of $2100, mortgage on two negro men named **Winston** and **Jacob**, one negro woman named **Fanny**, two negro girls named **Huldy** & **Mary**, and one negro boy named **Nelson**. Sd **JOHNSON** has sold to sd **OBANNON** a tract of land on which he now lives, and the title is disputed in a suit instituted by James **TANNER** and now pending. If sd **OBANNON** is be clear and free from all costs and in peacable possession, then this deed is null and void. Signed John **JOHNSON**. Wit James **RUSSELL**, William **CREATH** (JP). Rec 3 Mar 1821.

1785. Page 78. 14 Dec 1820. Commissioners to Partition Lands of the heirs of Louis **LORIMIER**, decd, to James **RAVENSCROFT**. For the sum of $43, Lot No. 12, Range D in Cape Girardeau; bounded on the E and fronted by Middle St, and S and fronted by Themis St. Sold as in F:20. Signed B. **COUSIN**, C. G. **ELLIS**, Wm. **KELSO**. Test John C. **HARBISON** (JP). Rec 3 Mar 1821.

1786. Page 79. 8 Dec 1820. Alexander **McNAIR**, Governor of Mo., to Isaac **SHEPPARD**, Esq. Appointment as Justice of the Cape Girardeau Co. Court for four years. Signed A. **McNAIR**. Wit Joshua **BARTON**, Sec. of State. Isaac **SHEPPARD** takes the oath of office. Signed Isaac **SHEPPARD**. Wit William **CREATH**. Rec 3 Mar 1821.

1787. Page 79. 8 Dec 1820. Alexander **McNAIR**, Governor of Mo., to Joseph **FRIZZLE**, Esq. Appointment as Justice of the Cape Girardeau Co. Court for four years. Signed A. **McNAIR**. Wit Joshua **BARTON**, Sec. of State. Joseph **FRIZZLE** takes the oath of office. Signed J. **FRISEL**. Wit William **CREATH**. Rec 3 Mar 1821.

1788. Page 80. 8 Dec 1820. Alexander **McNAIR**, Governor of Mo., to George H. **SCRIPPS**, Esq. Appointment as Justice of the Cape Girardeau Co. Court for four years. Signed A. **McNAIR**. Wit Joshua **BARTON**, Sec. of State. George H. **SCRIPPS** takes the oath of office. Signed Geo. H. **SCRIPPS**. Wit William **CREATH**. Rec 3 Mar 1821.

1789. Page 80. 25 Nov 1814. James **DOWTY** by Sheriff John **HAYS** to John **HAYS** and William J. **STEPHENSON**. For the sum of $40, 100 acres on the waters of White Water adjoining the Big Swamp and land of Ezekiel **ABLE**; being part of the head right of Andrew **FRANKS**. Sold on 24 Nov 1814 in execution of two writs dated 8 Oct 1814 against sd **DOWTY** and for the Cape Girardeau Dist; one for $5 fine and $26.55 costs in case of assault and battery against Samuel D. **STROTHER**; the other against sd **DOWTY** and John **SMITH** for $5 fine and $28.10 costs by reason of an affray against the peace. Signed John **HAYS**, Shff. Wit Joseph **McFERRON**, Clerk. Rec 5 Mar 1821.

1790. Page 81. 11 Oct 1820. Commissioners to Partition Lands of the heirs of Louis **LORIMIER**, decd, to Robert **GIBONEY**. For the sum of $24, Lot No. 9, Range I in Cape Girardeau; bounded on the E and fronted by Gravesend, W and fronted by Spanish St, S by Lot No. 8, and N by Lot No. 10. Sold as in F:20. Signed B. **COUSIN**, Wm. **KELSO**, W. **GARNER**. Test John C. **HARBISON** (JP). Rec 5 Mar 1821.

1791. Page 82. 11 Oct 1820. Same to Samuel **CUPPLES**. For the sum of $60, 10 acres, more or less, SW of Cape Girardeau, being Outlot No. 14; bounded on the N by Outlot No. 13, S by Outlot No. 24, W by Outlot No. 25, and E by Outlot No. 15. Sold as in F:20. Signed B. **COUSIN**, Wm. **KELSO**, W. **GARNER**. Test John C. **HARBISON** (JP). Rec 5 Mar 1821.

1792. Page 82. 11 Oct 1820. Same to Jacob **STAHL**. For the sum of $25, Lot No. 26, Range A; Lot No. 47, Range G; and Lot No. 38, Range H; all in Cape Girardeau. Sold as in F:20. Signed B. **COUSIN**, Wm. **KELSO**, C. G. **ELLIS**. Test John C. **HARBISON** (JP). Rec 7 Mar 1821.

1793. Page 83. 8 Mar 1821. John **BROWN**, adminr of Richard **McBRIDE**, decd, to Samuel G. **DUNN**. For the sum of $1821, three negroes or mulatteo slaves, **Sarah**, **Mariah**, and **Louis**. Sold on 7 Feb 1821 on two writs of execution to the constable of Bird Twp, directed from William **CREATH**'s docket, JP for Bird Twp, obtained at the suits of Joel **BLUNT** and Louis **LORIMIER**. Signed John **BROWN**, D. **CUNSBERL** [Deputy Constable?] Wit Joel **BLUNT**, John **JUDEN** Jr., Clerk. Rec 8 Mar 1821.

1794. Page 83. 13 Oct 1820. John **DRYBREAD** and Mary, his wife, of Ste. Genevieve Co. to Isaac **DEVORE**. For the sum of $400, 120 acres on the Big Swamp, being part of the head right of Andrew **FRANKS**; beginning at the SW corner of sd tract at a stake and stone near two elms; adjoining sd **DEVORE** on the W. Signed John (x) **DRYBREAD**, Mary (x) **DRYBREAD**. Wit Daniel **BARTLETT**, JP in Jefferson Co., Mo., Henry **BAILEY**. Rec 8 Mar 1821.

1795. Page 84. 4 Nov 1820. Alexander **McDONALD** to William **SHEPERD**. For the sum of $10, __ acres, being his preemption right on the Big Swamp; joining John **GIBONEY** on the E. Signed Alex. **McDONALD**. Wit William **MATTHEWS**, William **CREATH** (JP). Rec 8 Mar 1821.

1796. Page 84. 10 Mar 1821. Abraham **DAUGHERTY** and Margret, his wife, to John **SHEPPARD** Junr. For the sum of $500, 100 acres on the waters of **HUBBELL**'s Creek, E of sd creek, including a cabin; adjoining Lewis **TASH** and Thomas **BULL**; being the same claimed by sd **DAUGHERTY** in right of Medad **RANDOL**; beginning near the SE corner on the N side of a small brook on a water beech or ironwood. Signed Abm. **DAUGHERTY**, Margaret (x) **DAUGHERTY**. Wit Simon ( ) **POE** Senr, Jno. **ABERNETHIE** (JP). Rec 13 Mar 1821.

1797. Page. 85. 21 Feb 1820. Nathan **McCARTY**, William **McCARTY**, and John **HAYS** and Cynthia, his wife, to Christian **GATES**. For the sum of $48, 16 acres, more or less, on Byrd's Creek; beginning at a post corner on the W bank of sd creek, which is B. **COUSIN**'s land, and also bounded by land previously sold to sd **GATES** by the grantors. Signed Nathan **McCARTY**, John **HAYS**, William **McCARTY**, Cynthia **HAYS**. Wit W. **GARNER**, Moses **BYRD**, William **CREATH** (JP). Rec 19 Mar 1821.

1798. Page. 86. 19 Mar 1821. Thomas **NEALE** of Jackson to John **ROGERS** Junr and William **WARNOCK** of Greenup Co., Ken. For the sum of $800, Lot No. 75 and a frame house painted white in front on Main St in Jackson, now occupied as a store by Mr. **SMITH** and bounded on all sides by sd **NEALE**; being the next below a brick house occupied by Nathaniel **CREATH** as a saddler's shop and next above the one occupied by sd **NEALE**. Signed Thomas **NEALE**. Wit Beverley **ALLEN**, John **PAYNE** Jr., Wm. **CREATH** (JP). Ellen **NEALE**, wife of sd **NEALE**, RD. Rec 19 Mar 1821.

1799. Page. 87. 17 Mar 1821. John B. **FENAMORE** of Jackson to Lyne **STARLING** and Elias N. **DLASHMUTT**. For the sum of $213.91, mortgage on one beaurow; one small falling leaf table; two beds, bedsteads, and furniture; two stands of curtain furniture white(?); three bed spreads, three quilts, and other furniture belonging to the beds; two stand of window curtains; three sets of plates; four dishes; four sets of teacups and saucers; one lot of china teapots, cups, & saucers; one coffee mill; one tin bucket; one wooden bucket; one pitcher; two wash bowls; one pair of candlesticks; eight glass tumblers; one common teapot; three tin coffee pots; one looking glass; one wooden bowl; six split bottomed chairs; one Dutch oven; one skillet; one pair of pot hooks; one waiter; one set of knives & forks; one trunk; one set of carpenter's tools compleat, together with a number of other tools not belonging to the set; two tin pans; three tin cups; two block bottles; three candle mooles; one pair of snuffers; one clothes brush; one pair of shoe brushes; one French watch; two tea kettles; one ladies saddle & bridle; and one tea canister. A note for the amount is due by 1 Sep next. Signed John B. **FENNIMORE**. Test Lindsey J. **DLASHMUTT**, John W. **SIMPKINS**, David **ARMOUR** (JP). Rec 21 Mar 1821.

1800. Page 87. 19 Mar 1821. Wm. **SUBLETT** to John **ERWIN**. For the sum of $250, half now and half by an obligation, mortgage on a negro woman named **Milley** about age 21. The amount is due by 12 months from this date. Signed Wm. **SUBLETT**. Test Beverley **ALLEN**. Rec 26 Mar 1821.

1801. Page 88. 2 Feb 1821. Stephen **MALOAN** to same. For the sum of $400, __ acres on the waters of Byrd's Creek; being a preemption right on the NE ¼, Sec 5, Twp 32 N, Rng 12 E under the act of Congress passed 12 Apr 1814. Signed Stephen **MALON**. Wit Wm. **McGUIRE**, Wm. P. **LACEY**, William **CREATH** (JP). Rec 26 Mar 1821.

1802. Page 88. 8 Jan 1820. George **YOUNT** to John **YOUNT**. For the sum of $30, his claim to 300 arpens on the W fork of Whitewater; being an undivided tract that was the property of his father Jacob **YOUNT**, decd, and being where the widow of sd Jacob now lives. Signed George **YOUNT**. Wit William **TINNIN** (JP). Rec 29 Mar 1821.

1803. Page 89. 10 Jan 1821. Henry **YUNT** and Sophia, his wife; Asariah **TINNIN** and Susanah, his wife; Jacob **JAMES** and Caty, his wife; John **POLK** and Christeeny, his wife; David **YUNT** and Caty, his wife; and Rubin **FARMER** and Betsey, his wife; all legatees of Jacob **YUNT**, decd, to John **YUNT**. For the sum of $30 to each legatee, their claims to about 300 acres on the W fork of White water where Jacob **YUNT** senior lived and died, adjoining Henry **BOLLINGER** on the S and **ASHABRAND** on the NW; beginning on a white oak stake on sd **BOLLINGER**'s line. Signed Henery (o) **YUNT**, Sophia (o) **YUNT**, Asariah **TINNIN**, Susan (|) **TINNIN**, John **POLK**, Christeinee ( ) **POLK**, Jacob (x) **JAMES**, Catey ( ) **JAMES**, David (x) **YUNT**, Catey (o) **YUNT**, Rubin ( ) **FARMER**, Betsey (o) **FARMER**. Wit William **POLK** (JP). Rec 29 Mar 1821.

1804. Page. 89. 29 Jun 1818. Jason **CHAMBERLAIN** to James **RUSSELL**. For the sum of $340, mortgage on Lot No. 2 in Jackson; bounded on the W and fronted by High St, N and fronted by first north street, E by Lot No. 26, and S by Lot No. 23. A note for the amount bearing even date with this deed is due to sd **RUSSELL** six months after date with ten percent interest per annum. Signed Jason **CHAMBERLAIN**. Test John **JOHNSON**, Enoch **HUDSON**, John **JUDEN** Jr., Clerk. Rec 31 Mar 1821.

1805. Page 90. 3 Apr 1821. Commissioners of the Courthouse and Jail to Samuel **CUPPLES**. For the sum of $40, Lot No. 82 in Jackson; bounded on the W and fronted by second west street, N and fronted by third south street, E by Lot No. 70, and S by a fraction. Signed John **DAVIS**, John **SHEPPARD**, Samuel G. **DUNN**, Abraham **BYRD**, Benja. **SHELL**. Wit Theodore **JONES**, Henry (x) **BOLLINGER**, Claiborne S. **THOMAS**, Dep Clerk. Rec 3 Apr 1821.

1806. Page 90. 8 Oct 1820. Medad **RANDOL** to James **RANDOL**. For the sum of $307, mortgage on a negro boy named **Bill** about 9 years old. Medad **RANDOL** has agreed to pay James **RANDOL**, adminr of Enos **RANDOL**, decd, the sum by 8 Apr next. Signed Medad **RANDOL**. Test Elijah **RANDOL**, Cne. S. **THOMAS**, Dep Clerk. Rec 4 Apr 1821.

1807. Page 91. 30 Dec 1820. Samuel **RAVENSCROFT** and James **RAVENSCROFT** to Robert **SMITH** Senr. For the sum of $225, 160 acres, being a preemption right and the SW ¼, Sec 7, Twp 29, Rng 14 E. Signed Samuel **RAVENSCROFT**, James **RAVENSCROFT**. Wit Greer W. **DAVIS**, Thos. W. **GRAVES**, Wm. **CREATH** (JP). Rec 5 Apr 1821.

1808. Page 91. 8 Jan 1821. Peter **MIERS** to David **WAGENNEN**. For the sum of $100, __ acres, being an improvement and preemption on Painter Crick [Panther Creek]; just above Mr. **REISHER**'s improvement; except the house and yard where sd **MIERS** now lives. Signed Peter **MIERS**. Wit John **PATTERSON**, Semion ( ) **LEWIS**, John B. **WHEELER** (JP). Rec 5 Apr 1821.

1809. Page 92. 5 Apr 1821. Medad **RANDOL** to William **ROBERTS**. For the sum of $400, mortgage on two negro female slaves named **Cate**, aged about 15, and **Sues**, aged about 5. Sd **RANDOL** borrowed the amount from sd **ROBERTS**, due with interest in one year. Signed Medad **RANDOL**. Wit J. **RANNEY**, Christian **GATES**, Cne. S. **THOMAS**, Dep Clerk. Rec 6 Apr 1821.

1810. Page 92. 28 Jun 1820. Web **HAYDEN** and Elizabeth, his wife, to Hiram **HAYDEN**. For the sum of $680, 150 acres on the waters of Hubble's Creek; bounded on the W by Major **DAVIS**' mill tract, N by Joel **RENFROE**, E by Web **HAYDEN**, and S by Abraham **BYRD**. Signed Web **HAYDEN**, Elizabeth (x) **HAYDEN**. Wit

John **AKIN** (JP), George (x) **COX**, Thomas **SULLINGER**. Rec 9 Apr 1821.

1811. Page 93. 3 Apr 1821. Commissioners of the Courthouse and Jail to John **BURNS**. For the sum of $60, Lot No. 126 in Jackson; bounded on the N and fronted by first south street, E and fronted by second east street, S by Lot No. 127, and W by Lot No. 42. Signed John **DAVIS**, John **SHEPPARD**, Samuel G. **DUNN**, Abraham **BYRD**, Benja. **SHELL**. Wit Stephen **BYRD**, John **PRIM**, John **JUDEN** Jr., Clerk. Rec 10 Apr 1821.

1812. Page 93. 12 Dec 1820. Commissioners to Partition Lands of the heirs of Louis **LORIMIER**, decd, to Robert **SMITH** Senr. For the sum of $236, 14 town lots in Cape Girardeau; Lot Nos. 15, 16, 17, 18, 19, & 20 in Range D; Lot Nos. 27, 28, 31, 32, 33, & 34 in Range E; and Lot Nos. 29 & 30 in Range F. Sold as in F:20. Signed B. **COUSIN**, W. **GARNER**, Wm. **KELSO**. Test John C. **HARBISON** (JP). Rec 12 Apr 1821.

1813. Page 94. 15 Sep 1820. Ithamer **HUBBEL** and Catherine, his wife, to Peter **HUBBEL**. For the sum of $400, 300 arpens on the waters of Whitewater, being the same tract granted by the Board of Commissioners of the U. S. to Samuel **DORSEY** under Harris **AUSTON**. Signed Ithamer (x) **HUBBEL**, Catherina (x) **HUBBEL**. Test John **AKIN** (JP), Sarah (+) **AKIN**. Rec 12 Apr 1821.

1814. Page 95. 23 Dec 1820. Commissioners to Partition Lands of the heirs of Louis **LORIMIER**, decd, to Michael **TANEY** and Nathan **McCARTY**. For the sum of $525, 160 acres, more or less, being Outlot No. 81 about a mile and a half W of Cape Girardeau on Cape la Cruche Creek; bounded on the E by Outlot Nos. 58 & 59, S by Outlot No. 87, W by Outlot No. 82, and N by Outlot No. 80. Sold as in F:20. Signed B. **COUSIN**, Wm. **KELSO**, W. **GARNER**. Test George **HENDERSON** (JP). Rec 16 Apr 1821.

1815. Page 95. 12 Mar 1821. Michael **TANEY** to George **HENDERSON**. For the sum of $50, equal and undivided half of the outlot described in the preceding deed. Signed Michl. **TANEY**. Test James **THOMPSON**, Victor **LORIMIER**, D. F. **STEINBECK**, David **ARMOUR** (JP). Rec 16 Apr 1821.

1816. Page 96. 21 Feb 1821. Ezekiel **ABLE** by Sheriff John **HAYS** to John **CROSS** and

William **GARNER**. For the sum of $1300, three tracts; 640 acres on the waters of Hubble's Creek confirmed to William **HAND**'s representatives; 640 acres on the Mississippi above the old Cape confirmed to Stephen **CAVENDER**; and an improvement and preemption right in the Big Bend of the Mississippi River between the above claim of Stephen **CAVENDER** and a tract confirmed to Jabez **FISHER**, being first improved by Samuel **HINCH** and Marcus **STEPHENSON**, on which sd **ABLE** formerly lived. Sold on 22 Aug 1820 in execution of two writs issued by Circuit Court against sd **ABLE**; one dated 22 Feb 1820 for Rufus **EASTON** for $700 debt, $200.16 and five mills damages, $34.85 and five mills costs, and $16.90 for costs related to delays; and one dated 23 May 1820 for George **HENDERSON** for $370.94 damages and $22.45 costs. Signed John **HAYS**, Sheriff. Wit John **JUDEN** Jr., Clerk. Rec 16 Apr 1821.

1817. Page 97. 16 Apr 1821. William **HAND** by same to **STARLING & DLASHMUTT**. For the sum of $99, five town lots; Lot No. 111 in Jackson and four lots in Bainbridge. Sold on 19 Dec 1820 in execution of a writ issued by Circuit Court for Lewis **DICKSON** against sd **HAND** and Gilbert **HECTOR** for $325.87 and five mills, against Phineas **COBURN** for $427.32 for damages, and $22.50 costs. Signed John **HAYS**, Sheriff. Wit John **JUDEN** Jr., Clerk. Rec 16 Apr 1821.

1818. Page 98. 9 Jan 1821. William J. **STEPHENSON**, decd, by same to John **RODNEY**. For the sum of $256, the undivided half of 400 acres at the edge of the Big Swamp; part of 640 acres confirmed to Andrew **FRANKS**' representatives. Sold on 19 Dec 1820 in execution of a writ issued by Circuit Court for William **MONTGOMERY**, execr of James **MONTGOMERY**, decd, against Elizabeth **STEPHENSON**, adminr of William J. **STEPHENSON**, decd, dated 6 Sep 1820, for $200 debt, $21.98 and five mills damages, and $21.82 and five mills costs. Signed John **HAYS**, Sheriff. Wit John **JUDEN** Jr., Clerk. Rec 16 Apr 1821.

1819. Page 99. 9 Jan 1821. John **ARMSTRONG** by same to William **McGUIRE**, Nathaniel **WATKINS**, and James **BROOKS**. For the sum of $240, a lot on Main St in Jackson, occupied at present by Greer W. **DAVIS** and sd **ARMSTRONG**. Sold on 5 Apr 1821 in execution of a writ issued by Circuit Court for Joseph **FRIZEL** against sd **ARMSTRONG** dated 10 Mar 1821 for $135.13 damages and

$11.35 costs. Signed John **HAYS**, Sheriff. Wit John **JUDEN** Jr., Clerk. Rec 16 Apr 1821.

1820. Page 100. 16 Mar 1821. William **NEELY** and Rachel, his wife, to James **RUSSELL**. For the sum of $3000, 240 arpens, more or less, on the waters of Hubble's Creek where they now live, adjoining Jackson; being the same confirmed to William **DAUGHERTY** under **DEAKINS** and conveyed by sd **DAUGHERTY** to sd **NEELY**; bounded on the E by Henry **SHERIDEN**'s concession, now partly lots of Jackson and partly owned by Richard **THOMAS**, W by Jonathan **FORMAN**'s concession now owned by the heirs of John **MARTIN**, S by John **SHEPHERD** and Edward **CRIDDLE**, and N by James **ARRELL**'s concession now claimed by the heirs of Joseph **SEWELL** and by sd **FOREMAN**'s concession. Signed Wm. **NEELY**, Rachel **NEELY**. Wit David **ARMOUR** (JP), Robert **BUCKNER**, G. N. **OBANNON**. Rec 18 Apr 1821.

1821. Page 101. 20 Apr 1821. John **JUDEN** Jr., Samuel **CUPPLES**, and William **SURRELL** to Alexander **McNAIR**, Governor of Mo. For the sum of $2000, bond to guarantee that sd **JUDEN** shall discharge the duties of Clerk of the Cape Girardeau Co. Court, his having been appointed. Signed John **JUDEN** Jr., Saml. **CUPPLES**, William **SURRELL**. Wit Cne. S. **THOMAS**. Approved by Joseph **FRIZEL**, Geo. H. **SCRIPPS**, and Isaac **SHEPPARD**, Justices of the Co. Court. John **JUDEN** Jr. takes the oath of office. Signed John **JUDEN** Jr. Wit J. **FRIZEL**. Rec 23 Apr 1821.

1822. Page 101. 22 Apr 1819. John **HALL** and Rebecky, his wife, to Web B. **HAYDEN**, all of Cape New Madrid, Mo. For the sum of $375, 80 acres on the waters of Randol's Creek; bounded on the S by sd **HAYDEN**, N by Joel **RENFROE**, and E by James **COX**. Signed John **HALL**, Rebeckah **HALL** (RD). Wit Enoch **EVANS**, New Madrid Co. Clerk. Rec 23 Apr 1821.

1823. Page 102. 16 Feb 1821. Frank J. **ALLEN** to Wm. **ROBERTS**. For the sum of $500, mortgage on two negroes, boy **Fleming** aged about 18, and boy **Sam** aged about 10. The debt is due by 16 Feb 1822. Signed Frank J. **ALLEN**. Test Townsend **NICHOLS**, David **BIRDWELL**, William **CREATH** (JP). Rec 24 Apr 1821.

1824. Page 103. 28 Aug 1820. Commissioners of the Courthouse and Jail to Robert **SMITH** and

John J. **DELASHMUTT**. For the sum of $42, Lot No. 141 in Jackson; bounded on the E and fronted by third east street, S and fronted by second south street, W by Lot No. 139, and N by Lot No. 150. Signed John **DAVIS**, John **SHEPPARD**, Samuel G. **DUNN**, Abraham **BYRD**. Wit Stephen **MALON**, Henry **CRITS**, James **RUSSELL** (JP). Rec 25 Apr 1821.

1825. Page 103. 12 Dec 1820. Commissioners to Partition Lands of the heirs of Louis **LORIMIER**, decd, to Nathaniel W. **WATKINS**. For the sum of $21, Lot Nos. 25 & 26 in Range F in Cape Girardeau; bounded on the E and fronted by a street, W by an alley, and S and fronted by St Belleview. Sold as in F:20. Signed B. **COUSIN**, W. **GARNER**, Wm. **KELSO**. Test John C. **HARBISON** (JP). Rec 25 Apr 1821.

1826. Page 104. 25 Apr 1821. William G. **BYRD**, Stephen **BYRD**, and John **HAYS** to Alexander **McNAIR**, Governor of Mo. For the sum of $3000, bond to perform the office of Cape Girardeau County Collector, his having been appointed on 24 Apr 1821 for one year. Signed Wm. G. **BYRD**, Stephen **BYRD**, John **HAYS**. Wit John **JUDEN** Jr. Rec 25 Apr 1821.

1827. Page 104. 24 Apr 1821. Same, same, and same to William **CHRISTY**, Auditor of Mo. For the sum of $7000, bond to perform the office of Cape Girardeau County Collector, his having been appointed on 24 Apr 1821 for one year. Signed Wm. G. **BYRD**, Stephen **BYRD**, John **HAYS**. Wit John **JUDEN** Jr. Rec 25 Apr 1821.

1828. Page 104. 20 Apr 1821. Alexander **McNAIR**, Governor of Mo., to John **JUDEN** Jr. Appointment as Clerk of the Cape Girardeau County Court. Signed A. **McNAIR**. Wit Joshua **BARTON**, Sec. of State. John **JUDEN** Junr takes the oath of office. Signed John **JUDEN** Jr. Wit David **ARMOUR** (JP). Rec 27 Apr 1821.

1829. Page 105. 28 Apr 1821. Warren **DAVIS** to Elias **DAVIS**. For the sum of $1200, one negro woman named **Phillis** about 40 years old; three negro girls, **Sibina** about 10 years old, **Lucy** about 6 years old, and ___ about 4 years old; and all his household furniture, horses, cattle, and hogs. Signed Warren **DAVIS**. Test R. **SMITH** Senr, Robert **SMITH** Jn. Rec 30 Apr 1821.

1830. Page 105. 28 Apr 1821. Levi L. **LIGHTNER** to Daniel F. **STEINBECK**. For the sum of $720, Lot No. 6, Range E in Cape Girardeau; bounded on the N by St Bellevue, S

by Lot No. 5, E by German St, and W by Spanish St. Signed Levi L. **LIGHTNER**. Wit William **STEINBECK**, George **HENDERSON** (JP). Rec 3 May 1821.

1831. Page 106. 5 May 1821. Commissioners of the Courthouse and Jail to Richard S. **THOMAS** and William **McGUIRE**. For the sum of $169, two lots in Jackson; Lot No. 33, bounded on the E and fronted by first south street, S and fronted by third south street, W by Lot No. 9, and N by Lot No. 32; and Lot No. 161, bounded on the S and fronted by first south street, W and fronted by third east street, N by Lot No. 160, and E by Lot No. 172. Signed John **SHEPPARD**, Samuel G. **DUNN**, Abraham **BYRD**. Wit Wm. S. **GANTT**, John **JUDEN** Jr., Clerk. Rec 5 May 1821.

1832. Page 106. 11 Oct 1820. Commissioners to Partition Lands of the heirs of Louis **LORIMIER**, decd, to Thomas S. **RODNEY** and John **RODNEY**. For the sum of $972, 153 acres, more or less, being Outlot Nos. 57 & 58 a mile W of Cape Girardeau; bounded on the E by Outlot No. 41 & 42, N by other lands of the heirs of Louis **LORIMIER**, S by Outlot No. 56, and N by Outlot No. 59. Sold as in F:20. Signed B. **COUSIN**, Wm. **KELSO**, W. **GARNER**. Test John C. **HARBISON** (JP). Rec 8 May 1821.

1833. Page 107. 16 Apr 1821. John **RODNEY** and Rachel, his wife, to Thomas S. **RODNEY**. For the sum of $807, 77 acres, being Outlot No. 56 a mile W of Cape Girardeau, bounded on the S by Outlot No. 55 and N by Outlot No. 57; and his undivided half of Outlot Nos. 57 & 58 as described in the preceding deed (F:106). Signed John **RODNEY**, Rachel (x) **RODNEY**. Wit Michl. **RODNEY**, Martin **RODNEY**, John **AKIN** (JP). Rec 8 May 1821.

1834. Page 108. 14 Dec 1820. Commissioners to Partition Lands of the heirs of Louis **LORIMIER**, decd, to same. For the sum of $55, Lot Nos. 19 & 23, Range E in Cape Girardeau; the first on the SE corner of Block No. 5, the other on the NW corner of sd block. Sold as in F:20. Signed B. **COUSIN**, C. G. **ELLIS**, Wm. **KELSO**. Test John C. **HARBISON** (JP). Rec 8 May 1821.

1835. Page 108. 13 Oct 1820. Same to same. For the sum of $150, 10 acres, more or less, being Outlot No. 9 W of Cape Girardeau; bounded on the E by Outlots C & A, W by Outlot No. 27, N by Outlot No. 8, and S by Outlot No. 10. Sold as in F:20. Signed B. **COUSIN**, Wm. **KELSO**, C.

G. **ELLIS**. Wit John C. **HARBISON** (JP). Rec 8 May 1821.

1836. Page 109. 11 Oct 1820. Same to same. For the sum of $47, 3 ¼ acres, being Outlot No. D W of Cape Girardeau; bounded on the N by Outlot C, S by Outlot E, W by Outlot No. 9, and E by Pacific St. Sold as in F:20. Signed B. **COUSIN**, Wm. **KELSO**, W. **GARNER**. Wit John C. **HARBISON** (JP). Rec 8 May 1821.

1837. Page 109. 11 Oct 1820. Same to same. For the sum of $71, 6 acres, more or less, being Outlot No. 11 W of Cape Girardeau; bounded on the E by Outlot No. 9 and land formerly of John **SCRIPPS**, W by Outlot No. 26, N by Outlot No. 10, and S by Outlot No. 12, including a spring. Sold as in F:20. Signed B. **COUSIN**, Wm. **KELSO**, Wm. **GARNER**. Wit John C. **HARBISON** (JP). Rec 8 May 1821.

1838. Page 110. 20 Mar 1821. Richard **MENEFEE**, agent and attorney for Jarrot **MENEFEE**, to Joseph **GEISTWITE**, both of Pulaski Co., Ark. For the sum of $150, 100 arpens, more or less, being part of the settlement right of Ranney **BRUMMITT**, as described in a deed from George **RUDDELL** to Jonas N. **MENEFEE**, then agent and attorney for Jarrot **MENEFEE**. Signed Jarrot **MENEFEE** by his agent & attorney Richard **MENEFEE**. Wit J. B. **HIGGINBOTHAM**; James C. **NEWELL** (JP in Pulaski Co., Ark.); Alexander **RENNICK**, Clerk, by Richard **MENEFEE**, Dep Clerk of Pulaski Co., Ark. Court; James **LEMON**, Judge of the Court of Common Pleas in Pulaski Co., Ark. Rec 9 May 1821.

1839. Page 111. 30 Sep 1820. William **ROBERTS** and Nancy, his wife, to Joseph **OBANNON**. For the sum of $2400, __ acres, being an improvement and preemption right in the Big Bend of the Mississippi River in SE fractional ¼, Sec 7 & NE fractional ¼, Sec 18, Twp 31 N, Rng 15 E; settled, improved, and cultivated by sd **ROBERTS**, and being where they now live. Signed William **ROBERTS**, Nancy (x) **ROBERTS**. Wit Saml. **HUSTON**, John **JOHNSON**, James **RUSSELL**, Wm. **CREATH** (JP). Rec 10 May 1821.

1840. Page 112. 26 Aug 1807. Joseph **WORTHINGTON** to Joseph **THOMPSON** Senior. For the sum of $243, 284 arpens, 31 1/3 perches (or nearly 243 acres) surveyed for him on 20 Dec 1805 as assignee of Henry **HALL**'s claim or head right; bounded on the N by John **GUIBONY**, S by Jacob **JACOBS** and Terence

DIAL, E by unappropriated land, and W by Abraham & Thomson **BYRD**. Signed Jos. **WORTHINGTON**, Margarett (x) **WORTHINGTON**. Wit B. **COUSIN**, L. **LAPORTE**, Christr. **HAYS** (JCCP). Margarette **WORTHINGTON**, widow of Joseph **WORTHINGTON**, RD on 27 Aug 1817. Wit Enoch **EVANS** (JP). Rec 10 May 1821.

1841. Page 112. 14 Oct 1816. Rachel **THOMPSON** to William **THOMPSON**. For the sum of $100, relinquishment of her claim in the lands belonging to the estate of Joseph **THOMPSON**. Signed Rachel **THOMPSON**. Wit George **HENDERSON** (JP). Rec 10 May 1821.

1842. Page 112. 29 Feb 1820. Joseph **THOMPSON** and Margarett, his wife, to same. For the sum of $640, 240 acres, more or less, being originally the head right of Henry **HALL** and known as Poe Place; bounded on the S by Jacob **JACOBS** Sen, W by Abriham **BYRD**, and N by John **LANGDON**. Signed Joseph **THOMPSON**, Margaret **THOMPSON**. Wit John C. **HARBISON** (JP), Isaac **THOMPSON**. Rec 10 May 1821.

1843. Page 113. 29 Nov 1819. Isaac **THOMPSON** and Mary, his wife, to same. For the sum of $240, their ¼ interest in Pond Place, conveyed by Henry **HALL** to Joseph **WORTHINGTON**, by sd **WORTHINGTON** to Joseph **THOMPSON**, decd, and which Isaac **THOMPSON** holds as one of the heirs of the estate of Joseph **THOMPSON**. Signed Isaac **THOMPSON**, Mary A. **THOMPSON**. Wit John **AKIN** (JP). Rec 10 May 1821.

1844. Page 114. 14 May 1821. Edmund **RUTTER** to John **CROSS** and William **GARNER**, and Hugh **McELROY** and William **GRUNDY** of Union Co., Ken. For the sum of $1, deed of trust on Lot No. 49 in Jackson, all its appurtenances, and his dwelling house; the lot adjoining Lot No. 49 to the N, purchased of Joseph **SEWELL**, decd; part of lot No. 51 in Jackson, on which his brick storehouse stands on Main St; 173 1/3 acres about a mile S of Jackson, part of a 640-acre tract confirmed to Peter **BILLUE**; the W end of 303 1/3 acres sold to C. G. **HOUTS** by Jason **CHAMBERLAIN**, decd, and transferred to sd **RUTTER**, the E end having been conveyed by sd **RUTTER** to Thomas **HOUTS** of New Madrid Co.; the ½ of, and 1/16 part of 500 arpens purchased by sd **RUTTER** of John **WATERS** on the N side of the Missouri River, including fractional Sec 36 and part of Sec 25, Twp 45 N, Rng 12 W; nine negro slaves: a man **Jacob** age 55 years, woman **Nance** age 36, woman **Justian** age 17, boy **Tom** aged 15, girl **Sarah** age 13, boy **Bob** age 6, boy **Jim** age 4, boy **Barrett** age 6 months, and girl **Mary Jane** age 6 months; stock of merchandise in Morganfield, Ken.; pleasure carriage of four wheels and harness; small waggen and geare; a chesnut sorrel mare; two bay mares; two bay horses; grey horse; cow, calf, and bull yearling; six feather beds and under bed to each, and bolsters and pillows, with their summer and winter furniture of blankets, sheets, quilts, & counterpanes; six bedsteads and two sets of curtains; two sets of carpeting for floors; one common desk and sugar desk; three tables and writing desk; cotton wheel and sheck reel; six windsor and six common chairs; one pair brass headed and three pair brass fire irons; all other articles of household, table, and kitchen furniture and farming utensils; all corn left after delivering 34 ½ bushels to John **MITCHELL**, 100 bushels to Joel **BLUNT**, and 100 bushels to John **GLASSCOCK**; a quantity of soap; two sows and 11 shoats; hewed logs for two small buildings; some rafters, joists, and shingles, part in Jackson and part on the first tract of land; two man's saddles; two women's saddles; three trunks; all notes, bills, and book accounts not collected and monies arising from judgments and executions; and all other property of which sd **RUTTER** is seized. The property to be sold at public auction to pay debts in the order and manner specified by sd **RUTTER**. Sd debts include $3000 to Samuel **McELROY**, $1200 to the bank of Washington in Lebanon, Ken., $217 to David **PHILIPS**, $622 to Betsey **RODGERS**, $325 to Evan **YOUNG**, $300 to Nicholas **RAY**, $1000 to John **BARROTT**, $450 to **DICKSEN** & Joseph R. **GIVEN**, all of Ken.; $126.34 to James **CRISSON**, $1327.54 to Hall & Worley, $158.75 to Thomas **DARRACH**, $135.55 to Adam **EVERLY**, $232.50 to Adams, Knox & Nixon, $1104.55 to Moore, Myers, & Co., $420 to Geo. A. **BICKNELL**, $115.50 to Dallas & Wilcox, $49.15 to W. & S. **WORRELL**, $33.35 to Jacob **LIX**, $106.75 to L & S. **BROWN**, $361.25 to Jacob & G. M. **JUSTICE**, $193 to Sharfmook Destrout & Co., $1255.80 to William **TAYLOR** Jr., $180 to Charles **FOULKE**, and $16.10 to John **GILL** & Co., all of Philadelphia, Penn.; $294.28 to William **KIPNER** and $108.90 to Cramer & Spear, both of Pittsburg; and about $800 to Spencer **CROUCH** of Ark. Terr. The property is to be sold to pay these debts if they are not paid by 1 Sep next. Sd **RUTTER** shall direct what part of the property can be sold first and no more shall be sold than is necessary

to pay the debt. Signed Edmund **RUTTER**. Wit John **JUDEN** Jr., Clerk. Rec 14 May 1821.

1845. Page 116. 15 May 1821. Joel **BLUNT** of Jackson to David **ARMOUR** and John **JUDEN** Junior. For the sum of $200, mortgage on the E ½ of Lot No. 54 in Jackson, between Zenas **PRIEST** and Samuel **LOCKHART**, and the improvements on sd lot; three feather beds and bed furniture; one beawreau; two tables; one dresser and all shelfware; two pots; one oven; one skillet; one trunk; one horse, bridle, and saddle; one rifle gun; five chairs; and one teakettle. A note for the amount is due by 1 Jan next with interest. Signed Joel **BLUNT**. Wit Zenas **PRIEST**, William **CREATH** (JP). Rec 15 May 1821.

1846. Page 117. 27 Jan 1821. James M. **CROPPER** to William **ROBERTS**. For the sum of $600 with 10% interest, bond to make a deed on all his undivided interest and moiety in the town of Bainbridge; and __ acres on Whitewater joining Thos. **RODNEY**, it being the same tract he purchased of Medad **RANDOL** and part of a tract confirmed to Andrew **FRANKS**. Signed J. M. **CROPPER**. Wit Medad **RANDOL**, David **ARMOUR** (JP). Rec 19 May 1821. [Marginal note: Full satisfaction received on 17 Aug 1821. Signed William **ROBERTS**. Wit John **JUDEN** Jr., Clerk.]

1847. Page 117. 17 May 1821. Ignatius **WATHEN** and Mary Ann, his wife, of New Madrid Co., Mo. to James **RAVENSCROFT**. For the sum of $150, Lot No. 13, Range A in Cape Girardeau; bounded on the E by Indian St, W by Merewether St, and S & W by Lot Nos. 14 & 16; being the same he purchased of Chittenden **LYON**. Signed Igs. **WATHEN**, M. A. **WATHEN**. Wit John **WATHN**, John **WATERS**, Richard **WATHEN**, JP in New Madrid Co., Mo. Rec 19 May 1821.

1848. Page 117. 20 May 1821. Victor **LORIMIER** and Sally, his wife, to John **CROSS**. For the sum of $700, 301 acres, more or less, being Outlot Nos. 76 & 77 about two miles NW of Cape Girardeau; and Lot No. 6, Range G in Cape Girardeau, bounded on the N by Lot No. 5, S by St of Good Hope, E by St Aquamsi, and W by Lot No. 7. Signed Victor **LORIMIER**, Sally (x) **LORIMIER**. Wit George **HENDERSON** (JP). Rec 21 May 1821.

1849. Page 118. 21 May 1821. Victor **LORIMIER** to Daniel F. **STEINBECK**. For the sum of $1, deed of trust on five lots in Cape

Girardeau, being Lot Nos. 10, 11, and 19 in Range A, Lot No. 6, Range G, and Lot No. 21, Range B; 151 acres, being Outlot No. 76; 150 acres, being Outlot No. 77; and five negroes: a man named **Sorus** or **Louce**, a woman named **Sophia**, a man named **George**, a girl named **Sylva**, and a boy named **Augustus**. Sd **LORIMIER** is indebted to sd **STEINBECK** for several obligations totaling $3924.25 and due by 5 Jul 1821, or the property is to be sold at public sale. Signed Victor **LORIMIER**. Wit John **JUDEN** Jr., Clerk. Rec 21 May 1821.

1850. Page 119. 20 Apr 1821. Alexander **McNAIR**, Governor of Mo., to James **EVANS**, Esq. Appointment as Clerk of the Fourth Judicial Circuit. Signed A. **McNAIR**. Wit Joshua **BARTON**, Sec. of State. Rec 21 May 1821.

1851. Page 119. 20 Aug 1816. Web **HAYDEN** and Elizabeth, his wife, to William **HAYDEN**. For the sum of $300, 130 arpens on the waters of Randol's Creek; bounded on the S by Robert **ENGLISH**, W by **DESHAY**, N by Solomon **HAYDEN**, and E by Thomas **MORGAN**. Signed Web. **HAYDEN**, Elibeth **HAYDEN**. Wit Solomon **HAYDEN**, Hiram **HAYDEN**, Thomas **SULLINGER**, John **AKIN** (JP). Rec 25 May 1821.

1852. Page 120. 26 May 1821. Richard S. **THOMAS** and Frances, his wife, to Samuel **CUPPLES** and Mary, his wife (daughter of sd Richard and Frances). For natural love and affection towards their daughter Mary, 9 acres and 79 poles adjoining Jackson, being all that tract where sd **THOMAS** now lives beginning at a stake on the S side of fourth south street. Signed Richard S. **THOMAS**, Frances **THOMAS**. Wit Cne. S. **THOMAS**, Dep Clerk. Rec 26 May 1821.

1853. Page 121. 28 May 1821. Joseph **FRIZEL** and Sarah, his wife, to Henry **VON PHUL** of the firm of Joseph **FRIZEL** & Co. For the sum of $1, quit claim to two lots in Jackson; being Lot Nos. 64 & 65, bounded by Main St, first west street, and first south street. Signed Joseph **FRIZEL**, Sarah **FRIZEL**. Wit Stephen **BACON**, Wm. **CREATH** (JP). Rec 29 May 1821.

1854. Page 121. 10 Mar 1812. John **WILSON** and Sally, his wife, to John **BYRD**. For the sum of $450, 124 ½ acres and 3 poles, more or less, lying E of his own survey, being part of a tract granted and surveyed to Amos **BYRD**, decd, by the King of Spain and confirmed to the heirs of

Amos **BYRD**; beginning at a stake and stone. Signed John **WILSON**, Sally (+) **WILSON**. Test Robert **McWILLIAMS**, John **COCHRAN**, John **DAVIS** (JP). Rec 29 May 1821.

1855. Page 122. 30 May 1821. Robert **ENGLISH** to Alexander **NEELY**. For the sum of $1100, 150 acres, more or less, on the waters of Randol's Creek, being part of the tract where sd **ENGLISH** now lives; beginning at a stake in Thomas **MORGAN**'s north field on the S boundary of sd tract. There are some doubts respecting title of sd land, and if it shall be lost, sd **ENGLISH** agrees to give sd **NEELY** the tract he bought of **BLACKMORE**, known as Desha's old field tract, adjoining the first tract. Signed Robert **ENGLISH**. Test Thos. **MORGAN**, Anthony (x) **RANDOL**, John **JUDEN** Jr., Clerk. Rec 31 May 1821.

1856. Page 122. 11 May 1821. William **SMITH** of Randolph Co., Ill. to Matthew **DUNCAN** of Jackson Co., Ill. For the sum of $250, 640 acres on the waters of Whitewater that was granted and confirmed to sd **SMITH** as his settlement right. Signed Wm. (x) **SMITH**, Margonnet (x) **SMITH**. Wit Saml. **JOHNSTON**, Sarah **JOHNSTON**, Hilliard **FOWLER**, John W. **GILLISS**, JP in Randolph Co., Ill., William C. **GREENUP**, Clerk of Randolph Co., Ill. Circuit Court. Rec 2 Jun 1821.

1857. Page 123. 16 Apr 1821. William **HICKMAN** to Samuel G. **DUNN**. For the sum of $500, one negro man named **Daniel** of black complexion, about 20 years old. Signed Wm. **HICKMAN**. Test James **THOMPSON**, Elizabeth **THOMPSON**, John **JUDEN** Jr., Clerk. Rec 2 Jun 1821.

1858. Page 123. 29 Mar 1821. Justinian **WILLIAMS** of Cooper Co., Mo. to Abraham **NEWFIELD**. For the sum of $500, mortgage on a negro man named **Solomon** about 20 years of age and of black complexion. Sd **WILLIAMS** has borrowed the amount from sd **NEWFIELD**, to be paid one year from this date. Signed Justinian **WILLIAMS**. Wit David **ARMOUR** (JP), Solomon H. **ARMOUR**. Rec 2 Jun 1821. [Marginal note: Full satisfaction received on 16 Jul 1822. Signed Abraham **NEWFIELD**. Wit John **JUDEN** Jr., Clerk.]

1859. Page 124. 2 Jun 1821. Joel **BLUNT** to Charles **SEXTON**. For the sum of $98, mortgage on Lot No. 54 in Jackson. The amount is to be paid by 1 Jun 1822 with interest. Signed

Joel **BLUNT**. Test David **ARMOUR** (JP). Rec 5 Jun 1821.

1860. Page 124. 20 Mar 1806. James **WINCHESTER** of Sumner Co., Tenn. to Isaac **BLEDSOE**, son of Anthony **BLEDSOE**, and William **NEELY**. For the sum of $1, deed of trust to one negro woman slave named **Beck** and her children **Nelley**, **Ailey**, **Charles**, and **Harvey** and their future increase; two feather beds and furniture, six sheep, 17 head of hoggs and one cow. The grantees are to apply the annual profits of sd property to the separate use of Susanna **PENNEY**, without the interference of William **PENNEY** her husband, or any future husband, during her lifetime. Upon her death, the annual profits are to be applied to any surviving children of Susanna **PENNEY**. Signed James **WINCHESTER**. Wit David **SHELBY**, Clerk of Sumner Co., Tenn., James **DOUGLAS**, Register of Sumner Co., Tenn. by Thomas **CULBERT**, Dep Register. Rec 5 Jun 1821.

1861. Page 125. 12 Mar 1821. Enoch **EVANS** and Amelia, his wife, of New Madrid Co., Mo. to Benjamin M. **HORREL**. For the sum of $2000, 275 acres five chains and 2388/10000 of an acre in two tracts on the waters of Ramsey's Creek, being the tracts originally confirmed to Pierre **GODAIR** and William **BONER**; beginning at the NE corner at a stake. Signed Enoch **EVANS**, Amelia **EVANS** (RD). Wit A. **BUCKNER**, David **ARMOUR** (JP), William **KELSO** (JP). Rec 6 Jun 1821.

1862. Page 126. 9 Apr 1821. Jacob **SHEPPARD** to James **WILKERSON**. For the sum of $400, one negro man named **Noah**. Signed Jacob **SHEPHERD**. Test A. **BUCKNER**, Joel **BLUNT**, David **ARMOUR** (JP). Rec 11 Jun 1821.

1863. Page 126. 31 May 1821. David **DAVIS** of Bracken Co, Ken. to Lyne **STARLING** and Elias N. **DLASHMUTT**. For the sum of $450, the E part of Lot No. 51 in Jackson; beginning at the SE corner and adjoining the public square. Signed David **DAVIS**, Sarah **DAVIS**. Wit John **COLGLAZER**, Augustus **DAVIS**, John **PAYNE**, Clerk of Bracken Co, Ken. Court. Rec 12 Jun 1821.

1864. Page 127. 13 Dec 1820. Commissioners to Partition Lands of the heirs of Louis **LORIMIER**, decd, to Miles **DOYLE**. For the sum of $555, 145 acres, more or less, being Outlot No. 70, one mile above Cape Girardeau on the Mississippi River; bounded on the E by

the river, S by Outlot No. 69, W by Outlot No. 71, and N by the N boundary of Louis **LORIMIER**'s original survey. Sold as in F:20. Signed B. **COUSIN**, C. G. **ELLIS**, Wm. **KELSO**. Test John C. **HARBISON** (JP). Rec 12 Jun 1821.

1865. Page 128. 20 Dec 1816. Web **HAYDEN** and Elizabeth, his wife, to Solomon **HAYDEN**. For the sum of $330, 110 acres on the waters of Randol's Creek; bounded on the S & W by Joel **RENFROE**, N by William **HAYDEN**, and E by **DESHAY**. Signed Web **HAYDEN**, Elizabeth **HAYDEN**. Wit Hiram **HAYDEN**, William **HAYDEN**, Thomas **SULLINGER**, John **AKIN** (JP). Rec 15 Jun 1821.

1866. Page 128. 26 Dec 1816. Same and same to same. For the sum of $120, 40 acres on the waters of Randol's Creek; bounded on the E & N by Joel **RENFROE**, W by Thomas **SULLINGER**, and S by Web **HAYDEN**. Signed Elizabeth **HAYDEN**, Web **HAYDEN**. Wit William **HAYDEN**, Hiram **HAYDEN**, Thomas **SULLINGER**, John **AKIN** (JP). Rec 15 Jun 1821.

1867. Page 129. 25 Nov 1819. Commissioners to Partition Lands of the heirs of Louis **LORIMIER**, decd, to Richard **WATHIN** of New Madrid Co., Mo. For the sum of $385, the S ½ of Lot No. 10, Range B in Cape Girardeau; bounded on the E by Lorimier St and S by Meriwether St. Sold as in F:20. Signed B. **COUSIN**, Wm. **KELSO**, C. G. **ELLIS**. Test John C. **HARBISON** (JP). Rec 19 Jun 1821.

1868. Page 130. 25 Nov 1819. Same to same. For the sum of $545, the N ½ of Lot No. 2, Range B in Cape Girardeau; bounded on the N by Lot No. 1, E by Aquamsi or Front St, and W by Lot No. 3. Signed B. **COUSIN**, Wm. **KELSO**, W. **GARNER**. Test John C. **HARBISON** (JP). Rec 19 Jun 1821.

1869. Page 131. 12 Jun 1821. Richard **WATHAN** of New Madrid Co., Mo. to Thomas Jefferson **RODNEY** and Polly **RODNEY**, children of Thomas S. **RODNEY** and Maria Louisa, his first wife, formerly Maria Louisa **LORIMIER**. For the sum of $680, the N ½ of Lot No. 2, and S ½ of Lot No. 10, as described in the preceding two deeds (F:129, 130). Signed Richd. **WATHEN**. Wit James **EVANS**, Enoch **EVANS**, John **JUDEN** Jr., Clerk. Rec 19 Jun 1821.

1870. Page 131. 22 Mar 1821. Eli **SHELBY** to John **WEAVER**. For the sum of $250, quit claim to 135 acres, more or less, on Ramsey's Creek, being the S end of 270 acres that was the head right and improvement of Michael **BERGEN**, granted by the Spanish Government and sold by him to Samuel **BRADLEY**; bounded by Ann Eve **WEAVER**, widow of Peter **WEAVER**, decd, John **WEAVER**, the heirs of Joseph **THOMPSON**, decd, and public lands. Signed Eli **SHELBY**, Mary (x) **SHELBY**. Wit John C. **HARBISON**, John **MORRISSON**, George **HENDERSON** (JP). Rec 20 Jun 1821.

1871. Page 132. 1 Dec 1819. Commissioners to Partition Lands of the heirs of Louis **LORIMIER**, decd, to Victor **LORIMIER**. For the sum of $140, Lot No. 27, Range G in Cape Girardeau; bounded on the N by Lot No. 26, S by Lot No. 28, E by Lorimier St, and W by an alley. Sold as in F:20. Signed B. **COUSIN**, Wm. **KELSO**, W. **GARNER**. Test John C. **HARBISON** (JP). Title is conveyed to George **HENDERSON** for the sum of $140 on 1 Dec 1819. Signed Victor **LORIMIER**. Wit Thos. S. **RODNEY**, Jno. **ABERNETHIE** (JP). Rec 25 Jun 1821.

1872. Page 133. 14 May 1821. Victor **LORIMIER** and Sally, his wife, to George **HENDERSON**. For the sum of $266, two lots in Range G Cape Girardeau; Lot No. 27, bounded on the N by Lot No. 26, S by Lot No. 28, E by Lorimier's St, and W by an alley; and an equal and undivided part of Lot No. 1, purchased by sd **HENDERSON**, Nathan **McCARTY**, and sd **LORIMIER**; bounded on the E and fronted by the Mississippi River, N by Williams St, W by Lot No. 12, and S by Lot No. 2. Signed Victor **LORIMIER**, Sally (x) **LORIMIER**. Wit Wm. **STEINBECK**, R. V. **LORIMIER**, Jno. **ABERNETHIE** (JP). Rec 25 Jun 1821.

1873. Page 134. 14 Jun 1821. Morris **YOUNG** to Stepen **BYRD** and George **MEAIZE**. For the sum of $400, bond to make a deed on 25 acres in the NW ¼, Sec 36, Twp 31, Rng 11; beginning at Ithamer **HUBBLE**'s line; and including the mill seat. The deed to be made as soon as sd **YOUNG** obtains a right from Congress by a settlement right or preemption. Signed Morris **YOUNG**. Wit John **JUDEN** Jr., Clerk. Rec 25 Jun 1821. [Marginal note: Deed of conveyance received of Morris **YOUNG** and Hannah, his wife, on 22 Mar 1826. Signed Geo. **MAIZE**.]

1874. Page 134. 9 Jun 1821. Robert **CRAFTIN** of Union Co., Ill. to Samuel G. **DUNN**. For the sum of $800, one negro man named **Shaderick** of a black complexion, about 22 years of age. Signed Robert **CRAFTON**. Test Wm. **HICKMAN**, Paul (x) **CRAFTON**, John **JUDEN** Jr., Clerk. Rec 25 Jun 1821.

1875. Page 135. 18 Nov 1807. John **GUETHING** and James **DOWTY** to Medad **RANDOL**. For the sum of $1600, bond to make title to 410 arpents, bounded by David **PATTERSON** on the N and Jon **FORMAN** on the S, as soon as land claims are established. Signed John **GUETHING**, James **DOWTY**. Wit Wm. **GARNER**, John **HANNAH**. All right to the bond is signed over to Stephen **BYRD** on 12 Dec 1807. Signed Medad **RANDOL**. Test James **DOWTY**, James **WILKINSON**, John **BYRD** (JP), David **ARMOUR** (JP), Cne. S. **THOMAS**, Dep. Clerk. Rec 27 Jun 1821.

1876. Page 135. 30 Mar 1821. John **DAVIS** and Nancy, his wife, to John **BURNS**. For the sum of $1500, 150 acres, more or less, on the waters of Hubble's Creek; bounded on the N by the heirs of David **PATTERSON**, decd, and Andrew **BURNS**, E by Andrew **BURNS** and Erasmus **ELLIS**, S by John **BROWN** and John **DELAP**, and W by Edward **HAIL**; being part of a tract granted to Jonathan **FOREMAN**, where sd **DAVIS** and family now live. Title has not yet been confirmed by the commissioners, and if the claim is rejected, then sd **DAVIS** and wife convey the right of preemption to sd **BURNS**, and give him power of attorney to act in their behalf to secure the tract. Signed John **DAVIS**, Nancy **DAVIS**. Wit Peleg **FREEMAN**, Thomas R. **BOYCE**, John **JUDEN** Jr., Clerk. Rec 29 Jun 1821.

1877. Page 136. 23 Jun 1821. Richard S. **THOMAS** and Frances, his wife, to John **SHEPPARD**. For the sum of $400, 23 acres, 1 rood, and 12 poles, more or less, where sd **THOMAS** now lives; being the same originally confirmed to Henry **SHARADIN**; beginning at a stake at the NE corner of sd tract. Signed Richard S. **THOMAS**, Frances **THOMAS**. Wit John **JUDEN** Jr., Clerk. Rec 30 Jun 1821.

1878. Page 137. 12 Jan 1821. William A. **BULL** to William **McGUIRE**. For the sum of $50, Lot No. 175 in Jackson; bounded on the N and fronted by second south street, E and fronted by fourth east street, S by Lot No. 176, and W by Lot No. 164. Signed Wm. A. **BULL**. Wit William **CREATH**, William **FISHBACK**, John **JUDEN** Jr., Clerk. Rec 4 Jul 1821.

1879. Page 138. 11 Jul 1821. John **BURNS** and Mary, his wife, to Robert **PACKIE**. For the sum of $25, 2 ½ acres, more or less, on Randol's Creek; beginning at a stake on the original line, so as to include the spring; being part of a tract confirmed to Enos **RANDOL** Junr. and conveyed to sd **BURNS** by Uriah **BROCK** and wife on 17 Jul 1820. Signed John **BURNS**, Mary (x) **BURNS**. Wit Havens Clary (HCA) **ABERNETHIE**, Wylie A. **ABERNETHIE**, Jno. **ABERNETHIE** (JP). Rec 12 Jul 1821.

1880. Page 138. 11 Jul 1821. Robert **PACKIE** and Margret, his wife, to John **BURNS**. For the sum of $2200, two tracts in Cape Girardeau Twp, being where sd **PACKIE** and family now live, and where sd **BURNS** and family formerly lived, on a tract purchased by sd **BURNS** from Anthony **RANDOL** on 4 Aug 1816, and the other from Lewis **TASH** on 10 Dec 1814, and both sold by sd **BURNS** to sd **PACKIE** on 27 Dec 1819. The tract from sd **RANDOL**, 13 acres, more or less, beginning at the SE corner of the land purchased by sd **BURNS** of sd **TASH**, and also bounded by Abraham **BYRD**, sd **RANDOL**, and Franks' Creek. The other tract, 200 arpens, French measure, being the E end of a tract confirmed to sd **TASH**, so as to include the plantation where sd **PACKIE** and Jonathan **ANDREWS** now live, beginning at the SE corner at a stone near a pond. Signed Robert **PACKIE**, Margret **PACKIE**. Wit Havens Clary (HCA) **ABERNETHIE**, Wylie A. **ABERNETHIE**, Jno. **ABERNETHIE** (JP). Rec 12 Jul 1821.

1881. Page 139. 11 Oct 1820. Commissioners to Partition Lands of the heirs of Louis **LORIMIER**, decd, to Samuel **RAVENSCROFT**. For the sum of $40, 3 ¼ acres, more or less, being Outlot B NW of Cape Girardeau; bounded on the N by Outlot D, S by Outlot C, W by Outlot No. 8, and E by Pacific St. Sold as in F:20. Signed B. **COUSIN**, Wm. **KELSO**, W. **GARNER**. Wit John C. **HARBISON** (JP). Rec 13 Jul 1821.

1882. Page 140. 18 Jul 1821. Minor M. **WHITNEY** to Louis **LORIMIER**. For the sum of $143.33 1/3, the N ½ of Lot No. 12, Range E in Cape Girardeau; bounded on the N by St Bellevew and E by Lorimier St. Signed Minor M. **WHITNEY**. Wit James **EVANS**, John **JUDEN** Jr., Clerk. Rec 18 Jul 1821.

1883. Page 141. 14 Jul 1821. Thomas **BOLING** to Lewis **BOLING** and William **BOLING**. For ___, freedom to trade, deal, and contract for

themselves; and he is not accountable for any more of their conduct. Signed Thomas (x) **BOLING**. Wit Hezekiah F. **JENKINS**, Thomas **RAMSEY**. Rec 19 Jul 1821.

1884. Page 141. 24 Feb 1820. Adam **BROWN** to Henry **EAKER**. For the sum of $320, ___ acres, being an improvement and preemption right on the waters of Crooked Creek, German Twp, near Gasper **SCHELL**'s place, being where sd **BROWN** now resides. Signed Adam **BROWN**. Wit Barnet **SNIDER** (JP). Rec 23 Jul 1821.

1885. Page 142. 22 Feb 1817. Commissioners of the Courthouse and Jail to George F. **BOLLINGER**, adminr of David **BULLINGER**, decd. For the sum of $56, Lot No. 97 in Jackson; bounded on the S and fronted by first north street, W and fronted by third west street, N by Joseph **SEWEL**, and E by Lot No. 85. Signed John **DAVIS**, John **SHEPPARD**, Samuel G. **DUNN**, Abraham **BYRD**. Wit Jos. **SEAWELL**, William **NEELY**. Rec 27 Jul 1821.

1886. Page 143. 5 Jul 1821. Alexander **McNAIR**, Governor of Mo., to Robert **GREEN**. Appointment as a Commissioner of the Loan Office in the Fifth District; being Ste. Genevieve, Perry, Madison, Wayne, Cape Girardeau, and New Madrid counties; his having been appointed by vote of the General Assembly. Signed A. **McNAIR**. Wit Wm. G. **PETTUS**, Sec. of State. Robert **GREEN** takes the oath of office. Signed Robt. **GREEN**. Wit David **ARMOUR** (JP). Rec 31 Jul 1821.

1887. Page 143. 5 Jul 1821. Same to James **RAVENSCROFT**. Appointment as a Commissioner of the Loan Office in the Fifth District; being Ste. Genevieve, Perry, Madison, Wayne, Cape Girardeau, and New Madrid counties, his having been appointed by vote of the General Assembly. Signed A. **McNAIR**. Wit Wm. G. **PETTUS**, Sec. of State. James **RAVENSCROFT** takes the oath of office. Signed James **RAVENSCROFT**. Wit David **ARMOUR** (JP). Rec 31 Jul 1821.

1888. Page 144. 5 Jul 1821. Same to James **EVANS**. Appointment as a Commissioner of the Loan Office in the Fifth District; being Ste. Genevieve, Perry, Madison, Wayne, Cape Girardeau, and New Madrid counties, his having been appointed by vote of the General Assembly. Signed A. **McNAIR**. Wit Wm. G. **PETTUS**, Sec. of State. James **EVANS** takes the oath of office. Signed James **EVANS**. Wit David **ARMOUR** (JP). Rec 31 Jul 1821.

1889. Page 145. 31 Jul 1821. James **EVANS**, Robert **GREEN**, and James **RAVENSCROFT**, Commissioners of the Loan Office, to William **McGUIRE**. Appointment as Clerk of the Loan Office. William **McGUIRE** takes the oath of office. Signed Wm. **McGUIRE**. Wit David **ARMOUR** (JP). Rec 2 Aug 1821.

1890. Page 145. 1 Aug 1821. William **McGUIRE**, Elias N. **DLASHMUTT**, John **DANIEL**, Stephen **BYRD**, James **RUSSELL**, Thomas W. **GRAVES**, John **JOHNSON**, William P. **LACEY**, John P. **WRIGHT**, Robert **BUCKNER**, Lindsey J. **DLASHMUTT**, and Saml. **RAVENSCROFT** to the State of Mo. For the sum of $60,000, bond to guarantee that William **McGUIRE** will demean himself well as Clerk of the Loan Office for the Fifth District, as established by an act of the Legislature approved 27 Jun 1821. Signed Wm. **McGUIRE**, John **DANIEL**, James **RUSSELL**, John **JOHNSON**, John P. **WRIGHT**, L. J. **DLASHMUTT**, E. N. **DLASHMUTT**, Stephen **BYRD**, Thos. W. **GRAVES**, Wm. P. **LACEY**, R. **BUCKNER**, Samuel **RAVENSCROFT**. Wit James **EVANS**. Rec 2 Aug 1821.

1891. Page 146. 25 Dec 1820. Erasmus **ELLIS** to John G. **LOVE** of Ste. Genevieve Co. For the sum of $1000, his claim to a negro man named **Ralph** now in dispute between him and Charles G. **ELLIS**; three milch cows & calves; and two horses. Signed Erasmus **ELLIS**. Test John **RODNEY**, Zachariah **DOWTY**, David **ARMOUR** (JP). Rec 12 Aug 1821.

1892. Page 146. 17 January 1805. Dennis **SULLIVAN** to Abraham **BYRD**. For the sum of $400, __ acres adjoining William **RUSSELL** on the Water Fork of Byrd's Creek, which sd **SULLIVAN** has entered as his head right. Signed Dens. **SULLIVAN**. Test Saml. **COOPER**, John **ZELIFROW**, James **RUSSELL** (JP). Rec 14 Aug 1821.

1893. Page 147. 5 Apr 1821. John **PRIM** to Stephen **BYRD** Senior. For the sum of $320, a ½ interest in Certificate of New Location No. 17 issued by Frederick **BATES**, Recorder of Land Titles; sd certificate being in the name of Joseph **GENERUUEX** under the act of Congress passed 17 Feb 1815; being 160 acres laid out on Apple Creek, Lot Nos. 4 & 5, NE ¼, Sec 2, Twp 33 N, Rng 12 E. Signed John **PRIM**. Wit Wm. **CREATH** (JP). Rec 13 Aug 1821.

1894. Page 147. 14 Aug 1821. Joseph **ROGERS** to Henry **BOLLINGER**, son of Phillip **BOLLINGER**. For the sum of $585, 200 acres on the W fork of Whitewater, German Twp, where sd **ROGERS** now lives; being part of 640 acres granted to John **BOLLINGER** Senear by the King of Spain; beginning at the NE corner of sd survey at a stake and adjoining Jacob **BOLLINGER**, John **WILSON**, and U. S. land. Signed Joseph **RODGERS**. Wit. Benja. **SHELL**, Adolph **YODER**, Gorge F. **BOLLINGER**, William **TINNIN** (JP). Rec 20 Aug 1821.

1895. Page 148. 29 Aug 1821. Timothy **FLINT** and Abigail, his wife, to Samuel **CUPPLES**. For the sum of $215, 5 acres, more or less, near Hubble's Creek on the N side of Jackson where sd **FLINT** now resides, being part of a tract confirmed to **MILLS**; beginning at a post near a spring and including the buildings. Signed Timothy **FLINT**, Abigail **FLINT**. Wit John **GILLELAND**, M. P. **FLINT**, Wm. **CREATH** (JP). Rec 6 Sep 1821.

1896. Page 149. 2 Aug 1821. William **NEELY**, Anthony B. **NEELY**, Joseph **FRIZEL**, and John **RANNEY**, executors of the last will and testament of Joseph **SEAWELL**, decd, to Timothy **FLINT**. For the sum of $150, 5 acres of a tract confirmed to **MILLS'** representatives as described in the preceding deed (F:148). Signed Wm. **NEELY**, Joseph **FRIZEL**, A. B. **NEELY**, Johnson **RANNEY**. Wit Wm. **CREATH** (JP). Rec 6 Sep 1821.

1897. Page 150. 10 Sep 1821. Samuel **CUPPLES** and Mary, his wife, to Theodore **JONES**. For the sum of $40, Lot No. 82 in Jackson; bounded on the W and fronted by second west street, N and fronted by third south street, E by Lot No. 70, and S by a fraction. Signed Saml. **CUPPLES**, Mary **CUPPLES**. Wit C. S. **THOMAS**, Dep Clerk. Rec 10 Sep 1821.

1898. Page 151. 20 Apr 1821. Jeremiah **RANDOL** to his brother John **RANDOL**. For the sum of $800, ½ of 240 arpens on Randol's Mill Creek; adjoined by Col. Nicholas **BUCKNER**, Charles G. **ELLIS**, and John **HITT** Junr; being a tract confirmed in favor of Jeremiah **RANDOL** and John, his natural and older brother, as heirs of Samuel **RANDOL**, their father; and including the plantation made by sd Samuel **RANDOL**. Signed Jeremiah **RANDOL**. Wit James **RANDOL**, Miles **RANDOL**, John **JUDEN** Jr., Clerk. Rec 10 Sep 1821.

1899. Page 152. 10 Feb 1819. Rachel **LAUGHERTY**, adminr of the estate of Benijah **LAUGHERTY**, decd, to Michael **COLLIER**. For the sum of $500, __ acres, being an improvement and preemption right on Flora Creek in Cape Girardeau Twp, which sd **LAUGHERTY** settled in about 1810. Sold on 10 Feb 1819 at order of Circuit Court issued in Sep Term 1818, on petition of Rachel **LAUGHERTY**, adminr of Benijah **LAUGHERTY**, to raise a sufficient sum to satisfy creditors of sd estate. Signed Rachel **LAUGHERTY**. Wit J. **RANNEY**, Zenas **PRIEST** (JP). Rec 10 Sep 1821.

1900. Page 153. 17 Jun 1820. Commissioners of the Courthouse and Jail to Harison **YOUNG**. For the sum of $118, Lot No. 129 in Jackson; bounded on the E and fronted by second east street, S and fronted by third south street, W by Lot No. 45, and N by Lot No. 128. Signed John **DAVIS**, John **SHEPPARD**, Samuel G. **DUNN**, Abraham **BYRD**. Wit N. **BUCKNER**, Greer W. **DAVIS**, John **JUDEN** Jr., Clerk. Rec 10 Sep 1821.

1901. Page 154. 10 Jun 1818. Same to William **NEELY**. For the sum of $61, Lot No. 148 in Jackson; bounded on the N and fronted by Main St, E and fronted by third east street, S by Lot No. 149, and W by Lot No. 136. Signed John **DAVIS**, John **SHEPPARD**, Samuel G. **DUNN**. Wit John **RODNEY**, Chas. **MOTH[ERSHEAD]**, Wm. **CREATH** (JP). Rec 10 Sep 1821.

1902. Page 155. 24 Feb 1821. Same to Samuel **LOCKHART**. For the sum of $28, W ½ of Lot No. 54 in Jackson; bounded on the N and fronted by first south street, W and fronted by first west street, and S by Lot No. 55. Signed John **DAVIS**, John **SHEPPARD**, Samuel G. **DUNN**, Benja. **SHELL**. Test John **JUDEN** Jr., Cne. S. **THOMAS**, Wm. **CREATH** (JP). Rec 10 Sep 1821.

1903. Page 156. 5 Sep 1821. William **WILLIAMS** and Elizabeth, his wife, to John **JUDEN** Junr. For the sum of $300, 41 acres, more or less, on both sides of Randol's Creek; adjoining John **ABERNETHIE**, James **MASSEY** formerly James **DOWTY**, sd **WILLIAMS** formerly part of Joseph **WALLER's** tract, and Isaac **WILLIAMS** formerly sd **WALLER**; beginning at a white walnut. Signed William **WILLIAMS**, Elizabeth (x) **WILLIAMS**. Wit Philip **DAVIS**, Jno. **ABERNETHIE** (JP). Rec 10 Sep 1821.

1904. Page 157. 25 Aug 1821. Heirs of James **MILLS** to Joseph **SEAWELL's** executors, William **NEELY**, Anthony B. **NEELY**, Joseph **FRIZEL**, and John **RANNEY**. On order of the Superior Court of Chancery at Feb Term 1921, 150 arpens confirmed to James **MILLS'** representatives on Hubble's Creek in Byrd Twp; bounded on the W by a tract confirmed to James **EARL** under Abraham **BYRD**, S by a tract confirmed to William **ASHLEY** under Henry **SHARODEN**, E by a tract confirmed to Samuel **PEW**, and N by an unconfirmed tract in possession of John **DAVIS**. Sd transfer arises from a case heard in the Superior Court of Chancery, Sep Term 1819; Joseph **SEAWELL**, complainant, vs. James **MILLS**, Wm. **MILLS**, Sally **BOYD** & James **BOYD** her husband, Fanny **MILLS**, and Merville **MILLS**, heirs and legal representatives of James **MILLS**, decd; which was decided for sd **SEAWELL**, and the defendants to pay costs. Sd **SEAWELL** had died by Feb term 1820. Signed Peter R. **GARRETT**, Clerk of the Superior Court of Chancery. Rec 12 Sep 1821.

1905. Page 159. 10 Oct 1818. Ezekiel **ABLE** to Johnson **RANNEY**. For the sum of $500, 161 acres, being an undivided part of the settlement right of John **SHIELDS** on Hubble's Creek containing 640 acres; being in Twp 30 N, Rng 12 E; and part of the land conveyed to sd **ABLE** by Charles S. **HEMPSTEAD**. Signed Ezekiel **ABLE**. Wit James **BRADY**, Mary **FRIZEL**, Zenas **PRIEST** (JP). Rec 24 Sep 1821.

1906. Page 159. 9 May 1821. John **BROWN** to Mary **FRIZEL**. For the sum of $170, mortgage on part of Lot No. 28 in Jackson, that he purchased of George **FRICKE**; bounded on the E and fronted by first east street, S and fronted by Lot No. 29, W by by a piece of ground once purchased by Clifton **MOTHERSHEAD**, and N and fronted by Main St. The debt is due in two months. Signed John **BROWN**. Wit J. **RANNEY**, Saml. **LOCKHART**, C. S. **THOMAS**, Dep Clerk. Rec 28 Sep 1821.

1907. Page 160. 22 Sep 1821. Harrison **YOUNG** of Perry Co., Mo. to Lyne **STARLING** and Elias N. **DLASHMUTT** of Jackson. For the sum of $30, part of Lot No. 146 in Jackson. Signed Harrison **YOUNG**. Wit John W. **SIMPKINS**, Wm. A. **BULL**, Saml. **ANDERSON**, Esq., Justice of Perry Co., Mo. Court. Rec 28 Sep 1821.

1908. Page 161. 4 Sep 1821. William **NEELY**, Anthony B. **NEELY**, Joseph **FRIZEL**, and John

RANNEY, executors of the last will and testament of Joseph SEAWELL, decd, to Caleb P. FULENWIDER. For the sum of $2000, 200 acres, more or less, in Byrd Twp, being the whole of James EARLE's head right that remains unsold; beginning at the NE corner of sd tract, adjoining the tract confirmed to James MILLS' representatives, and also adjoining Thomas NEAL and Hubble Creek, S by Richard S. THOMAS and James RUSSELL, W by MARTIN and BYRD, and N by Edward HAIL and Stephen BYRD. Signed Wm. NEELY, J. FRIZEL, J. RANNEY. Wit George F. BOLLINGER, John PRIM, Wm. CREATH (JP). Rec 11 Oct 1821.

1909. Page 162. 12 Oct 1821. Robert MORRISSON and Elizabeth, his wife, to Elias N. BARBER. For the sum of $300, ½ of Lot No. 196 on first south street in Jackson. Signed Robert MORRISON, Elizabeth ( ) MORRISON. Wit Claiborne S. THOMAS, Dep Clerk, James WATTS. Rec 12 Oct 1821.

1910. Page 163. 20 Oct 1820. Harrison YOUNG and Sally, his wife, to Alexander BUCKNER. For the sum of $600, Lot No. 129 in Jackson; bounded on the E and fronted by second east street, S and fronted by third south street, W by Lot No. 45, and N by Lot No. 128. Signed Harrison YOUNG, Sally YOUNG. Wit Wm. S. GANTT, Wm. CREATH (JP). Rec 18 Oct 1821.

1911. Page 164. 10 Feb 1821. John JUDEN Junr. to Claiborne S. THOMAS. Appointment as Deputy Clerk of the Fourth Judicial Circuit. Signed John JUDEN Jr., Clerk of Circuit Court. Richard S. THOMAS, Judge of Fourth Judicial Circuit, approves the appointment. Signed R. S. THOMAS. Claiborne S. THOMAS takes the oath of office. Signed Cne. S. THOMAS. Wit R. S. THOMAS, Judge. Rec 24 Oct 1821.

1912. Page 164. 21 Jul 1821. Same to same. Appointment as Deputy Clerk of the Cape Girardeau County Court. Signed John JUDEN Jr., Clerk of County Court. Claiborne S. THOMAS takes the oath of office. Signed Cne. S. THOMAS. Wit David ARMOUR (JP). Isaac SHEPPARD and George H. SCRIPPS, Justices of County Court, approve the appointment. Signed Isaac SHEPPARD, Geo. H. SCRIPPS. Rec 24 Oct 1821.

1913. Page 165. 25 Oct 1821. William McLAIN and Elizabeth, his wife, to Jonathan BUIS. For the sum of $189.50, 75 acres, 3 roods, and 19 poles that fell to them as heirs of Amos BYRD, decd; being part of 600 arpens granted by the Spanish Government to sd BYRD and confirmed to him by the U. S. Commissioners; bounded on the W by the tract where sd BUIS now lives, N by one of the heirs of sd BYRD, S by part of the same tract sold to Joseph YOUNG. Signed William McLAIN, Elizabeth ( ) McLAIN. Wit Wm. CREATH (JP). Rec 25 Oct 1821.

1914. Page 166. 25 Oct 1821. Jonathan BUIS to the State of Mo. For the sum of $42.37 ½ at the rate of 6% per annum from 25 Oct 1822, mortgage on the tract described in the preceding deed (F:165). Signed Jonathan BUIS. Test Wm. McGUIRE, C. S. THOMAS, Dep Clerk. Rec 25 Oct 1821. [Marginal note: Full satisfaction received on 17 Aug 1822. Signed Wm. McGUIRE, Clerk of Loan Office.]

1915. Page 166. 26 Oct 1821. James EVANS to same. For the sum of $1000, mortgage on a house and lot in Jackson where he now lives. Signed James EVANS. Test C. S. THOMAS, Dep Clerk. Rec 26 Oct 1821.

1916. Page. 167. 26 Feb 1819. Ezekiel ABLE to William WILLIAMS. For the sum of $1, 160 acres on Hubble's Creek, being the ¼ part of an undivided tract, the settlement right of John SHIELDS, and a part of the land conveyed to sd ABLE by Charles S. HEMPSTEAD. This deed is given to perfect a former conveyance dated 26 Jul 1817, in which sd ABLE conveyed the land to sd WILLIAMS for $400. Signed Ezekiel ABLE. Wit George HENDERSON (JP). Rec 29 Oct 1821.

1917. Page 167. 31 Oct 1821. Enoch EVANS to the State of Mo. For the sum of $100 at the rate of 6% per annum from 31 Oct 1822, mortgage on a lot in Cape Girardeau he purchased of Andrew RAMSEY. Signed Enoch EVANS. Test John JUDEN Jr., Clerk. Rec 31 Oct 1821.

1918. Page 168. 1 Nov 1821. Jacob SHEPHERD and Nancy, his wife, to Thomas S. RODNEY. For the sum of $615, 156.90 acres in Rng 12 E, Twp 30 N; being part of a tract confirmed to John P. ADINER, and being where sd SHEPHERD now lives; to be taken off the SW end of the survey; beginning at the SW corner at a stake and stone where a redbud and hickory stand marked as bearing trees; adjoining John RODNEY on the SW. Signed Jacob SHEPHERD, Nancy (x) SHEPHARD (RD). Wit John AKIN (JP), John WRIGHT. Rec 1 Nov 1821.

1919. Page 169. 2 Nov 1821. John **PROPTZ** and Barbara, his wife, to Hiram **ESTES** and Polly, his wife and late Polly **PROPTZ**, daughter of sd John & Barbara. For love and natural affection, 140 acres, more or less, on both sides of Whitewater, being part of the land confirmed to sd **PROPTZ**; beginning at a Spanish oak. Signed John **PROPTZ**, Barbara (x) **PROPTZ**. Wit C. S. **THOMAS**, Dep Clerk. Rec 2 Nov 1821.

1920. Page 169. 5 Oct 1821. Moses **BYRNE** to Thompson **BIRD**. In consideration of a debt of $100 to be secured, 300 acres, more or less, being a farm and house in Cape Girardeau Twp where he now lives. Signed Moses **BYRNE**. Wit John **DAVIS**, John P. **WRIGHT**, John **AKIN** (JP). Rec 6 Nov 1821.

1921. Page 170. 21 Sep 1821. Alexander **McNAIR**, Governor of Mo., to Townsend **NICHOLS**. Appointment as a JP for Cape Girardeau Twp for four years. Signed A. **McNAIR**. Wit Wm. G. **PETTUS**, Sec. of State. Townsend **NICHOLS** takes the oath of office. Signed Townsend **NICHOLS**. Wit David **ARMOUR** (JP). Rec 14 Nov 1821. [Marginal note: Full satisfaction received on 5 Oct 1822. Signed Thompson **BIRD**. Wit John **JUDEN** Jr., Clerk.]

1922. Page 170. 3 Oct 1821. Harrison **YOUNG** and Sally, his wife, to Thomas **BLAIR**. For the sum of $20, Lot No. 146 in Jackson; fronting on first north street. Signed Harrison **YOUNG**, Sally **YOUNG**. Wit David **ARMOUR** (JP). Rec 20 Nov 1821.

1923. Page 171. 21 Nov 1821. Matthew **DUNCAN** of Jackson Co., Ill. to John **PAYNE** of Jackson. For the sum of $1800, 640 acres on the waters of Whitewater, being the same granted and confirmed to William **SMITH**, and transferred by sd **SMITH** to sd **DUNCAN** on 11 May 1821. Signed Matthew **DUNCAN**. Wit C. V. **FIELD**, James B. **McDONALD**, David **ARMOUR** (JP). Rec 22 Nov 1821.

1924. Page 172. 25 Nov 1819. Commissioners to Partition Lands of the heirs of Louis **LORIMIER**, decd, to Jenifer T. **SPRIGG**. For the sum of $785, Lot No. 3, Range B in Cape Girardeau; bounded on the N by Lot No. 4, S by Merriwether St, E by Lot No. 2, and W by Spanish St. Sold as in F:20. Signed B. **COUSIN**, W. **GARNER**, Wm. **KELSO**. Test John C. **HARBISON** (JP). Rec 23 Nov 1821.

1925. Page 173. 14 Jan 1820. Jenifer T. **SPRIGG** to Victor **LORIMIER**. For the sum of $785, Lot No. 3, Range B in Cape Girardeau, as described in the preceding deed (F:172). Signed Jenifer T. **SPRIGG**. Wit C. G. **ELLIS**, George **HENDERSON** (JP). Rec 23 Nov 1821.

1926. Page 173. 26 Jul 1820. Commissioners to Partition Lands of the heirs of Louis **LORIMIER**, decd, to same. For the sum of $56, three lots in Cape Girardeau; Lot No. 25, Range A, bounded on the E by Middle St and S by Williams St; Lot No. 21, Range B, bounded on the W by a street and S by Merriwether St; and Lot No. 23, Range B, bounded on the W by a street. Sold as in F:20. Signed B. **COUSIN**, C. G. **ELLIS**, Wm. **KELSO**. Wit John C. **HARBISON** (JP). Rec 23 Nov 1821.

1927. Page 174. 22 Nov 1819. Same to James **EVANS**. For the sum of $265, the N ½ of Lot No. 3, Range A in Cape Girardeau; bounded on the N by Lot No. 4, E by Lot No. 2, and W by Spanish St. Sold as in F:20. Signed B. **COUSIN**, C. G. **ELLIS**, Wm. **KELSO**, W. **GARNER**, Benjn. M. **HORRELL**. Test John C. **HARBISON** (JP). Rec 23 Nov 1821.

1928. Page 175. 22 Nov 1819. Same to same. For the sum of $655, N ½ of Lot No. 5, Range A in Cape Girardeau; bounded on the N by Merriwether St, E by Spanish St, and W by a lane. Sold as in F:20. Signed B. **COUSIN**, C. G. **ELLIS**, Wm. **KELSO**, W. **GARNER**, Benjn. M. **HORRELL**. Test John C. **HARBISON** (JP). Rec 23 Nov 1821.

1929. Page 176. 23 Nov 1819. Same to same. For the sum of $3000, Lot No. 17, Range A in Cape Girardeau; bounded on the N by Lot Nos. 2 & 3, S by Williams St, E by Aquamsi or Front St, and W by Lot No. 18. Sold as in F:20. Signed B. **COUSIN**, Wm. **KELSO**, C. G. **ELLIS**, W. **GARNER**, Benjn. M. **HORRELL**. Test John C. **HARBISON** (JP). Rec 23 Nov 1821.

1930. Page 177. 25 Nov 1819. Same to same. For the sum of $625, the S ½ of Lot No. 2, Range B in Cape Girardeau; bounded on the E by Aquamsi or Front St, W by Lot No. 3, and S by Merriwether St. Sold as in F:20. Signed B. **COUSIN**, W. **GARNER**, C. G. **ELLIS**, Wm. **KELSO**. Test John C. **HARBISON** (JP). Rec 23 Nov 1821.

1931. Page 178. 22 Nov 1819. Same to same. For the sum of $281, the N ½ of Lot No. 2, Range A in Cape Girardeau; bounded on the E by

Aquamsi or Front St, N by Lot No. 1, and W by Lot No. 3. Sold as in F:20. Signed B. **COUSIN**, C. G. **ELLIS**, William **KELSO**, W. **GARNER**, Benjn. M. **HORRELL**. Test John C. **HARBISON** (JP). Rec 23 Nov 1821.

1932. Page 179. 22 Nov 1819. Same to same. For the sum of $237, the N ½ of Lot No. 1, Range A in Cape Girardeau; bounded on the N by Merriwether St and E by Aquamsi or Front St. Sold as in F:20. Signed B. **COUSIN**, C. G. **ELLIS**, William **KELSO**, W. **GARNER**, Benjn. M. **HORRELL**. Test John C. **HARBISON** (JP). Rec 23 Nov 1821.

1933. Page 179. 3 Dec 1821. Victor **LORIMIER** and Sarah, his wife, heirs of Louis **LORIMIER**, decd, to Louis **LORIMIER**. For the sum of $1, their share of 1000 acres, more or less, on a small creek above the old Cape, including an old Indian field and lick or glase on sd stream; being originally granted to Louis **LORIMIER** (son of Louis) on 28 Dec 1799, and confirmed by the U. S., then conveyed by Louis **LORIMIER** (son of Louis) to his father on 18 Apr 1812. Signed Victor **LORIMIER**, Sally (x) **LORIMIER**. Wit Jacob **SHEPHERD**, Martin **RODNEY**, Joel **SHEPPARD**, David **ARMOUR** (JP). Rec 3 Dec 1821.

1934. Page 180. 24 Jul 1821. William P. **LACEY** and Emily, his wife, to John M. **DANIEL**. For the sum of $200, Block No. 7 in Cape Girardeau, including Lot Nos. 33, 34, 35, 36, 37, 38, 39, & 40, Range F; bounded on the N by North St, S by St Belleview, and E & W by two other streets. Signed Wm. P. **LACEY**, Emily (x) **LACEY**. Wit Peter R. **GARRETT**, C. A. **GARRETT**, Daniel **HOOSER**, C. S. **THOMAS**, Dep Clerk. Rec 4 Dec 1821.

1935. Page 181. 3 Dec 1821. Thomas **SULLINGER** to Samuel G. **DUNN**. For the sum of $600, one negro man named **Daniel**, of black complexion, about 34 years of age. Signed Thomas **SULLINGER**. Test William P. **DUNN**, Jared C. **MARTIN**, C. S. **THOMAS**, Dep Clerk. Rec 5 Dec 1821.

1936. Page 182. 7 Aug 1820. David **ARMOUR** and John **JUDEN** Jr. to Samuel **McFARLAND**. For the sum of $100, ½ of the S ½ of Lot No. 21; bounded on the E and fronted by High St, S and fronted by third south street, W by Lot No. 57, and N by the N ½ of sd lot. Signed David **ARMOUR**, John **JUDEN** Jr. Wit Joel **BLUNT**, George **FRICK**, Zenas **PRIEST** (JP). Rec 10 Dec 1821.

1937. Page 183. 11 Dec 1821. John **LOGAN** and Marie, his wife, to Gustavus A. **BIRD**, Atty at Law of Ste. Genevieve, Mo. In consideration for his prosecuting their claim to all of the estate of Louis **LORIMIER**, Senior, 1/3 of all of their share of sd estate, both real and personal, to which they are entitled. The sd Marie claims as wife and widow of sd **LORIMIER** by dower, marriage contract, and also as sole heir of Manuel **LORIMIER**, decd, son of herself and sd Louis & his sole heir; and sd John claims in right of his wife. Signed John **LOGAN**, Marie **LOGAN**. Wit Isaac **CADWALLADER**, Samuel **IRELAND**, Benjamin **DAVIS**, Esq, JP in Perry Co., Mo. Rec 11 Dec 1823. [Marginal note: I do hereby cancel this deed and am fully satisfied. No date. Signed G. A. **BIRD**. Test C. S. **THOMAS**, Clerk.]

1938. Page 183. 11 Dec 1821. John **PAYNE** to the State of Mo. For the sum of $500 with 6% interest per annum, beginning on 11 Dec 1822, mortgage on 640 acres on Whitewater, granted and confirmed to William **SMITH**, conveyed by him to Mathew **DUNCAN**, and by him to sd **PAYNE**. Signed John **PAYNE** Jr. Wit Wm. **McGUIRE**, C. S. **THOMAS**, Dep Clerk. Rec 12 Dec 1821.

1939. Page 184. 22 Dec 1815. William **GARNER** and John **HAYS** to Richard **WALLER**. For the sum of $1000, bond to make a deed on 240 French arpens on Randoll's Creek and the plantation and improvements, formerly belonging to James **DOWTY**, where he and his family lived, and granted to sd **DOWTY** by the Spanish Government; bounded by Charnal **GLASSCOCK** (formerly **WHITAKER**'s old place), William **WILLIAMS**, William **WILLIAMS** (formerly Joseph **WALLER**'s Spanish Grant), John **ABERNETHIE**, and some vacant land. The deed is to be made after right is obtained from the U. S. A. Signed W. **GARNER**, John **HAYS**. Wit John **MASSEY**, William (x) **MURPHY**. Rec 12 Dec 1821.

1940. Page 184. 5 Sep 1821. Richard **WALLER** to James **MASSEY**. For the sum of $1000, bond to make a deed on 240 French arpens described in the preceding deed (F:184); to be made within six months of the time sd **WALLER** receives a deed from William **GARNER**. Signed Richard **WALLER**. Wit Joshua **McDONALD**, Wm. **FISHBACK**, John **GLASSCOCK**. Rec 12 Dec 1821.

1941. Page 185. 11 Dec 1821. Samuel **McFARLAND** to the State of Mo. For the sum of $400 with 6% interest per annum from 11 Dec 1822, mortgage on a house and lot in Jackson. Signed Saml. **McFARLAND**. Wit Wm. **McGUIRE**, C. S. **THOMAS**, Dep Clerk. Rec 14 Dec 1821.

1942. Page 186. 22 Jul 1820. John **MASSEY** to John **BURNS**. For the sum of $1200, bond to make a deed for 120 French arpens on Randol's Creek by 1 Dec next; being ½ of the N end of a tract granted by the Spanish Government to James **DOWTY**; beginning on the boundary of the original survey at a stake. Signed John **MASSEY**. Test John **DAVIS**, John **GILES**, Richard **WALLER**, Wm. **CREATH** (JP). This original deed recorded in E:528. Wit B. **COUSIN**, Dep Clerk. Bond is assigned to Robert **PACKIE** for value received on 11 Jul 1821. Signed John **BURNS**. Wit Jno. **ABERNETHIE** (JP). Rec 14 Dec 1821.

1943. Page 187. 5 Sep 1821. Richard **WALLER** to James **MASSEY**. For the sum of $1000, bond to make a deed on 240 French arpens as described in E:184; sd deed to be made within six months of the date sd **WALLER** receives a deed for the tract from William **GARNER**, who purchased the tract from James **DOWTY**. Signed Richard **WALLER**. Wit Joshua **McDONALD**, Wm. **FISHBACK**, John **GLASSCOCK**, C. S. **THOMAS**, Dep Clerk. Rec 15 Dec 1821.

1944. Page 188. 20 Dec 1821. Parish **GREEN** and Clary, his wife, to William **HICKMAN**. For the sum of $2250, two tracts; an undivided 50 acres on the Mississippi River at a place known as Green's Ferry, formerly Waller's Ferry, including the ferry landing; and __ acres in Union Co., Ill., fronting on the bank of the Mississippi River ¼ of a mile, known as Green's Ferry, including the ferry landing. Signed Parish **GREEN**. Wit James **EVANS**, R. **DAUGHERTY**, C. S. **THOMAS**, Dep Clerk. Rec 20 Dec 1821.

1945. Page 189. 15 Dec 1821. Nathl. W. **WATKINS** to the State of Mo. For the sum of $166 with 6% interest per annum after 15 Dec 1822, mortgage on a lot in Jackson on Main St, occupied by James **BROOKS**, purchased by sd **WATKINS** under an execution against John **ARMSTRONG** in favor of Joseph **FRIZEL**. Signed N. W. **WATKINS**. Wit Wm. **McGUIRE**, C. S. **THOMAS**, Dep Clerk. Rec 22 Dec 1821.

1946. Page 189. 20 Dec 1821. William **HICKMAN** to same. For the sum of $500 with 6% interest per annum after 20 Dec 1822, mortgage on 49 ½ acres on the Mississippi River, known as Green's Ferry, including the ferry landing. Signed Wm. **HICKMAN**. Wit Wm. **McGUIRE**, C. S. **THOMAS**, Dep Clerk. Rec 22 Dec 1821.

1947. Page 190. 20 Dec 1821. James **TANNER** to same. For the sum of $500 with 6% interest per annum after 20 Dec 1822, mortgage on 640 acres on Whitewater that was confirmed to James **SMITH**, and by him transferred to John **BROWN** (D:464), and transferred by sd **BROWN** to sd **TANNER** on 25 Mar 1819. Signed James **TANNER**. Wit Wm. **McGUIRE**, C. S. **THOMAS**, Dep Clerk. Rec 22 Dec 1821.

1948. Page 190. 21 Dec 1821. John **JUDEN** Jur. to David **ARMOUR**. For the sum of $500, his part of Lot No. 6 in Jackson; bounded on the W and fronted by High St, N and fronted by first north street, E by Lot No. 30, and S by Lot No. 7. The lot was purchased by sd **JUDEN** and sd **ARMOUR** of the Commissioners of the Courthouse and Jail on 17 Dec 1818, and they had held it as joint tenants. Signed John **JUDEN** Jr. Wit C. S. **THOMAS**, Peter R. **GARRETT**, Wm. **CREATH** (JP). Rec 22 Dec 1821.

1949. Page 191. 21 Dec 1821. William **NEELY**, Anthony B. **NEELY**, Joseph **FRIZEL**, and John **RANNEY**, executors of the last will and testament of Joseph **SEAWELL**, decd, to Elizabeth **SEXTON**. For the sum of $35, a lot of ground confirmed to James **MILLS'** representatives; beginning on the NW corner of Lot No. 3 owned by Henry **CLINARD** on Seawell St. Signed Wm. **NEELY**, Johnson **RANNEY**, Joseph **FRIZEL**. Wit Edward **HOLLISTER**, Wm. **CREATH** (JP). Rec 22 Dec 1821.

1950. Page 192. 15 Jul 1819. Jesse B. **THOMAS** and Rebecca, his wife, of St. Clair Co., Ill. to George **BULLITT** of Ark. Terr. For the sum of $200, Lot No. 14 in Jackson; bounded on the E and fronted by High St, N and fronted by first north street, W by Lot No. 50, and S by Lot No. 15 appropriated to public use. The lot was purchased by sd **THOMAS** and sd **BULLITT** of the Commissioners of the Courthouse and Jail on 18 May 1816, and they held it as joint tenants. Signed Jesse B. **THOMAS**, Rebecca **THOMAS**. Wit A. M. **HAMTRAMCK**, A. W. **SNYDER**, Joseph **TROTIER**, JP in St. Clair

Co., Ill., Shadrach **BOND**, Governor of Ill. (as to Joseph **TROTIER**). Rec 23 Dec 1821.

1951. Page 193. 22 Dec 1821. George **BULLITT** to the State of Mo. For the sum of $800 with 6% interest per annum after 22 Dec 1822, mortgage on Lot No. 14 in Jackson. Signed Geo. **BULLITT**. Wit C. S. **THOMAS**, Dep Clerk. Rec 24 Dec 1821.

1952. Page 193. 2 Oct 1821. Enoch **EVANS** and Amelia, his wife, of New Madrid Co., Mo. to John **EVANS**. For love and affection they bear to their son John **EVANS**, 72 acres and 8 chain(?) on Ramsey Creek where John **EVANS** now lives; beginning at the NE corner of land claimed by Thomas **ENGLISH**. Signed Enoch **EVANS**. Wit Victor **LORIMIER**, George **HENDERSON** (JP). Rec 24 Dec 1821.

1953. Page 194. 13 Dec 1821. Richard S. **THOMAS** to the State of Mo. For the sum of $800 and 6% interest per annum after 13 Dec next, 4 acres, more or less, beginning on the E side of Hubble's Creek, and the corn cribs, dwelling house, kitchen, loom house, smoke house, and other buildings. Signed Richard S. **THOMAS**. Wit C. S. **THOMAS**, John **JUDEN** Jr., Clerk. Rec 24 Dec 1821.

1954. Page 195. 24 Nov 1819. Commissioners to Partition Lands of the heirs of Louis **LORIMIER**, decd, to **MENEFEE & ISOM**. For the sum of $157, Lot No. 20, Range A in Cape Girardeau; bounded on the N by Lot No. 7, S by Williams St, E by an alley, and W by Lorimier's St. Sold as in F:20. Signed B. **COUSIN**, Wm. **KELSO**, W. **GARNER**, Benjn. M. **HORRELL**. Test John C. **HARBISON** (JP). Rec 28 Dec 1821.

1955. Page 195. 26 Nov 1819. Same to Jonas N. **MENEFEE**. For the sum of $200, Lot No. 10, Range F in Cape Girardeau; bounded on the N by North St, S by Lot No. 9, and E by Lorimier's St. Sold as in F:20. Signed B. **COUSIN**, Wm. **KELSO**, C. G. **ELLIS**. Test John C. **HARBISON** (JP). Rec 28 Dec 1821.

1956. Page 196. 29 Dec 1821. Jonas N. **MENEFEE** to the State of Mo. For the sum of $224 with 6% interest per annum after 29 Dec 1822, mortgage on Lot No. 9, Range C in Cape Girardeau, and house on the same. Signed Jonas N. **MENEFEE**. Wit John **JUDEN** Jr., Clerk. Rec 29 Dec 1821.

1957. Page 197. 26 Oct 1821. William **CRACROFT** to James **EVANS**. For the sum of $130, mortgage on 84 acres adjoining where sd **CRACROFT** now lives; one rone mare; two featherbeds and furniture; one colt; about 30 head of hogs; and five head of sheep. The amount to be paid within one year. Signed William **CRACROFT**. Wit John **WATHN**, John **JUDEN** Jr., Clerk. Rec 29 Dec 1821.

1958. Page 197. 2 Jan 1822. William **HICKMAN** to David **ARMOUR** of Jackson. For the consideration of sd **ARMOUR** serving as security in two actions brought against sd **HICKMAN** by Parish **GREEN** and Merit **COTES**, and for the sum of $1, 120 acres in Union Co. Ill. fronting for ¼ mile on the Mississippi River, and which sd **HICKMAN** bought of sd **GREEN**, known as Green's Ferry. Signed Wm. **HICKMAN**. Wit James **EVANS**, W. P. **HICKMAN**, John **JUDEN** Jr., Clerk. Rec 2 Jan 1822.

1959. Page 198. 9 Nov 1821. William **WEBSTER** of Stewart Co., Tenn. to William P. **HICKMAN**, John W. **HICKMAN**, Peter T. **HICKMAN**, Thomas J. **HICKMAN**, and Mary **HICKMAN**; children of his sister Mary **HICKMAN**, and his nephews and niece. For love and esteem, and the sum of $100, the following negroes: **Sam, Randle, Harry, Jessee, Lidia, Mariah, Susan, Suckey, Ailsy, Linda, Ann, John, Katharine, & Addam**. Signed Wm. **WEBSTER**. Wit Alexander **FOWLER**, John **JUDEN** Jr., Clerk. Rec 2 Jan 1823.

1960. Page 198. 10 Nov 1821. Same to his nephew William P. **HICKMAN**. For diverse good causes and considerations, power of attorney to manage, hire, receive, and pay for the negroes named in the preceding deed (F:198). Signed Wm. **WEBSTER**. Wit Alexander **FOWLER**, Wm. **HICKMAN**, John **JUDEN** Jr., Clerk. Rec 2 Jan 1822.

1961. Page 199. 22 Dec 1815. William **GARNER** and John **HAYS** to Richard **WALLER**. For the sum of $1000, bond to make a deed on 240 French arpens on Randoll's Creek as described in F:184. Signed W. **GARNER**, John **HAYS**. Wit John **MASSEY**, William (x) **MURPHY**, C. S. **THOMAS**, Dep Clerk. Rec 7 Jan 1822. [see F:184]

1962. Page 200. 9 Jan 1822. Gilbert **HECTOR** to John M. **DANIEL**. For the sum of $100, 10 acres where sd **DANIEL** now lives; beginning at a sugar tree ten inches in diameter. Signed Gilbert ( ) **HECTOR**. Wit C. S. **THOMAS**, Dep Clerk. Rec 9 Jan 1822.

1963. Page 201. 21 Sep 1821. Alexander **McNAIR**, Governor of Mo., to John **McCOMBS**. Appointment as a JP for Byrd Twp for four years. Signed A. **McNAIR**. Wit Wm. G. **PETTUS**, Sec. of State. John **McCOMBS** takes the oath of office. Signed John **McCOMBS**. Wit Wm. **CREATH** (JP). Rec 9 Jan 1822.

1964. Page 201. 30 Oct 1817. Elijah **RANDOL** to John G. **LOVE**. For the sum of $100, Lot No. 125 in Jackson; bounded on the E and fronted by second east street, S and fronted by first south street, W by Lot No. 41, and N by Lot No. 124. Signed Elijah **RANDOL**, Penelope **RANDOL**. Test Chrs. **MOTHERSHEAD**, [illegible], Jno. **ABERNETHIE** (JP), Zenas **PRIEST** (JP). Rec 14 Jan 1822.

1965. Page 202. 5 Jan 1822. James **RAVENSCROFT** to the State of Mo. For the sum of $1000 with 6% interest per annum after 5 Jan 1823, mortgage on 500 arpens where he now lives. Signed James **RAVENSCROFT**. Wit C. S. **THOMAS**, Dep Clerk. Rec 18 Jan 1822.

1966. Page 203. 30 Jan 1822. Samuel **LOCKHART** to John **CROSS**. For the sum of $150, ½ of Lot No. 54 in Jackson; bounded on the N and fronted by first south street, W and fronted by first west street, S by Lot No. 55, and E by the other half of the lot. Signed Saml. **LOCKHART**. Wit C. S. **THOMAS**, Dep Clerk. Rec 30 Jan 1822.

1967. Page 203. 16 Nov 1821. Victor **LORIMIER** and Sally, his wife, to John **RODNEY**. For the sum of $20, Lot No. 25, Range A in Cape Girardeau; bounded on the E by Middle St and S by Williams St. Signed Victor **LORIMIER**, Salley (x) **LORIMIER** (RD). Wit Thos. S. **RODNEY**, Jacob **SHEPHERD**, John **AKIN** (JP). Rec 11 Feb 1822.

1968. Page 204. 6 Dec 1821. Charles S. **HEMPSTEAD** and Rachel, his wife, of St. Louis, Mo. to Richard **SEARCY** of Ark. Terr. For the sum of $300, 160 acres, being an undivided half of 320 acres that was the undivided moiety of 640 acres confirmed as the settlement and improvement right of John **SHIELDS**; conveyed by sd **SHIELDS** to sd **HEMPSTEAD**, and quit claimed by Ezekiel

ABLE (for the 320 acres). Signed Chs. S. **HEMPSTEAD**, R. **HEMPSTEAD**. Wit Thos. **McGUIRE**, JP in St. Louis Co., Mo. Rec 12 Feb 1822.

1969. Page 205. 8 Dec 1821. John **ARMSTRONG** and Eliza, his wife, of Jackson to Samuel R. **OBER** and Clement **MARCH** of St. Louis, Mo. For the sum of $75, ½ of Lot No. 63 in Jackson; bounded on the S and fronted by Main St, ground formerly owned by Joseph **THORN**, and William **SHEPPARD**. Signed John **ARMSTRONG**, Hulale **ARMSTRONG** (also for money received). Wit David **ARMOUR** (JP). Rec 14 Feb 1822.

1970. Page 205. 8 Dec 1821. Same and same to same and same. For the sum of $20, Lot No. 44 in Decatur. Signed John **ARMSTRONG**, Hulale **ARMSTRONG**. Wit David **ARMOUR** (JP). Rec 14 Feb 1822.

1971. Page 206. 23 Nov 1821. James **EVANS** and Susan, his wife, of Jackson to Thomas S. **RODNEY**. For the sum of $3100, six lots in Cape Girardeau: the N ½ of Lot Nos. 1, 2, 3, & 5 in Range A, S ½ of Lot No. 2 in Range B, and 1/3 part of Lot No. 17, Range A, being the lot on which stands what is called the Red House; and 240 arpens, more or less, on Ramsey's Creek, confirmed to John Bte. **GODAIR** and conveyed by him to sd **EVANS**. Signed James **EVANS**, Susan M. **EVANS**. Wit Wm. **CREATH** (JP). Rec 14 Feb 1822.

1972. Page 207. 30 Apr 1821. Thomas S. **RODNEY**, guardian of Thomas Jefferson **RODNEY** and Polly **RODNEY**, children of Thomas S. **RODNEY** and Maria Louisa, his wife and formerly Maria Louisia **LORIMIER**, to Thomas Jefferson **RODNEY** and Polly **RODNEY**. For the sum of $3627.66 2/3 received of the commissioners appointed to divide the estate of Louis **LORIMIER**, decd, several parcels of land in and near Cape Girardeau; 1/3 of Lot No. 11, Range D; Lot No. 23, Range E; 3 ¼ acres, being Outlot C; 3 ¼ acres, being Outlot D; 3 ¼ acres, being Outlot E; 10 acres, being Outlot No. 9; 214 ½ acres, being Outlot Nos. 56, 57, & 58; 160 acres, being Outlot No. 79; 70 acres, more or less, being Outlot No. 87. Signed Thos. S. **RODNEY**. Wit Joel **BLUNT**, Erasmus **ELLIS**, Wm. **CREATH** (JP). Rec 14 Feb 1822.

1973. Page 208. 20 Nov 1821. Victor **LORIMIER** and Sally, his wife, to Thomas S. **RODNEY**. For the sum of $75, two lots in Cape

Girardeau; Lot No. 3, Range B, bounded on the N by Lot No. 4, S by Merriweather St, E by Lot No. 2, and W by Spanish St; and Lot No. 23, Range B, bounded on the W by a street. Signed Victor **LORIMIER**, Sally (x) **LORIMIER** (RD). Wit John **AKIN** (JP), Sally **AKIN**. Rec 14 Feb 1822.

1974. Page 209. __ Jan 1820. Jacob **SHEPHERD** [and Nancy, his wife,] to Richard **WRIGHT**. For the sum of $300, 50 acres, being part of 255.90 acres sold by John P. **AIDENER** to sd **SHEPHERD**; beginning at an elm 10 inches diameter. Signed Jacob **SHEPHERD**, Nancy **SHEPPARD** (RD). Wit Victor **LORIMIER**, Zenas **PRIEST** (JP), George **HENDERSON** (JP). Rec 18 Feb 1822.

1975. Page 209. 11 Feb 1822. Same and same to Joel **SHEPHERD**. For the sum of $1000, 50 acres, being part of a tract of 255.90 acres sold by John P. **AIDENGER** of Ste. Genevieve Co. to Jacob **SHEPHERD**; beginning at a post on the NW boundary line of sd survey. Signed Jacob **SHEPHERD**, Nancy (x) **SHEPPERD**. Wit A. B. **PENNEY**, George **HENDERSON** (JP). Rec 18 Feb 1822.

1976. Page 210. 22 Nov 1821. Martin **COTNER** to John **PARINGER**. For the sum of $133.75, 107 ¼ acres, beginning on **WILBURN**'s line at a white oak. Signed Martin (x) **COTNER**, Maryat (x) **COTTNER**. Test William **POLK**, Isaac (x) **MIERS**. Rec 19 Feb 1822.

1977. Page 211. 20 Feb 1822. Lyne **STARLING** of Ohio to Elias N. **D'LASHMUTT** of Jackson. Appointment as true and lawful attorney to sell and convey every interest or claim to any lands or town lots. Signed Lyne **STARLING**. Wit C. S. **THOMAS**, Dep Clerk. Rec 20 Feb 1822.

1978. Page 211. 18 Jan 1820. Thomas S. **RODNEY** and Polly, his wife, to Erasmus **ELLIS**. For the sum of $800, 80 acres on the waters of Hubble's Creek, being part of the land granted to Henery **HAND** by the Spanish Government and confirmed by the U. S. Commissioners, and sold by William & Sarah **HAND** and Henry & Sarah **HAND** to sd **RODNEY**; beginning on the W line of sd tract. Signed Thos. S. **RODNEY**, Polly (x) **RODNEY**. Wit Thos. **SLOAN**, John **WILSON**, William **CREATH** (JP). Rec 21 Feb 1822.

1979. Page 212. 22 Dec 1821. Erasmus **ELLIS** to John G. **LOVE**. For the sum of $1200, 80 acres as described in the preceding deed (F:212).

Signed Erasmus **ELLIS**. Wit Wm. **CREATH** (JP). Rec 21 Feb 1822.

1980. Page 213. 15 Sep 1821. James **WHITESIDE** to T. **QUARLES**. For the sum of $5000, bond to convey 481.60 acres in Twp 32 N, Rng 13 E; including 131.80 acres, being SW fractional ¼, Sec 18; SW fractional ¼, Sec 19; and SE ¼, Sec 18 and W ½, NE ¼, Sec 19. Signed James **WHITESIDE**. Wit P. R. **GARRETT**, C. S. **THOMAS**, Dep Clerk. Rec 23 Feb 1822.

1981. Page 213. 15 Oct 1817. John **LOGAN** and Mary, his wife, to the adminrs of Louis **LORIMIER**, decd (by Danl. F. **STEINBECK**). Acknowledgment of receipt of $4720 in cash or personal property, as part of $8000 agreed for with and paid by sd **STEINBECK** in the name of the heirs of sd **LORIMIER**, as consideration in full for all claims and demands of sd Mary **LOGAN** against his estate; the residue of the sum, $3280, having been paid in negroes and surrender of a mortgage on Francois **BERTHIAUME**'s property. Signed John **LOGAN**, Marey **LOGAN**. Wit James **LOGAN**, Abel **LOGAN**. Rec 25 Feb 1822.

1982. Page 213. 20 Dec 1821. Alexander **McNAIR**, Governor of Mo., to James **RUSSELL**. Appointment as a Justice of the Cape Girardeau Co. Court for four years. Signed A. **McNAIR**. Wit Wm. G. **PETTUS**, Sec. of State. James **RUSSELL** takes the oath of office. Signed James **RUSSELL**. Wit Wm. **CREATH** (JP). Rec 25 Feb 1822.

1983. Page 214. 4 Aug 1819. Simon **POE** Junr and Martha, his wife, to William **MARTIN**. For the sum of $15.75, 5 acres and 37 poles, being part of a tract that sd **POE** purchased of Elijah **RANDOL**, part of Enos **RANDOL**'s settlement right; being the NE corner of sd **POE**'s land; beginning at a white oak at sd **MARTIN** and Priscilla **JOHNSON**'s corner on a bridge near Ste. Genevieve Rd leading to Cape Girardeau. Signed Simon **POE** Junr., Martha (x) **POE**. Wit Jeancy (x) **POE**, Christiana (x) **MURPHY**, Jno. **ABERNETHIE** (JP). Rec 26 Feb 1822.

1984. Page 215. 31 Jan 1822. Greer W. **DAVIS** and Eliza, his wife, to George **MORROW**, all of Jackson. For the sum of $282, part of Lot No. 17 in Jackson; beginning at the NE corner, and bounded on the E and fronted by High St, S by Lot No. 17 owned by sd **DAVIS**, W by Lot No. 53, and N by Lot No. 16. Signed Greer W.

DAVIS, Eliza DAVIS. Wit C. S. THOMAS, Dep Clerk. Rec 26 Feb 1822.

1985. Page 215. 5 May 1821. Hugh BRANNON of Pulaski Co., Ark. to Charles G. ELLIS. For the sum of $110, 250 arpens on the W bank of the Mississippi River about 2 ½ miles below Cape Girardeau, bounded by public lands on all sides; being the same granted to sd BRANNON by the Commissioners. Signed Hugh BRANNON. Wit Jesse JEFFRY, Thos. FLETCHER, Hy. SANFORD, Clerk of Court of Common Pleas, Lawrence Co., Ark. Rec 2 Mar 1822.

1986. Page 216. 29 Jan 1821. William NEELY, Anthony B. NEELY, Joseph FRIZEL, and John RANNEY, executors of the last will and testament of Joseph SEAWELL, decd, to Rene LEMELLIEUR. For the sum of $50, __ acres near Jackson on the road to Bollinger's Mill; beginning at a stake at the SE corner of sd land, on the N side of the road; being the same sd LEMELLEUR formerly sold to Samuel PUTNAM, and now occupied by the widow WALKER. Signed Wm. NEELY, Joseph FRIZEL, Johnson RANNEY. Wit William CREATH (JP). Rec 4 Mar 1822.

1987. Page 217. 31 Oct 1821. Rene LEMELLIEUR to Henry LITTLE and Caleb P. FULLENWIDER. For the sum of $30, __ acres as described in the preceding deed (F:216). Signed Rene LeMELLIOUR. Wit N. CREATH, Johnson RANNEY, Wm. CREATH (JP). Rec 4 Mar 1822.

1988. Page 217. 9 Feb 1822. Henry LITTLE to Caleb FULANWIDER. For the sum of $15, his part of __ acres as described in the preceding deeds (F:216, 217), formerly occupied by the widow WALKER. Signed Hy. LITTLE. Wit Wm. CREATH (JP), W. GARNER. Rec 4 Mar 1822.

1989. Page 218. 5 May 1821. Michael RODNEY and Matilda, his wife, to Louis LOROMIER. For the sum of $352, quit claim to the undivided 1/3 part of Lot No. 11, Range D in Cape Girardeau, as described in the deed to sd RODNEY, sd LORIMIER, and Thomas S. RODNEY by the commissioners of the estate of Louis LORIMIER, decd. Signed Michl. RODNEY, Matilda RODNEY. Wit Tho. RODNEY, John AKIN (JP). Rec 4 Mar 1822.

1990. Page 219. 27 Dec 1820. Morgan BYRNE (principal), and Robert GREEN and James

RAVENSCROFT (securities) to John SMITH and George CLEMER. For the sum of $3000, bond to transfer 640 acres on Apple Creek within 80 days of the issue of a patent for land in Cape Girardeau Co. Sd BYRNE owns a New Madrid Claim Certificate issued by the Recorder of Land Titles at St. Louis to Phillip SHACKLER, the original claimant, for 640 acres, dated 18 Aug 1818; and sd BYRNE agrees to locate the tract on Apple Creek so as to include the improvements of sd SMITH and sd CLEMER, whereon they and their families now reside. Signed Morgan BYRNE, Robt. GREEN, James RAVENSCROFT. Wit Johnson RANNEY, C. S. THOMAS, Dep Clerk. Sd BYRNE is not to be liable if the 640 acres is not located so as to include both improvements as a consequence of their being too far apart, or if he is unable to secure sd land, but shall locate the grant elsewhere on lands subject thereunto as sd SMITH and CLEMER may require. Signed John SMITH, George CLEMMER. Wit J. RANNEY, C. S. THOMAS, Dep Clerk. Right of this bond is assigned to John HOFMAN for $990 on 28 Jan 1822. Signed George CLEMMER. Wit Samuel L. MOORE, Isidore MOORE, C. S. THOMAS, Dep Clerk. Rec 9 Mar 1822.

1991. Page 220. 9 Mar 1822. John MASSEY to John LANDERS of Wayne Co., Mo. For the sum of $109.84 ½, mortgage on Lot No. 138 in Jackson; bounded on the E by Lot No. 150, S by Lot No. 139, W and fronted by second east street, and N and fronted by first south street. The debt is due by 1 Nov next. Signed John MASSEY. Wit Otheniel DAVIS, George HENDERSON (JP). Rec 9 Mar 1822.

1992. Page 221. 4 Mar 1822. William MARTIN and Anna, his wife, to John D. RUTAN. For the sum of $100, two tracts; 5 acres and 37 poles, being a tract purchased by sd MARTIN of Simon POE Junr on 4 Aug 1819, and by sd POE from Elijah RANDOL, being part of the head right of Enos RANDOL Junr, beginning at a white oak corner (Priscilla JOHNSON's corner) on a ridge near the old Ste. Genevieve Rd; and 12 acres, more or less, being part of sd Enos RANDOL's confirmed land, and sold by him to Elijah RANDOL, and by him to John EDWARDS and Priscilla JOHNSON, and by them to sd MARTIN, beginning at a stake at Simon POE's SE corner near the Ste. Genevieve Rd. Signed William MARTIN, Anna MARTIN. Wit Simon POE Junr, John EDWARDS, Jno. ABERNETHIE (JP). Rec 11 Mar 1822.

1993. Page 222. 25 Nov 1819. Commissioners to Partition Lands of the heirs of Louis **LORIMIER**, decd, to Andrew **GUIBONEY**. For the sum of $80, the S ½ of Lot No. 15, Range F in Cape Girardeau; bounded on the S by Lot No. 16, W by Middle St, and E by an alley. Sold as in F:20. Signed W. **GARNER**, C. G. **ELLIS**, B. **COUSIN**, Wm. **KELSO**. Test John C. **HARBISON** (JP). Rec 16 Mar 1822.

1994. Page 223. 10 Oct 1820. Same to same. For the sum of $35, Lot No. 8, Range H in Cape Girardeau; bounded on the W and fronted by Spanish St, E by Lot No. 5, N by Lot No. 9, and W by Lot No. 7. Sold as in F:20. Signed B. **COUSIN**, Wm. **KELSO**, W. **GARNER**, C. G. **ELLIS**. Test John C. **HARBISON** (JP). Rec 16 Mar 1822.

1995. Page 223. 18 Mar 1822. Louis **LORIMIER** and Peggy, his wife, to Polly **DUNHAM**. For the sum of $1070, 284 acres in the Big Bend of the Mississippi River, being part of a tract of 1006 arpens and 32 poles granted by the Spanish Government to sd **LORIMIER**, and confirmed by the U. S.; beginning at a stake and stone on the line of sd survey. Conveyed in accordance with a title bond dated 12 Apr 1819. Signed L. **LORIMIER**, Peggy (x) **LORIMIER**. Wit [illegible], Jno. **RODNEY**, Wm. **CREATH** (JP). Rec 18 Mar 1822.

1996. Page 224. 18 Mar 1822. William **WILLIAMS** and William **RUSSELL** of St. Louis Co. Partition of 640 acres originally granted and confirmed to Thomas **FOSTER**; in Twp 30 N, Rng 12 E; beginning at the corner represented by the letter E on the plat, which is the SW corner of a survey of 300 arpens confirmed to James **CAROTHERS**. Sd **WILLIAMS** has conveyed all but 340 French arpens to sd **RUSSELL**, and the division line begins at the letter F in the plat. Sd **RUSSELL** owns the N part, and sd **WILLIAMS** and other assignees of sd **FOSTER** own the S part, which contains 300 acres, or 352 arpens. Signed William **WILLIAMS**, Wm. **RUSSELL**. Wit James **RUSSELL**, CGCCJ, Richard **McCARTY**. Rec 21 Mar 1822. [see Figure 3]

1997. Page 227. 19 Jan 1822. Reubin **SMITH** of Washington Co., Mo. to John G. W. **McCABE** of Madison Co., Mo. For the sum of $1920, 640 acres, being the same tract purchased by sd **SMITH** of Burwell J. **THOMPSON** on 18 Jul 1820 (E:509). Signed Reubin **SMITH**. Wit Tom. **MOSELEY** Jr., Clerk of Madison Co., Mo. Rec 30 Mar 1822.

1998. Page 227. 30 Mar 1822. James **BURNS** of Perry Co., Mo. to Jesse **HAIL**. For the sum of $650, Lot No. 13 in Jackson; beginning at the SE corner on High St. Signed James **BURNS**. Wit Nathl. **CREATH**, Wm. **CREATH** (JP). Rec 30 Mar 1822.

1999. Page 228. 30 Mar 1822. Jesse **HAIL** to the State of Mo. For the sum of $426 plus 6% interest from 30 Mar 1823, mortgage on Lot No. 13 in Jackson. Signed Jesse **HAIL**. Wit Claiborne S. **THOMAS**, Dep Clerk. Rec 30 Mar 1822.

2000. Number not used.

2001. Page 229. 30 Mar 1822. John G. W. **McCABE** to the State of Mo. For the sum of $500 plus 6% interest from 30 Mar 1823, mortgage on 640 acres on Whitewater confirmed to Lemuel **HARGROVES**, conveyed by him to Burwell J. **THOMPSON**, by him to Reubin **SMITH**, and by him to sd **McCABE**. Signed John G. W. **McCABE**, Jesse **HAIL**. Wit Peter R. **GARRETT**, Claiborne S. **THOMAS**, Dep Clerk. Rec 30 Mar 1822.

2002. Page 229. 16 Jul 1817. Priscillar **JOHNSON** to Col. John **EDWARDS**, her worthy friend. Appointment as her attorney in fact to transact all her business, serve as guardian to her children, and purchase or exchange property. She reserves the right to dispose of any property. Signed Priscillar **JOHNSON**. Wit James **GRIBBIN**, William **WILLIAMS**. Rec 30 Mar 1822.

2003. Page 230. 30 Mar 1822. John **EDWARDS**, atty in fact for Precillar **JOHNSON**, to the State of Mo. For the sum of $130 with 6% interest after 13 Mar 1823, mortgage on 40 acres; beginning at a white oak, a corner of Scarlet **GLASSCOCK**'s in the old line of Enos **RANDOL**. Signed Preceller **JOHNSON** by her atty in fact John **EDWARDS**. Wit Peter R. **GARRETT**, Claiborne S. **THOMAS**, Dep Clerk. Rec 30 Mar 1822.

2004. Page 230. 6 Mar 1822. Henry **BOLLINGER** Sr. and Katharine, his wife, to Ephraim R. **CONRAD**. For the sum of $1000, 50 ½ acres, more or less, on Whitewater in the NE corner of a survey confirmed to sd **BOLLINGER** by the Spanish Government; beginning at a sycamore on the E bank of the river. Signed Heinrich **BOLLINGER**, Katharine **BOLLINGER** [both in German]. Wit

John **BOLLINGER**, William **POLK**, C. S. **THOMAS**, Dep Clerk. Rec 1 Apr 1822.

2005. Page 231. 1 Apr 1822. Ephraim R. **CONRAD** to the State of Mo. For the sum of $100 with 6% interest from 1 Apr 1823, mortgage on 50 ½ acres as described in the preceding deed (F:230). Signed Ephraim R. **CONRAD**. Wit Claiborne S. **THOMAS**, Dep Clerk. Rec 1 Apr 1822.

2006. Page 232. 4 Mar 1822. Tunstall **QUARLES** of Ken. to Lyne **STARLING** and Elias N. **D'LASHMUTT** of the firm of E. N. **DLASHMUTT** & Co. in Jackson. For the sum of $170, __ acres, being the E ½, SE ¼ and 24 acres off the N and W ½ of Sec 18, Twp 32 N, Rng 13 E. Signed T. **QUARLES**. Wit Pet. R. **GARRETT**, F. **CANNON**, Wm. **CREATH** (JP). Rec 1 Apr 1822.

2007. Page 232. 2 Jan 1822. Commissioners to divide the lands of Samuel **TIPTON**, decd, to William **TIPTON**. For the sum of $300, 240 arpens on the waters of Ramsay's Creek confirmed to the representatives of Samuel **TIPTON**, decd; adjoining the original survey of Louis **LORIMIER**, decd, and Andrew **RAMSEY**, decd. Sold on order of Circuit Court issued Aug term 1820 on petition for partition of sd lands. Signed Benjn. M. **HORRELL**, John C. **HARBISON**, D. F. **STEINBECK**, Alexander **MILLER**. Wit Claiborne S. **THOMAS**, Dep Clerk. Rec 8 Apr 1822.

2008. Page 233. 10 Apr 1822. Charles **MOTHERSHEAD** by Sheriff John **HAYS** to Alexander **BUCKNER**. For the sum of $200, lot and building in Jackson where Dr. Edward S. **GANTT** now resides. Sold on 20 Apr 1820 in execution of a writ issued on 5 Jan 1820 by Circuit Court in favor of Nicholas **PEAY** and against sd **MOTHERSHEAD** (impleaded with Daniel M. **STOUT**) for $1047.09 debt, $128.22 damages, and $21.47 and 5 mills costs. Signed John **HAYS**, Shff. Wit Claiborne S. **THOMAS**, Dep Clerk. Rec 8 Apr 1822.

2009. Page 235. 12 Apr 1822. John **GUETHING**, decd, by Court of Chancery to John **SHEPPARD**. Ordered by sd court in case of John **SHEPPARD**, complainant, against Catharine **GUETHING**, now Catharine **BROWN**, devisee of John **GUETHING**, decd, defendants. The sd bill is dismissed against William **CROUSE** and John **DUNN**. Signed Peter R. **GARRETT**, Clerk. Rec 13 Apr 1822.

2010. Page 236. 18 Feb 1822. Alexander **McNAIR**, Governor of Mo., to Edmund **RUTTER**. Appointment as a JP for Byrd Twp for four years. Signed A. **McNAIR**. Wit Wm. G. **PETTUS**, Sec. of State. Edmund **RUTTER** takes the oath of office. Signed Edmund **RUTTER**. Wit Wm. **CREATH** (JP). Rec 15 Apr 1822.

2011. Page 237. 10 Apr 1822. Stephen **BYRD**, adminr de bonis non of Jason **CHAMBERLAIN**, decd, to Lyne **STARLING** and Elias N. **DLASHMUTT**. For the sum of $1236, Lot No. 2 in Jackson; bounded on the N by first north street, E by Lot No. 26, S by the public square, and W by High St. Sold on order of Circuit Court issued at Dec 1821 term on petition of sd **BYRD** to sell sd lands to pay debts against the estate. Signed Stephen **BYRD**, adminr de bonis non of Jason **CHAMBERLAIN**, decd. Wit G. A. **BIRD**, Greer W. **DAVIS**, John **JUDEN** Jr., Clerk. Rec 17 Apr 1822.

2012. Page 238. 15 Mar 1822. David **HOLLEY** to John **GIBONEY**. For the sum of $450 plus interest, quit claim to 240 arpens deed to him by sd **GIBONEY**; adjoined on the N by William **MATHEWS**, E by the head right of James **HANAH**; supposed to be the original right of Thomas **FOSTER**, for which sd **HOLLEY** paid $450 to sd **GIBONEY** on 4 Oct 1818. Signed David **HOLLEY**. Test Samuel **WHITE**, Claiborne S. **THOMAS**, Dep Clerk. Rec 19 Apr 1822.

2013. Page 239. 19 Apr 1822. Lyne **STARLING** by Elias N. **DLASHMUTT**, his atty in fact, and Elias N. **D'LASHMUTT** and Ann, his wife, to John J. **DLASHMUTT**. For the sum of $100, part of Lot No. 51 in Jackson; adjoining the public square and beginning on the NE corner of sd lot. Signed Lyne **STARLING** by E. N. **DLASHMUTT** his atty in fact, Elias N. **DLASHMUTT**, Ann **DLASHMUTT**. Wit Wm. **CREATH** (JP). Rec 20 Apr 1822.

2014. Page 240. 19 Apr 1822. Same, same, and same to the Trustees of the Town of Jackson. For the recognition that alleys between adjoining lots in sd town would be of great utility and other good causes, a parcel of ground commencing at the NE corner of Lot No. 51. Signed Elias N. **DLASHMUTT**, Lyne **STARLING** by E. N. **DLASHMUTT** his atty in fact, Ann **DLASHMUTT**. Wit Wm. **CREATH** (JP). Rec 20 Apr 1822.

2015. Page 241. 30 Apr 1822. George W. **ROBERTS** of Jackson to Van B. **DLASHMUTT** and N. W. **WATKINS**. For the sum of $106, the frame of a one-story house on a lot owned by George **FRICKE** on Main St; all his stock of furs of racoon, beaver, muskrat, and rabitt; and all his tools for the hatter's trade. Signed George W. (x) **ROBERTS**. Wit F. **CANNON**, Wm. P. **LACEY**, Claiborne S. **THOMAS**, Dep Clerk. Van B. **DLASHMUTT** and N. W. **WATKINS** agree to relinquish the property to sd **ROBERTS** if he pays the amount to them by 1 Oct 1823. Signed Van B. **DLASHMUTT**, N. W. **WATKINS**. Test F. **CANNON**, Wm. P. **LACEY**, Claiborne S. **THOMAS**, Dep Clerk. Rec 1 May 1822.

2016. Page 242. 29 Apr 1822. John G. **LOVE** and [Rebecka], his wife, of Perry Co., Mo. to George **FRICKE**. For the sum of $225, Lot No. 125 in Jackson; bounded on the E and fronted by second east street, S and fronted by first south street, W by Lot No. 41, and N by Lot No. 124. Signed John G. **LOVE**, Rebecka (x) **LOVE** (RD). Test Benjamin **DAVIS**, JP in Perry Co., Mo., Isaac **CADWALLADER**. Rec 3 May 1822.

2017. Page 243. 3 May 1822. Andrew **FIGHT** of Ste. Genevieve Co., Mo. to James **RAVENSCROFT** and Thomas W. **GRAVES**. For the sum of $852.50, 240 arpens, more or less, on Hubble's Creek; bounded on the E by the mill tract of David **DAVIS**, N by sd **GRAVES**, W by Joseph **OBANNON** on which Lewis **MANSKER** now lives, and S by George **AIKIN** whereon John **AIKIN** now lives; being the head or settlement right of Joseph **FIGHT**, decd. Signed Andrew **FIGHT**. Wit Greer W. **DAVIS**, Charles **SEAVERS**, David **ARMOUR** (JP). Rec 4 May 1822.

2018. Page 244. 14 Feb 1822. Thomas S. **RODNEY** and Polly, his wife, to Michael **RODNEY**. For the sum of $1500, several parcels of land; 156.90 acres that Thomas S. **RODNEY** bought of Jacob **SHEPHERD** in the Great Swamp in Rng 12 E, Twp 30 N, adjoining John **RODNEY** on the SW; 131.40 acres, being SE fractional ¼, Sec 16, Twp 30 N, Rng 12 E; 41.97 acres where the schoolhouse stands, being fractional Sec 36, Twp 30 N, Rng 12 E; 6 ¼ acres, including a spring, being Outlot No. 11 W of Cape Girardeau; Lot Nos. 19 & 23 in Cape Girardeau. Signed Thos. S. **RODNEY**, Polly (x) **RODNEY** (RD). Wit Jno. **RODNEY**, A. B. **PENNEY**, R. **DOWTY**, John **AKIN** (JP). Rec 7 May 1822.

2019. Page 246. 6 May 1822. Elias N. **DLASHMUTT** and Ann, his wife, to Van B. **D'LASHMUTT**. For the sum of $577.50, equal and undivided ½ of 231 acres on Randoll's Creek, being the plantation where Van B. **D'LASHMUTT** now lives; adjoined on the W by John **ABERNETHIE**, Esq, S by John **HITT**, N by a division line between Isaac **WILLIAMS** and sd tract, and E by vacant land; being the same purchased by Van B. **DLASHMUTT** of Richard **WALLER**. Signed Elias N. **DLASHMUTT**, Ann **DLASHMUTT** (RD). Wit Jno. **ABERNETHIE** (JP). Rec 9 May 1822.

2020. Page 247. 2 Apr 1820. Benjamin **WILSON** and Virginia, his wife, to Maxamillian **HORRELL**. For the sum of $1000, 100 acres, more or less, beginning at the SW corner of **BOAD**'s(?) old survey. Sd **HORRELL** agrees that he will only demand the consideration money be refunded if he is dispossessed of the tract by agreeable title. Signed Benjamin **WILSON**, Virginia **WILSON**, Maxln. **HORRELL**. Wit Wm. **CREATH** (JP), J. **VINCENT**. Rec 25 May 1822.

2021. Page 248. 30 Jan 1819. Joseph **SEAWELL** and Rene **LeMEILLEUR**. Agreement to transfer to sd **LeMEILLEUR**, for the sum of $9000, 240 arpens, more or less, in Byrd Twp, being where sd **SEAWELL** resides; bounded on the N by Edward **HALE**, W by **MARTIN**, S by William **NEELY**, and E by the middle of the creek which runs on the W side of Jackson; being part of James **EARLE**'s head right; to be transferred to sd **LeMEILLEUR** in one year, and will be returned to sd **SEAWELL** if sd **LeMEILLEUR** fails to pay the purchase price in six years. Signed Jos. **SEAWELL**, Rene **LeMEILLEUR**. Wit **RANNEY**, Zenas **PRIEST**, David **ARMOUR**, Solomon R. **BOLIN** (JP). Recorded in D:427. Rene **LeMEILLEUR** of Ste. Genevieve to William **NEELY**, Anthony B. **NEELY**, Joseph **FRIZEL**, and John **RANNEY**, execrs of the last will and testament of Joseph **SEAWELL**, decd. For the sum of $240, the head right of James **EARL**'s, which was sold and transferred by Joseph **SEAWELL** in his lifetime to sd **LeMEILLEUR**. Signed Rene **LeMEILLEUR**. Wit James **EVANS**, William **CREATH** (JP). Rec 28 May 1822.

2022. Page 250. 29 May 1822. William P. **LACEY**, Alexander **BUCKNER**, Thomas W. **GRAVES**, William **McGUIRE**, James **RAVENSCROFT**, and Nathaniel W. **WATKINS** to William **CHRISTY**, Auditor of the State of Mo. For the sum of $7000, bond to guarantee that sd **LACEY** shall perform the duties of Cape Girardeau Co. Collector, his having been appointed by the County Court for one year. Signed Wm. P. **LACEY**, T. W. **GRAVES**, J. **RAVENSCROFT**, A. **BUCKNER**, Wm. **McGUIRE**, N. W. **WATKINS**. Wit John **JUDEN** Jr. Rec 29 May 1822.

2023. Page 251. 29 May 1822. William P. **LACEY**, Alexander **BUCKNER**, William **McGUIRE**, Thomas W. **GRAVES**, James **RAVENSCROFT**, and Nathaniel W. **WATKINS** to Alexander **McNAIR**, Governor of the State of Mo. For the sum of $3000, bond to guarantee that sd **LACEY** shall perform the duties of Cape Girardeau Co. Collector, his having been appointed by the County Court for one year. Signed Wm. P. **LACEY**, Wm. **McGUIRE**, James **RAVENSCROFT**, A. **BUCKNER**, T. W. **GRAVES**, N. W. **WATKINS**. Wit John **JUDEN** Jr. Rec 29 May 1822.

2024. Page 251. 4 Mar 1822. John **EDWARDS** and Priscilla **JOHNSON** to Simon **POE** Junr. For the sum of $5, 2 acres, more or less, adjoining sd **POE**; beginning at a red oak on sd **POE**'s line. Signed John **EDWARDS**, Preciller (x) **JOHNSON**. Wit William **MARTIN**, John D. **RUTAN**, Jno. **ABERNETHIE** (JP). Rec 1 Jun 1822.

2025. Page 252. 4 Jun 1822. John **BYRD** and Polly, his wife, to Jacob **DELPH**. For the sum of $500, 167 3/4 acres on the waters of Byrd's Creek, including one grist mill and all the works and implements; being part of a tract confirmed to John **BYRD** Senr, decd. Signed John **BYRD**, Polly (x) **BYRD**. Test James **RUSSELL** (JP), James **CRAWFORD**. Rec 4 Jun 1822.

2026. Page 253. 13 Feb 1822. Jacob **BOLLINGER**, son of John **BOLLINGER** senior, decd, of German Twp to John **WILSON**. For the sum of $420, 105 acres on the S fork of White Water Creek; being part of 640 acres granted and confirmed to John **BOLLINGER** Senior, decd, by the King of Spain; beginning at Joseph **ROGERS**' SE corner at a stake, white oak, and hickory. Signed Jacob **BOLLINGER**. Wit Wm. **CROWDER**, G. A. **BIRD**, William **TINNIN** (JP). Rec 4 Jun 1822.

2027. Page 254. 22 Oct 1821. John **RISHER** and Mary, his wife, to Daniel F. **STEINBECK**. For the sum of $60, Lot Nos. 15 & 17 in Decatur.

Signed John **RISHER**, Mary (x) **RISHER**. Wit Theodore **JONES**, George **HENDERSON** (JP). Rec 6 Jun 1822.

2028. Page 255. 15 Apr 1822. Lyne **STARLING** and Elias N. **DLASHMUTT** and Ann, his wife, trading as **STARLING & D'LASHMUTT**, by sd **D'LASHMUTT**, to same. For the sum of $850, 80 acres, being Lot No. 50 in Cape Girardeau and the outlots thereunto attached; being part of a tract granted by the Spanish Government to Louis **LORIMIER** and confirmed by the U. S. Signed Lyne **STARLING**, Elias N. **D'LASHMUTT**, Ann **D'LASHMUTT** (RD). Wit Wm. **CREATH** (JP). Rec 6 Jun 1822.

2029. Page 256. 11 Jun 1822. Charles **DEMOSS** of Cooper Co., Mo. to John **McCOMBS**. For the sum of $900, 300 acres, more or less, being part of 640 acres confirmed to sd **DEMOSS**; beginning at the NE corner of Nicholas **WHITELAW**'s survey. Signed Charles **DEMOSS**. Wit Peter R. **GARRETT**, Allen **MARTIN**. Wit James **RUSSELL**, County Court Justice. Rec 11 Jun 1822.

2030. Page 257. 8 Jun 1822. Lyne **STARLING** to Elias N. **DLASHMUTT**. For the sum of $4000, all his part of several lots and parcels; three lots in Jackson conveyed to them by the Commissioners on 9 May 1820: Lot No. 30, bounded on the N and fronted by first south street, E and fronted by first east street, and S by Lot No. 31; Lot No. 39, bounded on the S and fronted by Main St, N by Lot No. 38, E by Lot No. 123, and W and fronted by first east street; and part of Lot No. 146; also six tracts in or near Cape Girardeau: 10 acres, being Outlot No. 17; 20 acres, being Outlot No. 24; ½ of Lot No. 7, Range E; Lot Nos. 18 & 22, Range F; and Lot No. 27, Range A deeded by Van B. **DLASHMUTT** and wife to **STARLING & DLASHMUTT** on 15 Feb 1821; 80 acres, being E ½, NW ¼, Sec 20, Twp 31 N, Rng 14 E entered on 17 Sep 1820; ½ of 3.90 acres, being fractional Sec 30, Twp 32 N, Rng 15 E; Lot No. 2, bounded on the N by first north street, E by Lot No. 26, S by the public square, and W by High St, deeded to **STARLING & DLASHMUTT** by Stephen **BYRD**, adminr of Jason **CHAMBERLAIN**, decd, on 11 Apr 1822; E ½, SE ¼, Sec 10(?), Twp 32 N, Rng 13 E; and 24 acres off the N end of the W ½ of the same as described in a deed from Tunstall **QUARLES** on 4 Mar 1822. Signed Lyne **STARLING**. Wit Wm. **CREATH** (JP). Rec 15 Jun 1822.

2031. Page 258. 18 Apr 1822. Same and Elias N. **DLASHMUTT** by Elias N. **DLASHMUTT**, acting agent, to Henry **HAND**. For the sum of $40 and in consideration of a quit claim deed from John **HAYS**, Sheriff, dated 17 Apr 1821, quit claim to 4 lots in Bainbridge, taken as the property of William **HAND** to satisfy an execution in favor of Lewis **DICKSON** dated 6 Sep 1820. Signed Elias N. **DLASHMUTT**, Lyne **STARLING** by his acting agent. Test Wm. **CREATH** (JP). Ann **DLASHMUTT** RD. Rec 20 Jun 1822.

2032. Page 259. 22 Jun 1822. Henry **CLINARD** of Davidson Co., Tenn. to William P. **LACEY**. For the sum of $200, two lots: the undivided ½ of Lot No. 3 adjoining Jackson; bounded on the N by Seawell St, E by first west street, S by James H. **JENKINS** and Phinehas **COBURN**, and W by Lot No. 4, being the same sold by the executors of Joseph **SEAWELL**, decd, to John **BINKLEY** and sd **CLINARD** on 21 Feb 1820; and the equal and undivided ½ of part of Lot No. 27 in Jackson, so as to include all the buildings, and beginning at a stake on the E side of the public square, being the same conveyed by the Commissioners of the Courthouse and Jail to Anthony B. **NEELY**, by sd **NEELY** and Margaret, his wife, to Jonas **WHITTENBERG**, by sd **WHITTENBERG** to George **MORROW**, and by sd **MORROW** to sd **CLINARD**. Signed Henry **CLINARD**. Wit John **BROWN**, Ce. **THOMAS**, Dep Clerk. Rec 22 Jun 1822.

2033. Page 261. 20 Jun 1822. William A. **BULL** of Perry Co., Mo. to Henry **CLINARD** of Davidson Co., Tenn. For the sum of $300, Lot No. 114 in Jackson; bounded on the N and fronted by first south street, E and fronted by third west street, S by Lot No. 115, and W by Lot No. 195. This deed corrects the description of lot as recorded in C:262, dated 20 Mar 1820. Signed Wm. A. **BULL**. Wit Jinny **ANDERSON**, Miley **ANDERSON**, Saml. **ANDERSON**, Justice of Perry Co., Mo. Court. Rec 25 Jun 1822.

2034. Page 261. 7 Jun 1822. James **CRAWFORD** and Anny, his wife, to Stephen **BYRD** and Abraham **BYRD**, execr of the estate of John **BYRD**. For the sum of $551.94, mortgage on 200 acres on the waters of Byrd's Creek; joined on the N by Philip **YOUNG** and E & S by the heirs of John **BYRD**, decd. A promissory note dated 26 Sep 1818 is due. Signed James **CRAWFORD**, Annah (x) **CRAWFORD**. Test David **CRADER**, James **RUSSELL** (JP). Rec 4 Jul 1822.

2035. Page 263. 11 Mar 1822. John D. **RUTAN** to George H. **SCRIPPS**. For the sum of $48.50, mortgage on two tracts; 5 acres and 37 poles, part of Enos **RANDOL**'s head right, conveyed to sd **RUTAN** by William **MARTIN** & wife on 4 Mar 1822, beginning at a white oak corner, being Priscilla **JOHNSON**'s corner on a ridge near Ste. Genevieve Rd; and 12 acres, more or less, part of the same head right, and conveyed by sd **MARTIN** & wife to sd **RUTAN** on 4 Mar 1822, beginning at a stake at the S corner of Simion **POE**'s near sd road. Sd **RUTAN** agrees the pay the debt in good beef cattle or milk cows at appraised value, or in work done in any line of business at the following rates: plastering and lathing inside walls of a house $0.25 a yard, building the wall of a cellar $0.50 per perch (materials and board to be found by sd **SCRIPPS**). Signed John D. **RUTAN**. Test David **SAILER**, Ce. **THOMAS**, Dep Clerk. Rec 5 Jul 1822.

2036. Page 264. 29 Jun 1822. Joel **SHEPHERD** to Susannah **WRIGHT**. For the sum of $300, 50 acres, being part of a tract of 255.90 acres sold by John P. **ADINER** of Ste. Genevieve Co. to Jacob **SHEPHERD**; beginning at a post on the NW boundary line; adjoining Richard **WRIGHT** on the NE and Michael **RODNEY** on the SW. Signed Joel **SHEPPARD**. Wit Thos. S. **RODNEY**, Benjamin **WRIGHT**, Jno. **RODNEY**, David **ARMOUR** (JP). Rec 6 Jul 1822.

2037. Page 265. 31 May 1821. David **DAVIS** of Bracken Co., Ken. to Greer W. **DAVIS**. For the love and affection he has for Greer W. **DAVIS** and the sum of $1, Lot No. 17 in Jackson; bounded on the E and fronted by High St, W and fronted by Lot No. 53, S and fronted by first south street, and N by Lot No. 16. Signed David **DAVIS**, Sarah **DAVIS** (RD). Wit Augustus **DAVIS**, John **CALGLAZER**, John **PAYNE**, Clerk of Bracken Co., Ken. Court. Rec 29 Jul 1822.

2038. Page 266. 28 Jul 1822. John **PAYNE** of Jackson to Matthew **DUNCAN** of Jackson Co., Ill. For the sum of $1300, 320 acres on the waters of White Water, to be taken off the NW end of 640 acres, being Survey No. 2273 in the name of William **SMITH**; and ½ of the same conveyed from sd **SMITH** to sd **DUNCAN** on 11 May 1821, and by sd **DUNCAN** to sd **PAYNE** on 21 Nov 1821. Signed John **PAYNE** Jr. Wit Isaiah F. **HAMILTON**, John **WATHN**, Claiborne S. **THOMAS**, Dep Clerk. Rec 29 Jul 1822.

2039. Page 266. 4 Jul 1822. Alexander **McNAIR**, Governor of Mo., to Welton **OBANNON**. Appointment as a JP for Randol Twp, his having been appointed by the County Court. Signed A. **McNAIR**. Wit Wm. G. **PETTUS**, Sec. of State. Welton **OBANNON** takes the oath of office. Signed Welton **OBANNON**. Wit James **RUSSELL** (JP). Rec 7 Aug 1822.

2040. Page 268. 20 Mar 1820. John G. **LOVE** and Rebecca, his wife, to William A. **BULL**. For the sum of $250, Lot No. 114 in Jackson; bounded on the N and fronted by first south street, E and fronted by third east street, S by Lot No. 115, and W by Lot No. 195. Signed John G. **LOVE**, Rebecka (x) **LOVE**. Wit Wm. **CREATH** (JP), Chrs. **MOTHERSHEAD**, Greenip **HALL**, Isaac **CADWALLADER**. Rec 15 Aug 1822.

2041. Page 268. 14 Aug 1822. Gilbert **HECTOR** to Thomas W. **GRAVES** and Anthony **RANDOL**. For the consideration that sd **GRAVES** and sd **RANDOL** have entered security for sd **HECTOR** in an injunction bond to further proceedings at law on a judgment which Lewis **DICKSON** obtained against William **HAND**, mortgage on 215 acres, more or less, on the waters of Hubble's Creek where sd **HECTOR** now lives. To be void if the bond does not have to be paid. Signed Gilbert (x) **HECTOR**. Wit James **EVANS**, Michl. **RODNEY**, C. S. **THOMAS**, Dep Clerk. Rec 19 Aug 1822.

2042. Page 269. 28 May 1821. John **DELAP** to John **MITCHEL**. For the sum of $600, 24 acres and 75 poles that sd **DELAP** purchased on John **DAVIS**, being part of sd **DAVIS**'s preemption; beginning at a stake, a "hicre" and two dogwoods. Signed John **DELAP**. Test Samuel W. **MITCHEL**, C. S. **THOMAS**, Dep Clerk. Rec 19 Aug 1822.

2043. Page 270. 19 Aug 1822. William **TIPTON** of Hickman Co., Ken. to John **CROSS**. For the sum of $1924, two tracts; 240 arpens, more or less, on the waters of Ramsay's Creek, adjoining the original survey of Louis **LORIMIER** and Andrew **RAMSAY**, decd, being the same confirmed to the representatives of Samuel **TIPTON**, decd, and sold by court order and purchased by William **TIPTON**; and 54 ½ acres, more or less, being part of a tract granted by the Spanish Government to Andrew **RAMSEY** senior, and purchased by William **TIPTON** of William **RAMSAY** and Elizabeth, his wife

(E:8). The balance of the tract is claimed by Rebecca **HARBISON**. Signed William **TIPTON**. Test J. **RAVENSCROFT**, Will. T. **GRAHAM**, John **AKIN** (JP). Rec 19 Aug 1822.

2044. Page 271. 21 Aug 1822. Richard S. **THOMAS** and Frances, his wife, to Isidore **MOORE** and John **LAYTON** of Perry Co., Mo. For the sum of $1020, 300 acres, more or less, on the waters of Hubble's Creek adjoining Jackson, where sd **THOMAS** now lives and purchased by him of William H. **ASHLEY**; except what sd **THOMAS** has sold to John **SHEPPARD**, Samuel **CUPPLES** and Mary, his wife, and about 30 acres to George **BULLITT**. Signed Richard S. **THOMAS**, Frances **THOMAS**. Wit John **JUDEN** Jr., Clerk. Rec 21 Aug 1822.

2045. Page 272. 1 Jan 1821. George H. **SCRIPPS** to **George**, his negro slave. Emancipation after 4 Jul 1829. Sd **George** is said to be between 35 and 40 years old and is a shoemaker by trade. Signed Geo. H. **SCRIPPS**. Wit W. **SCRIPPS**, George **BAKER**, John **JUDEN** Jr., Clerk. Rec 24 Aug 1822.

2046. Page 272. 23 Apr 1822. Sally **WELKER**, widow of Peter **WELKER**, decd, and a lawful representative of Jacob **YOUNT**, decd, to John **YOUNT**. For the sum of $30, quit claim to 300 arpens on west White Water belonging to Jacob **YOUNT**, decd. Signed Saly (x) **WELKER**. Wit William **TINNIN** (JP). Rec 30 Aug 1822.

2047. Page 273. 27 Feb 1822. Jessee **YOUNT**, a lawful heir and representative of Jacob **YOUNT**, decd, to same. For the sum of $30, quit claim to 300 arpens on west White Water belonging to Jacob **YOUNT**, decd. Signed Jesse **YOUNT**, Seb[ley] (x) **YOUNT**. Wit William **TINNIN** (JP). Rec 30 Aug 1822.

2048. Page 273. 10 Apr 1822. Robert **SMITH** Senr to Robert **SMITH** Jur. For natural love and affection, two negro boys, **Andrew** about 18 years old, and **Edward**, alias Ned, about 8 years old. Signed R. **SMITH** Senr. Wit Wm. **McGUIRE**, P. R. **GARRETT**, C. S. **THOMAS**, Dep Clerk. Rec 3 Sep 1822.

2049. Page 274. 23 Aug 1822. Ezekiel **ABLE** by Sheriff John **HAYS** to Thomas **SUBLETT**. For the sum of $10, 640 acres on White Water, confirmed to Jacob **SHERIDEN** Senr.'s representatives. Sold on 16 Aug 1822 in execution of a writ issued by Circuit Court on 6 May 1822 for Hiram C. **DAVIS**, assignee of

William and Nelly **MOTHERSHEAD**, against sd **ABLE** and Jeremiah **ABLE** for $160.43 7 ½ mills for debt, $17.27 and 5 mills damages, and $26.87 costs. Signed John **HAYS**, Shff. Wit C. S. **THOMAS**, Dep Clerk. Rec 4 Sep 1822.

2050. Page 275. 21 Aug 1822. James **BRADY**, decd, by same to John **WATHEN**. For the sum of $20, Lot No. 88 in Jackson, lying on Main St opposite Nathan **VANHORN**. Sold on 16 Aug 1822 in execution of a writ issued by Circuit Court of New Madrid Co. on 7 Aug 1822 for John **WATHAN** and against Charles T. **RAMSEY**, execr of James **BRADY**, decd, for $599.49 debt, $29.59 damages, and costs. Signed John **HAYS**, Shff. Wit C. S. **THOMAS**, Dep Clerk. Rec 4 Sep 1822.

2051. Page 277. 23 Aug 1822. John **MASSEY** by same to Elias N. **DLASHMUTT**. For the sum of $50, a lot and improvements in Jackson on first south street. Sold on 9 Apr 1822 in execution of two writs issued by Circuit Court on 9 Feb 1822 in favor of sd **DLASHMUTT** before David **ARMOUR**, Esq, JP for Byrd Twp, and against sd **MASSEY**; one for $11.75 debt, $0.28 and 5 mills interest, and $0.50 costs, and $2.10 costs in court, less $5.17 for property sold; and one for $13.62 and 5 mills debt with $0.04 interest and $0.50 costs, and $2.10 costs in court, less $4.17 for property sold. Signed John **HAYS**, Shff. Wit C. S. **THOMAS**, Dep Clerk. Rec 4 Sep 1822.

2052. Page 279. 10 Sep 1822. John **PAYNE** Jun to Matthew **DUNCAN**. Correction of deed in F:266; to read: taken off the SW instead of the NW end, so as to make 320 acres. Signed John **PAYNE** Jun, Matthew **DUNCAN**. Wit C. S. **THOMAS**, Dep Clerk. Rec 10 Sep 1822.

2053. Page 279. 27 Dec 1811. Geo. W. **COCHRAN** and Betsey, his wife, to Jonathan **BUIS**. For the sum of $189.50, 75 acres, 3 roods, and 19 poles, being part of 600 arpens granted to Amos **BYRD**, decd, and confirmed to sd **BYRD**'s heirs; bounded on the N by one of the heirs of sd **BYRD** and S by part of the same tract sold by sd **COCHRAN** to Joseph **YOUNG**. Signed Geo. W. **COCHRAN**, Betsey **COCHRAN**. Wit John **WILSON**, Joseph **YOUNG**, Wm. **CREATH** (JP). Rec 12 Sep 1822.

2054. Page 280. 4 Sep 1822. Marie **LAPORTE**, widow, sole heiress, and adminr of Louis **LAPORTE**, decd, of Ste. Genevieve, Mo. to Daniel F. **STEINBECK**. For the sum of $295,

Lot No. 6, Range B in Cape Girardeau, purchased by Louis **LAPORTE** on 24 Nov 1819 for $290. Signed Marie (x) **LAPORTE**. Test John **RIBOUIT**, Timothy **DAVIS** & Thomas **OLIVER**, JP in Ste. Genevieve Co. Rec 13 Sep 1822.

2055. Page 281. 27 Aug 1822. Alexander **McNAIR**, Governor of Mo., to William **CREATH**. Commission as Sheriff of Cape Girardeau Co. for two years, his having been elected on the 1st Mon of Aug last. Signed A. **McNAIR**. Wit Wm. S. **PETTUS**, Secretary of State. William **CREATH** takes the oath of office. Signed William **CREATH**. Wit R. S. **THOMAS**, Judge of Fourth Judicial Circuit. Rec 14 Sep 1822.

2056. Page 281. 13 Sep 1822. William **CREATH**, John **PRIM**, Johnson **RANNEY**, and Ebenezar **FLINN** to Alexander **McNAIR**, Governor of Mo. For the sum of $12,000, bond to guarantee that sd **CREATH** shall faithfully discharge the duties of Sheriff of Cape Girardeau Co. Signed William **CREATH**, John **PRIM**, Johnson **RANNEY**, E. **FLINN**. Wit R. S. **THOMAS**, Judge of Fourth Judicial Circuit. Rec 14 Sep 1822.

2057. Page 282. 15 Sep 1822. Matthew **DUNCAN** of Jackson Co., Ill. to William P. **LACEY** of Jackson. For the sum of $500, three negroes: **Mariah**, **Eliza**, and **Diannah**; the oldest 20 years old, second about 2 years, and youngest an infant; being the same negroes transferred from Isaac **MURPHY**, who raised them in Sumner Co., Tenn., to sd **DUNCAN** on 28 Apr 1822. Signed Matthew **DUNCAN**. Test So. **DUNCAN**, E. **FENWICK**. Rec 17 Sep 1822.

2058. Page 282. 30 Jan 1822. John **SHEPPARD** and Nancy, his wife, to Alexander **BUCKNER**. For the sum of $3000, 300 arpens or 255.21 acres on Randoll's Creek in Twp 31 N, Rng 13 E, beginning on the E boundary of Enos **RANDOL** Senr's survey; bounded on the N by the heirs of Samuel **RANDOL**, S by Jeremiah **THOMPSON**'s grant, and W by Enos **RANDOL**'s original grant; and being the same conveyed to sd **SHEPPARD** by Samuel **RANDOL**, William **THOMPSON**, and Elizabeth **THOMPSON**, and confirmed to sd **SHEPPARD** under Samuel **RANDOL** sen. Signed John **SHEPPARD**, Nancy (x) **SHEPPARD**. Wit R. S. **THOMAS**, Judge of 4th Judicial Circuit, Francis **BROWN**. Rec 19 Sep 1822.

2059. Page 283. 27 Aug 1822. Alexander **McNAIR**, Governor of Mo., to Thomas **MORGAN**. Commission as Coroner of Cape Girardeau Co. for two years, his having been elected on the 1st Mon of Aug last. Signed A. **McNAIR**. Wit Wm. S. **PETTUS**, Secretary of State. Thomas **MORGAN** takes the oath of office. Signed Thomas **MORGAN**. Wit C. S. **THOMAS**, Dep Clerk. Rec 19 Sep 1822.

2060. Page 284. 23 Sep 1822. Thomas **MORGAN**, Elijah **RANDOL**, Robert **ENGLISH**, and Nicholas **SEAVERS** to Alexander **McNAIR**, Governor of Mo. For the sum of $5000, bond to guarantee that sd **MORGAN** shall faithfully discharge the duties of Coroner of Cape Girardeau Co. Signed Thos. **MORGAN**, Elijah **RANDOL**, Robert **ENGLISH**, Nicholas **SEAVERS**. Wit R. S. **THOMAS**, Judge of Fourth Judicial Circuit. Rec 23 Sep 1822.

2061. Page 284. 21 Sep 1820. James **EDMOND** to Wm. **CALDWELL** of Adair Co., Ken. For the sum of $270, one negro girl named **Fanney** about 8 years old. Signed James **EDMOND**. Test Thomas **STELEY**, C. S. **THOMAS**, Dep Clerk. Rec 25 Sep 1822.

2062. Page 285. __ ___ 1822. Frederick **LIMBAUGH** and Barbara, his wife, Daniel **CRADER** and Polly, his wife, and Samuel **CRADER** and Elizabeth, his wife, to Jacob **CRADER** and Samuel **CRADER**. For the sum of $500, 640 acres, being the same confirmed to the heirs of Jacob **CRATER**. Signed Frederek (x) **LIMBOCK**, Barbara (x) **LIMBOCK**, Daniel **CRATER**, Polly (x) **CRATER**, Samuel **GRADER**, Elizabeth (x) **CRADER**. Wit William **TINNIN** (JP), Barnet **SNIDER** (JP), John B. **WHEELER** (JP). Rec 7 Oct 1822.

2063. Page 287. 26 Jul 1822. Moses **BYRNE** and Rebecca, his wife, to George **BOHANNON**. For the sum of $450, 300 arpens on the waters of Ramsay's Creek; adjoined on the S by Eli **SHELBY** and by U. S. land on all other sides; being the same conveyed to sd **BYRNE** by John **WEAVER** and Mary, his wife, on 9 Oct 1815, and where sd **BYRNE** and family reside and have lived for a number of years. Signed Moses **BYRNE**, Rebecca (x) **BYRNE**. Wit Simon **BLACK** Jr, Jno. **ABERNETHIE** (JP). Rec 10 Oct 1822.

2064. Page 288. 20 Apr 1822. William **RUSSELL** of St. Louis Co., Mo. to Martha Jane **RUSSELL** and Joseph William **RUSSELL**,

infant children of James **RUSSELL** and Elizabeth Ann, his wife, of Jackson. For the sum of $5 and the affection, esteem, and high regard he has for them, seven tracts; 68.06 acres, being fractional Sec 18, Twp 31 N, Rng 13 E; 80 acres, being the W ½, NW ¼, Sec 13, Twp 31 N, Rng 13 E; 3.87 acres, being SW fractional ¼, Sec 13, Twp 31 N, Rng 14 E; 141.27 acres, being SE fractional ¼, Sec 14, Twp 31 N, Rng 14 E; 160 acres, being NE ¼, Sec 23, Twp 31 N, Rng 14 E; 48.78 acres, being NW fractional ¼, Sec 24, Twp 31 N, Rng 14 E; and 5 acres joining Jackson, being the same purchased by William **RUSSELL** from Joseph **SEAWELL** and Prudence, his wife, on 11 Feb 1817 (D:70). Should one of the children die before reaching age 21, without children, then all the property to go to the survivor; otherwise the children to receive an equal ½ of the property at age 21. If neither survives to age 21, but leave a child or children as lawful issue, then that child or children is to have full property rights. Signed Wm. **RUSSELL**. Wit Stephen **REMINGTON**, Wm. **NEILL**, R. S. **THOMAS**, Judge of 4th Judicial Circuit. Rec 18 Oct 1822.

2065. Page 290. 19 Oct 1822. Daniel F. **STEINBECK** to George **COLLIER** and Peter **POWELL**, merchants and partners in St. Louis, Mo., under the name of **COLLIER & POWELL**. For the sum of $2213.94 through their agent Robert **WASH**, mortgage on two lots; the corner square lot in Jackson, opposite the courthouse, whereupon are erected several tenements now occupied by several tenants, and a storehouse occupied by Kerr & Graham, adjoining the tavern lot occupied by **LOCKHART**; and about 2 arpens in Cape Girardeau immediately under the hill, with all the storehouses, warehouses, buildings, and improvements. Three promissory notes, each for $737.98, are due on 1 Oct 1823, 1 Oct 1824, and 1 Oct 1825, together with interest from this date. Should no payment of the principal be made, but the interest be paid when the first note and second note are due, then the grantees shall not foreclose and the grantor is to retain possession and rent on the property until the third note is due. Signed D. F. **STEINBECK**. Wit R. **WASH**, C. F. **THOMAS**, Dep Clerk. Rec 21 Oct 1822.

2066. Page 292. 12 Oct 1822. Andrew **BURNS** to Johnson **RANNEY**. For the sum of $500, a tract on Hubble's Creek in Byrd Twp, whereupon he now resides; being either a confirmed tract of 125 acres, or a preemption right entitled to entry of 185 acres. Signed A. **BURNS**. Wit Stephen

BACON, T. **CURTISS**, William **CREATH** (JP). Rec 26 Oct 1822.

2067. Page 292. 7 Aug 1822. Josiah **VINCENT** to Scarlet **GLASSCOCK**. For the sum of $460, mortgage on two negroes now in the possession of John J. **DLASHMUTT**; a young negro man named **Charles**, aged about 19 years; and a negro girl named **Hannah** aged about 19 years. The debt is due by 7 Oct next. Signed Josiah **VINCENT**. Wit Peter R. **GARRETT**, C. S. **THOMAS**, Dep Clerk. Rec 29 Oct 1822.

2068. Page 293. 3 Sep 1821. Thomas **SLOAN** and Catharine, his wife, to Elias **BARBER** and Robert **MORRISON**. For the sum of $80, the E ½ of Lot No. 112 in Jackson; beginning at the NE corner of sd lot on Main St. Signed Thos. **SLOAN**, Catharine (x) **SLOAN**. Wit J. **RANNEY**, C. S. **THOMAS**, Dep Clerk. Rec 31 Oct 1822.

2069. Page 294. 3 Oct 1822. Jonathan **BUIS** and Ann, his wife, to William **EVERET**. For the sum of $150, all their part of 102 acres on Byrd's Creek, being a tract confirmed to Eliga **EVERET**, adjoining a tract where sd **BUIS** now lives. Signed Jonathan **BUIS**, Ann (x) **BUIS**. Test James **RUSSELL** (JP), Abraham **BYRD**. Rec 1 Nov 1822.

2070. Page 294. 28 Oct 1822. Stephen **BYRD** and Catharine, his wife, to John **BYRD**. For the sum of $303, 101 ¼ acres, more or less, on the waters of Byrd's Creek, being part of a tract confirmed to the heirs of Amos **BYRD** Junior, decd, and joining John **BYRD**. Signed Stephen (x) **BYRD**, Catharine **BYRD**. Test James **RUSSELL** (JP). Rec 1 Nov 1822.

2071. Page 295. 1 Oct 1822. Michael **COLLIER** Jr. of Union Co., Ill. to John **LOGAN** Jr. of Shelbyville, Ken. For the sum of $1062.91, mortgage on two tracts; 147 acres and 70 poles, being a preemption right purchased by sd **COLLIER** from the heirs of Benijah **LAUGHERTY**; and 70 acres and 86 poles on Flora Creek, being part of the same preemption right. The debt is due in a note payable in four years. Signed M. **COLLIER** Jr. Wit Benj. W. **BROOKS**, Richd. M. **YOUNG**, Chas. **DUNN**, JP in Union Co., Ill., Abner **FIELDS**, Clerk of Union Co., Ill. Court, Jesse **ECHOLS**, Presiding Judge of Union Co., Ill. Court. Rec 2 Nov 1822.

2072. Page 296. 4 Jun 1822. Commissioners to divide the lands of Abraham **BIRD**, decd, to Thompson **BIRD**. For the sum of $32, Lot No. 5, Range D in Cape Girardeau; bounded on the N by Harmony St, S by the public square, E by Spanish St, and W by Lorimier St. Sold by order of Circuit Court issued Apr Term 1922, on petition for partition of lands belonging to Mary **BIRD**, Thompson **BIRD**, John **BIRD**, William **BIRD**, Abraham **BIRD**, and Samuel **NAIL** and Mary, his wife, all heirs of Abraham **BIRD**, decd. Signed D. F. **STEINBECK**, Joel **RENFROE**, Robert **GIBONEY**, John **CROSS**. Wit George **HENDERSON** (JP). Rec 8 Nov 1822.

2073. Page 297. 3 Jun 1822. Same to same. For the sum of $700, 560 arpens on the waters of Hubble's Creek, being the head right of Abraham **BIRD**, Senr; adjoining David **DAVIS**, Nicolas **SEAVERS**, and others. Sold by order of Circuit Court issued Apr Term 1922, on petition for partition of lands belonging to Mary **BIRD**, Thompson **BIRD**, John **BIRD**, William **BIRD**, Abraham **BIRD**, and Samuel **NAIL** and Mary, his wife, all heirs of Abraham **BIRD**, decd. Signed D. F. **STEINBECK**, Joel **RENFROE**, Robert **GIBONEY**. Wit George **HENDERSON** (JP). Rec 8 Nov 1822.

2074. Page 288. 8 Nov 1822. Franklin **CANNON** to Enoch **LARRABEE**. For the sum of $150, ½ of Lot No. 102; bounded on the W by third west street, N by first south street, E by E half of the lot, and S by Lot No. 103. Signed Franklin **CANNON**. Wit C. S. **THOMAS**, Dep Clerk. Rec 8 Nov 1822.

2075. Page 299. 25 Oct 1822. William P. **LACEY** and Emily, his wife, to Franklin **CANNON**. For the sum of $150, equal and undivided ½ of Lot No. 27 in Jackson, including the building on sd ground; beginning at a stake at the E side of the public square; being the same conveyed by the Commissioners to Anthony B. **NEELY**, by sd **NEELY** and Margaret, his wife, to James **WHITTENBURG**, and by sd **WHITTENBURG** to George **MORROW**, by sd **MORROW** to Henry **CLINARD**, and by sd **CLINARD** to sd **LACEY**. Signed Wm. P. **LACEY**, Emily M. **LACEY**. Wit C. S. **THOMAS**, Dep Clerk. Rec 9 Nov 1822.

2076. Page 300. 16 Nov 1822. William **GARNER** to the State of Mo. For the sum of $400 with 6 % interest from 16 Nov 1822, undivided ½ of 640 acres on White Water confirmed to Jacob **SHERIDAN**'s representatives. Signed W. **GARNER**. Wit C. S. **THOMAS**, Dep Clerk. Rec 16 Nov 1822. [Marginal note: Received $265.30 and 5 mills, the residue of this mortgage, and full satisfaction on 16 Mar 1827. Signed Hy. **SANFORD**, Dep Clerk.]

2077. Page 300. 13 Oct 1822. Alexander **McNAIR**, Governor of Mo., to Peter R. **GARRETT**. Appointment as JP for Byrd Twp for four years. Signed A. **McNAIR**. Wit Wm. S. **PETTUS**, Secretary of State. Peter R. **GARRETT** takes the oath of office. Signed Peter R. **GARRETT**. Wit David **ARMOUR** (JP). Rec 25 Nov 1822.

2078. Page 301. 28 Aug 1822. Thomas S. **RODNEY** to John **RODNEY**. For the sum of $1544, $1069 received previously and $475 in hand in round silver, mortgage on four negro slaves; a man named **Jim** 22 years old, a mulatto boy named **Stephen** 16 years old, a woman named **Dils**(?) about 19 years old, and her boy child named **Bill Allen** 3 years old. Signed Tho. S. **RODNEY**. Wit Thomas **TOWNSEND**, Jacob (x) **SHULTZ**. The sum is due with 6% interest, on 1 Jan 1825, and if paid this deed to be null and void. Signed John **RODNEY**. Wit Thomas **TOWNSEND**, Jacob (x) **SHULTZ**, Jno. **ABERNETHIE** (JP). Rec 27 Nov 1822.

2079. Page 302. 20 Nov 1822. George **TENNILLE** of Saline Co., Mo. to Robert G. **WATSON** of New Madrid Co., Mo. For the sum of $330, mortgage on two tracts; 250 arpens granted and confirmed to John **MAY**, and conveyed by him to sd **TENNILLE**; and 300 arpens granted to Cornelias **EVERET** and confirmed to John **MAY** under sd **EVERET**, conveyed to sd **TENNILLE** by sd **MAY**. Sd **WATSON** is security in the administration bond of sd **TENNILLE** on the estate of Richard Jones **WATERS**, decd, and on the last settlement of the estate at Nov Term of New Madrid Co. Court there was a surplus of $322.94. This mortgage guarantees sd **TENNILLE** will pay when legally required, and sd **WATSON** to be harmless from all responsibility. Signed George **TENNILLE**. Wit R. D. **DAWSON**, Christr. G. **HOUTS**, Clerk of New Madrid Co. Court. Rec 6 Dec 1822.

2080. Page 303. 15 Oct 1817. Commissioners of the Courthouse and Jail to James **RAVENSCROFT**. For the sum of $92, Lot No. 135 in Jackson; bounded on the S and fronted by Main St, W and fronted by second east street, N by Lot No. 134, and E by Lot No. 147. Signed John **DAVIS**, John **SHEPPARD**, Samuel G. **DUNN**, Abraham **BYRD**, Benja. **SHELL**. Wit J. **FRIZEL**, Jacob **MILLER**, Michl.

RODNEY, Wm. **CREATH** (JP). Rec 9 Dec 1822.

2081. Page 304. 17 Sep 1822. Henery **YUNT** [and Sofiah, his wife,] to Thomas **UNDERWOOD** and Valentine **UNDERWOOD**. For the sum of $100, 6 3/4 acres, more or less, on both sides of White Water in German and Byrd Twps; being part of 640 acres confirmed to Peter **GROUNDS** and conveyed to sd **YUNT**; beginning on a stake. Signed Henery **YUNT**, Sofiah **YUNT**. Test William **POLK** Sr., James **UNDERWOOD**, William **POLK** Jr, William **TINNIN** (JP). Rec 12 Dec 1822.

2082. Page 305. 19 Nov 1822. Stephen **BYRD** and Katherine, his wife, to Martin **THOMAS**. For the sum of $200, 97 or 98 acres, more or less, on the waters of Byrd's Creek; bounded on the S by John **PATTERSON**, W by Michael O. **HOGAN**, and N by James **WILKINSON**. Signed Stephen (x) **BYRD**, Catharine **BYRD**. Test James **RUSSELL** (JP). Rec 18 Dec 1822.

2083. Page 306. 20 Nov 1822. Parish **GREEN** and Clary, his wife, to Benjamin **HALL**. For the sum of $500, 49 ½ acres, being the lower ½ of the land at Hickman's, formerly sd Green's, Ferry on the Mississippi River, including ½ of ferry land, and extending the ½ of the 1/3 of a mile up or along the bank of the river, and to extend 1/3 mile back from the river to make 49 ½ acres; adjoining sd **HICKMAN**'s 49 ½ acres, the upper part of the ferry land. Signed Parish **GREEN**, Clary (x) **GREENE**. Wit Lineus B. **SUBLETT**, Harriet (x) **SUBLETT**, Jno. **ABERNETHIE** (JP). Rec 20 Dec 1822.

2084. Page 307. 12 Oct 1822. Obadiah **MALONE** and Thomas **MALONE** to Stephen **MALONE**. For the sum of $430, bond to make a title for 76 acres and 90 square poles, being where Thomas **MALONE** now lives; adjoining land granted to Abraham **HUGHES** and land where Obadiah **MALONE** now lives. Signed Obediah A. **MALOAN**, Thos. **MALOAN**. Wit Rezin L. **BISHOP**, Jacob **FULBRIGHT**, David **ARMOUR** (JP). Rec 26 Dec 1822.

2085. Page 308. 2 Dec 1822. Mary **BLACKMORE**, wife of Charles N. **BLACKMORE**, of Sumner Co., Tenn. acknowledged that the deed recorded in E:383 is her wish and will for the purposes therein mentioned. Signed James **CHARLTON**, JP in Sumner Co., Tenn. Rec 29 Dec 1822.

2086. Page 308. 10 Jan 1823. William **McMURTRY** of Madison Co. to John **GLASCOCK**. For the sum of $80, the SE corner of Lot No. 99 in Jackson, fronting on Main St. Signed Wm. **McMURTREY**. Wit N. W. **WATKINS**, Francis (x) **BLAIR**, John **JUDEN** Jr, Clerk. Rec 10 Jan 1823.

2087. Page 309. 24 Oct 1822. John **BURROWS** and Bethena, his wife, and Mary **HUBBELL** to Joel **RENFRO**. For the sum of $600, 189 acres, more or less, on the E side of Hubbell's Creek; adjoining Alexander **SUMMERS**, Joseph **WHITNEY** or Nathaniel **BULLARD**, Isaiah **POE**, and **DAVIS**'s mill tract, formerly Ithamar **HUBBELL**; being part of a tract confirmed to the heirs of Waters **BURROWS**, decd, and whereon John **BURROWS** and family now live; beginning at a rock on sd **SUMMERS**' line. Signed John **BURROWS**, Bethena (x) **BURROWS**, Mary (x) **HUBBELL**. Wit James **DOWTY**, Thomas **BURROWS**, Joseph (x) **WHITNEY**, Jn. **ABERNETHIE** (JP). Rec 11 Jan 1823.

2088. Page 310. 20 Dec 1822. Joseph **WHITNEY** and Rebecca, his wife, to same. For the sum of $300, 50 acres on the E side of Hubbell's Creek; beginning at the NE corner of sd tract at a stone and stake, Thomas **MORGAN**'s corner on Alexr. **SUMMERS**' line; being part of John **BORROWS'** land granted by him to sd **WHITNEY** on 20 Sep 1817; adjoining sd **RENFROE** formerly John **BURROWS**, Alexander **SUMMERS**, Isaiah **POE**, and sd **MORGAN**. Signed Joseph (x) **WHITNEY**, Rebecca (x) **WHITNEY**. Wit N. **BULLARD**, Isaiah **POE**, Jno. **ABERNETHIE** (JP). Rec 11 Jan 1823.

2089. Page 312. 1 Mar 1821. Medad **RANDOL** to Wm. **ROBERTS**. For the sum of $88, mortgage on two negro boys, one named **Bill** aged 9 years, the other named **Mose** about 5. The debt is due by 1 Mar 1823. Signed Medad **RANDOL**. Test Townsend **NICHOLS** (JP). Rec 16 Jan 1823.

2090. Page 312. 28 Oct 1822. Stephen **BYRD** and Katherine, his wife, to Henry **SHANER**. For the sum of $60, quit claim to 31 acres, on the waters of Byrd's Creek; being part of a tract confirmed to James **COOPER**; beginning 35 ¼ poles from the SE corner of sd tract. Signed Stephen (x) **BYRD**, Catharine **BYRD**. Test James **RUSSELL** (JP). Rec 18 Jan 1823.

2091. Page 313. 16 Apr 1821. Ezekiel **ABLE** by Sheriff John **HAYS** to William M. **PERRY** of Washington Co. For the sum of $31, 640 acres on White Water confirmed to Francis **MURPHY**'s representatives. Sold on 2 Aug 1820 in execution of two writs from Circuit Court dated 22 May 1820; one for Simon **WOODROW** at Court of Common Pleas against sd **ABLE** for $8.41 debt, $14.70 damages, and $16 and 5 mills costs; the other a writ of scire facias for Thomas **GREEN**, adminr with the will annexed of Thomas **STEVENS**, decd, against John **ABLE** for $127.69 damages by non performance of certain promises made by John **ABLE** to sd **STEVENS** in his lifetime, $25.86 costs, and $11.47 and 5 mills costs for the proceeding against Ezekiel **ABLE**. Signed John **HAYS**, Shff. Wit John **JUDEN** Jr, Clerk. Rec 19 Jan 1823.

2092. Page 315. 28 Oct 1822. John **PATTERSON** to Moses **BAILEY**. For the sum of $500, bond to make a deed to 80 acres on Hog Creek, being the W ½, SW ¼, Sec 25, Twp 31 N, Rng 10; to be made when sd **PATTERSON** gets the patent from the U. S. Signed John **PATTERSON**. Wit Rhua (x) **SNIDER** [now Rhua **CRITES**], Barnet **SNIDER**, John B. **WHEELER** (JP). Rec 24 Jan 1823.

2093. Page 316. 10 Dec 1822. Erasmus **ELLIS** by Sheriff William **CREATH** to Johnson **RANNEY**. For the sum of $57.50, a lot and tract of land; Lot No. 63 in Jackson on Main St, where sd **ELLIS** lately resided; and 80 acres near Jackson, being part of a tract confirmed to Henry **HAND**, and purchased of Thomas S. **RODNEY**. Sold on 9 Dec 1822 in execution of a writ issued by Circuit Court on 18 Oct 1822 on a judgment obtained against sd **ELLIS** before William **CREATH**, JP in Byrd Twp on 11 Jan 1821 and for **FRIZEL & VONPHUL** for $66.29 debt, $0.77 ¼ interest, $0.75 costs. Signed William **CREATH**, Shff. Wit C. Simms **THOMAS**, John **JUDEN** Jr., Clerk. Rec 31 Jan 1823.

2094. Page 317. 18 Dec 1822. Gilbert **HECTOR** by same to same. For the sum of $396, 234 acres, being part of a 400 arpen tract confirmed to sd **HECTOR**, where sd **HECTOR** now resides; adjoining John **HAYS**, John **DANIEL** and others. Sold on 14 Dec 1822 in execution of writ issued by Circuit Court on 2 Nov 1822 on a judgment in favor of Stephen **BACON** against sd **HECTOR** for $105.50, debt, $0.42 damages, and $13.20 costs. First sold on 13 Dec 1822 for $300 to William P. **LACEY**, but sd **LACEY** failed to pay the money. Signed William

CREATH, Sheriff. Wit John PRIM, S. REMINGTON, John JUDEN Jr., Clerk. Rec 31 Jan 1823.

2095. Page 318. 5 Nov 1822. Abraham HUGHES and Peggy, his wife, to William RUSSELL of St. Louis Co., Mo. For the sum of $50, 640 acres granted and confirmed to sd HUGHES on the waters of Apple Creek; being the same where sd HUGHES now resides; located in parts of Secs 19, 20, 28, 29, & 30, Twp 33 N, Rng 12 E. Signed Abraham HUGHES, Peggy (x) HUGHES. Wit Elizabeth Ann RUSSELL, Mary HOUSTEN, James RUSSELL (JP). Rec 3 Feb 1823.

2096. Page 320. 7 Apr 1822. Ludwell R. DAVIS to Timothy SHAW. For a valuable consideration, a preemption right to a certain improvement where sd SHAW now lives. Signed L. R. DAVIS. Wit Gamaliel PARKER, John JUDEN Jr., Clerk. Rec 11 Feb 1823.

2097. Page 320. 12 Feb 1823. Eliza CHAMBERLAIN, widow of Jason CHAMBERLAIN, decd, and Eliza CHAMBERLAIN and Ann Williams CHAMBERLAIN, children of sd decd, to Edmund RUTTER. By order of Circuit Court in Chancery, 303 ¼ acres; beginning at a stake on Richard S. THOMAS' line; also bounded by Thomas BULL, Lewis TASHE, and A. RANDOL. Signed John JUDEN Jr., Clerk. Rec 17 Feb 1823.

2098. Page 321. 17 Feb 1823. Edmund RUTTER and Betsy, his wife, to Thomas HOUTS of Scott Co., Mo. For the sum of $595, quit claim to 130 acres lying about 1 ½ miles SE of Jackson, being part of 640 acres granted to Peter BILLUE; beginning at an ash and hornbeam near the top of the dividing ridge; including the plantation whereon John C. HOUTS now lives. The tract passed to sd RUTTER for security of a debt for $595, and sd HOUTS agrees sd RUTTER is not accountable for any loss of the land by any other claim. Signed Edmund RUTTER, Betsey RUTTER. Wit John JUDEN Jr., Clerk. Rec 17 Feb 1833.

2099. Page 322. 2 Dec 1822. John BURNS and Mary A., his wife, to David G. L. CALDWELL. For the sum of $600, two tracts; 112 acres, part of a tract confirmed to Lewis TASH, beginning at the SE corner of sd tract at a stake near a pond, bounded on the E by Anthony RANDOL, N by sd BURNS, W by sd TASH's heirs, and S by Hugh CRESSWELL's confirmation; and 13

acres on Frank's Creek the waters of Randol's Creek, part of a tract where sd RANDOL now lives off the SW corner of sd tract, beginning at the SE corner of sd TASH's survey, bounded on the W & S by sd CRESSWELL's confirmation, and E & N by Anthony RANDOL's land. Signed John BURNS, Mary (x) BURNS. Test Anthony (*) RANDOL, Sarah CAMPBELL, Jno. ABERNETHIE (JP). Rec 22 Feb 1823.

2100. Page 323. 21 Feb 1823. Richard THOMAS and Francis, his wife, to John J. DLASHMUTT, all of Jackson. For the sum of $40, __ acres, being part of the tract on which sd THOMAS now lives; beginning at CUPPLES' SW corner of a tract conveyed by sd THOMAS to sd CUPPLES & wife. Signed Richard S. THOMAS, Frances THOMAS. Wit David ARMOUR (JP). Rec 22 Feb 1823.

2101. Page 324. 13 Dec 1822. Alexander McNAIR, Governor of Mo., to John HORRELL, Esq. Appointment as Justice of the Cape Girardeau County Court for four years. Signed A. McNAIR. Wit Wm. S. PETTUS, Secretary of State. John HORRELL takes the oath of office. Signed John HORRELL. Wit Isaac SHEPPARD, Count Court Justice. Rec 24 Feb 1823.

2102. Page 325. 10 Oct 1820. Commissioners to Partition Lands of the heirs of Louis LORIMIER, decd, to Joseph DORFEUILLE. For the sum of $22, Lot Nos. 29 & 30, Range E in Cape Girardeau; bounded on the E by a street and W by an alley, Lot No. 30 also fronting on St Bellview. Sold as in F:20. Signed B. COUSIN, W. GARNER, Wm. KELSO. Wit John C. HARBISON (JP). Rec 27 Feb 1823.

2103. Page 326. 4 Mar 1823. Thomas N. HARRIS to Solomon H. ARMOUR. For the sum of $35, one feather bed and bedding, one cherry breakfast table, one pair Britania tea pots, one looking glass, one pair andirons, one pair shovel & tongs, one cupboard cups & saucers, knives & forks, four chairs, one brace & bits, one pannel plow, one pair grooving plaines, one sashplane, one hand saw, one tennant saw, one doovetale saw, one saw, one hatchet, one hammer, one set bench planes, two augers, twelve moulding planes, some chisels, one pot and two ovens, one tea kettle, one tea caddy, one grindstone, one breeding sow, two shoats, and one skillit. Signed Thos. N. HARRIS. Wit George W. JUDEN, Saml. LOCKHART, David ARMOUR (JP). Rec 5 Mar 1823.

2104. Page 327. 21 Jun 1820. Commissioners of the Courthouse and Jail to Joel **BLUNT**. For the sum of $113, two lots in Jackson; Lot No. 55, bounded on the W and fronted by first west street, S and fronted by second south street, E by Lot No. 19, and N by Lot No. 54; and Lot No. 152, bounded on the N and fronted by second south street, E and fronted by third east street, S by Lot No. 53, and W by Lot No. 140. Signed John **DAVIS**, John **SHEPPARD**, Samuel G. **DUNN**, Abraham **BYRD**, Benja. **SHELL**. Wit Wm. S. **GANTT**, Edw. S. **GANTT**, David **ARMOUR** (JP). Rec 8 Mar 1823.

2105. Page 328. 27 Apr 1822. William B. **LITTLEJOHN** to N. W. **WATKINS** and William **CRACRAFT**. For the sum of $106, 38 arpens, more or less, on Hubble's Creek, being part of the head right of Lewis **LATHEUM**, adjoining the widow **SUMMERS** on the W and John **SOMERS** on the S. Signed William B. **LITTLEJOHN**. Test John **BROWN**, Townsend **NICHOLS**. It is agreed that is sd **LITTLEJOHN** pays $106 to sd **WATKINS** and sd **CRACRAFT** or the loan office at Jackson within 12 months, they will reconvey the tract to him. Signed N. W. **WATKINS**, William **CRACRAFT**. Wit Townsend **NICHOLS**, Medad **RANDOL**, John **JUDEN** Jr., Clerk. Rec 8 Mar 1823. [Marginal note: Full satisfaction received on 16 Nov 1827. This mortgage has been forfeited, see Sheriff's deed to James **LISHMAN**, H:247.]

2106. Page 329. 15 Feb 1821. Samuel **RAVENSCROFT** to **STARLING** & **DLASHMUTT**. For the sum of $250, undivided ½ of 250 arpens purchased by sd **RAVENSCROFT** of John **WEAVER** on 2 Dec 1820. If the title is not confirmed, then sd **RAVENSCROFT** agrees to enter two ¼ sections by preemption as equal partner with **STARLING** and **DLASHMUTT** by their furnishing ½ of the purchase price. Signed Samuel **RAVENSCROFT**. Test Lindsey J. **DLASHMUTT**. Title is assigned to E. N. **DLASHMUTT** on 8 Jun 1822. Signed Lyne **STARLING**. Rec 10 Mar 1823.

2107. Page 329. 13 Feb 1822. Scarlet **GLASSCOCK** to Lyne **STARLING** and Elias N. **DLASHMUTT**. For the sum of $98.62 ½, undivided ½ of 157 acres where Jont. **MALONE** Sr. formerly lived. The deed to be executed as soon as sd **GLASSCOCK** obtains a patent for the same from the U. S. Signed Scarlet **GLASSCOCK**. Test R. **DAUGHERTY**. Title is assigned to E. N. **DLASHMUTT** on 8 Jun

1822. Signed Lyne **STARLING**. Rec 10 Mar 1823.

2108. Page 329. 16 Dec 1822. John **BURNS** and Mary, his wife, to Margret **JONES**. For the sum of $269, Lot No. 126 in Jackson; bounded on the B and fronted by first south street, E and fronted by second east street, S by Lot No. 127, and W by Lot No. 42. Signed John **BURNS**, Mary A. (x) **BURNS**. Wit James **SMITH**, Antony (x) **RANDOL**, John **ABERNETHIE** (JP). Rec 13 Mar 1823.

2109. Page 330. 16 Dec 1822. Margret **JONES** to John **BURNS**. For the sum of $69, mortgage on ½ of Lot No. 126 in Jackson as described in the preceding deed (F:329). A note is due in bed furniture, payable by 1 Oct 1823. Signed Margret (x) **JONES**. Wit James **SMITH**, Antony (x) **RANDOL**, John **ABERNETHIE** (JP). Rec 13 Mar 1823. [Marginal note: Full satisfaction received on 16 Mar 1829. Signed John **BURNS**. Wit Fr. **FLACK**, Deputy Clerk.]

2110. Page 331. 18 Feb 1822. David **COTNER** of Union Co., Ill. to Jacob **COTNER**. For the sum of $100, all his right to __ acres on White Water, willed to him by his father Jacob **COTNER**, sd tract joining John **MILLER**. Signed David **COTNER**, Poley (x) **COTNER**. Wit Green H. **COLEMAN**, Abram **HUNSAKER**, JP in Union Co., Ill., Mary (x) **HUNSACKER**. Rec 13 Mar 1823.

2111. Page 332. 22 Mar 1823. Washington **STERIT** to Samuel G. **DUNN**. For the sum of $550, one negro man named **Samuel**, of a black complexion and 23 years old. Signed Washington **STERRET**. Wit John **JUDEN** Jr., Clerk, John **McCOMBS**. Rec 22 Mar 1823.

2112. Page 332. 15 Mar 1823. John **EVANS** to Joseph **ENGLISH**. For the sum of $400, 72 acres and 8 chains on Ramsey Creek; beginning at a stake at the NE corner of Thomas **ENGLISH**. Signed John **EVANS**. Wit George **HENDERSON** (JP). Rec 24 Mar 1823.

2113. Page 333. 14 Dec 1822. Heirs of Zilla **DICKSON** by Sheriff William **CREATH** to Lewis **DICKSON**. For the sum of $326, about 400 acres on Randol's Creek, being the same confirmed to Zilla **DICKSON** or Drusilla **DICKSON**. Sold on 12 Dec 1822 in execution of an order of Circuit Court in Chancery issued 23 Oct 1822 in favor of John **RANDOL** against Gilbert **HECTOR** and Ann, his wife, Lewis **DICKSON**, Frederick **DICKSON**, Nathaniel

DICKSON, Hezekiah DICKSON, Jonathan PURDY and Unis, his wife, David BRADY and Ester, his wife, and Arthur BURNS and Polly, his wife, all heirs and devisees of Zellah DICKSON, decd, for $39.42 costs in a certain cause in sd court. Signed William CREATH, Sheriff. Wit J. RANNEY, John JUDEN Jr., Clerk. Rec 24 Mar 1823.

2114. Page 335. 22 Dec 1820. Mathew HUBBELS to George STROUP. For the sum of $400, 300 acres on the waters of Crader's Creek and Hog Creek; beginning at a stake and black gum. Signed Mathew HUBBEL, Peggy HUBBEL. Wit Barnet SNIDER (JP), George SNIDER. Rec 25 Mar 1823.

2115. Page 336. 5 Jul 1822. William WALLACE to John HARRASS. For the sum of $186, quit claim to a negro boy named Bob, purchased at the sale of Robt. STEEL, decd. Signed William WALLACE. Test Saml. B. McKNIGHT. John WALLACE to same. For the sum of $151, quit claim to same. Signed John WALLACE. Test Saml. B. McKNIGHT, John JUDEN Jr., Clerk. Rec 26 Mar 1823.

2116. Page 336. 27 Jan 1823. Scarlett GLASSCOCK to John J. DLASHMUTT. For the sum of $1000, Lot No. 66 in Jackson; bounded on the N and fronted by first south street, E and fronted by first west street, S by Lot No. 67, and W by Lot No. 78. Signed Scarlett GLASSCOCK, Jane GLASSCOCK. Wit Peter R. GARRETT (JP). Rec 31 Mar 1823.

2117. Page 337. 14 Dec 1822. Victor LORIMIER by Sheriff John HAYS to Thomas W. GRAVES. For the sum of $200, 400 arpents on Hubble's Creek, confirmed to John STRONG under Ithamer HUBBLE, and known as Davis's Mill. Sold on 13 Aug 1822 in execution of two writs issued by Circuit Court against sd LORIMIER; one dated 8 Jul 1822 for Isaac RODGERS for $372 debt, $28.83 damages, and $17.85 costs; and one dated 29 Apr 1822 for Thomas W. GRAVES and Samuel RAVENSCROFT, adminr of Levi WOLVERTON, decd, for $750 debt, $175 damages, and $16.80 costs. Sd HAYS did not execute a deed at the time of sale, and sd GRAVES obtained a court order directing the present sheriff to execute a deed. Signed William CREATH, Sheriff. Wit J. RANNEY, John JUDEN Jr., Clerk. 4 Apr 1823. Thomas W. GRAVES to Daniel F. STEINBECK. For the sum of $225, the tract sold by Sheriff's deed above. Signed Thomas W. GRAVES. Wit J.

RANNEY, John JUDEN Jr., Clerk. Rec 4 Apr 1823.

2118. Page 339. 27 Feb 1823. Michael O. HOGAN and Elizabeth, his wife, to James WILKINSON. For the sum of $550, 390 acres, more or less, on the waters of Byrd's Creek; bounded on the E by Martin THOMAS, S by Jhn. PATTERSON, W by Philip YOUNG and U. S. lands, and N by public lands and Daniel CLIPPARD. Signed Michel O. HOGAN, Elizebeth O. (x) HOGAN. Test Philip YOUNG, John PATTERSON, John JUDEN Jr., Clerk. Rec 12 Mar 1823.

2119. Page 340. 26 Dec 1822. William NEELY and Rachel, his wife, to Joseph OBANNON. For the sum of $275, Lot No. 76 in Jackson; bounded on the N and fronted by Main St, W and fronted by second west street, S by Lot No. 77, and E by Lot No. 64. Signed Wm. NEELY, Rachel NEELY (RD). Wit James RUSSELL, JCGCC, Wm. JOHNSON. Rec 18 Mar 1823.

2120. Page 341. 23 Apr 1823. John PROPES and Barbara, his wife, to Jacob CRADER and Samuel CRADER. For the sum of $5, 1 acre, or 160 poles, on the waters of Caney Fork, being part of 640 arpens granted to sd PROPEST by the King of Spain and ratified by Congress; bounded on the E by Jacob & Samuel CRADER; beginning at a shugar tree on the dividing line between sd PROPEST and sd CRADERs. Signed John PROBST, Barbara (x) PROBS. Wit James RUSSELL (JP). Rec 5 May 1823.

2121. Page 342. 5 May 1823. William McGUIRE and Susan, his wife, to Henry STEELE. For diverse good considerations and the sum of $1500, 336 acres, two rood, and 39 poles; beginning on the E side of Stephen BYRD; also bounded by Hugh CONNELLY. Signed Wm. McGUIRE, Susan McGUIRE. Wit John JUDEN Jr., Clerk, Charles SEAVERS. Rec 5 May 1823.

2122. Page 343. 5 May 1823. Simon WHITTENBURGH, one of the heirs of John WHITTENBURGH, decd, to Wm. THOMPSON. For the sum of $700, all his right to land, negros, and other property that may come to him as a son of John WHITTENBURGH, decd. Signed Simon J. WHITTENBURGH. Wit J. RANNEY, Peter R. GARRETT (JP). Rec 5 May 1823.

2123. Page 344. 23 Nov 1822. Andrew **RAMSEY** to Margaret **GIBBONEY**. For the sum of $500, 200 arpents, being part of a tract granted by the Spanish Government to John **SIMPSON**; bounded on the E by sd **RAMSEY**, N by vacant lands, W by part of the grant conveyed to William **COX**, and S by vacant land. Signed Andrew **RAMSEY**. Wit Nicholas **SEAVERS**, Andrew **GIBONEY**, John **JUDEN** Jr., Clerk. Rec 6 May 1823.

2124. Page 345. 22 Jul 1820. John **MASSEY** to John **BURNS**. For the sum of $1200, bond to make a deed by 1 Dec next for ½ of 120 French arpens on Randol's Creek, being the N end of a tract granted by the Spanish Government to James **DOWTY**; beginning at a stake on the boundary of the original survey. Signed John **MASSEY**, Wit John **DAVIS**, John **GILES**, Wm. **CREATH** (JP). [E:528.] John **BURNS** to Robert **PACKIE**. Assignment of his right to sd tract, where he now lives and where sd **MASSEY** formerly lived, on 11 Jul 1821. Signed John **BURNS**. Wit Wylie A. **ABERNETHIE**, John **ABERNETHIE** (JP). [F:186] Robert **PACKIE** to John **BURNS**. Assignment of his interest in the tract on 8 Feb 1823. Signed Robert **PACKIE**. Wit Jno. **ABERNETHIE** (JP). Rec 8 May 1823.

2125. Page 346. 9 Jun 1823. Richard S. **THOMAS**, Judge of 4th Judicial Circuit, to Claiborne S. **THOMAS**. Appointment as Circuit Court Clerk for Cape Girardeau Co. in place of John **JUDEN** Junior. Signed R. S. **THOMAS**. Claiborne S. **THOMAS** takes the oath of office. Signed Claiborne S. **THOMAS**. Wit Peter R. **GARRETT** (JP). Rec 9 Jun 1823.

2126. Page 347. 9 Jun 1823. Claiborne S. **THOMAS**, Peter R. **GARRETT**, Charles **SEAVERS**, and George **BULLITT** to Alexander **McNAIR**, Governor of Mo. For the sum of $3000, bond to guarantee that sd **THOMAS** will perform the duties of Clerk of Circuit Court for Cape Girardeau Co. Signed Claibne. S. **THOMAS**, Peter R. **GARRETT**, Charles **SEAVERS**, Geo. **BULLITT**. Wit Richard S. **THOMAS**, Circuit Court Judge. Rec 9 Jun 1823.

2127. Page 347. 20 Apr 1822. Stephen **BYRD** to Christian **GATES**. For the sum of $300, mortgage on 600 arpens on Cain Creek; bounded on the N by Hennery **HOWARD**, E by William **McGUIRE**, S by William **RUSSELL**, John **HOREL**, and Isaac **SHEPARD**, and W by Mrs. **LOVE**. A promissory note dated 21 Mar is due

to sd **GATES**. Signed Stephen **BYRD**. Test Abraham **BYRD**, Wm. G. **BYRD**, James **RUSSELL** (JP). Rec 9 Jun 1823. [Marginal note: Full satisfaction received on 4 Jul 1833. Signed Christian **GATES**. Wit Hy. **SANFORD**, Clerk.]

2128. Page 348. 1 Mar 1823. Richard R. **PACE** to Joseph **OBANNON**. For the sum of $59.61, one sorrel mare five years old with a star and snip about 14 ½ hands high, one bay mare about eleven years old with a star and snip about 14 1/5 hands high, a gray mare colt about three years old about 13 ½ hands high, one iron gray horse about three years old about 13 hands high, one read and white cow marked crop and half crop in the right ear and a crop of the left, one black and white cow with a stump tail marked with a crop of each ear, one read cow with a white face marked with a crop and underbit in her left ear and crop and half crop in the right ear, one read heifer marked with a crop in the right ear, one oxecart, two beds and bed clothing, and part of a set of carpenter tools. Signed Richard R. **PACE**. Wit Welton **OBANNON**, James **RUSSELL** (JP). Rec 9 Jun 1823.

2129. Page 349. 19 Apr 1823. Thomas **GRAHAM** of Hamilton Co., Ohio to John **RAMSEY** of Scott Co., Mo. For the consideration of his having given a title bond to sd **RAMSEY**, 500 arpens, being part of a tract originally granted by the Spanish Government to Louis **LASEUR**; sold by the Sheriff to James **EVANS**, and by sd **EVANS** to sd **GRAHAM**. Signed Tho. **GRAHAM**. Wit James **EVANS**, Wm. **GRAHAM**, James **GRAHAM**, John **JUDEN** Jr., Clerk. Rec 9 Jun 1823.

2130. Page 350. 26 Feb 1823. John **McLANE** to Samuel **LOVE**. For the sum of $500, bond to make a deed to __ acres bought by sd **McLANE** of the U. S.; being part of the SE fractional ¼ and part of the NE ¼, Sec 19, Twp 32 N, Rng 13 E; beginning on the line of Christopher **HAYS'** original survey where the spring branch from John **WILSON'**s preemption right crosses sd line. The deed to be made as soon as sd **McLANE** gets the patent from the government. Signed Jno. **McLANE**. Test John G. **LOVE**, M. R. **McLANE**, Peter R. **GARRETT** (JP), John **PRIM**. Bond is assigned to Ebenezer **FLINN** for $325 on 3 Apr 1822. Signed Samuel **LOVE**. Wit Geo. H. **SCRIPPS**, George **BAKER**, P. R. **GARRETT** (JP). Rec 21 Jun 1823.

2131. Page 351. 8 Feb 1823. James **MASSEY** and John **BURNS** to Robert **PACKEY**. For the sum of $1200, bond to make a deed for __ acres, being ½ of a tract originally granted to James DOWTY; beginning at the boundary of the original survey at a stake. The deed to be made as soon as sd MASSEY can obtain title from Richard WALLER. Signed James MASSEY, John BURNS. Wit Jno. ABERNETHIE (JP). Rec 23 Jun 1823.

2132. Page 352. 23 Jun 1823. Frances JOHNSON to Anthony RANDOL. For the sum of $10.37 ½, 8.30 acres, being fractional Sec 17, Twp 31 N, Rng 14 E, and the same entered on 7 Jan 1822. Signed Frances JOHNSON. Wit C. S. THOMAS, Clerk. Rec 23 Jun 1823.

2133. Page 353. 11 Jul 1823. Alexander McNAIR, Governor of Mo., to Claiborne S. THOMAS. Commission as Circuit Court Clerk of Cape Girardeau Co. for two years, his having been elected on the 1st Mon of Aug last. Signed A. McNAIR. Wit Wm. S. PETTUS, Secretary of State. Claiborne S. THOMAS takes the oath of office. Signed C. S. THOMAS. Wit Peter R. GARRETT (JP). Rec 15 Jul 1823.

2134. Page 354. 8 Jun 1822. Elias N. DLASHMUTT and Ann, his wife, to Lyne STARLING. For the sum of $4000, several parcels; five lots in Jackson, being ½ of Lot No. 51, being the same sold to STARLING & DLASHMUTT by Edward McGUIRE and wife on 2 Jan 1819, the other ½ of Lot No. 51, except for the part conveyed to J. J. DLASHMUTT, being the same conveyed by David DAVIS and May, his wife, to STARLING & DLASHMUTT on 31 May 1821, Lot Nos. 69 & 81, being the same conveyed on 9 May 1820 to STARLING & DLASHMUTT by the Commissioners, and Lot No. 111, conveyed by Sheriff John HAYS to STARLING & DLASHMUTT on 16 Apr 1821; three outlots near Cape Girardeau, 50 acres, being Outlot No. 38, and 80 acres, being Outlot No. 52, both conveyed by Van B. DLASHMUTT and wife to STARLING & DLASHMUTT on 15 Feb 1821, and 10 acres, being Outlot No. 13, conveyed by John J. DLASHMUTT to STARLING & DLASHMUTT on 22 Jan 1821; 138.82 acres, being NW fractional ¼, Sec 17, Twp 30 N, Rng 14 E entered by STARLING & DLASHMUTT on 4 Dec 1821; and 160 acres, being SE ¼, Sec 32, Twp 31 N, Rng 11 E. Signed Elias N. DLASHMUTT, Ann D'LASHMUTT (RD). Wit J. BROWN & William PORTER, JP in Mason Co., Ken. (as to Ann DLASHMUTT),

Wm. CREATH (JP), Marshall KEY, Clerk of Mason Co., Ken. Rec 15 Jul 1823.

2135. Page 355. 16 Jul 1823. Greer W. DAVIS to George W. FRICKE. For the consideration of serving as principal and security for debts totaling $287, bond to release a mortgage on Lot No. 52 in Jackson. Sd FRICKE has obtained two notes from the State of Mo., one for $155.25 for which sd DAVIS is principal and Samuel LOCKHART is security, and one for $132.08 in which sd LOCKHART is principal and sd DAVIS is security; and if the notes are not paid, then sd DAVIS will sell the property to pay the debts. Signed Greer W. DAVIS. Wit John GLASSCOCK, James BRADLEY, C. S. THOMAS, Clerk. Rec 16 Jul 1823.

2136. Page 356. 16 Jul 1823. George FRICKE to Greer W. DAVIS. For the sum of $287, part of Lot No. 52 in Jackson; bounded on the N by Main St and beginning at the office of Johnson RANNEY; being the same sd FRICKE purchased of John BROWN. The debt is due in a writing obligatory by 13 Jul 1824. Signed George FRICKE. Wit John GLASSCOCK, James BRADLEY, C. S. THOMAS, Clerk. Rec 16 Jul 1823.

2137. Page 357. 2 Jun 1820. Samuel WARDEN to Daniel F. STEINBECK. For the sum of $235, quit claim to Lot Nos. 21 & 22, Range A in Cape Girardeau; bounded on the S by Williams St, E by Spanish St, and W by Lorimier's St; being the same purchased by sd WARDEN at the public sale on 23 Nov last. Signed Saml. WARDEN. Wit Elijah RANDOL, B. COUSIN, George HENDERSON (JP). Rec 31 Jul 1823.

2138. Page 358. 13 Apr 1823. Daniel F. STEINBECK (at the time of execution in Baltimore, Md.) to Anna D. STEINBECK, widow and sold executrix of the last will and testament of John C. STEINBECK, decd, of Baltimore, Md. For consideration of several promises the sum of $5, mortgage on 17 acres N of Cape Girardeau, bounded on the N by Outlot No. 34, S by Outlot No. 1 and the grave or churchyard, E by a vacant space on the river destined for a boatyard or other public uses, and W by Outlot No. 31; sold by William GARNER and other commissioners to sd STEINBECK on 30 Nov 1819 (E:232). Daniel F. STEINBECK owes $3000 to Anna D. STEINBECK within five years; he had a balance due to John C. STEINBECK upon liquidating accounts on 26 Aug 1816, for which he executed his promissory note. Signed D. F. STEINBECK. Wit Edwd.

JOHNSON, Mayor of Baltimore, Md., Fras. J. **DALLAN**. Rec 31 Jul 1828.

2139. Page 359. 13 Aug 1823. John **LOGAN** to the heirs of Louis **LORIMIER**, represented by Daniel F. **STEINBECK**. For the sum of $10,000, all of his share of the estate of Louis **LORIMIER**, Sr., the share of his wife, Marie **LOGAN**, widow of sd **LORIMIER**, and the share of Marie **LOGAN** as sole heir of Manuel **LORIMIER**, decd, child of Louis **LORIMIER**, decd, and Mary his wife. Signed John **LOGAN**. Wit L. L. **LIGHTNER**, James **EVANS**, David **ARMOUR** (JP). Rec 13 Aug 1823.

2140. Page 360. 12 Aug 1823. John **DAVIS** to Stephen **BIRD**. Power of attorney to proceed on obtaining title to 232 arpents on the fork of Hubble's Creek, and commence a suit against Benjamin **TENNELLE** for defect of title. Sd **TENNELLE** conveyed the tract sd **DAVIS** on 29 Oct 1806, and the title failed. Signed John **DAVIS**. Wit J. **RANNEY**, Claiborne S. **THOMAS**, Clerk. Rec 13 Aug 1823.

2141. Page 361. 15 Aug 1823. Nicholas **SEAVERS** to Charles **SEAVERS**. For the sum of $500, 170 acres, more or less, on Randle's Creek; beginning at the NW corner of Nicholas **SEAVERS** at a stake. Signed Nicholas **SEAVERS**. Wit N. W. **WATKINS**, Wm. P. **LACEY**, Claiborne S. **THOMAS**, Clerk. Rec 15 Aug 1823.

2142. Page 362. 10 Aug 1823. William **COX** to John **MAYFIELD**. For the sum of $80, mortgage on an improvement on both sides of White Water where both now live, a one-year-old horse colt, three head of sheep, 15 head of hogs, and all his household furniture. The debt is due in 12 months. Signed Wm. **COX**. Wit Robinson **STOE**, Abraham **HENDRICKS**, C. S. **THOMAS**, Clerk. Rec 16 Aug 1823.

2143. Page 363. 15 Aug 1823. Charles **SEAVERS** to Nicholas **SEAVERS**. For the sum of $500, 170 acres, more or less, on Randle's Creek; beginning at the SW corner of the E boundary line of **BYRD**'s survey. Signed Charles **SEAVERS**, Sarah **SEAVERS**. Wit N. W. **WATKINS**, Wm. P. **LACEY**, Peter R. **GARRETT** (JP). Rec 18 Aug 1823.

2144. Page 364. __ Nov 1822. William **TINNIN** [and Susanah, his wife,] to John **YUNT**. For the sum of $519, 519 arpents or 441 3/4 acres and 16 square poles, more or less, on the S fork of White Water, including all the improvements where

Jacob **YUNT**, decd, formerly lived; being the land confirmed to sd **TINNIN** and Jacob **YUNT**, decd; beginning at a stake on Henery **BOLLINGER**'s line. Signed William **TINNIN**, Susanah (x) **TINNIN**. Test John **BOLLINGER**, David **ARMOUR** (JP). Rec 25 Aug 1823.

2145. Page 365. 27 Aug 1823. Jonas N. **MENEFEE** by Sheriff William **CREATH** to John **PAYNE** Junr, Thomas W. **GRAVES**, and James **RAVENSCROFT**. For the sum of $104, brick house and Lot on the Hill, formerly the property of Louis **LORIMIER**, decd, sold by him to James **EVANS**, and by sd **EVANS** to sd **MENEFEE**. Sold on 11 Dec 1822 on two executions issued by Circuit Court against sd **MENEFEE**; one issued 16 Oct 1822 for Jacob **STAHL** against sd **MENEFEE** (impleaded with John **SHERRILL**) for $23.87 ½ costs; the other issued on 17 Sep 1822 for William **McGUIRE**, assignee of William **MONTGOMERY**, assignee of John **McELNNENY** for $250 debt, $4.37 damages, and $12.75 costs. Signed William **CREATH**, Sheriff. Wit Claiborne S. **THOMAS**, Clerk. Rec 27 Aug 1823.

2146. Page 367. 7 Jun 1823. George **BULLITT** to John **JUDEN** Junior. For the sum of $2600, mortgage on several items; the equal and undivided ½ of 640 acres confirmed to Benjamin **HARGRAVE**, and conveyed by sd **HARGRAVE** to sd **BULLITT** and Robert T. **BROWN**; 30 acres adjoining Jackson, being part of a tract transferred by William H. **ASHLEY** to Richard S. **THOMAS** , and by sd **THOMAS** to sd **BULLITT**, being the same where sd **BULLITT** now lives; Lot No. 14 in Jackson; one negro man named **Willis** about 28 years old; a negro boy named **Frank** about 17 years old; and one negro boy named **Joe** about 15 years old. Sd **BULLITT** has given four promissory notes, for $300, $300, $1000, and $1000; the first three due in one year, and the last payable in two years. Signed Geo. **BULLITT**. Wit Claiborne S. **THOMAS**, Clerk, Jesse B. **THOMAS** Jr. Rec 29 Aug 1823. [Marginal note: $1600 received on 27 Feb 1824. Signed John **JUDEN** Jr. Wit C. S. **THOMAS**, Clerk.]

2147. Page 368. 2 Sep 1823. David **DAVIS** by Sheriff William **CREATH** to John D. **COOK** and Morgan **BYRNE**. For the sum of $5, 640 acres on Hubble's Creek, on which is erected a grist and saw mill; confirmed to John **STRONG** under Ithamer **HUBBLE**. Sold on 16 Aug 1823 on an execution issued by Circuit Court on 21 Jul 1823 for sd **BYRNE** against sd **DAVIS**, on a case heard before George **HENDERSON**, JP, for $43.25 debt with interest from 25 Dec 1819, $3.46 and 5 mills costs, and $2.10 costs in Circuit Court. Signed Wm. **CREATH**, Sheriff. Wit Claiborne S. **THOMAS**, Clerk. Rec 2 Sep 1823.

2148. Page 369. 13 Aug 1823. Charles S. **HEMPSTEAD** by same to John **RISHER**. For the sum of $460 paid to former Sheriff John **HAYS**, 45 acres and 84 poles adjoining Cape Girardeau; beginning on the bank of the Mississippi River in the direction of Simeon **WOODROW**'s lower line. Sold on 13 Aug 1822 on a mortgage foreclosure issued by Circuit Court in Apr Term 1822. Signed William **CREATH**, Sheriff. Wit Claiborne S. **THOMAS**, Clerk. Rec 2 Sep 1823.

2149. Page 370. 8 Aug 1823. Jonas N. **MENEFEE** by same to John **PAYNE** Junr and Charles G. **ELLIS**. For the sum of $31, a shop, painted white and used by sd **MENEFEE** as a drug or apothecaries shop. Sold on 11 Dec 1822 on two executions issued by Circuit Court as described in F:365. Signed Wm. **CREATH**, Sheriff. Wit Claiborne S. **THOMAS**, Clerk. Rec 2 Sep 1823.

2150. Page 373. 2 Sep 1823. John G. **LOVE** by same to Christian **GATES**. For the sum of $82, ½ of a lot in Jackson, adjoining the public square on the W and Main St on the E, opposite where Dr. Edward S. **GANTT** then lived; and for the sum of $25, Lot No. 125 in Jackson on first south street. Sold on 12 Dec 1822 on two executions issued by Circuit Court on 28 Sep 1822 against Erasmus **ELLIS** and sd **LOVE**; one in favor of Johnson **RANNEY** for $334.93 damages for non-performance of a contract, and $18.75 costs; the other in favor of sd **GATES** for $284.08 damages for non-performance of a contact, and $18.75 costs. Signed Wm. **CREATH**, Sheriff. Wit Claiborne S. **THOMAS**, Clerk. Rec 2 Sep 1823.

2151. Page 375. 1 Sep 1823. Maurice **WILLIAMS** and John **LEMON**, otherwise called James **LEMON**, by same to Thomas **BYRNE**. For the sum of $25 received by former Sheriff John **HAYS**, undivided 2/3 of 720 arpens at the mouth of Cape la Cruche Creek, on which William **KELSO** formerly lived. Sold on 14 Aug 1822 on a writ of execution issued on 10 Jul 1822 by Circuit Court, in favor of Isaac **HODGES**, sole heir and legal representative of James **HODGE**, decd, and against sd **WILLIAMS** and sd **LEMON** for $522.65 damages, by reason of non-performance of certain promises and

undertakings, and $26.36 ¼ costs. Signed William **CREATH**, Sheriff. Wit Claiborne S. **THOMAS**, Clerk. Rec 3 Sep 1823.

2152. Page 376. 5 Sep 1823. Jacob **PROPST** and Sally, his wife, to Martain **TOMMIS**. For the sum of $200, 100 acres on the E side of the W fork of Whitewater, beginning on a heavy stake and rock; bounded on two sides by lands of sd **PROPST**, and being part of the tract where he now lives. Signed Jacob (x) **PROPST**, Sally (x) **PROPST**. Test David **ARMOUR** (JP), Polly **LEWIS**, Jacob **HARTLE**. Rec 8 Sep 1823.

2153. Page 377. 8 Sep 1823. Daniel F. **STEINBECK** and George **HENDERSON**, adminrs with the will annexed of Louis **LORIMIER** Senior, decd, to Ignatius **WATHEN** and Mary Ann, his wife, Alfred P. **ELLIS** and Fanny, his wife, William **SHAW** and Polly, his wife, Henry **WAIT** and Elanor, his wife, John **LARK** and Precious, his wife, Nancy **MIFFLIN**, and Amelia **DAVIS**, heirs of Thomas W. **WATERS**, decd. In consideration of the premises and the sum of $400 paid by sd **WATERS**, decd, during his lifetime, 400 arpens, more or less, on the waters of Randol's Creek about four miles from Jackson, being the original grant or settlement right of Andrew **FRANKS** and that sd **LORIMIER** purchased on 9 Mar 1805. Conveyed on a decree of Circuit Court in Chancery dated 5 Sep 1823, issued in case of the heirs of Thomas W. **WATERS**, decd, complainant, against sd **STEINBECK** and sd **HENDERSON**. Sd **WATERS** purchased the land in his lifetime, but did not receive legal title, and sd **LORIMIER** executed his bond for a deed and received the consideration money. Signed D. F. **STEINBECK**, George **HENDERSON**. Wit J. **RANNEY**, Thos. W. **GRAVES**, Claiborne S. **THOMAS**, Clerk. Rec 8 Sep 1823.

2154. Page 379. 11 Sep 1823. Edward **HAILE** to his children Jesse **HAIL** and John **ZILEFROE**. For love and affection and the sum of $400, about 250 arpents on Hubble's Creek near Jackson, being the same confirmed to him and being the plantation where he now resides. Signed Edward (x) **HAIL**. Wit John **HORRELL**, Peter R. **GARRETT** (JP). Rec 13 Sep 1823.

2155. Page 379. 24 Sep 1823. John **ROGERS** Junior of Greenup Co., Ken. to John **PAYNE** Jr. For the sum of $500, Lot No. 75 and a house in Jackson, fronting on Main St and including the alley between it and the brick building adjacent; being the same conveyed to sd **ROGERS** and

William **WARNOCK** by Thomas **NEAL** on 19 Mar 1821. Signed Jno. **ROGERS** Jr. Wit Peter R. **GARRETT** (JP). Rec 24 Sep 1823.

2156. Page 380. 24 Sep 1823. John **PAYNE** Jr. to John **ROGERS** Jr. of Greenup Co., Ken. For the sum of $100, an undivided ½ of a lot in Cape Girardeau, being the same on which is situated a small frame building painted white, late owned by Jonas N. **MENEFEE** and purchased by sd **PAYNE** and Charles G. **ELLIS** at Sheriff's sale on 28 Aug last. Signed John **PAYNE** Jr. Wit Peter R. **GARRETT** (JP). Rec 24 Sep 1823.

2157. Page 381. 17 Sep 1823. John **ROSS** to Thomas **BYRNE**. For the sum of $800, 210 arpens, more or less, on the Mississippi River where sd **ROSS** now lives; adjoining Robert **GIBBONEY** and John **BALDWIN**, and being the same willed to sd **ROSS** by William **ROSS**, decd; beginning at a hickory tree marked with a blaze on each side in the line between sd **ROSS** and John **BALDWIN**, in and near a wet place between the river and the hills. Signed John **ROSS**. Wit William **KELSO** (JP). Rec 30 Sep 1823.

2158. Page 382. 6 Oct 1823. John **ABERNETHIE** and Havens Clary, his wife, to John **JUDEN** Junior. For the sum of $200, 60 acres on both sides of the left hand fork of Randol's Creek, including part of the farm where Thomas **JUDEN** and family now reside, and where Charnal **GLASCOCK** and family formerly lived; adjoining James **MASSEY**, land John **JUDEN** Junr. got from William **WILLIAMS**, Isaac **WILLIAMS**, sd **ABERNETHIE**, Parish **GREEN**, etc.; being part of sd **ABERNETHIE**'s confirmed land, and part being 34 acres sold to William **WILLIAMS**, for which sd **ABERNETHIE** posted bond to make a deed; beginning at a stake on the NE corner of Isaac **WILLIAMS**' ten acre survey. Signed John **ABERNETHIE**, Havens Clary (x) **ABERNETHIE**. Wit C. S. **THOMAS**, Clerk. Rec 6 Oct 1823.

2159. Page 383. 6 Oct 1823. Same and same to Isaac **WILLIAMS**. For the sum of $80, 10 acres on the waters of Randol's Creek, being part of sd **ABERNETHIE**'s confirmed land, and including part of a field adjoining sd **WILLIAMS**' plantation whereon Robert **LOONEY** and family live; also adjoining sd **ABERNETHIE** and John **JUDEN** Junr; beginning at a stake on the road that leads from Jackson to Cape Girardeau near sd **WILLIAMS**' fence, where sd **ABERNETHIE**'s line crosses sd road, fence,

and field. Signed John **ABERNETHIE**, Havens Clary (x) **ABERNETHIE**. Wit C. S. **THOMAS**, Clerk. Rec 6 Oct 1823.

2160. Page 384. 15 Jul 1823. Charles **SEAVERS** and Sarah, his wife, to Louis **LORIMIER**. For the sum of $1195, two lots in Cape Girardeau; Lot No. 4, Range B, bounded on the N by Independence St, S by Lot No. 3, W by Spanish St, and E by Lot No. 1, sold to him on 24 Nov 1819; and Lot No. 15, Range E, bounded on the N by Lot No. 14, S by Lot No. 16, E by Spanish St, and W by an alley, sold to him on 3 Nov 1819. Signed Charles **SEAVERS**, Sarah **SAVERS**. Wit David **ARMOUR** (JP). Rec 7 Oct 1823.

2161. Page 385. 13 Dec 1822. William P. **LACEY** to John D. **RUTAN**. For the sum of $300, undivided ½ of Lot No. 3 adjoining Jackson; bounded on the N by Seawell St, E by first west street, S by James H. **JENKINS** and Phineas **COBURN**, and W by Lot No. 4; being the same sold by the execr of Joseph **SEAWELL**, decd, to John **BINKNEY**. Signed Wm. P. **LACEY**, Emily M. **LACEY**. Wit Peter R. **GARRETT** (JP), Morgan **BYRNE**. Rec 11 Oct 1823.

2162. Page 386. 20 Oct 1823. Same to David **ARMOUR**. For the sum of $492, mortgage on one negro woman slave named **Maria** about 20 years old, of black complexion. Sd **LACEY** owes sd **ARMOUR** two notes, one dated 31 May 1823 for $370 in Loan Office Certificates drawing 7 ½% interest in specie, and one dated 6 Oct 1823 payable in Loan Office Certificates bearing 7 ½% interest per annum; both due 1 Jan next. Signed Wm. P. **LACEY**. Wit C. S. **THOMAS**, Clerk. Rec 21 Oct 1823.

2163. Page 387. 6 Nov 1823. U. S. A. to James **WHITESIDE** of Tenn. For full payment under the Act of 24 Apr 1820, Patent #232 for 160 acres, being SE ¼, Sec 18, Twp 32, Rng 13 E. Signed James **MONROE**, President, George **GRAHAM**, Commissioner of the Genl. Land Off. Rec in [Vol. 1], page 227. Rec 7 Jan. [1824].

2164. Page 387. 26 Sep 1823. Jesse **HAIL** to David **ARMOUR** and Johnson **RANNEY**. For the sum of $146.54, mortgage on ½ of an undivided 250 arpents on Hubble's Creek; being the same confirmed to his father Edward **HAILE**, and whereon his father now resides and which he lately transferred to Jesse **HAIL** and John **ZILLEFROE**, jointly reserving a life lease. Jesse **HAILE** owes the amount in a writing obligatory to sd **ARMOUR** and sd

RANNEY. Signed Jesse HAILE. Wit Wm. CREATH, Saml. LOCKHART, Peter R. GARRETT (JP). Rec 26 Sep 1823. [Marginal note: Full satisfaction received on 1 Aug 1827. Signed David ARMOUR, Johnson RANNEY. Wit Hy. SANFORD, Clerk.]

2165. Page 388. 3 Sep 1822. Thomas S. RODNEY and Polly, his wife, to Thomas Jefferson RODNEY and Polly RODNEY. For the sum of $3100 to be accounted on final settlement of his guardianship for them, several parcels; 6 lots in Cape Girardeau obtained from the commissioners to partition the real estate of Louis LORIMIER, decd; the N ½ of Lot Nos. 1, 2, 3, & 5 in Range A; S ½ of Lot No. 2, Range A; and 1/3 part of Lot No. 17, Range A, on which stands what is called the Red House; and 240 arpens, more or less, on Ramsey's Creek, confirmed to John Bapts. GODAIR, conveyed by him to James EVANS, and by sd EVANS to Thomas S. RODNEY. Signed Thos. S. RODNEY, Polly (x) RODNEY (RD). Wit John RODNEY, Michl. RODNEY, David ARMOUR (JP). Rec 29 Nov 1823.

2166. Page 389. 10 Dec 1823. James BROOKS to Benjamin SCHELL. For the sum of $26, 1/3 part of an undivided lot in Jackson, being the same that Wm. M. McGUIRE, Nathaniel W. WATKINS, and sd BROOKS purchased at Sheriff's sale. Signed James BROOKS. Wit J. RANNEY, John EDWARDS, Peter R. GARRETT (JP). Rec 9 Dec 1823.

2167. Page 390. 9 Dec 1823. William SURRELL and Ann, his wife, to George HENDERSON. For the sum of $55, Block No. 8, Range C in Cape Girardeau; bounded on the W by Pacific St, E by another street, N by Themis St, and S by Independent St; being the same sd SURRELL purchased at public sale on 11 Oct 1820. Signed William SURRELL, Ann SURRELL. Wit David ARMOUR (JP). Rec 9 Dec 1823.

2168. Page 391. 15 Dec 1823. Anthony B. NEELY by Sheriff William CREATH to Samuel W. MITCHELL. For the sum of $11.50, lot on Main St in Jackson adjoining the public square on the W and Thomas BULL on the N; whereon a house formerly occupied by Dr. E. S. GANTT as a medical shop. Sold on 10 Dec 1823 on an execution issued on 6 Nov 1823 by Wayne Co., Mo. Circuit Court in favor of Peter HAHN and against sd NEELY and Robert RICKMAN for $112 debt, $11.30 damages, and costs. [Signed by Solomon R. BOLIN, Clerk of Wayne Co., Mo. Court.] Signed Wm. CREATH, Sheriff. Wit Peter R. GARRETT, Fkln. CANNON, Claiborne S. THOMAS, Clerk. Rec 16 Dec 1823.

2169. Page 393. 18 Dec 1823. Robert MORRISON and Elizabeth, his wife, to Elias BARBER. For the sum of $150, ½ of Lot No. 196 in Jackson on first south street. Signed Robert MORRISON, Elizabeth MORRISON. Wit Peter R. GARRETT (JP). Rec 20 Dec 1823.

2170. Page 393. 25 Dec 1823. Isidore MOORE and John LAYTON of Perry Co., Mo. to Richard S. THOMAS. For the sum of $1___, 300 acres, more or less, adjoining Jackson; being the same purchased by him on 21 Aug 1822. Signed Isidore MOORE, John LAYTON. Wit Nathan VANHORN, C. S. THOMAS, Clerk. Rec 25 Dec 1823.

2171. Page 394. 25 Dec 1823. Richard S. THOMAS and Frances, his wife, to Nathan VANHORN and John B. WHEELER. For the sum of $1000, 1 acre and 2 perches on Hubble's Creek, being part of where sd THOMAS now lives; beginning on sd THOMAS' line adjoining ___ street in Jackson; including the carding machines, building, and all things appertaining. Signed R. S. THOMAS, Frances THOMAS. Wit John SHEPPARD, John LAYTON, C. S. THOMAS, Clerk. Rec 25 Dec 1823.

2172. Page 395. 25 Dec 1823. Same and same to John SHEPPARD. For the sum of $400, 107 acres and 13 poles on the waters of Hubble's Creek, being part of a tract where sd THOMAS now lives, which he purchased of William H. ASHLEY; beginning at a stone corner, being the offset in the N and W line and cornering at sd SHEPPARD's land. Signed R. S. THOMAS, Frances THOMAS. Wit Nathan VANHORN, John B. WHEELER, C. S. THOMAS, Clerk. Rec 25 Dec 1823.

2173. Page 396. 15 Dec 1823. George MORROW by Sheriff William CREATH to Johnson RANNEY. For the sum of $18.12 ½, two lots in Jackson on the N side of first south street; Lot No. 41, where sd MORROW now resides; and part of Lot No. 17, whereon Greer W. DAVIS now resides on High St, being the same sd MORROW purchased of sd DAVIS. Sold on 10 Dec 1823 on an execution issued on 9 Sep 1823 by Circuit Court in favor of Christian GATES and against sd MORROW and Johnson RANNEY for $143 debt, $1.15 court costs, and $7.55 costs expended by sd GATES. Signed

Wm. **CREATH**, Sheriff. Wit C. S. **THOMAS**, Clerk. Rec 31 Dec 1823.

2174. Page 398. 12 Aug 1823. John **BROWN** by same to same. For the sum of $100, part of Lot No. 28 in Jackson, purchased of George **FRICKE**; bounded on the E and fronted by first east street, S and fronted by Lot No. 29, W by a piece of ground once purchased by Clifton **MOTHERSHEAD**, and N and fronted by Main St. Sold on 12 Aug 1823 on order of Circuit Court in foreclosure of a mortgage by sd **BROWN** to Mary **FRISEL** dated 9 May 1821. Signed Wm. **CREATH**, Sheriff. Wit C. S. **THOMAS**, Clerk. Rec 1 Jan 1824.

2175. Page 399. 1 Jan 1824. Phineas **COBURN** by same to Franklin **CANNON**. For the sum of $54.62 ½, Lot No. 61 in Jackson on first north and west streets. Sold on 14 Apr 1823 on an execution issued by Circuit Court on 20 Dec 1822 on a judgment in favor of Lewis **DICKSON** against William **HAND** and Gilbert **HECTOR** for $25.87 and 5 mills, and sd **COBURN** for $427.32 damages, and $25.10 costs in a case for breach of a covenant made between sd **DICKSON** and the defendants. Signed Wm. **CREATH**, Sheriff. Wit C. S. **THOMAS**, Clerk. Rec 1 Jan 1824.

2176. Page 401. 1 Jan 1824. James **TANNER** by same to Charles G. **ELLIS**. For the sum of $155 received by former Sheriff John **HAYS**, 640 acres on the Mississippi River confirmed to Jabez **FISHER**'s representatives on which Welton **OBANNON** lived at the time of sd sale. Sold on 15 Aug 1822 on a writ of execution from Madison Co., Mo. Circuit Court on a judgment in favor of William P. **LACEY**, John **JOHNSON**, and James **RUSSELL** against sd **TANNER** for $158.21 costs. Sd **ELLIS** petitioned the Court for a deed, and the Court so ordered. Signed Wm. **CREATH**, Sheriff. Wit C. S. **THOMAS**, Clerk. Rec 3 Jan 1824.

2177. Page 402. 3 Jan 1824. John **ARMSTRONG** by same to Franklin **CANNON**. For the sum of $5, undivided ½ of Lot No. 63 in Jackson on Main St between Dr. **ELLIS**' and the new frame house lately owned by **SHEPPARD**. Sold on 14 Dec 1822 on two executions issued by Circuit Court on 8 Nov 1822; one in favor of Henry **BOLLINGER** against sd **ARMSTRONG** and William **SHEPPARD** for $131.92 damages for breach of promise and $16.85 costs; the other in favor of Frederick **BOLLINGER** against sd **ARMSTRONG** and sd **SHEPPARD** for

$138.42 damages for failure to pay a note, and $16.75 costs. Signed Wm. **CREATH**, Sheriff. Wit C. S. **THOMAS**, Clerk. Rec 3 Jan 1824.

2178. Page 404. 2 Jan 1824. John **BROWN** by same to Scarlet **GLASSCOCK**. For the sum of $800 received by John **HAYS**, former Sheriff, part of Lot No. 52 in Jackson and a house on sd lot, on Main St, presently occupied by Samuel **LOCKHART** as a tavern. Sold on 14 Aug 1822 on two executions issued by Circuit Court; one dated 9 May 1822 in favor of Thomas **HALL** for the use of Asaph **JETTON** against A. **BRAVAIS** and sd **BROWN**, his security in the appeal bond, for $51.10 damages for non-payment of a note and $11.90 costs; the other dated 10 Apr 1822 in favor of George **FLEMING** against sd **BROWN** and Johnson **RANNEY** for $210 debt, $3.60 damages, and $3.60 costs. Sd **GLASSCOCK** petitioned the Court for a deed, and the Court so ordered. Signed Wm. **CREATH**, Sheriff. Wit C. S. **THOMAS**, Clerk. Rec 3 Jan 1824.

2179. Page 406. 4 Dec 1823. Claiborne S. **THOMAS** to Jesse B. **THOMAS** Junior. Appointment as Deputy Circuit Court Clerk. Signed Claiborne S. **THOMAS**, Clerk. Jesse B. **THOMAS** Junior takes the oath of office. Signed Jesse B. **THOMAS** Jr. Wit Richard S. **THOMAS**, Judge of 4th Judicial Circuit. Rec 3 Jan 1824.

2180. Page 407. 19 Jan 1824. John **McFARLAND** to John M. **DANIEL**. For the sum of $96, mortgage on 55.40 acres, more or less, being SW fractional ¼, Sec 34, Twp 31 N, Rng 12 E. Sd **McFARLAND** owes the debt in 12 months. Signed John (x) **McFARLAND**. Wit Peter R. **GARRETT**, Wm. **CREATH**, C. S. **THOMAS**, Clerk. Rec 3 Feb 1824.

2181. Page 408. 6 Nov 1823. U. S. A. to James **WHITESIDE** of Tenn. For full payment under the Act of 24 Apr 1820, Certificate #233 for 80 acres, being W ½, NE ¼, Sec 19, Twp 32, Rng 13 E. Signed James **MONROE**, President, George **GRAHAM**, Commissioner, Genl. Land Off. Rec in Vol. 1, page 228. Rec 6 Jan 1824.

2182. Page 408. 6 Nov 1823. Same to same. For full payment under the Act of 24 Apr 1820, Certificate #234 for 131.80 acres, being SW fractional ¼, Sec 18, Twp 32, Rng 13 E. Signed James **MONROE**, President, George **GRAHAM**, Commissioner, Genl. Land Off. Rec in Vol. 1, page 229. Rec 6 Jan 1824.

2183. Page 409. 6 Nov 1823. Same to same. For full payment under the Act of 24 Apr 1820, Certificate #235 for 109.80 acres, being SW fractional ¼, Sec 19, Twp 32, Rng 13 E. Signed James **MONROE**, President, George **GRAHAM**, Commissioner, Genl. Land Off. Rec in Vol. 1, page 230. Rec 6 Jan 1824.

2184. Page 410. 6 Nov 1823. U. S. A. to Robert A. **McBRIDE**. For full payment under the Act of 24 Apr 1820, Certificate # 9 for 80 acres, being N ½, SW ¼, Sec 35, Twp 32, Rng 14 E. Signed James **MONROE**, President, George **GRAHAM**, Commissioner, Genl. Land Off. Rec in Vol. 1, page 9. Rec 7 Jan 1824.

2185. Page 411. 6 Nov 1823. Same to same. For full payment under the Act of 24 Apr 1820, Certificate #10 for 160 acres, being NW ¼, Sec 35, Twp 32, Rng 14 E. Signed James **MONROE**, President, George **GRAHAM**, Commissioner, Genl. Land Off. Rec in Vol. 1, page 10. Rec 7 Jan 1824.

2186. Page 411. 6 Nov 1823. Same to William **ROBERTS** and J. T. **SPRIGG**. For full payment under the Act of 24 Apr 1820, Certificate #11 for 169.14 acres, being W fractional ½, Sec 31, Twp 32, Rng 15 E. Signed James **MONROE**, President, George **GRAHAM**, Commissioner, Genl. Land Off. Rec in Vol. 1, page 187. Rec 7 Jan 1824.

2187. Page 412. 6 Nov 1823. Same to John R. **CLARKE**. For full payment under the Act of 24 Apr 1820, Certificate #22 for 160 acres, being SE ¼, Sec 34, Twp 32, Rng 14 E. Signed James **MONROE**, President, George **GRAHAM**, Commissioner, Genl. Land Off. Rec in Vol. 1, page 22. Rec 7 Jan 1824.

2188. Page 413. 6 Nov 1823. Same to Nathan **VANHORN**. For full payment under the Act of 24 Apr 1820, Certificate #15 for 307.35 acres, being NE ¼ and SE fractional ¼, Sec 25, Twp 32, Rng 12 E. Signed James **MONROE**, President, George **GRAHAM**, Commissioner, Genl. Land Off. Rec in Vol. 1, page 15. Rec 8 Jan 1824.

2189. Page 414. 6 Nov 1823. Same to John R. **CLARKE**. For full payment under the Act of 24 Apr 1820, Certificate #23 for 80 acres, being E ½, SW ¼, Sec 34, Twp 32, Rng 14 E. Signed James **MONROE**, President, George **GRAHAM**, Commissioner, Genl. Land Off. Rec in Vol. 1, page 23. Rec 7 Jan 1824.

2190. Page 414. 6 Nov 1823. Same to John **WILSON**. For full payment under the Act of 24 Apr 1820, Certificate #263 for 80 acres, being W ½, NW ¼, Sec 24, Twp 33, Rng 12 E. Signed James **MONROE**, President, George **GRAHAM**, Commissioner, Genl. Land Off. Rec in Vol. 1, page 258. Rec 16 Jan 1824.

2191. Page 415. 22 Nov 1822. Daniel **HICKMON** to Micajah **HICKMON** and Ann **HICKMON**. For natural love and affection to his beloved son, 113 acres adjoining Daniel **DAVIS**; 75.27 acres adjoining John **JONSON**, sd **DAVIS**, and Moses **BYRNE**; 19 head of cattle; four head of horses; 30 head hogs; three sett of hores gears; four beds & furniture; 12 plates; set of knives & forks; two pots; one kittle; on woman saddle; two spinning wheels; one table; six cheers; and 200 bushels of corn. The aforementioned bed & furniture, six cheers, two yoke of steers, one cow, one table, two pots and one kittle, four head of horses, and five head of sheep, and 34 geese are to be delivered at the time of sealing and delivery. Signed Daniel (x) **HICKMAN**. Test Richard B. **NEWKIRK**, Margaret (+) **YOUNG**, Chs. **MOTHERSHEAD**. Rec 16 Jan 1824.

2192. Page 416. 1 Aug 1823. Peter **KIMMEL** of Jackson Co., Ill. to Allen W. **KIMMEL** of Ste. Genevieve Co., Mo. For the sum of $500, all his right to 6 acres adjoining Cape Girardeau, where Barnet **HYTE**, decd, lately occupied a tanyard. Signed Peter **KIMMEL**. Wit S. H. **KIMMEL**, ___?, A. **JONES**, Jas. D. **GRAFTON**, JP in Ste. Genevieve Co., Mo. Rec 19 Jan 1824.

2193. Page 417. 6 Nov 1823 U. S. A. to Thomas P. **GREEN**. For full payment under the Act of 24 Apr 1820, Certificate #68 for 80 acres, being E ½, SE ¼, Sec 15, Twp 31, Rng 13 E. Signed James **MONROE**, President, George **GRAHAM**, Commissioner, Genl. Land Off. Rec in Vol. 1, page 64. Rec 19 Jan 1824.

2194. Page 417. 20 Jan 1824. Isaac **WILLIAMS** to John **SCOTT** and Beverly **ALLEN**, his attorneys. In consideration of their trouble, labor, council, and advice, any land over 100 acres recovered by sd **WILLIAMS** in a suit he is filing for 640 acres confirmed to Joseph **WALLER**, and purchased by sd **WILLIAMS**, on the Mississippi River; known as Waller's Ferry, now Green's Ferry. Sd land is now held in adverse possession, and sd **WILLIAMS** is commencing a suit to recover the land. Signed Isaac (x) **WILLIAMS**. Wit John **JUDEN** Jr., Richd.

MADDNE, Peter R. **GARRETT** (JP). Rec 20 Jan 1824.

2195. Page 418. 17 Sep 1823. Joseph **WALLER** Junior and Polly, his wife, to Isaac **WILLIAMS**. For the sum of $400, 640 acres, more or less, on the Mississippi River about 3 ½ miles above Bainbridge; being the same confirmed to sd **WALLER** by the name of Joseph **WALLER**, and known as Green's Ferry or Waller's Ferry. Signed Joseph **WALLER**. Wit R. **DAUGHERTY**, Scarlet **GLASSCOCK**, Claiborne S. **THOMAS**, Clerk. Rec 20 Jan 1824.

2196. Page 419. 22 Jan 1824. John **PAYNE** Jr. to Levi L. **LIGHTNER**. For the sum of $80, 1/3 of a lot in Cape Girardeau, being the same purchased by James **EVANS** from Lewis **LORIMIER**, decd, sold by sd **EVANS** to Jonas N. **MENEFEE**, and purchased by sd **PAYNE**, Thomas W. **GRAVES**, and James **RAVENSCROFT** at sheriff's sale. Signed John **PAYNE** Jr. Wit Peter R. **GARRETT** (JP). Rec 23 Jan 1824.

2197. Page 420. 6 Nov 1823. U. S. A. to Robert **COWAN**. For full payment under the Act of 24 Apr 1820, Certificate #114 for 125.45 acres, being SE fractional ¼, Sec 26, Twp 32, Rng 11 E. Signed James **MONROE**, President, George **GRAHAM**, Commissioner, Genl. Land Off. Rec in Vol. 1, page 105. Rec 24 Jan 1824.

2198. Page 421. 18 Jul 1818. George C. **MILLER** and Catharine, his wife, to Barnet **SNIDER**. For the sum of $900, 350 acres on the middle fork of Crooked Creek; beginning at a white oak; being part of a tract purchased by sd **MILLER** from Robert **CRUMP**, being part of sd **CRUMP**'s settlement right. Signed George **MILLER**, Catrine **MILLER**. Test Peter (x) **CRITS** Junyer, Thomas **WELCH**, John B. **WHEELER** (JP). Rec 29 Jan 1824.

2199. Page 422. 6 Nov 1823. U. S. A. to Daniel **WELKER**. For full payment under the Act of 24 Apr 1820, Certificate #274 for 80 acres, being the E ½, NE ¼, Sec 7, Twp 33, Rng 12 E. Signed James **MONROE**, President, George **GRAHAM**, Commissioner, Genl. Land Off. Rec in Vol. 1, page 268. Rec 30 Jan 1824.

2200. Page 422. 6 Nov 1823. Same to same. For full payment under the Act of 24 Apr 1820, Certificate #55 for 80 acres, being the W ½, SW ¼, Sec 8, Twp 33, Rng 12 E. Signed James **MONROE**, President, George **GRAHAM**,

Commissioner, Genl. Land Off. Rec in Vol. 1, page 51. Rec 30 Jan 1824.

2201. Page 423. 6 Nov 1823. Same to Nicholas **SHRUM**. For full payment under the Act of 24 Apr 1820, Certificate #46 for 80 acres, being the E ½, NE ¼, Sec 11, Twp 31, Rng 9 E. Signed James **MONROE**, President, George **GRAHAM**, Commissioner, Genl. Land Off. Rec in Vol. 1, page 42. Rec 10 Feb 1824.

2202. Page 424. 6 Nov 1823. Same to Jacob **SHRUM**. For full payment under the Act of 24 Apr 1820, Certificate #108 for 80 acres, being the W ½, NW ¼, Sec 13, Twp 31, Rng 9 E. Signed James **MONROE**, President, George **GRAHAM**, Commissioner, Genl. Land Off. Rec in Vol. 1, page 101. Rec 10 Feb 1824.

2203. Page 425. 17 Dec 1814. Commissioners of the Courthouse and Jail to Philip **BOLLINGER**. For the sum of $34, Lot No. 1 in Jackson; bounded on the W and fronted by High St, S and fronted by first north street, E by Lot No. 25, and N by Joseph **SEAWELL**. Signed John **DAVIS**, John **SHEPPARD**, Samuel G. **DUNN**, Abraham **BYRD**, Benja. **SHELL**. Wit Thos. **NEALE**, A. P. **PATTERSON**, Jno. **ABERNETHIE** (JP). Rec 14 Feb 1824.

2204. Page 426. 18 Feb 1824. Ezekiel **FENWICK** and Isabella, his wife and formerly Isabella **GIBONY**, of Perry Co., Mo., to Margaret **GIBONEY** and Andrew **GIBONY**. For the sum of $155 cash and a negro girl named **Clara** valued at $300 from Andrew **GIBONY**, and $175 and a negro girl named **Lucy** valued at $275; all their claim to two tracts in Twp 30 N, Rng 13 E; 480 arpens confirmed to Alexander **GIBONEY**'s representatives, bounded on the N & W by Jonathan **STOKER**, E by Morgan **BYRNE** under Timothy **CONNELLY**, and S by public lands; and 350 arpens confirmed to Jonathan **STOKER**, bounded on the N by Robert **GIBONEY** and Charles **BRADLEY**'s representatives, E by Charles **BRADLEY**, S by Alexander **GIBONEY**'s representatives and public land, and W by John **SHIELDS** and Jesse **SCRUGGS** under Terence **DIGALL**. Sd Isabella and Margaret are daughters of Alexander **GIBONY**, decd, and were entitled to one equal and undivided share of the estate of their father. Signed E. **FENWICK**, Isabella **FENWICK**, Margaret **GIBONEY**. Wit C. S. **THOMAS**, Clerk. Rec 18 Feb 1824.

2205. Page 427. 6 Nov 1823. U. S. A. to Gasper **SHELL**. For full payment under the Act of 24

Apr 1820, Certificate #251 for 80 acres, being W ½, NE ¼, Sec 8, Twp 30, Rng 10 E. Signed James **MONROE**, President, George **GRAHAM**, Commissioner, Genl. Land Off. Rec in Vol. 1, page 246. Rec 20 Feb 1824.

2206. Page 428. 6 Nov 1823. Same to same. For full payment under the Act of 24 Apr 1820, Certificate #249 for 80 acres, being the E ½, SW ¼, Sec 8, Twp 30, Rng 10 E. Signed James **MONROE**, President, George **GRAHAM**, Commissioner, Genl. Land Off. Rec in Vol. 1, page 244. Rec 20 Feb 1824.

2207. Page 429. 6 Nov 1823. Same to Henry **HAHN**. For full payment under the Act of 24 Apr 1820, Certificate #72 for 80 acres, being W [½], SW ¼, Sec 9, Twp 30, Rng 10 E. Signed James **MONROE**, President, George **GRAHAM**, Commissioner, Genl. Land Off. Rec in Vol. 1, page 68. Rec 21 Feb 1824.

2208. Page 430. 6 Nov 1823. Same to Daniel **HAHN**. For full payment under the Act of 24 Apr 1820, Certificate #70 for 80 acres, being E ½, NE ¼, Sec 7, Twp 30, Rng 10 E. Signed James **MONROE**, President, George **GRAHAM**, Commissioner, Genl. Land Off. Rec in Vol. 1, page 66. Rec 21 Feb 1824.

2209. Page 430. 6 Nov 1823. Same to Henry **HAHN**. For full payment under the Act of 24 Apr 1820, Certificate #69 for 80 acres, being E ½, SE ¼, Sec 8, Twp 30, Rng 10 E. Signed James **MONROE**, President, George **GRAHAM**, Commissioner, Genl. Land Off. Rec in Vol. 1, page 65. Rec 23 Feb 1824.

2210. Page 431. 6 Nov 1823. Same to John **DECK**. For full payment under the Act of 24 Apr 1820, Certificate #90 for 177.40 acres, being Lot Nos. 2 & 3, NW ¼, Sec 6, Twp 30, Rng 10 E. Signed James **MONROE**, President, George **GRAHAM**, Commissioner, Genl. Land Off. Rec in Vol. 1, page 83. Rec 24 Feb 1824.

2211. Page 432. 6 Nov 1823. Same to Abraham **WHITENER**. For full payment under the Act of 24 Apr 1820, Certificate #60 for 160 acres, being the SE ¼, Sec 29, Twp 32, Rng 9 E. Signed James **MONROE**, President, George **GRAHAM**, Commissioner, Genl. Land Off. Rec in Vol. 1, page 56. Rec 24 Feb 1824.

2212. Page 433. 12 Sep 1823. William **NEELY** and Johnson **RANNEY**, surviving execrs of the last will and testament of Joseph **SEAWELL**, decd, to John **DAVIS**, John **SHEPPARD**, Samuel G. **DUNN**, Abraham **BYRD**, and Benjamin **SHELL**, Commissioners of the Courthouse and Jail. For the sum of $1 received by sd **SEAWELL** in his lifetime, 45 or 50 acres, more or less, being part of where Jackson now stands. Executed by decree of Court of Chancery; sd **SEAWELL** executed a deed to sd commissioners on 25 Mar 1814, believing that the title was in his name, and doubtful as to a suit in Chancery against the heirs of James **MILLS**, to whom the same was confirmed. Sd **SEAWELL**'s execrs, appointed by his last will and testament recorded on 26 Oct 1819, were given power to make deeds confirming each and every lot in sd town. Signed William **NEELY**, Johnson **RANNEY**. Wit John **McKENZIE**, Peter R. **GARRETT** (JP). Rec 24 Feb 1824.

2213. Page 434. 6 Nov 1823. U. S. A. to Joseph **BAKER**. For full payment under the Act of 24 Apr 1820, Certificate #441 for 138.22 acres, being SW fractional ¼, Sec 33, Twp 32, Rng 11 E. Signed James **MONROE**, President, George **GRAHAM**, Commissioner, Genl. Land Off. Rec in Vol. 1, page 397. Rec 26 Feb 1824.

2214. Page 435. 6 Nov 1823. Same to William **HITT**. For full payment under the Act of 24 Apr 1820, Certificate #145 for 80 acres, being E ½, SW ¼, Sec 28, Twp 31, Rng 13 E. Signed James **MONROE**, President, George **GRAHAM**, Commissioner, Genl. Land Off. Rec in Vol. 1, page 135. Rec 27 Feb 1824.

2215. Page 436. 6 Nov 1823. Same to Hiram **KINNISON**. For full payment under the Act of 24 Apr 1820, Certificate # 95 for 80 acres, being Lot No. 1, SE ¼, Sec 29, Twp 31, Rng 13 E. Signed James **MONROE**, President, George **GRAHAM**, Commissioner, Genl. Land Off. Rec in Vol. 1, page 88. Rec 27 Feb 1824.

2216. Page 436. 6 Nov 1823. Same to John **ROBERTS**. For full payment under the Act of 24 Apr 1820, Certificate #305 for 160 acres, being NW ¼, Sec 7, Twp 31, Rng 15 E. Signed James **MONROE**, President, George **GRAHAM**, Commissioner, Genl. Land Off. Rec in Vol. 1, page 300. Rec 27 Feb 1824.

2217. Page 437. 23 Feb 1824. Jacob **LIKE** and Barbara, his wife, to John **BYRD**. For the sum of $250, __ acres on the Water Fork of Byrd Creek; being No. 1, NW ¼, Sec 2, Twp 32, Rng 12 E. Signed Jacob **LAICK**, Barbara (|) **LIKE**. Wit James **RUSSELL** (JP). Rec 6 Mar 1824.

2218. Page 438. 2 Mar 1824. William **McGUIRE** and Susan, his wife, to James **RUSSELL**, all of Jackson. For the sum of $85, undivided ½ of Lot No. 100 in Jackson; bounded on the N and fronted by Main St, E by Lot No. 88, S by Lot No. 101, and W and fronted by third west street; being the same deeded from Samuel **PUTNAM** and wife to sd **McGUIRE** and Willis **McGUIRE** on 25 Jan 1820, and ½ being previously sold to sd **RUSSELL** by Willis **McGUIRE** on 1 Mar 1821. Signed William **McGUIRE**, Susan **McGUIRE**. Wit Peter R. **GARRETT** (JP), Jesse **MOORE** Jr. Rec 9 Mar 1824.

2219. Page 439. 22 Jun 1822. Henry **CLINARD** of Davidson Co., Tenn. to same. For the sum of $100, part of Lot No. 114 in Jackson; beginning at the NE corner at first south street and third west street, and also bounded by Lot No. 115. Signed Henry **CLINARD**. Wit N. W. **WATKINS**, Wm. **McGUIRE**, R. S. **THOMAS**, Judge of 4th Judicial Circuit. Rec 9 Mar 1824.

2220. Page 440. 20 Sep 1823. Enoch **LARIBEE** and Anna, his wife, to same. For the sum of $30, ½ of Lot No. 102 in Jackson; bounded on the W by third west street, N by first south street, E by the E ½ of sd lot, and S by Lot No. 103. Signed Enoch **LARRABEE**, Anna **LARRABEE**. Wit William **KELSO** (JP). Rec 9 Mar 1824.

2221. Page 441. 15 Nov 1823. Thomas **NEALE** and Ellen, his wife, to Joseph **OBANNON**. For the sum of $70, part of Lot No. 75 in Jackson, on the N side of Main St, with a 1-story brick house 21 ft long; located between the small yellow frame building of Edward **CRIDDLE** on the E and the frame building of John **PAYNE** on the W. Signed Th. **NEALE**, Ellen **NEALE**. Wit John **McKENZIE**, James **RUSSELL**, CGCCJ. Rec 9 Mar 1824.

2222. Page 442. 4 Mar 1824. Scarlet **GLASSCOCK** and Jane, his wife, to James **RUSSELL** and Welton **OBANNON**. For the sum of $1200, part of Lot No. 52 in Jackson, being where Samuel **LOCKHART** now lives and keeps a tavern; being formerly owned by John **BROWN** and sold at sheriff's sale to sd **GLASSCOCK**. Signed Scarlet **GLASSCOCK**, Jane **GLASSCOCK**. Wit Peter R. **GARRETT** (JP), John W. **McGUIRE**. Rec 9 Mar 1824.

2223. Page 443. 8 Mar 1824. Joseph **OBANNON** to Joseph Pressby Neville **OBANNON**. For natural affection for his son and the sum of $5, 154.22 acres in the Big Bend

of the Mississippi River; being the SE fractional ¼, Sec 7, Twp 31, Rng 15 E, and E ½, SW ¼, Sec 7 adjoining the first portion; and patented by Joseph **OBANNON** from the U. S. A. Signed Joseph **OBANNON**. Wit James **RUSSELL**, CGCCJ, James **DOWTY**. Rec 9 Mar 1824.

2224. Page 444. 3 Jan 1824. James **DOWTY** to James **RUSSELL**. For the sum of $1, deed of trust on 255 acres, more or less, where he now lives; bounded on the N by land originally owned by John **SUMMERS**, E by Edward **ROBERTSON**'s grant and Joshua **GOZA**, S by Rena **BRUMMIT**, and W by public lands. Executed in order to decrease the payment of $45 due to Joseph **OBANNON** by a note dated this date and due in three months with 10% interest per annum. Sd **RUSSELL** is to sell the land at public sale to pay the debt if sd **DOWTY** does not. Signed James **DOWTY**. Wit Wm. **JOHNSON**, Joseph **WHITTENBURGH**, R. S. **THOMAS**, Judge of 4th Judicial Circuit. Rec 9 Mar 1824.

2225. Page 445. 17 Dec 1814. Commissioners of the Courthouse and Jail to Joseph **SEAWELL**. For the sum of $85, Lot No. 52 in Jackson; bounded on the W and fronted by first west street, N and fronted by Main St, E by Lot No. 16, and S by Lot No. 53. Signed John **DAVIS**, John **SHEPPARD**, Samuel G. **DUNN**, Abraham **BYRD**, Benja. **SHELL**. Wit A. P. **PATTERSON**, Tho. **NEALE**, Jno. **ABERNETHIE** (JP). Rec 9 Mar 1824.

2226. Page 446. 9 Dec 1822. Richard S. **THOMAS** and Frances, his wife, to William **FISHBACK**. For the sum of $110, 2.47 acres on Hubble's Creek; being part of a tract originally granted to Henry **SHERIDAN**; beginning at a stake at the NE corner of sd tract at Samuel **PUGH**'s corner. Signed Richard S. **THOMAS**, Frances **THOMAS**. Wit John **JUDEN** Jr., Clerk. Rec 10 Mar 1824.

2227. Page 448. 31 Jan 1824. John D. **RUTAN** to George H. **SCRIPPS**. For the sum of $47.50, mortgage on Lot No. 3 adjoining Jackson, where sd **RUTAN** now lives, and a roan horse & saddle that sd **RUTAN** bought of Terry **POE** Senr. The debt is due by 15 Feb next. Signed John D. **RUTAN**. Wit David **ARMOUR** (JP), Jos. **ISBELL**. Rec 12 Mar 1824. [Marginal note: Full satisfaction received on 20 Oct 1826. Signed Geo. H. **SCRIPPS**. Wit C. S. **THOMAS**, Clerk.]

2228. Page 448. 31 Jan 1824. Same and Sarah, his wife, to Terry **POE**. For the sum of $100, two tracts; 5 acres and 37 poles, being purchased by William **MARTIN** from Simmon **POE** Jun and wife on 11 Aug 1819, by sd **POE** from Elijah **RANDOL**, and being the NE corner part of Enos **RANDOL** Junior's head right, beginning at a white oak at Priscilla **JOHNSON**'s corner; and 12 acres, more or less, being part of sd Enos **RANDOL**'s confirmation, sold by him to Elijah **RANDOL**, by sd **RANDOL** to John **EDWARDS** and Priscilla **JOHNSON**, by them to sd **MARTIN**, and by sd **MARTIN** and Anna, his wife, to sd **RUTAN** on 4 Mar 1822, beginning at a stake at the S corner of Simon **POE**'s. Signed John D. **RUTAN**, Sarah **RUTAN**. Wit Jos. **ISBELL**, David **ARMOUR** (JP). Rec 12 Mar 1824.

2229. Page 450. 6 Nov 1823. U. S. A. to Henry **BAKER**. For full payment under the Act of 24 Apr 1820, Certificate #94 for 80 acres, being the W ½, SW ¼, Sec 36, Twp 31, Rng 9 E. Signed James **MONROE**, President, George **GRAHAM**, Commissioner, Genl. Land Off. Rec in Vol. 1, page 87. Rec 13 Mar 1824.

2230. Page 451. 6 Nov 1823. Same to John **DAVENPORT**. For full payment under the Act of 24 Apr 1820, Certificate #343 for 80 acres, being the E ½, NE ¼, Sec 34, Twp 33, Rng 12 E. Signed James **MONROE**, President, George **GRAHAM**, Commissioner, Genl. Land Off. Rec in Vol. 1, page 336. Rec 13 Mar 1824.

2231. Page 451. 6 Nov 1823. Same to Jacob **RHODES**. For full payment under the Act of 24 Apr 1820, Certificate #118 for 80 acres, being the W ½, SW ¼, Sec 35, Twp 31, Rng 9 E. Signed James **MONROE**, President, George **GRAHAM**, Commissioner, Genl. Land Off. Rec in Vol. 1, page 109. Rec 13 Mar 1824.

2232. Page 452. 6 Nov 1823. Same to same. For full payment under the Act of 24 Apr 1820, Certificate #117 for 80 acres, being the E ½, SE ¼, Sec 34, Twp 31, Rng 9 E. Signed James **MONROE**, President, George **GRAHAM**, Commissioner, Genl. Land Off. Rec in Vol. 1, page 118. Rec 13 Mar 1824.

2233. Page 453. 6 Nov 1823. Same to Peter **BAKER**. For full payment under the Act of 24 Apr 1820, Certificate #162 for 80 acres, being Lot No. 2, NE ¼, Sec 6, Twp 30, Rng 10 E. Signed James **MONROE**, President, George **GRAHAM**, Commissioner, Genl. Land Off. Rec in Vol. 1, page 15. Rec 13 Mar 1824.

2234. Page 453. 6 Nov 1823. Same to Mary **BAKER**. For full payment under the Act of 24 Apr 1820, Certificate #84 for 85.36 acres, being Lot No. 3, NE ¼, Sec 6, Twp 30, Rng 10 E. Signed James **MONROE**, President, George **GRAHAM**, Commissioner, Genl. Land Off. Rec in Vol. 1, page 76. Rec 13 Mar 1824.

2235. Page 454. 6 Nov 1823. Same to Peter **BAKER**. For full payment under the Act of 24 Apr 1820, Certificate #426 for 80 acres, being Lot No. 1, NE ¼, Sec 6, Twp 30, Rng 10 E. Signed James **MONROE**, President, George **GRAHAM**, Commissioner, Genl. Land Off. Rec in Vol. 1, page 382. Rec 13 Mar 1824.

2236. Page 455. 6 Nov 1823. Same to John **LORANCE**. For full payment under the Act of 24 Apr 1820, Certificate #81 for 131.06 acres, being Lot No. 2, NE ¼, Sec 2, Twp 30, Rng 9 E. Signed James **MONROE**, President, George **GRAHAM**, Commissioner, Genl. Land Off. Rec in Vol. 1, page 75. Rec 13 Mar 1824.

2237. Page 456. 6 Nov 1823. Same to same. For full payment under the Act of 24 Apr 1820, Certificate #80 for 118.35 acres, being Lot No. 2, NW ¼, Sec 1, Twp 30, Rng 9 E. Signed James **MONROE**, President, George **GRAHAM**, Commissioner, Genl. Land Off. Rec in Vol. 1, page 74. Rec 13 Mar 1824.

2238. Page 457. 6 Nov 1823. Same to John **LORENS**. For full payment under the Act of 24 Apr 1820, Certificate #428 for 80 acres, being the E ½, SW ¼, Sec 2, Twp 30, Rng 10 E. Signed James **MONROE**, President, George **GRAHAM**, Commissioner, Genl. Land Off. Rec in Vol. 1, page 384. Rec 13 Mar 1824.

2239. Page 457. 11 Mar 1824. Benjamin **WILSON** and Virginia, his wife, to Bernard **LAYTON** of Perry Co., Mo. For the sum of $700, 160 acres, being the NW ¼, Sec 21, Twp 33 N, Rng 12 E. Signed Benjamin **WILSON**, Virginia **WILSON**. Wit Peter R. **GARRETT** (JP). Rec 15 Mar 1824.

2240. Page 458. 8 Feb 1819. Joseph **ANDREWS** and Catharine, his wife, to David **BRYANT**, all of Jefferson Co., Mo. For the sum of $418.25, ½ acre, being Lot No. 14, Rng E in Cape Girardeau; bounded on the S by Harmony St, W by Indian St, N by Charles G. **ELLIS**, and E by a lot deed to sd **BRYANT** by sd **ANDREWS**; being the same sd **ANDREWS** purchased from Louis **LORIMIER**, Esq, and Maria, his wife, on 3 Jul 1811, and mortgaged by sd **BRYANT** on 12

May 1812 in favor of sd **ANDREWS**. Signed Joseph **ANDREWS**, Catherine **ANDREWS**. Wit A. **RANKINS**, Zapher P. **EVENS**, Sam. **WOODSON**, Clerk of Jefferson Co. Court. Rec 16 Mar 1824.

2241. Page 459. 8 Jan 1824. John **RODNEY** and Rachel, his wife, to Thomas S. **RODNEY** in trust for John **RODNEY**, his son, until he reaches age 21. For natural love and affection for their nephew John **RODNEY** and the sum of $1, 159.91 acres on Whitewater, being the SE fractional ¼, Sec 31, Twp 30 N, Rng 12 E. Signed John **RODNEY**, Rachel (x) **RODNEY** (RD). Wit T. **DICKINSON**, Richard **BRAZIL**, JP in Wayne Co., Mo., Thos. **WHITTAKER**. Rec 16 Mar 1824.

2242. Page 461. 11 Sep 1823. John **WILSON** and Elizabeth, his wife, to William **NEELY** of Cape Girardeau Co. and Isaac **BLEDSOE** of Sumner Co., Tenn., both trustees for Susanna **PENNY** and for the heirs of her body. For the sum of $1000, 103 acres, more or less, on the waters of Randol's Creek, being the W ½ of Anthony **RANDOL**'s Spanish grant, which was purchased by James **MORRISON** and sd **WILSON** of sd **RANDOL**; beginning at the NW corner of the survey at a dogwood sapling and stone where a white oak and red oak are marked for bearing trees; adjoined on the S by Robert **ENGLISH**, W by John **SUMMERS** and the heirs of Thomas **ENGLISH**, N by Abraham **BYRD**, and E by William **PENNY**. Signed John **WILSON**, Elizabeth (|) **WILSON**. Wit David **ARMOUR** (JP). Rec 16 Mar 1824.

2243. Page 462. 6 Nov 1823. U. S. A. to Simon **HARTEL**. For full payment under the Act of 24 Apr 1820, Certificate #120 for 80 acres, being the W ½, SE ¼, Sec 35, Twp 33, Rng 10 E. Signed James **MONROE**, President, George **GRAHAM**, Commissioner, Genl. Land Off. Rec in Vol. 1, page 111. Rec 19 Mar 1824.

2244. Page 463. 6 Nov 1823. Same to same. For full payment under the Act of 24 Apr 1820, Certificate #121 for 94.28 acres, being Lot No. 3, NE ¼, Sec 2, Twp 32, Rng 10 E. Signed James **MONROE**, President, George **GRAHAM**, Commissioner, Genl. Land Off. Rec in Vol. 1, page 112. Rec 19 Mar 1824.

2245. Page 463. 6 Nov 1823. Same to George **KIBLER**. For full payment under the Act of 24 Apr 1820, Certificate #123 for 80 acres, being the W ½, SW ¼, Sec 2, Twp 32, Rng 10 E. Signed James **MONROE**, President, George

GRAHAM, Commissioner, Genl. Land Off. Rec in Vol. 1, page 114. Rec 20 Mar 1824.

2246. Page 464. 10 Mar 1824. Charles S. **HEMPSTEAD** of St. Louis, Mo. to Johnson **RANNEY**, Esq of Jackson. In consideration of the trust and confidence he has in sd **RANNEY** and the sum of $10, deed of trust on three tracts; 160 acres on the waters of Hubble's Creek, being the ¼ part of 640 acres confirmed to John **SHIELDS**, sold by sd **SHIELDS** to sd **HEMPSTEAD**; 410 arpens, more or less, on the waters of Whitewater, being part of a larger tract confirmed to Jeremiah **CONWAY**, who sold sd part to sd **HEMPSTEAD**; 320 acres in Twp 30, Rng 10, being the undivided ½ of a tract confirmed to William **PAGE**'s representatives, being the same sold to Richard **SEARCY** by sd **SHIELDS**, assignee of sd **PAGE**, and sold by sd **SEARCY** to sd **HEMPSTEAD**. Sd **HEMPSTEAD** has been sued in Ste. Genevieve Co. Circuit Court as security in a bond for Joel **CHILDRESS** by Henry **DODGE**, for use of Michael **GOZA**, and judgment recovered, on which sd **HEMPSTEAD** has obtained a supersedea with Horatio **COZENS** and the late Joshua **BORTONARCHIS**(?); and also sd **HEMPSTEAD** owes a debt to August **HAMMER**, adminr of Fredericker **HAMMER** of Baltimore, for $900. The land is to be sold to pay the security if sd **HEMPSTEAD** loses the suit, with the surplus to pay the debt; and should sd **HEMPSTEAD** win the suit, then the property is to be sold to pay the debt. Signed Chs. S. **HEMPSTEAD**. Wit Archibald **GAMBLE**, Clerk of St. Louis Co. Circuit Court. Rec 21 Mar 1824.

2247. Page 465. 14 Mar 1824. Webb **HAYDEN** and Elisabeth, his wife, to Webb B. **HAYDEN**. For the sum of $900, 190 acres on the waters of Randol's Creek, being part of a tract granted to Samuel **STROTHER** by the Spanish Government; bounded on the E by James **COX**, S by Charles **SEAVERS**, W by Hiram **HAYDEN**, and N by Joel **RENFROE**. Signed Web **HAYDEN**, Elizabeth **HAYDEN**. Wit Peter R. **GARRETT** (JP). Rec 23 Mar 1824.

2248. Page 466. 6 Nov 1823. U. S. A. to Henry **SHRUM**. For full payment under the Act of 24 Apr 1820, Certificate #241 for 80 acres, being Lot No. 3, NE ¼, Sec 3, Twp 33, Rng 11 E. Signed James **MONROE**, President, George **GRAHAM**, Commissioner, Genl. Land Off. Rec in Vol. 1, page 236. Rec 29 Mar 1824.

2249. Page 467. 6 Nov 1823. Same to same. For full payment under the Act of 24 Apr 1820, Certificate #242 for 80 acres, being Lot No. 2, NW ¼, Sec 2, Twp 33, Rng 11 E. Signed James **MONROE**, President, George **GRAHAM**, Commissioner, Genl. Land Off. Rec in Vol. 1, page 237. Rec 29 Mar 1824.

2250. Page 467. 6 Nov 1823. Same to same. For full payment under the Act of 24 Apr 1820, Certificate #295 for 50.84 acres, being Lot No. 3, NW ¼, Sec 2, Twp 33, Rng 11 E. Signed James **MONROE**, President, George **GRAHAM**, Commissioner, Genl. Land Off. Rec in Vol. 1, page 289. Rec 29 Mar 1824.

2251. Page 468. 6 Nov 1823. Same to James **HUGHES**. For full payment under the Act of 24 Apr 1820, Certificate #352 for 80 acres, being Lot No. 1, NE ¼, Sec 4, Twp 33, Rng 12 E. Signed James **MONROE**, President, George **GRAHAM**, Commissioner, Genl. Land Off. Rec in Vol. 1, page 345. Rec 31 Mar 1824.

2252. Page 468. 29 Mar 1824. Samuel **CUPPLES** and Mary, his wife, of Lawrence Co., Ark. to Richard S. **THOMAS**. For the sum of $100, 9 acres and 79 poles, more or less, in Jackson; beginning at a stake on the S side of fourth south street, and also bounded by High St; being the same conveyed by sd **THOMAS** and Frances, his wife, to sd **CUPPLES** on 26 May 1821 (F:120). Signed Samuel **CUPPLES**, Mary **CUPPLES**. Wit Thos. **MAXWELL**, Spencer **CROUCH**, JP in Spring River Twp, Lawrence Co., Ark., Hy. **SANFORD**, Clerk of Lawrence Co, Ark. Rec 5 Apr 1824.

2253. Page 470. 29 Mar 1824. Same and same to William **ROBINSON**. For the sum of $300, 5 acres, more or less, on the N side of Jackson, where sd **ROBINSON** now resides; being part of a tract confirmed to **MILLS**; beginning at a post near a spring. Signed Samuel **CUPPLES**, Mary **CUPPLES**. Wit Thos. **MAXWELL**, Spencer **CROUCH**, JP in Spring River Twp, Lawrence Co., Ark., Hy. **SANFORD**, Clerk of Lawrence Co, Ark. Rec 12 Apr 1824.

2254. Page 471. 20 Oct 1821. Nathan **McCARTY** to George **HENDERSON**. In consideration of sd **HENDERSON** paying notes that the representatives of the estate of Louis **LORIMIER**, decd, hold against sd **McCARTY** and sd **HENDERSON**, mortgage on two parcels; his ½ of Lot No. 1, Range G in Cape Girardeau, bounded on the E by Aquamsi St, W by Lot No. 12, N by William St, and S by Lot

No. 2, being the same purchased by Victor **LORIMIER**, sd **McCARTY**, and sd **HENDERSON** of the estate of Louis **LORIMIER**, decd, on 16 Dec 1820; and 160 acres, more or less, about a mile and a half W of Cape Girardeau on Cape la Cruche Creek, bounded on the E by Outlot Nos. 58 & 59, S by Outlot No. 87, W by Outlot No. 82, and N by Outlot No. 80, and being the same purchased by Michael **TANEY**, sd **McCARTY**, and sd **HENDERSON** from Victor **LORIMIER**. The debt is due by the date the last installment for sd lots is due. Signed Nathan **McCARTY**. Test Sophia **McCARTY**, Henry (x) **McCLESKEY**, Jno. **ABERNETHIE** (JP). Rec 13 Apr 1824.

2255. Page 472. 15 Apr 1824. Edmund **RUTTER** by Sheriff William **CREATH** to John J. **DLASHMUTT**. For the sum of $60, part of Lot No. 51 in Jackson, now occupied by William **STANHOPE**, on which is a brick storehouse; bounded on the S by Main St and W by first west street. Sold on 13 Apr 1824 on two writs of execution issued by Circuit Court on 19 Jan 1824; one in favor of Thomas W. **GRAVES** and Samuel **RAVENSCROFT**, adminr of Levi **WOLVERTON**, decd, against sd **RUTTER**, Christopher G. **HOUTS**, and Mark H. **STALCUP** for $140 damages for nonperformance of certain promises to sd **WOLVERTON** in his lifetime, and $35.86 ¼ costs; the other in favor of William **COWHERD** against sd **RUTTER** for $536.30 damages for nonpayment of certain promises and undertakings, and $19.34 and 5 mills costs. Signed Wm. **CREATH**, Sheriff. Wit C. S. **THOMAS**, Clerk. Rec 15 Apr 1824.

2256. Page 475. 19 Apr 1824. Johnson **RANNEY** to William **COWHERD**. For the sum of $100, part of Lot No. 28 in Jackson, on the S side of Main St; also bounded on the E and fronted by first east street, S by Lot No. 29, and W by part of a lot formerly owned by Clifton **MOTHERSHEAD**. Signed Johnson **RANNEY**. Wit Peter R. **GARRETT** (JP). Rec 19 Apr 1824.

2257. Page 475. 26 Apr 1824. John **HAYS** by Sheriff William **CREATH** to George **HENDERSON**. For the sum of $63, 285 arpens, being ½ of a tract whereon Sophia **McCARTY**, widow of John **McCARTY**, decd, formerly lived. Sold on 13 Apr 1824 on a writ of execution issued by Circuit Court on 12 Jan 1824 in favor of Benjamin **SHELL** and against sd **HAYS** (impleaded with Nathan **McCARTY** for $286.16 damages for failing to perform a covenant, and $7.19 costs. Signed Wm. **CREATH**, Sheriff. Wit C. S. **THOMAS**, Clerk. Rec 15 Apr 1824.

2258. Page 477. 26 Apr 1824. Clifton **MOTHERSHEAD** by same to Samuel **LOCKHART**. For the sum of $238, part of a lot in Jackson on the S side of Main St; bounded on the N by Main St, W by George F. **BOLLINGER**, E by part of the same lot, and being where a house and tavern occupied by Charles **SEAVERS** now stands. Sold on 14 Apr 1824 in execution of two writs from Circuit Court, issued on two judgments obtained against sd **MOTHERSHEAD** before Peter R. **GARRETT**, JP in Byrd Twp; one issued on 18 Feb 1824 in favor of **KERR & GRAHAM** for $64 debt and $1.68 3/4 costs of suit, and $2.54 further costs; the other issued 11 Dec 1823 in favor of Greer W. **DAVIS** for $49 debt, $1.50 costs of suit, and $2.35 further costs. Signed Wm. **CREATH**, Sheriff. Wit C. S. **THOMAS**, Clerk. Rec 20 Apr 1824.

2259. Page 479. 17 Feb 1824. Washington **STERRETT** to Elizabeth **THOMPSON**. For the sum of $300, one negro girl named **Milley** of a black complexion. Signed Washington **STERRET**. Test Samuel G. **DUNN**, Margaret **DUNN**, Peter G. **GARRETT** (JP). No recording date listed.

2260. Page 479. 1 May 1824. Edmund **RUTTER** by Sheriff William **CREATH** to William **ROBINSON**. For the sums of $77.12 and $27, two parcels; 1 acre, more or less, being a lot in Jackson N of and adjoining Lot No. 49; and 173 acres about one mile S of Jackson, being a tract confirmed to Peter **BELOW**, and located W of 160 acres that was part of sd confirmation and was sold by sd **RUTTER** to Thomas **HOUTS** of New Madrid Co. Sold on 13 Apr 1824 on two writs of execution issued by Circuit Court on 19 Jan 1824; one in favor of Thomas W. **GRAVES** and Samuel **RAVENSCROFT**, adminr of Levi **WOLVERTON**, decd, against sd **RUTTER**, Christopher G. **HOUTS**, and Mark H. **STALCUP** for $140 damages for nonperformance of certain promises to sd **WOLVERTON** in his lifetime, and $35.86 ¼ costs; the other in favor of William **COWHERD** against sd **RUTTER** for $536.30 damages for nonpayment of certain promises and undertakings, and $19.34 and 5 mills costs. Signed Wm. **CREATH**, Sheriff. Wit C. S. **THOMAS**, Clerk. Rec 1 May 1824.

2261. Page 482. 7 May 1824. Lyne **STARLING** and Elias N. **DLASHMUTT**, trading as **STARLING & DLASHMUTT**, by E. N. **DLASHMUTT** to Thomas W. **GRAVES**. For the sum of $560, bond to a deed for 40 acres, being Outlot No. 41 adjoining Cape Girardeau. Sd **GRAVES** is to pay for the lot in 3 payments; $93.33 1/3 due in six months, $93.33 1/3 due in 12 months, and $93.33 1/3 due in 18 months; then the deed will be executed. Signed **STARLING & DLASHMUTT** by E. N. **DLASHMUTT**, acting partner. Wit L. J. **DLASHMUTT**, C. S. **THOMAS**, Clerk. Rec 27 May 1824.

2262. Page 483. 6 Nov 1823. U. S. A. to Henry **WHITTENBURGH**. For full payment under the Act of 24 Apr 1820, Certificate #135 for 80 acres, being the E ½, NE ¼, Sec 28, Twp 33, Rng 12 E. Signed James **MONROE**, President, George **GRAHAM**, Commissioner, Genl. Land Off. Rec in Vol. 1, page 123. No recording date.

2263. Page 483. 6 Nov 1823. Same to same. For full payment under the Act of 24 Apr 1820, Certificate #133 for 80 acres, being the E ½, SE ¼, Sec 21, Twp 33, Rng 12 E. Signed James **MONROE**, President, George **GRAHAM**, Commissioner, Genl. Land Off. Rec in Vol. 1, page 124. No recording date.

2264. Page 484. 4 Jun 1824. Daniel F. **STEINBECK** and Agatha, his wife, to Benjamin **HALL**. For the sum of $400, 100 acres in the Big Bend of the Mississippi River on Felonia Creek, being part of a survey of 751 acres confirmed to Augustus B. **LORIMIER**; beginning at a post. Signed D. F. **STEINBECK**, Agatha **STEINBECK**. Wit George **HENDERSON** (JP). No recording date.

2265. Page 485. 24 May 1824. William H. **ASHLEY**, Lt. Governor of Mo., exercising the powers of Governor, to Robert A. **McBRIDE**. Appointment as JP for Randol Twp. Signed William H. **ASHLEY**, Governor. Wit Wm. G. **PETTUS**, Sec. of State. Robert A. **McBRIDE** takes the oath of office. Signed Ro. A. **McBRIDE**. Wit _____, JP in Byrd Twp. No recording date.

2266. Page 486. 13 Apr 1824. Robert **TROTTER** to William **TAYLOR**. For the sum of $28.09, bond to make a deed on 22 acres and 57 ½ rods, being the NW corner of the quarter section where he now dwells. Sd deed to be made as soon as he receives a patent. Signed Robert

TROTTER. Wit Samuel **LEGATE**, David **ARMOUR** (JP). No recording date.

2267. Page 486. 23 Aug 1824. Louis **LORIMIER** to Michael **RODNEY**. Power of attorney to receive monies, debts, and judgments, and interest recovered in the name of sd **LORIMIER**. Sd **LORIMIER** is about to take a journey and will be absent for a considerable time. Signed Louis **LORIMIER**. Wit Peter R. **GARRETT** (JP). No recording date.

2268. Page 487. 10 Jul 1824. Alexander **McNAIR**, Governor of Mo., to James **WILLIAMS**. Appointment as JP for Lorance Twp for four years. Signed A. **McNAIR**. Wit Wm. S. **PETTUS**, Secretary of State. James **WILLIAMS** takes the oath of office. Signed James **WILLIAMS**. Wit William **JOHNSON** (JP). Rec 15 Sep 1824.

2269. Page 487. 10 Jul 1824. Alexander **McNAIR**, Governor of Mo., to Barnet **SNIDER**. Appointment as JP for Lorance Twp. Signed A. **McNAIR**. Wit Wm. S. **PETTUS**, Secretary of State. Barnet **SNIDER** takes the oath of office. Signed Barnet **SNIDER**. Wit Davd. **ARMOUR** (JP). No recording date.

2270. Page 488. 10 Jul 1824. Alexander **McNAIR**, Governor of Mo., to James **FERGUSON**. Appointment as JP for Lorance Twp. Signed A. **McNAIR**. Wit Wm. S. **PETTUS**, Secretary of State. James **FERGUSON** takes the oath of office. Signed James **FERGUSON**. Wit Peter R. **GARRETT** (JP). No recording date.

2271. Page 488. 5 Aug 1824. John **HAYS**, Esq., to Levi L. **LIGHTNER**. For the sum of $705, 6 ½ acres, being No. 2 in Cape Girardeau; bounded on the N by the grave yard, W by No. 3, S by North St, and E by No. 1. Signed John **HAYES**. Wit James **BRALY**, George **HENDERSON** (JP). No recording date.

2272. Page 489. 10 Jul 1824. Alexander **McNAIR**, Governor of Mo., to William **JOHNSON**. Appointment as JP for Lorance Twp. Signed A. **McNAIR**. Wit Wm. S. **PETTUS**, Secretary of State. William **JOHNSON** takes the oath of office. Signed William **JOHNSON**. Wit James **FERGUSON** (JP). No recording date.

2273. Page 489. 11 Aug 1824. William **HICKMAN** by Sheriff William **CREATH** to

William P. **LACEY**. For the sum of $12, 50 acres on the Mississippi River known as Green's, formerly Waller's, Ferry, including the ferry landing. Sold on 10 Aug 1824 on an execution from Circuit Court issued 10 Jul 1824 in favor of William G. **BYRD**, assignee of Abraham **SMITH**, against sd **HICKMAN** for $650 debt, $33.60 damages, and $43.86 ¼ costs. Signed William **CREATH**, Sheriff. Wit John **JUDEN** Jr., Peter R. **GARRETT**, Claiborne S. **THOMAS**, Clerk. No recording date.

2274. Page 490. 17 Aug 1824. Michael **RODNEY** and Matilda, his wife, to Reuben **DOWTY** and Polly, his wife. For the sum of $600, 131.40 acres at the edge of the Great Swamp, being SE fractional ¼, Sec 16, Twp 30 N, Rng 12 E. Signed Michael **RODNEY**, Matilda (x) **RODNEY** (RD). Wit Thomas S. **RODNEY**, William **LORIMIER**, John **AKIN** (JP). No recording date.

2275. Page 491. 3 May 1823. Same and same to Reuben **DOWTY**. For the sum of $80, 41.97 acres on the waters of Hubble's Creek, being fractional Sec 36, Twp 30, Rng 12 E. Signed Michael **RODNEY**, Matilda (x) **RODNEY** (RD). Wit Thomas S. **RODNEY**, John **RODNEY**, John **AKIN** (JP). No recording date.

2276. Page 492. 29 May 1821. James **THOM[PSON]** and John **THOMPSON** to William **ROBERTS**. For the sum of $135, __ acres, being the tract of land on which Bainbridge is erected, including the dwelling house in which Medad **RANDOL** now lives; that sd **THOMPSON**s hold under a Sheriff's deed. Signed James **THOMPSON**, John **THOMPSON**. Wit William **CREATH** (JP). No recording date.

2277. Page 492. 26 Jul 1824. John **PROBST** [Senr] and Barbara, his wife, to Hiram **ESTES**. For the sum of $250, 199 acres, more or less; beginning at or adjoining **CRADER**, Josiah **LEE**, Joseph **NISWONGER**, and land deeded to sd **ESTES** by sd **PROPST**, also adjoining the widow **WELKER**. Signed John **PROBST**, Barbara **PROBST**. Wit John **JOHNSON** (JP), Joseph **BOVI**. No recording date.

2278. Page 493. 2 Aug 1824. William H. **MINTON** to Francis J. **ALLEN**. For the sum of $271, 80 acres on the SW side of Flora Creek, Randol Twp; being the S ½, SW ¼, Sec 35, Twp 32 N, Rng 14 E. Signed W. H. **MINTON**, Rhoda (x) **MINTON** (RD). Wit Ro. A. **McBRIDE** (JP), John R. **CLARK**. Rec 1 Oct 1824.

2279. Page 493. 26 Jul 1824. Hiram **ESTES** and Polly, his wife, to John **PROPTS** Junr. For the sum of $250, 140 acres, more or less, on both sides of White Water, being the same deeded to them by John **PROPTS** Senr; beginning at a Spanish oak. Signed Hiram (x) **ESTES**, Polly (x) **ESTES**. Wit Joseph **BAKER**, John **JOHNSON** (JP). Rec 5 Oct 1824.

2280. Page 494. 10 Jul 1824. Alexander **McNAIR**, Governor of Mo., to Jacob **ROADS**. Appointment as JP for Lorance Twp. Signed A. **McNAIR**. Wit Wm. S. **PETTUS**, Secretary of State. Jacob **RHODES** takes the oath of office. Signed Jacob **RHODES**. Wit James **WILLIAMS** (JP). Rec 15 Oct 1824.

2281. Page 495. 19 Oct 1824. Claiborne S. **THOMAS** resigns the office of Clerk of Circuit Court for Cape Girardeau Co. Signed Claiborne S. **THOMAS**. Wit Hon. R. S. **THOMAS**, Judge of 4th Judicial Circuit. No recording date.

2282. Page 495. 19 Oct 1824. Richard S. **THOMAS**, Judge of 4th Judicial Circuit, to Ralph **DAUGHERTY**. Appointment as Clerk of Circuit Court for Cape Girardeau Co. Signed R. S. **THOMAS**. No recording date.

2283. Page 495. 28 Oct 1824. Alexander **McNAIR**, Governor of Mo., to Ralph **DAUGHERTY**. Commission as Clerk of Circuit Court for Cape Girardeau Co., his having been appointed. Signed A. **McNAIR**. Wit Wm. S. **PETTUS**, Secretary of State. Ralph **DAUGHERTY** takes the oath of office. Signed Ralph **DAUGHERTY**. Wit Richard S. **THOMAS**, Judge of 4th Judicial Circuit. No recording date.

2284. Page 495. 21 Oct 1824. Ralph **DAUGHERTY**, Robert **GREEN**, John **HAYS**, William **GARNER**, and William **DAUGHERTY** to Alexander **McNAIR**, Governor of Mo. For the sum of $3000, bond to guarantee that Ralph **DAUGHERTY** will faithfully discharge the office of Clerk of Circuit Court for Cape Girardeau Co. Signed Ralph **DAUGHERTY**, Robert **GREEN**, John **HAYS**, William **GARNER**, William **DAUGHERTY** . Wit William S. **GANTT**, Edward **CRIDDLE**, R. S. **THOMAS**, Judge of 4th Judicial Circuit. No recording date.

2285. Page 496. 21 Oct 1824. Same, same, same, same, and same to same. For the sum of $6000, bond to guarantee that Ralph **DAUGHERTY** will faithfully discharge the duties of maintaining records of the Loan Office as directed by an act of the state of Mo. Signed Ralph **DAUGHERTY**, Robert **GREEN**, John **HAYS**, William **DAUGHERTY**, William **GARNER** . Wit Edward **CRIDDLE**, William S. **GANTT**, R. S. **THOMAS**, Judge of 4th Judicial Circuit. No recording date.

2286. Page 497. 5 Nov 1824. Parish **GREEN** and William **RUSSELL** of St. Louis Co. Deed of partition and division of 640 acres confirmed to Joseph **WALLER** on the W shore of the Mississippi River, including Waller's or Green's Ferry, in Twp 32 N, Rng 14 E; being the same conveyed by sd **WALLER** to sd **GREEN**. Part of the tract totaling 540 acres was sold by sd **GREEN** and Clary, his wife, to sd **RUSSELL** on 28 Jan 1819 (D:425). The whole of the 640 acres was patented to sd **GREEN** by the U. S. A. on 21 Jun 1824 (Vol. 4:438), and this deed confirms the conveyance to sd **RUSSELL** of the 540 acres and describes the 100 acres not conveyed to sd **RUSSELL**; to begin at a post corner on the margin of the Mississippi River. Signed Parish **GREEN**, William **RUSSELL**. Wit Joseph P. N. **OBANNON**, John **ABERNETHIE** (JP). Rec 6 Nov 1824.

2287. Page 498. 24 Sep 1824. Morgan **BYRNE** and Jane, his wife, to Barnet **SNYDER**. For the sum of $100, 50 acres, more or less, on the waters of Crooked Creek, being a part of the tract where sd **SNIDER** now lives, originally granted to Robert **CRUMP**; beginning at a stake corner on the N and S line dividing between sd **BYRNE** and sd **SNIDER**. Signed Morgan **BYRNE**, Jane **BYRNE**. Wit David **ARMOUR** (JP). Rec 10 Nov 1824.

2288. Page 499. 23 Aug 1824. Timothy **SHAW** and Polly, his wife, to William **HUTSON**. For the sum of $125, 80 acres, being the W ½, NE ¼, Sec 12, Twp 29 N, Rng 13 E. Signed Timothy **SHAW**, Polly **SHAW**. Wit William **KELSO** (JP). Rec 18 Nov 1824.

2289. Page 500. 23 Nov 1824. David **ARMOUR** to Mathew **ALLEN**. For the sum of $200, two tracts; 144.90 acres, being SE fractional ¼, Sec 7, Twp 31, Rng 13 E; and 11.44 acres, being SW fractional Sec 7, Twp 31, Rng 13 E; both having been conveyed to sd **ARMOUR** by Washington **STERRETT** on 6 Nov 1823, being #197 & #198. Signed David **ARMOUR**. Wit W. **ROBINSON**, Wm. P. **LACEY**, Ralph **DAUGHERTY**, Clerk. Rec 24 Nov 1824.

2290. Page 501. 10 Jul 1824. Alexander **McNAIR**, Governor of Mo., to Benjamin **BACON**. Appointment as JP for Apple Creek Twp for four years. Signed A. **McNAIR**. Wit William G. **PETTUS**, Secretary of State. Benjamin **BACON** takes the oath of office and swears he will not engage in a duel or aid or abet a duel. Signed Benjamin **BACON**. Wit David **ARMOUR** (JP). Rec 24 Nov 1824.

2291. Page 502. 10 Jul 1824. Alexander **McNAIR**, Governor of Mo., to Caleb P. **FULLENWIDER**. Appointment as CGCCJ, John **HORRELL**, Esq, having resigned. Signed A. **McNAIR**. Wit Wm. G. **PETTUS**, Secretary of State. Caleb P. **FULLENWIDER** takes the oath of office and swears he will not engage in a duel or aid or abet a duel. Signed C. P. **FULLENWIDER**. Wit Peter R. **GARRETT** (JP). Rec 25 Nov 1824.

2292. Page 502. 10 Jul 1824. Alexander **McNAIR**, Governor of Mo., to Elijah **HARRIS**. Appointment as CGCCJ, Isaac **SHEPPARD**, Esq, having resigned. Signed A. **McNAIR**. Wit Wm. G. **PETTUS**, Secretary of State. Elijah **HARRIS** takes the oath of office and swears he will not engage in a duel or aid or abet a duel. Signed Elij. **HARRIS**. Wit Peter R. **GARRETT** (JP). Rec 25 Nov 1824.

2293. Page 503. 23 Jul 1822. William **PATTERSON** and Jane, his wife, to George **CAVANER**. For the sum of $40, 28 acres on the waters of Byrd's Creek; beginning at a gum tree at the NE corner of Stephen **BYRD**'s portion of the Cooper Tract. Signed William **PATTERSON**, Jane (x) **PATTERSON**. Wit James **RUSSELL** (JP), Jacob **LIEUX**. Rec 30 Nov 1824.

2294. Page 504. 12 May 1824. Obadiah **MALONE** to Henry **SHANER**. For the sum of $200, 69 acres, more or less, in Rng 12 E, Twp 32 N, Sec 5, part of the SW ½; beginning at the NW corner of the SW half ¼. Signed Ob. A. **MALOAN**, Elisa **MALOAN**. Wit John **JOHNSON** (JP), Hortentia **JOHNSON**. Rec 1 Dec 1824.

2295. Page 504. 1 Dec 1824. William P. **LACEY** to Parish **GREEN**. For the sum of $29, 50 acres, more or less, on the Mississippi River, known as Green's Ferry and including the ferry landing on the W side of the river. Signed William P. **LACEY**. Wit N. W. **WATKINS**, R. **DAUGHERTY**, Clerk. Rec 1 Dec 1824.

2296. Page 505. 11 Sep 1823. John **ZELLEFROE** and Jesse **HAILE** to Edward **HAILE** Senior and Rachel, his wife. In consideration of the rents and services herein mentioned and diverse other good causes, 240 arpens on Hubble's Creek near Jackson confirmed to sd Edward **HAILE** and being whereon he now lives, which has this day been transferred to sd **ZILLEFROE** and Jesse **HAILE** by sd Edward on this date. Sd tract to be for the use of Edward & Rachel **HAILE** for their natural lives upon payment of $0.10 yearly. Should either of them die, then the survivor is to remain on the tract for the same rent. Signed Jesse **HAIL**, John **ZILEFROE**, Edwd. (x) **HAILE**, Rachel (x) **HAILE**. Wit John **HORRELL**, Peter R. **GARRETT** (JP). Rec 9 Dec 1824.

2297. Page 506. 17 Apr 1824. Lott **ABERNATHY** and Peggy, his wife, to John **McCOMBS**. For the sum of $200, 154.07 acres, being Lot No. 2, NW ¼, Sec 5, Twp 32, Rng 13 E. Signed Lott **ABERNATHY**, Margaret **ABERNATHY**. Wit John **LITTLE**, Benjamin **BACON** (JP). Rec 11 Dec 1824.

2298. Page 506. 13 Dec 1824. James **EVANS**, complainant, against Louis **LORIMIER**, Victor **LORIMIER**, Daniel F. **STEINBECK** and Argat, his wife, Polly **RODNEY**, and Thomas Jefferson **RODNEY**. Sd **EVANS** purchased of Louis **LORIMIER** in his lifetime, for $50, a lot in Cape Girardeau, on which he built a brick house. Victor **LORIMIER** has not appeared to answer the bill of complaint, so the Court decrees that the lot should go to sd **EVANS**, unless Victor **LORIMIER** shall bring a bill of review within five years. Sd defendants are to pay court costs. Signed R. **DAUGHERTY**, Clerk. Rec 13 Dec 1824.

2299. Page 507. 10 Nov 1824. John **ROBERTS** to Frank J. **ALLEN**. For the sum of $300 in Ill. State Paper, 160 acres in the bend of the Mississippi, being the NW ¼, Sec 7, Twp 31, Rng 15 E; adjoining Capt. **OBANNON**'s lands. Signed John **ROBERTS**. Wit William **LITTLETON**, Jacob **LITTLETON**, Peter R. **GARRETT** (JP). Rec 13 Dec 1824.

2300. Page 507. 14 Oct 1824. Katharine **BYRD** to Jacob **COTNER**. For the sum of $62.50, 50 acres on Whitewater, being the land willed to her by her father Jacob **COTNER**, decd, out of a tract confirmed to him. Signed Catharine (x) **BYRD**. Test John **JOHNSON** (JP), Hortentia **JOHNSON**. Rec 13 Dec 1824.

2301. Page 508. 16 Dec 1824. Greer W. **DAVIS** to Matthew **ALLEN**. For the sum of $40, part of Lot No. 13 in Jackson, beginning on High St and also bounded by first north street. Signed Greer W. **DAVIS**. Wit Z. **PRIEST**, H. **GANTT**, Ralph **DAUGHERTY**, Clerk. Rec 16 Dec 1824.

2302. Page 509. 27 Aug 1824. Isaac **WILLIAMS** and Susannah, his wife, to Ezekiel **HILE**. For the sum of $100, 80 acres, being the E ½, NE ¼, Sec 13, Twp 31, Rng 13 E; being the same patented to sd **WILLIAMS** by the U. S. A. on 6 Nov 1823. Signed Isaac (x) **WILLIAMS**, Susannah (x) **WILLIAMS**. Wit W. D. **WALLING**, John **ABERNATHIE** (JP). Rec 24 Dec 1824.

2303. Page 510. 19 Apr 1824. George F. **BOLLINGER** to John B. **WHEELER**. For the sum of $100, 80 acres, being the SE ¼, Sec 20, Twp 31, Rng 11 E. Signed George F. **BOLLINGER**. Wit W. **GARNER**, R. **DAUGHERTY**, Clerk. Rec 20 Dec 1824.

2304. Page 510. 27 Dec 1824. Benjamin **HALE** and Rebecca, his wife, to Parish **GREEN**. For the sum of $300, 49 ½ acres on the bank of the Mississippi River at Green's Ferry, west bank; being the lower ½ of the ferry land as conveyed by sd **GREEN** and Clary, his wife, to sd **HALE**. Signed Benja. (x) **HALE**, Rebecca **HALE**. Wit James **THOMPSON**, Jno. **ABERNATHIE**, Robert A. **McBRIDE** (JP). Rec 31 Dec 1824.

2305. Page 511. 16 Dec 1824. Jesse **HAIL** by Sheriff William **CREATH** to Greer W. **DAVIS**. For the sum of $26, Lot No. 13 in Jackson. Sold on 13 Dec 1824 on foreclosure of mortgage from the Circuit Clerk's Office; sd mortgage being was obtained by sd **HAIL** on 13 Mar 1822, for $426 at 2% interest per annum, due one year from date. Signed William **CREATH**, Sheriff. Wit R. **DAUGHERTY**, Clerk. Rec 16 Dec 1824.

2306. Page 513. 16 Dec 1824. Frederick **BATES**, Governor of Mo., to John **ABERNATHY**. Commission as JP for Cape Girardeau Twp, his former commission having expired. Signed Frederick **BATES**. Wit H. R. **GAMBLE**, Sec of State. John **ABERNATHY** takes the oath of office. Signed Jno. **ABERNETHIE**. Wit Peter R. **GARRETT** (JP). Rec 3 Jan 1825.

2307. Page 513. 16 Dec 1824. Frederick **BATES**, Governor of Mo., to John B. **WHEELER**. Commission as JP for German Twp, his former commission having expired. Signed Frederick **BATES**. Wit H. R. **GAMBLE**, Sec of State. John B. **WHEELER** takes the oath of office. Signed John B. **WHEELER**. Wit Peter R. **GARRETT** (JP). Rec 8 Jan 1825.

2308. Page 514. 8 Jan 1825. David G. L. **CALDWELL** to John **BURNS**. For the sum of $600, two tracts; 112 acres, being part of a tract confirmed to Lewis **TASH**, beginning at the SE corner of sd tract at a stake near a pond of water, bounded on the E by A. **RANDOL**, N by sd **BURNS**, W by the heirs of Lewis **TASH**, and S by Hugh **CRISWELL**; and 13 acres, being part of a tract whereon Anthony **RANDOL** now lives, off the SW corner of sd tract, beginning at the SE corner of sd **TASH**'s survey, bounded on the W & S by sd **CRISWELL**'s confirmation, and E & N by sd **RANDOL**. Signed David G. L. **CALDWELL**. Wit Jno. **ABERNATHIE** (JP). Rec 11 Jan 1825.

2309. Page 515. 24 Jan 1825. William **ROBINSON** and Elizabeth, his wife, to John **HAYS**. For the sum of $13, 1 acre, more or less, being a lot in Jackson, adjoining Lot No. 49 on the N, and formerly owned by Edmund **RUTTER**. Signed William **ROBINSON**, Elizabeth T. **ROBINSON**. Wit Peter R. **GARRETT** (JP). Rec 24 Jan 1825.

2310. Page 516. 8 Jan 1825. John **BURNS** and Mary, his wife, to Joseph **ISBELL**. For the sum of $775, two tracts on Franks Creek, a fork of Randol's Creek, where sd **BURNS** and his family now live and have lived for some time, part adjoining Abraham **BYRD**, Anthony **RANDOL**, John **HOUTS**, and the heirs of Lewis **TASH**, decd; the first tract of 13 acres purchased by sd **BURNS** of Anthony **RANDOL** on 10 Dec 1819, begins at the SE corner of a tract bought from Lewis **TASH**; and the other of 200 arpents, French measure, and taken off the E end of sd **TASH**'s confirmation, whereon William **POE** and family now live, beginning at a stake near a pond of water at the SE corner of sd survey, and being the same purchased by sd **BURNS** of sd **TASH** on 24 Aug 1816. Signed John **BURNS**, Mary (x) **BURNS**. Wit Jno. **ABERNATHIE** (JP). Rec 26 Jan 1825.

2311. Page 517. 4 Dec 1824. Ezekiel **HILE** and Rachel, his wife, to Hardy **BROOKS**. For the sum of $100, 80 acres, being the E ½, NE ¼, Sec 13, Twp 31, Rng 13 E; obtained by Isaac **WILLIAMS** from the U. S. A. by patent on 6 Nov 1823, and conveyed by him to sd **HILE** on 27 Aug 1824. Signed Ezekiel **HILE**, Rachel (x)

HILE. Wit David **HOLLEY**, Jno. **ABERNETHIE** (JP). Rec 28 Jan 1825.

2312. Page 518. 16 Dec 1824. Frederick **BATES**, Governor of Mo., to David **ARMOUR**. Commission as JP for Byrd Twp, his former commission having expired. Signed Frederick **BATES**. Wit H. R. **GAMBLE**, Sec of State. David **ARMOUR** takes the oath of office. Signed David **ARMOUR**. Wit Peter R. **GARRETT** (JP). Rec 28 Jan 1825.

2313. Page 519. 8 Jan 1825. John **RANDOL** and Margaret, his wife, to John **BURNS**. For the sum of $400, 240 arpens or 204.16 acres, being part of a tract confirmed to Zillah **DIXSON**; beginning on a divisional line between William **WILLIAMS** and **WHITAKER** at a stake corner with a poplar 36 inches in diameter. Signed John **RANDOL**, Margaret **RANDOL**. Wit James **MASSEY** (JP). Rec 12 Feb 1825.

2314. Page 520. 31 Jan 1825. William **EVERT** to John **BYRD**. For the sum of $270, 212 acres, more or less, on the waters of Byrd's Creek; bounded on the E by John **BYRD**, N by land confirmed to the heirs of Amos **BYRD**, decd, W & E by George **CAVENDER**, and S by unconfirmed lands. Signed William **EVRETT**. Test Abraham **BYRD**, John B. **YOUNG**, Peter R. **GARRETT** (JP). Rec 24 Feb 1825.

2315. Page 520. 28 Jan 1825. Peter R. **GARRETT**, William **CREATH**, David **ARMOUR**, and Thomas **NEALE** to Frederick **BATES**, Governor of Mo. For the sum of $1000, bond to guarantee that Peter R. **GARRETT** shall perform the duties of Clerk of the Cape Girardeau Co. Court, his having been appointed by the Justices of sd court. Signed Peter R. **GARRETT**, Wm. **CREATH**, David **ARMOUR**, and Th. **NEALE**. Wit C. P. **FULENWIDER**, Elijah **HARRIS**, CGCCJ. Rec 4 Mar 1825.

2316. Page 521. 4 Nov 1824. Nathan **VANHORN** and Clarissa, his wife, to John **THOMPSON**. For the sum of $1, quit claim to ½ of 194.89 acres, more or less, being that part of the NW ¼, SW fractional ¼, Sec 25, Twp 32, Rng 12 E, lying W of a line beginning on the ¼ section corner on the N side of Sec 25, and running S, ending on the N side of Robert **PATTERSON**'s survey. Sd **VANHORN** and sd **THOMPSON** obtained patent No. 16 from the U. S. A. on 6 Nov 1823 for the tract as tenants in common. Signed Nathan **VANHORN**, Clarissa

M. (x) **VANHORN**. Wit R. S. **THOMAS**, Judge of 4th Judicial Circuit. Rec 5 Mar 1825.

2317. Page 522. 13 Jan 1825. William **POLK** of Madison Co., Mo. to John **HOW** of Perry Co., Mo. For the sum of $2000, 640 acres, more or less, on the main stream of White Water, beginning at a stake near the stove chimney; being a tract confirmed to Henery **BOLLINGER**, son of Daniel **BOLLINGER** Sr.. Signed William **POLK**, Mary (\) **POLK**. Test Ellis M. **COFER**, Mary (x) **JOHNSON**, William **TINNIN** (JP). Rec 5 Mar 1825.

2318. Page 523. 16 Dec 1824. Frederick **BATES**, Governor of Mo., to William **TINNAN**. Commission as JP for German Twp, his former commission having expired. Signed Frederick **BATES**. Wit H. R. **GAMBLE**, Sec of State. William **TINNIN** takes the oath of office. Signed William **TINNIN**. Wit David **ARMOUR** (JP). Rec 9 Mar 1825.

2319. Page 524. 25 Nov 1824. Scarlet **GLASSCOCK** to Obe **MALONE**. For the sum of $60, an equal and undivided ½ of 157.28 acres; being the SW fractional ¼, Sec 28, Twp 33, Rng 12 E, and the same obtained by sd **GLASSCOCK** of the U. S. A. by patent on 6 Nov 1823. Signed Scarlet **GLASSCOCK**, Jane **GLASSCOCK**. Wit David **ARMOUR** (JP). Rec 9 Mar 1825.

2320. Page 525. 16 Dec 1824. Frederick **BATES**, Governor of Mo., to George **HENDERSON**. Commission as JP for Cape Girardeau Twp, his former commission having expired. Signed Frederick **BATES**. Wit H. R. **GAMBLE**, Sec of State. George **HENDERSON** takes the oath of office. Signed George **HENDERSON**. Wit Peter R. **GARRET** (JP). Rec 11 Mar 1825.

2321. Page 525. 21 Mar 1825. John **RISHER** to Martin **THOMAS**. For the sum of $220, mortgage on 40 acres, more or less, in Cape Girardeau Twp where he now lives. Sd **RISHER** owes a judgment from Circuit Court to sd **THOMAS**, to be paid within 12 months. Signed John **RISHER**. Test R. **DAUGHERTY**, Clerk. Rec 21 Mar 1825.

2322. Page 526. 4 Nov 1824. John **THOMPSON** and Jane Goodin, his wife, to Nathan **VANHORN**. For the sum of $1, quit claim to 59.19 acres, more or less, being that part of the NW ¼, SW fractional ¼, Sec 25, Twp 32, Rng 12 E, lying E of a line beginning on the ¼ section corner on the N side of Sec 25, and running S, ending on the N side of Robert **PATTERSON**'s survey. Sd **VANHORN** and sd **THOMPSON** obtained Patent No. 16 from the U. S. A. on 6 Nov 1823 for the tract as tenants in common. Signed John **THOMPSON**, Jane (x) Gooden **THOMPSON**. Wit R. S. **THOMAS**, Judge of 4th Judicial Circuit. Rec 30 Mar 1825.

2323. Page 527. 16 Aug 1824. Alexander **McNAIR**, Governor of Mo., to William **CREATH**. Commission as Sheriff of Cape Girardeau Co., his having been elected on the first Monday of Aug 1824. Signed A. **McNAIR**. Wit Wm. G. **PETTUS**, Secretary of State. William **CREATH** takes the oath of office. Signed William **CREATH**. Wit Peter R. **GARRETT** (JP). Rec 11 Apr 1825.

2324. Page 527. 11 Apr 1825. William **CREATH**, Alexander **BUCKNER**, Johnson **RANNEY**, David **ARMOUR**, and John **PRIM** to Frederick **BATES**, Governor of Mo. For the sum of $10,000, bond to guarantee that William **CREATH** will perform the duties of Sheriff of Cape Girardeau Co. Signed William **CREATH**, A. **BUCKNER**, David **ARMOUR**, Johnson **RANNEY**. Wit R. **DAUGHERTY**, Clerk. Rec 11 Apr 1825.

2325. Page 528. 13 Apr 1825. Samuel **CUPPLES** by Sheriff William **CREATH** to James **EVANS**. For the sum of $20, 8 acres, more or less, adjoining Cape Girardeau. Sold on 16 Dec 1824 on a writ of execution issued by Circuit Court on 12 Nov 1824 in favor of William **HOOD** and William **OLIVER**, assignees of the estate of **MANN & CUPPLES**, and against Samuel **CUPPLES** and Theodore **JONES**, for $2400 debt, $372 damages, and $19.57 ½ costs. Signed William **CREATH**, Shff. Wit R. **DAUGHERTY**, Clerk. Rec 12 Apr 1825.

2326. Page 529. 15 Apr 1825. Ezekiel **ABLE** by Sheriff John **HAYS** to Robert **GIBONEY**. For the sum of $10.12 ½, 640 acres on White Water confirmed to William **PAGE**'s representatives; adjoining John & Samuel G. **DUNN**. Sold on 8 Aug 1821 by on an execution of Circuit Court issued on 25 Apr 1820 in favor of Hiram C. **DAVIS**, assignee of William and Polly **MOTHERSHEAD**, against Ezekiel **ABLE** and Jeremiah **ABLE** for $177.81 2/3 debt and $25.52 costs. Sd **HAYS** did not make a deed, and this deed is executed on the petition of sd **GIBONEY**. Signed William **CREATH**, Shff.

Wit Johnson **RANNEY**, R. **DAUGHERTY**, Clerk. Rec 16 Apr 1825.

2327. Page 530. 15 Apr 1825. Erasmus **ELLIS** by same to Johnson **RANNEY**. For the sum of $71, three parcels; 80 acres, being part of the head right of Henry **HAND** near Jackson, originally purchased of sd **HAND** by **RODNEY**; a house and lot on Main St in Jackson, purchased of John **ARMSTRONG** by sd **ELLIS**; and Lot No. 10, Range E in Cape Girardeau, bounded on the W by Lorimier St and S by Harmony St. Sold on 8 Aug 1821 on four executions issued by Circuit Court against sd **ELLIS**; one issued 9 Apr 1821 in favor of John **RODNEY** for $1000.75 debt and damages and $9.85 costs; one issued 12 Apr 1821 in favor of Johnson **RANNEY** against sd **ELLIS** and Andrew **HAYNES** for $174.49 debt and $15 costs; one issued on 2 Apr 1821 in favor of James **ELLIS** for $128.32; and one issued 4 Apr 1821 in favor of James **ELLIS** for $142.80. Sd **HAYS** did not make a deed, and this deed is executed on the petition of sd **RANNEY**. Signed William **CREATH**, Shff. Wit Beverley **ALLEN**, R. **DAUGHERTY**, Clerk. Rec 16 Apr 1825.

2328. Page 532. 15 Apr 1825. Zenas **PRIEST** by same to John **ERWIN**. For the sum of $305, lot in Jackson on High St on which sd **PRIEST** then and now resides. Sold on 7 Aug 1821 on two executions of Circuit Court issued in Aug Term 1821 against sd **PRIEST**; one in favor of Robert **BUCKNER** for $330 debt and $5.30 costs; the other in favor of Christian **GATES** against sd **PRIEST** and William **NEELY** for $174 debt and $14.80 costs. Sd **HAYS** did not make a deed, sd **ERWIN** conveyed the lot to John **CROSS** on 25 Aug 1821, and this deed is executed on the petition of sd **CROSS**. Signed William **CREATH**, Shff. Wit Beverley **ALLEN**, R. **DAUGHERTY**, Clerk. Rec 16 Apr 1825.

2329. Page 533. 19 Apr 1825. Phineas **COBURN** by Sheriff William **CREATH** to David **HOLLY**. For the sum of $13.62 ½, 100 acres on the E side Hubble's Creek, being part of the head right of James **HANNAH**; beginning at a sugar tree. Sold on 16 Dec 1824 on a writ of execution issued 12 Nov 1824 by Circuit Court in Chancery in favor of sd **HOLLY** and against Charles G. **ELLIS** and William **NEELY** for $50, and Phinehas **COBOURN** for $50; being the amount sd **HOLLY** overpaid on a mortgage. Signed William **CREATH**, Sheriff. Wit R. **DAUGHERTY**, Clerk. Rec 19 Apr 1825.

2330. Page 534. 19 Apr 1825. James **RAVENSCROFT** by same to Greer W. **DAVIS**. For the sum of $5.50, 500 arpens on which sd **RAVENSCROFT** had lived. Sold on 13 Dec 1824 on an order of sale issued on 24 Aug 1824 by Circuit Court on a decree in favor of the State of Mo. for $1000 in foreclosure of mortgage. Signed William **CREATH**, Sheriff. Wit James **EVANS**, R. **DAUGHERTY**, Clerk. Rec 19 Apr 1825.

2331. Page 536. 11 Apr 1825. George **TENNELL** by same to John **THOMPSON**. For the sum of $351, two tracts; one of 250 arpens granted and confirmed to John **MAY**, and conveyed to sd **TENNELL**; the other of 300 arpens granted to Corelius **EVERET** and confirmed to sd **MAY** under sd **EVERET**, conveyed by sd **MAY** to sd **TENNELL**. Sold in Aug 1824 on two orders of Circuit Court in petition to foreclose a mortgage to Robert G. **WATSON** for $254 with 10% interest per annum. Signed William **CREATH**, Sheriff. Wit Johnson **RANNEY**, R. **DAUGHERTY**, Clerk. Rec 19 Apr 1825.

2332. Page 537. 1 Sep 1824. John **STUMP** of Pope Co., Ill. to Alexander P. **FIELD**. For the sum of $400, all his right to the estate of Henry **DOUGLAS**, decd, of Cape Girardeau Co. Signed John **STUMP**. Wit B. W. **BROOKS**, JP in Union Co., Ill., Winstead **DAVIE**, County Clerk of Union Co., Ill. Rec 21 Apr 1825.

2333. Page 538. 29 Apr 1825. David **HOLLEY** and Delilah, his wife, to Ezekiel **HILL**. For the sum of $133 1/3, 66 2/3 acres on the E side of Hubbell's Creek on which sd **HILL** and family now live; being part of 100 acres granted to James **HANNAH** as part of his head right, and being 2/3 of an undivided interest in sd 100 acres between sd **HOLLEY**, Charles G. **ELLIS**, and William **NEELY**; beginning at a sugar tree. Signed David **HOLLEY**, Delilah (x) **HOLLEY**. Wit Havens C. (x) **ABERNETHIE**, John **ABENETHIE** (JP). Rec 29 Apr 1825.

2334. Page 539. 30 Jan 1824. Tunstall **QUARLES** to William T. **GRAHAM**, both of Jackson. Power of attorney to convey 377.60 acres to Peter R. **GARRETT**; being the residue of land sd **QUARLES** bought of James **WHITESIDE**. Signed T. **QUARLES**. Wit William **McGUIRE** (JP), C. S. **THOMAS**, D. **ARMOUR** (JP). No recording date.

2335. Page 539. 30 Jan 1824. Same to Peter R. **GARRETT**. For the sum of $1000, bond to

make a deed on 377.60 acres; being the SW fractional ¼, Sec 19, Twp 32 N, Rng 13 E; SW fractional ¼, Sec 18, Twp 32 N, Rng 13 E; W ½, NE ¼, Sec 19, Twp 32 N, Rng 13 E; and 56 acres of the SE ¼, Sec 18, Twp 32 N, Rng 13 E, the last being the remainder of a tract he conveyed to **STARLING & DLASHMUTT**. The deed is to be executed as soon as sd **QUARLES** can get a decree for the tract, on a suit he brought against James **WHITESIDE** in Circuit Court in Chancery. Signed T. **QUARLES**. Wit William **McGUIRE** (JP), C. S. **THOMAS**, D. **ARMOUR** (JP). No recording date.

2336. Page 540. 23 Mar 1825. Same by William T. **GRAHAM**, his attorney in fact, to same. For the sum of $300, 377.60 acres as described in the preceding deed (F:539). Signed T. **QUARLES** by William T. **GRAHAM**, attorney in fact. Wit David **ARMOUR** (JP). Rec 20 May 1825.

2337. Page 541. 16 Jul 1824. Obediah **MALONE** to John **JOHNSON**. For the sum of $150, 250 acres on the waters of Apple Creek; beginning at the NE corner of Edward **McGUIRE**'s land deed to sd **McGUIRE** by sd **JOHNSON** to Abraham **HEWES**; also bounded by Abraham **BYRD**. Signed Obadiah A. **MALOAN**. Wit Elijah (x) **LOVENG**, Hortentia **JOHNSON**, Stephen **MALON**, John **JUDEN** Jr., Dep. Clerk. Rec 21 May 1825.

2338. Page 542. 16 Jul 1824. John **JOHNSON** to Obadiah **MALONE**. For the sum of $700, 229.16 acres, more or less, being S fractional ½, Sec 15, Twp 32, Rng 12 E. Signed John **JOHNSON**. Wit Elijah (x) **LOVEING**, Hortentia **JOHNSON**, Stephen **MALONE**, John **JUDEN** Jr., Dep. Clerk. Rec 21 May 1825.

2339. Page 542. 28 Feb 1825. William **McLAIN** to David Dixon **McLAIN**. For the sum of $67, 20 ½ acres, more or less; beginning at an elm and being the NE corner of the W ½, NE ¼, Sec 18, Twp 32, Rng 14 E; and being the same granted to William **McLAIN** by the U. S. A. on 6 Nov 1823. Signed William **McLAIN**, Betsey (x) **McLAIN**. Test James **RUSSELL**, Martin (x) **FOSTER**, John **McCOMBS** (JP). Rec __ May 1825.

2340. Page 543. 29 May 1825. Moses **NORMAN** to Thomas **WELCH**. For the sum of $83, __ acres, being the improvement where he now lives; the blacksmith tools; two horse cretures; nine hed of cattle; six hed of sheep; seven head of hogs; and farming tools; together with household property. The debt to be paid within 18 months. Signed Moses **NORMAN**. Wit David **ORR**, William **BAKER**, James **WILLIAMS** (JP). Rec 2 Jun 1825.

2341. Page 544. 23 Mar 1825. Peter R. **GARRETT** to John M. **DANIEL**. For the sum of $334.75, 267.80 acres; being part of a tract conveyed to sd **GARRETT** by Tunstall **QUARLES**, and that sd **QUARLES** purchased of James **WHITESIDE** and that was decreed to sd **QUARLES** in Circuit Court; being the SW fractional ¼, Sec 18, Twp 32 N, Rng 13 E; W ½, NE ¼, Sec 19, Twp 32, Rng 13 E; and 56 acres of the SE ¼, Sec 18, Twp 32 N, Rng 13 E, the last being the residue of a tract conveyed by sd **QUARLES** to **STARLING & DLASHMUTT**. Signed Peter R. **GARRETT**. Wit David **ARMOUR** (JP). Rec 3 Jun 1825.

2342. Page 544. 4 Apr 1825. William **MATHEWS** to Martin **RODNEY**. For the sum of $110 in round Spanish mill dollars, mortgage on a negro woman named **Nell** about 25 years old. The debt is due by 4 Oct next, and sd **MATHEWS** is still to owe the debt if the woman dies. Signed William **MATTHEWS**. Wit Thomas **MATTHEWS**, Michl. **RODNEY**, John **JUDEN** Jr., Dep Clerk. Rec 21 Jun 1825.

2343. Page 545. 11 Apr 1825. Thomas S. **RODNEY** to Thomas Jefferson **RODNEY**. For the sum of $1000 in the form of a negro man named **Jim** about 25 years old, and a negro woman named **Betsey** about 22 years old; bond to guarantee collection of a judgment obtained against Daniel F. **STEINBECK** in favor of Thomas S. **RODNEY** for the use of Thomas Jefferson **RODNEY**. As soon as Thomas Jefferson **RODNEY** attains the age of 21, he will clear Thomas S. **RODNEY**, his former guardian, and John **RODNEY**, his present guardian, of their guardianship of his estate. If the judgment is less than the value of one negro, then the sale is to be void for one negro at the option of Thomas S. **RODNEY**; sd **Jim** valued at $600, and sd **Betsey** at $400. Signed Thos. S. **RODNEY**, Thos. Jefferson **RODNEY**. Wit P. R. **PITMAN**, John **RODNEY**, John **JUDEN** Jr., Dep Clerk. Rec 21 Jun 1825.

2344. Page 547. 25 Jun 1824. Oliver **HARRIS** and Marggret, his wife, to Robert W. **HARRIS**. For the sum of $100, 80 acres, being the W ½, SW ¼, Sec 9, Twp 33 N, Rng 13 E. Signed Oliver **HARRIS**, Margaret (x) **HARRIS**. Wit Benjamin **BACON** (JP), Mathew **HENDERSON**. Rec 25 Jun 1825.

2345. Page 548. 11 Oct 1824. Obadiah **MALONE** to John **HENDRICKS**. For the sum of $300, 160 acres on the waters of Byrd's Creek, being the balance of the fractional ½, Sec 5, Twp 32, Rng 12 E; and the balance of a tract, after deducting 69 acres, deeded by sd **MALONE** to Henry **SHANER**. Signed Ob. A. **MALONE**. Wit Jacob **FULBRIGHT**, George (|) **LEGATE**, John **JOHNSON** (JP). Rec 25 Jun 1825.

2346. Page 549. 10 Feb 1819. Commissioners of the Courthouse and Jail to Benjamin **SHELL**. For the sum of $72, Lot No. 80 in Jackson; bounded on the N and fronted by first south street, W and fronted by second west street, S by Lot No. 81, and E by Lot No. 68. Signed John **SHEPPARD**, Samuel G. **DUNN**, Abraham **BYRD**. Wit John W. **SIMPKINS**, Zenas **PRIEST** (JP). Rec 27 Jun 1825.

2347. Page 550. 6 Nov 1823. U. S. A. to John **PERKINS**. For full payment under the Act of 24 Apr 1820, Certificate #254 for 80 acres, being the E ½, NW ¼, Sec 15, Twp 30, Rng 10 E. Signed James **MONROE**, President, Geo. **GRAHAM**, Commissioner, Genl. Land Off. Rec in Vol. 1, page 249. Rec 23 Jul 1825.

2348. Page 550. 1 Sep 1819. Michael **COLLIER** Jr. of Ill. to Albert **BRITE** and Geo. P. **MILLER**, merchants trading as **BRITE & MILLER**; John **HALL** and James **MALONE**, merchants trading as **HALL & MALONE**; and David **ROBERTSON**; all of Shelbyville, Ken. For the sum of $1 and securing debts, mortgage on three parcels; __ acres, being his preemption right on Flora Creek and being the same purchased of the heirs of Benjamin **LAFERTY**; two lots in Jonesborough, Union Co., Ill., being the same deeded by sd **COLLIER** by John **HUCKY** and Urssell E. **HEACOCK**; and ½ of a lot in sd town deeded to sd **COLLIER** by _____ **HUTCHINS**. Sd **COLLIER** owes debts as follows: $395 to **BRITE & MILLER** due 12 months after date, $672.66 to **HALL & MALONE** payable 12 months after date, $188.99 to sd **ROBERTSON** due 12 months from date. Signed Michael **COLLIER** Jr. Wit P. **EUBANK**, Geo. **WOOLFORD**, _____, JP in Union Co., Ill. Mortgage is assigned to Joseph W. **McKNIGHT** and John **LOGAN** Jr. for value received on __ Mar 1822. Signed Albert **BRIGHT** (also for George P. **MILLER**). Wit Winstead **DAVIE**, Clerk. Rec 29 Jul 1825.

2349. Page 552. 6 Aug 1825. Richard S. **THOMAS** and Frances, his wife, to George **BULLITT**. For the sum of $900, 104 acres two roods and 32 poles, more or less, on a branch of Hubble's Creek; beginning at the SE corner of land sd **THOMAS** heretofore conveyed to William **FISHBACK**; being part of a tract confirmed to William H. **ASHLEY** as assignee of Henry **SHERIDAN**; bounded in part by a line run by William B. **BYRD** between sd **THOMAS** and John **SHEPPARD**. Signed Richard S. **THOMAS**, Frances **THOMAS**. Test R. **DAUGHERTY**, Clerk. Rec 6 Aug 1825.

2350. Page 554. 8 Aug 1825. Same and same to John **JUDEN** Junior. For the sum of $900, three parcels; the undivided ½ of Lot Nos. 33 & 161 in Jackson, being the same purchased of the Commissioners of the Courthouse and Jail by sd **THOMAS** and William **McGUIRE** on 5 May 1821; and 120 acres, more or less, confirmed to William H. **ASHLEY**, assignee of Henry **SHAREDAN**, bounded on the E by George **BULLITT**, S by John **SHEPPARD**, W by James **RUSSELL**, N by the town of Jackson except for 4 acres mortgaged to the State of Mo., 1 acre sold to Nathan **VANHORN** and John B. **WHEELER**, and ¼ acre sold to John J. **DLASHMUTT**. Signed R. S. **THOMAS**, Frances **THOMAS**. Test R. **DAUGHERTY**, Clerk. Rec 8 Aug 1825.

2351. Page 556. 29 Jun 1822. Itharmer **HUBBLE** of Byrd Twp to Stephen **BYRD** and George **MEAIZE**. For the sum of $5, 3 acres, more or less, on the E side of Whitewater adjoining the mill seat; being part of 640 acres confirmed to sd **HUBBLE**; and beginning against the lower end of the butment. Signed Ithamer (x) **HUBBLE**, Catharine (x) **HUBBLE**. Wit John **MORRISSON**, Andrue (x) **PEW**, R. **DAUGHERTY**, Clerk. Rec 9 Aug 1825.

2352. Page 557. 13 Aug 1825. James **RUSSELL** to James **DOWTY**. For the sum of $45, 255 acres, more or less, being all that tract whereon sd **DOWTY** now lives; bounded on the N by lands originally owned by John **SUMMERS**, E by land granted to Edward **ROBERTSON** and Joshua **GOZA**, S by Renna **BRUMMETT**, and W by public lands; being the same tract conveyed to sd **RUSSELL** by sd **DOWTY** on 3 Jan 1824 by deed of trust. The conditions of the earlier deed have been complied with, as endorsed on sd deed on 28 May 1824. Signed James **RUSSELL**. Test R. **DAUGHERTY**, Clerk, David **HILE**. Rec 13 Aug 1825.

2353. Page 558. 20 Aug 1825. Ithamer **HUBBLE** [and Catherine, his wife] to Ebenezer **HUBBLE** and his son William **HUBBLE**, all of Byrd Twp. For the sum of $450, 120 acres, more or less, in Byrd Twp, being part of a tract confirmed to Ithamer **HUBBLE**; beginning 6 ft W of the spring used by sd Ebenezer, which is the beginning corner of J. **LANGDON**. The land to go to sd Ebenezer during his lifetime, then to his son William. Signed Ithamer (x) **HUBBLE**, Catherine (x) **HUBBLE**. Wit J. **LANGDON**, R. **DAUGHERTY**, Clerk. Rec 20 Aug 1825.

2354. Page 560. 15 Apr 1824. John J. **DLASHMUTT** of New Madrid Co., Mo. to John **HAYS**. For the sum of $85, part of Lot No. 51 in Jackson, formerly owned by Edmund **RUTTER**, on which there is a brick storehouse occupied by sd **HAYS** as an office for the Receiver of Public Monies; bounded on the S by Main St and W by first west street; being the same he purchased at Sheriff's sale in Apr 1824 of William **CREATH**, Sheriff. Signed John J. **DLASHMUTT**. Wit W. **GARNER**, John **SHEPPARD**, Ralph **DAUGHERTY**, Clerk. Rec 20 Aug 1825.

2355. Page 561. 23 Aug 1825. Joel **BLUNT** by Sheriff William **CREATH** to William **SURRELL**. For the sum of $25, the E ½ of Lot No. 54 in Jackson, lying between Zenas **PRIEST** and Samuel **LOCKHART**. Sold on 5 Jan 1824 on an order of Circuit Court issued 19 Sep 1823 in favor of David **ARMOUR** and John **JUDEN** Junior and against sd **BLUNT** in a petition for mortgage foreclosure. Sd mortgage was executed on 15 May 1821 to sd **ARMOUR** and sd **JUDEN** on sd lot for $200 and three feather beds and bed furniture, one beaureau, two tables, one dresser and all shelfware, two pots, one oven, one skillet, one trunk, one horse bridle and saddle, one rifle gun, five chairs and one tea kettle. Signed William **CREATH**, Sheriff. Wit Ralph **DAUGHERTY**, Clerk. Rec 23 Aug 1825.

2356. Page 564. 2 Jun 1825. William **ROBERSON** of New Madrid Co., Mo. to Ralph **DAUGHERTY**, surviving partner of **FRIZEL** & **DAUGHERTY**. For the sum of $104, mortgage on 5 acres, more or less, on Hubble's Creek on the N side of Jackson on which William **ROBISON** lately resided; being part of a tract confirmed to **MILLS**; beginning at a post near a spring. Sd note is dated 31 Jan 1825 and is due by 1 Sep next with interest. Signed Wm. **ROBINSON**. Wit John **JUDEN** Junr., William S. **GANTT**, John D. **COOK**, Judge of 4th Judicial Circuit. Rec 25 Aug 1825.

2357. Page 565. 6 Aug 1825. Joseph **GEISTWITE** of Ark. Terr. to James A. **ATKINS**. For the sum of $100, 100 arpens, more or less, being part of the head settlement right of Ranney **BRUMMETT**, as described in a deed from George **RUDDLE** to Jonas N. **MENEFEE**, agent for Jarrot **MENEFEE**. Signed Joseph **GEISTWITE**. Wit R. **DAUGHERTY**, Clerk, C. S. **THOMAS**, George **FRICKE**. Rec 26 Aug 1825.

2358. Page 566. 16 Aug 1825. Jonas N. **MENEFEE** by Sheriff William **CREATH** to Levi L. **LIGHTNER**. For the sum of $10, Lot No. 10, Range F in Cape Girardeau, fronting on North St and Lorimier St. Sold in Aug 1825 on an order of Circuit Court issued 15 Apr 1825 in favor of Louis **LORIMIER**, Daniel F. **STEINBECK**, Victor **LORIMIER**, Thomas Jefferson **RODNEY** by John **RODNEY**, his guardian, and Polly **RODNEY** by Thomas **BYRNE**, her guardian, for the use of Levi L. **LIGHTNER** and against sd **MENEFEE** in a petition for mortgage foreclosure. Signed William **CREATH**, Shff. Wit Ralph **DAUGHERTY**, Clerk. Rec 23 Aug 1825.

2359. Page 568. 23 Aug 1825. Simon J. **WHITTENBURGH** by same to William **THOMSON**. For the sum of $5.06 ¼, 400 acres whereon the widow **WHITTENBURGH** now lives, being part of a tract confirmed to Jeremiah **THOMSON**. Sold on 20 Apr 1824 on an execution from Circuit Court issued on 20 Jan 1824 in favor of the State of Mo. and against sd **WHITTENBURGH** and John **PAYNE**, impleaded with William G. **SHORDE**(?), for $175.95 damages by reason of sd **WHITTENBURGH** and sd **PAYNE** not having kept a covenant, and $10.60 costs. Signed William **CREATH**, Sheriff. Wit Ralph **DAUGHERTY**, Clerk. Rec 23 Aug 1825.

2360. Page 570. 23 Aug 1825. 23 Aug 1825. John P. **WRIGHT** and the heirs of Samuel **WRIGHT** by same to David **ARMOUR**. For the sum of $53, the undivided 1/3 of 280 3/4 acres on the River Zenon, alias Hubble's Creek, known as Ramsey's and Cracroft's mill tract. Sold in May 1824 on an order of Circuit Court issued 27 Dec 1823 in favor of Andrew **RAMSEY** for the use of David **ARMOUR** and against John P. **WRIGHT**, Sarah **WRIGHT**, Alexander **WRIGHT**, Allison **WRIGHT**, Betsey **WRIGHT**, Sarah **WRITE**, Nancy **WRIGHT**, Mariah **WRIGHT**, Jane **WRIGHT**, and Emily **WRIGHT** in a petition for mortgage foreclosure. Sd John P. **WRIGHT** and one

Samuel **WRIGHT** executed the mortgage on 2 Mar 1820 to secure payment of four obligations, and sd Samuel died soon after, leaving Sarah **WRIGHT**, his widow, and eight infant heirs (Alexander, Allison, Betsey, Sarah, Nancy, Maria, Jane, and Emily **WRIGHT**), without having paid the sum of $1666.65 plus interest. Signed William **CREATH**, Shff. Wit Ralph **DAUGHERTY**, Clerk. Rec 24 Aug 1825.

2361. Page 572. 3 Sep 1825. James A. **ATKINS** to Leavin **WADKINS**. For the sum of $100, 100 arpens, more or less, being part of the head settlement right of Ranny **BRUMMET**, as described in a deed from George **RUDDLE** to Jonas N. **MENEFEE**. Signed James A. **ATKINS**. Wit Ralph **DAUGHERTY**, Clerk. Rec 3 Sep 1825.

2362. Page 574. 19 Sep 1825. John **HAYS** to Betsey **LOVE**. For the sum of $___, 240 arpens, more or less, being where Edward F. **BOND** once lived, adjoined on the W by Colo. Stephen **BYRD**, N by the heirs of Joseph **YOUNG**, decd, S by Maximilian **HORRELL**, and E by public lands. Sd tract was conveyed by sd **HAYS** in 1805 or 1806 to sd **BOND**. Sd **BOND** conveyed the same to Betsey **GIBSON**, who has since intermarried with _____ **LOVE** and resides in Davidson Co., Tenn., on 26 Dec 1806. The deed was not recorded in Cape Girardeau Co., but with the Register of Land Titles in St. Louis, and doubts have arisen as to the right of Betsey **LOVE** to the tract. This deed removes those doubts. Signed John **HAYS**. Wit Claib. Simms **THOMAS**, Th. **NEALE** (JP). Rec 19 Sep 1825.

2363. Page 575. 23 Sep 1825. William **CREATH** and Martha P., his wife, to Nathan **VANHORN**, all of Jackson. For the sum of $93.90, undivided ½ of 122.74 acres, being fractional ¼, Sec 30, Twp 32, Rng 13 E; being the same patented to Nathaniel & William **CREATH** as No. 338. Signed Wm. **CREATH**, M. P. **CREATH**. Wit David **ARMOUR** (JP). Rec 26 Sep 1825.

2364. Page 576. 22 Oct 1822. Daniel F. **STEINBECK** to Alexander **MacDONALD** and Nicholas **RIDGELY** of Baltimore. For the sum of $1009, mortgage on 1000 arpens known as the concession of Louis **LONGEARE**. A note dated 1 Dec 1819 is due with interest. Signed D. F. **STEINBECK**. Wit David **ARMOUR** (JP). Rec 29 Sep 1825.

2365. Page 577. 23 Aug 1825. Enoch **EVANS** by Sheriff William **CREATH** to Alfred P.

ELLIS. For the sum of $30.50, Lot No. 7 in Jackson, being the same purchased by sd **EVANS** of Andrew **RAMSEY**. Sold on 8 Dec 1824 on order of Circuit Court issued at Aug Term 1824 in favor of the State of Mo. and against sd **EVANS** in a petition for mortgage foreclosure on the sum of $100. Signed William **CREATH**, Sheriff. Wit Ralph **DAUGHERTY**, Clerk. Rec 29 Sep 1825.

2366. Page 578. 24 Aug 1825. Jenifer T. **SPRIGG** by same to Charles G. **ELLIS**. For the sum of $28, two tracts; 10 acres, being Outlot No. 1, bounded on the N by Outlot No. 32, S by North St, E by vacant space destined for a public boat yard, and W by Outlot No. 2 and the grave yard; and 10 acres, more or less, being Outlot No. 5 adjoining Cape Girardeau, bounded on the N by Outlot No. 30, S by North St, E by Outlot No. 4, and W by Outlot No. 6. Sold on 10 Aug 1825 on first pluries execution of Circuit Court in favor of Louis **LORIMIER**, Daniel F. **STEINBECK**, Victor **LORIMIER**, Thomas Jefferson **RODNEY** and Polly **RODNEY** for the use of August **HAMMER**, and against sd **ELLIS** and sd **SPRIGG** for $1170 debt, $148.23 damages, and $15.51 costs. Signed Wm. **CREATH**, Sheriff. Wit Ralph **DAUGHERTY**, Clerk. Rec 29 Sep 1825.

2367. Page 580. 30 Apr 1824. Martin B. **LAWRENCE** and Mariah, his wife, to John C. **WATSON**. For the sum of $16, the NW corner of Block No. 5, Range C in Cape Girardeau; being one of two lots sd **LAWRENCE** purchased at public sale from the Commissioners on 14 Dec 1820. Signed Martin B. **LAWRENCE**, Mariah **LAWRENCE**. Test George **HENDERSON** (JP). Rec 1 Oct 1825.

2368. Page 581. 28 May 1824. James **DOWTY** to Reuben **DOWTY**. For the sum of $50, 300 acres, more or less, being all the tract where he now lives; bounded on the S by Joseph **OBANNON**, E by Thomas W. **GRAVES**, and E & N by David **ARMOUR**. Signed James **DOWTY**. Wit John **RODNEY**, David **ARMOUR** (JP). Rec 12 Nov 1825.

2369. Page 582. 22 Jan 1825. William **ROBINSON** and Elizabeth T., [his wife,] to John **SHEPPARD** Senr. For the sum of $120, 173 1/3 acres about one mile S of Jackson, being part of a tract confirmed to Peter **BELEW**; adjoining **BULL**, **TASH**, **THOMAS**, and **HOUTS**. Signed Wm. **ROBINSON**, Elizabeth T. **ROBINSON**. Wit Peter R. **GARRETT** (JP). Rec 15 Nov 1825.

2370. Page 583. 28 Nov 1825. Daniel **BOLLINGER** Senior, late of Cape Girardeau Co., to Polly **HUDSON**, widow of Enoch **HUDSON**, decd. For love and natural affection toward his daughter and the sum of $250, a negro girl called **Cinta**, alias **Cynthia**, aged about 12 years, of tolerable black complexion. Signed Daniel **BOLLINGER**. Wit Claibne. S. **THOMAS**, R. **DAUGHERTY**, Clerk. Rec 28 Nov 1825.

2371. Page 584. 17 Nov 1825. Stephen **BYRD**, adminr de bonis non of Jason **CHAMBERLAIN**, decd, to George **BULLITT**. For the sum of $805, 337 3/4 acres, more or less, being part of a tract confirmed to Peter **BILLEW**; beginning at the NW corner of sd tract, which is also the SW corner of Samuel **PEW**'s survey; also bounded by Richard S. **THOMAS** and Edmund **RUTTER**. Sd **BULLITT** executed a note with sd **THOMAS** as security to sd **BYRD** on 10 Apr 1822, payable in one year; sd **BYRD** executed a bond of $1610 to make a deed to the tract; and this deed discharges that bond. Sold on ___ at order of Circuit Court issued in Dec Term 1821 to sell the land of sd **CHAMBERLAIN**. Signed Stephen **BYRD**, adminr de bonis non of Jason **CHAMBERLAIN**, decd. Wit R. S. **THOMAS**, R. **DAUGHERTY**, Clerk. Rec 2 Dec 1825.

2372. Page 586. 6 Nov 1823. U. S. A. to James **HOLCOMB**. For full payment under the Act of 24 Apr 1820, Certificate #142 for 80 acres, being E ½, NE ¼, Sec 21, Twp 31, Rng 13 E. Signed James **MONROE**, President, George **GRAHAM**, Commissioner, Genl. Land Off. Rec in Vol. 1, page 132. Title is assigned to Edward F. **EVANS** for value received on 10 Dec 1825. Signed James **HOLCOMB**. Wit C. S. **THOMAS** (JP), John **JUDEN** Jr. Rec 10 Dec 1825.

2373. Page 587. 23 Aug 1825. John P. **WRIGHT** and the heirs of Samuel **WRIGHT** by Sheriff William **CREATH** to David **ARMOUR**. For the sum of $53, the undivided 2/3 of 280 3/4 acres on the River Zenon, alias Hubble's Creek, known as Ramsey's and Cracroft's mill tract. Sold in May 1824 on an order of Circuit Court issued 27 Dec 1823 as described in F:570. Signed Wm. **CREATH**, Shff. Wit Ralph **DAUGHERTY**, Clerk. Rec 24 Aug 1825.

2374. Page 590. 15 Dec 1825. Frederick **LIMBAUGH** and Catharine, his wife, to Jacob **LIMBEAUGH**. For love and affection for their son and for the sum of $100, 500 acres, more or less, in German Twp whereon they now reside; being the same confirmed to sd Frederick. Signed Frederick (O) **LIMBEAUGH**, Catharine (   ) **LIMBEAUGH**. Wit J. **RANNEY**, D. **ARMOUR**, Th. **NEALE** (JP). Rec 16 Dec 1825.

2375. Page 591. 14 Dec 1825. Stephen **BYRD** to John **LANGDON** and John **WHITTENBURGH**. For the sum of $200, undivided ½ of two tracts sd **BYRD** jointly owns with George **MEAIZE**, including the mills; 25 acres in the NW ¼, Sec 36, Twp 31 N, Rng 11 E, purchased of Morris **YOUNG**, including the mill seat, beginning at Ithamer **HUBBLE**'s; and 3 acres purchased from Ithamer **HUBBLE** and wife, part of 640 acres confirmed to sd **HUBBLE** on the E side of White Water, adjoining the mill seat, beginning at the lower end of the butment. Sd **MEAIZE** has also conveyed his ½ to sd **LANGDON** and sd **WHITTENBURGH**. Signed Stephen **BYRD**. Wit John **JUDEN** Jr., R. **DAUGHERTY**, Clerk. Rec 15 Dec 1825.

2376. Page 593. 1 Sep 1824. John D. **COOK** to John **CROSS** and William **GARNER**, trustees of Edmund **RUTTER**. For the sum of $40, quit claim to Lot No. 49 in Jackson, being where he now lives and which he purchased at sheriff's sale at the last Apr term. Signed John D. **COOK**. Wit Thomas P. **GREEN**, R. **DAUGHERTY**, Clerk. Rec 21 Dec 1825.

2377. Page 593. no date. James **EVANS** of Jackson to **GREGOIRE & PRATT** of Ste. Genevieve. For the sum of $212, mortgage on an itemized list of law books; three feather beds, bedsteads & furniture of every description belonging to the same; ½ dozen windsor chairs; five large tables & 2 small do; all his cubbard furniture, including large silver table spoons, ½ dozen plated, 16 silver tea spoons, 1 large silver soop spoon, china tea cups & saucors, coffie do, tea pots & coffe do, plates do, cut and plaine glass, delph ware, plates, tea cups & saucers, knives & forks; household & kitchen furniture of every description; 2 mares, 1 sorrel, the other brown; 3 cows & calves; 1 large looking glass & 2 small do; 1 secretary; 3 beaureaus; 1 old desk; 1 work do; 1 sugar chest; and one negro man named **Corminete**. Sd **EVANS** owes the debt in a note due in 12 months, with 10% interest, and is to keep possession of the property until then. Signed James **EVANS**. Wit R. **DAUGHERTY**, Clerk. Rec 24 Dec 1825.

2378. Page 595. 26 Dec 1825. William **MORRISON** by Sheriff William **CREATH** to Henry **CLAY**, execr of James **MORRISON**, decd. For the sum of $70, 640 acres on White Water in Twp 30 & 31 N, Rng 11 E, confirmed to William **MORRISON** under Jonathan **HUBBLE**; being Claim No. 2256; beginning at the upper corner on White Water of Claim No. 1816; also bounded by Claim Nos. 2227 & No. 816, and the line between Sec Nos. 2 & 11. Sold on 19 Dec 1825 on a writ of execution from the Supreme Court, 3rd Judicial Dist, issued 19 Nov 1825 in favor of sd **CLAY**, execr of James **MORRISON**, and against William **MORRISON** for $8000 damages and $6.30 costs, for non-performance of certain premises and undertakings. Signed Wm. **CREATH**, Shff. Wit Ralph **DAUGHERTY**, Clerk. Rec 26 Dec 1825.

2379. Page 598. 26 Dec 1825. Same by same to same. For the sum of $99, 640 acres confirmed to William **MORRISON** under Daniel **HUBBLE**, and being Claim No. 2253 in Twp 29 & 30 N, Rng 12 E; beginning at a post where the W boundary of Survey No. 792 intersects the Twp line; also bounded by the E boundary of Sec 1, Twp 30 N, Rng 11 E and Survey Nos. 2284 & 792. Sold on a writ of execution as described in the preceding deed (F:595). Signed Wm. **CREATH**, Shff. Wit Ralph **DAUGHERTY**, Clerk. Rec 26 Dec 1825.

2380. Page 601. 26 Dec 1825. George **FRICKE** by Sheriff William **CREATH** to Samuel **LOCKHART**. For the sum of $99, part of Lot No. 52 in Jackson; bounded on the N by Main St and beginning at the office of Johnson **RANNEY**; also bounded by James **RUSSELL**. Sold in Aug 1825 at order of Circuit Court issued 3 Jun 1825 on petition of Greer W. **DAVIS** to foreclose a mortgage for $287. Signed Wm. **CREATH**, Shff. Wit R. **DAUGHERTY**, Clerk. Rec 26 Dec 1825.

2381. Page 603. 15 Dec 1825. William **CRACROFT** by same to James **EVANS**. For the sum of $41.25, 84 acres, more or less. Sold on 22 Sep 1825 at order of Circuit Court issued 20 Aug 1825 on petition of sd **EVANS** to foreclose a mortgage for $130 plus interest. Signed Wm. **CREATH**, Shff. Wit R. **DAUGHERTY**, Clerk. Rec 27 Dec 1825.

2382. Page 605. 26 Dec 1825. Charles C. **JACKSON** by same to Andrew **RAMSEY**. For the sum of $51, __ acres, being 1/3 of a tract in Byrd Twp known as Wright's Mill Tract. Sold to

David **ARMOUR** on 9 Aug 1824 on an execution issued by Circuit Court on 26 Apr 1824 in favor of Charles **CRACROFT**, assignee of John **CRACROFT**, and against sd **JACKSON** for $261.62 and 5 mills debt, $59.68 ¼ damages, and $80.75 costs. Sd **ARMOUR** petitioned on 22 Dec 1825 to have the title transferred to Andrew **RAMSEY**, and relinquished his right to the tract. Signed Wm. **CREATH**, Shff. Wit R. **DAUGHERTY**, Clerk. Rec 27 Dec 1825.

2383. Page 607. 26 Sep 1825. Thomas **HOUTS** and Sally, his wife, of Scott Co., Mo. to Albert G. **CREATH**. For the sum of $400, 130 acres about 1 ½ mile SE of Jackson, on which sd **HOUTS** now resides; being part of a tract of 640 acres granted to Peter **BILLUE**; beginning at an ash and hornbeam near the top of the dividing ridge. Signed Thomas **HOUTS**, Sally **HOUTS**. Wit John P. **RUTTER**, Scott Co., Mo. Clerk. Rec 28 Dec 1825.

2384. Page 609. 27 Dec 1825. William **CREATH**, adminr of Nathaniel **CREATH**, decd, to Nathan **VANHORN**. In consideration of money given to Nathaniel **CREATH** by William **CREATH**, 122.74 acres; being NW fractional ¼, Sec 30, Twp 32 N, Rng 13. Conveyed at order of Circuit Court in Chancery issued in Dec Term 1825. Nathaniel **CREATH**, in his lifetime, conveyed the tract to William **CREATH**, and executed a bond of $500 on 24 Feb 1823 to execute a deed. The bond was transferred by sd William to Nathan **VANHORN**, and Nathaniel **CREATH** died without complying with the contract, and sd **VANHORN** brought suit against sd **CREATH**. Signed Wm. **CREATH**, adminr of Nathaniel **CREATH**, decd. Wit R. **DAUGHERTY**, Clerk. Rec 29 Dec 1825.

2385. Page 610. 3 May 1825. Mary **FRIZEL** to George F. **BOLLINGER**. In consideration of the great trust and confidence she has in him and for diverse good causes, power of attorney to transact all business in Missouri, especially to take possession of 160 acres purchased by her of the U. S. A., about five miles N of Jackson; being SW ¼, Sec 10, Twp 32, Rng 13 E. Sd **BOLLINGER** may rent or dispose of sd land on the terms he judges best. Signed Mary **FRIZEL**. Wit R. **DAUGHERTY**, Clerk. Rec 2 Jan 1826.

2386. Page 611. 2 Nov 1825. John **SCRIPPS** and Agnes, his wife, to Aaron **PAINTER**. For the sum of $300, 6 acres near Cape Girardeau, being the same of which sd **PAINTER** has

possession and is working a tanyard. Signed John **SCRIPPS**, Agnes **SCRIPPS**. Wit John **RANDOL**, Thomas **BYRNE**, David **ARMOUR** (JP). George H. **SCRIPPS**, brother of John **SCRIPPS**, had executed a bond to convey sd tract, and sd John is unwilling to have any writings between him and sd George; so sd George binds himself to defend title to sd **PAINTER** on 7 Nov 1825. Signed Geor. H. **SCRIPPS**. Test George **BAKER**, George **HENDERSON** (JP). Rec 17 Jan 1826.

2387. Page 614. 28 Dec 1825. Michael **KNOX** of Byrd Twp to Elem Lewis **ADAMS**. For the sum of $310, 160 acres, being NE ¼, Sec 19, Twp 33, Rng 13 E; being Patent No. 315 issued to sd **KNOX** on 6 Nov 1823 by the U. S. A. Signed Michael **KNOX**. Wit Adlai O. **BREVARD**, Eliza S. **BACON**, Benjamin **BACON** (JP). Rec 19 Jan 1826.

2388. Page 615. 22 Jan 1826. John **RISHER** to Benjamin **SHELL** and Christopher **EDINGER**. For the consideration that they have become his securities in an appeal bond in chancery in case of sd **RISHER** vs. George **ROUSH**, 40 acres, more or less, where sd **RISHER** now resides and called Decatur; a set of blacksmith tools; two cows; and one horse. Signed John **RISHER**. Wit G. A. **BIRD**, David **ARMOUR** (JP). Rec 23 Jan 1826.

2389. Page 616. 15 Mar 1825. John McLANE to Joseph R. McLANE. For the sum of $500, 225 acres, more or less, being part of Sec Nos. 19 & 20, Twp 32, Rng 13 E; beginning at Ebenezer **FLINN's** corner on **HAYES'** line at or near the spring branch in Sec 19; also bounded by the line between Sec Nos. 17 & 20, the corner dividing the NW ¼ of Sec 20, and **HARRIS**. Signed Jno. **McLANE**. Wit Charles **TUCKER**, David **EVANS**, David **ARMOUR** (JP). Rec 8 Feb 1826.

2390. Page 617. 8 Mar 1825. Same to same. For the sum of $100, 90 acres, more or less, beginning at the SE corner of Sec 20, Twp 32, Rng 13 E. Signed Jno. **McLANE**. Wit Charles **TUCKER**, David **EVANS**, David **ARMOUR** (JP). Rec 8 Feb 1826.

2391. Page 618. 8 Feb 1826. Matthew **ALLEN** to Frances, his wife and late Francis **JOHNSON**. For the love and affection he feels toward his wife and the sum of $40, part of Lot No. 13 in Jackson, beginning on High St. Signed Matthew **ALLEN**. Wit John D. **COOK**, David **ARMOUR** (JP). Rec 11 Feb 1826.

2392. Page 620. 7 Sep 1824. Lewis **RANDOL** to Jacob **LITTLETON** of Union Co., Ill. For the sum of $1000, bond to make a deed on Lot No. 2 and 3/4 of Lot No. 1 in Bainbridge on the Mississippi River; being 5 ½ acres to be taken off a fraction of land between Sec Nos. 25 & 36, running down the river with the N and S lines so as to include the town of Bainbridge. The deed to be made on or before 15 Oct 1825, but not until title is obtained from the adminr of William **ROBERTS**, decd; and sd **LITTLETON** is to have the privilege of the ferry at Bainbridge sold by Medad **RANDOL** to James **EDMONDS**. Signed Lewis **RANDOL**. Test R. A. **McBRIDE**. The obligation is assigned to William **LITTLETON** for $570 on 19 Jul 1825. Signed Jacob **LITTLETON**. Test Frank J. **ALLEN**, R. A. **McBRIDE** (JP). Rec 1 Mar 1826.

2393. Page 621. 1 Mar 1826. John **ERWIN** to same. For the sum of $30, Lot Nos. 15 & 13 in Bainbridge. Signed John **ERWIN**. Wit Peter R. **GARRETT** (JP). Rec 1 Mar 1826.

2394. Page 621. 1 Feb 1826. William **WALLACE** and Jane, his wife, to John **MATTHEWS**. For the sum of $100, 80 acres, being the E ½, SE ¼, Sec 24, Twp 33 N, Rng 12 E. Signed William **WALLACE**, Jane **WALLACE**. Wit Wm. A. **BULL**, Matthew **SMITH**, Benjamin **BACON** (JP). Rec 2 Mar 1826.

2395. Page 622. 14 Mar 1825. John **McLANE** to John Anson **McLANE**. For the sum of $100, 80 acres on the waters of Buckeye, being the E ½, NW ¼, Sec 14, Twp 33, Rng 12 E. Signed Jn. **McLANE**. Wit Charles **TUCKER**, David **EVANS**, Benjamin **BACON** (JP). Rec 4 Mar 1826.

2396. Page 623. 2 Jan 1826. Francis **BLAIR** to his black man **Peter**. For the sum of $600, his freedom. Signed Francis **BLAIR**. Wit J. **RANNEY**, Jesse **HAIL**, Th. **NEALE**, Judge of Probate. Rec 11 Mar 1826.

2397. Page 623. 7 Feb 1826. Henry **HAHN** to Thomas **BRADY**. For the sum of $66 and 4 shillings, __ acres on the S side of Crooked Creek, being part of the E end, SW half ¼, Sec 9, Twp 30, Rng 10 E; beginning at the S section line at a sassafras 40 rods from the W corner. Sd **HAHN** agreed to make this deed on 20 Dec 1821, and this confirms that agreement. Signed Henry (x) **HAHN**, Lavina (x) **HAHN**. Wit James **WILLIAMS** (JP). Rec 11 Mar 1826.

2398. Page 625. 7 Jan 1826. Edmund **RUTTER** by trustees John **CROSS** and William **GARNER** of Cape Girardeau Co., and Hugh **McELROY** and William **GRUNDY** of Union Co., Ken. to John **SHEPPARD** Senior. For the sum of $80, 173 1/3 acres, being part of a tract confirmed to Peter **BELEW**, adjoining Thomas **BULL** and others. Sold on 14 Dec 1824 to pay debts according to the provisions of a deed of trust dated 14 May 1821 (F:114). Signed John **CROSS**, W. **GARNER**, Hugh **McELROY**, William **GRUNDY**. Wit George **HENDERSON** (JP), Edwd. **WILLETTE**, JP in Union Co., Ken., James **TOWNSEND**, JP in Union Co., Ken., James R. **HUGHES**, Clerk of Union Co., Ken. (as to **WILLETTE** and **TOWNSEND**), Robert **GILCHRIST**, Presiding Justice of Union Co., Ken. Rec 24 Mar 1826.

2399. Page 628. 7 Feb 1826. Ralph **DAUGHERTY**, Circuit Court Clerk, to Henry **SANFORD**. Appointment as Deputy Clerk. Signed R. **DAUGHERTY**. Wit D. **ARMOUR** (JP), John D. **COOK**, Judge of 4th Judicial Circuit. Rec 24 Mar 1826.

2400. Page 628. 23 Aug 1821. Jenifer T. **SPRIGG**, William **ROBERTS**, and Thomas **MOSLEY** Jr. to John **ERVIN**. For the sum of $663.99, Lot Nos. 70, 73, 15 & 13 in Bainbridge. Signed J. T. **SPRIGG**, William **ROBERTS**, Thomas **MOSLEY** Jr. Wit Wm. **McGUIRE**, Saml. **LOCKHART**, Theodore **JONES**, Abraham **BYRD**, Joseph **BENNETT**, JP in Madison Co., Mo. (as to Thomas **MOSELEY** Jr.), David **ARMOUR** (JP). Rec 25 Mar 1826.

2401. Page 629. 22 Dec 1824. Elizabeth **POWELL** to Winston **WHITWORTH**. For the sum of $100, 80 acres, being the W ½, SE ¼, Sec 24, Twp 33, Rng 9 E; being the same purchased by her of the U. S. A., Patent No. 378. Signed Elizabeth (x) **POWELL**. Wit Peter R. **GARRETT** (JP), John **YONT**. Rec 25 Mar 1826.

2402. Page 630. 29 Mar 1826. Thomas **MORGAN** to John **HALL** and Andrew **RAMSEY**. For the sum of $390, two tracts; 240 arpens, French measure, on the waters of Frank's Creek, a fork of Ramsey's Mill Creek, being all the tract whereon sd **MORGAN** now lives, and being the same bid off to sd **RAMSEY** and sd **HALL** for $350 on 24 Mar 1826, adjoining Robert **ENGLISH**, Alexander **SUMMERS**, and William **HAYDEN**, and being the same purchased by sd **MORGAN** of Allen **McKENZIE**, and which was the Spanish grant of sd **McKENZIE**; and a lot in Cape Girardeau, bounded on the N by the public square, S by a street, E by a street that also bounds the lots of B. **COUSIN**, and W by an improved lot sold by **LORIMIE** to sd **MORGAN** on 17 Jun 1806, and being the same bid off to sd **RAMSEY** and sd **HALL** at public sale on 24 Mar 1826 for $40. Signed Thos. **MORGAN**. Wit N. W. **WATKINS**, Robt. **IRWIN**, Peter R. **GARRETT** (JP). Rec 29 Mar 1826.

2403. Page 632. 29 Mar 1826. 29 Mar 1826. Thomas W. **GRAVES** and Mary Ann, his wife, to Frederick **OVERFIELD** and Mary, his wife. For the sum of $280, 40 acres in Cape Girardeau, being Outlot No. 42; part of a tract belonging to Louis **LORIMIER**, decd, sold by order of Circuit Court to Van B. **DLASHMUTT**, and by **STARLING & DLASHMUTT** to sd **GRAVES** on 25 Jul 1823. Signed Thomas W. **GRAVES**, Mary Ann **GRAVES** (RD). Wit Peter R. **GARRETT** (JP). Rec 31 Mar 1826.

2404. Page 633. 1 Apr 1826. John **ERWIN** to his children. For natural love and affection and toward their better support; to William, all his silversmith and mechanical tools, all his books, and $100; to Olivia, one bed and beadcloths and $100; to Teresa, one bed and bedclothes and $100; to Mary Ann, one bed and bedcloths and $100; to Orilla, one bed and bedcloths and $100; to John, 47 ½ acres in Ill. and $100; and to Columbus, 47 ½ acres of the same tract in Ill. as recorded in the General Land Office, $100, and all his household and kitchen furniture. Signed John **ERWIN**. Wit Thos. W. **GRAVES**, N. **WHITELOW**, George **FRICKE**, Hy. **SANFORD**, Peter R. **GARRETT** (JP). Rec 1 Apr 1826.

2405. Page 634. 7 Apr 1826. Martin **COTNER** and Mary, his wife, to John **COTNER**. For the sum of $50, 280 acres, more or less, being part of a tract confirmed to Martin **COTNER**; beginning at a post at the NE corner of sd survey. Signed Martin (x) **COTNER**, Mary (x) **COTNER** (RD). Wit Benja. **SHELL** (JP). Rec 8 Apr 1826.

2406. Page 637 [should be 635, but is mislabeled]. 6 Jan 1826. Lewis **DICKSON** to William **CREATH**. For the sum of $110, about 400 acres on Hubble's Creek, being part of 640 acres confirmed to Drusella **DICKSON**, excepting 240 arpents heretofore sold to John **RANDOL**; being the same he purchased at sheriff's sale on a execution against the heirs of Drusilla **DICKSON**. Signed Lewis **DIXON**.

Wit J. **RANNEY**, David **ARMOUR** (JP). Rec 17 Apr 1826.

2407. Page 636. 26 Dec 1825. Matthew **ALLEN** and Frances, his wife, to same. For the sum of $100, two tracts; 144.90 acres, being the SE fractional ¼, Sec 7, Twp 31, Rng 13 E; and 11.54 acres, being the SW fractional ¼, Sec 7, Twp 31, Rng 13 E. Both tracts were conveyed to sd **ALLEN** on 23 Nov 1824 by David **ARMOUR**, and to sd **ARMOUR** by Washington **STERRETT** on 4 Jun 1824, and originally patented to sd **STERRETT** on 7 Nov 1823 in Patent Nos. 197 & 198. Signed Matthew **ALLEN**, Frs. **ALLEN** (RD). Wit David **ARMOUR** (JP). Rec 17 Apr 1826.

2408. Page 637. 7 Apr 1826. John **SUMMERS** and Sarah, his wife, to Alexander **SUMMERS**. For the sum of $325, 640 acres, more or less, on the waters of Hubble's Creek, being all of a tract confirmed to John **SUMMERS** Junr.; bounded on the S by the confirmation of John **SUMMERS** Senr., N by Elijah **DAUGHERTY** and the heirs of Andrew **SUMMERS**, decd, and W by public lands. Signed John **SUMMERS**, Sarah **SUMMERS** (RD). Wit Hy. **SANFORD**, A. **GIBONEY**, David **ARMOUR** (JP). Proved by David **HOLLEY** and Daniel **STRINGER**. Rec 18 Apr 1826.

2409. Page 638. 7 Aug 1821. Martha **WHITE** to Wright **DANIEL**, both of Pulaski Co., Ark. Terr. For the sum of $600, 170 arpens, more or less, adjoining the heirs of **SUMMERS**, decd, and Thomas **ENGLISH**, decd; being part of 200 arpens confirmed to Lewis **LATHAM**, conveyed by him to Robert **CRAWFORD**, by sd **CRAWFORD** to James **McCLAIG**, by sd **McCLAIG** to Elisha **WHITE**, and willed by sd **WHITE** to Martha **WHITE**. Signed Martha (x) **WHITE**, Wright **DANIEL**. Wit Thos. P. **ESKRIDGE**, B. S. **COSTILLO**, Andrew **SCOTT**, Judge of Superior Court in Ark. Terr. Rec 10 May 1826.

2410. Page 639. 30 Oct 1824. Asaph **JETTON** to John **HELDERMAN**. For the sum of $160, 80 acres, being the W ½, NE ¼, Sec 25, Twp 31, Rng 11 E. Signed Asaph **JETTON**. Wit James O. **MORRISON**, John **MILLER**, George (x) **PROFFER**, David **ARMOUR** (JP). Rec 13 May 1826.

2411. Page 640. 25 Apr 1826. Ignatius **WATHEN** and Mary Ann, his wife and formerly Mary Ann **WATERS**, to Nathaniel **WICKLIFFE** of Nelson Co., Ken. For the sum of $1500, two tracts and other property; 200 arpens in Tywappity Bottom in Scott Co. Mo. in two parcels, one bounded on the E by the Mississippi River, S by the head right of Stephen **QUIMSBY**, W by public land, and N by Robert **LURER**(?) and being the same purchased by sd **WATHEN** and James **BRADY** of James **CURRAN** and Essey, his wife, the other adjoining the first and being ½ of the head right of Stephen **QUIMSBY**, purchased by sd **WATHEN** of James **BRADY**; their share of 400 arpens in Cape Girardeau Co., now in dispute in a suit brought by the heirs of Thomas W. **WATERS** against Robert **ENGLISH**, it being the interest to the tract of sd **WATHEN** and his wife Mary Ann, as one of the heirs of sd **WATERS**, with sd **WICKLIFFE** to be refunded the money for this tract if sd **ENGLISH** wins the suit; also their interest in 12 negroes held by Charles **ELLIS**, adminr de bonis non of the estate of sd **WATERS**, and their share of the hire of sd negroes since they have been in the possession of sd **ELLIS**; and all of their share of any other property belonging to the estate of sd **WATERS**. Signed Igs. **WATHEN**, M. A. **WATHEN**. Wit Hy. **SANFORD**, Dep Clerk. Rec 13 May 1826.

2412. Page 643. 21 Apr 1825. Benjamin **CARPENTER** and Sarah, his wife, to Samuel **MATTERSON**. For the sum of $190, 80 acres, more or less, being the W ½, SW ¼, Sec 13, Twp 31 N, Rng 13 E; being the same sd **CARPENTER** purchased of the U. S. on 6 Nov 1823. Signed Benjamin **CARPENTER**, Sarah **CARPENTER** (RD). Wit George **HENDERSON** (JP). Rec 15 May 1826.

2413. Page 644. 8 May 1826. Jenifer T. **SPRIGG** by Sheriff William **CREATH** to Johnson **RANNEY**. For the sum of $51.25, two tracts on or near the Mississippi River; about 160 acres, being the NE ¼, Sec 36, Twp 32 N, Rng 14 E, entered by William **ROBERTS**, sd **SPRIGG**, and Nathaniel W. **WATKINS**; and about 169.14 acres, being the W portion or ½ of Sec 31, Twp 32 N, Rng 15 E, entered by sd **ROBERTS** and sd **SPRIGG**. Sold on 14 Dec 1825 on an execution issued by Circuit Court on 2 Nov 1825 in favor of Lewis **DIXON** against Thomas **MOSELY**, James M. **CROPPER**, sd **SPRIGG**, and Medad **RANDOL** for $206.99 debt, $105.62 damages, and costs. Signed Wm. **CREATH**, Shff. Wit Hy. **SANFORD**, Dep Clerk. Rec 16 May 1826.

2414. Page 646. 15 Apr 1826. Daniel **WILLS** and John **SMITH**, execr of the last will and testament of Martin **RHYNE**, decd, to John **RHYNE**. On decree of Circuit Court in Chancery issued 15 Apr 1826, 80 acres, being the E ½, SE ¼, Sec 5, Twp 33 N, Rng 12 E. John **RHYNE** filed a bill of complaint in Circuit Court in Chancery on 11 Feb 1826 against sd **WILLS** and sd **SMITH**, claiming he purchased an improvement on public land in 1821; and being only age 20, Martin **RHYNE**, his father, purchased sd land with $100 provided by John **RHYNE** on 11 Sep 1821, and promised to convey the land to his son as soon as legal title could be obtained. Martin **RHYNE** assigned the receiver's receipt to John **RHYNE** on 27 Jan 1823, but did not transfer the land to John **RHYNE** before the patent was obtained. Signed Daniel **WILLS**, John **SMITH**, execr of the last will and testament of Martin **RHYNE**, decd. Wit Hy. **SANFORD**, Dep Clerk. Rec 11 May 1826.

2415. Page 649. 11 Apr 1826. Thomas **BYRNE**, execr of D. F. **STEINBECK**, decd, to David **DAVIS**. For the sum of $__ and on decree of Circuit Court in Chancery issued Apr Term 1826, 465 acres on the waters of Hubble's Creek, confirmed to John **STRONG** and Ithama **HUBBLE**; bounded on the W by John **AIKIN** and the **FITE** farm now owned by **RAVENSCROFT** and **GRAVES**, N by the **BURROWS** now owned by **RENFROE** and Isaiah **POE**, E by Joel **RENFROE** and the school tract, and S by Hiram **HADIN**, **BIRD**, sd **DAVIS**. Sd **STEINBECK**, in his lifetime, posted a bond for $12,000 on 26 May 1818 to make a deed, and died before doing so. This deed discharges that bond. Signed Thomas **BYRNE**, execr of D. F. **STEINBECK**. Wit J. **RANNEY**, Hy. **SANFORD**, Dep Clerk. Rec 17 May 1826.

2416. Page 650. 12 Apr 1826. Thomas **BYRNE**, execr of D. F. **STEINBECK**, decd, to Moses **McLAIN**. For the sum of $150 in leather and on decree of Circuit Court in Chancery issued 12 Apr 1826, the S ½, Lot No. 5 in Cape Girardeau, including **KIBLER**'s old tanyard, fronting on Spanish St. Sd **STEINBECK**, in his lifetime, posted a bond 2 Jul 1821 to make a deed to the lot after receiving the leather, and died before doing so. This deed discharges that bond. Signed Thomas **BYRNE**, execr of D. F. **STEINBECK**. Wit J. **RANNEY**, Hy. **SANFORD**, Dep Clerk. Rec 17 May 1826.

2417. Page 652. 22 Mar 1826. Morris **YOUNG** and Hannah, his wife, to George **MAIZE** and Stephen **BYRD**. For the sum of $200, 25 acres on the margin of White Water in the NW ¼, Sec 36, Twp 31 N, Rng 11 E, including Byrd's and

Maize's Mill; beginning at Ithamer **HUBBLE**'s line. Signed Morris **YOUNG**, Hannah **YOUNG**. Wit Hy. **SANFORD**, Wm. G. **BYRD**, John **PRIM**, John D. **COOK**, Judge of 4th Judicial Circuit. Rec 22 May 1826.

[End of Deed Book F]

INDEX

This index includes every name mentioned in the deed abstracts, as well as locations mentioned in the deeds. **Numbers refer to the numbers assigned to each deed for indexing purposes--not page numbers.** Grantees and grantors for each deed are boldfaced. In some cases where indexing names would be highly repetitive, names are not indexed. Examples include the Commmissioners of the Courthouse and Jail for Jackson (John Davis, John Sheppard, Samuel G. Dunn, Abraham Byrd, and Benjamin Shell), Commissioners to Partition Lands of the Heirs of Louis Lorimier (Bartholomew Cousin, William Kelso, and William Garner), and the heirs of Louis Lorimier (Daniel F. and Agatha Steinbeck, Victor Lorimier, Thomas Jefferson and Polly Rodney, and Augustus B. Lorimier).

Andrews, Alexr. 127
Andrews, Catharine **2240**
Andrews, Elisth. **95**
Andrews, Jonathan 1880
Andrews, Joseph **529**, **558**, **579**, **2240**
Anthony, Benjamin **182**, **241**, **723**
Anthony, George **896**
Armour, David (D.) **1105**, 1115, 1117, **1129-1130**, **1185**, 1235, **1390**, 1474, **1700**, 1702-1704, 1707-1708, 1715, **1768**, 1772-1773, 1775, 1799, 1815, 1820, 1828, **1845**, 1846, 1858-1859, 1861-1862, 1875, 1886-1889, 1891, 1912, 1921-1923, 1933, **1936**, **1948**, **1958**, 1969-1970, 2017, 2021, 2036, 2051, 2077, 2084, 2100, 2103-2104, 2139, 2144, 2152, 2160, **2162**, **2164**, 2165, 2167, 2227-2228, 2242, 2266, 2269, 2287, **2289**, 2290, **2312**, **2315**, 2318-2319, **2324**, 2334-2336, 2341, 2355, **2360**, **2373**, 2374, 2363-2364, 2368, 2373, 2382, 2386, 2388-2391, 2399-2400, 2406-2408, 2410
Armour, Solomon H. 1772, 1858, **2103**
Armstrong, Elisa (Eliza, Hulale) **1263**, **1455**, **1969-1970**
Armstrong, John **1230**, **1263**, **1410**, **1455**, 1479, **1819**, 1945, **1969-1970**, **2177**, 2327
Armstrong, Thomas 50
Arrel (Arel, Arrele, Arle, Arrell, Erles), James (see Earl) 8-9, **42**, 96, 152, 154, 211, 248, 256, **278**, **409-411**, 505-506, 627, 868, 1820
Arrel, Mary **410**
Arril, ___ 1147
Ashabrand, ___ 1803
Ashabranner (Ashembraner), Daniel (Danile) **14**, **104**
Ashabranner, Urbin 104
Ashley, Mary **694**, **714**
Ashley, Mr. 505
Ashley, William 1904
Ashley, William H. (Wm. H.) **256**, 269, **297**, **694**, **714**, 792,

905, 957, **1128**, 1180, 1466, 1609, 2044, 2146, 2172, **2265**, 2349-2350
Atkins, Henry 650
Atkins, James A. **2357**, **2361**
Austin, Ch. A. 579
Austin (Ausen, Auston), Harris 1172, 1262, 1813
Austin, Horrace 62-63, **65**
Austin, James 351
Averitt see Everett
Axley, Elisha 1188
Bacon, Benjamin **2290**, 2297, 2344, 2387, 2394, 2395
Bacon, Eliza S. 2387
Bacon, Stephen 1178, 1216, 1853, 2066, 2094
Bacon, William **929**, **1074**
Bagley, Asher 769
Bailey, Henry 1794
Bailey, Isaac **1698**
Bailey, John 463
Bailey, Moses **2092**
Bailey, Nathiel **1698**
Bailey (Baily, Baley, Baly, Bayles, Bemrie), Reason (Reson, Rezin, Rozein) 66, **124**, 169, **272**, 375, 937
Baker, Ewel 1706
Baker, George 2045, 2130, 2386
Baker, Henry **2229**
Baker, John **515**
Baker (Bakar), Joseph **101**, **797**, 1485, **2213**, 2279
Baker, Mary **2234**
Baker, Peter **2233**, **2235**
Baker, William 2340
Baldwin, John 501, **546**, **650**, 995, 1137, 1646, 2157
Baldwin, Samuel (Saml.) **361**, **384**, 1022
Ballew, ___ (see Bellew) 118
Ballew (Belew), Thomas (Thos.) 7, 58, 60, 62, 64, 68-70, 110, **117**, 129, 132, 135, **156-157**, 163, 249, **277**, 320, **380**, 388, 741-742
Ballinger, John **340**
Banigh (Benigh, Bennick, Bonig), Jeremiah 14, **108**, **182**, **241**, 723
Banigh (Bennick), Margaretha 182
Barber, Elias **1764**, **2068**, **2169**
Barber, Elias N. **1909**
Barker, Samuel 522
Barker, Samuel P. 728

Barnhart, Christopher 769
Barrott, John 1844
Bartlett, Daniel 1794
Barton, D. 714, 752, 805
Barton, David 793
Barton, Joshua 1682-1683, 1695, 1697 1700, 1702-1704, 1707-1709, 1711, 1716, 1765, 1776, 1786-1787, 1828, 1850
Bates, Edw. 787
Bates, Frederick 221-222, **234**, **306**, **308**, **309**, **310**, **311**, **315**, **318**, **335**, **343**, 344, **358**, **360**, 390, **397**, **423-424**, **426**, **449**, 475, 539, 545, 552, 562, 567, 586, 588, **595-607**, **611**, 613, **615**, 617, 632-635, **638**, 640-641, 643, 645, 662, **675**, 690, 695, 702, 705-706, 711, 720, 727, 729, 731-732, 753, 777, 782, 784-785, 799, 836, 857, 865, 874, 882, 942, 985-986, 997, 1036, 1046, **1206**, **1260**, **1264**, **1413**, 1487, 1518, 1893, **2306-2307**, **2312**, **2315**, **2318**, **2320**, **2324**
Bates, Robert **1569**, **1655**, 1658
Beardsley, John 581-582, 685
Beasly, James 848
Beaty, Adam **961**
Beaty, Francis 961, 1035
Beaty, John **961**
Beaty, Joseph **961**
Beaty, Mary **961**
Bellew (Belew, Below, Billew, Billue, Blew), Peter (see Ballew) 42, **57**, 166, 769, 822, 1101, **1149**, 1180, 1197, **1243**, 1605, 1609, 1844, 2098, 2260, 2369, 2371, 2383, 2398
Bellew, Polly **1149**, 1243, 1609
Bennett (Bennette), Levi **1117**
Bennett, Joseph 2400
Bent, Silas 739
Bergan (Bergen, Burgen, Burgon), Michael **130**, 285, 1870
Bergin, ___ 122
Berry, John 1417
Berry, Margart 910
Berthiaume, Francois **294**, **965**, 1981
Best, Catharine **1699**
Best, John **1699**

Bettis, Elijah 649, **703**, **843-844**
Bettis, Elijah Jr. **842**
Bettis, Overton 703
Bibb, George 668
Bibb, Thomas 658
Bicknell, Geo. A. 1844
Bilderback, Ephraim **432**, 787, **1159**
Bilderback, John **432**, **786**, 787, **1159**, **1481**
Binkley, Adam 548
Binkley, John **1216**, **1478**, 2032, 2161
Bird (see Byrd)
Bird, ___ 143, 2415
Bird, A. 956
Bird, G. A. 2011, 2026, 2388
Bird, Gustavus A. **1937**
Bird, Mary 2072-2073
Bird, S. A. 1607
Birdwell, David 1823
Bishop, Rezin L. 2084
Black William **1089**
Black, John Sr. **763**
Black, Simon Jr. 2063
Blackman, C. N. 1224-1225
Blackmore, ___ 1855
Blackmore, C. N. 788
Blackmore, C. W. 892
Blackmore, Charles N. **1437**, 2085
Blackmore, Charles W. **1502**
Blackmore, Mary 1502, **2085**
Blair, Francis 2086, **2396**
Blair, R. 366
Blair, Robert (Robt.) 214-216, 224, **234**, 242-245, 257, 276-277, 284, 287, 289-293, 313, 332, 378, 380-382, 386, 390, 394, **407**, 414, 418, 419, **423**, 429, 437, 440, 484, 618, 771
Blair, Thomas **1922**
Blanks, Jesse 350
Bledsoe, Anthony 1860
Bledsoe, Caty **521**
Bledsoe, Isaac **742**, **1860**, **2242**
Bledsoe, Isaac M. **297**, 345, 393, **434**, 445, 474, 521
Bledsoe, William Lytle **521**
Block, Simmons Jr. **1592**
Blundridge, Simeon 87
Blunt, Joel 756, 798, 931, 956, 1109, 1235, 1793, 1844, **1845**, **1859**, 1862, 1936, 1972, **2104**, **2355**
Blythe, Sth. 1437
Boad(?), ___ 2020

Bogard, Jacob 223, 1518
Bohannon, George **2063**
Bolduc, Agathe **1058**
Bolin, S. R. 1105, 1127
Bolin (Bolen), Solomon R. 817, 954, **1036**, 1039, 1041, 1046, 1050, 1069, 1072-1075, 1107, 1115-1116, 2021, 2168
Bolin, William 884, **1107**
Boling, Lewis **1883**
Boling, Thomas **1489**, **1883**
Boling, William **1883**
Bollinger, Aaron 1055
Bollinger, Andrew 1468
Bollinger, Catharine (Katharine) **104**, **2004**
Bollinger (Bullinger, Bullingor), Daniel (Danil) 14, 113, 241, 469, 723, 834, 1041
Bollinger, Daniel Sr. (Danil Sr.) 1041, 2317, **2370**
Bollinger (Bullinger), David 74, **1885**
Bollinger, Elizabeth, widow 1596
Bollinger (Bullinger), Frederick (Frederic) **340**, 2177
Bollinger (Bullinger), Frederick G. **766**
Bollinger (Bolinger), George Frederick (F.) **767**, **829-830**, 856, **973**, 819, 895, 969, 1067, **1489**, **1885**, 1894, 1908, 2258, **2303**, **2385**
Bollinger (Bullinger), Henry (Heinrich, Henary, Henery) 113, **425**, 840, **841**, **872**, **1041**, 1803, 1805, **1894**, 2144, 2177, 2317
Bollinger, Henry Sr. **2004**
Bollinger (Bullinger), Jacob 872, **1381**, 1894, **2026**
Bollinger (Bullinger), John 104, 345, **425**, 840-841, 1089, 2004, 2144
Bollinger (Bullinger), John Sr. (Johannes) 425, **840**, 872, 2026
Bollinger, Mathias **1067**
Bollinger, Phillip (Philip) 14, **834**, 1699, **2203**, 1894
Bollinger, Phillip, heirs of 1104, 1597
Bollinger (Bullinger), Solomon (Sollomon) 840, **1089-1093**

Bond, Edward F. (Edwd. F, Edw. F) 1, 5, 17, 25, 76, 78, 82, 110, **111**, 115, 117, 131, **134**, **151**, **208**, 213, 375, 507, 544, 547, 673, 1106, **1110**, 1118, 1155, 2362
Bond, Shadrach 1157, 1159, 1188, 1950
Boner (Bonner), Catherine **292**, **419**
Boner (Bonar, Bonner), William (Willm.) 13, **22**, 235, 284, **292**, **366**, **419**, 808, **1253**, 1861
Boon, William 280
Boran, Bazel 507, 518, 554
Bortonarchis(?), Joshua 2246
Bounes, ___ 526
Bovey, Louis 769
Bovi, Joseph 2277
Bowden, Catherine 593
Bowden, Jesse **66**, 139, 201, 203, 348, 386, **593**
Bower, Reubn. H. 1047
Bowie (Booy, Boyei), Reece 139-140, 251, 592, 593
Boyce, ___ 1452
Boyce, Benjamin **1164**
Boyce, George 719
Boyce, George W. **1388**, 1428
Boyce (Boice, Byse), Jonathan (Johnathan) 1229, 1451, 1453-1454
Boyce, Susanna R. 825, 894, 1183
Boyce, Thomas 1007, 1086, 1164
Boyce, Thomas R. 1876
Boyd, Elizabeth 517
Boyd, J. 26, 132, 797
Boyd, James (Jas., Js.) 4, **24**, 42, 57, 61, 69, 71, 124, 264, 269, 271-272, 321, 338, 458-459, 461-462, 465, 470, 486, 497, **507**, 517, **518**, 527, 542, 544, 564, 648, 708-709, 772, 860, 1095, 1106, 1128, **1142**, 1904
Boyd, John (Jno., Joh., Jon) 41, 45, 55, 64, **95**, 254, 321, 379, 414, **517**, 526, **564**, 648, 1095
Boyd, Poly **321**
Boyd, Sally (Sallay) **507**, 544, 1904
Boyd, Sarah **518**, **1142**
Boyer, Henry 1462
Bradley, ___ 902-903

Chandler & Price 477-**478**

Chaney (Chany, Cheney),
Lemuel 79, **87**, 120-121,
138, 142-143, 237, 253, 301,
320, 408

Charlton, James 2085

Cheek, James 935-936

Chevalier, Andre 35

Chevalier, P. 35

Chevaliers, Joseph **35**

Chevaliers, Joseph Jr. 35

Childress, Joel 2246

Christy, W. 694

Christy, William 1022, **1827**,
2022

Christy, Wm. Jr. 1688

Clark, Francis **697**

Clark, John 1426, 1432

Clark (Clarke), John R. **2187**,
2189, 2278

Clark, Robert P. 1170

Clark, Sally 1426

Clark, William **632-637, 640-
641, 643, 645, 662, 690-691,
695, 702, 705-706, 711-713,
720, 727, 729, 731-732, 734,
753, 777, 782, 784-785, 799,
836, 857-858, 865, 874, 889,
985-986, 997, 1003-1004,
1036, 1046, 1162-1163,
1267, 1461, 1470-1472,
1477, 1525**

Clay, Henry **2378-2379**

Clemmer, George **1990**

Clinard, Henry **1216, 1478-
1479**, 1764, 1949, **2032-
2033**, 2075, **2219**

Clingingsmith, Daniel 1045,
1446, 1485

Clippard (Clipperd), Daniel
1111, 1269, 2118

Cobb, F. W. 293

Coburn, Phineas (Phinehas)
921, 930, 1066, 1263, 1478,
1817, 2032, 2161, **2175, 2329**

Cochran, Betsey (Betcy) **671,
2053**

Cochran, G. W. 500

Cochran, George W. (Geo. W.)
609, 671, 980, **1022**, 1052,
2053

Cochran, John 726, 1854

Cochrun, Jos. 104

Cocke, Mary 754

Cocke, R. 754

Cockerham, Henry (Hy.) **289**,
408, 451, **587**

Cockerham, John Y. 587

Cofer, Ellis M. 2317

Coleman, Green H. 2110

Colglazer, John 1863

Collier & Powell **2065**

Collier, George **2065**

Collier, Michael **1899**

Collier, Michael Jr. **2071, 2348**

Collins, Samuel 1147

Colwell, Caty 1045

Commans, William 1034

Commissioners of the
Courthouse and Jail **663,
694, 701, 737, 743-745, 747,
749, 755, 766, 779, 791, 806,
812, 817, 819, 824-827, 829-
830, 894, 899, 901, 906, 918,
927, 960, 962, 971, 982,
1010, 1013, 1066, 1073,
1101, 1105, 1124, 1127,
1129-1130, 1132, 1134,
1145, 1168, 1178, 1183,
1220, 1246-1247, 1274,
1377, 1436, 1466-1469,
1475-1476, 1499, 1689-1691,
1694, 1777, 1805, 1811,
1824, 1831, 1885, 1900-
1902, 2080, 2104, 2203,
2212, 2225, 2346**

Commissioners to Partition
Land of the Heirs of Louis
Lorimier **1277, 1287-1289,
1358-1376, 1379, 1384-1385,
1395, 1398-1400, 1412,
1415, 1418-1425, 1443,
1445, 1504-1506, 1508-1511,
1513-1514, 1520-1524, 1575-
1578, 1582-1591, 1593-1595,
1598-1604, 1610, 1615-1618,
1621, 1623-1635, 1639-1640,
1642-1644, 1680, 1684-1687,
1693, 1701, 1712-1713,
1717-1732, 1734-1736, 1760-
1762, 1769, 1779, 1785,
1790-1792, 1812, 1814,
1825, 1832, 1834-1837,
1864, 1867-1868, 1871,
1881, 1924, 1926-1932,
1954-1955, 1993-1994, 2102**

Conaway (Conway), Jeremiah
(Gerry, Jerry) **57**, 218, **219**,
263, 313, 409, **514, 557, 563**,
772, **822**, 883, 1070-1072,
1605, 2246

Conaway, Mr. 246

Conaway, Rachel **822**

Condelet, Baronade 751

Connelly (Conely), Hugh 4,
43, 726, 2121

Connelly (Conely), Hugh Sr.
1027

Connelly, Timothy **12**, 31, 657,
2204

Conrad, Ephraim R. **2004-2005**

Conway, Jas. S. 1114

Conyers, James **491, 502**

Conyers, John **490-491, 528**

Conyers, Mary (Polley) **502**

Cook, George K. **1542**

Cook, John D. 1001, **2147**,
2356, **2376**, 2391, 2399, 2417

Cooper, ___ 609

Cooper (Coopers), James (Jas.)
42, 43, **44**, 170, 671, 673,
2090

Cooper, Robert 650

Cooper, Saml. 1892

Cooper, Thomas 767

Corman(?), John 831

Cornelius, Jeptha **36**

Cornelius, Joseph 769

Costillo, B. S. 1048, 1191-
1194, 1282, 2409

Costillo, Burrell (Burrel) S.
925, **1061, 1195**, 1409, **1411**

Cotes, Merit 1958

Cotner, ___ 1489

Cotner, David **2110**

Cotner, Jacob 2110, **2300**

Cotner, John **2405**

Cotner, Martin 717, **1976**,
2405

Cotner, Mary **2405**

Cotner, Poley 2110

Cottle, James **122**, 130, 362,
688

Cottle, Susana **688**

Cottner, Maryat 1976

Coursang, Mr. 52

Cousant, ___ 233

Cousants, ___ 339

Cousin (Cousins, Cousung,
Cozen), B. 15, 18-20, 23-24,
26, 31, 41, 45, 49, 54, 56, 70,
73, 77, 80, 86, 94-95, 108,
123, 137, 146, 159, 174-175,
177, 184-196, 225-226, 252,
258, 284, 292, 294-295, 303-
304, 325, 332, 373, 378, 389,
407, 435, 468, 483-484, 497,
498-499, 504, 507, 511-513,
517-518, 529, 544, 554, 568,
577, 619, 627, 639, 659-661,
665, 686, 808, 978, 990, 998,
1014-1017, 1031-1032, 1053,
1106, 1156, 1161, 1254,
1460, 1463, 1481, 1493,

1526, 1608, 1797, 1840, 1942, 2137, 2402
Cousin (Cousins), Bartholomew (Barthe., Bartholimew, Barthelemi, Bmy.) 8-9, 12-13, **21**, 27, 71, 107, **197**, **198**, 254, 326, 379, 452, **453-456**, **675-676**, 556, 587, **987**, **1008**, **1097**, 1255, **1492**, 1494, **1547**, **1629**, **1636**, **1720-1722**, **1730**, **1780**
Cowan, Robert **2197**
Cowherd, William 2255, **2256**, 2260
Cox, ___ 86
Cox, Anna **912**
Cox, Elizabeth **699**, **913**, **1414**
Cox, George 1810
Cox, James (Jas.) 47, 56, 213, 870, 951, 976, 1822, 2247
Cox, James Jr. 240, 320, **527**, 628, **699-700**, **912**, 913, **1198**, 1250
Cox, James Sr. 55, **699**, 700, **907**, **912-913**, **974**, 1198, 1226, **1414**, **1780**
Cox, John Jr. 1592
Cox, William (Wm.) 341, 462, 884, **1414**, 2123, **2142**
Cox, William W. (Wm. W.) 526, 653
Cozens, Horatio 2246
Cracraft (Cracroft), Elizabeth **1239**, 1692
Cracraft (Cracroft, Craycraft), William 422, **425**, **540**, **696**, **798**, 826, 855, 907, 1002, **1012**, **1054**, 1065, **1213**, 1215, **1239**, 1387, **1388-1389**, 1414, **1692**, **1957**, **2105**, **2381**
Cracroft, Charles 1002, 2382
Cracroft, John 2382
Crader, ___ 2277
Crader (Greder), Abraham **1043-1044**
Crader (Greter), Daniel **339**, **2062**
Crader, David 2034
Crader, Elizabeth **2062**
Crader, Jacob **1043-1044**, **2120**
Crader, Jacob [Jr.] **2062**
Crader (Crater), Jacob [Sr.] 2062
Crader, Polly **2062**
Crader (Grader), Samuel **1043-1044**, **2062**, **2120**
Crader, Susanah 1205

Craft, William 1426
Craftin, Paul 1874
Craftin, Robert **1874**
Craig, P. 371
Craig, Peter 276, 287, **438-439**, 646, **664**, **763**, **820**
Cramer & Spear 1844
Crath, George 114
Cravens, Jeremiah **961**, **1035**
Cravens, W. 961
Cravens, William **1035**
Crawford, Ann (Anny) **443**, **2034**
Crawford, Elizabeth **620**, **656**, **767**, **851-852**, **856**
Crawford, James 414, **856**, 1228, 2025, **2034**
Crawford, Moses **1284**
Crawford, Robert **537-538**, 574, **620**, **656**, 699, **767**, 798, **851-852**, **856**, 1226, 2409
Crawford, Thompson 767
Crawford, William 442
Creatch, George 114
Creath, Albert G. **2383**
Creath, Martha P. **2363**
Creath, N. 1987
Creath, Nathaniel (Nathl.) 1645, 1798, 1998, **2384**
Creath, William (Wm.) **1206**, 1234, 1241, 1247, 1262, 1269, 1271-1273, 1281, 1377-1378, 1386, 1404, 1409-1410, 1417, 1426, 1429-1430, 1434-1435, 1455-1456, 1478-1480, 1482, 1490-1491, 1494, 1496-1497, 1503, 1512, 1516, 1606, 1614, 1622, 1636, 1638, 1641, 1645, 1648, **1681**, **1707**, 1765-1766, 1774-1775, 1783-1784, 1786-1788, 1793, 1795, 1797-1798, 1801, 1807, 1823, 1839, 1845, 1853, 1878, 1893, 1895-1896, 1901-1902, 1908, 1910, 1913, 1942, 1948-1949, 1963, 1971-1972, 1978-1979, 1982, 1986, 1987-1988, 1995, 1998, 2006, 2010, 2013-2014, 2020-2021, 2028, 2030-2031, 2040, 2053, **2055-2056**, 2066, 2080, 2093-2094, 2113, 2117, 2124, 2134, 2145, 2147-2151, 2164, 2168, 2173-2178, 2180, 2255, 2257-2258, 2260,

2273, 2276, 2305, 2315, **2323-2324**, 2325-2331, 2354-2355, 2358-2360, **2363**, 2365-2366, 2373, 2378-2379-2382, **2384**, **2406-2407**, 2413
Cresswell (Creswell), ___ 728, 818, 823, 908
Cresswell (Chriswell, Creswell, Crisswell, Criswell, Curswell), Hugh **118**, 152-153, **154**, 254, **258**, 384, 388, 438, 717, **877**, 1012, **1023**, 1026, **1064**, 2099, 2308
Creswell, Nancy **877**, **1064**
Criddle, E. 1042
Criddle, Edward **735**, 863, 1409, 1433, 1438-1440, **1455**, 1820, 2221, 2284-2285
Crisson, James 1844
Crites, Elizabeth 736
Crites, Mary **736**
Crites, Peter **736**
Crites, Rhua 2092
Crits, Henry 1824
Crits, Peter Jr. 2198
Crize, Davald 14
Cromwell, John **394**, 440
Cropper (Crooper), James M. **1232**, **1435**, **1452**, **1454**, **1696**, **1846**, 2413
Cropper, Jm. 1401, 1444
Crosby, Thomas W. 933
Cross, John 474, 616, 625, **1141**, **1265-1266**, **1448-1450**, 1459, **1567**, **1636**, **1639-1640**, **1653**, **1816**, **1844**, **1848**, **1966**, **2043**, 2072, 2328, **2376**, 2398
Cross, Maria J. **1332**, **1400**, **1701**, **1739**
Crouch, Spencer 1844, 2252-2253
Crouse, ___ 477-478, 551
Crouse, William (Wm.) 2009, 2026
Crowley, Fanny **948**
Crowley, Samuel **948**
Crowtz, William 505
Crump, Robert **132**, 161, 724, 821, 2198, 2287
Crump, Robert [Jr.] 377
Crump, Robert Sr. **377**
Crutchelow (Critchlow, Crutchlow, Schchelou), Joseph **48**, **53**, 127, 487
Culbert, Thomas 1860
Cummins, Nancy 563
Cunsberl, D. 1793

Garrett, Jacob **795**, **814**, **882**, 1091-1093
Garrett, P. R. 1980, 2048, 2130, 2006
Garrett (Garret), Peter R. 1904, 1934, 1948, 2001, 2003, 2009, 2029, 2067, **2077**, 2116, 2122, 2125, **2126**, 2130, 2133, 2143, 2154-2156, 2161, 2164, 2166, 2168-2169, 2180, 2194, 2196, 2212, 2218, 2222, 2239, 2247, 2256, 2258-2259, 2267, 2270, 2273, 2291-2292, 2296, 2299, 2306-2307, 2309, 2312, 2314, 2312, **2315**, 2320, 2323, 2334, **2335**, **2341**, 2369, 2393, 2401, 2402-2404
Gates, Christian **469**, **1010**, **1434**, **1494**, **1797**, 1809, **2127**, **2150**, 2173, 2328
Gates, Samuel 1428
Geistwite, Joseph **1838**, **2357**
Genereux (Generuuex), Joseph 1487, 1893
Gibbins, A. E. 754
Gibbonee, ___ 40
Gibbs, Samuel **1432**
Gibler, Frederick (Frederck) 163, 167, **225-226**, 284, 328, 351, **383**, 445, **498-499**, **629**
Giboney, A. 2408
Giboney (Guibony), Alexander 12, 27, 519, 657, 987, 2204
Giboney (Gibony, Guiboney), Andrew **1408**, **1626**, **1651**, **1668**, **1993-1994**, 2123, **2204**
Giboney (Gibboney), Elizabeth 976, **1285-1286**
Giboney (Gibboney, Gibbony, Gibbonie, Guiboney, Guibony), John 27, **31**, 55-56, **110**, 148-149, 195, 199, 213, **244-245**, 357, **460**, **563**, **576**, **581-582**, 772, 822, 902, 913, **976**, **987-988**, **1148**, 1174, **1285-1286**, 1611, 1795, 1840, **2012**
Giboney (Gibboney), Margaret **2123**, **2204**
Giboney (Gibony), Rebecca 938
Giboney (Gibboney, Gibbony, Gibony, Guibony), Robert **31**, **244-245**, **276**, 345, 523, 573, 655, 819, 939, 955, 976, 987, 1039, **1148**, 1182, **1505-**

1507, **1544**, **1553**, **1657**, **1790**, 2072-2073, 2157, 2204, **2326**
Gibony, Isabell **2204**
Gibson, Arra Minter 111
Gibson, Betsey (Betsy) 82, 111, 151, **208**, 2362
Gibson, Jno. 312, 323, 324
Gilbreth, James **280**
Gilchrist, Robert 2398
Giles, John 861, **1190**, 1637-1638, 1942, 2124
Gill, John & Co. 1844
Gillaspie, Andrew P. 1172, **1518**, 1609
Gilleland, John 1895
Gilliss, John W. 1856
Gitt, W. 1649-1650
Gitt, William W. 1540, 1737, 1752
Given, Joseph R. 1844
Glasscock (Glascock), Charnal **1183**, **1402**, **1648**, 1939, 2158
Glasscock (Glascock), Fieldin (Feeling) **1125-1126**, 1177
Glasscock (Glascock), Jane 2116, **2222**, 2319
Glasscock (Glascock), John 1192-1193, 1648, 1844, 1940, 1943, **2086**, 2135-2136
Glasscock, Polly **1402**
Glasscock (Glascock), Scarlet (Scarlett) **1168**, 1176, 1224, **1235-1236**, **1391**, **1405**, 1478, **1648**, 2003, **2067**, **2107**, **2116**, **2178**, 2195, **2222**, **2319**
Gobeau, Jno. B **114**
Godair, Batist 911
Godair, Essix **197**
Godair, John Baptiste (Bapts., Batiste, Bte.) 780, **839**, 1971, 2165
Godair (Godaire, Godar), Peter (Pierre) **22**, **31**, **197**, 242, **284**, 292, 402, 419, **476**, 572, 614, 618, 627, 670, **682**, 683, **1252**, 1253, 1861
Goings, C. S. 814
Goodin, Ben 29-30, 454
Goosing, Mr. 53
Gordon, Geo. 692
Gordon, Robert 1181
Gordon, William **884-885**, **1114**, 1706, 1778
Goulke, Charles 1844
Goza, James 1258
Goza, John 463

Goza, Joshua 271, **273**, 463, **526**, 651, 696, 2224, 2352
Goza (Gosey), Mary **875**
Goza, Michael 2246
Goza (Gozy), Polly **862**
Grafton, Jas. D. 2192
Graham, Aaron 432, 787
Graham, George (Geo.) 2163, 2181-2190, 2193, 2197, 2199-2202, 2205-2211, 2213-2216, 2229-2238, 2243-2245, 2248-2251, 2262-2263, 2347, 2372
Graham, James 2129
Graham (Grayham), Thomas **207**, **330**, 416, **2129**
Graham, William T. (Will. T.) 2043, **2334**, **2336**
Graham, Wm. 2129
Graves, ___ 2415
Graves, John 557
Graves, Mary **1240**
Graves, Mary Ann **2403**
Graves, Thomas W. (Thos. W.) 651, **696**, **698**, **858**, 859, 1214, 1239, **1240**, 1438, **1565**, **1577**, 1807, **1890**, **2017**, **2022-2023**, **2041**, **2117**, **2145**, 2153, 2196, 2255, 2260, **2261**, 2368, **2403**, 2404
Gray, A. 1619
Gray, John C. 1609
Green, ___ 155
Green, Clary **1113**, **1944**, **2083**, 2286
Green, David 51, 55, 477-478, **500**, 551, **606**, 665, 735, **863**, **1082**, 1144
Green, Elizabeth **1082**, 1403
Green, Jane 500
Green, Parish 628, **790**, **796**, 801, 809, **1113**, 1144, 1229, **1944**, 1958, **2083**, 2158, **2286**, **2295**, **2304**
Green, Robert (Robt.) 16, **17**, 26, 28, 51, 73, 146, 152-154, 161, 164-165, 172, 206, 229, 253-255, 259-261, 263, 268, 270, 281, 285-286, 294-296, 298-299, 300-302, 321, 325-326, 328, **335**, 359, 363, 391-392, 453, 477-478, 481, **500**, 509, **545**, 551, **613**, **632**, 636-637, 644, **665**, 666, 676-677, **702**, 707-709, 713, 735, 757, 890, 914, 968, **1267**, **1886**, **1889**, 1990, **2284-2285**

612, 616, 619, 624-626, 627-
628, 654, 657, 660-661, 659,
673, 683, 686, 689, 693, 698,
725, 1031, 1140
Henderson, George (Geo.) 1-3,
6, 33-34, 51, 149, 184, 193,
205, 211, 217, 257, **296**, 301,
307, **309**, **310**, **311**, 317, 327,
344, 345-346, 350, 351, 352,
354-357, 361, 363-374, 377,
379, 383, **385**, **386**, 387-389,
390, **392**, 393, 395-396, 398-
399, 400-401, 402, 405-406,
409-412, 414, 416-417, 420-
422, 430-431, 433-436, 438-
440, 443-445, 448, 450-451,
458-462, 465, 466, 470-471,
474, 476, 477-478, **481**, 482,
484, 487-488, 494, 496, 498-
499, **504**, **539**, **552-553**, 555,
598, **602-603**, **611**, 615, 639,
646, 648, 665-666, **667**, 668,
681, **707-709**, 718, 771, **774**,
775, **778**, **782**, 808, 816, 834-
835, 839, 845, 866, 873, 884-
885, **880**, 891, 896, 909, 915,
924, 935-936, 940-941, 950-
951, 955, 958, 965, 967, 970,
976-978, 983, 990, 992-994,
996, 1006, 1008-1009, 1014-
1017, 1030, 1032, **1037**,
1053, 1076-1077, 1079-1080,
1096, 1097, 1100, 1110,
1122-1123, 1140-1141, 1174,
1148, 1153, 1150, 1169,
1222-1223, 1251-1255, **1256**,
1259, 1276, **1334**, 1382,
1385, 1392-1394, 1414,
1442, 1459-1460, **1513-1514**,
1515, 1524, **1530**, **1548**,
1579, 1580-1581, 1613,
1615, **1660**, **1682**, **1684-
1686**, 1693, 1695, 1697,
1700, 1717-1719, 1731-1733,
1745, **1753**, **1757**, 1778-
1779, 1814, **1815**, 1816,
1830, 1841, 1848, 1870-
1871, **1872**, 1916, 1925,
1952, 1974-1975, 1991,
2027, 2072-2073, 2112,
2137, 2147, **2153**, **2167**,
2254, **2257**, 2264, 2271,
2320, 2367, 2386, 2398, 2412
Henderson, John, Capt. 718
Henderson, Mathew 2344
Hendrick, Henry 470, 486
Hendricks, ___ 1431
Hendricks, Abraham 2142

Hendricks, John **2345**
Henry, F. M. 214, 215, 216, 375
Henthorn, John **428**
Herbert, John 920
Herbert, John & Co. **1059-1061**, **1236**, **1681**
Hew, Ilsey 491
Hewitt, Homan 1282
Hickman, ___ 1431
Hickman, Austin **1151**
Hickman, Daniel **1151**, **2191**
Hickman, James 667-668
Hickman, John W. **1959**
Hickman, Mary **1959**(2)
Hickman, Peter T. **1959**
Hickman, Robert **1151**
Hickman, Theophilus 280
Hickman, Thomas J. **1959**
Hickman, W. P. 1958
Hickman, William (Wm.) 591,
1857, **1874**, **1944**, **1946**,
1958, 1960, **2273**
Hickman, William P. **1959-1960**
Hickmon, Ann **2191**
Hickmon, Micajah **2191**
Higginbotham, J. B. 1838
Hightower, Charnal **1098**
Hile, David 2352
Hile, Ezekiel **2302**, **2311**
Hile, Rachel **2311**
Hiler, David 877, **1121**
Hill, Ezekiel **1094**, **2333**
Hill, Isaac 502
Hill, John 958
Hill, Mary **516**
Hill, William 8, 155
Hill, William Sr. **516**, **531**
Hinck (Hinch), Samuel 1449, 1816
Hinkle (Hincle), Peter **1503**
Hitt, Benjamin 527, 628, 699-700, **911**, 912, 1198
Hitt, Frances **818**, **1198**
Hitt, John **178**, 436, **531**, 612,
628, **818**, 1144, **1198**, 1212,
1227, 1771, 2019
Hitt, John Jr. **1250**, 1898
Hitt, John Sr. **913**, **1250**, 1592
Hitt, William 168, 699, 912, **2214**
Hoble, Eithamore 176
Hodges (Hodge), Isaac **1465**, 2151
Hodges (Hodge), James 1465, 2151
Hofman, John 1990

Hogan, David 650
Hogan, Edmond (Edmd, Edmund) 31, 238-239, 342,
347, 348-349, **358**, 403-404,
408, 415, 501, **546**, **650**,
1137, 1427-1428
Hogan, Edwd. 331
Hogan, Patsey (Patsy) 501, **650**
Holcomb, James **2372**
Holley (Holly), David 240,
679, 1028, 1188, **1285-1286**,
2012, 2311, **2329**, **2333**, 2408
Holley, Delilah **2333**
Hollister, Edward 1949
Holmes, William 682
Hood, William 2325
Hooker, Geo. 574
Hoover, Felix (Felex, Philix)
432, **786**, 787, 1159, 1481
Horn, Joseph 1410
Horrell (Horrel), Benjamin **1233**
Horrell, Benjamin (Benjn.) M.
1182, 1265, 1592, **1861**, 2007
Horrell (Horel), John **1158**,
1190, **1441**, **2101**, 2127,
2154, 2291, 2296
Horrell, Maximilian
(Maxamillian) **1106**, **2020**, 2362
Horsley, Thomas Y. 420
Horton, Elihu 371
Hotchkiss, Miles 280
Houk, John 964
Houser (Hooser), Daniel **1029**,
1099, 1934
Housten, Mary 2095
Houts, ___ 1024, 2369
Houts, C. G. 1844
Houts (Hauts), Christr
(Christo.) G. 1224, **1681**
Houts (Hautz), Christopher
1021, **1058**, **1066**, 1178,
1234, **1271-1272**, **1497**,
2079, 2255, 2260
Houts, John 2310
Houts, John C. 2098
Houts, Letitia G. **1271-1272**
Houts, Rutter 1211
Houts, Sally **2383**
Houts, Thomas 1844, **2098**,
2260, **2383**
How, John **2317**
Howard, Benjamin 475, **539**,
545, **552-553**, **562**, **567**, **586**,
588, **613**
Howard, Henry (Hennery) **37**,
994, 2127

1290, **1298**, 1299, 1308,
1328, **1331**, 1332, **1341**,
1350-1351, **1374-1376, 1534**,
1573, **1580-1581**, 1674-1677,
1686, 1717, 1744, **1757**,
1758, 1815, **1848-1849**,
1871-1872, 1925-1926, 1933,
1952, **1967, 1973**, 1974,
2117, 2254, **2298**, 2358, 2366
Lorimier, William (Gm., Gme.)
206, 299, 328, **367**, 368, 437,
440, 467, 616, 661, 754, 978,
1276, 2274-2275
Lorimier, William Jr. **1719**,
1781
Losla, John 619, **659**
Loslea, ___ 721
Love, ___ 2362
Love, Betsey **2362**
Love, John G. 921, **1028**,
1099, **1124, 1126-1127**,
1189, **1218, 1891, 1964**,
1979, 2016, 2040, 2130, **2150**
Love, Mrs. 2127
Love, Rebecca (Rebecka)
1218, 2016, 2040
Love, Samuel **848, 2130**
Loveing (Loveng), Elijah
2337-2338
Lowr (Lohr), Valetine **233**
Lowrie, Mathew B. 1465
Lowry (Lowery, Lowrey),
William (Wm.) 64, 70, 454,
532, **627**
Loyd, Delily **202-203**
Loyd, John 7, 144-145, 201,
202-203, 348, **493, 566**, 578
Loyd, W. 203
Loyd, Wm. 202
Lucas (Lucus), Charles (Chas.)
372, 590, 697, 708, 787, 910,
1134
Lucas, James 120
Lucas, John (Jno.) B. C. 128,
240, 617, 769, 787
Lunceford, Wm. 429
Lurer(?), Robert 2411
Luslay, John 680
Lusley, ___ 526
Lyon, Chittenden (Chittendan)
482, 488, 513, 524, 1847
Mabry (Mayberry), Benjamin
(Benjn.) **1102-1103**
MacDonald, Alexander **2364**
Maddne, Richd. 2194
Madison, John H. **640**, 643,
1020

Magee, Joseph (Jos.) (see
McGee) **144-145**, 589
Magness, Morgan 1018
Maize (Meaize), George **1873**,
2351, 2375, **2417**
Maloan, Elisa 2294
Malone, James 2348
Malone, Jonathan (Jont.) **1160**,
2107
Malone, Obadiah (Obe.) **1380**,
1464, 2294, 2319, 2337-
2338, **2345**
Malone, Obadiah A. **2084**
Malone (Maloan, Malon),
Stephen 125, 1431, 1464,
1801, 1824, **2084, 2337-2338**
Malone (Maloan), Thomas
(Thos.) 1160, **2084**
Mann & Cupples 2325
Mansker, Lewis 2017
March, Clement **1969-1970**
Marote, Hippolite (Hippt.,
Hippte., Hypolite, Polite) 8,
20-21, 119, 197, **295**, 437,
452-453, 454-455, 1157,
1526
Marrasse, Pierre 437
Martin, ___ 1115, 1908, 2021
Martin, Allen 1147, 2029
Martin, Andrew (Andw.) 748,
869, **1037, 1073**, 1129, 1147,
1380
Martin, Anna 1217, **1992**, 2228
Martin, Catherine 92
Martin, Elisabeth **92**
Martin, Harry 786
Martin, James Huchinson **1147**
Martin, Jared C. 1935
Martin, John **155, 158**, 254,
319, 516, 815
Martin, John [Jr.] **1147**
Martin, John Sr. 1147
Martin, John, heirs of 505, 735,
881, 1158, 1820
Martin, Margret T. 319
Martin, Sally **1037**
Martin, Widow 477-478, 551
Martin (Martain), William
(Wm.) 693, **1175**, 1217,
1983, 1992, 2024, 2035, 2228
Mason, Isaac 394
Mason, Joseph 750-751
Massey, James 1155, **1940**,
1943, 2131, 2158, 2313
Massey, John (Jno.) 679, 756,
1155, 1451, **1499**, 1637,
1638, 1774, 1903, 1939,
1942, 1961, **1991, 2051, 2124**

Massie, Peter 762, 859
Mast, John **1538**
Masters, Henry 942
Masterson, Enos 653
Masterson, Jeremiah 728
Masterson, William **897**
Mathews, Edw. 253
Mathews, John 565
Mattack (Matlock, Metlock),
White **73**, 155, 477, **478**,
550-551
Matterson, Samuel **2412**
Matthews, Charity 574
Matthews, Edward **644**
Matthews, Edward H. **795, 814**
Matthews, Edward W. **644**
Matthews, John **2394**
Matthews, Mary **642, 644**
Matthews, Thomas 2342
Matthews (Mathews), William
(Wm.) **172**, 316, 320, 359,
392, 433, 468, **470**, 486, 489,
495, 497, 535-536, **574**, 614,
689, **813**, 979, 1108, 1181,
1226-1227, 1286, 1795,
2012, **2342**
Maulsby, Lemuel (Leml.) H.
1197, 1271
Mauphet (Morefoot,
Manheaut), William 92
Maxwell, Hugh H. 765
Maxwell, Thos. 2252-2253
May, John **828**, 2079, 2331
May, Mary Ann **828**
Mayberry, Benjamin 1103
Mayfield, John **2142**
McBride, R. A. 2392
McBride, Richard **1793**
McBride, Robert (Ro.) A.
2184-2185, 2265, 2278, 2304
McCabe, John G. W. **1997**,
2001
McCabe, Thomas **820**
McCallister, Robert 576
McCarey, John 321
McCartee (McArtee), James
1246, 1436, 1467
McCarty, Eliza **361**, 525
McCarty, John **38-40**, 41, 52-
53, **54, 64**, 68, **69-70**, 71-72,
86, 99, **127, 164, 254**, 261,
379, 395, 396, **398**, 487, 525,
666, 708, 896, 2257
McCarty, Lucy 525
McCarty, Matilda 525
McCarty, Nathan 55, **127**, 183,
205, **395-396, 448, 487, 525**,
666, 673, 824, 889, 1061,

Medley, Joseph 760
Melloy, John 108
Menard, Angelique 1157
Menard, Pierre **437**, 295, **325-326**, 452, 1014, 1016, **1157**
Menefee & Isom **1305**, **1954**
Menefee, Jarrot **679**, **1278**, **1838**, 2357
Menefee, Jonas **679**
Menefee (Manefee, Mennefee), Jonas N. **756**, **771**, **802**, **845**, 859, **909**, 924, 970, 977, **983**, 991, **1096**, 1100, 1305, **1324**, 1517, 1838, **1955-1956**, **2145**, **2149**, 2156, 2196, 2357, **2358**, 2361
Menefee, Richard 1131, 1138, 1158, **1278**, **1838**
Meredith, Daniel **868**
Meredith, Reese (Rees) **258**, 264, 868, 1462-1463
Meredith (Merideth), Roland **32-34**, **205**, **258**, **868**, 1462, **1463**
Merit, John 415
Michel, Joseph 623
Miers, Isaac 1976
Miers, Peter **1808**
Mifflin, John H. **408**
Mifflin, Nancy **2153**
Milburn (Millburn), William **884-885**, 1114, 1706, **1778**
Miller, Alexander 2007
Miller, Andrew **413**
Miller, Catharine **2198**
Miller, Caty **914**
Miller, George **132**
Miller, George C. **914**, 1091-1093, **2198**
Miller, George P. **2348**
Miller, Jacob 1483, **1485**, 2080
Miller, John **684**, 718, 1022, **1146**, **1283**, 2110, 2410
Miller, John S. 756, 880, 1188
Miller, Joseph 1091-1093
Miller, Junius Brutus **794**
Miller, Martin **863**, **914**, **1447**
Miller, Robert **413**
Miller, Valentine (Voluntine) **1723-1724**, **1740**, **1749**
Millican, Robert 1042
Millikin, Alex. Andrew 546
Millikin, Alexander **201**, 202-203, **204**, 347-348, 441, 642, 650. **1137**, 1231
Millis, Thomas (Thos.) **909**, 1256, **1742**

Mills, ___ 1895-1896, 2253, 2356
Mills, ___, heirs of 1273
Mills, Fanny 1904
Mills, James (Santiago) 29, **258**, 1026, 1462-1463, 1908, 2212
Mills, James, heirs of **1904**
Mills, James [Jr.] 1904
Mills, Lavina (Lavena, Levina, Levinah, Leviney) 154, **468**, 469, 538, **564**, 1023, **1026**, 1388
Mills, Manul(?) 1026
Mills, Merville 1904
Mills, Richard (Richd.) **424**, 430, 451, 485, 488, 490
Mills, Roswell 1149, 1243
Mills, Thos. 1221
Mills, Widow 118, 153, 494, 648, 856, 1012
Mills, Wm. 1904
Minton, Rhoda 2278
Minton, William H. 1442, **2278**
Mitchell (Mitchel), John 1844, **2042**
Mitchell (Mitchel), Samuel W. **1491**, 2042, **2168**
Moffett, J. A. 1171
Monday, Norris **165**, **316**
Monroe, James 2163, 2181-2190, 2193, 2197, 2199-2202, 2205-2211, 2213-2216, 2229-2238, 2243-2245, 2248-2251, 2262-2263, 2347, 2372
Montgomery, Barbary **228**
Montgomery, James **227-229**, 238, 334, **350**, 385, **406**, 479, 1818
Montgomery, John **1207**, 1208, **1297**, **1303**, **1325**
Montgomery (Montgumry), Sammuel **878**
Montgomery, William **1050**, 1818, 2145
Montgomery, Wilson 227, 228
Montooth, Adly 1465
Mooney (Moonay), James **1462-1463**
Moore, Fras. 290, 291
Moore, Geo. W. 975
Moore, Isidore 1033, 1990, **2044**, **2170**
Moore, Jesse, Jr. 2218
Moore, Jos. 795, 814, 851, 856
Moore, Myers, & Co. 1844
Moore, Samuel L. 1990

Moosly, Thomas **1435**
Morales, Don Juan 444
Morefoot, William 12, **92**
Morgan, Benn. (Ben) 157, 627
Morgan, George 169, **218**, 263, 278, **563**, 822, 832
Morgan, Thomas (Thos.) 42, 247, **303**, 371, 378, **417**, 672, 801, 855, **879**, **897-898**, **1436**, **1705**, **1776**, 1851, 1855, **2059-2060**, 2088, **2402**
Morrison, ___ 118, 338, 542
Morrison, Elizabeth **1909**, **2169**
Morrison (Morison), Fergus S. 846, **996**
Morrison, Isabella **742**
Morrison, J. Jr. 367, 741
Morrison (Morrisson, Morroson), James 117, **156-157**, 163, 277, 388, **728**, **740-741**, 2242, **2378-2379**
Morrison, James O. 2410
Morrison, James Sr. 469
Morrison, Jas. Jr. 443
Morrison, Joshua 740-741
Morrison, Robert 282, 290, 432, **1085**, 1404, **1405**, **1512**, **1909**, **2068**, **2169**
Morrison, Samuel **740-742**
Morrison, William (Wm.) **56**, 62-63, 65, **290-291**, **2378-2379**
Morrisson, John 581-582, **1094**, 1870, 2351
Morrow, George **971-972**, 1028, **1042**, **1216**, 1622, **1984**, 2032, 2075, **2173**
Morrow, Susan **1216**
Morrow, Susannah **1042**
Mosby, Joseph 415
Moseley & Cropper **1453**
Mosely (Moseley, Mosley), Thomas (Tom) Jr. **1232**, **1413**, **1452**, **1454**, 1696, 1997, **2400**, 2413
Moss, Marget 1201
Moth[ershead], Chas. 1901
Mothershead, Charles (Chas., Chrs., Chs.) 954, 973, 1246-1247, 1436, 1467, **1473**, 1681, 1964, **2008**, 2040, 2191
Mothershead, Clifton **895**, 956, 1199, 1906, 2174, 2256, **2258**
Mothershead, Nelly 2049
Mothershead, Polly **800**, 895, **1247**, 2326

Rodney, J. 1258
Rodney, John (Jno.) 463-465,
 489, 497, 512, 515, 530, 532-
 533, **534-535**, 536, **541**, **559**,
 580, **594**, **689**, **716**, 762, 855,
 859, **864**, 884-885, 966, 979,
 1054, 1135, **1196**, 1239-
 1240, 1248-1249, **1517**,
 1573, **1610**, 1611, **1675**,
 1773, **1818**, **1832-1833**,
 1891, 1901, 1918, **1967**,
 1995, 2018, 2036, **2078**,
 2165, **2241**(2), 2327, 2343,
 2358, 2368
Rodney, Lewis **511**
Rodney, Louisa (Louise) **159**,
 495, **511-512**
Rodney, M. 1244
Rodney, Maria (M., Mary)
 Louisa 1014, 1016, 1781,
 1869, 1972
Rodney, Marie 102, 1157
Rodney, Martin 133, **160**, 172,
 176, 179, **433**, **463**, 464, 465,
 489, **495**, **530**, **533-536**, **541**,
 619, **689**, 716, 864, 1196,
 1500, 1833, 1933, **2342**
Rodney, Matilda **783**, **1989**,
 2274-2275
Rodney, Michael (Mich.,
 Michl.) 489, 515, 532, **533**,
 534-535, **536**, 541, 559, 594,
 610, 689, **772**, **783**, 864, 966,
 1196, 1261, **1316**, **1423**,
 1515, **1611**, 1833, **1989**,
 2018, 2036, 2041, 2080,
 2165, **2267**, **2274-2275**, 2342
Rodney, **Polly 511**, **813**, **1248-
 1249**, **1261**, 1573, **1611**,
 1773, **1869**, **1972**, **1978**,
 2018, **2165**(2), **2298**, 2358,
 2366
Rodney, Rachel **1196**, **1517**,
 1833, **2241**
Rodney, Thomas (Tho., Thos.)
 159, 470, 486, 574, 581, **627**,
 1222, 1846, 1989
Rodney, Thomas J. 1293,
 1295, 1032, 1304
Rodney, Thomas (Thos.)
 Jefferson **511**, 1573, **1869**,
 1972, **2165**, **2298**, **2343**,
 2358, 2366
Rodney, Thomas (Thos.) S.
 133, 272, 298, 431, **433**, 456,
 463-464, 489, **495**, 497, **511-
 512**, **515**, 530, **532**, 535-536,
 555, 559, **565**, 580, 594, **610**,

772, **813**, 859, 864, **966**, 978,
 1166, **1196**, **1224-1225**,
 1234, **1248-1249**, **1258**,
 1261, 1281, **1316**, **1350-
 1351**, **1423-1425**, **1456**,
 1501, 1573, **1611**, **1674-
 1677**, **1744**, **1758**, **1773**,
 1832-1837, 1869, 1871,
 1918, 1967, **1971-1973**,
 1978, 1989, **2018**, 2036,
 2078, 2093, **2165**, **2241**,
 2274-2275, **2343**
Rodregas, Peyroud ne 325
Rogers, Adenston (Adence)
 128, 179
Rogers, John Jr. **1798**, **2155-
 2156**
Rogers (Rodgers), Joseph **872**,
 1381, **1894**, 2026
Rogers, Thomas 943
Rose (Roze), Benjamin (Benj.)
 77, **79**, **253**, 288, 408, 587
Ross, Bird William 120, 121
Ross, Elisabeth **415**
Ross, J. T. 1450
Ross, Jane **1646**
Ross, John **2157**
Ross, Phillip **1142**
Ross, Stephen 341
Ross, William **31**, 60, **415**,
 546, 650, **853-854**, **1646**,
 2157
Rosse, Benjn. **142**
Roush, George **2388**
Rouzer, John 649
Rozen, James **107**
Rubottom, Ezekiel (Ezek.)
 662, 842-844, **874**, 961,
 1049, 1056-1057
Rucker, Morton A. **1197**
Ruddell (Ruddle), George **679-
 680**, **721**, 1152, 1838, 2357,
 2361
Ruddell, Isaac 679
Russell, Clair 1043-1044
Russell, Elizabeth Ann 2064,
 2095
Russell (Russel), James **706**,
 730, 767, 826-827, 832, 840-
 841, 856, 860, 964, 998,
 1022, 1033, 1043-1044,
 1102, 1120-1121, 1127,
 1167, 1179, 1183, 1202-
 1205, 1220, 1228, 1275,
 1477, **1480**, **1516**, **1518-
 1524**, **1529**, **1535-1536**,
 1545, **1559**, **1568**, 1641,
 1688, **1765**, 1766, **1773**,

1775, **1783**, 1784, **1804**,
 1820, 1824, 1839, **1890**,
 1892, 1908, **1982**, 1996,
 2025, 2029, 2034, 2039,
 2064, 2069-2070, 2082,
 2090, 2095, 2119-2120,
 2127-2128, 2176, 2217,
 2218-2220, 2221, **2222**,
 2223, **2224**, 2293, 2339,
 2350, **2352**, 2380
Russell, Jesse I. 571
Russell, Joseph William **2064**
Russell, Magdalen 94
Russell, Martha Jane **2064**
Russell (Russel), William
 (Wm.) **649**, **697**, **724**, **739**,
 761, **769**, **787-789**, 790, 796,
 881, 1026, **1113**, 1158, **1179-
 1180**, **1427**, 1892, **1996**,
 2064, **2095**, 2127, **2286**
Rust (Roost), John Nicholas
 1353
Rutan, John D. **1992**, 2024,
 2035, **2161**, **2227-2228**
Rutan, Sarah **2228**
Rutter, ___ 1024
Rutter, Betsey **2098**
Rutter, Edmund **1021**, **1058**,
 1271-1272, **1458**, 1490,
 1844, **2010**, **2097-2098**,
 2255, **2260**, 2309, 2354,
 2371, **2376**, **2398**
Rutter, Houts, & Stallcup **1058**
Rutter, John P. 2383
Sadler, George 202-203
Sailer, David 2035
Sanderson, Jno. A. 1114
Sandord, Hy. 279
Sanford, H. 1087
Sanford, Henry (Hy.) 1295,
 1302, 1304, 1353, 1540,
 1569, 1655, 1737, 1742,
 1755, 1985, 2076, 2127,
 2164, 2252-2253, **2399**,
 2404, 2408, 2411, 2413-2417
Saul, Benjn. J. 1211
Savage, Nicholas 941
Saxon, Daniel 408
Schrader, Otho 432, 452, 454,
 456
Schultz, Jacob 2078
Scott & Pope 752
Scott, Alexander (Alex.) 214,
 216, 504
Scott, Alexander St. **445**
Scott, Andrew 2409
Scott, Elizabeth **445**
Scott, James 66-67, 197, 883

Woodson, Sam. 2240
Woolford, Geo. 2348
Worley, Isaac 681
Worrell, W. & S. 1844
Worth, Rachel **514-515**, 813
Worthington, James **775**, 838,
  870
Worthington, Joseph (Jos.) **26**,
  49, 116, **149-150**, **199**, **338**,
  364, 386, **542**, 543, 867,
  1840, 1843
Worthington, Margarett 1840,
  1842
Worthington, Phebe **775**, **870**
Worthington, R. 9, 83, 297,
  362, 370, 372, 380-381, 589
Worthington, Robert 119
Woth, Lewis 148
Wright, Alexander 2360, 2373
Wright, Allison 2360, 2373
Wright, Benjamin 2036
Wright, Betsey 2360, 2373
Wright, David 1112
Wright, Emily 2360, 2373
Wright, Jane 2360, 2373
Wright, John 1918
Wright, John P. **1438-1440**,
  1625, **1671**, **1890**, 1920,
  2360, **2373**
Wright, Mariah 2360, 2373
Wright, Nancy 2360, 2373
Wright, Richard 810, 956,
  1974, 2036
Wright, Samuel **1438-1440**,
  2360, 2373
Wright, Samuel, heirs of **2360**,
  2373
Wright (Write), Sarah 2360(2),
  2373
Wright, Susannah **2036**
Write, James 684
Yansey, Sandford **1622**
Yoder, Adolph 1894
Young, A. G. 1646
Young, Austin 36, 561, 730
Young, Evan 1844
Young, Hannah 1873, **2417**
Young, Harrison (Harison)
  1900, **1907**, **1910**, **1922**
Young, James 883
Young, John B. 2314
Young, Joseph **36-37**, 43, 46,
  47, 49, 50, **94**, 103, 125, 379,
  443, **671**, **673**, 1052, 1203,
  1228, 1913, 2053
Young, Joseph, heirs of 2362
Young, Margaret 2191

Young, Morris (Maurice) **209**,
  1168, 1447, **1873**, 2375, **2417**
Young, Phillip (Philip) 36,
  964, 1228, 2034, 2118
Young, Richd. M. 2071
Young, Sally **1228**, **1910**, **1922**
Yount (Yunt), Caty **1803**
Yount (Yunt), Charity 1055
Yount (Yunt), David **1803**
Yount, George **1802**
Yount (Yunt), Henry (Henery)
  1055, **1803**, **2081**
Yount (Yunt), Jacob 872,
  1802, 2046-2047, 2144
Yount (Yunt), Jacob Sr. 841,
  1803
Yount, Jesse **2047**
Yount (Yont, Yunt), **John**
  1802-1803, **2046**, **2144**, 2401
Yount, Sebley 2047
Yount (Yunt), Sophia (Sofiah)
  1803, **2081**
Zachery, Bartlet **928**
Zenoe, Jacob **142**
Zillefroe (Zelifrow, Zilefroe,
  Zellefroe), John (Jno.) 44,
  1892, **2154**, 2164, **2296**
Zoeller, C. E. 1579

Index of Enslaved Persons

Abraham (Abram) 243, 947
Addam 1959
Ailey (Ailsy) 1860, 1959
Alesey 472
Alexander 171
Amy (Ame) 243, 520
Andrew 82, 2048
Ann (Anne) 450, 1959
Anthony 1698
Augustus 1849
Ause(?) 698
Barrett 1844
Beck 1860
Betsey 2343
Bill 1806, 2089
Bill Allen 2078
Bob 243, 831, 1844, 2115
Boy 136
Cate 243, 1809
Caty 704
Charity 243
Charles 837, 1447, 1698, 1860,
  2067
child 400
Cinta 2370
Clara 2204
Clory 243
Corminete 2377

Cynthia 794, 2370
Dan 541
Daniel 780, 1698, 1857, 1935
Darcus 243, 481
Diannah 2057
Dick 243, 381
Dils(?) 2078
Diner 171, 400
Eady 762
Easter 685
Edmund 523
Edward 520, 2048
Eliza 2057
Ezbal 780
Fanny (Fanney) 243, 1784,
  2061
Fleming 1823
Frances 1153
Frank 171, 2146
Franny 380
Frederic 243
Gabriel 949
Genny 243
George 340, 1123, 1698, 1766,
  1849, **2045**
Girl 139
Hannah 949, 2067
Harriett 427
Harry 243, 1959
Harvey 1860
Huldy 1784
Isaac 243, 530, 580, 770, 815,
  1053
Isabella 704
Jack 948
Jacob 243, 1784, 1844
James 520
Jannet 243
Jefferson 530
Jeffry 216
Jenny 1766
Jerry 533
Jesse (Jessee) 243, 704, 1959
Jim 565, 1844, 2078, 2343
Joe 183, 2146
John 520, 1959
Joseph 472
Joshua 472
Justian 1844
Katharine 1959
Liddy 1123
Lidia 1959
Linda 1959
Louce 1849
Louis 1793
Lucy 1829, 2204
Lydia 82, 1122
Maria 472, 2162

Lot No. 10, Range D 1315, 1320
Lot No. 10, Range E 185, 2327
Lot No. 10, Range F 1324, 1955, 2358
Lot No. 10, Range G 1730
Lot No. 10, Range H 1623, 1654
Lot No. 10, Range I 1506, 1553
Lot No. 11, Range A 1298, 1375, 1849
Lot No. 11, Range B 1313, 1323, 1379, 1412
Lot No. 11, Range D 1316, 1423, 1972, 1989
Lot No. 11, Range E 184
Lot No. 11, Range F 1325
Lot No. 11, Range G 1333
Lot No. 11, Range H 1523, 1559
Lot No. 11, Range I 1616, 1656
Lot No. 12, Range B 196, 304
Lot No. 12, Range C 445
Lot No. 12, Range D 1513, 1530, 1747, 1785
Lot No. 12, Range E 1319-1320, 1882
Lot No. 12, Range F 1320
Lot No. 12, Range G 1685, 1753
Lot No. 12, Range H 1640, 1653
Lot No. 12, Range I 1556, 1595
Lot No. 13, Range A 513, 524, 1847
Lot No. 13, Range B 434-435, 474, 754
Lot No. 13, Range C 504
Lot No. 13, Range F 1320, 1326, 1415
Lot No. 13, Range G 1334, 1385
Lot No. 13, Range I 1655
Lot No. 14, Range A 1304, 1590
Lot No. 14, Range C 1313, 1412
Lot No. 14, Range D 1513, 1530, 1684, 1745
Lot No. 14, Range E 187, 529, 558, 568, 579, 681, 2240
Lot No. 14, Range F 1325
Lot No. 14, Range G 1685, 1753

Lot No. 14, Range H 1618, 1665
Lot No. 14, Range I 1555, 1575
Lot No. 15, Range A 1302, 1589
Lot No. 15, Range B 1314
Lot No. 15, Range C 1748
Lot No. 15, Range D
Lot No. 15, Range E 2160
Lot No. 15, Range F 1327, 1395, 1408, 1993
Lot No. 15, Range G 1335
Lot No. 15, Range H 1506, 1553
Lot No. 15, Range I 1730
Lot No. 15-20, Range D 1737
Lot No. 16, Range A 1303
Lot No. 16, Range B 1314
Lot No. 16, Range C 1520, 1529
Lot No. 16, Range F 1320
Lot No. 16, Range G 1730
Lot No. 16, Range H 1722
Lot No. 16, Range I 1557
Lot No. 17, Range A 1299, 1929, 1971, 2165
Lot No. 17, Range B 1533, 1760
Lot No. 17, Range C 1684, 1745
Lot No. 17, Range F 1736
Lot No. 17, Range G 1336, 1443
Lot No. 17, Range H 1554, 1600
Lot No. 17, Range I 1755
Lot No. 18, Range A 1300, 1358
Lot No. 18, Range B 1724, 1749
Lot No. 18, Range C 1513, 1530
Lot No. 18, Range F 1508, 1528, 1770
Lot No. 18, Range G 1728, 1754
Lot No. 18, Range H 1722
Lot No. 18, Range I 1558
Lot No. 19 2018
Lot No. 19, Range A 1295, 1586, 1849
Lot No. 19, Range B 1521, 1535
Lot No. 19, Range C 1748
Lot No. 19, Range E 1744, 1834
Lot No. 19, Range F 1736

Lot No. 19, Range G 1337, 1373
Lot No. 19, Range I 1558
Lot No. 20, Range A 1305, 1954
Lot No. 20, Range B 1736
Lot No. 20, Range C 1520, 1529
Lot No. 20, Range E 1531, 1598
Lot No. 20, Range F 1527, 1601
Lot No. 20, Range G 1730
Lot No. 20, Range H 1722
Lot No. 20, Range I 1755
Lot No. 21, Range A 1301
Lot No. 21, Range B 1534, 1849, 1926
Lot No. 21, Range C 1734
Lot No. 21, Range D 1625
Lot No. 21, Range E 1684, 1745
Lot No. 21, Range F 1736
Lot No. 21, Range G 1338, 1371
Lot No. 21, Range H 1552
Lot No. 21, Range I 1523, 1559
Lot No. 21-22, Range A 2137
Lot No. 21-26, Range D 1671
Lot No. 22, Range A 1301, 1608
Lot No. 22, Range B 1726, 1750
Lot No. 22, Range C 1608
Lot No. 22, Range D 1625
Lot No. 22, Range E 1513, 1530
Lot No. 22, Range F 1508, 1528, 1770
Lot No. 22, Range G 1730
Lot No. 22, Range H 1722
Lot No. 22, Range I 1685, 1753
Lot No. 23 2018
Lot No. 23, Range A 1295, 1583
Lot No. 23, Range B 1534, 1926, 1973
Lot No. 23, Range D 1625
Lot No. 23, Range E 1744, 1834, 1972
Lot No. 23, Range F 1743
Lot No. 23, Range G 1339, 1365
Lot No. 23, Range H 1506, 1553
Lot No. 23, Range I 1560

Lot No. 50, Range E 1630
Lot No. 51, Range A 1629
Lot No. 52, Range A 1629
Lot No. 53, Range A 1629
Lot No. 54, Range A 1629
Lot No. 55, Range H 1626
Lot No. 55-58, Range H 1668
Lot No. 55-64, Range A 1666
Lot No. 56, Range H 1626
Lot No. 57, Range H 1626
Lot No. 57-64, Range G 1672
Lot No. 58, Range H 1626
Lot No. 65, Range G 1624
Lot No. 65-72, Range G 1663
Lot No. 66, Range G 1624
Lot No. 67, Range G 1624
Lot No. 68, Range G 1624
Lot No. 69, Range G 1624
Lot No. 70, Range G 1624
Lot No. 71, Range G 1624
Lot No. 72, Range G 1624
Lot Nos 27-28, Range F 1649
Lot Nos. 1-3, Range A 1971
Lot Nos. 15-16, Range B 1399
Lot Nos. 15-20, Range D 1812
Lot Nos. 21-22, Range A 1398
Lot Nos. 23-30, Range C 1742
Lot Nos. 25-26, Range F 1825
Lot Nos. 27-28, Range E 1812
Lot Nos. 27-32, Range D 1664
Lot Nos. 29-30, Range F 1737, 1812
Lot Nos. 31-32, Range F 1649
Lot Nos. 31-34, Range E 1737, 1812
Lot Nos. 31-38, Range C 1729
Lot Nos. 33-40, Range F 1687, 1934
Lot Nos. 39-46, Range C 1665
Lot Nos. 41-48, Range F 1663
Lot Nos. 57-64, Range G 1729
Outlot No. 1 1346, 2366
Outlot No. 2 1347, 1608
Outlot Nos. 3-4 1347
Outlot No. 5 1346, 2366
Outlot No. 6 1422

Outlot Nos. 7-8 1509, 1537, 1770
Outlot No. 9 1677, 1835, 1972
Outlot No. 10 1514, 1548
Outlot No. 11 1676, 1837, 2018
Outlot No. 12 1621, 1667
Outlot No. 13 1549, 1713-1715, 2134
Outlot No. 14 1662, 1791
Outlot No. 15 1511, 1570, 1770
Outlot No. 16 1666
Outlot No. 17 1511, 1570, 1770, 2030
Outlot No. 18 1574, 1644
Outlot No. 22 1571, 1576
Outlot No. 23 1633
Outlot No. 24 1511, 1570, 1770, 2030
Outlot No. 25 1701, 1739
Outlot No. 26 1511, 1570, 1770
Outlot No. 27 1631
Outlot No. 28-29 1509, 1537, 1770
Outlot No. 30 1353
Outlot No. 31 1354
Outlot No. 32 1355, 1363, 1608, 1731
Outlot No. 33-34 1356, 1367
Outlot No. 35-36 1277, 1357
Outlot No. 37 1541, 1603
Outlot No. 38 1509, 1537, 2134
Outlot No. 39 1550, 1594
Outlot No. 40 1615, 1660
Outlot No. 41 1514, 1548, 2261
Outlot No. 42 1673, 1769-1770, 2403
Outlot No. 43 1701, 1739
Outlot No. 44 1572, 1634
Outlot No. 45 1701, 1739
Outlot No. 46 1571, 1576
Outlot Nos. 47 1633
Outlot No. 48 1571. 1576
Outlot No. 49 1735
Outlot No. 50 1511, 1570, 1770
Outlot No. 51 1723, 1740
Outlot No. 52 1511, 1570, 1770, 2134
Outlot No. 53 1701, 1739
Outlot No. 54 1524, 1568
Outlot No. 55 1735

Outlot No. 56 1573, 1610, 1833, 1972
Outlot No. 57 1675, 1832-1833, 1972
Outlot No. 58 1675, 1972
Outlot No. 59 1551, 1604
Outlot No. 60 1628
Outlot No. 61 1701, 1739
Outlot No. 62 1735
Outlot No. 63 1344, 1359
Outlot No. 64-65 1735
Outlot No. 66 1344, 1348, 1360
Outlot Nos. 67-68 1345, 1362
Outlot No. 69 1701, 1739
Outlot No. 70 1864
Outlot No. 71-73 1701, 1739
Outlot No. 74 1680, 1741
Outlot No. 75 1732
Outlot No. 76-77 1717, 1848-1849
Outlot No. 78a 1732
Outlot No. 78b 1732
Outlot No. 79 1758, 1972
Outlot No. 80 1718
Outlot No. 81 1759, 1814-1815
Outlot No. 82 1732
Outlot No. 83 1732
Outlot No. 84 1779
Outlot No. 85 1782
Outlot No. 86 1719, 1781
Outlot No. 87 1758, 1972
Outlot No. A 1352, 1421
Outlot No. B 1661, 1881
Outlot No. C 1351, 1424, 1972
Outlot No. D 1674, 1836, 1972
Outlot No. E 1350, 1425, 1972
Outlot No. F 1615, 1660
Outlot No. G 1349
Outlot No. H 1608
Outlot No. I 1524, 1568
Outlot No. K 1627, 1659
Outlot No. L 1569
Outlot No. M 1658
Square No. 8, Range C 1617
MO, Cape New Madrid 1822
MO, Cooper Co. 1170, 1858, 2029
MO, Decatur 968, 2388
MO, Decatur
Lot No. 2 1100
Lot No. 3 1100
Lot No. 4 970
Lot No. 5 970, 1279